P9-CAO-328

$9\frac{1}{2}'' \times 14\frac{1}{2}''$

3

10

Student
Solutions Manual

Doreen Kelly
Mesa Community College

$96'' \times 48$

Elementary Algebra
for College Students

Sixth Edition

Allen R. ANGEL

PEARSON

Prentice
Hall

Upper Saddle River, NJ 07458

Editor-in-Chief: Chris Hoag
Senior Acquisitions Editor: Paul Murphy
Supplement Editor: Kerri-Ann O'Donnell
Assistant Managing Editor: John Matthews
Production Editor: Donna Crilly
Supplement Cover Manager: Paul Gourhan
Supplement Cover Designer: Joanne Alexandris
Manufacturing Buyer: Ilene Kahn

© 2004 by Pearson Education, Inc.
Pearson Education, Inc.
Upper Saddle River, NJ 07458

Pearson Prentice Hall. All rights reserved. Printed in the United States of America. This publication is protected by Copyright and permission should be obtained from the publisher prior to any prohibited reproduction, storage in a retrieval system or transmission in any form or by any means, electronic, mechanical, photocopying, recording, or likewise. For information regarding permission(s), write to: Rights and Permissions Department.

Pearson Prentice Hall is a trademark of Pearson Education, Inc.

Printed in the United States of America

10 9 8 7 6 5 4 3

ISBN 0-13-140025-8

Pearson Education Ltd., *London*
Pearson Education Australia Pty. Ltd., *Sydney*
Pearson Education Singapore, Pte. Ltd.
Pearson Education North Asia Ltd., *Hong Kong*
Pearson Education Canada, Inc., *Toronto*
Pearson Educación de Mexico, S.A. de C.V.
Pearson Education—Japan, *Tokyo*
Pearson Education Malaysia, Pte. Ltd.
Pearson Education, *Upper Saddle River, New Jersey*

Table of Contents

Chapter 1

Exercise Set 1.1

11. To prepare properly for this class, you need to do all the homework carefully and preview the new material that is to be covered in class.

13. At least 2 hours of study and homework time for each hour of class time is generally recommended.

15. a. You need to do the homework in order to practice what was presented in class.

   b. When you miss class, you miss important information, Therefore it is important that you attend class regularly.

17. Answers will vary.

Exercise Set 1.2

1. Understand, translate, calculate, check, state answer

3. Substitute smaller or larger numbers so that the method becomes clear.

5. Rank the data. The median is the value in the middle.

6. We usually think of the mean as the average.

7. The mean is greater since it takes the value of 30 into account.

9. A mean average of 80 corresponds to a total of 800 points for the 10 quizzes. Pat's mean average of 79 corresponds to a total of 790 points for the 10 quizzes. Thus, he actually missed a B by 10 points.

11. a. $\dfrac{78 + 97 + 59 + 74 + 74}{5} = \dfrac{382}{5} = 76.4$
   The mean grade is 76.4.

   b. 59, 74, 74, 78, 97
   The middle value is 74.
   The median grade is 74.

13. a. $\dfrac{204.83 + 153.85 + 210.03 + 119.76 + 128.38}{5} = \dfrac{816.85}{5} = 163.37$
   The mean bill is \$163.37.

   b. \$119.76, \$128.38, \$153.85, \$204.83, \$210.03
   The middle value is \$153.85.
   The median bill is \$153.85.

15. a. $\dfrac{10.63 + 10.67 + 10.68 + 10.83 + 11.6 + 11.76 + 11.87 + 12.18 + 12.8 + 12.91}{10}$

   $= \dfrac{115.93}{10} \approx 11.593$
   The mean inches for rainfall for the 10 years is 11.593.

   b. 10.63, 10.67, 10.68, 10.83, 11.6, 11.76, 11.87, 12.18, 12.8, 12.91
   The middle values are 11.6 and 11.76.

   $\dfrac{11.6 + 11.76}{2} = \dfrac{23.36}{2} = 11.68$

   The median inches for rainfall for the 10 years is 11.68.

17.   Barbara's earnings = 5% of sales
Barbara's earnings = 0.05(9400)
                                    = 470
Her week's earnings were $470.

19. a.   sales tax = 7% of price
sales tax = 0.07(16,700)
                        = 1169
The sales tax was $1,169.

   b.   Total cost = price + tax
Total cost = 16,700 + 1,169
                        = 17,869
The total cost was $17,869.

21. a.   total cost with payments = down payment + (number of months)(monthly payment)
total cost with payments = 200 + 24(33)
                                              = 200 + 792
                                              = 992
Making monthly payments, it costs $992.

   b.   savings = total cost with payments – total cost at purchase
savings = 992 - 950
                = 42
He saves $42 by paying the total at the time of purchase.

23.   Women enlisted in the army = 45% of total
enlisted women = .45(91,600) = 41,220

Women enlisted in the navy = 24% of total
enlisted women = .24(91,600) = 21984

Army Women – Navy Women

= 41,220- 21,984 = 19,236

There are approximately 19,236 more women enlisted in the army than the navy.

25.   miles per gallon $= \dfrac{\text{number of miles}}{\text{number of gallons}}$

$= \dfrac{16,935.4 - 16,741.3}{10.5}$

$= \dfrac{194.1}{10.5}$

≈ 18.49

His car gets about 18.49 miles per gallon.

27.   savings = local cost – mail order cost
local cost $= \$425 + (0.08)(\$425)$
                  $= \$425 + \$34$
                  $= \$459$

mail cost $= 4(\$62.30 + \$6.20 + \$8)$
                  $= 4(\$76.50)$
                  $= \$306$
savings $= \$459 - \$306$
              $= \$153$
Eric saved $153.

29.a.   taxes = 15% of income
taxes = 0.15($34,612)
            = $5191.80
Their taxes were $5191.80

   b.   taxes
$= \$6780 + 27.5\%$ of (income $- \$45,200) \cdot$ taxes
$= \$6780 + 0.275(\$53,710 - \$45,200)$
$= \$6780 + 0.275(\$8510)$
$= \$6780 + \$2340.25$
$= \$9120.25$

Their taxes were $9120.25.

31. a.   gallons per year = 365(gallons per day)
         gallons per year = 365(11.25 gallons)
               = 4106.25 gallons

       additional money spent
       = (cost)(gallons wasted)
       additional money spent

$$= \frac{\$5.20}{1000 \text{ gallons}} \cdot 4106.25 \text{ gallons}$$

$$\approx \$21.35$$

33.   Cost = Flat Fee + .30(each quarter mile traveled)
                + .20(each 30 seconds stopped in traffic)
           = 2.00 + .30(12) = .20(3)
           = 6.20
      His ride cost $6.20.

35. a.   difference in cost = cost in Santa Monica – cost in Austin
                     = 480(number of weeks) + 109(number of weeks)
                     = 480(20) – 109(20)
                     = 9600 – 2180
                     = 7420
      It costs $7420 more for daycare in Santa Monica.

b.   hour of evening babysitting = $\dfrac{\text{total amount one can spend}}{\text{cost per hour of babysitter}}$

$$= \frac{132}{6}$$

$$= 22$$

      You can obtain 22 hours of babysitting.

37.   A single green block should be placed on the 3 on the right.

39.   mean = $\dfrac{\text{total cost}}{\text{number of nights spent in a hotel}}$

      mean = $\dfrac{1470.72}{8}$

           = $183.84 per night

41. a.   mean = $\dfrac{\text{sum of grades}}{\text{number of exams}}$

      $60 = \dfrac{50 + 59 + 67 + 80 + 56 + \text{ last}}{6}$

      360 = 312 + last
      last = 360 – 312
           = 48
      Lamond needs at least a 48 on the last exam.

b. $70 = \dfrac{312 + \text{ last}}{6}$

      420 = 312 + last
      last = 420 – 312
           = 108
      Lamond would need 108 points on the last exam, so he cannot get a C.

43.   Answers will vary.

Exercise Set 1.3

1. **a.**   Variables are letters that represent numbers.

   b.   Letters often used to represent variables are x, y, and z.

3. $5(x), (5)x, (5)(x), 5x, 5 \cdot x$

5. Divide out factors that are common to both the numerator and the denominator.

7. **a.** The least common denominator is the smallest number divisible by he two denominators.
   b. Answers will vary.

9. Part b) shows simplifying a fraction. In part a) common factors are divided out of two fractions.

11. Part a) is incorrect because you cannot divide out common factors when adding.

13. c); $\frac{4}{5} \cdot \frac{1}{4} = \frac{1}{5} \cdot \frac{1}{1} = \frac{1}{5}$. Divide out the common factor, 4. This process can be used only when multiplying fractions and so cannot be used for a) or b). Part d) becomes $\frac{4}{5} \cdot \frac{4}{1}$ so no common factor can be divided out.

15. Multiply numerators and multiply denominators.

17. Write fractions with a common denominator, add or subtract numerators, keep the common denominator.

19. Yes, it is simplified because the greatest common divisor of the numerator and denominator is 1.

21. The greatest common factor of 3 and 12 is 3.
$$\frac{3}{12} = \frac{3 \div 3}{12 \div 3} = \frac{1}{4}$$

23. The greatest common factor of 10 and 15 is 5.
$$\frac{10}{15} = \frac{10 \div 5}{15 \div 5} = \frac{2}{3}$$

25. The greatest common factor of 17 and 17 is 17.
$$\frac{17}{17} = \frac{17 \div 17}{17 \div 17} = \frac{1}{1} = 1$$

27. The greatest common factor of 36 and 76 is 4.
$$\frac{36}{76} = \frac{36 \div 4}{76 \div 4} = \frac{9}{19}$$

29. The greatest common factor of 40 and 264 is 8.
$$\frac{40}{264} = \frac{40 \div 8}{264 \div 8} = \frac{5}{33}$$

31. 12 and 25 have no common factors other than 1. Therefore, the fraction is already simplified.

33. $2\frac{3}{5} = \frac{10+3}{5} = \frac{13}{5}$

35. $2\frac{13}{15} = \frac{30+13}{15} = \frac{43}{15}$

37. $4\frac{3}{4} = \frac{16+3}{4} = \frac{19}{4}$

39. $4\frac{13}{19} = \frac{76+13}{19} = \frac{89}{19}$

41. $\frac{7}{4} = 1\frac{3}{4}$ because $7 \div 4 = 1$ R 3

43. $\frac{15}{4} = 3\frac{3}{4}$ because $15 \div 4 = 3$ R 3

45. $\frac{110}{20} = 5\frac{10}{20} = 5\frac{1}{2}$ because $110 \div 20 = 5$ R 10

47. $\frac{32}{7} = 4\frac{4}{7}$ because $32 \div 7 = 4$ R 4

49. $\frac{2}{3} \cdot \frac{4}{5} = \frac{2 \cdot 4}{3 \cdot 5} = \frac{8}{15}$

51. $\frac{5}{12} \cdot \frac{4}{15} = \frac{1}{12} \cdot \frac{4}{3} = \frac{1}{3} \cdot \frac{1}{3} = \frac{1 \cdot 1}{3 \cdot 3} = \frac{1}{9}$

53. $\frac{3}{4} \div \frac{1}{2} = \frac{3}{4} \cdot \frac{2}{1} = \frac{3}{2} \cdot \frac{1}{1} = \frac{3}{2}$ or $1\frac{1}{2}$

55. $\frac{3}{8} \div \frac{3}{4} = \frac{3}{8} \cdot \frac{4}{3} = \frac{1}{2} \cdot \frac{1}{1} = \frac{1 \cdot 1}{2 \cdot 1} = \frac{1}{2}$

57. $\frac{5}{12} \div \frac{4}{3} = \frac{5}{12} \cdot \frac{3}{4} = \frac{5}{4} \cdot \frac{1}{4} = \frac{5 \cdot 1}{4 \cdot 4} = \frac{5}{16}$

59. $\frac{10}{3} \div \frac{5}{9} = \frac{10}{3} \cdot \frac{9}{5} = \frac{2}{3} \cdot \frac{9}{1} = \frac{2}{1} \cdot \frac{3}{1} = \frac{2 \cdot 3}{1 \cdot 1} = \frac{6}{1} = 6$

61. $\left(2\frac{1}{5}\right)\frac{7}{8}$

$2\frac{1}{5} = \frac{10+1}{5} = \frac{11}{5}$

$\left(2\frac{1}{5}\right)\frac{7}{8} = \left(\frac{11}{5}\right)\frac{7}{8} = \frac{11 \cdot 7}{5 \cdot 8} = \frac{77}{40}$ or $1\frac{37}{40}$

63. $5\dfrac{3}{8}$ $1\dfrac{1}{4}$

$$5\frac{3}{8} = \frac{40+3}{8} = \frac{43}{8}$$

$$1\frac{1}{4} = \frac{4+1}{4} = \frac{5}{4}$$

$$5\frac{3}{8} \; 1\frac{1}{4} = \frac{43}{8} \; \frac{5}{4}$$

$$= \frac{43}{8} \cdot \frac{4}{5}$$

$$= \frac{43}{2} \cdot \frac{1}{5}$$

$$= \frac{43 \cdot 1}{2 \cdot 5}$$

$$= \frac{43}{10} \text{ or } 4\frac{3}{10}$$

65. $\dfrac{1}{4} + \dfrac{3}{4} = \dfrac{1+3}{4} = \dfrac{4}{4} = 1$

67. $\dfrac{5}{12} - \dfrac{1}{12} = \dfrac{5-1}{12} = \dfrac{4}{12} = \dfrac{1}{3}$

69. $\dfrac{8}{17} + \dfrac{2}{34}$

$$\frac{8}{17} = \frac{8}{17} \cdot \frac{2}{2} = \frac{16}{34}$$

$$\frac{8}{17} + \frac{2}{34} = \frac{16}{34} + \frac{2}{34} = \frac{16+2}{34} = \frac{18}{34} = \frac{9}{17}$$

71. $\dfrac{4}{5} + \dfrac{6}{15}$

$$\frac{4}{5} = \frac{4}{5} \cdot \frac{3}{3} = \frac{12}{15}$$

$$\frac{4}{5} + \frac{6}{15} = \frac{12}{15} + \frac{6}{15} = \frac{12+6}{15} = \frac{18}{15} = \frac{6}{5} \text{ or } 1\frac{1}{5}$$

73. $\dfrac{1}{6} - \dfrac{1}{18}$

$$\frac{1}{6} = \frac{1}{6} \cdot \frac{3}{3} = \frac{3}{18}$$

$$\frac{1}{6} - \frac{1}{18} = \frac{3}{18} - \frac{1}{18} = \frac{3-1}{18} = \frac{2}{18} = \frac{1}{9}$$

75. $\dfrac{5}{12} - \dfrac{1}{8}$

$$\frac{5}{12} = \frac{5}{12} \cdot \frac{2}{2} = \frac{10}{24}$$

$$\frac{1}{8} = \frac{1}{8} \cdot \frac{3}{3} = \frac{3}{24}$$

$$\frac{5}{12} - \frac{1}{8} = \frac{10}{24} - \frac{3}{24} = \frac{10-3}{24} = \frac{7}{24}$$

77. $\dfrac{7}{12} - \dfrac{2}{9}$

$$\frac{7}{12} = \frac{7}{12} \cdot \frac{3}{3} = \frac{21}{36}$$

$$\frac{2}{9} = \frac{2}{9} \cdot \frac{4}{4} = \frac{8}{36}$$

$$\frac{7}{12} - \frac{2}{9} = \frac{21}{36} - \frac{8}{36} = \frac{21-8}{36} = \frac{13}{36}$$

79. $\dfrac{5}{9} - \dfrac{4}{15}$

$$\frac{5}{9} = \frac{5}{9} \cdot \frac{5}{5} = \frac{25}{45} \quad \frac{5}{9} = \frac{5}{9} \cdot \frac{5}{5} = \frac{25}{45}$$

$$\frac{4}{15} = \frac{4}{15} \cdot \frac{3}{3} = \frac{12}{45}$$

$$\frac{5}{9} - \frac{4}{15} = \frac{25}{45} - \frac{12}{45} = \frac{25-12}{45} = \frac{13}{45}$$

81. $6\dfrac{1}{3} - 3\dfrac{1}{5}$

$$6\frac{1}{3} = \frac{18+1}{3} = \frac{19}{3} = \frac{19}{3} \cdot \frac{5}{5} = \frac{95}{15}$$

$$3\frac{1}{5} = \frac{15+1}{5} = \frac{16}{5} \cdot \frac{3}{3} = \frac{48}{15}$$

$$6\frac{1}{3} - 3\frac{1}{5} = \frac{95}{15} - \frac{48}{15} = \frac{95-48}{15} = \frac{47}{15} \text{ or } 3\frac{2}{15}$$

83. $5\dfrac{3}{4} - \dfrac{1}{3}$

$$5\frac{3}{4} = \frac{20+3}{4} = \frac{23}{4} = \frac{23}{4} \cdot \frac{3}{3} = \frac{69}{12}$$

$$\frac{1}{3} = \frac{1}{3} \cdot \frac{4}{4} = \frac{4}{12}$$

$$5\frac{3}{4} - \frac{1}{3} = \frac{69}{12} - \frac{4}{12} = \frac{65}{12} \text{ or } 5\frac{5}{12}$$

85. $55\dfrac{3}{16} - 46\dfrac{1}{4}$

$$55\frac{3}{16} = \frac{880+3}{16} = \frac{883}{16}$$

$$46\frac{1}{4} = \frac{184+1}{4} = \frac{185}{4} = \frac{185}{4} \cdot \frac{4}{4} = \frac{740}{16}$$

$$53\frac{3}{16} - 46\frac{1}{4} = \frac{883}{16} - \frac{740}{16} = \frac{143}{16} = 8\frac{5}{16}$$

Kim has grown $8\dfrac{5}{16}$ inches.

87. $1 - \dfrac{25}{36} = \dfrac{36}{36} - \dfrac{25}{36} = \dfrac{36-25}{36} = \dfrac{11}{36}$

About $\dfrac{\mathbf{11}}{\mathbf{36}}$ of all U.S. employees were not online.

89. $1 - \dfrac{39}{50} = \dfrac{50}{50} - \dfrac{39}{50} = \dfrac{50-39}{50} = \dfrac{11}{50}$

About $\dfrac{11}{50}$ of sales were for imported vehicles in 2001.

91. $4\dfrac{1}{2} = \dfrac{8+1}{2} = \dfrac{9}{2} = \dfrac{9}{2} \cdot \dfrac{6}{6} = \dfrac{54}{12}$

$1\dfrac{1}{6} = \dfrac{6+1}{6} = \dfrac{7}{6} = \dfrac{7}{6} \cdot \dfrac{2}{2} = \dfrac{14}{12}$

$1\dfrac{3}{4} = \dfrac{4+3}{4} = \dfrac{7}{4} = \dfrac{7}{4} \cdot \dfrac{3}{3} = \dfrac{21}{12}$

$4\dfrac{1}{2} + 1\dfrac{1}{6} + 1\dfrac{3}{4} = \dfrac{54}{12} + \dfrac{14}{12} + \dfrac{21}{12} = \dfrac{89}{12} = 7\dfrac{5}{12}$

The total weight is $7\dfrac{5}{12}$ tons.

93. 15 feet $2\dfrac{1}{2}$ in. - 3 feet $3\dfrac{1}{4}$ in.

$= 14$ feet $14\dfrac{2}{4}$ in. - 3 feet $3\dfrac{1}{4}$ in.

$= 11$ feet $11\dfrac{1}{4}$ in. or

$11(12) + 11\dfrac{1}{4} = 132 + 11\dfrac{1}{4} = 143\dfrac{1}{4}$ in. or

$143\dfrac{1}{4} \quad 12 = \dfrac{572+1}{4} \cdot \dfrac{1}{12} = \dfrac{573}{48} \approx 11.9$ ft.

95. $3\dfrac{1}{8} = \dfrac{24+1}{8} = \dfrac{25}{8}$

$3\dfrac{1}{8} \quad 2 = 3\dfrac{1}{8} \cdot \dfrac{2}{1} = \dfrac{25}{8} \cdot \dfrac{1}{2} = \dfrac{25}{16}$ or $1\dfrac{9}{16}$

Each piece is $\dfrac{25}{16}$ or $1\dfrac{9}{16}$ inches long.

97. $5\dfrac{1}{2} = \dfrac{10+1}{2} = \dfrac{11}{2}$

$5\dfrac{1}{2} \cdot \dfrac{1}{4} = \dfrac{11}{2} \cdot \dfrac{1}{4} = \dfrac{11 \cdot 1}{2 \cdot 4} = \dfrac{11}{8}$ or $1\dfrac{3}{8}$

$1\dfrac{3}{8}$ cups of chopped onions are needed.

99. $15 \quad \dfrac{3}{8} = \dfrac{15}{1} \cdot \dfrac{8}{3} = \dfrac{5}{1} \cdot \dfrac{8}{1} = \dfrac{5 \cdot 8}{1 \cdot 1} = \dfrac{40}{1} = 40$

Tierra can wash her hair 40 times.

101. $\dfrac{1}{4} + \dfrac{1}{4} + 1 = \dfrac{1}{4} + \dfrac{1}{4} + \dfrac{4}{4} = \dfrac{6}{4} = \dfrac{3}{2}$ or $1\dfrac{1}{2}$

The total thickness is $1\dfrac{1}{2}$ inches.

103. $4\dfrac{2}{3} = \dfrac{12+2}{3} = \dfrac{14}{3}$

$28 \quad \dfrac{14}{3} = \dfrac{28}{1} \cdot \dfrac{3}{14} = \dfrac{2}{1} \cdot \dfrac{3}{2} = \dfrac{6}{1} = 6$

There will be 6 whole strips of wood.

105. a. Total height of computer + monitor

$= 7\dfrac{1}{2}$ in. $+ 14\dfrac{3}{8}$ in.

$7\dfrac{1}{2} = \dfrac{15}{2} = \dfrac{15}{2} \cdot \dfrac{4}{4} = \dfrac{60}{8}$

$14\dfrac{3}{8} = \dfrac{112+3}{8} = \dfrac{115}{8}$

$7\dfrac{1}{2} + 14\dfrac{3}{8} = \dfrac{60}{8} + \dfrac{115}{8} = \dfrac{175}{8}$ or $21\dfrac{7}{8}$

Total height of computer and monitor is $\dfrac{175}{8}$ or $21\dfrac{7}{8}$ inches, so there is sufficient room.

b. $22\dfrac{1}{2} = \dfrac{44+1}{2} = \dfrac{45}{2} = \dfrac{45}{2} \cdot \dfrac{4}{4} = \dfrac{180}{8}$

$22\dfrac{1}{2} - 21\dfrac{7}{8} = \dfrac{180}{8} - \dfrac{175}{8} = \dfrac{5}{8}$

There will be $\dfrac{5}{8}$ inch of extra height.

c. $22\dfrac{1}{2} = \dfrac{44+1}{2} = \dfrac{45}{2} = \dfrac{45}{2} \cdot \dfrac{2}{2} = \dfrac{90}{4}$

$26\dfrac{1}{2} = \dfrac{52+1}{2} = \dfrac{53}{2} = \dfrac{53}{2} \cdot \dfrac{2}{2} = \dfrac{106}{4}$

$2\dfrac{1}{2} = \dfrac{4+1}{2} = \dfrac{5}{2} = \dfrac{5}{2} \cdot \dfrac{2}{2} = \dfrac{10}{4}$

$1\dfrac{1}{4} = \dfrac{4+1}{4} = \dfrac{5}{4}$

$22\dfrac{1}{2} + 26\dfrac{1}{2} + 2\dfrac{1}{2} + 1\dfrac{1}{4}$

$= \dfrac{90}{4} + \dfrac{106}{4} + \dfrac{10}{4} + \dfrac{5}{4}$

$= \dfrac{211}{4}$ or $52\dfrac{3}{4}$

The height of the desk is $52\dfrac{3}{4}$ in.

107. a. $\dfrac{*}{a} + \dfrac{?}{a} = \dfrac{*+?}{a}$

6

b. $\dfrac{\odot}{?} - \dfrac{\square}{?} = \dfrac{\odot - \square}{?}$

c. $\dfrac{\Delta}{\square} + \dfrac{4}{\square} = \dfrac{\Delta + 4}{\square}$

d. $\dfrac{x}{3} - \dfrac{2}{3} = \dfrac{x - 2}{3}$

e. $\dfrac{12}{x} - \dfrac{4}{x} = \dfrac{12 - 4}{x} = \dfrac{8}{x}$

109. number of pills

$= \dfrac{(\text{mg per day})(\text{days per month})(\text{number of months})}{\text{mg per pill}}$

$\text{number of pills} = \dfrac{(450)(30)(6)}{300}$

$= 270$

Dr. Highland should prescribe 270 pills

111. Answers will vary.

112. $\dfrac{9 + 8 + 15 + 32 + 16}{5} = \dfrac{80}{5} = 16$

The mean is 16.

113. In order, the values are: 8, 9, 15, 16, 32. The median is 15.

114. Variables are letters used to represent numbers.

Exercise Set 1.4

1. A set is collection of elements.

3. Answers will vary. One possible answer is the set of all natural numbers less than 0.

5. The set of whole numbers contains the natural numbers and zero which is not a natural number.

7. a. A rational number is any number that can be expressed as a quotient of two integers, denominator not 0.

b. Any integer can be expressed as a quotient of two integers by writing it with a denominator of 1. Therefore every integer is a rational number.

9. a. yes

b. no

b. no

c. yes

11. The integers are $\{\ldots, -3, -2, -1, 0, 1, 2, 3, \ldots\}$.

13. The whole numbers are $\{0, 1, 2, \ldots\}$.

15. The negative integers are $\{\ldots, -3, -2, -1\}$.

17. True; the whole numbers are $\{0, 1, 2, \ldots\}$.

19. True; any number that can be represented on a real number line is a real number.

21. False; the integers are $\{\ldots, -2, -1, 0, 1, 2, \ldots\}$.

23. False; $\sqrt{2}$ cannot be expressed as the quotient of two integers.

25. True; $-\dfrac{1}{5}$ is a quotient of two integers, $\dfrac{-1}{5}$.

27. True; 0 can be expressed as a quotient of two integers, $\dfrac{0}{1}$.

29. False; $4\dfrac{5}{8}$ is rational since it can be expressed as a quotient of two integers.

31. False; $-\dfrac{5}{3}$ is rational since it is a quotient of two integers.

33. True, either $\varnothing$ or $\{\ \}$ is used.

35. False; irrational numbers are real but not rational.

37. True; any rational number can be represented on a real number line and is therefore real.

39. True; irrational numbers are real numbers which are not rational.

41. True; the counting numbers are $\{1, 2, 3, \ldots\}$, the whole numbers are $\{0, 1, 2, \ldots\}$.

43. True; the symbol R represents the set of real numbers.

45. False; every number greater than zero is positive but not necessarily an integer.

47. True; the integers are

$$\left\{ \underbrace{\ldots, -2, -1}_{\text{negative integers}}, \underbrace{0}_{\text{zero}}, \underbrace{1, 2, \ldots}_{\text{positive integers}} \right\}.$$

49. a. 0 is an integer.

b.   0 and $2\frac{1}{2}$ are rational numbers.

c.   0 and $2\frac{1}{2}$ are real numbers.

51. a.   3 and 77 are positive integers.

b.   0, 3, and 77 are whole numbers

c.   0, –2, 3, and 77 are integers.

d. $-\frac{5}{7}$, 0, – 2, 3, $6\frac{1}{4}$, 1.63, and   77 are rational numbers.

e. $\sqrt{7}$ and $-\sqrt{3}$ are irrational numbers.

f. $-\frac{5}{7}$, 0, – 2, 3, $6\frac{1}{4}$, $\sqrt{8}$, $-\sqrt{7}$, 1.63, and 77 are real numbers.

For Exercises 53–64, answers will vary. One possible answer is given.

53.   0, 3, 1

55. $\sqrt{3}$, $\sqrt{7}$, π

57. $\frac{1}{2}$, 6.4, –2.6

59.   –1, –7, –24

61.   0, $\sqrt{2}$, –5

63.   –7, 1, 5

65.   {8, 9, 10, 11, …, 94}
94-8+1=86+1=87
The set has 87 elements.

67. a. $A = \{1, 3, 4, 5, 8\}$

b. $B = \{2, 5, 6, 7, 8\}$

c. A and $B = \{5, 8\}$

d. A or $B = \{1, 2, 3, 4, 5, 6, 7, 8\}$

69. a.   Set B continues beyond 4.

b.   Set A has 4 elements.

c.   Set B has an infinite number of elements.

d.   Set B is an infinite set.

71. a.   There are an infinite number of fractions between any 2 numbers.

b.   There are an infinite number of fractions between any 2 numbers.

73. $5\frac{2}{5} = \frac{5\cdot 5 + 2}{5} = \frac{25 + 2}{5} = \frac{27}{5}$

74. $\frac{16}{3} = 5\frac{1}{3}$ because $16 \div 3 = 5 \text{ R } 1$

75. $\frac{3}{5} + \frac{5}{8}$
$\frac{3}{5} = \frac{3}{5} \cdot \frac{8}{8} = \frac{24}{40}$
$\frac{5}{8} \cdot \frac{5}{5} = \frac{25}{40}$
$\frac{3}{5} + \frac{5}{8} = \frac{24}{40} + \frac{25}{40} = \frac{49}{40}$ or $1\frac{9}{40}$

76. $\left(\frac{5}{9}\right)\left(4\frac{2}{3}\right)$
$4\frac{2}{3} = \frac{12 + 2}{3} = \frac{14}{3}$
$\left(\frac{5}{9}\right)\left(4\frac{2}{3}\right) = \frac{5}{9} \cdot \frac{14}{3} = \frac{70}{27}$ or $2\frac{16}{27}$

Exercise Set 1.5

1. a.
$-6\ -5\ -4\ -3\ -2\ -1\ \ 0\ \ 1\ \ 2\ \ 3\ \ 4\ \ 5\ \ 6$

b.
$-6\ -5\ -4\ -3\ -2\ -1\ \ 0\ \ 1\ \ 2\ \ 3\ \ 4\ \ 5\ \ 6$

c.   –2 is greater than –4 because it is farther to the right on the number line.

d. $-4 < -2$

e. $-2 > -4$

3. a.   4 is 4 units from 0 on a number line.

b.   –4 is 4 units from 0 on a number line.

c.   0 is 0 units from 0 on a number line.

5.   Yes; for example, $5 > 3$ and $3 < 5$. Also, $-2 > -5$ and $-5 < -2$.

7.   No, $-3 > -4$ but $|-3| < |-4|$.

9.   No, $|-4| > |-3|$ but $-4 < -3$.

11. $|7| = 7$

13. $|-15| = 15$

15. $|0| = 0$

17. $-|-5| = -(5) = -5$

19. $-|21| = -(21) = -21$

21. $5 > 2$; 5 is to the right of 2 on a number line.

23. $-6 < 0$; -6 is to the left of 0 on a number line.

25. $\frac{1}{2} > -\frac{2}{3}$; $\frac{1}{2}$ is to the right of $-\frac{2}{3}$ on a number line.

27. $0.7 < 0.8$; 0.7 is to the left of 0.8 on a number line.

29. $-\frac{1}{2} > -1$; $-\frac{1}{2}$ is to the right of -1 on a number line.

31. $3 > -3$; 3 is to the right of -3 on a number line.

33. $-2.1 < -2$; -2.1 is to the left of -2 on a number line.

35. $\frac{4}{5} > -\frac{4}{5}$; $\frac{4}{5}$ is to the right of $-\frac{4}{5}$ on a number line.

37. $-\frac{3}{8} < \frac{3}{8}$; $-\frac{3}{8}$ is to the left of $\frac{3}{8}$ on a number line.

39. $0.49 > 0.43$; 0.49 is to the right of 0.43 on a number line.

41. $5 > -7$; 5 is to the right of -7 on a number line.

43. $-0.006 > -0.007$; -0.006 is to the right of -0.007 on a number line.

45. $\frac{5}{8} > 0.6$ because $\frac{5}{8} = 0.625$ and 0.625 is to the right of 0.6 on a number line.

47. $-\frac{2}{3} < -\frac{1}{3}$; $-\frac{2}{3}$ is to the left of $-\frac{1}{3}$ on a number line.

49. $-\frac{1}{2} > -\frac{3}{2}$; $-\frac{1}{2}$ is to the right of $-\frac{3}{2}$ on a number line.

51. $0.3 < \frac{1}{3}$; 0.3 is to the left of .333... on a number line.

53. $\frac{13}{15} < \frac{8}{9}$; $\frac{39}{45}$ is to the left of $\frac{40}{45}$ on a number line.

55. $-(-6) > -(-5)$; 6 is to the right of 5 on a number line.

57. $3 > |-2|$ since $|-2| = 2$

59. $|-4| > \frac{2}{3}$ since $|-4| = 4$

61. $|0| < |-4|$ since $|0| = 0$ and $|-4| = 4$

63. $4 < \left|-\frac{9}{2}\right|$ since $\left|-\frac{9}{2}\right| = \frac{9}{2}$ or $4\frac{1}{2}$

65. $\left|-\frac{4}{5}\right| < \left|-\frac{5}{4}\right|$ since $\left|-\frac{4}{5}\right| = \frac{4}{5} = \frac{16}{20}$ and $\left|-\frac{5}{4}\right| = \frac{5}{4} = \frac{25}{20}$

67. $|-4.6| = \left|-\frac{23}{5}\right|$ since $|-4.6| = 4.6$ and $\left|-\frac{23}{5}\right| = \frac{23}{5} = 4.6$

69. $\frac{2}{3} + \frac{2}{3} + \frac{2}{3} + \frac{2}{3} = 4 \cdot \frac{2}{3}$ since $\frac{2}{3} + \frac{2}{3} + \frac{2}{3} + \frac{2}{3} = \frac{2+2+2+2}{3} = \frac{8}{3}$ and $4 \cdot \frac{2}{3} = \frac{4}{1} \cdot \frac{2}{3} = \frac{8}{3}$

71. $\frac{1}{2} \cdot \frac{1}{2} < \frac{1}{2}$ since $\frac{1}{2} \cdot \frac{1}{2} = \frac{1 \cdot 1}{2 \cdot 2} = \frac{1}{4}$ and $\frac{1}{2} \div \frac{1}{2} = \frac{1}{2} \cdot \frac{2}{1} = \frac{1}{1} \cdot \frac{1}{1} = 1$

73. $\frac{5}{8} - \frac{1}{2} < \frac{5}{8} \div \frac{1}{2}$ since $\frac{5}{8} - \frac{1}{2} = \frac{5}{8} - \frac{4}{8} = \frac{1}{8}$ and $\frac{5}{8} \div \frac{1}{2} = \frac{5}{8} \cdot \frac{2}{1} = \frac{10}{8}$

75. $-|-8|, .38, \frac{4}{9}, \frac{3}{5}, |-6|$ because $-|8| = -8$, $\frac{4}{9} = 0.444...$, $\frac{3}{5} = 0.6$ and $|-6| = 6$.

77. $\frac{5}{12}$, 0.6, $\frac{2}{3}$, $\frac{19}{25}$, |-2.6| because $\frac{5}{12}$ = .416416...,

$\frac{2}{3}$ = .666..., $\frac{19}{25}$ = .76 and |-2.6| = 2.6.

79. 4 and –4 since |4| = |–4| = 4

For Exercises 81-87, answers will vary. One possible answer is given.

81. Three numbers greater than 4 and less than 6 are $4\frac{1}{2}$, 5, 5.5.

83. Three numbers less than –2 and greater than –6 are –3, –4, –5.

85. Three numbers greater than –3 and greater than 3 are 4, 5, 6.

87. Three numbers greater than |–2| and less than |–6| are 3, 4, 5.

89. **a.** Between does not include endpoints.

   b. Three real numbers between 4 and 6 are 4.1, 5, and $5\frac{1}{2}$.

   c. No, 4 is an endpoint.

   d. Yes, 5 is greater than 4 and less than 6.

   e. True

91. **a.** The taxes were less than 50 cents all the time

   b. In March 2000 the gasoline was greater than $1.50 for the firs time.

   c. Gas was less than $1.00 from January to March, 1999.

   d. March 2000 – May 2001, except for June 2000

93. The result of dividing a number by itself is 1. Thus, the result of dividing a number between 0 and 1 by itself is a number, 1, which is greater than the original number.

95. Yes, 0 since |0| = 0 and –|0| = –(0) = 0

98. $1\frac{2}{3} - \frac{3}{8}$

$1\frac{2}{3} = \frac{3+2}{3} = \frac{5}{3} = \frac{5}{3} \cdot \frac{8}{8} = \frac{40}{24}$

$\frac{3}{8} = \frac{3}{8} \cdot \frac{3}{3} = \frac{9}{24}$

$1\frac{2}{3} - \frac{3}{8} = \frac{40}{24} - \frac{9}{24} = \frac{31}{24}$ or $1\frac{7}{24}$

99. The set of whole numbers is {0, 1, 2, 3, ...}.

100. The set of counting numbers is {1, 2, 3, 4, ...}.

101. **a.** 5 is a natural number.

   b. 5 and 0 are whole numbers.

   c. 5, –2, and 0 are integers.

   d. 5, –2, 0, $\frac{1}{3}$, $-\frac{5}{9}$, and 2.3 are rational numbers.

   e. $\sqrt{3}$ is an irrational number.

   f. 5, –2, 0, $\frac{1}{3}$, $\sqrt{3}$, $-\frac{5}{9}$, and 2.3 are real numbers.

Exercise Set 1.6

1. The 4 basic operations of arithmetic are addition, subtraction, multiplication, and division.

   b. One example is 3 and –3.

3. **a.** No; $-\frac{2}{3} + \frac{3}{2}$ does not equal 0.

   b. The opposite of $-\frac{2}{3}$ is $\frac{2}{3}$ because $-\frac{2}{3} + \frac{2}{3} = 0$.

5. The sum of a positive number and a negative number can be either positive or negative. The sum of a positive number and a negative number has the same sign as the number that has larger absolute value.

7. Answers will vary.

9. **a.** He owed 175, a negative, and then paid a positive amount, 93, toward his debt.

   b. –175 + 93
   The numbers have different signs so find the difference between the absolute values.
   |–175| – |93| = 82

$|-175|$ is greater so sum is negative.
$-175 + 93 = -82$

c.   Answers will vary.

11. Yes, it is correct.

13. The opposite of 9 is -9 since $9 + (-9) = 0$.

15. The opposite of -28 is 28 since $-28 + 28 = 0$.

17. The opposite of 0 is 0 since $0 + 0 = 0$.

19. The opposite of $\dfrac{5}{3}$ is $-\dfrac{5}{3}$ since $\dfrac{5}{3} + \left(-\dfrac{5}{3}\right) = 0$.

21. The opposite of $2\dfrac{3}{5}$ is $-2\dfrac{3}{5}$ since
$2\dfrac{3}{5} + \left(-2\dfrac{3}{5}\right) = 0$.

23. The opposite of 3.72 is -3.72 since
$3.72 + (-3.72) = 0$.

25. Numbers have same sign, so add absolute values.
$|5| + |6| = 5 + 6 = 11$
Numbers are positive so sum is positive.
$5 + 6 = 11$

27. Numbers have different signs so find difference
between larger and smaller absolute values.
$|4| - |-3| = 4 - 3 = 1$. $|4|$ is greater than $|-3|$ so the
sum is positive.
$4 + (-3) = 1$

29. Numbers have same sign, so add absolute values.
$|-4| + |-2| = 4 + 2 = 6$.
Numbers are negative, so sum is negative.
$-4 + (-2) = -6$

31. Numbers have different signs, so find difference
between absolute values.
$|6| - |-6| = 6 - 6 = 0$
$6 + (-6) = 0$

33. Numbers have different signs, so find difference
between absolute values.
$|-4| - |4| = 4 - 4 = 0$
$-4 + 4 = 0$

35. Numbers have same sign, so add absolute values.
$|-8| + |-2| = 8 + 2 = 10$. Numbers are negative, so
sum is negative.
$-8 + (-2) = -10$

37. Numbers have different signs, so find difference
between absolute values.
$|-6| - |6| = 6 - 6 = 0$
$-6 + 6 = 0$

39. Numbers have same sign, so add absolute values.
$|-8| + |-5| = 8 + 5 = 13$
Numbers are negative, so sum is negative.
$-8 + (-5) = -13$

41. $0 + 0 = 0$

43. $-6 + 0 = -6$

45. Numbers have different signs, so find difference
between larger and smaller absolute values.
$|18| - |-9| = 18 - 9 = 9$. $|18|$ is greater than $|-9|$ so
sum is positive.
$18 + (-9) = 9$

47. Numbers have same sign, so add absolute values.
$|-33| + |-31| = 33 + 31 = 64$
Numbers are negative, so sum is negative.
$-33 + (-31) = -64$

49. Numbers have same sign, so add absolute values.
$|-42| + |-9| = 42 + 9 = 51$
Numbers are negative, so sum is negative.
$-42 + (-9) = -51$

51. Numbers have different signs, so find difference
between larger and smaller absolute values.
$|-30| - |4| = 30 - 4 = 26$. $|-30|$ is greater than $|4|$ so
sum is negative.
$4 + (-30) = -26$

53. Numbers have different signs, so find difference
between larger and smaller absolute values.
$|40| - |-35| = 40 - 35 = 5$. $|40|$ is greater than $|-35|$
so sum is positive.
$-35 + 40 = 5$

55. Numbers have different signs, so take difference
between larger and smaller absolute values.
$|6.5| - |-4.2| = 6.5 - 4.2 = 2.3$. $|6.5|$ is greater than
$|-4.2|$ so sum is positive.
$-4.2 + 6.5 = 2.3$

57. Numbers have same sign, so add absolute values.
$|-9.7| + |-5.4| = 9.7 + 5.4 = 15.1$. Numbers are
negative, so sum is negative..
$-9.7 + (-5.4) = -15.1$

59. Numbers have different signs, so find difference
between larger and smaller absolute values.

$|-200| - |180| = 200 - 180 = 20$. $|-200|$ is greater than $|180|$ so sum is negative.
$180 + (-200) = -20$

61. Numbers have different signs, so find difference between larger and smaller absolute values.
$|-67| - |28| = 67 - 28 = 39$. $|-67|$ is greater than $|28|$ so sum is negative.
$-67 + 28 = -39$

63. Numbers have different signs, so find difference between larger and smaller absolute values.
$|184| - |-93| = 184 - 93 = 91$. $|184|$ is greater than $|-93|$ so sum is positive.
$184 + (-93) = 91$

65. Numbers have different signs, so find difference between larger and smaller absolute values.
$|-452| - |312| = 452 - 312 = 140$. $|-452|$ is greater than $|312|$ so sum is negative.
$-452 + 312 = -140$

67. Numbers have same sign, so add absolute values.
$|-26| + |-79| = 26 + 79 = 105$. Numbers are negative so sum is negative.
$-26 + (-79) = -105$

69. Numbers have same sign, so add absolute values.
$|-24.6| + |-13.9| = 24.6 + 13.9 = 38.5$. Numbers are negative so sum is negative.
$-24.6 + (-13.9) = -38.5$

71. Numbers have different signs, so find difference between larger and smaller absolute values.
$|110.9| - |106.3| = 110.9 - 106.3 = 4.6$. $|-110.9|$ is greater than $|106.3|$ so sum is negative.
$106.3 + (-110.9) = -4.6$

73. $\dfrac{3}{5} + \dfrac{1}{7} = \dfrac{21}{35} + \dfrac{5}{35} = \dfrac{21+5}{35} = \dfrac{26}{35}$

75. $\dfrac{5}{12} + \dfrac{6}{7} = \dfrac{35}{84} + \dfrac{72}{84} = \dfrac{35+72}{84} = \dfrac{107}{84}$

77. Numbers have different signs, so find difference between larger and smaller absolute values.
$-\dfrac{8}{11} + \dfrac{4}{5} = -\dfrac{40}{55} + \dfrac{44}{55} = \left|\dfrac{44}{55}\right| - \left|-\dfrac{40}{55}\right| = \dfrac{44}{55} - \dfrac{40}{55} = \dfrac{4}{55}$
$\left|\dfrac{44}{55}\right|$ is greater than $\left|-\dfrac{40}{55}\right|$ so sum is positive.
$-\dfrac{8}{11} + \dfrac{4}{5} = \dfrac{4}{55}$

79. Numbers have different signs, so find difference between larger and smaller absolute values.
$-\dfrac{7}{10} + \dfrac{11}{90} = \left|-\dfrac{63}{90}\right| - \left|\dfrac{11}{90}\right| = \dfrac{63}{90} - \dfrac{11}{90} = \dfrac{63-11}{90} = \dfrac{52}{90} = \dfrac{26}{45}$
$\left|-\dfrac{63}{90}\right|$ is greater than $\left|\dfrac{11}{90}\right|$ so sum is negative.
$-\dfrac{7}{10} + \dfrac{11}{90} = -\dfrac{26}{45}$

81. Numbers have different signs, so find difference between larger and smaller absolute values
$\dfrac{9}{25} + \left(-\dfrac{3}{50}\right) = \left|\dfrac{18}{50}\right| - \left|-\dfrac{3}{50}\right| = \dfrac{18}{50} - \dfrac{3}{50} = \dfrac{18-3}{50} = \dfrac{15}{50} = \dfrac{3}{10}$
$\left|\dfrac{18}{50}\right|$ is greater than $\left|-\dfrac{3}{50}\right|$ so sum is positive.
$\dfrac{9}{25} + \left(-\dfrac{3}{50}\right) = \dfrac{3}{10}$

83. Numbers have same sign, so add absolute values.
$-\dfrac{7}{30} + \left(-\dfrac{5}{6}\right) = \left|-\dfrac{7}{30}\right| + \left|-\dfrac{25}{30}\right| = \dfrac{7}{30} + \dfrac{25}{30} = \dfrac{7+25}{30} = \dfrac{32}{30} = \dfrac{16}{15}$
Numbers are negative so sum is negative.
$-\dfrac{7}{30} + \left(-\dfrac{5}{6}\right) = -\dfrac{16}{15}$

85. Numbers have same sign, so add absolute values.
$-\dfrac{4}{5} + \left(-\dfrac{5}{75}\right) = \left|-\dfrac{60}{75}\right| + \left|-\dfrac{5}{75}\right| = \dfrac{60}{75} + \dfrac{5}{75} = \dfrac{60+5}{75} = \dfrac{65}{75} = \dfrac{13}{15}$
Numbers are negative so sum is negative.
$-\dfrac{4}{5} + \left(-\dfrac{5}{75}\right) = -\dfrac{13}{15}$

87. Numbers have different signs, so find difference between larger and smaller absolute values.
$\dfrac{5}{36} + \left(-\dfrac{5}{24}\right) = \dfrac{10}{72} + \left(-\dfrac{15}{72}\right) = \left|-\dfrac{15}{72}\right| - \left|\dfrac{10}{72}\right| = \dfrac{15}{72} - \dfrac{10}{72} = \dfrac{5}{72}$
$\left|-\dfrac{15}{72}\right|$ is greater than $\left|\dfrac{10}{72}\right|$ so sum is negative.
$\dfrac{5}{36} + \left(-\dfrac{5}{24}\right) = -\dfrac{5}{72}$

89. Numbers have same sign, so add absolute values.

$$-\frac{5}{12} + \left(-\frac{3}{10}\right) = -\frac{25}{60} + \left(-\frac{18}{60}\right) = -\left|\frac{25}{60}\right| + \left|-\frac{18}{60}\right| =$$

$$\frac{25}{60} + \frac{18}{60} = \frac{43}{60}$$

Numbers are negative so sum is negative.

$$-\frac{5}{12} + \left(-\frac{3}{10}\right) = -\frac{43}{60}$$

91. Numbers have same sign, so add absolute values.

$$-\frac{13}{14} + \left(-\frac{7}{42}\right) = -\frac{39}{42} + \left(-\frac{7}{42}\right) = -\left|\frac{39}{42}\right| + \left|-\frac{7}{42}\right| =$$

$$\frac{39}{42} + \frac{7}{42} = \frac{39+7}{42} = \frac{46}{42} = \frac{23}{21}$$

Numbers are negative so sum is negative.

$$-\frac{13}{14} + \left(-\frac{7}{42}\right) = -\frac{23}{21}$$

93. a. Positive; |587| is greater than |−197| so sum will be positive.

  b. $587 + (-197) = 390$

  c. Yes; By part a) we expect a positive sum. The magnitude of the sum is the difference between the larger and smaller absolute values.

95. a. Negative; the sum of 2 negative numbers is always negative.

  b. $-84 + (-289) = -373$

  c. Yes; the sum of 2 negative numbers should be (and is) a larger negative number.

97. a. Negative; |−947| is greater than |495| so sum will be negative.

  b. $-947 + 495 = -452$

  c. Yes; by part a) we expect a negative sum. Magnitude of the sum is the difference between the larger and smaller absolute values.

99. a. Negative; the sum of 2 negative numbers is always negative.

  b. $-496 + (-804) = -1300$

  c. Yes; the sum of 2 negative numbers should be (and is) a larger negative number.

101. a. Negative; |-375| is greater than |263| so sum will be negative.

  b. $-375 + 263 = -112$

  c. Yes; by part a) we expect a negative sum. The magnitude of the sum is the difference between the larger and smaller absolute values.

103. a. Negative; the sum of 2 negative numbers is always negative.

  b. $-1833 + (-2047) = -3880$

  c. Yes; The sum of 2 negative numbers should be (and is) a larger negative number.

105. a. Positive; |3124| is greater than |−2013| so sum will be positive.

  b. $3124 + (-2013) = 1111$

  c. Yes; by part a) we expect a positive sum. Magnitude of sum is difference between larger and smaller absolute values.

107. a. Negative; the sum of 2 negative numbers is always negative.

  b. $-1025 + (-1025) = -2050$

  c. Yes; the sum of 2 negative numbers should be (and is) a larger negative number.

109. True

111. True; the sum of two positive numbers is always positive.

113. False; the sum has the sign of the number with the larger absolute value.

115. Mr. Peter's balance was –$94. His new balance can be found by adding. $-94 + (-183) = -277$
Mr. Peter owes the bank $277.

117. Total loss can be represented as $-18 + (-3)$.
$|-18| + |-3| = 18 + 3 = 21$. The total loss in yardage is 21 yards.

119. The depth of the well can be found by adding $-27 + (-34) = -61$. The well is 61 feet deep.

121. Distance from sea level to place on mountain can be represented by $-267 + 198$.
$|-267| - |198| = 267 - 198 = 69$

$|-267| > |198|$ so $-267 + 198 = -69$
Their vertical distance is 69 feet below sea level.

123. a. In 2001, the Postal Service will have a net loss of $3 billion.

   b. 1999: 0,4 billion dollars
   2000: - 0.3 billion dollars
   2001: -3 billion dollars
   0.4+(-0.3)+(-3)= -2.9 billion dollars
   From 1999 through 2001, the Postal Service had a net loss of $2.9 billion.

125. $(-4) + (-6) + (-12) = (-10) + (-12) = -22$

127. $29 + (-46) + 37 = (-17) + 37 = 20$

129. $(-12) + (-10) + 25 + (-3) = (-22) + 25 + (-3)$
$$= 3 + (-3)$$
$$= 0$$

131. $\dfrac{1}{2} + \left(-\dfrac{1}{3}\right) + \dfrac{1}{5} = \left(\dfrac{3}{6} - \dfrac{2}{6}\right) + \dfrac{1}{5}$
$$= \dfrac{1}{6} + \dfrac{1}{5}$$
$$= \dfrac{5}{30} + \dfrac{6}{30}$$
$$= \dfrac{11}{30}$$

133. $1 + 2 + 3 + \cdots + 10 = (1 + 10) + (2 + 9) \cdots + (5 + 6)$
$$= (5)(11)$$
$$= 55$$

135. $1\dfrac{2}{3} = \dfrac{3+2}{3} = \dfrac{5}{3}$
$$\left(\dfrac{3}{5}\right)\left(1\dfrac{2}{3}\right) = \left(\dfrac{3}{5}\right)\left(\dfrac{5}{3}\right) = \dfrac{1}{1} \cdot \dfrac{1}{1} = 1$$

136. $3 = \dfrac{3}{1} \cdot \dfrac{16}{16} = \dfrac{48}{16}$
$$3 - \dfrac{5}{16} = \dfrac{48}{16} - \dfrac{5}{16} = \dfrac{48-5}{16} = \dfrac{43}{16} \text{ or } 2\dfrac{11}{16}$$

137. $\{1, 2, 3, 4, \ldots\}$

138. $|-3| > 2$ since $|-3| = 3$

139. $8 > |-7|$ since $|-7| = 7$

Exercise Set 1.7

1. 2 - 7

3. $\ast - \square$

5. a. to subtract b from a, add the opposite of b to a.

   b. $5 + (-14)$

   c. $5 + (-14) = -9$

7. a. $a - (+b) = a - b$

   b. $7 - (+9) = 7 - 9$

   c. $7 - 9 = 7 + (-9) = -2$

9. a. $3 - (-6) + (-5) = 3 + 6 - 5$

   b. $3 + 6 - 5 = 9 - 5 = 4$

11. Yes it is correct.

13. $12 - 5 = 12 + (-5) = 7$

15. $8 - 9 = 8 + (-9) = -1$

17. $-4 - 2 = -4 + (-2) = -6$

19. $-4 - (-3) = -4 + 3 = -1$

21. $-4 - 4 = -4 + (-4) = -8$

23. $0 - 7 = 0 + (-7) = -7$

25. $8 - 8 = 8 + (-8) = 0$

27. $-3 - 1 = -3 + (-1) = -4$

29. $5 - 3 = 5 + (-3) = 2$

31. $6 - (-3) = 6 + 3 = 9$

33. $0 - (-5) = 0 + 5 = 5$

35. $-9 - 11 = -9 + (-11) = -20$

37. $(-4) - (-4) = -4 + 4 = 0$

39. $-8 - (-12) = -8 + 12 = 4$

41. $-6 - (-2) = -6 + 2 = -4$

43. $-9 - 2 = -9 + (-2) = -11$

45. $-35 - (-8) = -35 + 8 = -27$

47. $-90 - 60 = -90 + (-60) = -150$

49. $-45 - 37 = -45 + (-37) = -82$

51. $70 - (-70) = 70 + 70 = 140$

53. $42.3 - 49.7 = 42.3 + (-49.7) = -7.4$

55. $-7.85 - (-3.92) = -7.85 + 3.92 = -3.93$

57. $-20 - 9 = -20 + (-9) = -29$

59. $-8 - 8 = -8 + (-8) = -16$

61. $-5 - (-3) = -5 + 3 = -2$

63. $9 - (-4) = 9 + 4 = 13$

65. $13 - 24 = 13 + (-24) = -11$

67. $-6.3 - (-12.4) = -6.3 + 12.4 = 6.1$

69. $\dfrac{4}{5} - \dfrac{5}{6} = \dfrac{24}{30} - \dfrac{25}{30} = \dfrac{24 - 25}{30} = -\dfrac{1}{30}$

71. $\dfrac{8}{15} - \dfrac{7}{45} = \dfrac{24}{45} - \dfrac{7}{45} = \dfrac{24 - 7}{45} = \dfrac{17}{45}$

73. $-\dfrac{1}{4} - \dfrac{2}{3} = -\dfrac{3}{12} - \dfrac{8}{12} = \dfrac{-3 - 8}{12} = -\dfrac{11}{12}$

75. $-\dfrac{4}{15} - \dfrac{3}{20} = -\dfrac{16}{60} - \dfrac{9}{60} = \dfrac{-16 - 9}{60} =$
$-\dfrac{25}{60} = -\dfrac{5}{12}$

77. $\dfrac{3}{8} - \dfrac{6}{48} = \dfrac{18}{48} - \dfrac{6}{48} = \dfrac{18 - 6}{48} = \dfrac{12}{48} = \dfrac{1}{4}$

79. $-\dfrac{7}{12} - \dfrac{5}{40} = -\dfrac{70}{120} - \dfrac{15}{120} = \dfrac{-70 - 15}{120}$
$= -\dfrac{85}{120} = -\dfrac{17}{24}$

81. $\dfrac{3}{16} - \left(-\dfrac{5}{8}\right) = \dfrac{3}{16} + \dfrac{10}{16} = \dfrac{3 + 10}{16} = \dfrac{13}{16}$

83. $-\dfrac{5}{12} - \left(-\dfrac{3}{8}\right) = -\dfrac{10}{24} + \dfrac{9}{24} = \dfrac{-10 + 9}{24} = -\dfrac{1}{24}$

85. $\dfrac{4}{7} - \dfrac{7}{9} = \dfrac{36}{63} - \dfrac{49}{63} = \dfrac{36 - 49}{63} = -\dfrac{13}{63}$

87. $-\dfrac{5}{12} - \left(-\dfrac{3}{10}\right) = -\dfrac{25}{60} + \dfrac{18}{60} = \dfrac{-25 + 18}{60} = -\dfrac{7}{60}$

89. a. Positive; $378 - 279 = 378 + (-279)$
|378| is greater than |-279| so the sum will be positive.

   b. $378 + (-279) = 99$

   c. Yes; by part a) we expect a positive sum. The size of the sum is the difference between the absolute values of the 2 numbers.

91. a. Negative; $-482 - 137 = -482 + (-137)$
The sum of 2 negative numbers is always negative.

   b. $-482 + (-137) = -619$

   c. Yes; the sum of two negative numbers should be (and is) a larger negative number.

93. a. Positive; $843 - (-745) = 843 + 745$.
The sum of 2 positive numbers is always positive.

   b. $843 + 745 = 1588$

   c. Yes; by part a) we expect a positive answer. The size of the sum is the sum of the absolute values of the numbers.

95. a. Positive; $-408 - (-604) = -408 + 604$.
|604| is greater than |−408| so the sum will be positive.

   b. $-408 + 604 = 196$

   c. Yes; by part a) we expect a positive answer. The size of the answer is the difference between the larger and smaller absolute values.

97. a. Negative; $-1024 - (-576) = -1024 + 576$.
|−1024| is greater than |576| so the sum will be negative.

   b. $-1024 + 576 = -448$

   c. Yes; by part a) we expect a negative answer. The size of the answer is the difference between the larger and the smaller absolute values.

99. a. Positive; $165.7 - 49.6 = 165.7 + (-49.6)$.
|165.7| is greater than |−49.6| so the sum will be positive.

   b. $165.7 + (-49.6) = 116.1$

c. Yes; by part a) we expect a negative answer. The size of the answer is the difference between the larger and the smaller absolute values.

101. a. Negative; $295 - 364 = 295 + (-364)$.
Since $|-364|$ is greater than $|295|$ the answer will be negative.

b. $295 + (-364) = -69$

c. Yes; by part a) we expect a negative answer. The size of the answer is the difference between the larger and the smaller absolute values.

103. a. Negative; $-1023 - 647 = -1023 + (-647)$. The sum of two negative numbers is always negative.

b. $-1023 + (-647) = -1670$

c. Yes; the sum of two negative numbers should be (and is) a larger negative number.

105. a. Zero; $-7.62 - (-7.62) = -7.62 + 7.62$. The sum of two opposite numbers is always zero.

b. $-7.62 + 7.62 = 0$

c. Yes; by part a) we expect zero.

107. $7 + 5 - (+8) = 7 + 5 + (-8) = 12 + (-8) = 4$

109. $-6 + (-6) + 6 = -12 + 6 = -6$

111. $-13 - (+5) + 3 = -13 + (-5) + 3 = -18 + 3 = -15$

113. $-9 - (-3) + 4 = -9 + 3 + 4 = -6 + 4 = -2$

115. $5 - (-9) + (-1) = 5 + 9 + (-1) = 14 + (-1) = 13$

117. $17 + (-8) - (+14) = 17 + (-8) + (-14)$
$$= 9 + (-14)$$
$$= -5$$

119. $-36 - 5 + 9 = -36 + (-5) + 9 = -41 + 9 = -32$

121. $-2 + 7 - 9 = -2 + 7 + (-9) = 5 + (-9) = -4$

123. $25 - 19 + 3 = 25 + (-19) + 3 = 6 + 3 = 9$

125. $(-4) + (-6) + 5 - 7 = (-4) + (-6) + 5 + (-7)$
$$= -10 + 5 + (-7)$$
$$= -5 + (-7)$$
$$= -12$$

127. $17 + (-3) - 9 - (-7) = 17 + (-3) + (-9) + 7$
$$= 14 + (-9) + 7$$
$$= 5 + 7$$
$$= 12$$

129. $-9 + (-7) + (-5) - (-3) = -9 + (-7) + (-5) + 3$
$$= -16 + (-5) + 3$$
$$= -21 + 3$$
$$= -18$$

131. a. $300 - 343 = 300 + (-343) = -43$
They had 43 sweaters on back order.

b. $43 + 100 = 143$
They would need to order 143 sweaters.

133. $42 - 58 = 42 + (-58) = -16$
The bottom of the well is 16 feet below sea level.

135. $44 - (-56) = 44 + 56 = 100$
Thus the temperature dropped 100°F.

137. a. $288 + (-12) = 276$
In 2002, his score was 276.

b. $-12 - (-4) = -12 + 4 = -8$
He had 8 strokes less in 2002 than in 2000.

c. 2000 stroke score: $288 + (-4) = 284$
2001 stroke score: $288 + (-16) = 272$
2002 stroke score: $288 + (-12) = 276$

Average $= \dfrac{284 + 272 + 276}{3} = \dfrac{832}{3} \approx 277.33$

His average stroke score was 277.33.

139. $1 - 2 + 3 - 4 + 5 - 6 + 7 - 8 + 9 - 10$
$$= (1 - 2) + (3 - 4) + (5 - 6) + (7 - 8) + (9 - 10)$$
$$= (-1) + (-1) + (-1) + (-1) + (-1)$$
$$= -5$$

141. a. 7 units

b. $5 - (-2) = 7$

143. a. $3 + 2 + 2 + 1 + 1 = 9$
The ball travels 9 feet vertically.

b. $-3 + 2 + (-2) + 1 + (-1) = -3$
The net distance is –3 feet.

144. The integers are $\{\ldots, -2, -1, 0, 1, 2, \ldots\}$.

145. The set of rational numbers together with the set of irrational numbers forms the set of real numbers.

146. $|-3| > -5$ since $|-3| = 3$

147. $|-6| < |-7|$ since $|-6| = 6$ and $|-7| = 7$

148. $\dfrac{4}{5} - \dfrac{3}{8} = \dfrac{32}{40} - \dfrac{15}{40} = \dfrac{32-15}{40} = \dfrac{17}{40}$

Exercise Set 1.8

1. Like signs: product is positive. Unlike signs: product is negative.

3. The product of 0 and any real number is 0

5. A fraction of the form $\dfrac{a}{-b}$ is generally written $-\dfrac{a}{b}$ or $\dfrac{-a}{b}$.

7. a. With $3 - 5$ you subtract, but with $3(-5)$ you multiply.

    b. $3 - 5 = 3 + (-5) = -2$
       $3(-5) = -15$

9. a. With $x - y$ you subtract, but with $x(-y)$ you multiply.

    b. $x - y = 5 - (-2) = 5 + 2 = 7$

    c. $x(-y) = [-(-2)] = 5(2) = 10$

    d. $-x - y = -5 - (-2) = -5 + 2 = -3$

11. The product $(8)(4)(-5)$ is negative since there is an odd number (1) of negatives

13. The product $(-102)(-16)(24)(19)$ is positive since there is an even number of negatives.

15. The product $(-40)(-16)(30)(50)(-13)$ is negative since there is an odd number (3) of negatives.

17. Since the numbers have like signs, the product is positive. $(-5)(-4) = 20$

19. Since the number have unlike signs, the product is negative. $6(-3) = -18$

21. Since the numbers have unlike signs, the product is negative. $(-2)(4) = -8$

23. Zero multiplied by any real number equals zero. $0(-5) = 0$

25. Since the numbers have like signs, the product is positive. $6(7) = 42$

27. Since the numbers have unlike signs, the product is negative. $(7)(-8) = -56$

29. Since the numbers have like signs, the product is positive. $(-5)(-6) = 30$

31. Zero multiplied by any real number equals zero. $0(3)(8) = 0(8) = 0$

33. Since there is one negative number (an odd number), the product will be negative. $(21)(-1)(4) = (-21)(4) = -84$

35. Since there are three negative numbers (an odd number), the product will be negative. $-1(-3)(3)(-8) = 3(3)(-8) = 9(-8) = -72$

37. Since there are two negative numbers (an even number), the product will be positive. $(-4)(5)(-7)(1) = (-20)(-7)(1) = (140)(1) = 140$

39. Zero multiplied by any real number equals zero. $(-1)(3)(0)(-7) = (-3)(0)(-7) = 0(-7) = 0$

41. $\left(\dfrac{-1}{2}\right)\left(\dfrac{3}{5}\right) = \dfrac{(-1)(3)}{2 \cdot 5} = \dfrac{-3}{10} = -\dfrac{3}{10}$

43. $\left(\dfrac{-5}{9}\right)\left(\dfrac{-7}{15}\right) = \dfrac{(-5)(-7)}{9 \cdot 15} = \dfrac{(-1)(-7)}{9 \cdot 3} = \dfrac{7}{27}$

45. $\left(\dfrac{6}{-3}\right)\left(\dfrac{4}{-2}\right) = \left(\dfrac{2}{-1}\right)\left(\dfrac{2}{-1}\right) = \dfrac{(2)(2)}{(-1)(-1)} = \dfrac{4}{1} = 4$

47. $\left(\dfrac{-3}{8}\right)\left(\dfrac{5}{6}\right) = \left(\dfrac{-1}{8}\right)\left(\dfrac{5}{2}\right) = \dfrac{(-1)(5)}{(8)(2)} = \dfrac{-5}{16} = -\dfrac{5}{16}$

49. Since the numbers have like signs, the quotient is positive. $\dfrac{10}{5} = 2$

51. Since the numbers have like signs, the quotient is positive. $-16 \div (-4) = \dfrac{-16}{-4} = 4$

53. Since the numbers have like signs, the quotient is positive. $\dfrac{-36}{-9} = 4$

55. Since the numbers have unlike signs, the quotient is negative. $\dfrac{36}{-2} = -18$

57. Since the numbers have like signs, the quotient is positive. $\dfrac{-12}{-1} = 12$

59. Since the numbers have unlike signs, the quotient is negative. $40/(-4) = \dfrac{40}{-4} = -10$

61. Since the numbers have unlike signs, the quotient is negative. $\dfrac{-42}{7} = -6$

63. Since the numbers have unlike signs, the quotient is negative. $\dfrac{36}{-4} = -9$

65. Since the numbers have like signs, the quotient is positive. $-64 \div (-8) = \dfrac{-64}{-8} = 8$

67. Zero divided by any nonzero number is zero. $\dfrac{0}{4} = 0$

69. Since the numbers have unlike signs, the quotient is negative. $\dfrac{30}{-10} = -3$

71. Since the numbers have unlike signs, the quotient is negative. $\dfrac{-120}{30} = -4$

73. $\dfrac{3}{12} \div \left(\dfrac{-5}{8}\right) = \dfrac{3}{12} \cdot \left(\dfrac{8}{-5}\right)$
$= \dfrac{1}{1} \cdot \left(\dfrac{2}{-5}\right)$
$= \dfrac{1 \cdot 2}{1(-5)}$
$= \dfrac{2}{-5}$
$= -\dfrac{2}{5}$

75. $\dfrac{-5}{12} \div (-3) = \dfrac{-5}{12} \cdot \dfrac{1}{-3} = \dfrac{-5(1)}{12(-3)} = \dfrac{-5}{-36} = \dfrac{5}{36}$

77. $\dfrac{-15}{21} \div \left(\dfrac{-15}{21}\right) = \dfrac{-15}{21} \cdot \dfrac{21}{-15}$
$= \dfrac{-1}{1} \cdot \dfrac{1}{-1}$
$= \dfrac{(-1)(1)}{(1)(-1)}$
$= \dfrac{-1}{-1}$
$= 1$

79. $-12 \div \dfrac{5}{12} = \dfrac{-12}{1} \cdot \dfrac{12}{5}$
$= \dfrac{(-12)(12)}{(1)(5)}$
$= \dfrac{-144}{5}$
$= -\dfrac{144}{5}$

81. Since the numbers have unlike signs, the product is negative. $-4(8) = -32$

83. Since the numbers have unlike signs, the quotient is negative. $\dfrac{100}{-5} = -20$

85. Since the numbers have unlike signs, the product is negative. $-7(2) = -14$

87. Since the numbers have unlike signs, the quotient is negative. $27 \div (-3) = \dfrac{27}{-3} = -9$

89. Since the numbers have unlike signs, the quotient is negative. $\dfrac{-100}{5} = -20$

91. Since the numbers have unlike signs, the quotient is negative. $\dfrac{60}{-60} = -1$

93. Zero divided by any nonzero number is zero. $0 \div 6 = \dfrac{0}{6} = 0$

95. Any nonzero number divided by zero is undefined. $\dfrac{5}{0}$ is undefined.

97. Zero divided by any nonzero number is zero. $\dfrac{0}{1} = 0$

99. Any nonzero number divided by zero is undefined. $\dfrac{8}{0}$ is undefined.

101. a. Since the numbers have unlike signs, the product will be negative.

  b. $92(-38) = -3496$

  c. Yes; as expected the product is negative.

103. a. Since the numbers have unlike signs, the quotient will be negative.

  b. $-240 / 15 = \dfrac{-240}{15} = -16$

  c. Yes; as expected the quotient is negative.

105. a. Since the numbers have unlike signs, the quotient will be negative.

  b. $243 \div (-27) = \dfrac{243}{-27} = -9$

  c. Yes; as expected the quotient is negative.

107. a. Since the numbers have like signs, the product will be positive.

  b. $(-49)(-126) = 6174$

  c. Yes; as expected the product is positive.

109. a. The quotient will be zero; zero divided by any nonzero number is zero.

  b. $\dfrac{0}{5335} = 0$

  c. Yes; as expected the answer is zero.

111. a. Undefined; any nonzero number divided by 0 is undefined.

  b. $7.2 \div 0 = \dfrac{7.2}{0}$ is undefined

  c. Yes; as expected the quotient is undefined.

113. a. Since the numbers have like signs, the quotient will be positive.

  b. $8 \div 2.5 = \dfrac{8}{2.5} = 3.2$

  c. Yes; as expected the quotient is positive.

115. a. Since there are two negative numbers (an even number), the product will be positive.

  b. $(-3.0)(4.2)(-18) = 226.8$

  c. Yes; as expected the product is positive.

117. False; the product of two numbers with like signs is a positive number

119. False; the quotient of two numbers with unlike signs is a negative number.

121. True

123. False; zero divided by any nonzero number is zero.

125. False; zero divided by 1 is zero.

127. True

129. $4(-15) = -60$
The total loss was 60 yards.

131. a. $\dfrac{1}{3}(450) = \dfrac{450}{3} = 150$
She paid back $150.

  b. $-450 + 150 = -300$
Her new balance is $-\$300$.

133. $3\left(-1\dfrac{1}{2}\right) = \dfrac{3}{1}\left(-\dfrac{3}{2}\right) = -\dfrac{9}{2}$ or $-4\dfrac{1}{2}$
It has lost $4\dfrac{1}{2}$ points.

135. a. $\dfrac{\text{change in October}}{\text{change in September}} = \dfrac{-415,000}{-200,000} \approx 2.075$
The change in October was about 2.075 times larger than in September.

  b. $\dfrac{\text{change in October}}{\text{change in July}} = \dfrac{-415,000}{-50,000} \approx 8.3$
The change in October was about 8.3 times larger than in July.

  d. You get an error message.

137. a. $220 - 50 = 170$
60% of $170 = 0.6(170) = 102$
75% of $170 = 0.75(170) = 127.5$
Target heart rate is 102 to 128 beats per minute.

  b. Answers will vary.

139. $(-2)^3 = (-2)(-2)(-2) = 4(-2) = -8$

141. $1^{100} = 1$

143. The product $(-1)(-2)(-3)(-4)\cdots(-10)$ will be positive because there are an even number (10) of negative numbers.

145. The country will start with D. Most students will select Denmark. They will most likely select kangaroo which leads to orange.

146. $\dfrac{5}{7} \div \dfrac{1}{5} = \dfrac{5}{7} \cdot \dfrac{5}{1} = \dfrac{5 \cdot 5}{7 \cdot 1} = \dfrac{25}{7}$ or $3\dfrac{4}{7}$

147. $-20 - (-18) = -20 + 18 = -2$

148. $6 - 3 - 4 - 2 = 3 - 4 - 2 = -1 - 2 = -3$

149. $\begin{aligned} 5 - (-2) + 3 - 7 &= 5 + 2 + 3 - 7 \\ &= 7 + 3 - 7 \\ &= 10 - 7 \\ &= 3 \end{aligned}$

150. $-40 \div (-8) = 5$

Exercise Set 1.9

1. In the expression a^b, a is the base and b is the exponent.

3. a. Every number has an understood exponent of 1.

    b. In $5x^3y^2z$, 5 has exponent of 1, x has an exponent of 3, y has an exponent of 2, and z has an exponent of 1.

5. a. $x + x + x + x + x = 5x$

    b. $x \cdot x \cdot x \cdot x \cdot x = x^5$

7. The order of operations are parentheses, exponents, multiplication or division, then addition or subtraction.

9. No; $4 + 5 \times 2 = 4 + 10 = 14$, on a scientific calculator.

11. a. $20 \div 5 - 3 = 4 - 3 = 1$

    b. $20 \div (5 - 3) = 20 \div 2 = 10$

    c. The keystrokes in b) are used since the fraction bar is a grouping symbol.

13. b. $\begin{aligned} \left[10 - (16 \div 4)\right]^2 - 6^3 &= \left[10 - 4\right]^2 - 6^3 \\ &= 6^2 - 6^3 \\ &= 36 - 216 \\ &= -180 \end{aligned}$

15. b. When $x = 5$:
$$\begin{aligned} -4x^2 + 3x - 6 &= -4(5)^2 + 3(5) - 6 \\ &= -4(25) + 3(5) - 6 \\ &= -100 + 15 - 6 \\ &= -85 - 6 \\ &= -91 \end{aligned}$$

17. $5^2 = 5 \cdot 5 = 25$

19. $1^7 = 1 \cdot 1 \cdot 1 \cdot 1 \cdot 1 \cdot 1 \cdot 1 = 1$

21. $-5^2 = -(5)(5) = -25$

23. $(-3)^2 = (-3)(-3) = 9$

25. $(-1)^3 = (-1)(-1)(-1) = -1$

27. $(-9)^2 = (-9)(-9) = 81$

29. $(-6)^2 = (-6)(-6) = 36$

31. $4^1 = 4$

33. $(-4)^4 = (-4)(-4)(-4)(-4) = 256$

35. $-2^4 = -(2)(2)(2)(2) = -16$

37. $\left(\dfrac{3}{4}\right)^2 = \dfrac{3}{4} \cdot \dfrac{3}{4} = \dfrac{9}{16}$

39. $\left(-\dfrac{1}{2}\right)^5 = \left(-\dfrac{1}{2}\right)\left(-\dfrac{1}{2}\right)\left(-\dfrac{1}{2}\right)\left(-\dfrac{1}{2}\right)\left(-\dfrac{1}{2}\right) = -\dfrac{1}{32}$

41. $5^2 \cdot 3^2 = 5 \cdot 5 \cdot 3 \cdot 3 = 225$

43. $4^3 \cdot 3^2 = 4 \cdot 4 \cdot 4 \cdot 3 \cdot 3 = 576$

45. a. Positive; a positive number raised to any power is positive.

    b. $7^3 = 343$

    c. Yes; as expected the answer is positive.

47. a. Positive; a positive number raised to any power is positive.

b. $5^4 = 625$

c. Yes; as expected the answer is positive.

49. a. Negative; a negative number raised to an odd power is negative.

b. $(-3)^5 = -243$

c. Yes; as expected the answer is negative.

51. a. Positive; a negative number raised to an even power is positive.

b. $(-5)^4 = 625$

c. Yes; as expected the answer is positive.

53. a. Positive; a positive number raised to any power is positive.

b. $(4.6)^4 = 447.7456$

c. Yes; as expected the answer is positive.

55. a. Negative; $\left(\dfrac{7}{8}\right)^2$ is positive therefore,

$-\left(\dfrac{7}{8}\right)^2$ is negative.

b. $-\left(\dfrac{7}{8}\right)^2 = -0.765625$

c. Yes; as expected the answer is negative.

57. $3 + 2 \cdot 6 = 3 + 12 = 15$

59. $6 - 6 + 8 = 0 + 8 = 8$

61. $1 + 3 \cdot 2^2 = 1 + 3 \cdot 4 = 1 + 12 = 13$

63. $-3^3 + 27 = -27 + 27 = 0$

65. $(4 - 3) \cdot (5 - 1)^2 = (1) \cdot (4)^2 = 1 \cdot 16 = 16$

67. $3 \cdot 7 + 4 \cdot 2 = 21 + 8 = 29$

69. $5 - 2(7 + 5) = 5 - 2(12) = 5 - 24 = -19$

71. $-32 - 5(7 - 10)^2 = -32 - 5(-3)^2 = -32 - 5(9) = -32 - 45 = -77$

73. $\dfrac{3}{4} + 2\left(\dfrac{1}{5}\right)^2 = \dfrac{3}{4} + 2\left(\dfrac{1}{25}\right) = \dfrac{3}{4} + \dfrac{2}{25} =$

$\dfrac{75}{100} + \dfrac{8}{100} = \dfrac{83}{100}$

75. $4^2 - 3 \cdot 4 - 6 = 16 - 3 \cdot 4 - 6$
$= 16 - 12 - 6$
$= 4 - 6$
$= -2$

77. $(6 \div 3)^3 + 4^2 \div 8 = (2)^3 + 4^2 \div 8$
$= 8 + 16 \div 8$
$= 8 + 2$
$= 10$

79. $\left[-8(-2 + 5)\right]^2 = \left[-8(3)\right]^2$
$= (-24)^2$
$= 576$

81. $(3^2 - 1) \div (3 + 1)^2 = (9 - 1) \div (3 + 1)^2$
$= 8 \div (4)^2$
$= 8 \div 16$
$= \dfrac{8}{16}$
$= \dfrac{1}{2}$

83. $[4 + ((5 - 2)^2 \div 3)^2]^2 = [4 + ((3)^2 \div 3)^2]^2$
$= [4 + (9 \div 3)^2]^2$
$= [4 + (3)^2]^2$
$= [4 + 9]^2$
$= (13)^2$
$= 169$

85. $2.5 + 7.56 \div 2.1 + (9.2)^2$
$= 2.5 + 7.56 \div 2.1 + 84.64$
$= 2.5 + 3.6 + 84.64$
$= 6.1 + 84.64$
$= 90.74$

87. $2\left[1.55 + 5(3.7)\right] - 3.35 = 2[1.55 + 18.5] - 3.35$
$= 2(20.05) - 3.35$
$= 40.1 - 3.35$
$= 36.75$

89. $\left(\dfrac{2}{5}+\dfrac{3}{8}\right)-\dfrac{3}{20}=\left(\dfrac{16}{40}+\dfrac{15}{40}\right)-\dfrac{3}{20}$

$$=\dfrac{31}{40}-\dfrac{3}{20}$$

$$=\dfrac{31}{40}-\dfrac{6}{40}$$

$$=\dfrac{25}{40}=\dfrac{5}{8}$$

91. $\dfrac{3}{4}-4\cdot\dfrac{5}{40}=\dfrac{3}{4}-\dfrac{4}{1}\cdot\dfrac{5}{40}=\dfrac{3}{4}-\dfrac{4}{8}=\dfrac{3}{4}-\dfrac{2}{4}=\dfrac{1}{4}$

93. $\dfrac{4}{5}+\dfrac{3}{4}\div\dfrac{1}{2}-\dfrac{2}{3}=\dfrac{4}{5}+\dfrac{3}{4}\cdot\dfrac{2}{1}-\dfrac{2}{3}$

$$=\dfrac{4}{5}+\dfrac{3}{2}-\dfrac{2}{3}$$

$$=\dfrac{24}{30}+\dfrac{45}{30}-\dfrac{20}{30}$$

$$=\dfrac{49}{30}$$

95. $\dfrac{5-[3(6\div3)-2]}{5^2-4^2\div2}=\dfrac{5-[3(2)-2]}{25-16\div2}$

$$=\dfrac{5-[6-2]}{25-8}$$

$$=\dfrac{5-4}{25-8}$$

$$=\dfrac{1}{17}$$

97. $\dfrac{-[4-(6-12)^2]}{[(9\div3)+4]^2+2^2}=\dfrac{-[4-(-6)^2]}{(3+4)^2+4}$

$$=\dfrac{-[4-36]}{7^2+4}$$

$$=\dfrac{-(-32)}{49+4}$$

$$=\dfrac{32}{53}$$

99. $\left\{5-2[4-(6\div2)]^2\right\}^2=\left\{5-2[4-3]^2\right\}^2$

$$=\left\{5-2(1)^2\right\}^2$$

$$=\left\{5-2(1)\right\}^2$$

$$=\left\{5-2\right\}^2$$

$$=(3)^2$$

$$=9$$

101. $-\left\{4-[-3-(2-5)]^2\right\}=-\left\{4-[-3-(-3)]^2\right\}$

$$=-\left\{4-[-3+3]^2\right\}$$

$$=-\left\{4-[0]^2\right\}$$

$$=-\left\{4-0\right\}$$

$$=-(4)$$

$$=-4$$

103. Substitute 3 for x

 a. $x^2=3^2=3\cdot3=9$

 b. $-x^2=-3^2=-(3)(3)=-9$

 c. $(-x)^2=(-3)^2=(-3)(-3)=9$

105. Substitute -4 for x

 a. $x^2=(-4)^2=(-4)(-4)=16$

 b. $-x^2=-(-4)^2=-(-4)(-4)=-(16)=-16$

 c. $(-x)^2=4^2=4\cdot4=16$

107. Substitute 6 for x

 a. $x^2=6^2=6\cdot6=36$

 b. $-x^2=-6^2=-(6\cdot6)=-36$

 c. $(-x)^2=(-6)^2=(-6)(-6)=36$

109. Substitute $-\dfrac{1}{3}$ for x

 a. $x^2=\left(-\dfrac{1}{3}\right)^2=\left(-\dfrac{1}{3}\right)\left(-\dfrac{1}{3}\right)=\dfrac{1}{9}$

 b. $-x^2=-\left(-\dfrac{1}{3}\right)^2=-\left(-\dfrac{1}{3}\right)\left(-\dfrac{1}{3}\right)=-\dfrac{1}{9}$

 c. $(-x)^2=\left(\dfrac{1}{3}\right)^2=\left(\dfrac{1}{3}\right)\left(\dfrac{1}{3}\right)=\dfrac{1}{9}$

111. Substitute -2 for x in the expression.
 $x+6=-2+6=4$

113. Substitute 4 for z in the expression.
$$5z - 2 = 5(4) - 2 = 20 - 2 = 18$$

115. Substitute -3 for a in the expression.
$$a^2 - 6 = (-3)^2 - 6 = 9 - 6 = 3$$

117. Substitute -1 for each x in the expression.
$$-4x^2 - 2x + 1 = -4(-1)^2 - 2(-1) + 1$$
$$= -4(1) - 2(-1) + 1$$
$$= -4 + 2 + 1$$
$$= -2 + 1$$
$$= -1$$

119. Substitute 2 for each p in the expression.
$$3p^2 - 6p - 4 = 3(2)^2 - 6(2) - 4$$
$$= 3(4) - 12 - 4$$
$$= 12 - 12 - 4$$
$$= 0 - 4$$
$$= -4$$

121. Substitute $\frac{1}{2}$ for each x in the expression.
$$-x^2 - 2x + 5 = -(\tfrac{1}{2})^2 - 2(\tfrac{1}{2}) + 5$$
$$= -\frac{1}{4} - 1 + 5$$
$$= -\frac{1}{4} - \frac{4}{4} + \frac{20}{4}$$
$$= -\frac{5}{4} + \frac{20}{4}$$
$$= \frac{15}{4}$$

123. Substitute 5 for each x in the expression.
$$4(3x + 1)^2 - 6x = 4(3(5) + 1)^2 - 6(5)$$
$$= 4(15 + 1)^2 - 30$$
$$= 4(16)^2 - 30$$
$$= 4(256) - 30$$
$$= 1024 - 30$$
$$= 994$$

125. Substitute 3 for s and 4 for t in the expression.
$$-3s + 2t = -3(3) + 2(4) = -9 + 8 = -1$$

127. Substitute -2 for r and -3 for s in the expression.
$$r^2 - s^2 = (-2)^2 - (-3)^2 = 4 - 9 = -5$$

129. Substitute 2 for x and -3 for y in the expression.
$$2(x + 2y) + 4x - 3y = 2[2 + 2(-3)] + 4(2) - 3(-3)$$
$$= 2(2 + (-6)) + 8 - (-9)$$
$$= 2(-4) + 8 + 9$$
$$= -8 + 8 + 9$$
$$= 0 + 9$$
$$= 9$$

131. Substitute 2 for x and -3 for y in the expression.
$$6x^2 + 3xy - y^2 = 6(2)^2 + 3(2)(-3) - (-3)^2$$
$$= 6(4) + 3(2)(-3) - 9$$
$$= 24 + (-18) - 9$$
$$= 6 - 9$$
$$= -3$$

133. $6 \cdot 3$ Multiply 6 by 3
$(6 \cdot 3) - 4$ Subtract 4 from the product
$[(6 \cdot 3) - 4] - 2$ Subtract 2 from the difference
Evaluate:
$$[(6 \cdot 3) - 4] - 2 = [18 - 4] - 2 = 14 - 2 = 12$$

135. $18 \div 3$ Divide 18 by 3
$(18 \div 3) + 9$ Add 9 to the quotient
$[(18 \div 3) + 9] - 8$ Subtract 8 from the sum
$9\{[(18 \div 3) + 9] - 8\}$ Multiply the difference by 9
Evaluate:
$$9\{[(18 \div 3) + 9]\} - 8 = 9\{[6 + 9] - 8\}$$
$$= 9[15 - 8]$$
$$= 9(7)$$
$$= 63$$

137. $\frac{4}{5} + \frac{3}{7}$ Add $\frac{4}{5}$ to $\frac{3}{7}$
$\left(\frac{4}{5} + \frac{3}{7}\right) \cdot \frac{2}{3}$ Multiply the sum by $\frac{2}{3}$
Evaluate:
$$\left(\frac{4}{5} + \frac{3}{7}\right) \cdot \frac{2}{3} = \left(\frac{28}{35} + \frac{15}{35}\right) \cdot \frac{2}{3}$$
$$= \left(\frac{43}{35}\right) \cdot \left(\frac{2}{3}\right)$$
$$= \frac{86}{105}$$

139. $-\left(x^2\right) = -x^2$ is true for all real numbers.

141. When $d = 15.99$, $0.07d = 0.07(15.99) \approx 1.12$. The sales tax is $1.12.

143. When $d = 15,000$,
$$d + 0.07d = 15,000 + 0.07(15,000)$$
$$= 15,000 + 1050$$
$$= 16,050$$
The total cost is $16,050.

145. a. $2 \div 5^2 = 2 \div 25 = 0.08$

b. $(2 \div 5)^2 = (0.4)^2 = 0.16$

147. When $R = 2$ and $T = 70$,
$$0.2R^2 + 0.003RT + 0.0001T^2$$
$$= 0.02(2)^2 + 0.003(2)(70) + 0.0001(70)^2$$
$$= 0.2(4) + 0.003(2)(70) + 0.0001(4900)$$
$$= 0.8 + 0.42 + 0.49 = 1.71$$
The growth is 1.71 inches.

149. $12 - (4 - 6) + 10 = 24$

155. a. There are 4 houses with 3 occupants.

b.

Occupants	Number of Houses
1	3
2	5
3	4
4	6
5	2

c. $3(1) + 5(2) + 4(3) + 6(4) + 2(5)$
$$= 3 + 10 + 12 + 24 + 10$$
$$= 13 + 12 + 24 + 10$$
$$= 25 + 24 + 10$$
$$= 49 + 10$$
$$= 59$$
There are 59 occupants in all.

d. Number of houses $= 3 + 5 + 4 + 6 + 2$
$$= 8 + 4 + 6 + 2$$
$$= 12 + 6 + 2$$
$$= 18 + 2$$
$$= 20$$
$$\text{mean} = \frac{\text{number of occupants}}{\text{number of houses}} = \frac{59}{20} = 2.95$$
There is a mean of 2.95 people per house.

156. $3 = \dfrac{6}{2} = \dfrac{1}{2} + \dfrac{5}{2} = \dfrac{1}{2} + \dfrac{20}{8}$
Cost $= \$2.40 + 20(0.20) = \$2.40 + \$4.00 = \$6.40$

157. $(-2)(-4)(6)(-1)(-3) = (8)(6)(-1)(-3)$
$$= (48)(-1)(-3)$$
$$= (-48)(-3)$$
$$= 144$$

158. $\left(\dfrac{-5}{7}\right) \div \left(\dfrac{-3}{14}\right) = \left(\dfrac{-5}{7}\right) \cdot \left(\dfrac{14}{-3}\right)$
$$= \dfrac{-5}{1} \cdot \dfrac{2}{-3}$$
$$= \dfrac{(-5)(2)}{(1)(-3)}$$
$$= \dfrac{10}{3} \text{ or } 3\dfrac{1}{3}$$

Exercise Set 1.10

1. The commutative property of addition states that the sum of two numbers is the same regardless of the order in which they are added. One possible example is $3 + 4 = 4 + 3$.

3. The associative property of addition states that the sum of 3 numbers is the same regardless of the way the numbers are grouped. One possible example is $(2 + 3) + 4 = 2 + (3 + 4)$.

5. a. In $x + (y + z)$ the sum of y and z is added to x whereas in $x(y + z)$, x is multiplied by the sum.

b. When $x = 4$, $y = 5$, and $z = 6$,
$$x + (y + z) = 4 + (5 + 6) = 4 + 11 = 15.$$

c. When $x = 4$, $y = 5$, and $z = 6$,
$$x(y + z) = 4(5 + 6) = 4(11) = 44.$$

7. The associative property involves changing parentheses with one operation whereas the distributive property involves distributing a multiplication over an addition.

9. 0

11. a. -6 **b.** $\dfrac{1}{6}$

13. a. 3 **b.** $-\dfrac{1}{3}$

15. a. $-x$ **b.** $\dfrac{1}{x}$

17. a. -1.6 **b.** $\dfrac{1}{1.6}$ or 0.625

19. a. $-\dfrac{1}{5}$ **b.** 5

21. a. $\dfrac{3}{5}$ **b.** $-\dfrac{5}{3}$

23. Associative property of addition

25. Distributive property

27. Commutative property of multiplication

29. Associative property of multiplication

31. Distributive property

33. Identity property for addition

35. Inverse property for multiplication

37. $6 + x$

39. $(-6 \cdot 4) \cdot 2$

41. $x + y$

43. $y \cdot x$

45. $3y + 4x$

47. $a + (b + 3)$

49. $3x + (4 + 6)$

51. $(m + n)3$

53. $4x + 4y + 12$

55. 0

57. $\dfrac{5}{2}n$

59. Yes; the order does not affect the outcome so the process is commutative.

61. No; the order affects the outcome, so the process is not commutative.

63. No; the order affects the outcome, so the process is not commutative.

65. Yes; the outcome is not affected by whether you do the first two items first or the last two first, so the process is associative.

67. No; the outcome is affected by whether you do the first two items first or the last two first, so the process is not associative.

69. No; the outcome is affected by whether you do the first two items first or the last two first, so the process is not associative.

71. In $(3 + 4) + x = x + (3 + 4)$ the $(3 + 4)$ is treated as one value.

73. This illustrates the commutative property of addition because the change is $3 + 5 = 5 + 3$.

75. No; it illustrates the associative property of addition since the grouping is changed.

77. $2\dfrac{3}{5} + \dfrac{2}{3}$

$2\dfrac{3}{5} = \dfrac{13}{5} = \dfrac{3}{3} \cdot \dfrac{13}{5} = \dfrac{39}{15}$

$\dfrac{2}{3} = \dfrac{2}{3} \cdot \dfrac{5}{5} = \dfrac{10}{15}$

$2\dfrac{3}{5} + \dfrac{2}{3} = \dfrac{39}{15} + \dfrac{10}{15} = \dfrac{49}{15}$ or $3\dfrac{4}{15}$

78. $3\dfrac{5}{8} - 2\dfrac{3}{16}$

$3\dfrac{5}{8} = \dfrac{29}{8} = \dfrac{2}{2} \cdot \dfrac{29}{8} = \dfrac{58}{16}$

$2\dfrac{3}{16} = \dfrac{35}{16}$

$3\dfrac{5}{8} - 2\dfrac{3}{16} = \dfrac{58}{16} - \dfrac{35}{16} = \dfrac{23}{16}$ or $1\dfrac{7}{16}$

79. $12 - 24 \div 8 + 4 \cdot 3^2 = 12 - 24 \div 8 + 4 \cdot 9$

$= 12 - 3 + 36$

$= 9 + 36$

$= 45$

80. Substitute 2 for x and -3 for y.

$-4x^2 + 6xy + 3y^2$

$= -4(2)^2 + 6(2)(-3) + 3(-3)^2$

$= -4(4) + 6(2)(-3) + 3(9)$

$= -16 + (-36) + 27$

$= -52 + 27$

$= -25$

Review Exercises

1. $60(12) - (162 + 187 + 196 + 95) = 720 - 640$

$= 80$

He had 80 hotdogs left over.

2. $1.05\left[1.05(500.00)\right] = 1.05\left[525\right] = 551.25$

In 2 years the goods will cost \$551.25.

3. Less than; the increase of 20% of the original price is less than the decrease of 20% of the higher price.

4. $\left[30 + 12(25)\right] - 300 = \left[30 + 300\right] - 300$
$$= 330 - 300$$
$$= 30$$

5. a. mean $= \dfrac{75 + 79 + 86 + 88 + 64}{5}$
$$= \dfrac{392}{5}$$
$$= 78.4$$
The mean grade is 78.4.

   b. 64, 75, 79, 86, 88
The middle number is 79. The median grade is 79.

6. a. mean $= \dfrac{76 + 79 + 84 + 82 + 79}{5} = \dfrac{400}{5} = 80$
The mean temperature is 80°F.

   b. 76, 79, 79, 82, 84
The middle number is 79. The median temperature is 79°F.

7. a. Profit = 18.2% of $45.79
$$= (0.182)(45.79)$$
$$= 8.33$$
The drug manufacturer makes $8.33 profit on the average U.S. prescription.

   b. Selling price = Original cost + (Original cost times Markup)
$$= 60 + 60(0.22)$$
$$= 60 + 13.2$$
$$= 73.2$$
The pharmacist will sell the drug for $73.20.

8. a. U.S. oil reserves – Canadian oil reserves
$$= 21.8 - 4.7$$
$$= 17.1$$
The U.S. has 17.1 billions of barrels of oil reserves more than Canada.

   b. Middle East oil reserves ÷ North American oil reserves $= 683.5 \div 54.7 \approx 12.5$
The Middle East has about 12.5 times more oil reserves than in North America.

   c. $54.8 + 95.2 + 17.2 + 59.0 + 74.9 + 683.6 + 44.1 = 1028.8$ billion barrels
The world's oil reserves total 1028.8 billion barrels.

9. $\dfrac{3}{5} \cdot \dfrac{5}{6} = \dfrac{1}{1} \cdot \dfrac{1}{2} = \dfrac{1 \cdot 1}{1 \cdot 2} = \dfrac{1}{2}$

10. $\dfrac{2}{5} \div \dfrac{10}{9} = \dfrac{2}{5} \cdot \dfrac{9}{10} = \dfrac{1}{5} \cdot \dfrac{9}{5} = \dfrac{1 \cdot 9}{5 \cdot 5} = \dfrac{9}{25}$

11. $\dfrac{5}{12} \div \dfrac{3}{5} = \dfrac{5}{12} \cdot \dfrac{5}{3} = \dfrac{5 \cdot 5}{12 \cdot 3} = \dfrac{25}{36}$

12. $\dfrac{5}{6} + \dfrac{1}{3} = \dfrac{5}{6} + \dfrac{1}{3} \cdot \dfrac{2}{2} = \dfrac{5}{6} + \dfrac{2}{6} = \dfrac{7}{6}$ or $1\dfrac{1}{6}$

13. $\dfrac{3}{8} - \dfrac{1}{9} = \dfrac{3}{8} \cdot \dfrac{9}{9} - \dfrac{1}{9} \cdot \dfrac{8}{8} = \dfrac{27}{72} - \dfrac{8}{72} = \dfrac{19}{72}$

14. $2\dfrac{1}{3} - 1\dfrac{1}{5}$

$2\dfrac{1}{3} = \dfrac{6+1}{3} = \dfrac{7}{3} = \dfrac{7}{3} \cdot \dfrac{5}{5} = \dfrac{35}{15}$

$1\dfrac{1}{5} = \dfrac{5+1}{5} = \dfrac{6}{5} = \dfrac{6}{5} \cdot \dfrac{3}{3} = \dfrac{18}{15}$

$2\dfrac{1}{3} - 1\dfrac{1}{5} = \dfrac{35}{15} - \dfrac{18}{15} = \dfrac{17}{15}$ or $1\dfrac{2}{15}$

15. The natural numbers are $\{1, 2, 3, ...\}$.

16. The whole numbers are $\{0, 1, 2, 3, ...\}$.

17. The integers are $\{..., -3, -2, -1, 0, 1, 2, ...\}$.

18. The set of rational numbers is the set of all numbers which can be expressed as the quotient of two integers, denominator not zero.

19. a. 3 and 426 are positive integers.

   b. 3, 0, and 426 are whole numbers.

   c. 3, −5, −12, 0, and 426 are integers.

   d. $3, -5, -12, 0, \dfrac{1}{2}, -0.62, 426,$ and $-3\dfrac{1}{4}$ are rational numbers.

   e. $\sqrt{7}$ is an irrational number.

   f. $3, -5, -12, 0, \dfrac{1}{2}, -0.62, \sqrt{7}, 426,$ and $-3\dfrac{1}{4}$ are real numbers.

20. a. 1 is a natural number.

   b. 1 is a whole number.

   c. −8 and −9 are negative numbers.

   d. −8, −9, and 1 are integers.

    e. $-2.3, -8, -9, 1\frac{1}{2}, 1,$ and $-\frac{3}{17}$ are rational

       numbers.

    f. $-2.3, -8, -9, 1\frac{1}{2}, \sqrt{2}, -\sqrt{2}, 1,$ and $-\frac{3}{17}$

       are real numbers.

21. $-7 < -5$; -7 is to the left of -5 on a number line.

22. $-2.6 > -3.6$; -2.6 is to the right of -3.6 on a number line.

23. $0.50 < 0.509$; 0.50 is to the left 0.509 on a number line.

24. $4.6 > 4.06$; 4.6 is to the right of 4.06 on a number line.

25. $-3.2 < -3.02$; -3.2 is to the left of -3.02 on a number line.

26. $5 > |-3|$ since $|-3|$ equals 3.

27. $-9 < |-7|$ since $|-7|$ equals 7.

28. $|-2.5| = \left|\frac{5}{2}\right|$ since $|-2.5| = \left|\frac{5}{2}\right| = 2.5$.

29. $-9 + (5) = -14$

30. $-6 + 6 = 0$

31. $0 + (-3) = -3$

32. $-10 + 4 = -6$

33. $-8 - (-2) = -8 + 2 = -6$

34. $-2 - (-4) = -2 + 4 = 2$

35. $4 - (-4) = 4 + 4 = 8$

36. $12 - 12 = 12 + (-12) = 0$

37. $7 - (-7) = 7 + 7 = 14$

38. $2 - 7 = 2 + (-7) = -5$

39. $0 - (-4) = 0 + 4 = 4$

40. $-7 - 5 = -7 + (-5) = -12$

41. $\dfrac{4}{3} - \dfrac{3}{4} = \dfrac{16}{12} - \dfrac{9}{12} = \dfrac{16 - 9}{12} = \dfrac{7}{12}$

42. $\dfrac{1}{2} + \dfrac{3}{5} = \dfrac{5}{10} + \dfrac{6}{10} = \dfrac{5 + 6}{10} = \dfrac{11}{10}$

43. $\dfrac{5}{9} - \dfrac{3}{4} = \dfrac{20}{36} - \dfrac{27}{36} = \dfrac{20 - 27}{36} = -\dfrac{7}{36}$

44. $-\dfrac{5}{7} + \dfrac{3}{8} = -\dfrac{40}{56} + \dfrac{21}{56} = \dfrac{-40 + 21}{56} = -\dfrac{19}{56}$

45. $-\dfrac{5}{12} - \dfrac{5}{6} = -\dfrac{5}{12} - \dfrac{10}{12} = \dfrac{-5 - 10}{12} = -\dfrac{15}{12} = -\dfrac{5}{4}$

46. $-\dfrac{6}{7} + \dfrac{5}{12} = -\dfrac{72}{84} + \dfrac{35}{84} = \dfrac{-72 + 35}{84} = -\dfrac{37}{84}$

47. $\dfrac{2}{9} - \dfrac{3}{10} = \dfrac{20}{90} - \dfrac{27}{90} = \dfrac{20 - 27}{90} = -\dfrac{7}{90}$

48. $\dfrac{7}{15} - \left(-\dfrac{7}{60}\right) = \dfrac{28}{60} + \dfrac{7}{60} = \dfrac{28 + 7}{60} = \dfrac{35}{60} = \dfrac{7}{12}$

49. $9 - 4 + 3 = 5 + 3 = 8$

50. $-5 + 7 - 6 = 2 - 6 = -4$

51. $-5 - 4 - 3 = -9 - 3 = -12$

52. $-2 + (-3) - 2 = -5 - 2 = -7$

53. $7 - (+4) - (-3) = 7 - 4 + 3 = 3 + 3 = 6$

54. $4 - (-2) + 3 = 4 + 2 + 3 = 6 + 3 = 9$

55. Since the numbers have unlike signs, the product is negative; $-3(9) = -27$

56. Since the numbers have like signs, the product is positive; $(-8)(-5) = 40$

57. Since there are an odd number (3) of negatives the product is negative;
$(-4)(-5)(-6) = (20)(-6) = -120$

58. $\left(\dfrac{3}{5}\right)\left(\dfrac{-2}{7}\right) = \dfrac{3(-2)}{5 \cdot 7} = \dfrac{-6}{35} = -\dfrac{6}{35}$

59. $\left(\dfrac{10}{11}\right)\left(\dfrac{3}{-5}\right) = \dfrac{2}{11} \cdot \dfrac{3}{-1} = \dfrac{2 \cdot 3}{(11)(-1)} = \dfrac{6}{-11} = -\dfrac{6}{11}$

60. $\left(\dfrac{-5}{8}\right)\left(\dfrac{-3}{7}\right) = \dfrac{(-5)(-3)}{8 \cdot 7} = \dfrac{15}{56}$

61. Zero multiplied by any real number is zero.
$0 \cdot \dfrac{4}{9} = 0$

62. Since there are four negative numbers (an even number), the product is positive.
$(-4)(-6)(-2)(-3) = (24)(-2)(-3) = (-48)(-3) = 144$

63. Since the numbers have unlike signs, the quotient is negative; $15 \div (-3) = \dfrac{15}{-3} = -5$

64. Since the numbers have unlike signs, the quotient is negative; $12 \div (-2) = \dfrac{12}{-2} = -6$

65. Since the numbers have unlike signs, the quotient is negative; $-20 \div 5 = \dfrac{-20}{5} = -4$

66. Zero divided by any nonzero number is zero;
$0 \div 4 = \dfrac{0}{4} = 0$

67. Since the numbers have unlike signs, the quotient is negative; $90 \div (-9) = \dfrac{90}{-9} = -10$

68. $-4 \div \left(\dfrac{-4}{9}\right) = \dfrac{-4}{1} \cdot \dfrac{9}{-4} = \dfrac{-1}{1} \cdot \dfrac{9}{-1} = \dfrac{-9}{-1} = 9$

69. $\dfrac{28}{-3} \div \left(\dfrac{9}{-2}\right) = \left(\dfrac{28}{-3}\right) \cdot \left(\dfrac{-2}{9}\right) = \dfrac{-56}{-27} = \dfrac{56}{27}$

70. $\dfrac{14}{3} \div \left(\dfrac{-6}{5}\right) = \dfrac{14}{3} \cdot \left(\dfrac{5}{-6}\right) = \dfrac{7}{3} \cdot \dfrac{5}{-3} = \dfrac{35}{-9} = -\dfrac{35}{9}$

71. Zero divided by any nonzero number is zero;
$0 \div 5 = \dfrac{0}{5} = 0$

72. Zero divided by any nonzero number is zero;
$0 \div (-6) = \dfrac{0}{-6} = 0$

73. Any real number divided by zero is undefined;
$8 \div 0 = \dfrac{8}{0}$ is undefined.

74. Any real number divided by zero is undefined;
$-4 \div 0 = \dfrac{-4}{0}$ is undefined.

75. Any real number divided by zero is undefined;
$\dfrac{8}{0}$ is undefined

76. Zero divided by any nonzero number is zero;
$\dfrac{0}{-5} = 0$

77. $-5(3 - 8) = -5(-5) = 25$

78. $2(4 - 8) = 2(-4) = -8$

79. $(3 - 6) + 4 = -3 + 4 = 1$

80. $(-4 + 3) - (2 - 6) = (-1) - (-4) = -1 + 4 = 3$

81. $[6 + 3(-2)] - 6 = [6 + (-6)] - 6 = 0 - 6 = -6$

82. $(-4 - 2)(-3) = (-6)(-3) = 18$

83. $[12 + (-4)] + (6 - 8) = 8 + (-2) = 6$

84. $9[3 + (-4)] + 5 = 9(-1) + 5 = -9 + 5 = -4$

85. $-4(-3) + [4 \div (-2)] = (12) + (-2) = 10$

86. $(-3 \cdot 4) \div (-2 \cdot 6) = -12 \div (-12) = 1$

87. $(-3)(-4) + 6 - 3 = 12 + 6 - 3 = 18 - 3 = 15$

88. $[-2(3) + 6] - 4 = [-6 + 6] - 4 = 0 - 4 = -4$

89. $7^2 = (7)(7) = 49$

90. $9^3 = (9)(9)(9) = 729$

91. $3^4 = (3)(3)(3)(3) = 81$

92. $(-3)^3 = (-3)(-3)(-3) = -27$

93. $(-1)^9 = (-1)(-1)(-1)(-1)(-1)(-1)(-1)(-1)(-1)$
$= -1$

94. $(-2)^5 = (-2)(-2)(-2)(-2)(-2) = -32$

95. $\left(\dfrac{-4}{5}\right)^2 = \left(\dfrac{-4}{5}\right)\left(\dfrac{-4}{5}\right) = \dfrac{16}{25}$

96. $\left(\dfrac{2}{5}\right)^3 = \left(\dfrac{2}{5}\right)\left(\dfrac{2}{5}\right)\left(\dfrac{2}{5}\right) = \dfrac{8}{125}$

97. $xxy = x^2 y$

98. $2 \cdot 2 \cdot 3 \cdot 3 \cdot 3xyy = 2^2 \cdot 3^3 xy^2$

99. $5 \cdot 7 \cdot 7 \cdot xxy = 5 \cdot 7^2 x^2 y$

100. $xyxyz = x^2 y^2 z$

101. $x^2 y = xxy$

102. $xz^3 = xzzz$

103. $y^3 z = yyyz$

104. $2x^3 y^2 = 2xxxyy$

105. $3 + 5 \cdot 4 = 3 + 20 = 23$

106. $4 \cdot 6 + 4 \cdot 2 = 24 + 8 = 32$

107. $(3 - 7)^2 + 6 = (-4)^2 + 6 = 16 + 6 = 22$

108. $10 - 36 \div 4 \cdot 3 = 10 - 9 \cdot 3 = 10 - 27 = -17$

109. $6 - 3^2 \cdot 5 = 6 - 9 \cdot 5 = 6 - 45 = -39$

110. $\left[6 - (3 \cdot 5)\right] + 5 = \left[6 - 15\right] + 5 = -9 + 5 = -4$

111. $3[9(4^2 + 3)] \cdot 2 = 3[9 - (16 + 3)] \cdot 2$
$= 3[9 - 19] \cdot 2$
$= 3 \cdot (-10) \cdot 2$
$= -30 \cdot 2$
$= -60$

112. $(-3^2 + 4^2) + (3^2 \div 3) = (-9 + 16) + (9 \div 3)$
$= (7) + (3)$
$= 10$

113. $2^3 \div 4 + 6 \cdot 3 = 8 \div 4 + 6 \cdot 3 = 2 + 18 = 20$

114. $(4 \div 2)^4 + 4^2 \div 2^2 = (2)^4 + 16 \div 4$
$= 16 + 16 \div 4$
$= 16 + 4$
$= 20$

115. $\left(8 - 2^2\right)^2 - 4 \cdot 3 + 10 = (8 - 4)^2 - 4 \cdot 3 + 10$
$= (4)^2 - 4 \cdot 3 + 10$
$= 16 - 4 \cdot 3 + 10$
$= 16 - 12 + 10$
$= 4 + 10$
$= 14$

116. $4^3 \div 4^2 - 5(2 - 7) \div 5 = 64 \div 16 - 5(-5) \div 5$
$= 4 - (-25) \div 5$
$= 4 - (-5)$
$= 4 + 5$
$= 9$

117. Substitute 5 for x;
$6x - 6 = 6(5) - 6 = 30 - 6 = 24$

118. Substitute -5 for x;
$6 - 4x = 6 - 4(-5) = 6 - (-20) = 6 + 20 = 26$

119. Substitute 6 for x;
$2x^2 - 5x + 3 = 2(6)^2 - 5(6) + 3$
$= 2(36) - 30 + 3$
$= 72 - 30 + 3$
$= 42 + 3$
$= 45$

120. Substitute -1 for y;
$5y^2 + 3y - 2 = 5(-1)^2 + 3(-1) - 2$
$= 5(1) - 3 - 2$
$= 5 - 3 - 2$
$= 2 - 2$
$= 0$

121. Substitute 2 for x;
$-x^2 + 2x - 3 = -2^2 + 2(2) - 3$
$= -4 + 4 - 3$
$= 0 - 3$
$= -3$

122. Substitute -2 for x;
$-x^2 + 2x - 3 = -(-2)^2 + 2(-2) - 3$
$= -4 + (-4) - 3$
$= -8 - 3$
$= -11$

123. Substitute 1 for x;
$-3x^2 - 5x + 5 = -3(1)^2 - 5(1) + 5$
$= -3(1) - 5 + 5$
$= -3 - 5 + 5$
$= -8 + 5$
$= -3$

124. Substitute -3 for x and -2 for y;
$-x^2 - 8x - 12y = -(-3)^2 - 8(-3) - 12(-2)$
$= -9 - (-24) + 24$
$= -9 + 24 + 24$
$= 15 + 24$
$= 39$

125. a. $278 + (-493) = -215$

    b. $|{-}493|$ is greater than $|278|$ so the sum should be (and is) negative.

126. a. $324 - (-29.6) = 324 + 29.6 = 353.6$

   b. The sum of two positive numbers is always positive. As expected, the answer is positive.

127. a. $\dfrac{-17.28}{6} = -2.88$

   b. Since the numbers have unlike signs, the quotient is negative, as expected.

128. a. $(-62)(-1.9) = 117.8$

   b. Since the numbers have like signs, the product is positive, as expected.

129. a. $(-3)^6 = 729$

   b. A negative number raised to an even power is positive. As expected, the answer is positive.

130. a. $-(4.2)^3 = -74.088$

   b. Since $(4.2)^3$ is positive, $-(4.2)^3$ should be (and is) negative.

131. Associative property of addition

132. Commutative property of multiplication

133. Distributive property

134. Commutative property of multiplication

135. Commutative property of addition

136. Associative property of addition

Practice Test

  1. a. $2(1.30) + 4.75 + 3(1.10)$
       $= 2.60 + 4.75 + 3.30$
       $= 7.35 + 3.30$
       $= 10.65$
       The bill is $10.65 before tax.

   b. $0.07(3.30) \approx 0.23$
       The tax on the soda is $0.23.

   c. $10.65 + 0.23 = 10.88$
       The total bill is $10.88.

   d. $50 - 10.88 = 39.12$
       Her change will be $39.12.

2. a. The average cost, per employee, for employers in 2002 was about $4400.

   b. $4400 - $3000 = $1400
       The difference in average cost, per employee, for employers from 1997 to 2002 was $1400.

3. a. $\dfrac{\text{Population}}{\text{Average family size}} = \dfrac{281 \text{ million}}{2.59}$
                     $\approx 108.5 \text{ million}$
       There were about 108.5 million households in the U.S. in 2000.

   b. This means half the population was above and half was below this age.

4. a. 42 is a natural number.

   b. 42 and 0 are whole numbers.

   c. $-6, 42, 0, -7,$ and -1 are integers.

   d. $-6, 42, -3\dfrac{1}{2}, 0, 6.52, \dfrac{5}{9}, -7,$ and -1 are rational numbers.

   e. $\sqrt{5}$ is an irrational number.

   f. $-6, 42, -3\dfrac{1}{2}, 0, 6.52, \sqrt{5}, \dfrac{5}{9}, -7,$ and -1 are real numbers.

5. $-9 > -12; -9$ is to the right of -12 on a number line.

6. $|-3| > |-2|$ since $|-3| = 3$ and $|-2| = 2$.

7. $-7 + (-8) = -15$

8. $-6 - 5 = -6 + (-5) = -11$

9. $15 - 12 - 17 = 3 - 17 = -14$

10. $(-4 + 6) - 3(-2) = (2) - (-6) = 2 + 6 = 8$

11. $(-4)(-3)(2)(-1) = (12)(2)(-1) = (24)(-1) = -24$

12. $\left(\dfrac{-2}{9}\right) \div \left(\dfrac{-7}{8}\right) = \dfrac{-2}{9} \cdot \dfrac{8}{-7} = \dfrac{-16}{-63} = \dfrac{16}{63}$

13. $\left(-18 \cdot \dfrac{1}{2}\right) \div 3 = \left(\dfrac{-18}{1} \cdot \dfrac{1}{2}\right) \div 3$

    $= \left(\dfrac{-9}{1} \cdot \dfrac{1}{1}\right) \div 3$

    $= -9 \div 3$

    $= -3$

14. $-\dfrac{3}{8} - \dfrac{4}{7} = -\dfrac{21}{56} - \dfrac{32}{56} = \dfrac{-21 - 32}{56} = -\dfrac{53}{56}$

15. $-6(-2 - 3) \div 5 \cdot 2 = -6(-5) \div 5 \cdot 2$

    $= 30 \div 5 \cdot 2$

    $= 6 \cdot 2$

    $= 12$

16. $\left(\dfrac{3}{5}\right)^3 = \left(\dfrac{3}{5}\right)\left(\dfrac{3}{5}\right)\left(\dfrac{3}{5}\right) = \dfrac{27}{125}$

17. $2 \cdot 2 \cdot 5 \cdot 5 \cdot yyzzz = 2^2 5^2 y^2 z^3$

18. $2^2 3^3 x^4 y^2 = 2 \cdot 2 \cdot 3 \cdot 3 \cdot 3xxxxyy$

19. Substitute -4 for x;
    $5x^2 - 8 = 5(-4)^2 - 8 = 5(16) - 8 = 80 - 8 = 72$

20. Substitute 3 for x and -2 for y;
    $6x - 3y^2 + 4 = 6(3) - 3(-2)^2 + 4$

    $= 6(3) - 3(4) + 4$

    $= 18 - 12 + 4$

    $= 6 + 4$

    $= 10$

21. Substitute -2 for each x;
    $-x^2 - 6x + 3 = -(-2)^2 - 6(-2) + 3$

    $= -4 - (-12) + 3$

    $= -4 + 12 + 3$

    $= 8 + 3$

    $= 11$

22. Substitute 1 for x and -2 for y;
    $-x^2 + xy + y^2 = -(1)^2 + (1)(-2) + (-2)^2$

    $= -1 + (-2) + 4$

    $= -3 + 4$

    $= 1$

23. Commutative property of addition

24. Distributive property

25. Associative property of addition

Chapter 2

Exercise Set 2.1

1. a. The terms of an expression are the parts that are added.

b. The terms of $3x - 4y - 5$ are $3x$, $-4y$, and -5.

c. The terms of $6xy + 3x - y - 9$ are $6xy$, $3x$, $-y$, and -9.

3. a. The factors of an expression are the parts that are multiplied.

b. In $3x$, 3 and x are factors because they are multiplied together.

c. In $5xy$, 5, x and y are factors because they are multiplied together.

5. a. The numerical part of a term is the numerical coefficient or coefficient of the term.

b. The coefficient of $4x$ is 4.

c. Since $x = 1x$, the coefficient of x is 1.

d. Since $-x = -1x$, the coefficient of $-x$ is -1.

e. Since $\dfrac{3x}{5} = \dfrac{3}{5}x$, the coefficient of $\dfrac{3x}{5}$ is $\dfrac{3}{5}$.

f. Since $\dfrac{4}{7}(3t - 5) = \dfrac{12t}{7} - \dfrac{20}{7} = \dfrac{12}{7}t - \dfrac{20}{7}$, the coefficient of $\dfrac{4}{7}(3t - 5)$ is $\dfrac{12}{7}$.

7. a. The signs of all the terms inside the parentheses are changed when the parentheses are removed.

b. $-(x - 8) = -x + 8$

9. $5x + 3x = 8x$

11. $4x - 5x = -x$

13. $y + 3 + 4y = y + 4y + 3$
$= 5y + 3$

15. $-2x + 5x = 3x$

17. $2 - 6x + 5 = -6x + 2 + 5$
$= -6x + 7$

19. $-2w - 3w + 5 = -5w + 5$

21. $-x + 2 - x - 2 = -x - x + 2 - 2$
$= -2x$

23. $3 + 6x - 3 - 6x = 6x - 6x + 3 - 3 = 0$

25. $5 + 2x - 4x + 6 = 2x - 4x + 5 + 6$
$= -2x + 11$

27. $4r - 6 - 6r - 2 = -4r - 6r - 6 - 2$
$= -2r - 8$

29. $2 - 3x - 2x + y = -3x - 2x + y + 2$
$= -5x + y + 2$

31. $-2x + 4x - 3 = 2x - 3$

33. $b + 4 + \dfrac{3}{5} = b + \dfrac{20}{5} + \dfrac{3}{5}$
$= b + \dfrac{23}{5}$

35. $5.1n + 6.42 - 4.3n = 5.1n - 4.3n + 6.42$
$= 0.8n + 6.42$

37. There are no like terms.
$\dfrac{1}{2}a + 3b + 1$

39. $2x^2 + 3y^2 + 4x + 5y^2 = 2x^2 + 4x + 3y^2 + 5y^2$
$= 2x^2 + 4x + 8y^2$

41. $-x^2 + 2x^2 + y = x^2 + y$

43. $2x - 7y - 5x + 2y = 2x - 5x - 7y + 2y$
$= -3x - 5y$

45. $4 - 3n^2 + 9 - 2n = -3n^2 - 2n + 4 + 9$
$= -3n^2 - 2n + 13$

46. $9x + y - 2 - 4x = 9x - 4x + y - 2$
$= 5x + y - 2$

47. $-19.36 + 40.02x + 12.25 - 18.3x$
$= 40.02x - 18.3x - 19.36 + 12.25$
$= 21.72x - 7.11$

49. $\frac{3}{5}x - 3 - \frac{7}{4}x - 2 = \frac{3}{5}x - \frac{7}{4}x - 3 - 2$

$$= \frac{12}{20}x - \frac{35}{20}x - 5$$

$$= -\frac{23}{20}x - 5$$

51. There are no like terms.
$5w^3 + 2w^2 + w + 3$

53. $2z - 5z^3 - 2z^3 - z^2 = -5z^3 - 2z^3 - z^2 + 2z$
$$= -7z^3 - z^2 + 2z$$

55. There are no like terms.
$6x^2 - 6xy + 3y^2$

57. $4a^2 - 3ab + 6ab + b^2 = 4a^2 + 3ab + b^2$

59. $2(x + 6) = 2x + 2(6)$
$$= 2x + 12$$

61. $5(x + 4) = 5x + 5(4)$
$$= 5x + 20$$

63. $-2(x - 4) = -2[x + (-4)]$
$$= -2x + (-2)(-4)$$
$$= -2x + 8$$

65. $-\frac{1}{2}(2x - 4) = -\frac{1}{2}[2x + (-4)]$

$$= -\frac{1}{2}(2x) + \left(-\frac{1}{2}\right)(-4)$$

$$= -x + 2$$

67. $1(-4 + x) = 1(-4) + 1(x)$
$$= -4 + x$$
$$= x - 4$$

69. $\frac{4}{5}(s - 5) = \frac{4}{5}s - \frac{4}{5}(5)$

$$= \frac{4}{5}s - 4$$

71. $-0.3(3x + 5) = -0.3(3x) + (-0.3)(5)$
$$= -0.9x + (-1.5)$$
$$= -0.9x - 1.5$$

73. $\frac{1}{3}(3r - 12) = \frac{1}{3}(3r) + \frac{1}{3}(-12)$

$$= r - 4$$

75. $0.7(2x + 0.5) = 0.7(2x) + 0.7(0.5)$
$$= 1.4x + 0.35$$

77. $-(-x + y) = -1(-x + y)$
$$= -1(-x) + (-1)(y)$$
$$= x + (-y)$$
$$= x - y$$

79. $-(2x + 4y - 8) = -1[2x + 4y + (-8)]$
$$= -1(2x) + (-1)(4y) + (-1)(-8)$$
$$= -2x - 4y + 8$$
$$= -2x - 4y + 8$$

81. $1.1(3.1x - 5.2y + 2.8)$
$$= 1.1[3.1x + (-5.2y) + 2.8]$$
$$= (1.1)(3.1x) + (1.1)(-5.2y) + (1.1)(2.8)$$
$$= 3.41x + (-5.72y) + 3.08$$
$$= 3.41x - 5.72y + 3.08$$

83. $2\left(3x - 2y + \frac{1}{4}\right) = 2\left[3x + (-2y) + \frac{1}{4}\right]$

$$= 2(3x) + 2(-2y) + 2\left(\frac{1}{4}\right)$$

$$= 6x + (-4y) + \frac{1}{2}$$

$$= 6x - 4y + \frac{1}{2}$$

85. $(x + 3y - 9) = 1[x + 3y + (-9)]$
$$= 1(x) + 1(3y) + (1)(-9)$$
$$= x + 3y + (-9) = x + 3y - 9$$

87. $-3(-x + 2y + 4) = -3(-x) + (-3)(2y) + (-3)(4)$
$$= 3x + (-6y) + (-12)$$
$$= 3x - 6y - 12$$

89. $3(x - 5) - x = 3x - 15 - x$
$$= 3x - x - 15$$
$$= 2x - 15$$

91. $-2(3 - x) + 7 = -6 + 2x + 7$
$$= 2x - 6 + 7$$
$$= 2x + 1$$

93. $6x + 2(4x + 9) = 6x + 8x + 18$
$$= 14x + 18$$

95. $2(x - y) + 2x + 3 = 2x - 2y + 2x + 3$
$$= 2x + 2x - 2y + 3$$
$$= 4x - 2y + 3$$

97. $4(2c - 3) - 3(c - 4) = 8c - 12 - 3c + 12$
$$= 8c - 3c - 12 + 12$$
$$= 5c$$

99. $8x - (x - 3) = 8x - x + 3$
$$= 7x + 3$$

101. $2(x - 3) - (x + 3) = 2x - 6 - x - 3$
$$= 2x - x - 6 - 3$$
$$= x - 9$$

103. $4(x - 1) + 2(3 - x) - 4 = 4x - 4(1) + 2(3) - 2x - 4$
$$= 4x - 4 + 6 - 2x - 4$$
$$= 4x - 2x - 4 + 6 - 4$$
$$= 2x - 2$$

105. $-(3s + 4) - (s + 2) = -3s - 4 - s - 2$
$$= -3s - s - 4 - 2$$
$$= -4s - 6$$

107. $-3(x + 1) + 5x + 6 = -3x - 3 + 5x + 6$
$$= -3x + 5x - 3 + 6$$
$$= 2x + 3$$

109. $4(m + 3) - 4m - 12 = 4m + 4(3) - 4m - 12$
$$= 4m + 12 - 4m - 12$$
$$= 4m - 4m + 12 - 12$$
$$= 0$$

111. $0.4 + (y + 5) + 0.6 - 2 = 0.4 + y + 5 + 0.6 - 2$
$$= y + 0.4 + 5 + 0.6 - 2$$
$$= y + 4$$

113. $4 + (3x - 4) - 5 = 4 + 3x - 4 - 5$
$$= 3x + 4 - 4 - 5$$
$$= 3x - 5$$

115. $4(x + 2) - 3(x - 4) - 5$
$$= 4x + 4(2) - 3x - 3(-4) - 5$$
$$= 4x + 8 - 3x + 12 - 5$$
$$= 4x - 3x + 8 + 12 - 5$$
$$= x + 15$$

117. $-0.2(6 - x) - 4(y + 0.4)$
$$= -0.2(6) - 0.2(-x) - 4y - 4(0.4)$$
$$= -1.2 + 0.2x - 4y - 1.6$$
$$= 0.2x - 4y - 1.2 - 1.6$$
$$= 0.2x - 4y - 2.8$$

119. $-6x + 7y - (3 + x) + (x + 3)$
$$= -6x + 7y - 3 - x + x + 3$$
$$= -6x - x + x + 7y - 3 + 3$$
$$= -6x + 7y$$

121. $\frac{1}{2}(x + 3) + \frac{1}{3}(3x + 6) = \frac{1}{2}x + \frac{3}{2} + \frac{3}{3}x + \frac{6}{3}$
$$= \frac{1}{2}x + \frac{3}{2} + x + 2$$
$$= \frac{1}{2}x + x + \frac{3}{2} + 2$$
$$= \frac{3}{2}x + \frac{7}{2}$$

123. $\square + \ominus + \ominus + \square + \ominus = 2\square + 3\ominus$

125. $x + y + \Delta + \Delta + x + y + y$
$$= x + x + y + y + y + \Delta + \Delta$$
$$= 2x + 3y + 2\Delta$$

127. $1 \cdot 12, \ 2 \cdot 6, \ 3 \cdot 4$
positive factors: 1, 2, 3, 4, 6, 12

129. $3\Delta + 5\square - \Delta - 3\square = 3\Delta - \Delta + 5\square - 3\square$
$$= 2\Delta + 2\square$$

131. $4x^2 + 5y^2 + 6(3x^2 - 5y^2) - 4x + 3$
$$= 4x^2 + 5y^2 + 18x^2 - 30y^2 - 4x + 3$$
$$= 4x^2 + 18x^2 - 4x + 5y^2 - 30y^2 + 3$$
$$= 22x^2 - 25y^2 - 4x + 3$$

133. $2x^2 - 4x + 8x^2 - 3(x + 2) - x^2 - 2$
$$= 2x^2 - 4x + 8x^2 - 3x - 6 - x^2 - 2$$
$$= 2x^2 + 8x^2 - x^2 - 4x - 3x - 6 - 2$$
$$= 9x^2 - 7x - 8$$

135. $|-7| = 7$

136. $-|-16| = -(16) = -16$

137. $-4 - 3 - (-6) = -4 - 3 + 6$
$$= -7 + 6$$
$$= -1$$

138. Answers will vary. The answer should include that the order is parentheses, exponents, multiplication and division from left to right, and addition and subtraction from left to right.

139. Substitute -1 for each x in the expression.
$$-x^2 + 5x - 6 = -(-1)^2 + 5(-1) - 6$$
$$= -1 + (-5) - 6$$
$$= -6 - 6$$
$$= -12$$

Exercise Set 2.2

1. An equation is a statement that shows two algebraic expressions are equal.

3. A solution to an equation may be checked by substituting the value in the equation and determining if it results in a true statement.

5. Equivalent equations are two or more equations with the same solution.

7. Add 4 to both sides of the equation to get the variable by itself.

9. One example is $x + 2 = 1$.

11. Subtraction is defined in terms of addition.

13. Substitute 2 for $x = 2$.
$$4x - 3 = 5$$
$$4(2) - 3 = 5$$
$$8 - 3 = 5$$
$$5 = 5 \qquad \text{True}$$
Since we obtain true statement, 2 is a solution.

15. Substitute -3 for x, $x = -3$.
$$2x - 5 = 5(x + 2)$$
$$2(-3) - 5 = 5[(-3) + 2]$$
$$-6 - 5 = 5(-1)$$
$$-11 = -5 \quad \text{False}$$
Since we obtain a false statement, -3 is not a solution.

17. Substitute 0 for p, $p = 0$.
$$3p - 4 = 2(p + 3) - 10$$
$$3(0) - 4 = 2(0 + 3) - 10$$
$$0 - 4 = 2(3) - 10$$
$$-4 = 6 - 10$$
$$-4 = -4 \text{ True}$$
Since we obtain a true statement, 0 is a solution.

19. Substitute 3.4 for x, $x = 3.4$.
$$3(x + 2) - 3(x - 1) = 9$$
$$3(3.4 + 2) - 3(3.4 - 1) = 9$$
$$3(5.4) - 3(2.4) = 9$$
$$16.2 - 7.2 = 9$$
$$9 = 9 \text{ True}$$
Since we obtain a true statement, 3.4 is a solution.

21. Substitute $\dfrac{1}{2}$ for x, $x = \dfrac{1}{2}$.
$$4x - 4 = 2x - 2$$
$$4\left(\frac{1}{2}\right) - 4 = 2\left(\frac{1}{2}\right) - 2$$
$$2 - 4 = 1 - 2$$
$$-2 = -1 \text{ False}$$
Since we obtain a false statement, $\dfrac{1}{2}$ is not a solution.

23. Substitute $\dfrac{11}{2}$ for x, $x = \dfrac{11}{2}$.
$$3(x + 2) = 5(x - 1)$$
$$3\left(\frac{11}{2} + 2\right) = 5\left(\frac{11}{2} - 1\right)$$
$$3\left(\frac{15}{2}\right) = 5\left(\frac{9}{2}\right)$$
$$\frac{45}{2} = \frac{45}{2} \text{ True}$$
Since we obtain a true statement, $\dfrac{11}{2}$ is a solution.

25. $x + 5 = 8$
$$x + 5 - 5 = 8 - 5$$
$$x + 0 = 3$$
$$x = 3$$
Check: $x + 5 = 8$
$$3 + 5 = 8$$
$$8 = 8 \text{ True}$$

27. $x + 1 = -6$
$$x + 1 - 1 = -6 - 1$$
$$x + 0 = -7$$
$$x = -7$$
Check: $x + 1 = -6$
$$-7 + 1 = -6$$
$$-6 = -6 \text{ True}$$

29. $x + 4 = -5$
$x + 4 - 4 = -5 - 4$
$x + 0 = -9$
$x = -9$
Check: $x + 4 = -5$
$-9 + 4 = -5$
$-5 = -5$ True

31. $x + 9 = 52$
$x + 9 - 9 = 52 - 9$
$x + 0 = 43$
$x = 43$
Check: $x + 9 = 52$
$43 + 9 = 52$
$52 = 52$ True

33. $-6 + w = 9$
$-6 + 6 + w = 9 + 6$
$0 + w = 15$
$w = 15$
Check: $-6 + w = 9$
$-6 + 15 = 9$
$9 = 9$ True

35. $27 = x + 16$
$27 - 16 = x + 16 - 16$
$11 = x + 0$
$11 = x$
Check: $27 = x + 16$
$27 = 11 + 16$
$27 = 27$ True

37. $-18 = -14 + x$
$-18 + 14 = -14 + 14 + x$
$-4 = 0 + x$
$-4 = x$
Check: $-18 = -14 + x$
$-18 = -14 + (-4)$
$-18 = -18$ True

39. $9 + x = 4$
$9 - 9 + x = 4 - 9$
$0 + x = -5$
$x = -5$
Check: $9 + x = 4$
$9 + (-5) = 4$
$4 = 4$ True

41. $4 + x = -9$
$4 - 4 + x = -9 - 4$
$0 + x = -13$
$x = -13$
Check: $4 + x = -9$
$4 + (-13) = -9$
$-9 = -9$ True

43. $7 + r = -23$

$7 + r = -23$
$7 - 7 + r = -23 - 7$
$0 + r = -30$
$r = -30$

Check: $7 + r = -23$
$7 + (-30) = -23$
$-23 = -23$ True

45. $8 = 8 + v$
$8 - 8 = 8 - 8 + v$
$0 = 0 + v$
$0 = v$
Check: $8 = 8 + v$
$8 = 8 + 0$
$8 = 8$ True

47. $-4 = x - 3$
$-4 + 3 = x - 3 + 3$
$-1 = x + 0$
$-1 = x$
Check: $-4 = x - 3$
$-4 = -1 - 3$
$-4 = -4$ True

49. $12 = 16 + x$
$12 - 16 = 16 - 16 + x$
$-4 = 0 + x$
$-4 = x$
Check: $12 = 16 + x$
$12 = 16 + (-4)$
$12 = 12$ True

51. $15 + x = -5$
$15 - 15 + x = -5 - 15$
$0 + x = -20$
$x = -20$
Check: $15 + x = -5$
$15 + (-20) = -5$
$-5 = -5$ True

53. $-10 = -10 + x$
$-10 + 10 = -10 + 10 + x$
$0 = 0 + x$
$0 = x$
Check: $-10 = -10 + x$
$-10 = -10 + 0$
$-10 = -10$ True

55. $5 = x - 12$
$5 + 12 = x - 12 + 12$
$17 = x + 0$
$17 = x$
Check: $5 = x - 12$
$5 = 17 - 12$
$5 = 5$ True

57. $-50 = x - 24$
$-50 + 24 = x - 24 + 24$
$-26 = x + 0$
$-26 = x$
Check: $-50 = x - 24$
$-50 = -26 - 24$
$-50 = -50$ True

59. $43 = 15 + p$
$43 - 15 = 15 - 15 + p$
$28 = 0 + p$
$28 = p$
Check: $43 = 15 + p$
$43 = 15 + 28$
$43 = 43$ True

61. $40.2 + x = -5.9$
$40.2 - 40.2 + x = -5.9 - 40.2$
$0 + x = -46.1$
$x = -46.1$
Check: $40.2 + x = -5.9$
$40.2 + (-46.1) = -5.9$
$-5.9 = -5.9$ True

63. $-37 + x = 9.5$
$-37 + 37 + x = 9.5 + 37$
$0 + x = 46.5$
$x = 46.5$
Check: $-37 + x = 9.5$
$-37 + 46.5 = 9.5$
$9.5 = 9.5$ True

65. $x - 8.77 = -17$
$x - 8.77 + 8.77 = -17 + 8.77$
$x + 0 = -8.23$
$x = -8.23$
Check: $x - 8.77 = -17$
$-8.23 - 8.77 = -17$
$-17 = -17$ True

67. $9.32 = x + 3.75$
$9.32 - 3.75 = x + 3.75 - 3.75$
$5.57 = x + 0$
$5.57 = x$
Check: $9.32 = x + 3.75$
$9.32 = 5.57 + 3.75$
$9.32 = 9.32$ True

69. No; there are no real numbers that can make
$x + 1 = x + 2$.

71. $x - \Delta = \square$
$x - \Delta + \Delta = \square + \Delta$
$x = \square + \Delta$

73. $\smiley = \square + \Delta$
$\smiley - \Delta = \square + \Delta - \Delta$
$\smiley - \Delta = \square$

76. Substitute 4 for each x in the expression.
$3x + 4(x - 3) + 2 = 3(4) + 4(4 - 3) + 2$
$= 12 + 4(1) + 2$
$= 12 + 4 + 2$
$= 16 + 2$
$= 18$

77. Substitute -3 for x in the expression.
$6x - 2(2x + 1) = 6(-3) - 2\left[2(-3) + 1\right]$
$= -18 - 2(-6 + 1)$
$= -18 - 2(-5)$
$= -18 + 10$
$= -8$

78. $4x + 3(x - 2) - 5x - 7 = 4x + 3x - 6 - 5x - 7$
$= 4x + 3x - 5x - 6 - 7$
$= 2x - 13$

79. $-(2t + 4) + 3(4t - 5) - 3t = -2t - 4 + 12t - 15 - 3t$
$= -2t + 12t - 3t - 4 - 15$
$= 7t - 19$

Exercise Set 2.3

1. Answers will vary. Answer should include that both
sides of an equation can be multiplied by the same
nonzero number without changing the solution to the
equation.

3. a. $-x = a$
$-1x = a$
$(-1)(-1x) = (-1)a$
$1x = -a$
$x = -a$

   b. $-x = 5$
$-1x = 5$
$(-1)(-1x) = (-1)5$
$1x = -5$
$x = -5$

c.
$$-x = -5$$
$$-1x = -5$$
$$(-1)(-1x) = (-1)(-5)$$
$$1x = 5$$
$$x = 5$$

5. Divide by -2 to isolate the variable.

7. Multiply both sides by 3 because $3 \cdot \dfrac{x}{3} = x$.

9. $4x = 12$
$$\frac{4x}{4} = \frac{12}{4}$$
$$x = 3$$
Check: $4x = 12$
$$4(3) = 12$$
$$12 = 12 \ \text{True}$$

11. $\dfrac{x}{2} = 4$
$$2\left(\frac{x}{2}\right) = 2(4)$$
$$x = 8$$
Check: $\dfrac{x}{2} = 4$
$$\frac{8}{2} = 4$$
$$4 = 4 \ \text{True}$$

13. $-4x = 12$
$$\frac{-4x}{-4} = \frac{12}{-4}$$
$$x = -3$$
Check: $-4x = 12$
$$-4(-3) = 12$$
$$12 = 12 \ \text{True}$$

15. $\dfrac{x}{4} = -2$
$$4\left(\frac{x}{4}\right) = 4(-2)$$
$$x = 4(-2)$$
$$x = -8$$
Check: $\dfrac{x}{4} = -2$
$$\frac{-8}{4} = -2$$
$$-2 = -2 \ \text{True}$$

17. $\dfrac{x}{5} = 1$
$$5\left(\frac{x}{5}\right) = 5(1)$$
$$x = 5$$
Check: $\dfrac{x}{5} = 1$
$$\frac{5}{5} = 1$$
$$1 = 1 \ \text{True}$$

19. $-27n = 81$
$$\frac{-27n}{-27} = \frac{81}{-27}$$
$$n = -3$$
Check: $-27n = 81$
$$-27(-3) = 81$$
$$81 = 81 \ \text{True}$$

21. $-7 = 3r$
$$\frac{-7}{3} = \frac{3r}{3}$$
$$-\frac{7}{3} = r$$
Check: $-7 = 3r$
$$-7 = 3\left(-\frac{7}{3}\right)$$
$$-7 = -7 \ \text{True}$$

23.
$$-x = -11$$
$$-1x = -11$$
$$(-1)(-1x) = (-1)(-11)$$
$$1x = 11$$
$$x = 11$$
Check: $-x = -11$
$$-11 = -11 \ \text{True}$$

25.
$$10 = -y$$
$$10 = -1y$$
$$(-1)(10) = (-1)(-1y)$$
$$-10 = 1y$$
$$-10 = y$$
Check: $10 = -y$
$$10 = -(-10)$$
$$10 = 10 \ \text{True}$$

27.
$$-\frac{w}{3} = -13$$

$$\frac{w}{-3} = -13$$

$$(-3)\left(\frac{w}{-3}\right) = (-3)(-13)$$

$$w = 39$$

Check: $-\dfrac{w}{3} = -13$

$$-\frac{39}{3} = -13$$

$$-13 = -13 \text{ True}$$

29.
$$4 = -12x$$

$$\frac{4}{-12} = \frac{-12x}{-12}$$

$$-\frac{1}{3} = x$$

Check: $4 = -12x$

$$4 = -12\left(-\frac{1}{3}\right)$$

$$4 = 4 \text{ True}$$

31.
$$-\frac{x}{3} = -2$$

$$\frac{x}{-3} = -2$$

$$(-3)\left(\frac{x}{-3}\right) = (-3)(-2)$$

$$x = 6$$

Check: $-\dfrac{x}{3} = -2$

$$-\frac{6}{3} = -2$$

$$-2 = -2 \text{ True}$$

33.
$$43t = 26$$

$$\frac{43t}{43} = \frac{26}{43}$$

$$t = \frac{26}{43}$$

Check: $43t = 26$

$$43\left(\frac{26}{43}\right) = 26$$

$$26 = 26 \text{ True}$$

35.
$$-4.2x = -8.4$$

$$\frac{-4.2x}{-4.2} = \frac{-8.4}{-4.2}$$

$$x = 2$$

Check: $-4.2x = -8.4$

$$-4.2(2) = -8.4$$

$$-8.4 = -8.4 \text{ True}$$

37.
$$7x = -7$$

$$\frac{7x}{7} = \frac{-7}{7}$$

$$x = -1$$

Check: $7x = -7$

$$7(-1) = -7$$

$$-7 = -7 \text{ True}$$

39.
$$5x = -\frac{3}{8}$$

$$\frac{1}{5} \cdot 5x = \left(\frac{1}{5}\right) \cdot \left(-\frac{3}{8}\right)$$

$$x = \frac{(1) \cdot (-3)}{(5) \cdot (8)}$$

$$x = -\frac{3}{40}$$

Check: $5x = -\dfrac{3}{8}$

$$5\left(-\frac{3}{40}\right) = -\frac{3}{8}$$

$$-\frac{3}{8} = -\frac{3}{8} \text{ True}$$

41.
$$15 = -\frac{x}{4}$$

$$15 = \frac{x}{-4}$$

$$(-4)(15) = (-4) \cdot \left(\frac{x}{-4}\right)$$

$$-60 = x$$

Check: $15 = -\dfrac{x}{4}$

$$15 = -\frac{(-60)}{4}$$

$$15 = 15 \text{ True}$$

43.
$$-\frac{b}{4} = -60$$
$$\frac{b}{-4} = -60$$
$$-4\left(\frac{b}{-4}\right) = (-4)(-60)$$
$$b = 240$$

Check: $-\frac{b}{4} = -60$
$$-\frac{240}{4} = -60$$
$$-60 = -60 \text{ True}$$

45.
$$\frac{x}{5} = -7$$
$$5\left(\frac{x}{5}\right) = 5(-7)$$
$$x = -35$$

Check: $\frac{x}{5} = -7$
$$\frac{-35}{5} = -7$$
$$-7 = -7 \text{ True}$$

47.
$$5 = \frac{x}{4}$$
$$4 \cdot 5 = 4\left(\frac{x}{4}\right)$$
$$20 = x$$

Check: $5 = \frac{x}{4}$
$$5 = \frac{20}{4}$$
$$5 = 5 \text{ True}$$

49.
$$\frac{3}{5}d = -30$$
$$\frac{5}{3} \cdot \frac{3}{5}d = \frac{5}{3}(-30)$$
$$d = -50$$

Check: $\frac{3}{5}d = -30$
$$\frac{3}{5}(-50) = -30$$
$$-30 = -30 \text{ True}$$

51.
$$\frac{y}{-2} = 0$$
$$(-2)\left(\frac{y}{-2}\right) = (-2)(0)$$
$$y = 0$$

Check: $\frac{y}{-2} = 0$
$$\frac{0}{-2} = 0$$
$$0 = 0 \text{ True}$$

53.
$$\frac{-7}{8}w = 0$$
$$\frac{8}{-7}\left(\frac{-7}{8}w\right) = \frac{8}{-7} \cdot 0$$
$$w = 0$$

Check: $\frac{-7}{8}w = 0$
$$\frac{-7}{8}(0) = 0$$
$$0 = 0 \text{ True}$$

55.
$$\frac{1}{5}x = 4.5$$
$$5\left(\frac{1}{5}x\right) = 5(4.5)$$
$$x = 22.5$$

Check: $\frac{1}{5}x = 4.5$
$$\frac{1}{5}(22.5) = 4.5$$
$$4.5 = 4.5 \text{ True}$$

57.
$$-4 = -\frac{2}{3}z$$
$$\left(-\frac{3}{2}\right)(-4) = \left(-\frac{3}{2}\right)\left(-\frac{2}{3}\right)z$$
$$6 = z$$

Check: $-4 = -\frac{2}{3}z$
$$-4 = -\frac{2}{3} \cdot 6$$
$$-4 = -4 \text{ True}$$

59.
$$-1.4x = 28.28$$
$$\frac{-1.4x}{-1.4} = \frac{28.28}{-1.4}$$
$$x = -20.2$$

Check: $-1.4x = 28.28$
$$-1.4(-20.2) = 28.28$$
$$28.28 = 28.28 \text{ True}$$

61.
$$-4w = \frac{7}{12}$$
$$-\frac{1}{4} \cdot -4w = -\frac{1}{4} \cdot \frac{7}{12}$$
$$w = -\frac{7}{48}$$

Check: $\quad -4w = \frac{7}{12}$
$$-4\left(-\frac{7}{48}\right) = \frac{7}{12}$$
$$\frac{28}{48} = \frac{7}{12}$$
$$\frac{7}{12} = \frac{7}{12} \text{ True}$$

63.
$$\frac{2}{3}x = 6$$
$$\frac{3}{2} \cdot \frac{2}{3}x = \frac{3}{2} \cdot 6$$
$$x = 9$$

Check: $\quad \frac{2}{3}x = 6$
$$\frac{2}{3}(9) = 6$$
$$6 = 6 \text{ True}$$

65. a. In $5 + x = 10$, 5 is added to the variable, whereas in $5x = 10$, 5 is multiplied by the variable.

b.
$$5x = 10$$
$$5 + x - 5 = 10 - 5$$
$$x = 5$$

c.
$$5x = 10$$
$$\frac{5x}{5} = \frac{10}{5}$$
$$x = 2$$

67. Multiplying by $\frac{3}{2}$ is easier because the equation involves fractions.
$$\frac{2}{3}x = 4$$
$$\left(\frac{3}{2}\right)\left(\frac{2}{3}\right)x = \left(\frac{3}{2}\right)\left(\frac{4}{1}\right)$$
$$x = \frac{12}{2}$$
$$x = 6$$

69. Multiplying by $\frac{7}{3}$ is easier because the equation involves fractions.
$$\frac{3}{7}x = \frac{4}{5}$$
$$\left(\frac{7}{3}\right)\frac{3}{7}x = \left(\frac{7}{3}\right)\frac{4}{5}$$
$$x = \frac{28}{15}$$

71. a. ▣

b. Divide both sides of the equation by Δ.

c.
$$☺ = \Delta▣$$
$$\frac{☺}{\Delta} = \frac{\Delta▣}{\Delta}$$
$$\frac{☺}{\Delta} = ▣$$

73. $-8 - (-4) = -8 + 4$
$$= -4$$

74. $6 - (-3) - 5 - 4 = 6 + 3 - 5 - 4$
$$= 9 - 5 - 4$$
$$= 4 - 4$$
$$= 0$$

75. $4^2 - 2^3 \cdot 6 \div 3 + 6 = 16 - 8 \cdot 6 \div 3 + 6$
$$= 16 - 48 \div 3 + 6$$
$$= 16 - 16 + 6$$
$$= 0 + 6$$
$$= 0$$

76. $-(x + 3) - 5(2x - 7) + 6 = -x - 3 - 10x + 35 + 6$
$$= -x - 10x - 3 + 35 + 6$$
$$= -11x + 38$$

77.
$$-48 = x + 9$$
$$-48 - 9 = x + 9 - 9$$
$$-57 = x + 0$$
$$-57 = x$$

Exercise Set 2.4

1. No; the variable x is on both sides of the equal sign.

3. $x = \frac{1}{3}$ because $1x = x$.

5. $x = -\frac{1}{2}$ because $-x = -1x$.

7. $x = \frac{3}{5}$ because $-x = -1x$.

9. You solve an equation. An equation that contains a variable is true for certain values of that variable. We solve an equation to find those values.

11. **a.** Answers will vary.

   b. Answers will vary.

13. **a.** Use the distributive property.
   Subtract 8 from both sides of the equation.
   Divide both sides of the equation by 6.

   b. $2(3x+4) = -4$
   $$6x + 8 = -4$$
   $$6x + 8 - 8 = -4 - 8$$
   $$6x = -12$$
   $$\frac{6x}{6} = -\frac{12}{6}$$
   $$x = -2$$

15. $3x + 6 = 12$
   $$3x + 6 - 6 = 12 - 6$$
   $$3x = 6$$
   $$\frac{3x}{3} = \frac{6}{3}$$
   $$x = 2$$

17. $-4w - 5 = 11$
   $$-4w - 5 + 5 = 11 + 5$$
   $$-4w = 16$$
   $$\frac{-4w}{-4} = \frac{16}{-4}$$
   $$w = -4$$

19. $5x - 6 = 19$
   $$5x - 6 + 6 = 19 + 6$$
   $$5x = 25$$
   $$\frac{5x}{5} = \frac{25}{5}$$
   $$x = 5$$

21. $5x - 2 = 10$
   $$5x - 2 + 2 = 10 + 2$$
   $$5x = 12$$
   $$\frac{5x}{5} = \frac{12}{5}$$
   $$x = \frac{12}{5}$$

23. $-2t + 9 = 21$
   $$-2t + 9 - 9 = 21 - 9$$
   $$-2t = 12$$
   $$\frac{-2t}{-2} = \frac{12}{-2}$$
   $$t = -6$$

25. $12 - x = 9$
   $$12 - 12 - x = 9 - 12$$
   $$-x = -3$$
   $$(-1)(-x) = (-1)(-3)$$
   $$x = 3$$

27. $8 + 3x = 19$
   $$8 - 8 + 3x = 19 - 8$$
   $$3x = 11$$
   $$\frac{3x}{3} = \frac{11}{3}$$
   $$x = \frac{11}{3}$$

29. $16x + 5 = -14$
   $$16x + 5 - 5 = -14 - 5$$
   $$16x = -19$$
   $$\frac{16x}{16} = \frac{-19}{16}$$
   $$x = -\frac{19}{16}$$

31. $-4.2 = 3x + 25.8$
   $$-4.2 - 25.8 = 3x + 25.8 - 25.8$$
   $$-30 = 3x$$
   $$\frac{-30}{3} = \frac{3x}{3}$$
   $$-10 = x$$

33. $7r - 16 = -2$
   $$7r - 16 + 16 = -2 + 16$$
   $$7r = 14$$
   $$\frac{7r}{7} = \frac{14}{7}$$
   $$r = 2$$

35. $60 = -5s + 9$
   $$60 - 9 = -5s + 9 - 9$$
   $$51 = -5s$$
   $$\frac{51}{-5} = \frac{-5s}{-5}$$
   $$-\frac{51}{5} = s$$

37.
$$-2x - 7 = -13$$
$$-2x - 7 + 7 = -13 + 7$$
$$-2x = -6$$
$$\frac{-2x}{-2} = \frac{-6}{-2}$$
$$x = 3$$

38.
$$-2 - x = -12$$
$$-2 + 2 - x = -12 + 2$$
$$-x = -10$$
$$(-1)(-x) = (-1)(-10)$$
$$x = 10$$

39.
$$2.3x - 9.34 = 6.3$$
$$2.3x - 9.34 + 9.34 = 6.3 + 9.34$$
$$2.3x = 15.64$$
$$\frac{2.3x}{2.3} = \frac{15.64}{2.3}$$
$$x = 6.8$$

41.
$$x + 0.07x = 16.05$$
$$1.07x = 16.05$$
$$\frac{1.07x}{1.07} = \frac{16.05}{1.07}$$
$$x = 15$$

43.
$$28.8 = x + 1.40x$$
$$28.8 = 2.40x$$
$$\frac{28.8}{2.40} = \frac{2.40x}{2.40}$$
$$12 = x$$

45.
$$\frac{x - 4}{6} = 9$$
$$6\left(\frac{x - 4}{6}\right) = 6(9)$$
$$x - 4 = 54$$
$$x - 4 + 4 = 54 + 4$$
$$x = 58$$

47.
$$\frac{d + 3}{7} = 9$$
$$7\left(\frac{d + 3}{7}\right) = 7(9)$$
$$d + 3 = 63$$
$$d + 3 - 3 = 63 - 3$$
$$d = 60$$

49.
$$\frac{1}{3}(t - 5) = -6$$
$$\frac{1}{3}t - \frac{5}{3} = -6$$
$$3\left(\frac{1}{3}t - \frac{5}{3}\right) = 3(-6)$$
$$1t - 5 = -18$$
$$1t - 5 + 5 = -18 + 5$$
$$1t = -13$$
$$t = -13$$

51.
$$\frac{3}{4}(x - 5) = -12$$
$$\frac{3}{4}x - \frac{15}{4} = -12$$
$$4\left(\frac{3}{4}x - \frac{15}{4}\right) = 4(-12)$$
$$3x - 15 = -48$$
$$3x - 15 + 15 = -48 + 15$$
$$3x = -33$$
$$\frac{3x}{3} = \frac{-33}{3}$$
$$x = -11$$

53.
$$\frac{1}{4} = \frac{z + 1}{4}$$
$$4\left(\frac{1}{4}\right) = 4\left(\frac{z + 1}{4}\right)$$
$$1 = z + 1$$
$$1 - 1 = z + 1 - 1$$
$$0 = z$$

55.
$$\frac{3}{4} = \frac{4m - 5}{6}$$
$$12\left(\frac{3}{4}\right) = 12\left(\frac{4m - 5}{6}\right)$$
$$9 = 2(4m - 5)$$
$$9 = 8m - 10$$
$$9 + 10 = 8m - 10 + 10$$
$$19 = 8m$$
$$\frac{19}{8} = \frac{8m}{8}$$
$$\frac{19}{8} = m$$

57.
$$4(n+2) = 8$$
$$4n + 8 = 8$$
$$4n + 8 - 8 = 8 - 8$$
$$4n = 0$$
$$\frac{4n}{4} = \frac{0}{4}$$
$$n = 0$$

59.
$$5(3 - x) = 15$$
$$15 - 5x = 15$$
$$15 - 15 - 5x = 15 - 15$$
$$-5x = 0$$
$$\frac{-5x}{-5} = \frac{0}{-5}$$
$$x = 0$$

61.
$$-4 = -(x + 5)$$
$$-4 = -x - 5$$
$$-4 + 5 = -x - 5 + 5$$
$$1 = -x$$
$$(-1)(1) = (-1)(-x)$$
$$-1 = x$$

63.
$$12 = 4(x - 3)$$
$$12 = 4x - 12$$
$$12 + 12 = 4x - 12 + 12$$
$$24 = 4x$$
$$\frac{24}{4} = \frac{4x}{4}$$
$$6 = x$$

65.
$$22 = -(3x - 4)$$
$$22 = -3x + 4$$
$$22 - 4 = -3x + 4 - 4$$
$$18 = -3x$$
$$\frac{18}{-3} = \frac{-3x}{-3}$$
$$-6 = x$$

67.
$$-3r + 4(r + 2) = 11$$
$$-3r + 4r + 8 = 11$$
$$r + 8 = 11$$
$$r + 8 - 8 = 11 - 8$$
$$r = 3$$

69.
$$x - 3(2x + 3) = 11$$
$$x - 6x - 9 = 11$$
$$-5x - 9 = 11$$
$$-5x - 9 + 9 = 11 + 9$$
$$-5x = 20$$
$$\frac{-5x}{-5} = \frac{20}{-5}$$
$$x = -4$$

71.
$$5x + 3x - 4x - 7 = 9$$
$$4x - 7 = 9$$
$$4x - 7 + 7 = 9 + 7$$
$$4x = 16$$
$$\frac{4x}{4} = \frac{16}{4}$$
$$x = 4$$

73.
$$0.7(x - 3) = 1.4$$
$$0.7x - 2.1 = 1.4$$
$$0.7x - 2.1 + 2.1 = 1.4 + 2.1$$
$$0.7x = 3.5$$
$$\frac{0.7x}{0.7} = \frac{3.5}{0.7}$$
$$x = 5$$

75.
$$2.5(4q - 3) = 0.5$$
$$10q - 7.5 = 0.5$$
$$10q - 7.5 + 7.5 = 0.5 + 7.5$$
$$10q = 8$$
$$\frac{10q}{10} = \frac{8}{10}$$
$$q = 0.8$$

77.
$$3 - 2(x + 3) + 2 = 1$$
$$3 - 2x - 6 + 2 = 1$$
$$-2x - 1 = 1$$
$$-2x - 1 + 1 = 1 + 1$$
$$-2x = 2$$
$$\frac{-2x}{-2} = \frac{2}{-2}$$
$$x = -1$$

79.
$$1 + (x + 3) + 6x = 6$$
$$1 + x + 3 + 6x = 6$$
$$7x + 4 = 6$$
$$7x + 4 - 4 = 6 - 4$$
$$7x = 2$$
$$\frac{7x}{7} = \frac{2}{7}$$
$$x = \frac{2}{7}$$

81.
$$4.85 - 6.4x + 1.11 = 22.6$$
$$-6.4x + 5.96 = 22.6$$
$$-6.4x + 5.96 - 5.96 = 22.6 - 5.96$$
$$-6.4x = 16.64$$
$$\frac{-6.4x}{-6.4} = \frac{16.64}{-6.4}$$
$$x = -2.6$$

83.
$$7 = 8 - 5(m + 3)$$
$$7 = 8 - 5m - 15$$
$$7 = -5m - 7$$
$$7 + 7 = -5m - 7 + 7$$
$$14 = -5m$$
$$\frac{14}{-5} = \frac{-5m}{-5}$$
$$-\frac{14}{5} = m$$

85.
$$10 = \frac{2s + 4}{5}$$
$$5(10) = 5\left(\frac{2s + 4}{5}\right)$$
$$50 = 2s + 4$$
$$50 - 4 = 2s + 4 - 4$$
$$46 = 2s$$
$$\frac{46}{2} = \frac{2s}{2}$$
$$23 = s$$

87.
$$x + \frac{2}{3} = \frac{3}{5}$$
$$15\left(x + \frac{2}{3}\right) = 15\left(\frac{3}{5}\right)$$
$$15x + 10 = 9$$
$$15x + 10 - 10 = 9 - 10$$
$$15x = -1$$
$$\frac{15x}{15} = \frac{-1}{15}$$
$$x = -\frac{1}{15}$$

89.
$$\frac{t}{4} - t = \frac{3}{2}$$
$$4\left(\frac{t}{4} - t\right) = 4\left(\frac{3}{2}\right)$$
$$t - 4t = 6$$
$$-3t = 6$$
$$\frac{-3t}{-3} = \frac{6}{-3}$$
$$t = -2$$

91.
$$\frac{3}{7} = \frac{3t}{4} + 1$$
$$28\left(\frac{3}{7}\right) = 28\left(\frac{3t}{4} + 1\right)$$
$$12 = 21t + 28$$
$$12 - 28 = 21t + 28 - 28$$
$$-16 = 21t$$
$$\frac{-16}{21} = \frac{21t}{21}$$
$$-\frac{16}{21} = t$$

93.
$$\frac{1}{2}r + \frac{1}{5}r = 7$$
$$10\left(\frac{1}{2}r + \frac{1}{5}r\right) = 10(7)$$
$$5r + 2r = 70$$
$$7r = 70$$
$$\frac{7r}{7} = \frac{70}{7}$$
$$r = 10$$

95.
$$\frac{x}{3} - \frac{3x}{4} = \frac{1}{12}$$
$$12\left(\frac{x}{3} - \frac{3x}{4}\right) = 12\left(\frac{1}{12}\right)$$
$$4x - 9x = 1$$
$$-5x = 1$$
$$\frac{-5x}{-5} = \frac{1}{-5}$$
$$x = -\frac{1}{5}$$

97.
$$\frac{1}{2}x + 4 = \frac{1}{6}$$
$$6\left(\frac{1}{2}x + 4\right) = 6\left(\frac{1}{6}\right)$$
$$3x + 24 = 1$$
$$3x + 24 - 24 = 1 - 24$$
$$3x = -23$$
$$\frac{3x}{3} = \frac{-23}{3}$$
$$x = -\frac{23}{3}$$

99.
$$\frac{4}{5}s - \frac{3}{4}s = \frac{1}{10}$$
$$20\left(\frac{4}{5}s - \frac{3}{4}s\right) = 20\left(\frac{1}{10}\right)$$
$$16s - 15s = 2$$
$$s = 2$$

101.
$$\frac{4}{9} = \frac{1}{3}(n - 7)$$
$$\frac{4}{9} = \frac{1}{3}n - \frac{7}{3}$$
$$9\left(\frac{4}{9}\right) = 9\left(\frac{1}{3}n - \frac{7}{3}\right)$$
$$4 = 3n - 21$$
$$4 + 21 = 3n - 21 + 21$$
$$25 = 3n$$
$$\frac{25}{3} = \frac{3n}{3}$$
$$\frac{25}{3} = n$$

103.
$$-\frac{3}{5} = -\frac{1}{9} - \frac{3}{4}x$$
$$180\left(-\frac{3}{5}\right) = 180\left(-\frac{1}{9} - \frac{3}{4}x\right)$$
$$-108 = -20 - 135x$$
$$-108 + 20 = -20 + 20 - 135x$$
$$-88 = -135x$$
$$\frac{-88}{-135} = \frac{-135x}{-135}$$
$$\frac{88}{135} = x$$

105. a. By subtracting first, you will not have to work with fractions.

b.
$$3x + 2 = 11$$
$$3x + 2 - 2 = 11 - 2$$
$$3x = 9$$
$$\frac{3x}{3} = \frac{9}{3}$$
$$x = 3$$

107. $3(x - 2) - (x + 5) - 2(3 - 2x) = 18$
$$3x - 6 - x - 5 - 6 + 4x = 18$$
$$3x - x + 4x - 6 - 5 - 6 = 18$$
$$6x - 17 = 18$$
$$6x - 17 + 17 = 18 + 17$$
$$6x = 35$$
$$\frac{6x}{6} = \frac{35}{6}$$
$$x = \frac{35}{6}$$

109. $4[3 - 2(x + 4)] - (x + 3) = 13$
$$4(3 - 2x - 8) - x - 3 = 13$$
$$4(-2x - 5) - x - 3 = 13$$
$$-8x - 20 - x - 3 = 13$$
$$-9x - 23 = 13$$
$$-9x - 23 + 23 = 13 + 23$$
$$-9x = 36$$
$$\frac{-9x}{-9} = \frac{36}{-9}$$
$$x = -4$$

111. a. Let x = cost of one box of stationery
$$3x + 6 = 42$$

b.
$$3x + 6 = 42$$
$$3x + 6 - 6 = 42 - 6$$
$$3x = 36$$
$$x = 12$$
A box of stationery costs $12.00.

113. $\left[5(2 - 6) + 3\left(8\quad 4\right)^2\right]^2 = \left[5(-4) + 3(2)^2\right]^2$
$$= \left[-20 + 3(4)\right]^2$$
$$= \left[-20 + 12\right]^2$$
$$= \left[-8\right]^2$$
$$= 64$$

114. Substitute 5 for x in the expression.
$$-2x^2 + 3x - 12$$
$$-2(5)^2 + 3(5) - 12$$
$$-2(25) + 15 - 12$$
$$-50 + 15 - 12$$

$-35 - 12$

-47

115. To solve an equation, we need to isolate the variable on one side of the equation.

116. To solve the equation, we divide both sides of the equation by –4.

Exercise Set 2.5

1. Answers will vary.

3. a. An identity is an equation that is true for infinitely many values of the variable.

   b. The solution is all real numbers.

5. The equation is an identity because both sides of the equation are identical.

7. An equation has no solution if it simplifies to a false statement.

9. a. Use the distributive property.
Subtract $4x$ from both sides of the equation.
Add 30 to both sides of the equation.
Divide both sides of the equation by 2.

   b. $4(x + 3) = 6(x - 5)$
$4x + 12 = 6x - 30$
$12 = 2x - 30$
$42 = 2x$
$21 = x$ or $x = 21$

11. $3x = -2x + 15$
$3x + 2x = -2x + 2x + 15$
$5x = 15$
$\dfrac{5x}{5} = \dfrac{15}{5}$
$x = 3$

13. $-4x + 10 = 6x$
$-4x + 4x + 10 = 6x + 4x$
$10 = 10x$
$\dfrac{10}{10} = \dfrac{10x}{10}$
$1 = x$

15. $5x + 3 = 6$
$5x + 3 - 3 = 6 - 3$
$5x = 3$
$\dfrac{5x}{5} = \dfrac{3}{5}$
$x = \dfrac{3}{5}$

17. $21 - 6p = 3p - 2p$
$21 - 6p = p$
$21 - 6p + 6p = p + 6p$
$21 = 7p$
$\dfrac{21}{7} = \dfrac{7p}{7}$
$3 = p$

19. $2x - 4 = 3x - 6$
$2x - 2x - 4 = 3x - 2x - 6$
$-4 = x - 6$
$-4 + 6 = x - 6 + 6$
$2 = x$

21. $6 - 2y = 9 - 8y + 6y$
$6 - 2y = 9 - 2y$
$6 - 2y + 2y = 9 - 2y + 2y$
$6 = 9$ False

Since a false statement is obtained, there is no solution.

23. $9 - 0.5x = 4.5x + 8.50$
$9 - 0.5x + 0.5x = 4.5x + 0.5x + 8.50$
$9 = 5x + 8.50$
$9 - 8.50 = 5x + 8.50 - 8.50$
$0.5 = 5x$
$\dfrac{0.5}{5} = \dfrac{5x}{5}$
$0.1 = x$

25. $0.62x - .065 = 9.75 - 2.63x$
$0.62x + 2.63x - 0.65 = 9.75 - 2.63x + 2.63x$
$3.25x - 0.65 = 9.75$
$3.25x - 0.65 + 0.65 = 9.75 + 0.65$
$3.25x = 10.4$
$\dfrac{3.25x}{3.25} = \dfrac{10.4}{3.25}$
$x = 3.2$

27.
$$5x + 3 = 2(x + 6)$$
$$5x + 3 = 2x + 12$$
$$5x - 2x + 3 = 2x - 2x + 12$$
$$3x + 3 = 12$$
$$3x + 3 - 3 = 12 - 3$$
$$3x = 9$$
$$\frac{3x}{3} = \frac{9}{3}$$
$$x = 3$$

29.
$$x - 25 = 12x + 9 + 3x$$
$$x - 25 = 15x + 9$$
$$x - x - 25 = 15x - x + 9$$
$$-25 = 14x + 9$$
$$-25 - 9 = 14x + 9 - 9$$
$$-34 = 14x$$
$$\frac{-34}{14} = \frac{14x}{14}$$
$$-\frac{17}{7} = x$$

31.
$$2(x - 2) = 4x - 6 - 2x$$
$$2x - 4 = 2x - 6$$
$$2x - 2x - 4 = 2x - 2x - 6$$
$$-4 = -6 \quad \text{False}$$
Since a false statement is obtained, there is no solution.

33.
$$-(w + 2) = -6w + 32$$
$$-w - 2 = -6w + 32$$
$$-w + w - 2 = -6w + w + 32$$
$$-2 = -5w + 32$$
$$-2 - 32 = -5w + 32 - 32$$
$$-34 = -5w$$
$$\frac{-34}{-5} = \frac{-5w}{-5}$$
$$\frac{34}{5} = w$$

35.
$$5 - 3(2t - 5) = 3t + 13$$
$$5 - 6t + 15 = 3t + 13$$
$$-6t + 20 = 3t + 13$$
$$-6t + 6t + 20 = 3t + 6t + 13$$
$$20 = 9t + 13$$
$$20 - 13 = 9t + 13 - 13$$
$$7 = 9t$$
$$\frac{7}{9} = \frac{9t}{9}$$
$$\frac{7}{9} = t$$

37.
$$\frac{a}{5} = \frac{a - 3}{2}$$
$$10\left(\frac{a}{5}\right) = 10\left(\frac{a - 3}{2}\right)$$
$$2a = 5(a - 3)$$
$$2a = 5a - 15$$
$$2a - 5a = 5a - 5a - 15$$
$$-3a = -15$$
$$\frac{-3a}{-3} = \frac{-15}{-3}$$
$$a = 5$$

39.
$$6 - \frac{x}{4} = \frac{x}{8}$$
$$8\left(6 - \frac{x}{4}\right) = 8\left(\frac{x}{8}\right)$$
$$48 - 2x = x$$
$$48 - 2x + 2x = x + 2x$$
$$48 = 3x$$
$$\frac{48}{3} = \frac{3x}{3}$$
$$16 = x$$

41.
$$\frac{5}{2} - \frac{x}{3} = 3x$$
$$6\left(\frac{5}{2} - \frac{x}{3}\right) = 6(3x)$$
$$15 - 2x = 18x$$
$$15 - 2x + 2x = 18x + 2x$$
$$15 = 20x$$
$$\frac{15}{20} = \frac{20x}{20}$$
$$\frac{15}{20} = x$$
$$\frac{3}{4} = x$$

43.

$$\frac{5}{8} + \frac{1}{4}a = \frac{1}{2}a$$

$$8\left(\frac{5}{8} + \frac{1}{4}a\right) = 8\left(\frac{1}{2}a\right)$$

$$5 + 2a = 4a$$

$$5 + 2a - 2a = 4a - 2a$$

$$5 = 2a$$

$$\frac{5}{2} = \frac{2a}{2}$$

$$\frac{5}{2} = a$$

45.

$$0.1(x + 10) = 0.3x - 4$$

$$0.1x + 1 = 0.3x - 4$$

$$0.1x - 0.1x + 1 = 0.3x - 0.1x - 4$$

$$1 + 4 = 0.2x - 4 + 4$$

$$5 = 0.2x$$

$$\frac{5}{0.2} = \frac{0.2x}{0.2}$$

$$25 = x$$

47.

$$2(x + 4) = 4x + 3 - 2x + 5$$

$$2x + 8 = 4x + 3 - 2x + 5$$

$$2x + 8 = 2x + 8$$

Since the left side of the equation is identical to the right side, the equation is true for all values of x. Thus the solution is all real numbers.

49.

$$5(3n + 3) = 2(5n - 4) + 6n$$

$$15n + 15 = 10n - 8 + 6n$$

$$15n + 15 = 16n - 8$$

$$15n - 15n + 15 = 16n - 15n - 8$$

$$15 = n - 8$$

$$15 + 8 = n - 8 + 8$$

$$23 = n$$

51.

$$-(3 - p) = -(2p + 3)$$

$$-3 + p = -2p - 3$$

$$-3 + p + 2p = -2p + 2p - 3$$

$$-3 + 3p = -3$$

$$-3 + 3 + 3p = -3 + 3$$

$$3p = 0$$

$$\frac{3p}{3} = \frac{0}{3}$$

$$p = 0$$

53.

$$-(x + 4) + 5 = 4x + 1 - 5x$$

$$-x - 4 + 5 = 4x + 1 - 5x$$

$$-x + 1 = -x + 1$$

Since the left side of the equation is identical to

the right side, the equation is true for all values of x. Thus the solution is all real numbers.

55.

$$35(2x - 1) = 7(x + 4) + 3x$$

$$70x - 35 = 7x + 28 + 3x$$

$$70x - 35 = 10x + 28$$

$$70x - 10x - 35 = 10x - 10x + 28$$

$$60x - 35 = 28$$

$$60x - 35 + 35 = 28 + 35$$

$$60x = 63$$

$$\frac{60x}{60} = \frac{63}{60}$$

$$x = \frac{21}{20}$$

57.

$$0.4(x + 0.7) = 0.6(x - 4.2)$$

$$0.4x + 0.28 = 0.6x - 2.52$$

$$0.4x - 0.4x + 0.28 = 0.6x - 0.4x - 2.52$$

$$0.28 = 0.2x - 2.52$$

$$0.28 + 2.52 = 0.2x - 2.52 + 2.52$$

$$2.8 = 0.2x$$

$$\frac{2.8}{0.2} = \frac{0.2x}{0.2}$$

$$14 = x$$

59.

$$\frac{3}{5}x + 4 = \frac{1}{5}x + 5$$

$$5\left(\frac{3}{5}x + 4\right) = 5\left(\frac{1}{5}x + 5\right)$$

$$3x + 20 = x + 25$$

$$3x - x + 20 = x - x + 25$$

$$2x + 20 = 25$$

$$2x + 20 - 20 = 25 - 20$$

$$2x = 5$$

$$\frac{2x}{2} = \frac{5}{2}$$

$$x = \frac{5}{2}$$

61. $\dfrac{3}{4}(2x-4)=4-2x$

$$\dfrac{6}{4}x-3=4-2x$$

$$4\left(\dfrac{6}{4}x-3\right)=4(4-2x)$$

$$6x-12=16-8x$$

$$6x+8x-12=16-8x+8x$$

$$14x-12=16$$

$$14x-12+12=16+12$$

$$14x=28$$

$$\dfrac{14x}{14}=\dfrac{28}{14}$$

$$x=2$$

63. $3(x-4)=2(x-8)+5x$

$$3x-12=2x-16+5x$$

$$3x-12=7x-16$$

$$3x-3x-12=7x-3x-16$$

$$-12=4x-16$$

$$-12+16=4x-16+16$$

$$4=4x$$

$$\dfrac{4}{4}=\dfrac{4x}{4}$$

$$1=x$$

65. $3(x-6)-4(3x+1)=x-22$

$$3x-18-12x-4=x-22$$

$$-9x-22=x-22$$

$$-9x+9x-22=x+9x-22$$

$$-22=10x-22$$

$$-22+22=10x-22+22$$

$$0=10x$$

$$\dfrac{0}{10}=\dfrac{10x}{10}$$

$$0=x$$

67. $5+2x=6(x+1)-5(x-3)$

$$5+2x=6x+6-5x+15$$

$$5+2x=x+21$$

$$5+2x-x=x-x+21$$

$$5+x=21$$

$$5-5+x=21-5$$

$$x=16$$

69. $7-(-y-5)=2(y+3)-6(y+1)$

$$7+y+5=2y+6-6y-6$$

$$12+y=-4y$$

$$12+y-y=-4y-y$$

$$12=-5y$$

$$\dfrac{12}{-5}=\dfrac{-5y}{-5}$$

$$-\dfrac{12}{5}=y$$

71. $\dfrac{1}{2}(2d+4)=\dfrac{1}{3}(4d-4)$

$$d+2=\dfrac{4d}{3}-\dfrac{4}{3}$$

$$3(d+2)=3\left(\dfrac{4d}{3}-\dfrac{4}{3}\right)$$

$$3d+6=4d-4$$

$$3d-3d+6=4d-3d-4$$

$$6=d-4$$

$$6+4=d-4+4$$

$$10=d$$

73. $\dfrac{3(2r-5)}{5}=\dfrac{3r-6}{4}$

$$\dfrac{6r-15}{5}=\dfrac{3r-6}{4}$$

$$20\left(\dfrac{6r-15}{5}\right)=20\left(\dfrac{3r-6}{4}\right)$$

$$4(6r-15)=5(3r-6)$$

$$24r-60=15r-30$$

$$24r-15r-60=15r-15r-30$$

$$9r-60=-30$$

$$9r-60+60=-30+60$$

$$9r=30$$

$$\dfrac{9r}{9}=\dfrac{30}{9}$$

$$r=\dfrac{30}{9}=\dfrac{10}{3}$$

75.
$$\frac{2}{7}(5x+4)=\frac{1}{2}(3x-4)+1$$
$$\frac{10x}{7}+\frac{8}{7}=\frac{3x}{2}-2+1$$
$$\frac{10x}{7}+\frac{8}{7}=\frac{3x}{2}-1$$
$$14\left(\frac{10x}{7}+\frac{8}{7}\right)=14\left(\frac{3x}{2}-1\right)$$
$$20x+16=21x-14$$
$$20x-20x+16=21x-20x-14$$
$$16=x-14$$
$$16+14=x-14+14$$
$$30=x$$

77.
$$\frac{a-5}{2}=\frac{3a}{4}+\frac{a-25}{6}$$
$$12\left(\frac{a-5}{2}\right)=12\left(\frac{3a}{4}+\frac{a-25}{6}\right)$$
$$6(a-5)=9a+2(a-25)$$
$$6a-30=9a+2a-50$$
$$6a-30=11a-50$$
$$6a-6a-30=11a-6a-50$$
$$-30=5a-50$$
$$-30+50=5a-50+50$$
$$20=5a$$
$$\frac{20}{5}=\frac{5a}{5}$$
$$4=a$$

79. a. One example is $x+x+1=x+2$.

   b. It has a single solution.

   c. Answers will vary. For equation given in part **a**):
$$x+x+1=x+2$$
$$2x+1=x+2$$
$$2x-x+1=x-x+2$$
$$x+1=2$$
$$x+1-1=2-1$$
$$x=1$$

81. a. One example is $x+x+1=2x+1$.

   b. Both sides simplify to the same expression.

   c. The solution is all real numbers.

83. a. One example is $x+x+1=2x+2$.

   b. It simplifies to a false statement.

   c. The solution is that there is no solution.

85.
$$5*-1=4*+5$$
$$5*-4*-1=4*-4*+5$$
$$*-1=5$$
$$*-1+1=5+1$$
$$*=6$$

87.
$$3\odot-5=2\odot-5+\odot$$
$$3\odot-5=3\odot-5$$
The left side of the equation is identical to the right side. The solution is all real numbers.

89.
$$4-\left[5-3(x+2)\right]=x-3$$
$$4-(5-3x-6)=x-3$$
$$4-5+3x+6=x-3$$
$$3x+5=x-3$$
$$3x-x+5=x-x-3$$
$$2x+5=-3$$
$$2x+5-5=-3-5$$
$$2x=-8$$
$$\frac{2x}{2}=\frac{-8}{2}$$
$$x=-4$$

91. a. $|4|=4$

   b. $|-7|=7$

   c. $|0|=0$

92. $\left(\frac{2}{3}\right)^5\approx0.131687243$

93. Factors are expressions that are multiplied together; terms are expressions that are added together.

94. $2(x-3)+4x-(4-x)=2x-6+4x-4+x$
$$=7x-10$$

95.
$$2(x-3)+4x-(4-x)=0$$
$$2x-6+4x-4+x=0$$
$$7x-10=0$$
$$7x-10+10=0+10$$
$$7x=10$$
$$\frac{7x}{7}=\frac{10}{7}$$
$$x=\frac{10}{7}$$

96. $(x+4)-(4x-3)=16$
$$x+4-4x+3=16$$
$$-3x+7=16$$
$$-3x+7-7=16-7$$
$$-3x=9$$
$$\frac{-3x}{-3}=\frac{9}{-3}$$
$$x=-3$$

Exercise Set 2.6

1. A ratio is a quotient of two quantities.

3. The ratio of c to d can be written as c to d, c:d, and $\frac{c}{d}$.

5. To set up and solve a proportion, we need a given
ratio and one of the two parts of a second ratio.

7. No, similar figures have the same shape but not necessarily the same size.

9. Yes; the terms in each ratio are in the same order.

11. No; The terms in each ratio are not in the same order.

13. $6:9 = 2:3$

15. $3:6 = 1:2$

17. Total grades $= 6+4+9+3+2=24$
Ratio of total grades to D's $= 24:3 = 8:1$

19. $7:4$

21. $5:15 = 1:3$

23. 3 hours $= 3\times60 = 180$ minutes
Ratio is $\frac{180}{30}=\frac{6}{1}$ or $6:1$.

25. 4 pounds is $4\times16 = 64$ ounces
Ratio is $\frac{26}{64}=\frac{13}{32}$ or $13:32$.

27. Gear ratio $= \dfrac{\text{number of teeth on driving gear}}{\text{number of teeth on driven gear}}$
$$=\frac{40}{5}=\frac{8}{1}$$
Gear ratio is $8:1$.

29. a. $199:140$

b. Since $199140 \approx 1.42$, $199:140 \approx 1.42:1$.

31. a. $1.13:0.38$

b. Since $1.130.38 \approx 2.97$, $1.13:0.38 \approx 2.97:1$.

33. a. $434:174$ or $217:87$

b. $374:434$ or $187:217$

35. a. $40:32$ or $5:4$

b. $15:11$

37. $\dfrac{3}{x}=\dfrac{5}{20}$
$$3\cdot20=x\cdot5$$
$$60=5x$$
$$\frac{60}{5}=x$$
$$12=x$$

39. $\dfrac{5}{3}=\dfrac{75}{a}$
$$5\cdot a=3\cdot75$$
$$5a=225$$
$$a=\frac{225}{5}=45$$

41. $\dfrac{90}{x}=\dfrac{-9}{10}$
$$90\cdot10=x(-9)$$
$$900=-9x$$
$$\frac{900}{-9}=x$$
$$-100=x$$

43. $\dfrac{15}{45}=\dfrac{x}{-6}$
$$45\cdot x=-6\cdot15$$
$$45x=-90$$
$$x=\frac{-90}{45}=-2$$

45. $\dfrac{3}{z}=\dfrac{-1.5}{27}$
$$-1.5\cdot z=3\cdot27$$
$$-1.5z=81$$
$$z=\frac{81}{-1.5}=-54$$

47. $\dfrac{15}{20} = \dfrac{x}{8}$

$15 \cdot 8 = 20 \cdot x$

$120 = 20x$

$\dfrac{120}{20} = x$

$6 = x$

49. $\dfrac{3}{12} = \dfrac{8}{x}$

$3x = (8)(12)$

$3x = 96$

$x = \dfrac{96}{3} = 32$

Thus the side is 32 inches in length.

51. $\dfrac{4}{7} = \dfrac{9}{x}$

$4x = (7)(9)$

$4x = 63$

$x = \dfrac{63}{4} = 15.75$

Thus the side is 15.75 inches in length.

53. $\dfrac{16}{12} = \dfrac{26}{x}$

$16x = (12)(26)$

$16x = 312$

$x = \dfrac{312}{16} = 19.5$

Thus the side is 19.5 inches in length.

55. Let x = number of loads one bottle can do.

$\dfrac{4 \text{ fl ounces}}{1 \text{ load}} = \dfrac{100 \text{ fl ounces}}{x \text{ loads}}$

$\dfrac{4}{1} = \dfrac{100}{x}$

$4x = 100$

$x = \dfrac{100}{4} = 25$

One bottle can do 25 loads.

57. Let x = number of miles that can be driven with a full tank.

$\dfrac{23 \text{ miles}}{1 \text{ gallon}} = \dfrac{x}{15.7 \text{ gallons}}$

$\dfrac{23}{1} = \dfrac{x}{15.7}$

$x = 23 \cdot 15.7$

$x = 361.1$

It can travel 361.1 miles on a full tank.

59. Let x = length of model in feet.

$\dfrac{1 \text{ foot model}}{20 \text{ foot train}} = \dfrac{x \text{ foot model}}{30 \text{ foot train}}$

$\dfrac{1}{20} = \dfrac{x}{30}$

$20x = 30$

$x = \dfrac{30}{20} = 1.5$

The model should be 1.5 feet long.

61. Let x = number of teaspoons needed for sprayer.

$\dfrac{3 \text{ teaspoons}}{1 \text{ gallon water}} = \dfrac{x \text{ teaspoons}}{8 \text{ gallons water}}$

$\dfrac{3}{1} = \dfrac{x}{8}$

$3 \cdot 8 = 1 \cdot x$

$24 = x$

Thus 24 teaspoons are needed for the sprayer.

63. Let x = length of beak of blue heron in inches.

$\dfrac{3.5 \text{ inches in photo}}{3.75 \text{ feet}} = \dfrac{0.4 \text{ inches in photo}}{x \text{ feet}}$

$\dfrac{3.5}{3.75} = \dfrac{0.4}{x}$

$3.5x = 3.75 \cdot 0.4$

$3.5x = 1.5$

$x \approx 0.43$

It's beak is about 0.43 feet long..

65. Let x = length on a map in inches.

$\dfrac{0.5 \text{ inches}}{22 \text{ miles}} = \dfrac{x \text{ inches}}{55 \text{ miles}}$

$\dfrac{0.5}{22} = \dfrac{x}{55}$

$0.5 \cdot 55 = 22 \cdot x$

$27.5 = 22x$

$1.25 = x$

The length on the map will be 1.25 inches.

67. Let x = length of the model bull in feet.

$\dfrac{2.95 \text{ feet metal bull}}{1 \text{ feet real bull}} = \dfrac{28 \text{ feet metal bull}}{x \text{ feet real bull}}$

$\dfrac{2.95}{1} = \dfrac{28}{x}$

$2.95 \cdot x = 1 \cdot 28$

$2.95x = 28$

$x \approx 9.49$

The model bull is about 9.49 feet long.

69. Let x = number of milliliters to be given.

$$\frac{1 \text{ milliliter}}{400 \text{ micrograms}} = \frac{x \text{ milliliter}}{220 \text{ micrograms}}$$

$$\frac{1}{400} = \frac{x}{220}$$

$$1 \cdot 220 = 400 \cdot x$$

$$220 = 400x$$

$$\frac{220}{400} = x$$

$$0.55 = x$$

Thus 0.55 milliliter should be given.

71. Let x = time, in minutes, it takes Jason to swim 30 laps.

$$\frac{3 \text{ laps}}{2.3 \text{ minutes}} = \frac{30 \text{ laps}}{x \text{ minutes}}$$

$$\frac{3}{2.3} = \frac{30}{x}$$

$$3 \cdot x = 2.3 \cdot 30$$

$$3x = 69$$

$$x = 23$$

It will take him 23 minutes.

73. Let x = number of children born with Prader-Willi Syndrome.

$$\frac{12,000 \text{ births}}{1 \text{ baby with syndrome}} = \frac{4,063,000 \text{ births}}{x \text{ babies with syndrome}}$$

$$\frac{12,000}{1} = \frac{4,063,000}{x}$$

$$12,000x = 4,063,000$$

$$x = \frac{4,063,000}{12,000} \approx 339$$

Thus, about 339 children were born with Prader-Willi Syndrome.

75.

$$\frac{12 \text{ inches}}{1 \text{ foot}} = \frac{78 \text{ inches}}{x \text{ feet}}$$

$$\frac{12}{1} = \frac{78}{x}$$

$$12x = 78$$

$$x = \frac{78}{12} = 6.5$$

Thus 42 inches equals 6.5 feet.

77.

$$\frac{9 \text{ square feet}}{1 \text{ square yard}} = \frac{26.1 \text{ square feet}}{x \text{ square yards}}$$

$$\frac{9}{1} = \frac{26.1}{x}$$

$$9x = 26.1$$

$$x = \frac{26.1}{9} = 2.9$$

Thus 26.1 square feet equals 2.9 square yards.

79.

$$\frac{2.54 \text{ cm}}{1 \text{ inch}} = \frac{50.8 \text{ cm}}{x \text{ inches}}$$

$$\frac{2.54}{1} = \frac{50.8}{x}$$

$$2.54x = 50.8$$

$$x = \frac{50.8}{2.54} = 20$$

Thus the length of the newborn is 20 inches.

81. Let x = number of home runs needed to be on schedule to break Bond's record.

$$\frac{73 \text{ home runs}}{162 \text{ games}} = \frac{x}{50 \text{ games}}$$

$$\frac{73}{162} = \frac{x}{50}$$

$$162 \cdot x = 73 \cdot 50$$

$$162x = 3650$$

$$x = \frac{3650}{162} \approx 22.53$$

A player would need to hit 23 home runs.

83.

$$\frac{480 \text{ grains}}{408 \text{ dollars}} = \frac{1 \text{ grain}}{x \text{ dollars}}$$

$$\frac{480}{408} = \frac{1}{x}$$

$$480x = 408$$

$$x = \frac{408}{480} = 0.85$$

Thus the cost per grain is 0.85.

85.

$$\frac{3.75 \text{ standard deviations}}{15 \text{ points}} = \frac{1 \text{ standard deviation}}{x \text{ points}}$$

$$\frac{3.75}{15} = \frac{1}{x}$$

$$3.75x = 15$$

$$x = \frac{15}{3.75} = 4$$

Thus 1 standard deviation equals 4 points.

87. The ratio of Mrs. Ruff's low density to high density cholesterol is $\dfrac{127}{60}$. If we divide 127 by 60 we obtain approximately 2.12. Thus Mrs. Ruff's ratio is approximately equivalent to 2.12:1. Therefore her ratio is less than the desired 4:1 ratio.

89. In $\dfrac{a}{b} = \dfrac{c}{d}$, if b and d remain the same while a increases, then c increases because $ad=bc$. If a increases ad increases so bc must increase by increasing c.

91. Let x = number of miles remaining on the life of each tire.
Inches remaining on the life of each tire:
$$0.31 - 0.06 = 0.25$$
$$\frac{0.03 \text{ inches}}{5000 \text{ miles}} = \frac{0.25 \text{ miles}}{x \text{ miles}}$$
$$\frac{0.03}{5000} = \frac{0.25}{x}$$
$$0.03x = 5000 \cdot 0.25$$
$$0.03x = 1250$$
$$x = \frac{1250}{0.03}$$
$$x \approx 41{,}667$$
The tires will last about 41,667 more miles.

93. Let x = number of cubic centimeters of fluid needed.
$$\frac{1}{40} = \frac{x}{25}$$
$$40x = 25$$
$$x = \frac{25}{40}$$
$$x = 0.625$$
0.625 cubic centimeters of fluid should be drawn up into a syringe.

97. Commutative property of addition

98. Associative property of multiplication

99. Distributive property

100.
$$-(2x + 6) = 2(3x - 6)$$
$$-2x - 6 = 6x - 12$$
$$-2x + 2x - 6 = 6x + 2x - 12$$
$$-6 = 8x - 12$$
$$-6 + 12 = 8x - 12 + 12$$
$$6 = 8x$$
$$\frac{6}{8} = \frac{8x}{8}$$
$$\frac{3}{4} = x$$

101.
$$3(4x - 3) = 6(2x + 1) - 15$$
$$12x - 9 = 12x + 6 - 15$$
$$12x - 9 = 12x - 9$$
$$12x - 12x - 9 = 12x - 12x - 9$$
$$-9 = -9 \quad \text{True}$$
Since a true statement is obtained, the solution is all real numbers.

Exercise Set 2.7

1. >: is greater than;
≥: is greater than or equal to;
<: is less than;
≤: is less than or equal to

3. a. $3 > 3$ is false because 3 is not greater than 3.

   b. $3 \geq 3$ is true because 3 is greater than or equal to 3.

5. The direction of the inequality symbol is changed when multiplying or dividing by a negative number.

7. Since 3 is always less than 5, the solution is all real numbers.

9. Since 5 is never less than 2, the answer is no solution.

11.
$$x + 2 > 6$$
$$x + 2 - 2 > 6 - 2$$
$$x > 4$$

13. $x + 9 \geq 6$

$x + 9 - 9 \geq 6 - 9$

$x \geq -3$

-3

15. $-x + 3 < 8$

$-x + 3 - 3 < 8 - 3$

$-x < 5$

$(-1)(-x) > (-1)(5)$

$x > -5$

-5

17. $8 \leq 2 - r$

$8 - 2 \leq 2 - r - 2$

$6 \leq -r$

$(-1)(6) \geq (-1)(-r)$

$-6 \geq r$

$r \leq -6$

-6

19. $-2x < 3$

$\dfrac{-2x}{-2} > \dfrac{3}{-2}$

$x > -\dfrac{3}{2}$

$-\dfrac{3}{2}$

21. $2x + 3 \leq 5$

$2x + 3 - 3 \leq 5 - 3$

$2x \leq 2$

$\dfrac{2x}{2} \leq \dfrac{2}{2}$

$x \leq 1$

1

23. $6n - 12 < -12$

$6n - 12 + 12 < -12 + 12$

$6n < 0$

$\dfrac{6n}{6} < \dfrac{0}{6}$

$n < 0$

0

25. $4 - 6x > -5$

$4 - 4 - 6x > -5 - 4$

$-6x > -9$

$\dfrac{-6x}{-6} < \dfrac{-9}{-6}$

$x < \dfrac{3}{2}$

$\dfrac{3}{2}$

27. $15 > -9x + 50$

$9x + 15 > -9x + 9x + 50$

$9x + 15 > 50$

$9x + 15 - 15 > 50 - 15$

$9x > 35$

$\dfrac{9x}{9} > \dfrac{35}{9}$

$x > \dfrac{35}{9}$

$\dfrac{35}{9}$

29. $6 < 3x + 10$

$6 - 10 < 3x + 10 - 10$

$-4 < 3x$

$\dfrac{-4}{3} < \dfrac{3x}{3}$

$\dfrac{-4}{3} < x$

$x > -\dfrac{4}{3}$

$-\dfrac{4}{3}$

56

31.
$$6s + 2 \le 6s - 9$$
$$6s + 2 - 2 \le 6s - 9 - 2$$
$$6s \le 6x - 11$$
$$6s - 6s \le 6s - 6s - 11$$
$$0 \le -11 \quad \text{False}$$
Since a false statement is obtained, there is no solution.

33.
$$x - 4 \le 3x + 8$$
$$x - 4 - 8 \le 3x + 8 - 8$$
$$x - 12 \le 3x$$
$$x - x - 12 \le 3x - x$$
$$-12 \le 2x$$
$$\frac{-12}{2} \le \frac{2x}{2}$$
$$-6 \le x$$
$$x \ge -6$$

35.
$$-x + 4 < -3x + 6$$
$$-x + 4 - 4 \le -3x + 6 - 4$$
$$-x < -3x + 2$$
$$-x + 3x < -3x + 3x + 2$$
$$2x < 2$$
$$\frac{2x}{2} < \frac{2}{2}$$
$$x < 1$$

37.
$$6(2m - 4) \ge 2(6m - 12)$$
$$12m - 24 \ge 12m - 24$$
$$12m - 12m - 24 \ge 12m - 12m - 24$$
$$-24 \ge -24 \quad \text{True}$$
Since a true statement is obtained, the solution is all real numbers.

39.
$$x + 3 < x + 4$$
$$x - x + 3 < x - x + 4$$
$$3 < 4$$
Since 3 is always less than 4, the solution is all real numbers.

41.
$$6(3 - x) < 2x + 12$$
$$18 - 6x < 2x + 12$$
$$18 - 12 - 6x < 2x + 12 - 12$$
$$6 - 6x < 2x$$
$$6 - 6x + 6x < 2x + 6x$$
$$6 < 8x$$
$$\frac{6}{8} < \frac{8x}{8}$$
$$\frac{3}{4} < x$$
$$x > \frac{3}{4}$$

43.
$$4x - 4 < 4(x - 5)$$
$$4x - 4 < 4x - 20$$
$$4x - 4x - 4 < 4x - 4x - 20$$
$$-4 < -20$$
Since −4 is never less than −20, there is no solution.

45.
$$5(2x + 3) \ge 6 + (x + 2) - 2x$$
$$10x + 15 \ge 6 + x + 2 - 2x$$
$$10x + 15 \ge 8 - x$$
$$10x + 15 - 15 \ge 8 - 15 - x$$
$$10x \ge -7 - x$$
$$10x + x \ge -7 - x + x$$
$$11x \ge -7$$
$$\frac{11x}{11} \ge \frac{-7}{11}$$
$$x \ge -\frac{7}{11}$$

47.
$$1.2x + 3.1 < 3.5x - 3.8$$
$$1.2x - 1.2x + 3.1 < 3.5x - 1.2x - 3.8$$
$$3.1 < 2.3x - 3.8$$
$$3.1 + 3.8 < 2.3x - 3.8 + 3.8$$
$$6.9 < 2.3x$$
$$\frac{6.9}{2.3} < \frac{2.3x}{2.3}$$
$$3 < x$$
$$x > 3$$

49.
$$1.2(m-3) \geq 4.6(2-m) + 1.7$$
$$1.2m - 3.6 \geq 9.2 - 4.6m + 1.7$$
$$1.2m - 3.6 \geq 10.9 - 4.6m$$
$$1.2m + 4.6m - 3.6 \geq 10.9 - 4.6m + 4.6m$$
$$5.8m - 3.6 \geq 10.9$$
$$5.8m - 3.6 + 3.6 \geq 10.9 + 3.6$$
$$5.8m \geq 14.5$$
$$\frac{5.8m}{5.8} \geq \frac{14.5}{5.8}$$
$$m \geq 2.5$$

51.
$$\frac{x}{3} \leq \frac{x}{4} + 4$$
$$12\left(\frac{x}{3}\right) \leq 12\left(\frac{x}{4} + 4\right)$$
$$4x \leq 3x + 48$$
$$4x - 3x \leq 3x - 3x + 48$$
$$x \leq 48$$

53.
$$t + \frac{1}{6} > \frac{2}{3}t$$
$$6\left(t + \frac{1}{6}\right) > 6\left(\frac{2}{3}t\right)$$
$$6t + 1 > 4t$$
$$6t - 6t + 1 > 4t - 6t$$
$$1 > -2t$$
$$\frac{1}{-2} < \frac{-2t}{-2}$$
$$-\frac{1}{2} < t$$
$$t > -\frac{1}{2}$$

55.
$$\frac{1}{8}(4 - r) \leq \frac{1}{4}$$
$$\frac{4}{8} - \frac{1}{8}r \leq \frac{1}{4}$$
$$8\left(\frac{4}{8} - \frac{1}{8}r\right) \leq 8\left(\frac{1}{4}\right)$$
$$4 - r \leq 2$$
$$4 - 4 - r \leq 2 - 4$$
$$-r \leq -2$$
$$(-1)(-r) \geq (-1)(-2)$$
$$r \geq 2$$

57.
$$\frac{2}{3}(t + 2) \leq \frac{1}{4}(2t - 6)$$
$$\frac{2}{3}t + \frac{4}{3} \leq \frac{1}{2}t - \frac{3}{2}$$
$$6\left(\frac{2}{3}t + \frac{4}{3}\right) \leq 6\left(\frac{1}{2}t - \frac{3}{2}\right)$$
$$4t + 8 \leq 3t - 9$$
$$4t - 3t + 8 \leq 3t - 3t - 9$$
$$t + 8 \leq -9$$
$$t + 8 - 8 \leq -9 - 8$$
$$t \leq -17$$

59. a. The average high temperature was greater than 65°F in May, June, July, August, and September.

b. The average high temperature was less than or equal to 59°F in January, February, March, April, November, and December.

c. The average low temperature was less than 29°F in January, February, and December.

d. The average low temperature was greater than or equal to 58°F in June, July, and August.

61. $\neq$

63. We cannot divide both sides of an inequality by y because we do not know that y is positive. If y is negative, we must reverse the sign of the inequality.

65. $6x - 6 > -4(x + 3) + 5(x + 6) - x$
$6x - 6 > -4x - 12 + 5x + 30 - x$
$6x - 6 > 18$
$6x - 6 + 6 > 18 + 6$
$6x > 24$
$\dfrac{6x}{6} > \dfrac{24}{6}$
$x > 4$

66. Substitute 3 for x.
$-x^2 = -(3)^2$
$= -(3)(3)$
$= -9$

67. Substitute -5 for x.
$-x^2 = -(-5)^2$
$= -(-5)(-5)$
$= -25$

68. $4 - 3(2x - 4) = 5 - (x + 3)$
$4 - 6x + 12 = 5 - x - 3$
$-6x + 16 = 2 - x$
$-6x + 6x + 16 = 2 - x + 6x$
$16 = 2 + 5x$
$16 - 2 = 2 - 2 + 5x$
$14 = 5x$
$\dfrac{14}{5} = \dfrac{5x}{5}$
$\dfrac{14}{5} = x$
$x = \dfrac{14}{5}$ or $2\dfrac{4}{5}$

69. Let x = number of kilowatt-hours of electricity used.
$$\dfrac{\$0.174}{1 \text{ kilowatt - hour}} = \dfrac{\$87}{x \text{ kilowatt - hours}}$$
$$\dfrac{0.174}{1} = \dfrac{87}{x}$$
$$0.174x = 87$$
$$x = \dfrac{87}{0.174} = 500$$
Thus the Vega's used 500 kilowatt-hours of electricity in July.

Review Exercises

1. $3(x + 4) = 3x + 3(4)$
$= 3x + 12$

2. $3(x - 2) = 3[x + (-2)]$
$= 3x + 3(-2)$
$= 3x + (-6)$
$= 3x - 6$

3. $-2(x + 4) = -2x + (-2)(4)$
$= -2x + (-8)$
$= -2x - 8$

4. $-(x + 2) = -1(x + 2)$
$= (-1)(x) + (-1)(2)$
$= -x + (-2)$
$= -x - 2$

5. $-(m + 3) = -1(m + 3)$
$= (-1)(m) + (-1)(3)$
$= -m - 3$

6. $-4(4 - x) = -4[4 + (-x)]$
$= (-4)(4) + (-4)(-x)$
$= -16 + 4x$

7. $5(5 - p) = 5[5 + (-p)]$
$= 5(5) + 5(-p)$
$= 25 + (-5p)$
$= 25 - 5p$

8. $6(4x - 5) = 6(4x) - 6(5)$
$= 24x - 30$

9. $-5(5x - 5) = -5[5x + (-5)]$
$= -5(5x) + (-5)(-5)$
$= -25x + 25$

10. $4(-x + 3) = 4(-x) + 4(3)$
$= -4x + 12$

11. $\dfrac{1}{2}(2x + 4) = \left(\dfrac{1}{2}\right)(2x) + \left(\dfrac{1}{2}\right)(4)$
$= x + 2$

12. $-(3 + 2y) = -1(3 + 2y)$
$= (-1)(3) + (-1)(2y)$
$= -3 + (-2y)$
$= -3 - 2y$

13. $-(x + 2y - z) = -1[x + 2y + (-z)]$
$= -1(x) + (-1)(2y) + (-1)(-z)$
$= -x + (-2y) + z$
$= -x - 2y + z$

14. $-3(2a - 5b + 7) = -3[2a + (-5b) + 7]$
    $$= -3(2a) + (-3)(-5b) + (-3)(7)$$
    $$= -6a + 15b + (-21)$$
    $$= -6a + 15b - 21$$

15. $7x - 3x = 4x$

16. $5 - 3y + 3 = -3y + 5 + 3$
    $$= -3y + 8$$

17. $1 + 3x + 2x = 1 + 5x$
    $$= 5x + 1$$

18. $-2x - x + 3y = -3x + 3y$

19. $4m + 2n + 4m + 6n = 4m + 4m + 2n + 6n$
    $$= 8m + 8n$$

20. There are no like terms.
    $9x + 3y + 2$ cannot be further simplified.

21. $6x - 2x + 3y + 6 = 4x + 3y + 6$

22. $x + 8x - 9x + 3 = 9x - 9x + 3$
    $$= 3$$

23. $-4z - 8z + 3 = -12z + 3$

24. $-2(3a^2 - 4) + 6a^2 - 8 = -6a^2 + 8 + 6a^2 - 8$
    $$= -6a^2 + 6a^2 + 8 - 8$$
    $$= 0$$

25. $2x + 3(x + 4) - 5 = 2x + 3x + 12 - 5$
    $$= 5x + 7$$

26. $4(3 - 2b) - 2b = 12 - 8b - 2b$
    $$= -8b - 2x + 12$$
    $$= -10b + 12$$

27. $6 - (-x + 6) - x = 6 + x - 6 - x$
    $$= x - x + 6 - 6$$
    $$= 0$$

28. $2(2x + 5) - 10 - 4 = 4x + 10 - 10 - 4$
    $$= 4x - 4$$

29. $-6(4 - 3x) - 18 + 4x = -24 + 18x - 18 + 4x$
    $$= 18x + 4x - 24 - 18$$
    $$= 22x - 42$$

30. $4y - 3(x + y) + 6x^2 = 4y - 3x - 3y + 6x^2$
    $$= 6x^2 - 3x + 4y - 3y$$
    $$= 6x^2 - 3x + y$$

31. $\frac{1}{4}d + 2 - \frac{3}{5}d + 5 = \frac{1}{4}d - \frac{3}{5}d + 2 + 5$
    $$= \frac{5}{20}d - \frac{12}{20}d + 7$$
    $$= -\frac{7}{20}d + 7$$

32. $3 - (x - y) + (x - y) = 3 - x + y + x - y$
    $$= -x + x + y - y + 3$$
    $$= 3$$

33. $\frac{5}{6}x - \frac{1}{3}(2x - 6) = \frac{5}{6}x - \frac{2}{3}x + 2$
    $$= \frac{5}{6}x - \frac{4}{6}x + 2$$
    $$= \frac{1}{6}x + 2$$

34. $\frac{2}{3} - \frac{1}{4}n - \frac{1}{3}(n + 2) = \frac{2}{3} - \frac{1}{4}n - \frac{1}{3}n - \frac{2}{3}$
    $$= -\frac{1}{4}n - \frac{1}{3}n + \frac{2}{3} - \frac{2}{3}$$
    $$= -\frac{3}{12}n - \frac{4}{12}n + 0$$
    $$= -\frac{7}{12}n$$

35. $6x = 6$
    $$\frac{6x}{6} = \frac{6}{6}$$
    $$x = 1$$

36. $x + 6 = -7$
    $$x + 6 - 6 = -7 - 6$$
    $$x = -13$$

37. $x - 4 = 7$
    $$x - 4 + 4 = 7 + 4$$
    $$x = 11$$

38. $\frac{x}{3} = -9$
    $$3\left(\frac{x}{3}\right) = 3(-9)$$
    $$x = -27$$

39.
$$2x + 4 = 8$$
$$2x + 4 - 4 = 8 - 4$$
$$2x = 4$$
$$\frac{2x}{2} = \frac{4}{2}$$
$$x = 2$$

40.
$$14 = 3 + 2x$$
$$14 - 3 = 3 - 3 + 2x$$
$$11 = 2x$$
$$\frac{11}{2} = \frac{2x}{2}$$
$$\frac{11}{2} = x$$

41.
$$4c + 3 = -21$$
$$4c + 3 - 3 = -21 - 3$$
$$4c = -24$$
$$\frac{4c}{4} = \frac{-24}{4}$$
$$c = -6$$

42.
$$4 - 2a = 10$$
$$4 - 4 - 2a = 10 - 4$$
$$-2a = 6$$
$$\frac{-2a}{-2} = \frac{6}{-2}$$
$$a = -3$$

43.
$$-x = -12$$
$$-1x = -12$$
$$(-1)(-1x) = (-1)(-12)$$
$$1x = 12$$
$$x = 12$$

44.
$$3(x - 2) = 6$$
$$3x - 6 = 6$$
$$3x - 6 + 6 = 6 + 6$$
$$3x = 12$$
$$\frac{3x}{3} = \frac{12}{3}$$
$$x = 4$$

45.
$$-12 = 3(2x - 8)$$
$$-12 = 6x - 24$$
$$-12 + 24 = 6x - 24 + 24$$
$$12 = 6x$$
$$\frac{12}{6} = \frac{6x}{6}$$
$$2 = x$$

46.
$$4(6 + 2x) = 0$$
$$24 + 8x = 0$$
$$24 - 24 + 8x = 0 - 24$$
$$8x = -24$$
$$\frac{8x}{8} = \frac{-24}{8}$$
$$x = -3$$

47.
$$-6n + 2n + 6 = 0$$
$$-4n + 6 = 0$$
$$-4n + 6 - 6 = 0 - 6$$
$$-4n = -6$$
$$\frac{-4n}{-4} = \frac{-6}{-4}$$
$$n = \frac{6}{4} = \frac{3}{2}$$

48.
$$-3 = 3w - (4w + 6)$$
$$-3 = 3w - 4w - 6$$
$$-3 = -1w - 6$$
$$-3 + 6 = -1w - 6 + 6$$
$$3 = -1w$$
$$\frac{3}{-1} = \frac{-1w}{-1}$$
$$-3 = w$$

49.
$$6 - (2n + 3) - 4n = 6$$
$$6 - 2n - 3 - 4n = 6$$
$$6 - 3 - 2n - 4n = 6$$
$$3 - 6n = 6$$
$$3 - 3 - 6n = 6 - 3$$
$$-6n = 3$$
$$\frac{-6n}{-6} = \frac{3}{-6}$$
$$n = -\frac{3}{6} = -\frac{1}{2}$$

50.
$$4x + 6 - 7x + 9 = 18$$
$$-3x + 15 = 18$$
$$-3x + 15 - 15 = 18 - 15$$
$$-3x = 3$$
$$\frac{-3x}{-3} = \frac{3}{-3}$$
$$x = -1$$

51. $4 + 3(x + 2) = 10$
$4 + 3x + 6 = 10$
$3x + 10 = 10$
$3x + 10 - 10 = 10 - 10$
$3x = 0$
$\dfrac{3x}{3} = \dfrac{0}{3}$
$x = 0$

52. $-3 + 3x = -2(x + 1)$
$-3 + 3x = -2x - 2$
$-3 + 3x + 3 = -2x - 2 + 3$
$3x = -2x + 1$
$3x + 2x = -2x + 1 + 2x$
$5x = 1$
$\dfrac{5x}{5} = \dfrac{1}{5}$
$x = \dfrac{1}{5}$

53. $8.4r - 6.3 = 6.3 + 2.1r$
$8.4r - 2.1r - 6.3 = 6.3 + 2.1r - 2.1r$
$6.3r - 6.3 = 6.3$
$6.3r - 6.3 + 6.3 = 6.3 + 6.3$
$6.3r = 12.6$
$\dfrac{6.3r}{6.3} = \dfrac{12.6}{6.3}$
$r = 2$

54. $19.6 - 21.3t = 80.1 - 9.2t$
$19.6 - 21.3t + 21.3t = 80.1 - 9.2t + 21.3t$
$19.6 = 80.1 + 12.1t$
$19.6 - 80.1 = 80.1 - 80.1 + 12.1t$
$-60.5 = 12.1t$
$\dfrac{-60.5}{12.1} = \dfrac{12.1t}{12.1}$
$-5 = t$

55. $0.35(c - 5) = 0.45(c + 4)$
$0.35c - 1.75 = 0.45c + 1.8$
$0.35c - 0.35c - 1.75 = 0.45c - 0.35c + 1.8$
$-1.75 = 0.10c + 1.8$
$-1.75 - 1.8 = 0.10c + 1.8 - 1.8$
$-3.55 = 0.10c$
$\dfrac{-3.55}{0.10} = \dfrac{0.10c}{0.10}$
$-35.5 = c$

56. $-2.3(x - 8) = 3.7(x + 4)$
$-2.3x + 18.4 = 3.7x + 14.8$
$-2.3x + 2.3x + 18.4 = 3.7x + 2.3x + 14.8$
$18.4 = 6.0x + 14.8$
$18.4 - 14.8 = 6.0x + 14.8 - 14.8$
$3.6 = 6.0x$
$\dfrac{3.6}{6.0} = \dfrac{6.0x}{6.0}$
$0.6 = x$

57. $\dfrac{p}{3} + 2 = \dfrac{1}{4}$
$12\left(\dfrac{p}{3} + 2\right) = 12\left(\dfrac{1}{4}\right)$
$4p + 24 = 3$
$4p + 24 - 24 = 3 - 24$
$4p = -21$
$\dfrac{4p}{4} = \dfrac{-21}{4}$
$p = -\dfrac{21}{4}$

58. $\dfrac{d}{6} + \dfrac{1}{7} = 2$
$42\left(\dfrac{d}{6} + \dfrac{1}{7}\right) = 42(2)$
$7d + 6 = 84$
$7d + 6 - 6 = 84 - 6$
$7d = 78$
$\dfrac{7d}{7} = \dfrac{78}{7}$
$d = \dfrac{78}{7}$

59. $\dfrac{3}{5}(r-6)=3r$

$$\dfrac{3}{5}r-\dfrac{18}{5}=3r$$

$$5\left(\dfrac{3}{5}r-\dfrac{18}{5}\right)=5(3r)$$

$$3r-18=15r$$

$$3r-3r-18=15r-3r$$

$$-18=12r$$

$$\dfrac{-18}{12}=\dfrac{12r}{12}$$

$$-\dfrac{18}{12}=r$$

$$-\dfrac{3}{2}=r$$

60. $\dfrac{2}{3}w=\dfrac{1}{7}(w-2)$

$$\dfrac{2}{3}w=\dfrac{1}{7}w-\dfrac{2}{7}$$

$$21\left(\dfrac{2}{3}w\right)=21\left(\dfrac{1}{7}w-\dfrac{2}{7}\right)$$

$$14w=3w-6$$

$$14w-3w=3w-3w-6$$

$$11w=-6$$

$$\dfrac{11w}{11}=\dfrac{-6}{11}$$

$$w=-\dfrac{6}{11}$$

61. $9x-6=-3x+30$

$$9x+3x-6=-3x+3x+30$$

$$12x-6=30$$

$$12x-6+6=30+6$$

$$12x=36$$

$$\dfrac{12x}{12}=\dfrac{36}{12}$$

$$x=3$$

62. $-(w+2)=2(3w-6)$

$$-w-2=6w-12$$

$$-w-2+12=6w-12+12$$

$$-w+10=6w$$

$$-w+w+10=6w+w$$

$$10=7w$$

$$\dfrac{10}{7}=\dfrac{7w}{7}$$

$$\dfrac{10}{7}=w$$

63. $2x+6=3x+9-3$

$$2x+6=3x+6$$

$$2x-2x+6=3x-2x+6$$

$$6=x+6$$

$$6-6=x+6-6$$

$$0=x$$

64. $-5a+3=2a+10$

$$-5a+3-10=2a+10-10$$

$$-5a-7=2a$$

$$-5a+5a-7=2a+5a$$

$$-7=7a$$

$$\dfrac{-7}{7}=\dfrac{7a}{7}$$

$$-1=a$$

65. $3x-12x=24-9x$

$$-9x=24-9x$$

$$-9x+9x=24-9x+9x$$

$$0=24\quad\text{False}$$

Since a false statement is obtained, there is no solution.

66. $5p-2=-2(-3p+6)$

$$5p-2=6p-12$$

$$5p-5p-2=6p-5p-12$$

$$-2=p-12$$

$$-2+12=p-12+12$$

$$10=p$$

67. $4(2x-3)+4=8x-8$

$$8x-12+4=8x-8$$

$$8x-8=8x-8$$

Since the equation is true for all values of x, the solution is all real numbers.

68. $4 - c - 2(4 - 3c) = 3(c - 4)$

$$4 - c - 8 + 6c = 3c - 12$$
$$5c - 4 = 3c - 12$$
$$5c - 3c - 4 = 3c - 3c - 12$$
$$2c - 4 = -12$$
$$2c - 4 + 4 = -12 + 4$$
$$2c = -8$$
$$\frac{2c}{2} = \frac{-8}{2}$$
$$c = -4$$

69. $2(x + 7) = 6x + 9 - 4x$

$$2x + 14 = 6x + 9 - 4x$$
$$2x + 14 = 2x + 9$$
$$2x - 2x + 14 = 2x - 2x + 9$$
$$14 = 9 \text{ False}$$

Since a false statement is obtained, there is no solution.

70. $-5(3 - 4x) = -6 + 20x - 9$

$$-15 + 20x = -6 + 20x - 9$$
$$-15 + 20x = -15 + 20x$$

The statement is true for all values of x, thus the solution is all real numbers.

71. $4(x - 3) - (x + 5) = 0$

$$4x - 12 - x - 5 = 0$$
$$3x - 17 = 0$$
$$3x - 17 + 17 = 0 + 17$$
$$3x = 17$$
$$\frac{3x}{3} = \frac{17}{3}$$
$$x = \frac{17}{3}$$

72. $-2(4 - x) = 6(x + 2) + 3x$

$$-8 + 2x = 6x + 12 + 3x$$
$$-8 + 2x = 9x + 12$$
$$-8 - 12 + 2x = 9x + 12 - 12$$
$$-20 + 2x = 9x$$
$$-20 + 2x - 2x = 9x - 2x$$
$$-20 = 7x$$
$$\frac{-20}{7} = \frac{7x}{7}$$
$$-\frac{20}{7} = x$$

73. $\dfrac{x + 3}{2} = \dfrac{x}{2}$

$$2(x + 3) = 2x$$
$$2x + 6 = 2x$$
$$2x - 2x + 6 = 2x - 2x$$
$$6 = 0 \quad \text{False}$$

Since a false statement is obtained, there is no solution.

74. $\dfrac{x}{6} = \dfrac{x - 4}{2}$

$$2 \cdot x = 6(x - 4)$$
$$2x = 6x - 24$$
$$2x - 6x = 6x - 6x - 24$$
$$-4x = -24$$
$$\frac{-4x}{-4} = \frac{-24}{-4}$$
$$x = 6$$

75. $\dfrac{1}{5}(3s + 4) = \dfrac{1}{3}(2s - 8)$

$$\frac{3}{5}s + \frac{4}{5} = \frac{2}{3}s - \frac{8}{3}$$
$$15\left(\frac{3}{5}s + \frac{4}{5}\right) = 15\left(\frac{2}{3}s - \frac{8}{3}\right)$$
$$9s + 12 = 10s - 40$$
$$9s - 9s + 12 = 10s - 9s - 40$$
$$12 = s - 40$$
$$12 + 40 = s - 40 + 40$$
$$52 = s$$

76. $\dfrac{2(2t - 4)}{5} = \dfrac{3t + 6}{4} - \dfrac{3}{2}$

$$\frac{4t - 8}{5} = \frac{3t + 6}{4} - \frac{3}{2}$$
$$20\left(\frac{4t - 8}{5}\right) = 20\left(\frac{3t + 6}{4} - \frac{3}{2}\right)$$
$$4(4t - 8) = 5(3t + 6) - 30$$
$$16t - 32 = 15t + 30 - 30$$
$$16t - 32 = 15t + 0$$
$$16t - 16t - 32 = 15t - 16t$$
$$-32 = -1t$$
$$\frac{-32}{-1} = \frac{-1t}{-1}$$
$$32 = t$$

77. $\dfrac{2}{5}(2 - x) = \dfrac{1}{6}(-2x + 2)$

$\dfrac{4}{5} - \dfrac{2}{5}x = -\dfrac{2}{6}x + \dfrac{2}{6}$

$\dfrac{4}{5} - \dfrac{2}{5}x = -\dfrac{1}{3}x + \dfrac{1}{3}$

$15\left(\dfrac{4}{5} - \dfrac{2}{5}x\right) = 15\left(-\dfrac{1}{3}x + \dfrac{1}{3}\right)$

$12 - 6x = -5x + 5$

$12 - 6x + 6x = -5x + 6x + 5$

$12 = x + 5$

$12 - 5 = x + 5 - 5$

$7 = x$

78. $\dfrac{x}{4} + \dfrac{x}{6} = \dfrac{1}{2}(x + 3)$

$\dfrac{x}{4} + \dfrac{x}{6} = \dfrac{x}{2} + \dfrac{3}{2}$

$12\left(\dfrac{x}{4} + \dfrac{x}{6}\right) = 12\left(\dfrac{x}{2} + \dfrac{3}{2}\right)$

$3x + 2x = 6x + 18$

$5x = 6x + 18$

$5x - 6x = 6x - 6x + 18$

$-1x = 18$

$\dfrac{-1x}{-1} = \dfrac{18}{-1}$

$x = -18$

79. $12 : 20 = 3 : 5$

80. $80 \text{ ounces} = \dfrac{80}{16} = 5 \text{ pounds}$

The ratio of 80 ounces to 12 pounds is thus 5:12.

81. $32 \text{ ounces} = \dfrac{32}{16} = 2 \text{ pounds}$

The ratio of 32 ounces to 2 pounds is $\dfrac{2}{2} = \dfrac{1}{1}$.

The ratio is 1:1.

82. $\dfrac{x}{4} = \dfrac{8}{16}$

$16 \cdot x = 8 \cdot 4$

$16x = 32$

$x = \dfrac{32}{16} = 2$

83. $\dfrac{5}{20} = \dfrac{x}{80}$

$20 \cdot x = 80 \cdot 5$

$20x = 400$

$x = \dfrac{400}{20} = 20$

84. $\dfrac{3}{x} = \dfrac{15}{45}$

$3 \cdot 45 = 15 \cdot x$

$135 = 15x$

$\dfrac{135}{15} = x$

$9 = x$

85. $\dfrac{20}{45} = \dfrac{15}{x}$

$20 \cdot x = 15 \cdot 45$

$20x = 675$

$x = \dfrac{675}{20} = \dfrac{135}{4}$

86. $\dfrac{6}{5} = \dfrac{-12}{x}$

$6 \cdot x = -12 \cdot 5$

$6x = -60$

$x = \dfrac{-60}{6} = -10$

87. $\dfrac{b}{6} = \dfrac{8}{-3}$

$-3 \cdot b = 6 \cdot 8$

$-3b = 48$

$x = \dfrac{48}{-3} = -16$

88. $\dfrac{-4}{9} = \dfrac{-16}{x}$

$-4 \cdot x = -16 \cdot 9$

$-4x = -144$

$x = \dfrac{-144}{-4} = 36$

89. $\dfrac{x}{-15} = \dfrac{30}{-5}$

$-5 \cdot x = -15 \cdot 30$

$-5x = -450$

$x = \dfrac{-450}{-5} = 90$

90. $\dfrac{6}{8} = \dfrac{30}{x}$

$6 \cdot x = 8 \cdot 30$

$6x = 240$

$x = \dfrac{240}{6} = 40$

The length of the side is thus 40 in.

91. $\dfrac{7}{3.5} = \dfrac{2}{x}$

$7 \cdot x = 2 \cdot 3.5$

$7x = 7$

$x = \dfrac{7}{7} = 1$

The length of the side is thus 1 ft.

92. $3x + 4 \geq 10$

$3x + 4 - 4 \geq 10 - 4$

$3x \geq 6$

$\dfrac{3x}{3} \geq \dfrac{6}{3}$

$x \geq 2$

93. $-4a - 6 > 4a - 14$

$-4a + 4a - 6 > 4a + 4a - 14$

$-6 > 8a - 14$

$-6 + 14 > 8a - 14 + 14$

$8 > 8a$

$\dfrac{8}{8} > \dfrac{8a}{8}$

$1 > a$

$a < 1$

94. $5 - 3r \leq 2r + 15$

$5 - 15 - 3r \leq 2r + 15 - 15$

$-10 - 3r \leq 2r$

$-10 - 3r + 3r \leq 2r + 3r$

$-10 \leq 5r$

$\dfrac{-10}{5} \leq \dfrac{5r}{5}$

$-2 \leq r$

$r \geq -2$

95. $2(x + 4) \leq 2x - 5$

$2x + 8 \leq 2x - 5$

$2x - 2x + 8 \leq 2x - 2x - 5$

$8 \leq -5$

Since 8 is never less than or equal to –5, there is no solution.

96. $2(x + 3) > 6x - 4x + 4$

$2x + 6 > 6x - 4x + 4$

$2x + 6 > 2x + 4$

$2x - 2x + 6 > 2x - 2x + 4$

$6 > 4$

Since 6 is always greater than 4, the answer is all real numbers.

97. $x + 6 > 9x + 30$

$x + 6 - 30 > 9x + 30 - 30$

$x - 24 > 9x$

$x - x - 24 > 9x - x$

$-24 > 8x$

$\dfrac{-24}{8} > \dfrac{8x}{8}$

$-3 > x$

$x < -3$

98. $x - 2 \leq -4x + 7$

$x - 2 + 2 \leq -4x + 7 + 2$

$x \leq -4x + 9$

$x + 4x \leq -4x + 4x + 9$

$5x \leq 9$

$\dfrac{5x}{5} \leq \dfrac{9}{5}$

$x \leq \dfrac{9}{5}$

99. $-(x + 2) < -2(-2x + 5)$

$$-x - 2 < 4x - 10$$
$$-x - 2 + 10 < 4x - 10 + 10$$
$$-x + 8 < 4x$$
$$-x + x + 8 < 4x + x$$
$$8 < 5x$$
$$\frac{8}{5} < \frac{5x}{5}$$
$$\frac{8}{5} < x$$
$$x > \frac{8}{5}$$

100. $\dfrac{x}{2} < \dfrac{2}{3}(x + 3)$

$$\frac{x}{2} < \frac{2}{3}x + 2$$
$$6\left(\frac{x}{2}\right) < 6\left(\frac{2}{3}x + 2\right)$$
$$3x < 4x + 12$$
$$3x - 4x < 4x - 4x + 12$$
$$-1x < 12$$
$$\frac{-1x}{-1} > \frac{12}{-1}$$
$$x > -12$$

101. $\dfrac{3}{10}(t - 2) \le \dfrac{3}{4}(4 + 2t)$

$$\frac{3}{10}t - \frac{6}{10} \le 3 + \frac{6}{4}t$$
$$20\left(\frac{3}{10}t - \frac{6}{10}\right) \le 20\left(3 + \frac{6}{4}t\right)$$
$$6t - 12 \le 60 + 30t$$
$$6t - 6t - 12 \le 60 + 30t - 6t$$
$$-12 \le 60 + 24t$$
$$-12 - 60 \le 60 - 60 + 24t$$
$$-72 \le 24t$$
$$\frac{-72}{24} \le \frac{24t}{24}$$
$$-3 \le t$$
$$t \ge -3$$

102. Let x = time in hours it takes the ship to travel 140 miles

$$\frac{40 \text{ miles}}{1.8 \text{ hours}} = \frac{140 \text{ miles}}{x \text{ hours}}$$
$$\frac{40}{1.8} = \frac{140}{x}$$
$$40 \cdot x = 1.8 \cdot 140$$
$$40x = 252$$
$$\frac{40x}{40} = \frac{252}{40}$$
$$x = 6.3$$

It will take 6.3 hours to travel 140 miles.

103. Let x = number of calories in a 6-ounce piece of cake.

$$\frac{4 \text{ ounces}}{160 \text{ calories}} = \frac{6 \text{ ounces}}{x \text{ calories}}$$
$$\frac{4}{160} = \frac{6}{x}$$
$$4 \cdot x = 160 \cdot 6$$
$$4x = 960$$
$$x = \frac{960}{4} = 240$$

Thus, a 6-ounce piece of cake has 240 calories.

104. Let x = number of pages that can be copied in 22 minutes.

$$\frac{1 \text{ minutes}}{20 \text{ pages}} = \frac{22 \text{ minutes}}{x \text{ pages}}$$
$$\frac{1}{20} = \frac{22}{x}$$
$$1 \cdot x = 22 \cdot 20$$
$$x = 440$$

440 pages can be copied in 22 minutes.

105. Let x = number of inches representing 380 miles.

$$\frac{60 \text{ miles}}{1 \text{ inch}} = \frac{380 \text{ miles}}{x \text{ inches}}$$
$$\frac{60}{1} = \frac{380}{x}$$
$$60 \cdot x = 380 \cdot 1$$
$$60x = 380$$
$$x = \frac{380}{60} = 6\frac{1}{3}$$

$6\frac{1}{3}$ inches on the map represent 380 miles.

106. Let x = size of actual car in feet

$$\frac{1 \text{ inch}}{1.5 \text{ feet}} = \frac{10.5 \text{ inches}}{x \text{ feet}}$$

$$\frac{1}{1.5} = \frac{10.5}{x}$$

$$1 \cdot x = 1.5 \cdot 10.5$$

$$x = 15.75$$

The size of the actual car is 15.75 ft.

107. Let x = the value of 1 peso in terms of U.S. dollars.

$$\frac{\$1 \text{ U.S.}}{9.165 \text{ pesos}} = \frac{x \text{ dollars}}{1 \text{ peso}}$$

$$\frac{1}{9.165} = \frac{x}{1}$$

$$9.165 \cdot x = 1 \cdot 1$$

$$9.165x = 1$$

$$x = \frac{1}{9.165} \approx 0.109$$

1 peso equals about 0.109.

108. Let x = number of bottles the machine can fill and cap in 2 minutes.

2 minutes = 120 seconds

$$\frac{50 \text{ seconds}}{80 \text{ bottles}} = \frac{120 \text{ seconds}}{x \text{ bottles}}$$

$$\frac{50}{80} = \frac{120}{x}$$

$$50 \cdot x = 80 \cdot 120$$

$$50x = 9600$$

$$x = \frac{9600}{50} = 192$$

The machine can fill and cap 192 bottles in 2 minutes.

Practice Test

1. $-3(4 - 2x) = -3[4 + (-2x)]$

$$= -3(4) + (-3)(-2x)$$

$$= -12 + 6x \text{ or } 6x - 12$$

2. $-(x + 3y - 4) = -\left[x + 3y + (-4)\right]$

$$= -1\left[x + 3y + (-4)\right]$$

$$= (-1)(x) + (-1)(3y) + (-1)(-4)$$

$$= -x + (-3y) + 4$$

$$= -x - 3y + 4$$

3. $5x - 8x + 4 = -3x + 4$

4. $4 + 2x - 3x + 6 = 2x - 3x + 4 + 6$

$$= -x + 10$$

5. $-y - x - 4x - 6 = -x - 4x - y - 6$

$$= -5x - y - 6$$

6. $a - 2b + 6a - 6b - 3 = a + 6a - 2b - 6b - 3$

$$= 7a - 8b - 3$$

7. $2x^2 + 3 + 2(3x - 2) = 2x^2 + 3 + 6x - 4$

$$= 2x^2 + 6x + 3 - 4$$

$$= 2x^2 + 6x - 1$$

8. $2.4x - 3.9 = 3.3$

$$2.4x - 3.9 + 3.9 = 3.3 + 3.9$$

$$2.4x = 7.2$$

$$\frac{2.4x}{2.4} = \frac{7.2}{2.4}$$

$$x = 3$$

9. $\dfrac{5}{6}(x - 2) = x - 3$

$$\frac{5}{6}x - \frac{10}{6} = x - 3$$

$$6\left(\frac{5}{6}x - \frac{10}{6}\right) = 6(x - 3)$$

$$5x - 10 = 6x - 18$$

$$5x - 5x - 10 = 6x - 5x - 18$$

$$-10 = x - 18$$

$$-10 + 18 = x - 18 + 18$$

$$8 = x$$

10. $6m - (4 - 2m) = 0$

$$6m - 4 + 2m = 0$$

$$6m + 2m - 4 = 0$$

$$8m - 4 = 0$$

$$8m - 4 + 4 = 0 + 4$$

$$8m = 4$$

$$\frac{8m}{8} = \frac{4}{8}$$

$$m = \frac{4}{8} = \frac{1}{2}$$

11.
$$3w + 2(2w - 6) = 4(3w - 3)$$
$$3w + 4w - 12 = 12w - 12$$
$$7w - 12 = 12w - 12$$
$$7w - 7w - 12 = 12w - 7w - 12$$
$$-12 = 5w - 12$$
$$-12 + 12 = 5w - 12 + 12$$
$$0 = 5w$$
$$\frac{0}{5} = \frac{5w}{5}$$
$$0 = w$$

12.
$$2x - 3(-2x + 4) = -13 + x$$
$$2x + 6x - 12 = -13 + x$$
$$8x - 12 = -13 + x$$
$$8x - 12 + 12 = -13 + 12 + x$$
$$8x = -1 + x$$
$$8x - x = -1 + x - x$$
$$7x = -1$$
$$\frac{7x}{7} = \frac{-1}{7}$$
$$x = -\frac{1}{7}$$

13.
$$3x - 4 - x = 2(x + 5)$$
$$3x - 4 - x = 2x + 10$$
$$2x - 4 = 2x + 10$$
$$2x - 2x - 4 = 2x - 2x + 10$$
$$-4 = 10 \text{ False}$$
Since a false statement is obtained, there is no solution.

14.
$$-3(2x + 3) = -2(3x + 1) - 7$$
$$-6x - 9 = -6x - 2 - 7$$
$$-6x - 9 = -6x - 9$$
Since the equation is true for all values of x, the solution is all real numbers.

15.
$$\frac{9}{x} = \frac{3}{-15}$$
$$9(-15) = 3x$$
$$-135 = 3x$$
$$\frac{-135}{3} = x$$
$$-45 = x$$

16.
$$\frac{1}{7}(2x - 5) = \frac{3}{8}x - \frac{5}{7}$$
$$\frac{2}{7}x - \frac{5}{7} = \frac{3}{8}x - \frac{5}{7}$$
$$56\left(\frac{2}{7}x - \frac{5}{7}\right) = 56\left(\frac{3}{8}x - \frac{5}{7}\right)$$
$$16x - 40 = 21x - 40$$
$$16x - 16x - 40 = 21x - 16x - 40$$
$$-40 = 5x - 40$$
$$-40 + 40 = 5x - 40 + 40$$
$$0 = 5x$$
$$\frac{0}{5} = \frac{5x}{5}$$
$$0 = x$$

17. a. An equation that has exactly one solution is a conditional equation.

    b. An equation that has no solution is a contradiction.

    c. An equation that has all real numbers as its solution is an identity.

18.
$$2x - 4 < 4x + 10$$
$$2x - 4 - 10 < 4x + 10 - 10$$
$$2x - 14 < 4x$$
$$2x - 2x - 14 < 4x - 2x$$
$$-14 < 2x$$
$$\frac{-14}{2} < \frac{2x}{2}$$
$$-7 < x$$
$$x > -7$$

19.
$$3(x + 4) \geq 5x - 12$$
$$3x + 12 \geq 5x - 12$$
$$3x + 12 + 12 \geq 5x - 12 + 12$$
$$3x + 24 \geq 5x$$
$$3x - 3x + 24 \geq 5x - 3x$$
$$24 \geq 2x$$
$$\frac{24}{2} \geq \frac{2x}{2}$$
$$12 \geq x$$
$$x \leq 12$$

20. $4(x+3)+2x < 6x-3$

$4x+12+2x < 6x-3$

$6x+12 < 6x-3$

$6x-6x+12 < 6x-6x-3$

$12 < -3$

Since 12 is never less than –3, the answer is no solution.

21. $-(x-2)-3x = 4(1-x)-2$

$-x+2-3x = 4-4x-2$

$-4x+2 = -4x+2$ True

This equation is true for all real numbers.

22. $\dfrac{3}{4} = \dfrac{8}{x}$

$3x = 4 \cdot 8$

$3x = 32$

$x = \dfrac{32}{3}$

The length of side x is $\dfrac{32}{3}$ feet or $10\dfrac{2}{3}$ feet.

23. Let x = number of gallons needed.

$\dfrac{3 \text{ acres}}{6 \text{ gallons}} = \dfrac{75 \text{ acres}}{x \text{ gallons}}$

$\dfrac{3}{6} = \dfrac{75}{x}$

$3x = 6 \cdot 75$

$3x = 450$

$x = \dfrac{450}{3} = 150$

150 gallons are needed to treat 75 acres.

24. Let x = number of gallons he needs to sell.

$\dfrac{\$0.40}{1 \text{ gallon}} = \dfrac{\$20,000}{x \text{ gallons}}$

$\dfrac{0.40}{1} = \dfrac{20,000}{x}$

$0.40x = 20,000$

$x = \dfrac{20,000}{0.40} = 50,000$

He needs to sell 50,000 gallons.

25. Let x = number of minutes it will take.

$\dfrac{25 \text{ miles}}{35 \text{ minutes}} = \dfrac{125 \text{ miles}}{x \text{ minutes}}$

$\dfrac{25}{35} = \dfrac{125}{x}$

$25x = 35 \cdot 125$

$25x = 4375$

$x = \dfrac{4375}{25} = 175$

It would take 175 minutes or 2 hours 55 minutes.

Cumulative Review Test

1. $\dfrac{52}{15} \cdot \dfrac{10}{13} = \dfrac{4}{3} \cdot \dfrac{2}{1}$

$= \dfrac{4 \cdot 2}{3 \cdot 1}$

$= \dfrac{8}{3}$

2. $\dfrac{5}{24} \div \dfrac{2}{9} = \dfrac{5}{24} \cdot \dfrac{9}{2}$

$= \dfrac{5}{8} \cdot \dfrac{3}{2}$

$= \dfrac{5 \cdot 3}{8 \cdot 2}$

$= \dfrac{15}{16}$

3. $|-2| > 1$ since $|-2| = 2$ and $2 > 1$.

4. $-5-(-4)+12-8 = -5+4+12-8$

$= -1+12-8$

$= 11-8$

$= 3$

5. $-7-(-6) = -7+6$

$= -1$

6. $20-6 \div 3 \cdot 2 = 20 - 2 \cdot 2$

$= 20-4$

$= 16$

7. $3\left[6-\left(4-3^2\right)\right]-30 = 3[6-(4-9)]-30$

$= 3[6-(-5)]-30$

$= 3[6+5]-30$

$= 3(11)-30$

$= 33-30$

$= 3$

8. Substitute –2 for each x.

$$-2x^2 - 6x + 8 = -2(-2)^2 - 6(-2) + 8$$
$$= -2(4) - (-12) + 8$$
$$= -8 + 12 + 8$$
$$= 4 + 8$$
$$= 12$$

9. Associative property of addition

10. $8x + 2y + 4x - y = 8x + 4x + 2y - y$
$$= 12x + y$$

11. $9 - \dfrac{2}{3}x + 16 + \dfrac{3}{4}x = \dfrac{3}{4}x - \dfrac{2}{3}x + 9 + 16$

$$= \dfrac{9}{12}x - \dfrac{8}{12}x + 25$$

$$= \dfrac{1}{12}x + 25$$

12. $\quad 6x + 2 = 10$

$$6x + 2 - 2 = 10 - 2$$
$$6x = 8$$
$$\dfrac{6x}{6} = \dfrac{8}{6}$$
$$x = \dfrac{8}{6} = \dfrac{4}{3}$$

13. $\quad \dfrac{1}{4}x = -10$

$$4\left(\dfrac{1}{4}x\right) = 4(-10)$$
$$x = -40$$

14. $\quad -6x - 5x + 6 = 28$

$$-11x + 6 = 28$$
$$-11x + 6 - 6 = 28 - 6$$
$$-11x = 22$$
$$\dfrac{-11x}{-11} = \dfrac{22}{-11}$$
$$x = -2$$

15. $\quad \dfrac{40}{30} = \dfrac{3}{x}$

$$40 \cdot x = 30 \cdot 3$$
$$40x = 90$$
$$\dfrac{40x}{40} = \dfrac{90}{40}$$
$$x = \dfrac{90}{40} = \dfrac{9}{4} \text{ or } 2.25$$

16. $\qquad \dfrac{3}{4}n - \dfrac{1}{5} = \dfrac{2}{3}n$

$$60\left(\dfrac{3}{4}n - \dfrac{1}{5}\right) = 60\left(\dfrac{2}{3}n\right)$$
$$45n - 12 = 40n$$
$$45n - 45n - 12 = 40n - 45n$$
$$-12 = -5n$$
$$\dfrac{-12}{-5} = \dfrac{-5n}{-5}$$
$$\dfrac{12}{5} = n$$

17. $\quad x - 3 > 7$

$$x - 3 + 3 > 7 + 3$$
$$x > 10$$

18. $\qquad 2x - 7 \le 3x + 5$

$$2x - 7 - 5 \le 3x + 5 - 5$$
$$2x - 12 \le 3x$$
$$2x - 2x - 12 \le 3x - 2x$$
$$-12 \le x$$
$$x \ge -12$$

19. Let x = number of pounds of fertilizer needed.

$$\dfrac{5000 \text{ square feet}}{36 \text{ pounds}} = \dfrac{22{,}000 \text{ square feet}}{x \text{ pounds}}$$
$$\dfrac{5000}{36} = \dfrac{22{,}000}{x}$$
$$5000x = (36)(22{,}000)$$
$$5000x = 792{,}000$$
$$x = \dfrac{792{,}000}{5000} = 158.4$$

158.4 pounds are needed to fertilize a 22,000-square-foot lawn.

20. Let x = amount he earns after 8 hours.

$$\dfrac{2 \text{ hours}}{\$10.50} = \dfrac{8 \text{ hours}}{x \text{ dollars}}$$
$$\dfrac{2}{10.5} = \dfrac{8}{x}$$
$$2x = (10.5)(8)$$
$$2x = 84$$
$$x = \dfrac{84}{2} = 42$$

He earns $42 after 8 hours.

Chapter 3

Exercise Set 3.1

1. A formula is an equation used to express a relationship mathematically.

3. The simple interest formula is:
$i = prt$ where i is interest, p is principle, r is the interest rate, and t is time.

5. The diameter of a circle is 2 times its radius.

7. When you multiply a unit by the same unit, you get a square unit.

9. Substitute 6 for s.
$P = 4s$
$P = 4(6)$
$P = 24$

11. Substitute 7 for s.
$A = s^2$
$A = (7)^2 = 49$

13. Substitute 8 for l and 5 for w.
$P = 2l + 2w$
$P = 2(8) + 2(5)$
$P = 16 + 10$
$P = 26$

15. Substitute 5 for r.
$A = \pi r^2$
$A = \pi(5)^2$
$A = 25\pi \approx 78.54$

17. Substitute 100 for x, 80 for m, and 10 for s.
$z = \dfrac{x - m}{s}$
$z = \dfrac{100 - 80}{10}$
$z = \dfrac{20}{10} = 2$

19. Substitute 60 for V and 12 for B.
$V = \dfrac{1}{3}Bh$
$60 = \dfrac{1}{3}(12)h$
$60 = 4h$
$\dfrac{60}{4} = \dfrac{4h}{4}$
$15 = h$

21. Substitute 36 for A and 16 for m.
$A = \dfrac{m + n}{2}$
$36 = \dfrac{16 + n}{2}$
$2(36) = 2\left(\dfrac{16 + n}{2}\right)$
$72 = 16 + n$
$72 - 16 = n$
$56 = n$

23. Substitute 15 for C.
$F = \dfrac{9}{5}C + 32$
$F = \dfrac{9}{5}(15) + 32$
$F = 27 + 32 = 59$

25. Substitute 678.24 for V, and 6 for r.
$V = \pi r^2 h$
$678.24 = \pi(6)^2 h$
$678.24 = 36\pi h$
$\dfrac{678.24}{36\pi} = \dfrac{36\pi h}{36\pi}$
$\dfrac{678.24}{36\pi} = h$
$6.00 \approx h$

27. Substitute 24 for B and 61 for h.
$B = \dfrac{703w}{h^2}$
$24 = \dfrac{703w}{(61)^2}$
$24(61)^2 = \dfrac{703w}{61^2}(61)^2$
$89,304 = 703w$
$\dfrac{89,304}{703} = \dfrac{703w}{703}$
$127.03 \approx w$

29. Substitute 160 for C and 0.12 for r.
$S = C + rC$
$S = 160 + (0.12)(160)$
$S = 160 + 19.20 = 179.20$

31. Substitute 6 for b and 4 for h.

$$A = \frac{1}{2}bh$$

$$A = \frac{1}{2}(6)(4)$$

$$A = (3)(4)$$

$$A = 12 \text{ in}^2$$

33. Substitute 4 for r and 9 for h.

$$V = \pi r^2 h$$

$$V = \pi(4)^2(9)$$

$$V = \pi(16)(9)$$

$$V = 144\pi \approx 452.39 \text{ cm}^3$$

35. Substitute 3 for h, 4 for b and 7 for d.

$$A = \frac{1}{2}h(b + d)$$

$$A = \frac{1}{2}(3)(4 + 7)$$

$$A = \frac{1}{2}(3)(11)$$

$$A = \frac{1}{2}(33)$$

$$A = 16.5 \text{ ft}^2$$

37. $P = 4s$

$$\frac{P}{4} = \frac{4s}{4}$$

$$\frac{P}{4} = s$$

39. $d = rt$

$$\frac{d}{r} = \frac{rt}{r}$$

$$\frac{d}{r} = t$$

41. $V = lwh$

$$\frac{V}{wh} = \frac{lwh}{wh}$$

$$\frac{V}{wh} = l$$

43. $A = \frac{1}{2}bh$

$$2A = 2\left(\frac{1}{2}bh\right)$$

$$2A = bh$$

$$\frac{2A}{h} = \frac{bh}{h}$$

$$\frac{2A}{h} = b$$

45. $P = 2l + 2w$

$$P - 2l = 2l - 2l + 2w$$

$$P - 2l = 2w$$

$$\frac{P - 2l}{2} = \frac{2w}{2}$$

$$\frac{P - 2l}{2} = w$$

47. $5 - 2t = m$

$$5 - 5 - 2t = m - 5$$

$$-2t = m - 5$$

$$\frac{-2t}{-2} = \frac{m - 5}{-2}$$

$$t = -\frac{m - 5}{2} = \frac{-m + 5}{2}$$

49. $y = mx + b$

$$y - mx = mx - mx + b$$

$$y - mx = b$$

51. $y = mx + b$

$$y - b = mx + b - b$$

$$y - b = mx$$

$$\frac{y - b}{m} = \frac{mx}{m}$$

$$\frac{y - b}{m} = x$$

53. $ax + by = c$

$$ax - ax + by = -ax + c$$

$$by = -ax + c$$

$$\frac{by}{b} = \frac{-ax + c}{b}$$

$$y = \frac{-ax + c}{b}$$

55. $V = \pi r^2 h$

$$\frac{V}{\pi r^2} = \frac{\pi r^2 h}{\pi r^2}$$

$$\frac{V}{\pi r^2} = h$$

57. $A = \dfrac{m+d}{2}$

$$2A = 2\left(\frac{m+d}{2}\right)$$

$$2A = m + d$$

$$2A - d = m + d - d$$

$$2A - d = m$$

59. $R = \dfrac{l+3w}{2}$

$$2R = 2\left(\frac{l+3w}{2}\right)$$

$$2R = l + 3w$$

$$2R - l = l - l + 3w$$

$$2R - l = 3w$$

$$\frac{2R-l}{3} = \frac{3w}{3}$$

$$\frac{2R-l}{3} = w$$

61. $3x + y = 5$
   a. $3x + y - 3x = 5 - 3x$
                $y = 5 - 3x$
   b.   Substitute 2 for x.
            $y = 5 - 3(2) = 5 - 6 = -1$

63. $4x = 6y - 8$

   a. $4x + 8 = 6y - 8 + 8$
              $4x + 8 = 6y$
           $2(2x + 4) = 6y$

$$\frac{2(2x+4)}{6} = \frac{6y}{6}$$

$$\frac{2x+4}{3} = y$$

b. Substitute 10 for *x*.

$$y = \frac{2(10)+4}{3}$$

$$= \frac{20+4}{3}$$

$$= \frac{24}{3}$$

$$= 8$$

65. $5y = -12 + 3x$

   a. $5y = -12 + 3x$

$$\frac{5y}{5} = \frac{-12+3x}{5}$$

$$y = \frac{3x-12}{5}$$

   b.   Substitute 4 for *x*.

$$y = \frac{3(4)-12}{5} = \frac{12-12}{5} = \frac{0}{5} = 0$$

67. $-3x + 5y = -10$

   a. $-3x + 5y + 3x = -10 + 3x$
               $5y = -10 + 3x$

$$\frac{5y}{5} = \frac{-10+3x}{5}$$

$$y = \frac{-10+3x}{5}$$

   b.   Substitute 4 for *x*.

$$y = \frac{-10+3(4)}{5}$$

$$= \frac{-10+12}{5}$$

$$= \frac{2}{5}$$

69. $15 - 3x = -6y$

   a. $15 - 3x = -6y$

$$\frac{15-3x}{-6} = \frac{-6y}{-6}$$

$$\frac{-3x+15}{-6} = y$$

$$\frac{-3(x-5)}{-6} = y$$

$$\frac{x-5}{2} = y$$

b. Substitute 0 for *x*.

$$y = \frac{0-5}{2} = \frac{-5}{2}$$

71. $-8 = -x - 2y$

a.
$$x - 8 = x - x - 2y$$
$$x - 8 = -2y$$
$$\frac{x-8}{-2} = \frac{-2y}{-2}$$
$$\frac{-x+8}{2} = y$$

b. Substitute -4 for *x*.

$$y = \frac{-(-4)+8}{2} = \frac{4+8}{2} = \frac{12}{2} = 6$$

73. a. $y + 3 = -\frac{1}{3}(x-4)$

$$y + 3 = -\frac{1}{3}x + \frac{4}{3}$$
$$y + 3 - 3 = -\frac{1}{3}x + \frac{4}{3} - 3$$
$$y = -\frac{1}{3}x + \frac{4}{3} - \frac{9}{3}$$
$$y = -\frac{1}{3}x - \frac{5}{3} = \frac{-x-5}{3}$$

b. Substitute 6 for *x*.

$$y = \frac{-(6)-5}{3} = \frac{-6-5}{3} = \frac{-11}{3}$$

75. a. $y - \frac{1}{5} = 2\left(x + \frac{1}{3}\right)$

$$y - \frac{1}{5} = 2x + \frac{2}{3}$$
$$y - \frac{1}{5} + \frac{1}{5} = 2x + \frac{2}{3} + \frac{1}{5}$$
$$y = 2x + \frac{10}{15} + \frac{3}{15}$$
$$y = 2x + \frac{13}{15} = \frac{30x}{15} + \frac{13}{15} = \frac{30x+13}{15}$$

b. Substitute 4 for *x*.

$$y = \frac{30(4)+13}{15} = \frac{120+13}{15} = \frac{133}{15}$$

77. Substitute 10 for *n*.

$$d = \frac{1}{2}n^2 - \frac{3}{2}n$$
$$d = \frac{1}{2}(10)^2 - \frac{3}{2}(10)$$
$$= \frac{1}{2}(100) - 15$$
$$= 50 - 15$$
$$= 35$$

79. Substitute 50 for *F*.

$$C = \frac{5}{9}(F - 32)$$
$$C = \frac{5}{9}(50 - 32)$$
$$= \frac{5}{9}(18)$$
$$= 10$$

The equivalent temperature is 10°C.

81. Substitute 25 for *C*.

$$F = \frac{9}{5}C + 32$$
$$F = \frac{9}{5}(25) + 32$$
$$= 45 + 32$$
$$= 77$$

The equivalent temperature is 77°F.

83. $P = \frac{KT}{V}$

$$P = \frac{(2)(20)}{1} = \frac{40}{1} = 40$$

85. $P = \frac{KT}{V}$

$$80 = \frac{K(100)}{5}$$
$$80 = 20K$$
$$\frac{80}{20} = \frac{20K}{20}$$
$$4 = K$$

87. $A = s^2$

$$A = (2s)^2 = 4s^2$$

The area is 4 times as large as the original area.

89. Substitute 6 for *n*.

$$S = n^2 + n$$
$$S = (6)^2 + 6 = 36 + 6 = 42$$

91. $i = prt$
$i = (6000)(0.08)(3) = 1440$
He will pay $1440 interest.

93. $i = prt$
$450 = p(0.03)(3)$
$450 = 0.09p$
$\dfrac{450}{0.09} = \dfrac{0.09p}{0.09}$
$5000 = p$
She placed $5000 in the savings account.

95. $P = a + b + c$
$P = 5 + 12 + 8 = 25$
The perimeter of the table top is 25 feet.

97. $A = \dfrac{1}{2}bh$
$A = \dfrac{1}{2}(36)(31) = 558$
The area is 558 square inches.

99. $A = \pi r^2$
$A = \pi(1.5)^2$
$A = \pi(2.25) \approx 7.07$
The area of the tabletop is about 7.07 square feet.

101. Total area = Area of top triangle + area of bottom triangle
Total Area = $.5b_1\, h_1 + .5b_2\, h_2$
Total Area = $.5(2)(1) + .5(2)(2)$
Total Area = $1 + 2 = 3$
The area of the kite is 3 square feet.

103. $V = \pi r^2 h$
$= \pi(4)^2(3)$
$= \pi(16)(3)$
$= 48\pi \approx 150.80$
The volume of water in the Jacuzzi is about 150.80 cubic feet.

105. $A = \dfrac{1}{2}h(b + d)$
$A = \dfrac{1}{2}(100)(80 + 200)$
$= \dfrac{1}{2}(100)(280)$
$= (50)(280)$
$= 14,000$
The seating area is 14,000 square feet.

107. The radius is half the diameter, so
$r = \dfrac{3}{2} = 1.5$ inches.

$V = \dfrac{1}{3}\pi r^2 h$

$V = \dfrac{1}{3}\pi(1.5)^2(5)$

$= \dfrac{1}{3}\pi(2.25)5$

$= 3.75\pi$

≈ 11.78
The volume of the cone is about 11.78 cubic inches.

109. a. $B = \dfrac{703w}{h^2}$

b. 5 feet 3 inches $= 5(12) + 3$
$= 60 + 3$
$= 63$ inches
$B = \dfrac{703(135)}{(63)^2} = \dfrac{94,905}{3969} \approx 23.91$

111. a. $V = lwh$
$V = (3x)(x)(6x - 1)$
$= 3x^2(6x - 1)$
$= 18x^3 - 3x^2$

b. $V = 18x^3 - 3x^2$
$V = 18(7)^3 - 3(7)^2$
$= 6174 - 147$
$= 6027$
Volume is 6027 cm^3.

c. $S = 2lw + 2lh + 2wh$
$S = 2(3x)(x) + 2(3x)(6x - 1) + 2(x)(6x - 1)$
$= 6x^2 + 36x^2 - 6x + 12x^2 - 2x$
$= 54x^2 - 8x$

d. $S = 54x^2 - 8x$
$S = 54(7)^2 - 8(7)$
$= 2646 - 56$
$= 2590$
Surface area is 2590 cm^2.

113. $\left[4\left(12 \div 2^2 - 3\right)^2\right]^2 = \left[4\left(12 \div 4 - 3\right)^2\right]^2$

$$= \left[4(3-3)^2\right]^2$$
$$= \left[4(0)^2\right]^2$$
$$= [0]^2$$
$$= 0$$

114. $\dfrac{6}{4} = \dfrac{3}{2}$ so the ratio of Arabians to Morgans is 3:2.

115. Let x = number of minutes to siphon 13,500 gallons

$$\dfrac{25 \text{ gallons}}{3 \text{ minutes}} = \dfrac{13,500 \text{ gallons}}{x \text{ minutes}}$$
$$\dfrac{25}{3} = \dfrac{13,500}{x}$$
$$25 \cdot x = 3(13,500)$$
$$25x = 40,500$$
$$x = \dfrac{40,500}{25} = 1620$$

It will take 1620 minutes or 27 hours to empty the pool.

116. $2(x-4) \geq 3x + 9$

$$2x - 8 \geq 3x + 9$$
$$2x - 17 \geq 3x$$
$$-17 \geq x$$
$$x \leq -17$$

Exercise Set 3.2

1. Added to, more than, increased by, and sum indicate the operation of addition.

3. Multiplied by, product of, twice, and three times indicate the operation of multiplication.

5. The cost is increased by 25% of the cost, so the expression needs $0.25c$.

7. $n + 7$

9. $4x$

11. $\dfrac{x}{2}$

13. $h + 0.8$

15. $p - 0.08$

17. $\dfrac{1}{10}n - 5$

19. $\dfrac{8}{9}m + 16{,}000$

21. $45 + 0.40x$

23. $25x$

25. $16x + y$

27. $n + 0.04n$

29. $p - 0.02p$

31. $220 + 80x$

33. $275x + 25y$

35. Three less than a number

37. One more than four times a number

39. Seven less than six times a number

41. Four times a number, decreased by two

43. Three times a number subtracted from two

45. Twice the difference between a number and one

47. $s + 5$

49. $b - 6$

51. $600 - a$

53. $100 - m$

55. $\dfrac{2}{3}m - 6$

57. $2r - 673$

59. $2p - 2.7$

61. $3n - 15$

63. $2n - 67{,}109$

65. $s + 0.20s$

67. $s + 0.15s$

69. $f - 0.12f$

71. $c + 0.07c$

73. $p - 0.50p$

75. a. Let x = first number, then $4x$ = second number.

   b. First number + second number = 20
   $x + 4x = 20$

77. a. Let x = smaller integer, then
   $x + 1$ = larger consecutive integer.

   b. Smaller + larger = 41
   $x + (x + 1) = 41$

79. a. Let x = the number.

   b. Twice the number decreased by 8 is 12.
   $2x - 8 = 12$

81. a. Let x = the number.

   b. One-fifth of the sum of the number and 10 is 150.
   $\dfrac{1}{5}(x + 10) = 150$

83. a. Let s = the distance traveled by the Southern Pacific train.

   b. $s + (2s - 4) = 890$

85. a. Let c = the cost of the car.

   b. $c + 0.07c = 32{,}600$

87. a. Let c = the cost of the meal.

   b. $c + 0.15c = 42.50$

89. a. Let f = the average salary in San Francisco.

   b. $1.28f - f = 16{,}762$

91. a. Let s = number of laser vision surgeries in 1999.

   b. $s + (s + 0.55) = 2.45$

93. Two more than a number is five.

95. Three times a number, decreased by one, is four more than twice the number.

97. Four times the difference between a number and one is six.

99. Six more than five times a number is the difference between six times the number and one.

101. The sum of a number and the number increased by four is eight.

103. The sum of twice a number and the number increased by three is five.

105. Answers will vary.

107. a. 1 minute = 60 seconds
   1 hour = 60 minutes = 3600 seconds
   1 day = 24 hours
   $\qquad$ = 1440 minutes
   $\qquad$ = 86,400 seconds
   $86{,}400d + 3600h + 60m + s$

   b. $86{,}400d + 3600h + 60m + s$
   $= 86{,}400(4) + 3600(6) + 60(15) + 25$
   $= 368{,}125$ seconds

109. $30 = 6t$

111. $3\left[(4 - 16) \div 2\right] + 5^2 - 3$
   $3\left[(-12) \div 2\right] + 25 - 3$
   $3(-6) + 25 - 3$
   $-18 + 25 - 3$
   $7 - 3$
   4

112. $\dfrac{3.6}{x} = \dfrac{10}{7}$
   $3.6 \cdot 7 = 10 \cdot x$
   $25.2 = 10x$
   $\dfrac{25.2}{10} = \dfrac{10x}{10}$
   $2.52 = x$

113. $2x - 4 > 3$
   $2x - 4 + 4 > 3 + 4$
   $\qquad 2x > 7$
   $\qquad x > \dfrac{7}{2}$

114. Substitute 40 for P and 5 for w.

$P = 2l + 2w$

$40 = 2l + 2(5)$

$40 = 2l + 10$

$30 = 2l$

$15 = l$

115.

$3x - 2y = 6$

$3x - 3x - 2y = -3x + 6$

$-2y = -3x + 6$

$\dfrac{-2y}{-2} = \dfrac{-3x + 6}{-2}$

$y = \dfrac{3x - 6}{2}$

$y = \dfrac{3}{2}x - 3$

Substitute 6 for x.

$y = \dfrac{3(6) - 6}{2} = \dfrac{18 - 6}{2} = \dfrac{12}{2} = 6$

Exercise Set 3.3

1. Answers will vary.

3. Let x = smaller integer, then

$x + 1$ = next consecutive integer.

Smaller number + larger number = 85.

$x + (x + 1) = 85$

$2x + 1 = 85$

$2x = 84$

$x = 42$

Smaller number = 42

Larger number = $x + 1 = 42 + 1 = 43$

5. Let x = smaller odd integer, then

$x + 2$ = next consecutive odd integer.

Sum of integers = 104.

$x + (x + 2) = 104$

$2x + 2 = 104$

$2x = 102$

$x = 51$

Smaller integer = 51

Larger integer = $51 + 2 = 53$

7. Let x = one number.

Then $2x + 3$ = second number.

First number + second number = 27

$x + (2x + 3) = 27$

$3x + 3 = 27$

$3x = 24$

$x = 8$

First number = 8

Second number = $2x + 3 = 2(8) + 3 = 19$

9. Let x = smaller integer, then

larger integer = $2x - 8$.

Larger integer − smaller integer = 17

$(2x - 8) - x = 17$

$2x - 8 - x = 17$

$x - 8 = 17$

$x = 25$

Smaller number = 25

Larger number = $2x - 8 = 2(25) - 8 = 42$

11. Let x = the life expectancy, in years, for men in the U.S. in 1900, then $2x - 19$ is the life expectancy, in years, for men in the U.S. in 2000.

Life expectancy in 2000 − Life expectancy in 1900 = 27.3

$(2x - 19) - x = 27.3$

$x - 19 = 27.3$

$x = 46.3$

$2x - 19 = 2(46.3) - 19 = 73.6$

The life expectancy of men in the U.S. in 2000 is 73.6 years old.

13. Let x = the number of DVD players sold in 2001, then $2x + 20$ = number of DVD players sold in 2002.

DVD players sold in 2001 + DVD players sold in 2002 = 3260

$x + (2x + 20) = 3260$

$3x + 20 = 3260$

$3x = 3240$

$x = 1080$

$2x + 20 = 2(1080) + 20 = 2180$

In 2002, 2,180 DVD players were sold.

15. Let x = the number of baseball cards given to Richey, then $3x$ = number of baseball cards given to Erin.

Number of cards given to Richey + Number of cards given to Erin = 260

$x + 3x = 260$

$4x = 260$

$4x = 260$

$x = 65$

Grandma gave 65 baseball cards to Richey.

17. Let x = the number of hours it takes to design a horse, then $2x + 1.4$ = the number of hours it takes to attach the gloves to the horse.

Time to design horse + Time to attach gloves to horse = 32.6

$x + (2x + 1.4) = 32.6$

$3x + 1.4 = 32.6$

$3x = 31.2$

$x = 10.4$

$2x + 1.4 = 2(10.4) + 1.4 = 22.3$
It took him 22.2 hours to attach the gloves to the horse.

19. Let x = the number of weeks, then $6x$ = the amount she wishes to add to her collection over x weeks.
Amount started with in collection + Amount added each week to the collection over x weeks = Total number in collection
$624 + 6x = 1000$
$6x = 376$
$x \approx 62.7$
It will take her about 62.7 weeks to get 1000 frogs in her collection.

21. Let x = the time in years, then $1200x$ = the increase in population over x years.
Current population + Increase in population over x years = Future population
$6500 + 1200x = 20,600$
$1200x = 14,100$
$x = 11.75$
In 11.75 years, the population will reach 20,600.

23. Let x = the number of weeks, then $120x$ = the number of computers shipped after x weeks.
Current supply of computers – Number of computers shipped over x weeks = Future inventory
$3600 - 120x = 2000$
$-120x = -1600$
$x \approx 13.3$
It will take about 13.3 weeks for the computer inventory to drop to 2000.

25. Let x = the number of miles, then $0.30x$ = the cost of driving over x miles.
Daily cost + Mileage cost = Total cost
$50 + 0.30x = 92$
$0.30x = 42$
$x = 140$
Lori can drive a maximum of 140 miles.

27. Let x the number of copies made, then $0.02x$ = the cost to make x number of copies.
Cost of machine + Cost of copies made = Total cost
$2100 + 0.02x = 2462$
$0.02x = 362$
$x = 18,100$
In one year, 18,100 copies were made.

29. Let x = the number of minutes, then $x - 500$ = the number of minutes talked over 500 minutes and $0.40(x - 500)$ = the cost to talk after 500 minutes.
Monthly fee + Cost of talk time over 500

minutes = Total cost
$25.95 + 0.40(x - 500) = 61.95$
$25.95 + 0.40x - 200 = 61.95$
$0.40x - 174.05 = 61.95$
$0.40x = 236$
$x = 590$
$x - 500 = 590 - 500 = 90$
Anke used 90 minutes over and above the 500 minutes of free time.

31. Let x = the time before the costs are the same.
Total cost for Kenmore = total cost for Neptune
Price of Kenmore + energy costs = Price of Neptune + energy costs
$362 + 84x = 454 + 38x$
$362 + 46x = 454$
$46x = 92$
$x = 2$
It will take 2 years before the total cost is the same for both machines.

33. Let x = number of years until the salaries are the same.
yearly salary = base salary + (yearly increase) · (number of years)
yearly salary at Data Tech. = yearly salary at Nuteck
$40,000 + 2400x = 49,600 + 800x$
$40,000 + 1600x = 49,600$
$1600x = 9600$
$x = 6$
It will take 6 years for the two salaries to be the same.

35. Let x = the number of pages, then $0.02x$ = the cost of printing x pages on the HP and $0.03x$ = the cost of printing x pages on the Lexmark.

Cost of the HP printer + Cost of printing x pages on the HP = Cost of the Lexmark printer + Cost of printing x pages on the Lexmark

$149 + 0.02x = 99 + 0.03x$
$50 = 0.01x$
$5000 = x$

For the two printers to have the same cost, 5000 pages would have to be printed.

37. Let x = the number of months, then $980x$ = the monthly payments in x months with First Union and $910x$ = the monthly payments in x months with Kensington.
First Union monthly payments = Kensington monthly payments + fees
$980x = 910x + 2000$
$70x = 2000$
$x \approx 28.6$

In about 28.6 months the total cost of both mortgages would be the same.

39. Let x = amount of assets Greg manages for Judy.
(Assets)(percentage) = fee
$(x)(0.01) = 620$
$0.01x = 620$
$x = 62,000$
Greg manages $62,000 in assets for Judy.

41. Let x = the cost of the flight before tax, then $0.07x$ = the sales tax on the flight.
Cost of flight before tax + Sales tax on flight = Total cost
$x + 0.07x = 280$
$1.07x = 280$
$x = 261.68$
The cost of the flight before taxes was $261.68.

43. Let x = Zhen's present salary, then $x + 0.30x$ = Zhen's salary at his new job.
New salary = 30,200
$x + 0.30x = 30,200$
$1.3x = 30,200$
$x = 23230.77$
Zhen's present salary is $23,230.77.

45. Let x = the size of former house in square feet, then $x - 0.18x$ = the size of the new house in square feet.
Size of new house = 2200 square feet
$x - 0.18x = 2200$
$0.82x = 2200$
$x = 2682.93$
The size of the former house was about 2682.93 square feet.

47. Let x = total amount collected at door;
3000 + 3% of admission fees = total amount received.
$3000 + 0.03x = 3750$
$0.03x = 750$
$x = \dfrac{7.50}{0.03} = 25,000$
The total amount collected at the door was $25,000.

49. Let x = average salary before wage cut.
(average salary before cut) − (decrease in salary) = average salary after wage cut
$x - 0.02x = 28,600$
$0.98x = 28,600$
$x \approx 29,183.67$
The average salary before the wage cut was $29,183.67.

51. Let x = total dollar volume in a week.
Then $0.06x$ = commission.
Salary + commission = 710
$350 + 0.06x = 710$
$0.06x = 360$
$x = \dfrac{360}{0.06} = 6000$
His dollar volume in a week must be $6000.

53. Let x = the amount of sales in dollars, then $600 + 0.02x$ = Plan 1 salary and $0.10x$ = Plan 2 salary.
Plan 1 salary = Plan 2 salary
$600 + 0.02x = 0.10x$
$600 = 0.08x$
$7500 = x$
Sales of $7,500 will result in the same salary from both plans.

55. Let x = customer assets in dollar, then $1000 + 0.01x$ = Plan 1 charges and $500 + 0.02x$ = Plan 2 charges.
Plan 1 charges = Plan 2 charges
$1000 + 0.01x = 500 + 0.02x$
$1000 = 500 + 0.01x$
$500 = 0.01x$
$50,000 = x$
Customer assets of $50,000 would result in both plans having the same total cost.

57. Let x = regular membership fee, then amount of reduction = $0.10x$.
regular fee − reduction − 20 = new fee on a Monday
$x - 0.10x - 20 = 250$
$x - 0.10x = 270$
$0.90x = 270$
$x = \dfrac{270}{0.90} = 300$
Regular fee is $300.

59. Let x = the amount in dollars Phil's daughter receives, then x + 0.25x = amount in dollars Phil's wife receives.
Daughter's share + Wife's share = $140,000
$x + (x + 0.25x) = 140,000$
$2x + 0.25x = 140,000$
$2,25x = 140,000$
$x = 62,222.22$
$x + 0.25x = 62,222.22 + (0.25)(62,222.22)$
$\qquad\qquad = 77,777.78$
Phil's wife will receive $77,777.78.

61. a. $\dfrac{74 + 88 + 76 + x}{4} = 80$

b. $\dfrac{74 + 88 + 76 + x}{4} = 80$

$74 + 88 + 76 + x = 320$

$238 + x = 320$

$x = 82$

Paul must receive an 82 on his fourth exam.

63. a. Yearly cost with 10% discount
$= 600 - 0.10(600) = \$540$. Let $x =$ the number of years it will take for the costs to be equal.
Total cost with driver's ed = Total cost without driver's ed.
$45 + 540x = 600x$

$45 = 60x$

$0.75 = x$

It will take 0.75 years, or 9 months for the costs to be equal.

b. $25 - 18 = 7$ years. The cost with driver's ed is $45 + 540(7) = \$3825$. The cost without driver's ed is $600 \cdot (7) = \$4200$. He will save $4200 - 3825 = \$375$.

65. $\dfrac{1}{4} + \dfrac{3}{4} \div \dfrac{1}{2} - \dfrac{1}{3} = \dfrac{3}{12} + \dfrac{9}{12} \div \dfrac{6}{12} - \dfrac{4}{12}$

$= \dfrac{3}{12} + \dfrac{9}{12} \cdot \dfrac{12}{6} - \dfrac{4}{12}$

$= \dfrac{3}{12} + \dfrac{9}{6} - \dfrac{4}{12}$

$= \dfrac{3}{12} + \dfrac{18}{12} - \dfrac{4}{12}$

$= \dfrac{21}{12} - \dfrac{4}{12}$

$= \dfrac{17}{12}$

66. Associative property of addition

67. Commutative property of multiplication

68. Distributive property

69. Let $x =$ number of pounds of coleslaw needed.

$\dfrac{5 \text{ people}}{\frac{1}{2} \text{ pound coleslaw}} = \dfrac{560 \text{ people}}{x \text{ pounds coleslaw}}$

$\dfrac{5}{\frac{1}{2}} = \dfrac{560}{x}$

$5x = \left(\dfrac{1}{2}\right)(560)$

$5x = 280$

$x = \dfrac{280}{5} = 56$

He will need 56 pounds of coleslaw.

70. $A = \dfrac{1}{2}bh$

$2A = 2(\dfrac{1}{2}bh)$

$2A = bh$

$\dfrac{2A}{h} = \dfrac{bh}{h}$

$\dfrac{2A}{h} = b$

Exercise Set 3.4

1. $A = (2l) \cdot \left(\dfrac{w}{2}\right) = lw$

The area remains the same

3. $V = 2l \cdot 2w \cdot 2h = 8(lwh)$
The volume is eight times as great.

5. $A = \pi r^2 = \pi(3r)^2 = \pi(9r^2) = 9\pi r^2$
The area is nine times as great.

7. An isosceles triangle is a triangle with 2 equal sides.

9. The sum of the measures of the angles in a triangle is 180°.

11. Let $x =$ the measure of the two equal angles, then $x + 42 =$ the measure of the third angle.
Sum of the three angles = 180°
$x + x + (x + 42) = 180$

$3x + 42 = 180$

$3x = 138$

$x = 46$

The two equal angles are each 46°. The third angle is $x + 42° = 46° + 42° = 88°$.

13. Let x = length of each side of the triangle, then
$P = x + x + x = 3x$.
Perimeter = 28.5
$$x = \frac{28.5}{3} = 9.5$$
The length of each side is 9.5 inches.

Let x = length of each side of the triangle, then
$P = x + x + x = 3x$.
Perimeter = 48.6 cm.
$$3x = 48.6$$
$$x = 16.2$$
The length of each side is 16.2 cm.

15. Let x = measure of angle B. Then
$2x + 21$ = measure of angle A.
Sum of the 2 angles = 90
$$x + (2x + 21) = 90$$
$$3x + 21 = 90$$
$$3x = 69$$
$$x = 23$$
Measure of angle $A = 2(23) + 21 = 67°$
Measure of angle $B = 23°$

17. Let x = measure of angle A, then
$3x - 8$ = measure of angle B.
Sum of the 2 angles = 180
$$x + (3x - 8) = 180$$
$$4x - 8 = 180$$
$$4x = 188$$
$$x = \frac{188}{4} = 47$$
Measure of angle $A = 47°$
Measure of angle $B = 3(47) - 8 = 141 - 8 = 133°$

19. The two angles have equal measures.
$$2x + 50 = 4x + 12$$
$$38 = 2x$$
$$19 = x$$
$2x + 50 = 2(19) + 50 = 38 + 50 = 88°$
$4x + 12 = 4(19) + 12 = 76 + 12 = 88°$
Each angle measures 88°.

21. Let x = measure of smallest angle. Then second
angle = $x + 10$ and third angle = $2x - 30$.
Sum of the 3 angles = 180
$$x + (x + 10) + (2x - 30) = 180$$
$$4x - 20 = 180$$
$$4x = 200$$
$$x = \frac{200}{4} = 50$$
The first angle is 50°.
The second angle is 50 + 10 = 60°.
The third angle is 2(50) − 30 = 70°.

23. Let x = width of rectangle. Then $x + 8$ = length of
rectangle.
$$P = 2l + 2w$$
$$48 = 2(x + 8) + 2x$$
$$48 = 2x + 16 + 2x$$
$$48 = 4x + 16$$
$$32 = 4x$$
$$8 = x$$
Width is 8 feet and length is 8 + 8 = 16 feet.

25. Let x = width of tennis court.
Then $2x + 6$ = length of tennis court.
$$P = 2l + 2w$$
$$228 = 2(2x + 6) + 2x$$
$$228 = 4x + 12 + 2x$$
$$228 = 6x + 12$$
$$216 = 6x$$
$$36 = x$$
The width is 36 feet and the length is
$2(36) + 6 = 78$ feet.

27. Let x = measure of each smaller angle.
Then $3x - 20$ = measure of each larger angle.
(measure of the two smaller angles) + (measure
of the two larger angles) = 360°
$$x + x + (3x - 20) + (3x - 20) = 360$$
$$8x - 40 = 360$$
$$8x = 400$$
$$x = 50$$
Each smaller angle is 50°. Each larger angle is
$3(50) - 20 = 130°$.

29. Let x = measure of the smallest angle.
Then $x + 10$ = measure of the second angle,
$2x + 14$ = measure of third angle, and
$x + 21$ = measure of fourth angle.
Sum of the four angles = 360°
$$x + (x + 10) + (2x + 14) + (x + 21) = 360$$
$$5x + 45 = 360$$
$$5x = 315$$
$$x = 63$$
Thus the angles are 63°, 63 + 10 = 73°
$2(63) + 14 = 140°$ and 63 + 21 = 84°.

31. Let x = width of bookcase shelf.
Then $x + 3$ = height of bookcase.
4 shelves + 2 sides = total lumber available.
$$4x + 2(x + 3) = 30$$
$$4x + 2x + 6 = 30$$
$$6x + 6 = 30$$
$$6x = 24$$
$$x = 4$$

The width of each shelf is 4 feet and the height is $4 + 3 = 7$ feet.

33. Let x = length of a shelf.
    Then $2x$ = height of bookcase.
    4 shelves + 2 sides = total lumber available
    $$4x + 2(2x) = 20$$
    $$4x + 4x = 20$$
    $$8x = 20$$
    $$x = \frac{20}{8} = 2.5$$
    The width of the bookcase is 2.5 feet. The height of the bookcase is $2(2.5) = 5$ feet.

35. Let x = width of fenced in area.
    Then $x + 4$ = length of fenced in area
    Five "widths" + one "length" = total fencing
    $$5x + (x + 4) = 64$$
    $$6x + 4 = 64$$
    $$6x = 60$$
    $$x = 10$$
    Width is 10 feet and length is $10 + 4 = 14$ feet.

37. $ac + ad + bc + bd$

39. $-|-6| < |-4|$ since $-|-6| = -6$ and $|-4| = 4$

40. $|-3| > -|3|$ since $|-3| = 3$ and $-|3| = -3$

41. $-6 - (-2) + (-4) = -6 + 2 + (-4)$
    $$= -4 + (-4)$$
    $$= -8$$

42. $-6y + x - 3(x - 2) + 2y$
    $$= -6y + x - 3x + 6 + 2y$$
    $$= x - 3x - 6y + 2y + 6$$
    $$= -2x - 4y + 6$$

43.
    $$2x + 3y = 9$$
    $$2x - 2x + 3y = -2x + 9$$
    $$3y = -2x + 9$$
    $$\frac{3y}{3} = \frac{-2x + 9}{3}$$
    $$y = \frac{-2x + 9}{3} \text{ or } y = -\frac{2}{3}x + 3$$
    Substitute 3 for x.
    $$y = \frac{-2x + 9}{3} = \frac{-6 + 9}{3} = \frac{3}{3} = 1$$

Exercise Set 3.5

1. Rate $= \dfrac{\text{distance}}{\text{time}} = \dfrac{150}{3} = 50$. Therefore, her average speed was 50 mph.

3. Thickness = rate · time = $(0.2)(12) = 2.4$. The door is 2.4 cm thick.

5. Time $= \dfrac{\text{amount}}{\text{rate}} = \dfrac{420}{30} = 14$. It will take 14 hours to lay the tile.

7. Rate $= \dfrac{\text{volume}}{\text{time}} = \dfrac{1500}{6} = 250$.
   Therefore, the flow rate should be 250 cm^3/hr.

9. Time $= \dfrac{\text{distance}}{\text{rate}} = \dfrac{5280}{4} = 1320$ seconds
   or $\dfrac{1320}{60} = 22$ minutes
   It will take about 22 minutes.

11. Rate $= \dfrac{\text{distance}}{\text{time}} = \dfrac{500}{2.635} \approx 189.75$. His average speed was approximately 189.75 mph.

13. Let t be the time it takes for Willie and Shanna to be 16.8 miles apart.

Person	Rate	Time	Distance
Willie	3	t	$3t$
Shanna	4	t	$4t$

$$3t + 4t = 16.8$$
$$7t = 16.8$$
$$t = 2.4$$
It will take 2.4 hours.

15. Let r be the second rate of the machine.

Machine	Rate	Time	Distance
First	60	7.2	432
Second	r	6.8	$6.8r$

$$432 + 6.8r = 908$$
$$6.8r = 476$$
$$r = 70$$
The second speed the machine was set at was 70 miles per hour.

17. Let t be the time they have been walking.

Walker	Rate	Time	Distance
Sadie	220	t	$220t$
Dale	100	t	$100t$

$$220t - 100t = 600$$
$$120t = 600$$
$$t = 5$$

They have been walking for 5 minutes.

19. a. Let r be the speed of the cutter coming from the east (westbound). Then $r + 5$ is the speed of the cutter coming from the west (eastbound).

Cutter	Rate	Time	Distance
Eastbound	$r + 5$	3	$3(r + 5)$
Westbound	r	3	$3r$

$$3(r + 5) + 3r = 225$$
$$3r + 15 + 3r = 225$$
$$6r = 210$$
$$r = 35$$

The speed of the westbound cutter is 35 mph and the speed of the eastbound cutter is 40 mph.

21. a. Distance = rate · time = $(2.38)(1.01) \approx 2.4$ miles

    b. Distance = rate · time = $(21.17)(5.29) \approx 112.0$ miles

    c. Distance = rate · time = $(8.32)(3.15) \approx 26.2$ miles

    d. $2.4 + 112.0 + 26.2 = 140.6$ miles

    e. $1.01 + 5.29 + 3.15 = 9.45$ hours

23. Let r be the rate of *Apollo*. Then $r + 4$ is the rate of *Pythagoras*.

Boat	Rate	Time	Distance
Apollo	r	0.7	$0.7r$
Pythagoras	$r + 4$	0.7	$0.7(r + 4)$

$$0.7r + 0.7(r + 4) = 9.8$$
$$0.7r + 0.7r + 2.8 = 9.8$$
$$1.4r = 7$$
$$r = 5$$

The speed of *Apollo* is 5 mph, and the speed of *Pythagoras* is 9 mph.

25. a. Let t be the time it takes for the Coast Guard to catch the bank robber.

Boat	Rate	Time	Distance
Robber	25	$t + \frac{1}{2}$	$25\left(t + \frac{1}{2}\right)$
Coast Guard	35	t	$35t$

$$25\left(t + \frac{1}{2}\right) = 35t$$
$$25t + \frac{25}{2} = 35t$$
$$\frac{25}{2} = 10t$$
$$1.25 = t$$

It will take 1.25 hours for the Coast Guard to catch the bank robber.

    b. Distance = rate · time = $(35)(1.25) = 43.75$ miles.

27. a. Let t be the time it takes for Phil's pass to reach Pete.

Player	Rate	Time	Distance
Pete	25	$t + 2$	$25(t + 2)$
Phil	50	t	$50t$

$$25(t + 2) = 50t$$
$$25t + 50 = 50t$$
$$50 = 25t$$
$$2 = t$$

It will take 2 seconds for Phil's pass to reach Pete.

    b. Distance = rate · time = $50 \cdot 2 = 100$ feet

29. Let t = time, in hours, Betty was traveling at 50 mph.

Speed	Rate	Time	Distance
Faster	70 mph	$t - 0.5$	$70(t - 0.5)$
Slower	50 mph	t	$50t$

    a. $50t - 70t + 35 = 5$
$$-20t = -30$$
$$t = 1.5$$

    b. Betty traveled for 1.5 hours at 50 mph.

31. Let r be the planned speed of the plane. Then $r + 30$ is the new speed of the plane.

Speed	Rate	Time	Distance
Planned	r	4	$4r$
New	$r + 30$	$4 - 0.2$	$3.8(r + 30)$

$$4r = 3.8(r + 30)$$
$$4r = 3.8r + 114$$
$$0.2r = 114$$
$$r = 570$$

The plane's planned speed is 570 miles per hour. The plane's new speed is 600 miles per hour.

33. Let r be the rate of clearing the bridge. Then $1.2 + r$ is the rate of clearing the road.

	Rate	Time	Distance
Road	$1.2 + r$	20	$20(1.2 + r)$
Bridge	r	60	$60r$

$$20(1.2 + r) + 60r = 124$$
$$24 + 20r + 60r = 124$$
$$80r = 100$$
$$r = 1.25$$

The crew will clear the bridge at a rate of 1.25 feet/day, and they will clear the road at a rate of 2.45 feet/day.

35. Let x be the amount invested at 5%. Then $9400 - x$ is the amount invested at 7%.

Principal	Rate	Time	Interest
x	5%	1	$0.05x$
$9400 - x$	7%	1	$0.07(9400 - x)$

$$0.05x + 0.07(9400 - x) = 610$$
$$0.05x + 658 - 0.07x = 610$$
$$-0.02x = -48$$
$$x = 2400$$

They invested $2400 at 5% and $7000 at 7%.

37. Let x be the amount invested at 6%. Then $6000 - x$ is the amount invested at 4%.

Principal	Rate	Time	Interest
x	6%	1	$0.06x$
$6000 - x$	4%	1	$0.04(6000 - x)$

$$0.06x = 0.04(6000 - x)$$
$$0.06x = 240 - 0.04x$$
$$0.10x = 240$$
$$x = 2400$$

She invested $2400 at 6% and $3600 at 4%.

39. Let x be the amount invested at 4%. Then $10,000 - x$ is the amount invested at 5%.

Principal	Rate	Time	Interest
x	4%	1	$0.04x$
$10,000 - x$	5%	1	$0.05(10,000 - x)$

$$0.05(10,000 - x) - 0.04x = 320$$
$$500 - 0.05x - 0.04x = 320$$
$$-0.09x = -180$$
$$x = 2000$$

She invested $2,000.00 at 4% and $8,000.00 at 5%.

41. Let t be the time, in months, during which Patricia paid $17.10 per month. Then $12 - t$ is the time during which she paid $18.40 per month.

Rate	Time	Amount
17.10	t	$17.10t$
18.40	$12 - t$	$18.40(12 - t)$

$$17.10t + 18.40(12 - t) = 207.80$$
$$17.10t + 220.80 - 18.40t = 207.80$$
$$-1.30t = -13$$
$$t = 10$$

She paid $17.10 for the first 10 months of the year, and paid $18.40 for the remainder of the year. The rate increase took effect in November.

43. Let x be the number of hours worked at Home Depot ($6.50 per hour). Then $18 - x$ is the number of hours worked at the veterinary clinic ($7.00 per hour).

Rate	Hours	Total
$6.50	x	$6.5x$
$7.00	$18 - x$	$7(18 - x)$

$$6.5x + 7(18 - x) = 122$$
$$6.5x + 126 - 7x = 122$$
$$-0.5x = -4$$
$$x = 8$$

Mihly worked 8 hours at Home Depot and 10 hours at the clinic.

45. Let t be the number of $1550 computer systems sold. Then $200 - t$ is the number of $1320 computer systems sold.

Rate	Amount /sold	Money collected
1550	t	1550
1320	$200 - t$	$1320(200 - t)$

$$1320(200 - t) + 1550t = 282{,}400$$
$$264{,}000 - 1320t + 1550t = 282{,}400$$
$$230t = 18{,}400$$
$$t = 80$$

There were 80 of the $1,550 Computer systems sold.

47. a. Let x be the number of shares of General Electric. Then $5x$ is the number of shares of PepsiCo.

Stock	Price	Shares	Total
GE	$74	x	$74x$
PepsiCo	$35	$5x$	$35 \cdot 5x$

$$74x + 35 \cdot 5x = 8000$$
$$74x + 175x = 8000$$
$$249x = 8000$$
$$x \approx 32.1$$

Since only whole shares can be purchased, he will purchase 32 shares of GE and 160 shares of PepsiCo.

b. Mr. Gilbert spent $32 \cdot 74 + 160 \cdot 35 = \$7968$. He has $8000 - \$7968 = \$32$ left over.

49. Let x be the amount of Family grass seed. Then $10 - x$ is the amount of Spot Filler grass seed.

Seed	Price	Amount	Total
Family	$2.45	x	$2.45x$
Filler	$2.10	$10 - x$	$2.10(10 - x)$
Mixture	$2.20	10	22

$$2.45x + 2.10(10 - x) = 22$$
$$2.45x + 21 - 2.10x = 22$$
$$0.35x = 1$$
$$x \approx 2.86$$

2.86 pounds of Family grass seed and 7.14 pounds of Spot Filler grass seed should be mixed together.

51. Let x be the number of gallons of regular gasoline.

Gas Type	Cost	Gallons	Total
Regular	$1.20	x	$1.20x$
Premium Plus	$1.35	$500 - x$	$1.35(500\text{-}x)$
Premium	126	500	1.26(500)

$$1.20x + 1.35(500 - x) = 126(500)$$
$$1.20x + 675 - 1.35x = 630$$
$$-.15x = -45$$
$$x = 300$$

He should mix 300 gallons of regular and 200 gallons of premium plus.

53. Let x be the cost per pound of the mixture.

Type	Cost	Pounds	Total
Good & Plenty	$2.49	3	$2.49(3)
Sweet Treats	$2.89	5	$2.89(5)
Mixture	x	8	$8x$

$$2.49(3) + 2.89(5) = 8x$$
$$7.47 + 14.45 = 8x$$
$$21.92 = 8x$$
$$2.74 = x$$

The mixture should sell for $2.74 per pound.

55. Let x be the percentage of alcohol in the mixture.

Percentage	Liters	Amount of Alcohol
12%	5	0.6
9%	2	0.18
x%	7	$\left(\frac{x}{100}\right) \cdot 7$

$$\left(\frac{x}{100}\right) \cdot 7 = 0.6 + 0.18$$
$$0.07x = 0.78$$
$$x \approx 11.1$$

The alcohol content of the mixture is about 11.1%.

57. Let x be the amount of 12 % sulfuric acid solution.

Solution	Strength	Liters	Amount
20%	0.20	1	0.20
12%	0.12	x	$0.12x$
Mixture	0.15	$x + 1$	$0.15(x + 1)$

$0.20 + 0.12x = 0.15(x + 1)$
$0.20 + 0.12x = 0.15x + 0.15$
$-0.03x = -0.05$
$$x = \frac{5}{3}$$

$1\frac{2}{3}$ liters of 12% sulfuric acid should be used.

59. Let x be the amount of the swimming pool shock treatment to be added to a quart of water.

Product	Percentage	Ounces	Amount
Clorox	5.25%	8	$(0.0525) \cdot 8$
Shock Treatment	10.5%	x	$0.105x$

$(0.0525)\cdot 8 = 0.105x$
$0.42 = 0.105x$
$4 = x$

Add 4 ounces of the shock treatment to a quart of water.

61. Let x be the percentage of milkfat in whole milk.

Type	Percentage	Gallons	Amount
Whole	$x\%$	4	$\left(\frac{x}{100}\right) \cdot 4$
Low fat	1%	5	$(0.01) \cdot 5$
Reduced fat	2%	9	$(0.02) \cdot 9$

$\left(\dfrac{x}{100}\right) \cdot 4 + (0.01) \cdot 5 = (0.02) \cdot 9$

$$\frac{4x}{100} + 0.05 = 0.18$$

$$\frac{4x}{100} = 0.13$$

$$4x = 13$$

$$x = 3.25$$

The milkfat content of whole milk is 3.25%.

63. Let x be the percent of orange juice in the new mixture.

Percentage of water without salt	Gallons	Amount
99.1%	50,000	0.991(50,000)
100%	x	$1x$
99.2%	$x + 50{,}000$	$0.992(x + 50{,}000$

$0.991(50{,}000) + 1x = 0.992(x + 50{,}000)$
$49{,}550 + 1x = 0.992x + 49{,}600$
$\phantom{49{,}550 + }0.008x = 50$
$\phantom{49{,}550 + 0.00}x = 6{,}250$

To lower the salt concentration, 6,250 gallons of 0% salt content has to be added.

65. Let x be the number of gallons of Prestone antifreeze added.

Brand	Percentage of antifreeze	Gallons	Amount
Prestone	12%	x	$0.12x$
Xeres	9%	1	$(0.09)(1)$
Mixture	10%	$x + 1$	$(0.10)(x+1)$

$0.12x + 0.09 = 0.10(x + 1)$
$0.12x + 0.09 = 0.10x + 0.10$
$0.02x = 0.01$
$x = 0.5$

Nina added 0.5 gallons of Prestone antifreeze.

67. The time it takes for the transport to make the trip is:
$$\text{Time} = \frac{\text{Distance}}{\text{Rate}} = \frac{1720}{370} \approx 4.65 \text{ hours}$$
The time it takes for the Hornets to make the trip is:
$$\text{Time} = \frac{\text{Distance}}{\text{Rate}} = \frac{1720}{900} \approx 1.91 \text{ hours}$$
It takes the transport $4.65 - 1.91 = 2.74$ hours longer to make the trip. Since it needs to arrive 3 hours before the Hornets, it should leave about $2.74 + 3 = 5.74$ hours before them.

71. a. $2\dfrac{3}{4} \div 1\dfrac{5}{8} = \dfrac{11}{4} \div \dfrac{13}{8}$

$\phantom{2\dfrac{3}{4} \div 1\dfrac{5}{8}} = \dfrac{11}{4} \cdot \dfrac{8}{13}$

$\phantom{2\dfrac{3}{4} \div 1\dfrac{5}{8}} = \dfrac{22}{13} \text{ or } 1\dfrac{9}{13}$

b. $2\dfrac{3}{4} + 1\dfrac{5}{8} = \dfrac{11}{4} + \dfrac{13}{8}$

$$= \dfrac{22}{8} + \dfrac{13}{8}$$

$$= \dfrac{35}{8} \text{ or } 4\dfrac{3}{8}$$

72. $6(x - 3) = 4x - 18 + 2x$
$6x - 18 = 6x - 18$
All real numbers are solutions.

73. $\dfrac{6}{x} = \dfrac{72}{9}$
$6 \cdot 9 = 72x$
$54 = 72x$
$x = \dfrac{54}{72} = \dfrac{3}{4} \text{ or } 0.75$

74. $3x - 4 \le -4x + 3(x - 1)$
$3x - 4 \le -4x + 3x - 3$
$3x - 4 \le -x - 3$
$4x \le 1$
$x \le \dfrac{1}{4}$

Review Exercises

1. Substitute 6 for r.
$C = 2\pi r$

$C = 2\pi(6)$

$= 12\pi$

≈ 37.70

2. Substitute 4 for l and 5 for w.
$P = 2l + 2w$

$P = 2(4) + 2(5) = 8 + 10 = 18$

3. Substitute 8 for b and 12 for h.
$A = \dfrac{1}{2}bh$

$A = \dfrac{1}{2}(8)(12) = 48$

4. Substitute 200 for K and 4 for v.
$K = \dfrac{1}{2}mv^2$

$200 = \dfrac{1}{2}m(4)^2$

$200 = \dfrac{1}{2}m(16)$

$200 = 8m$

$\dfrac{200}{8} = \dfrac{8m}{8}$

$25 = m$

5. Substitute 15 for y, 3 for m, and -2 for x.
$y = mx + b$

$15 = (3)(-2) + b$

$15 = -6 + b$

$15 + 6 = -6 + 6 + b$

$21 = b$

6. Substitute 4716.98 for P and 0.06 for i.
$P = \dfrac{f}{1 + i}$

$4716.98 = \dfrac{f}{1 + 0.06}$

$4716.98 = \dfrac{f}{1.06}$

$1.06 \times 4716.98 = \dfrac{f}{1.06} \times 1.06$

$5000 \approx f$

7. a. $\qquad 2x = 2y + 4$

$2x - 4 = 2y + 4 - 4$

$2x - 4 = 2y$

$\dfrac{2x - 4}{2} = \dfrac{2y}{2}$

$\dfrac{2x}{2} - \dfrac{4}{2} = y$

$x - 2 = y$

b. Substitute 10 for x.
$10 - 2 = y$

$8 = y$

8. a. $\qquad 6x + 3y = -9$

$6x - 6x + 3y = -9 - 6x$

$3y = -9 - 6x$

$\dfrac{3y}{3} = \dfrac{-9 - 6x}{3}$

$y = \dfrac{-9}{3} - \dfrac{6x}{3}$

$y = -3 - 2x$

b. Substitute 12 for x.
$$y = -3 - 2(12) = -3 - 24 = -27$$

9. a. $5x - 2y = 16$
$$5x - 5x - 2y = 16 - 5x$$
$$-2y = 16 - 5x$$
$$\frac{-2y}{-2} = \frac{16 - 5x}{-2}$$
$$y = \frac{16 - 5x}{-2}$$
$$y = \frac{5}{2}x - 8$$

b. Substitute 2 for x.
$$y = \frac{5}{2}(2) - 8 = 5 - 8 = -3$$

10. a. $2x = 3y + 12$
$$2x - 12 = 3y + 12 - 12$$
$$2x - 12 = 3y$$
$$\frac{2x - 12}{3} = \frac{3y}{3}$$
$$\frac{2x - 12}{3} = y$$
$$y = \frac{2}{3}x - 4$$

b. Substitute –6 for x.
$$y = \frac{2}{3}(-6) - 4$$
$$= -4 - 4$$
$$= -8$$

11. $A = lw$
$$\frac{A}{l} = \frac{lw}{l}$$
$$\frac{A}{l} = w$$

12. $A = \frac{1}{2}bh$
$$2A = 2\left(\frac{1}{2}bh\right)$$
$$2A = bh$$
$$\frac{2A}{b} = \frac{bh}{b}$$
$$\frac{2A}{b} = h$$

13. $i = prt$
$$\frac{i}{pr} = \frac{prt}{pr}$$
$$\frac{i}{pr} = t$$

14. $P = 2l + 2w$
$$P - 2l = 2l - 2l + 2w$$
$$P - 2l = 2w$$
$$\frac{P - 2l}{2} = \frac{2w}{2}$$
$$\frac{P - 2l}{2} = w$$

15. $V = \pi r^2 h$
$$\frac{V}{\pi r^2} = \frac{\pi r^2 h}{\pi r^2}$$
$$\frac{V}{\pi r^2} = h$$

16. $V = \frac{1}{3}Bh$
$$3V = 3(\frac{1}{3}Bh)$$
$$3V = Bh$$
$$\frac{3V}{B} = \frac{Bh}{B}$$
$$\frac{3V}{B} = h$$

17. Substitute 600 for p, 0.09 for r, and 2 for t.
$$i = prt$$
$$i = (600)(0.09)(2) = 108$$
Tom will pay \$108 interest.

18. $P = 2l + 2w$
$$16 = 2l + 2(2)$$
$$16 = 2l + 4$$
$$12 = 2l$$
$$6 = l$$
The length of the rectangle is 6 inches.

19. The sum of a number and the number increased by 5 is 9.

20. The sum of a number and twice the number decreased by 1 is 10.

21. Let x = the smaller number.
Then $x + 8$ = the larger number.
Smaller number + larger number = 74

$$x + (x + 8) = 74$$
$$2x + 8 = 74$$
$$2x = 66$$
$$x = 33$$

The smaller number is 33 and the larger number is $33 + 8 = 41$.

22. Let x = smaller integer.
    Then $x + 1$ = next consecutive integer.
    Smaller number + larger number = 237
    $$x + (x + 1) = 237$$
    $$2x + 1 = 237$$
    $$2x = 236$$
    $$x = 118$$
    The smaller number is 118 and the larger number is $118 + 1 = 119$.

23. Let x = the smaller integer.
    Then $5x + 3$ = the larger integer
    Larger number – smaller number = 31
    $$(5x + 3) - x = 31$$
    $$4x + 3 = 31$$
    $$4x = 28$$
    $$x = 7$$
    The smaller number is 7 and the larger number is $5(7) + 3 = 38$.

24. Let x = cost of car before tax.
    Then $0.07x$ = amount of tax.
    Cost of car before tax + tax on car
    = cost of car after tax
    $$x + 0.07x = 23,260$$
    $$1.07x = 23,260$$
    $$x = \frac{23,260}{1.07} = 21,738.32$$
    The cost of the car before tax is $21,738.32.

25. Let x = the number of months, then $20x$ = the increase in production of bagels over x months.
    Current production + Increase in production = Future production
    $$520 + 20x = 900$$
    $$20x = 380$$
    $$x = 19$$
    It will take 19 months.

26. Let x = weekly dollar sales that would make total salaries from both companies the same.
    The commission at present company = $0.03x$ and commission at new company = $0.08x$
    Salary + commission for present company = salary + commission for new company

$$500 + 0.03x = 400 + 0.08x$$
$$100 + 0.03x = 0.08x$$
$$100 = 0.05x$$
$$\frac{100}{0.05} = x$$
$$2000 = x$$

Ron's weekly sales would have to be $2000 for the total salaries from both companies to be the same.

27. Let x = original price of camcorder. Then $0.20x$ = reduction during first week.
    Original price – first reduction – second reduction = price during second week
    $$x - 0.20x - 25 = 495$$
    $$0.8x - 25 = 495$$
    $$0.8x = 520$$
    $$x = \frac{520}{0.8} = 650$$
    The original price of the camcorder was $650.

28. Let x = the number of months for the total payments for both banks to be the same.
    First Federal = Internet Bank
    $$900 + 889x = 1200 + 826x$$
    $$900 + 63x = 1200$$
    $$63x = 300$$
    $$x \approx 4.76$$
    It will take about 4.76 months.

29. Let x = measure of the smallest angle. Then $x + 10$ = measure of second angle and $2x - 10$ = measure of third angle.
    Sum of the three angles = 180°
    $$x + (x + 10) + (2x - 10) = 180$$
    $$4x = 180$$
    $$x = 45$$
    The angles are 45°, $45 + 10 = 55$°, and $2(45) - 10 = 80$°.

30. Let x = measure of the smallest angle. Then $x + 10$ = measure of second angle, $5x$ = measure of third angle, $4x + 20$ = measure of the fourth angle.
    Sum of the four angles = 360°
    $$x + (x + 10) + 5x + (4x + 20) = 360$$
    $$11x + 30 = 360$$
    $$11x = 330$$
    $$x = \frac{330}{11} = 30$$
    The angles are 30°, $30 + 10 = 40$°.
    $5(30) = 150$°, and $4(30) + 20 = 140$°.

31. Let w = width of garden. Then $w + 4$ = length of garden.

$$P = 2l + 2w$$
$$70 = 2(w + 4) + 2w$$
$$70 = 4w + 8$$
$$62 = 4w$$
$$15.5 = w$$

The width is 15.5 feet and the length is
15.5 + 4 = 19.5 feet.

32. Let x = the width of the room. Then
$x + 30$ = the length of the room. The amount of
string used is the perimeter of the room plus the
wall separating the two rooms.
$$P = 2l + 2w + w$$
$$P = 2l + 3w$$
$$310 = 2(x + 30) + 3x$$
$$310 = 2x + 60 + 3x$$
$$310 = 5x + 60$$
$$250 = 5x$$
$$50 = x$$
The width of the room is 50 feet and the length is
50 + 30 = 80 feet.

33. Let r be the flow rate of the water.
Amount = rate · time
$$105 = r \cdot (3.5)$$
$$\frac{105}{3.5} = \frac{r \cdot (3.5)}{3.5}$$
$$30 = r$$
The flow rate of the water is 30 gallons per hour.

34. Speed = $\dfrac{\text{distance}}{\text{time}} = \dfrac{26}{4} = 6.5$ mph

35. Let t be the time it takes for the joggers to be 4
kilometers apart.

Jogger	Rate	Time	Distance
Harold	8	t	$8t$
Susan	6	t	$6t$

$$8t - 6t = 4$$
$$2t = 4$$
$$t = 2$$
It takes the joggers 2 hours to be 4 kilometers
apart.

36. Let t be the amount of time it takes for the trains
to be 440 miles apart.

Train	Rate	Time	Distance
First	50	t	$50t$
Second	60	t	$60t$

$$50t + 60t = 440$$
$$110t = 440$$
$$t = 4$$
After 4 hours, the two trains will be 440 miles
apart.

37. Rate = $\dfrac{\text{Distance}}{\text{Time}} = \dfrac{200 \text{ feet}}{22.73 \text{ seconds}} \approx 8.8$ ft / sec
The cars travel at about 8.8 ft/sec.

38. Let x be the amount invested at 8%. Then
$12,000 - x$ is the amount invested at $7\frac{1}{4}$%.

Principal	Rate	Time	Interest
x	8%	1	$0.08x$
$12,000 - x$	$7\frac{1}{4}$%	1	$0.0725(12,000 - x)$

$$0.08x + 0.0725(12,000 - x) = 900$$
$$0.08x + 870 - 0.0725x = 900$$
$$0.0075x = 30$$
$$x = 4000$$
Tatiana should invest \$4000 at 8% and \$8000 at
$7\frac{1}{4}$%.

39. Let x be the amount invested at 3%. Then
$4,000 - x$ is the amount invested at 3.5%.

Principal	Rate	Time	Interest
x	3%	1	$0.03x$
$4,000 - x$	3.5%	1	$0.035(4,000 - x)$

$$0.03x + 94.50 = 0.035(4,000 - x)$$
$$0.03x + 94.50 = 140 - .035x$$
$$0.065x = 45.5$$
$$x = 700$$
Aimee invested \$700 in the 3% account and
\$3300 in the 3.5% account.

40. Let x be the number of gallons of pure punch.
Then $2 - x$ is the number of liters of the 5% acid
solution.

Punch Solution	Strength	Gallons	Amount
98%	0.98	2	0.98(2)
100%	1	x	$1x$
98.5%	0.985	$x + 2$	$0.985(x + 2)$

$$1.96 + x = 0.985(x + 2)$$
$$1.96 + x = 0.985x + 1.97$$

$0.015x = 0.01$

$x \approx 0.67$

Marcie should add about 0.67 gallons of pure punch.

41. Let x be the number of small wind chimes sold..

Type	Price	Number Sold	Amount
Small	$8	x	$8x$
Large	$20	$30 - x$	$20(30 - x)$

$8x + 20(30 - x) = 492$

$8x + 600 - 20x = 492$

$-12x = -108$

$x = 9$

He sold 9 small and 21 large wind chimes

42. Let x be the number of liters of the 10% solution. Then $2 - x$ is the number of liters of the 5% acid solution.

Solution	Strength	Liters	Amount
10%	0.10	x	$0.10x$
5%	0.05	$2 - x$	$0.05(2 - x)$
Mixture	0.08	2	0.16

$0.10x + 0.05(2 - x) = 0.16$

$0.10x + 0.10 - 0.05x = 0.16$

$0.05x = 0.06$

$x = 1.2$

The chemist should mix 1.2 liters of 10% solution with 0.8 liters of 5% solution.

43. Let $x =$ smaller odd integer. Then $x + 2 =$ next consecutive odd integer. Smaller number + larger number = 208

$x + (x + 2) = 208$

$2x + 2 = 208$

$2x = 206$

$x = 103$

The smaller number is 103 and the larger number is $103 + 2 = 105$.

44. Let $x =$ cost of television before tax. Then amount of tax $= 0.06x$. Cost of television before tax + tax on television = cost of television after tax.

$x + 0.06x = 477$

$1.06x = 477$

$x = \dfrac{477}{1.06} = 450$

The cost of the television before tax is $450.

45. Let $x =$ his dollar sales.
Then $0.05x =$ amount of commission.
Salary + commission = 900

$300 + 0.05x = 900$

$0.05x = 600$

$x = \dfrac{600}{0.05} = 12,000$

His sales last week were $12,000.

46. Let $x =$ measure of the smallest angle. Then $x + 8 =$ measure of second angle and $2x + 4 =$ measure of third angle.
Sum of the three angles $= 180°$

$x + (x + 8) + (2x + 4) = 180$

$4x + 12 = 180$

$4x = 168$

$x = 42$

The angles are $42°$, $42 + 8 = 50°$, and $2(42) + 4 = 88°$.

47. Let $t =$ number of years. Then $25t =$ increase in employees over t years
Present number of employees + increase in employees = future number of employees

$427 + 25t = 627$

$25t = 200$

$t = \dfrac{200}{25} = 8$

It will take 8 years before they reach 627 employees.

48. Let $x =$ measure of each smaller angle. Then $x + 40 =$ measure of each larger angle
(measure of the two smaller angles)
+(measure of the two larger angles) $= 360°$

$x + x + (x + 40) + (x + 40) = 360$

$4x + 80 = 360$

$4x = 280$

$x = 70$

Each of the smaller angles is $70°$ and each of the two larger angles is $70 + 40 = 110°$.

49. a. Let $x =$ number of copies that would result in both centers charging the same. Then charge for copies at Copy King $= 0.04x$ and charge for copies at King Kopie $= 0.03x$
Monthly fee + charge for copies at Copy King = monthly fee + charge for copies at King Kopie.

$20 + 0.04x = 25 + 0.03x$

$0.04x = 5 + 0.03x$

$0.01x = 5$

$x = \dfrac{5}{0.01} = 500$

500 copies would result in both centers charging the same.

50. a. Let t = time the sisters meet after Chris starts swimming.

Person	Rate	Time	Distance
Chris	60	t	$60t$
Kathy	50	$t + 2$	$50(t + 2)$

$60t = 50(t + 2)$

$60t = 50t + 100$

$10t = 100$

$t = 10$

The sisters will meet 10 minutes after Chris starts swimming.

b. rate $\cdot$ time = distance

$60 \cdot 10 = 600$

The sisters will be 600 feet from the boat when they meet.

51. Let x be the amount of \$3.50 per pound ground beef. Then $80 - x$ is the amount of \$4.10 per pound of ground beef.

Ground Beef	Price	Amount	Total
\$3.50	3.50	x	$3.50x$
\$4.10	4.10	$80 - x$	$4.10(80 - x)$
Mixture	3.65	80	292

$3.50x + 4.10(80 - x) = 292$

$3.50x + 328 - 4.10x = 292$

$-0.60x = -36$

$x = 60$

The butcher mixed 60 lbs of \$3.50 per pound ground beef with 20 lbs of \$4.10 per pound ground beef.

52. Let x = the rate the older brother travels. Then $x + 5$ = the rate the younger brother travels.

Brother	Rate	Time	Distance
Younger	$x + 5$	2	$2(x + 5)$
Older	x	2	$2x$

Younger brother's distance + older brother's distance = 230 miles.

$2(x + 5) + 2x = 230$

$2x + 10 + 2x = 230$

$4x + 10 = 230$

$4x = 220$

$x = 55$

The older brother travels at 55 miles per hour and the younger brother travels at $55 + 5 = 60$ miles per hour.

53. Let x = the number of liters of 30% solution.

Percent	Liters	Amount
30%	x	$0.30x$
12%	2	$(0.12)(2)$
15%	$x + 2$	$0.15(x + 2)$

$0.30x + (0.12)(2) = 0.15(x + 2)$

$0.30x + 0.24 = 0.15x + 0.30$

$0.15x + 0.24 = 0.30$

$0.15x = 0.06$

$x = 0.4$

0.4 liters of the 30% acid solution need to be added.

Practice Test

1. Let r = interest rate in decimal form.

$i = prt$

$3240 = (12,000)(r)(3)$

$3240 = 36,000r$

$\dfrac{3240}{36,000} = r$

$0.09 = r$

The interest rate is 9%.

2. $P = 2l + 2w$

$P = 2(6) + 2(3) = 12 + 6 = 18$

The perimeter is 18 feet.

3. $A = P + Prt$

$A = 100 + (100)(0.15)(3)$

$= 100 + 45$

$= 145$

4. $A = \dfrac{m + n}{2}$

$79 = \dfrac{73 + n}{2}$

$2 \times 79 = \left(\dfrac{73 + n}{2}\right) \times 2$

$158 = 73 + n$

$85 = n$

5. $C = 2\pi r$

$50 = 2\pi r$

$\dfrac{50}{2\pi} = \dfrac{2\pi r}{2\pi}$

$7.96 \approx r$

6. a. $4x = 3y + 9$

$4x - 9 = 3y + 9 - 9$

$4x - 9 = 3y$

$\dfrac{4x - 9}{3} = \dfrac{3y}{3}$

$\dfrac{4x - 9}{3} = y$

$y = \dfrac{4}{3}x - 3$

   b.   Substitute 12 for x.

$y = \dfrac{4}{3}(12) - 3$

$= 4(4) - 3$

$= 16 - 3$

$= 13$

7. $P = IR$

$\dfrac{P}{I} = \dfrac{IR}{I}$

$\dfrac{P}{I} = R$

8. $A = \dfrac{a + b}{3}$

$3A = 3\left(\dfrac{a + b}{3}\right)$

$3A = a + b$

$3A - b = a + b - b$

$3A - b = a$

9. $A = \dfrac{1}{2}h(b + d)$

$= \dfrac{1}{2}(4)[5 + 9]$

$= \dfrac{1}{2}(4)(14)$

$= 2(14)$

$= 28$

The area of the trapezoid is 28 square feet.

10. The area of the skating rink is the area of a rectangle plus the area of two half circles, or one full circle. The radius of the circle is $\dfrac{30}{2} = 15$ feet.

Area of rectangle $= l \cdot w = 80 \cdot 30 = 2400$ ft^2

Area of circle

$= \pi r^2 = \pi(15)^2 = 225\pi \approx 706.86$ ft^2

Total area $= 2400 + 706.86 = 3106.86$ ft^2

11. $500 - n$

12. $2f + 6000$

13. The sum of a number and the number increased by 4 is 9.

14. Let $x =$ smaller integer.

Then $2x - 10 =$ larger integer.

Smaller number + larger number $= 158$

$x + (2x - 10) = 158$

$3x - 10 = 158$

$3x = 168$

$x = 56$

The smaller number is 56 and the larger number is $2(56) - 10 = 102$

15. Let $x =$ smallest integer.

Then $x + 1$ is the consecutive integer.

Sum of the two integers $= 43$

$x + (x + 1) = 43$

$2x + 1 = 43$

$2x = 42$

$x = 21$

The integers are 21 and $21 + 1 = 22$.

16. Let $c =$ the cost of the furniture before tax

Tax amount $=$ (cost) $\cdot$ (tax rate) $= 0.06c$

Total cost $=$ cost before tax + tax amount

$2650 = c + 0.06c$

$2640 = 1.06c$

$\dfrac{2650}{1.06} = \dfrac{1.06c}{1.06}$

$2500 = c$

The cost of the furniture before tax was $2500.

17. Let $x =$ price of most expensive meal he can order.

Then $0.15x =$ tip and $0.07x =$ tax

Price of meal + tip + tax $= 40$

$x + 0.15x + 0.07x = 40$

$1.22x = 40$

$$x = \frac{40}{1.22} \approx 32.79$$

The price of the most expensive meal he can order is $32.79.

18. Let x = the amount of money Peter invested.
Then $2x$ = the amount of money Julie invested.
Then $2x$ = the amount of profit Julie receives.
Peter's profit + Julie's profit
= Total profit
$x + 2x = 120,000$
$3x = 120,000$

$x = 40,000$

Peter will receive $40,000 and Julie receives
2($40,000) = $80,000.

19. Let x = the number of times the plow is needed for the costs to be equal.
Elizabeth's charge = $80 + 5x$
Jan charge = $50 + 10x$
The charges are equal when:
$80 + 5x = 50 + 10x$
$30 + 5x = 10x$

$30 = 5x$

$6 = x$

The snow would need to be plowed 6 times for the costs to be the same.

20. Let x = number of months for the total cost of both mortgages to be equal.
Then $980x$ = monthly payments for x months at Bank of Washington,
and $1025x$ = monthly payments for x months at First Trust.
Bank of Washington = First Trust
$980x + 1500 = 1025x$
$1500 = 45x$
$33.3 \approx x$
It would take about 33.3 months for the costs to be the same.

21. Let x = length of smallest side.
Then $x + 15$ = length of second side and
$2x$ = length of third side.
Sum of the three sides = perimeter
$x + (x + 15) + 2x = 75$
$4x + 15 = 75$

$4x = 60$

$x = 15$

The three sides are 15 inches,
$15 + 15 = 30$ inches, and $2(15) = 30$ inches.

22. Let w = width of flag
Then $2w - 4$ = length of flag.
$2l + 2w$ = perimeter
$2(2w - 4) + 2w = 28$
$4w - 8 + 2w = 28$
$6w - 8 = 28$
$6w = 36$
$w = 6$
The width is 6 feet and the length is 8 feet.

23. Let x = the rate Harlene digs.
Then $x + 0.2$ is the rate Ellis digs.

Name	Rate	Time	Distance
Harlene	x	84	$84x$
Ellis	$x + 0.2$	84	$84(x + 0.2)$

Distance Harlene digs + distance Ellis digs
= total length of trench
$84x + 84(x + 0.2) = 67.2$
$84x + 84x + 16.8 = 67.2$
$168x = 50.4$
$x = 0.3$
Harlene digs at 0.3 feet per minute and Ellis digs at $0.3 + 2 = 0.5$ feet per minute.

24. Let x be the number of pounds of Jelly Belly candy. Then $3 - x$ is the number of pounds of Kit candy.

Type	Cost	Pounds	Total
Jelly Belly	$2.20	x	$2.20(x)$
Kits	$2.75	$3 - x$	$2.75(3 - x)$
Mixture	$2.40	3	$2.40(3)$

$2.20x + 2.75(3 - x) = 2.40(3)$
$2.2x + 8.25 - 2.75x = 7.2$
$-0.55x + 8.25 = 7.2$
$-0.55x = -1.05$
$x \approx 1.91$
The mixture should contain about 1.91 pounds of Jelly Belly candy and about 1.09 pounds of Kits candy.

25. Let x = amount of 20% salt solution to be added.

Percent	Liters	Amount
20%	x	$0.20x$
40%	60	$(0.40)(60)$
35%	$x + 60$	$0.35(x + 60)$

$$0.20x + (0.40)(60) = 0.35(x + 60)$$
$$0.20x + 24 = 0.35x + 21$$
$$-0.15x + 24 = 21$$
$$-0.15x = -3$$
$$x = 20$$

20 liters of 20% solution must be added.

Cumulative Review Test

1. 40% of $40,000 per year = $(0.40)(40,000)$
$$= 16,000$$
Emily receives $16,000 in social security.

2. a. 42.3 million – 35.4 million = 6.9 million

   b. $\dfrac{42.3}{35.4} \approx 1.19$ times greater

3. a. $\dfrac{5 + 6 + 8 + 12 + 5}{5} = 7.2$

   The mean level was 7.2 parts per million.

   b. Carbon dioxide levels in order: 5, 5, 6, 8, 12
   The median is 6 parts per million.

4. $\dfrac{5}{12} \div \dfrac{3}{4} = \dfrac{5}{12} \cdot \dfrac{4}{3} = \dfrac{20}{36} = \dfrac{5}{9}$

5. $\dfrac{2}{3} - \dfrac{3}{8} = \dfrac{2 \cdot 8}{3 \cdot 8} - \dfrac{3 \cdot 3}{8 \cdot 3} = \dfrac{16}{24} - \dfrac{9}{24} = \dfrac{7}{24}$
$\dfrac{2}{3}$ inch is $\dfrac{7}{24}$ inch greater than $\dfrac{3}{8}$ inch.

6. a. $\{1, 2, 3, 4, \ldots\}$

   b. $\{0, 1, 2, 3, \ldots\}$

   c. A rational number is a quotient of two integers, denominator not 0.

7. a. $|-9| = 9$

   b. $|-5| = 5$ and $|-3| = 3$. Since $5 > 3$, $|-5| > |-3|$.

8. $2 - 6^2 \div 2 \cdot 2 = 2 - 36 \div 2 \cdot 2$
$$= 2 - 18 \cdot 2$$
$$= 2 - 36$$
$$= -34$$

9. $4(2x - 3) - 2(3x + 5) - 6 = 8x - 12 - 6x - 10 - 6$
$$= 2x - 28$$

10. $4x - 6 = x + 12$
$$4x - 6 - x = x - x + 12$$
$$3x - 6 = 12$$
$$3x - 6 + 6 = 12 + 6$$
$$3x = 18$$
$$\dfrac{3x}{3} = \dfrac{18}{3}$$
$$x = 6$$

11. $6r = 2(r + 3) - (r + 5)$
$$6r = 2r + 6 - r - 5$$
$$6r = r + 1$$
$$6r - r = r - r + 1$$
$$5r = 1$$
$$\dfrac{5r}{5} = \dfrac{1}{5}$$
$$r = \dfrac{1}{5}$$

12. $2(x + 5) = 3(2x - 4) - 4x$
$$2x + 10 = 6x - 12 - 4x$$
$$2x + 10 = 2x - 12$$
$$2x - 2x + 10 = 2x - 2x - 12$$
$$10 = -12$$
The equation has no solution.

13. $\dfrac{50 \text{ miles}}{2 \text{ gallons}} = \dfrac{225 \text{ miles}}{x \text{ gallons}}$
$$\dfrac{50}{2} = \dfrac{225}{x}$$
$$50x = 450$$
$$x = 9$$
It will need 9 gallons.

14. $3x - 4 \le -1$
$$3x - 4 + 4 \le -1 + 4$$
$$3x \le 3$$
$$\dfrac{3x}{3} \le \dfrac{3}{3}$$
$$x \le 1$$

15. Substitute 6 for r.
$$A = \pi r^2$$
$$A = \pi(6)^2 = 36\pi \approx 113.10$$

16. a.
$$4x + 8y = 16$$
$$4x - 4x + 8y = 16 - 4x$$
$$8y = 16 - 4x$$
$$\frac{8y}{8} = \frac{16 - 4x}{8}$$
$$y = \frac{16}{8} - \frac{4x}{8}$$
$$y = 2 - \frac{1}{2}x$$
$$y = -\frac{1}{2}x + 2$$

b. Substitute –4 for x.
$$y = -\frac{1}{2}(-4) + 2 = 2 + 2 = 4$$

17.
$$P = 2l + 2w$$
$$P - 2l = 2l - 2l + 2w$$
$$P - 2l = 2w$$
$$\frac{P - 2l}{2} = \frac{2w}{2}$$
$$\frac{P - 2l}{2} = w$$

18. Let x = smaller number.
Then $2x + 11$ = larger number.
smaller number + larger number = 29
$$x + (2x + 11) = 29$$
$$3x + 11 = 29$$
$$3x = 18$$
$$x = 6$$
The smaller number is 6 and the larger number is $2(6) + 11 = 23$.

19. Let x = number of minutes for the two plans to have the same cost.
Cost for Plan A = $19.95 + 0.35x$
Cost for Plan B = $29.95 + 0.10x$
The costs will be equal when the cost for Plan A = cost for Plan B.
$$19.95 + 0.35x = 29.95 + 0.10x$$
$$0.35x = 10 + 0.10x$$
$$0.25x = 10$$
$$x = 40$$
Lori would need to talk 40 minutes in a month for the plans to have the same cost.

20. Let x = smallest angle. Then $x + 5$ = second angle, $x + 50$ = third angle, and $4x + 25$ = fourth angle. Sum of the angle measures = 360°
$$x + (x + 5) + (x + 50) + (4x + 25) = 360$$
$$7x + 80 = 360$$
$$7x = 280$$
$$x = 40$$
The angle measures are 40°, $40 + 5 = 45°$, $40 + 50 = 90°$, and $4(40) + 25 = 185°$.

Chapter 4

Exercise Set 4.1

1. In the expression c^r, c is the base, r is the exponent.

3. a. $\dfrac{x^m}{x^n} = x^{m-n}$, $x \neq 0$

    b. Answers will vary.

5. a. $\left(x^m\right)^n = x^{m \cdot n}$

    b. Answers will vary.

7. $x^0 \neq 1$ when $x = 0$.

9. $x^5 \cdot x^4 = x^{5+4} = x^9$

11. $z^4 \cdot z = z^{4+1} = z^5$

13. $3^2 \cdot 3^3 = 3^{2+3} = 3^5 = 243$

15. $y^3 \cdot y^2 = y^{3+2} = y^5$

17. $z^3 \cdot z^5 = z^{3+5} = z^8$

19. $y^6 \cdot y = y^6 \cdot y^1 = y^{6+1} = y^7$

21. $\dfrac{6^2}{6} = \dfrac{6^2}{6^1} = 6^{2-1} = 6^1 = 6$

23. $\dfrac{x^{10}}{x^3} = x^{10-3} = x^7$

25. $\dfrac{3^5}{3^2} = 3^{5-2} = 3^3 = 27$

27. $\dfrac{y^4}{y^6} = \dfrac{y^4}{y^4 \cdot y^2} = \dfrac{1}{1 \cdot y^2} = \dfrac{1}{y^2}$

29. $\dfrac{c^4}{c^4} = c^{4-4} = c^0 = 1$

31. $\dfrac{a^3}{a^7} = \dfrac{a^3}{a^3 \cdot a^4} = \dfrac{1}{1 \cdot a^4} = \dfrac{1}{a^4}$

33. $x^0 = 1$

35. $3x^0 = 3 \cdot 1 = 3$

37. $4(5d)^0 = 4(5^0 d^0) = 4(1 \cdot 1) = 4 \cdot 1 = 4$

39. $-3(-4x)^0 = -3(-4)^0 \cdot x^0$

                   $= -3(1 \cdot 1)$

                   $= -3(1)$

                   $= -3$

41. $5x^3 yz^0 = 5x^3 y(1) = 5x^3 y$

43. $-5r(st)^0 = -5rs^0 t^0 = -5r \cdot 1 \cdot 1 = -5r$

45. $\left(x^4\right)^2 = x^{4 \cdot 2} = x^8$

47. $\left(x^5\right)^5 = x^{5 \cdot 5} = x^{25}$

49. $\left(x^3\right)^1 = x^{3 \cdot 1} = x^3$

51. $\left(x^4\right)^3 = x^{4 \cdot 3} = x^{12}$

53. $\left(n^6\right)^3 = n^{6 \cdot 3} = n^{18}$

55. $(1.3x)^2 = (1.3)^2 x^2 = 1.69x^2$

57. $\left(-3x^3\right)^3 = (-3)^3 x^{3 \cdot 3} = (-27)x^9$

59. $\left(3a^2 b^4\right)^3 = 3^3 \cdot a^{2 \cdot 3} b^{4 \cdot 3} = 27a^6 b^{12}$

61. $\left(\dfrac{x}{3}\right)^2 = \dfrac{x^2}{3^2} = \dfrac{x^2}{9}$

63. $\left(\dfrac{y}{x}\right)^4 = \dfrac{y^4}{x^4}$

65. $\left(\dfrac{6}{x}\right)^3 = \dfrac{6^3}{x^3} = \dfrac{216}{x^3}$

67. $\left(\dfrac{3x}{y}\right)^3 = \dfrac{3^3 x^3}{y^3} = \dfrac{27x^3}{y^3}$

69. $\left(\dfrac{4p}{5}\right)^2 = \dfrac{4^2 p^2}{5^2} = \dfrac{16p^2}{25}$

71. $\left(\dfrac{2y^3}{x}\right)^4 = \dfrac{2^4 y^{3\cdot 4}}{x^4} = \dfrac{16y^{12}}{x^4}$

73. $\dfrac{x^6 y}{xy^3} = \dfrac{x \cdot x^5 \cdot y}{x \cdot y \cdot y^2} = \dfrac{x^5}{y^2}$

75. $\dfrac{10x^3 y^8}{2xy^{10}} = \dfrac{2 \cdot 5 \cdot x \cdot x^2 \cdot y^8}{2 \cdot x \cdot y^8 \cdot y^2} = \dfrac{5x^2}{y^2}$

77. $\dfrac{3ab}{27a^3 b^4} = \dfrac{3 \cdot a \cdot b}{3 \cdot 9 \cdot a \cdot a^2 \cdot b \cdot b^3} = \dfrac{1}{9a^2 b^3}$

79. $\dfrac{35x^4 y^9}{15x^9 y^{12}} = \dfrac{5 \cdot 7 \cdot x^4 \cdot y^9}{5 \cdot 3 \cdot x^4 \cdot x^5 \cdot y^9 \cdot y^3} = \dfrac{7}{3x^5 y^3}$

81. $\dfrac{-36xy^7 z}{12x^4 y^5 z} = -\dfrac{3 \cdot 12 \cdot x \cdot y^5 \cdot y^2 \cdot z}{12 \cdot x \cdot x^3 \cdot y^5 \cdot z} = -\dfrac{3y^2}{x^3}$

83. $-\dfrac{6x^2 y^7 z}{3x^5 y^9 z^6} = -\dfrac{2 \cdot 3 \cdot x^2 \cdot y^7 \cdot z}{3 \cdot x^2 \cdot x^3 \cdot y^7 \cdot y^2 \cdot z \cdot z^5}$

$= -\dfrac{2}{x^3 y^2 z^5}$

85. $\left(\dfrac{10x^4}{5x^6}\right)^3 = \left(\dfrac{10}{5} \cdot \dfrac{x^4}{x^6}\right)^3$

$= \left(\dfrac{2}{x^2}\right)^3$

$= \dfrac{2^3}{x^{2\cdot 3}}$

$= \dfrac{8}{x^6}$

87. $\left(\dfrac{6y^6}{2y^3}\right)^3 = \left(\dfrac{6}{2} \cdot \dfrac{y^6}{y^3}\right)^3$

$= \left(3y^3\right)^3$

$= 3^3 y^{3\cdot 3}$

$= 27y^9$

89. $\left(\dfrac{9a^2 b^4}{3a^2 b^9}\right)^0 = 1$

91. $\left(\dfrac{x^4 y^3}{x^2 y^5}\right)^2 = \left(\dfrac{x^4}{x^2} \cdot \dfrac{y^3}{y^5}\right)^2$

$= \left(\dfrac{x^2}{y^2}\right)^2$

$= \dfrac{x^{2\cdot 2}}{y^{2\cdot 2}}$

$= \dfrac{x^4}{y^4}$

93. $\left(\dfrac{9y^2 z^7}{18y^9 z}\right)^4 = \left(\dfrac{9}{18} \cdot \dfrac{y^2}{y^9} \cdot \dfrac{z^7}{z}\right)^4$

$= \left(\dfrac{z^6}{2y^7}\right)^4$

$= \dfrac{z^{6\cdot 4}}{2^4 y^{7\cdot 4}}$

$= \dfrac{z^{24}}{16y^{28}}$

95. $\left(\dfrac{4xy^5}{y}\right)^3 = \left(4x \cdot \dfrac{y^5}{y}\right)^3$

$= (4xy^4)^3$

$= 4^3 x^3 y^{4\cdot 3}$

$= 64x^3 y^{12}$

97. $\left(5xy^4\right)^2 = 5^2 x^2 y^{4\cdot 2} = 25x^2 y^8$

99. $\left(2x^4 y\right)\left(-y^5\right) = -2x^4\left(y^{5+1}\right) = -2x^4 y^6$

101. $(-2xy)(3xy) = (-2\cdot 3)\left(x^{1+1}\right)\left(y^{1+1}\right)$

$= -6x^2 y^2$

103. $\left(5x^2 y\right)\left(3xy^5\right) = (5\cdot 3)\left(x^{2+1}\right)\left(y^{1+5}\right) = 15x^3 y^6$

105. $\left(-3p^2 q\right)^2\left(-pq\right) = [(-3)^2 p^{2\cdot 2} q^2](-p^2 q)$

$= (9p^4 q^2)(-pq)$

$= (9 \cdot -1)(p^{4+2})(q^{2+1})$

$= -9p^6 q^3$

107. $\left(5r^3 s^2\right)^2\left(5r^3 s^4\right)^0 = (5^2 \cdot r^{3\cdot 2} s^{2\cdot 2})(1) = 25r^6 s^4$

109. $(-x)^2 = (-x)(-x) = x^2$

111.
$$\left(\frac{x^5 y^5}{xy^5}\right)^3 = \left(\frac{x^5}{x} \cdot \frac{y^5}{y^5}\right)^3$$
$$= \left(x^4 \cdot 1\right)^3$$
$$= \left(x^4\right)^3$$
$$= x^{4\cdot 3} = x^{12}$$

113. $\left(2.5x^3\right)^2 = 2.5^2 \cdot x^{3\cdot 2} = 6.25x^6$

115. $\dfrac{x^7 y^2}{xy^6} = \dfrac{x^7}{x} \cdot \dfrac{y^2}{y^6} = \dfrac{x^6}{y^4}$

117. $\left(\dfrac{-m^4}{n^3}\right)^3 = \dfrac{(-1)^3 m^{4\cdot 3}}{n^{3\cdot 3}} = -\dfrac{m^{12}}{n^9}$

119. $\left(-6x^3 y^2\right)^3 = (-6)^3 x^{3\cdot 3} y^{2\cdot 3} = -216x^9 y^6$

121. $\left(-2x^4 y^2 z\right)^3 = (-2)^3 x^{4\cdot 3} y^{2\cdot 3} z^{1\cdot 3} = -8x^{12} y^6 z^3$

123. $\left(9r^4 s^5\right)^3 = 9^3 \cdot r^{4\cdot 3} \cdot s^{5\cdot 3} = 729r^{12} s^{15}$

125.
$$\left(4x^2 y\right)\left(3xy^2\right)^3 = \left(4x^2 y\right)\left(3^3 x^3 y^{2\cdot 3}\right)$$
$$= \left(4x^2 y\right)\left(27x^3 y^6\right)$$
$$= 4\cdot 27 x^{2+3} y^{1+6}$$
$$= 108x^5 y^7$$

127. $\left(7.3x^2 y^4\right)^2 = 7.3^2 x^{2\cdot 2} y^{4\cdot 2} = 53.29x^4 y^8$

129.
$$\left(x^7 y^5\right)\left(xy^2\right)^4 = \left(x^7 y^5\right)\left(x^{1\cdot 4} y^{2\cdot 4}\right)$$
$$= \left(x^7 y^5\right)\left(x^4 y^8\right)$$
$$= x^{7+4} y^{5+8}$$
$$= x^{11} y^{13}$$

131.
$$\left(\frac{-x^4 z^7}{x^2 z^5}\right)^4 = \left(-1 \cdot \frac{x^4}{x^2} \cdot \frac{z^7}{z^5}\right)^4$$
$$= (-x^2 z^2)^4$$
$$= (-1)^4 x^{2\cdot 4} z^{2\cdot 4}$$
$$= x^8 z^8$$

133. $\dfrac{x+y}{x}$ cannot be simplified.

135. $\dfrac{y^2 + 3}{y}$ cannot be simplified.

137. $\dfrac{6yz^4}{yz^2} = 6y^{1-1} \cdot z^{4-2} = 6z^2$

139. $\dfrac{x}{x+1}$ cannot be simplified.

141. $x^2 y = 4^2 \cdot 2 = 16 \cdot 2 = 32$

143. $\left(xy\right)^0 = (2\cdot 4)^0 = 8^0 = 1$

145. The sign will be negative because a negative number with an odd number for an exponent will be negative. This is because $(-1)^m = -1$ when m is odd.

147. Area $= $ Length $\times$ Width $= 7x \cdot x = 7x^2$

149. Area $= $ (Area of Shape 1) $+$ (Area of Shape 2)
$$= x \cdot 3x + x \cdot 2y + xy + xy$$
$$= 3x^2 + 2xy + 2xy$$
$$= 3x^2 + 4xy$$

151. $\left(\dfrac{3x^4y^5}{6x^6y^8}\right)^3\left(\dfrac{9x^7y^8}{3x^3y^5}\right)^2 = \left(\dfrac{3}{6}\cdot\dfrac{x^4}{x^6}\cdot\dfrac{y^5}{y^8}\right)^3\left(\dfrac{9}{3}\cdot\dfrac{x^7}{x^3}\cdot\dfrac{y^8}{y^5}\right)^2$

$= \left(\dfrac{1}{2x^2y^3}\right)^3\left(\dfrac{3x^4y^3}{1}\right)^2$

$= \dfrac{1^3}{2^3x^{2\cdot3}y^{3\cdot3}}\cdot\dfrac{3^2\,x^{4\cdot2}y^{3\cdot2}}{1^2}$

$= \dfrac{9x^8y^6}{8x^6y^9}$

$= \dfrac{9x^2}{8y^3}$

154. $3^4\div3^3-(5-8)+7=81\div27-(-3)+7$

$= 3-(-3)+7$

$= 6+7$

$= 13$

155. $-4(x-3)+5x-2=-4x+12+5x-2$

$= -4x+5x+12-2$

$= x+10$

156. $2(x+4)-3=5x+4-3x+1$

$2x+8-3=2x+5$

$2x+5=2x+5$

All real numbers are solutions to this equation.

157. a. $P=2l+2w$

$26=2(x+5)+2(x)$

$26=2x+10+2x$

$26=4x+10$

$16=4x$

$4=x$

$x+5=4+5=9$

The sides are 4 and 9 inches long.

b. $P=2l+2w$

$P-2l=2l+2w-2l$

$P-2l=2w$

$\dfrac{P-2l}{2}=w$

Exercise Set 4.2

1. Answers will vary.

3. No, it is not simplified because of the negative exponent.

$x^5y^{-3}=\dfrac{x^5}{y^3}$

5. The given simplification is not correct since $\left(y^4\right)^{-3}=y^{4\cdot(-3)}=y^{-12}=\dfrac{1}{y^{12}}$.

7. a.   The numerator has one term, x^5y^2.

b.   The factors of the numerator are x^5 and y^2.

9. The sign of the exponent changes when a factor is moved from the numerator to the denominator of a fraction.

11. $x^{-6}=\dfrac{1}{x^6}$

13. $5^{-1}=\dfrac{1}{5}$

15. $\dfrac{1}{x^{-3}}=x^3$

17. $\dfrac{1}{x^{-1}}=x^1=x$

19. $\dfrac{1}{6^{-2}}=6^2=36$

21. $\left(x^{-2}\right)^3=x^{-2\cdot3}=x^{-6}=\dfrac{1}{x^6}$

23. $\left(y^{-5}\right)^4=y^{-5\cdot4}=y^{-20}=\dfrac{1}{y^{20}}$

25. $\left(x^4\right)^{-2} = x^{4(-2)} = x^{-8} = \dfrac{1}{x^8}$

27. $\left(2^{-2}\right)^{-3} = 2^{(-2)(-3)} = 2^6 = 64$

29. $y^4 \cdot y^{-2} = y^{4+(-2)} = y^2$

31. $x^7 \cdot x^{-5} = x^{7-5} = x^2$

33. $3^{-2} \cdot 3^4 = 3^{-2+4} = 3^2 = 9$

35. $\dfrac{r^5}{r^6} = r^{5-6} = r^{-1} = \dfrac{1}{r}$

37. $\dfrac{p^0}{p^{-3}} = p^{0-(-3)} = p^3$

39. $\dfrac{x^{-7}}{x^{-3}} = x^{-7-(-3)} = x^{-4} = \dfrac{1}{x^4}$

41. $\dfrac{3^2}{3^{-1}} = 3^{2-(-1)} = 3^3 = 27$

43. $3^{-3} = \dfrac{1}{3^3} = \dfrac{1}{27}$

45. $\dfrac{1}{z^{-9}} = z^9$

47. $\left(p^{-4}\right)^{-6} = p^{-4(-6)} = p^{24}$

49. $\left(y^{-2}\right)^{-3} = y^{(-2)(-3)} = y^6$

51. $x^3 \cdot x^{-7} = x^{3-7} = x^{-4} = \dfrac{1}{x^4}$

53. $x^{-8} \cdot x^{-7} = x^{-8-7} = x^{-15} = \dfrac{1}{x^{15}}$

55. $-4^{-2} = -\dfrac{1}{4^2} = -\dfrac{1}{16}$

57. $-(-4)^{-2} = -\dfrac{1}{(-4)^2} = -\dfrac{1}{16}$

59. $(-4)^{-3} = \dfrac{1}{(-4)^3} = -\dfrac{1}{64}$

61. $(-6)^{-2} = \dfrac{1}{(-6)^2} = \dfrac{1}{36}$

63. $\dfrac{x^{-5}}{x^5} = x^{-5-5} = x^{-10} = \dfrac{1}{x^{10}}$

65. $\dfrac{n^{-5}}{n^{-7}} = n^{-5-(-7)} = n^2$

67. $\dfrac{2^{-3}}{2^{-3}} = 2^{-3-(-3)} = 2^0 = 1$

69. $\left(2^{-1} + 3^{-1}\right)^0 = 1$

71. $\dfrac{2}{2^{-5}} = 2^{1-(-5)} = 2^6 = 64$

73. $\left(x^{-4}\right)^{-2} = x^{(-4)(-2)} = x^8$

75. $\left(x^0\right)^{-2} = (1)^{-2} = 1$

77. $2^{-3} \cdot 2 = 2^{-3+1} = 2^{-2} = \dfrac{1}{2^2} = \dfrac{1}{4}$

79. $6^{-4} \cdot 6^2 = 6^{-4+2} = 6^{-2} = \dfrac{1}{6^2} = \dfrac{1}{36}$

81. $\dfrac{x^{-1}}{x^{-4}} = x^{-1-(-4)} = x^3$

83. $\left(4^2\right)^{-1} = 4^{2 \cdot -1} = 4^{-2} = \dfrac{1}{4^2} = \dfrac{1}{16}$

85. $\dfrac{5}{5^{-2}} = 5^{1-(-2)} = 5^3 = 125$

87. $\dfrac{3^{-4}}{3^{-2}} = 3^{-4-(-2)} = 3^{-2} = \dfrac{1}{3^2} = \dfrac{1}{9}$

89. $\dfrac{7^{-1}}{7^{-1}} = 7^{-1-(-1)} = 7^0 = 1$

91. $\left(6x^2\right)^{-2} = 6^{-2} x^{2(-2)} = 6^{-2} x^{-4} = \dfrac{1}{6^2 x^4} = \dfrac{1}{36 x^4}$

93. $3x^{-2} y^2 = 3 \cdot \dfrac{1}{x^2} \cdot y^2 = \dfrac{3y^2}{x^2}$

95. $\left(\dfrac{1}{2}\right)^{-2} = \left(\dfrac{2}{1}\right)^{2} = 2^2 = 4$

97. $\left(\dfrac{5}{4}\right)^{-3} = \left(\dfrac{4}{5}\right)^{3} = \dfrac{4^3}{5^3} = \dfrac{64}{125}$

99. $\left(\dfrac{x^2}{y}\right)^{-2} = \left(\dfrac{y}{x^2}\right)^{2} = \dfrac{y^2}{x^{2\cdot2}} = \dfrac{y^2}{x^4}$

101. $-\left(\dfrac{r^4}{s}\right)^{-4} = -\left(\dfrac{s}{r^4}\right)^{4} = -\dfrac{s^4}{r^{4\cdot4}} = -\dfrac{s^4}{r^{16}}$

103. $7a^{-3}b^{-4} = 7 \cdot \dfrac{1}{a^3} \cdot \dfrac{1}{b^4} = \dfrac{7}{a^3 b^4}$

105. $\left(x^5 y^{-3}\right)^{-3} = x^{5(-3)} y^{(-3)(-3)} = x^{-15} y^9 = \dfrac{y^9}{x^{15}}$

107. $\left(4y^{-2}\right)\left(5y^{-3}\right) = 4 \cdot 5 \cdot y^{-2} \cdot y^{-3} = 20y^{-5} = \dfrac{20}{y^5}$

109. $4x^4\left(-2x^{-4}\right) = 4 \cdot (-2) \cdot x^4 \cdot x^{-4} = -8x^0 = -8$

111. $\left(4x^2 y\right)\left(3x^3 y^{-1}\right) = 4 \cdot 3 \cdot x^2 \cdot x^3 \cdot y \cdot y^{-1} = 12x^5$

113. $\left(5y^2\right)\left(4y^{-3}z^5\right) = 5 \cdot 4 \cdot y^2 \cdot y^{-3} \cdot z^5$
$$= 20y^{-1}z^5$$
$$= \dfrac{20z^5}{y}$$

115. $\dfrac{12c^9}{4c^4} = \dfrac{12}{4} \cdot c^{\,9-4} = 3c^5$

117. $\dfrac{36x^{-4}}{9x^{-2}} = \dfrac{36}{4} \cdot \dfrac{x^{-4}}{x^{-2}} = 4 \cdot \dfrac{1}{x^2} = \dfrac{4}{x^2}$

119. $\dfrac{3x^4 y^{-2}}{6y^3} = \dfrac{3}{6} \cdot x^4 \cdot \dfrac{y^{-2}}{y^3} = \dfrac{1}{2} \cdot x^4 \cdot \dfrac{1}{y^5} = \dfrac{x^4}{2y^5}$

121. $\dfrac{32x^4 y^{-2}}{4x^{-2}y^0} = \left(\dfrac{32}{4}\right)x^{4-(-2)}y^{-2-0}$
$$= 8x^6 y^{-2}$$
$$= \dfrac{8x^6}{y^2}$$

123. $\left(\dfrac{2x^2 y^{-3}}{z}\right)^{-4} = \left(\dfrac{z}{2x^2 y^{-3}}\right)^{4}$
$$= \dfrac{z^4}{2^4 x^{2\cdot4} y^{-3\cdot4}}$$
$$= \dfrac{z^4}{16x^8 y^{-12}}$$
$$= \dfrac{y^{12}z^4}{16x^8}$$

125. $\left(\dfrac{2r^{-5}s^9}{t^{12}}\right)^{-4} = \left(\dfrac{t^{12}}{2r^{-5}s^9}\right)^{4}$
$$= \dfrac{t^{12\cdot4}}{2^4 r^{-5\cdot4} s^{9\cdot4}}$$
$$= \dfrac{t^{48}}{16r^{-20}s^{36}}$$
$$= \dfrac{r^{20}t^{48}}{16s^{36}}$$

127. $\left(\dfrac{x^3 y^{-4}z}{y^{-2}}\right)^{-6} = \left(\dfrac{y^{-2}}{x^3 y^{-4}z}\right)^{6}$
$$= \dfrac{y^{-2\cdot6}}{x^{3\cdot6} y^{-4\cdot6} z^6}$$
$$= \dfrac{y^{-12}}{x^{18} y^{-24} z^6}$$
$$= \dfrac{y^{-12-(-24)}}{x^{18}z^6}$$
$$= \dfrac{y^{12}}{x^{18}z^6}$$

129. $\left(\dfrac{a^2 b^{-2}}{3a^4}\right)^{3} = \left(\dfrac{a^{2-4}b^{-2}}{3}\right)^{3}$
$$= \left(\dfrac{a^{-2}b^{-2}}{3}\right)^{3}$$
$$= \dfrac{a^{-2\cdot3}b^{-2\cdot3}}{3^3}$$
$$= \dfrac{a^{-6}b^{-6}}{27}$$
$$= \dfrac{1}{27a^6 b^6}$$

131. a. Yes, $a^{-1}b^{-1} = \dfrac{1}{a} \cdot \dfrac{1}{b} = \dfrac{1}{ab}$.

    b. No, $a^{-1} + b^{-1} = \dfrac{1}{a} + \dfrac{1}{b} \neq \dfrac{1}{a+b}$.

133. $4^2 + 4^{-2} = 16 + \dfrac{1}{4^2} = 16 + \dfrac{1}{16} = 16\dfrac{1}{16}$

135. $2^2 + 2^{-2} = 4 + \dfrac{1}{2^2} = 4 + \dfrac{1}{4} = 4\dfrac{1}{4}$

137. $5^0 - 3^{-1} = 1 - \dfrac{1}{3^1} = 1 - \dfrac{1}{3} = \dfrac{2}{3}$

139.
$$2 \cdot 4^{-1} + 4 \cdot 3^{-1} = 2\left(\dfrac{1}{4^1}\right) + 4\left(\dfrac{1}{3^1}\right)$$
$$= 2\left(\dfrac{1}{4}\right) + 4\left(\dfrac{1}{3}\right)$$
$$= \dfrac{2}{4} + \dfrac{4}{3}$$
$$= \dfrac{6}{12} + \dfrac{16}{12}$$
$$= \dfrac{22}{12}$$
$$= \dfrac{11}{6}$$

141.
$$2 \cdot 4^{-1} - 3^{-1} = 2 \cdot \dfrac{1}{4} - \dfrac{1}{3}$$
$$= \dfrac{2 \cdot 1}{4} - \dfrac{1}{3}$$
$$= \dfrac{2}{4} - \dfrac{1}{3}$$
$$= \dfrac{6}{12} - \dfrac{4}{12}$$
$$= \dfrac{2}{12} = \dfrac{1}{6}$$

143.
$$3 \cdot 5^0 - 5 \cdot 3^{-2} = 3 \cdot 1 - 5 \cdot \dfrac{1}{3^2}$$
$$= 3 - 5 \cdot \dfrac{1}{9}$$
$$= 3 - \dfrac{5}{9}$$
$$= \dfrac{27}{9} - \dfrac{5}{9}$$
$$= \dfrac{22}{9}$$

145. The missing number is –2 since
$$3^{-2} = \dfrac{1}{3^2} = \dfrac{1}{9}.$$

147. The missing number is –2 since $\dfrac{1}{3^{-2}} = 3^2 = 9$.

149. The missing number is –2 since
$$(x^{-2})^{-2} = x^{(-2)(-2)} = x^4.$$

151. The missing number is –3 since
$$(x^4)^{-3} = x^{4(-3)} = x^{-12} = \dfrac{1}{x^{12}} \text{ and}$$
$$(y^{-3})^{-3} = y^{(-3)(-3)} = y^9.$$

155. Let x = the number of miles.
$$\dfrac{3 \text{ miles}}{48 \text{ minutes}} = \dfrac{x}{80 \text{ minutes}}$$
$$\dfrac{3}{48} = \dfrac{x}{80}$$
$$48x = 240$$
$$x = 5$$
It will sail 5 miles.

156. Substitute 5 for r and 12 for h.
$$V = \pi r^2 h$$
$$= \pi(5)^2(12)$$
$$= \pi(25)(12)$$
$$\approx 942.48$$
The volume is about 942.48 cubic inches.

157. Let x = the larger integer.
Then $37 - x$ = the smaller integer.
$$x = 3(37 - x) + 1$$
$$x = 111 - 3x + 1$$
$$4x = 112$$
$$x = 28$$
The numbers are 28 and $37 - 28 = 9$.

158. Let p = price of the item before the increase.
$$p + .20p = 150$$
$$1.20p = 150$$
$$p = 125$$
The item cost \$125 before the increase.

159. Let n = the first integer, then $n + 1$ is the next integer.
$$n + (n + 1) = 75$$
$$2n + 1 = 75$$
$$2n = 74$$
$$n = 37$$
The integers are 37 and 38.

Exercise Set 4.3

1. A number in scientific notation is written as a number greater than or equal to 1 and less than 10 that is multiplied by some power of 10.

3. **a.** Answers will vary.

 b. 0.00568 in scientific notation is 5.68×10^{-3}

5. You will move the decimal point 5 places to the left.

7. The exponent will be negative when the number is less than 1.

9. The exponent will be negative since $0.00734 < 1$.

11. $0.000001 = 1 \times 10^{-6}$

13. $350,000 = 3.5 \times 10^5$

15. $450 = 4.5 \times 10^2$

17. $0.053 = 5.3 \times 10^{-2}$

19. $19,000 = 1.9 \times 10^4$

21. $0.00000186 = 1.86 \times 10^{-6}$

23. $0.00000914 = 9.14 \times 10^{-6}$

25. $220,300 = 2.203 \times 10^5$

27. $.005104 = 5.104 \times 10^{-3}$

29. $4.3 \times 10^4 = 43,000$

31. $5.43 \times 10^{-3} = .00543$

33. $2.13 \times 10^{-5} = 0.0000213$

35. $6.25 \times 10^5 = 625,000$

37. $9 \times 10^6 = 9,000,000$

39. $5.35 \times 10^2 = 535$

41. $6.201 \times 10^{-4} = 0.0006201$

43. $1 \times 10^4 = 10,000$

45. 8 micrometers $= 8 \times 10^{-6} = 0.000008$ meters.

47. 125 gigawatts $= 125 \times 10^9 = 125,000,000,000$ watts.

49. 15.3 km $= 15.3 \times 10^3 = 15,300$ meters.

51. 15 micrograms $= 15 \times 10^{-6} = 0.000015$ grams.

53. $(2 \times 10^2)(3 \times 10^5) = (2 \times 3)(10^2 \times 10^5)$
$$= 6 \times 10^7$$
$$= 60,000,000$$

55. $(2.7 \times 10^{-6})(9 \times 10^4) = (2.7 \times 9)(10^{-6} \times 10^4)$
$$= 24.3 \times 10^{-2}$$
$$= 0.243$$

57. $(1.3 \times 10^{-8})(1.74 \times 10^6) = (1.3 \times 1.74)(10^{-8} \times 10^6)$
$$= 2.262 \times 10^{-2}$$
$$= 0.02262$$

59. $\dfrac{8.4 \times 10^6}{2 \times 10^3} = \left(\dfrac{8.4}{2}\right)\left(\dfrac{10^6}{10^3}\right) = 4.2 \times 10^3 = 4,200$

61. $\dfrac{7.5 \times 10^6}{3 \times 10^3} = \left(\dfrac{7.5}{3}\right)\left(\dfrac{10^6}{10^3}\right) = 2.5 \times 10^3 = 2500$

63. $\dfrac{4 \times 10^2}{8 \times 10^5} = \left(\dfrac{4}{8}\right)\left(\dfrac{10^2}{10^5}\right) = .5 \times 10^{-3} = 0.0005$

65. $(700,000)(6,000,000) = (7 \times 10^5)(6 \times 10^6)$
$$= (7 \times 6)(10^5 \times 10^6)$$
$$= 42 \times 10^{11}$$
$$= 4.2 \times 10^{12}$$

67. $(500,000)(25,000) = (5 \times 10^5)(2.5 \times 10^4)$
$$= (5 \times 2.5)(10^5 \times 10^4)$$
$$= 12.5 \times 10^9$$
$$= 1.25 \times 10^{10}$$

69. $\dfrac{1,400,000}{700} = \dfrac{1.4 \times 10^6}{7 \times 10^2}$
$$= \left(\dfrac{1.4}{7}\right)\left(\dfrac{10^6}{10^2}\right)$$
$$= 0.2 \times 10^4$$
$$= 2 \times 10^3$$

71. $\dfrac{0.00035}{0.000002} = \dfrac{3.5 \times 10^{-4}}{2.0 \times 10^{-6}}$

$$= \left(\dfrac{3.5}{2.0}\right)\left(\dfrac{10^{-4}}{10^{-6}}\right)$$

$$= 1.75 \times 10^2$$

73. $8.3 \times 10^{-4}, \ 3.2 \times 10^{-1}, \ 4.6, \ 4.8 \times 10^5$

75. a. $\left(6.20 \times 10^9\right) - \left(2.81 \times 10^8\right) = \left(62.0 \times 10^8\right) - \left(2.81 \times 10^8\right)$

$$= \left(62.0 - 2.81\right) \times 10^8$$

$$= 59.19 \times 10$$

$$= 5{,}919{,}000{,}000$$

The people that live outside the U.S. total about 5,919,000,000.

    b. $\dfrac{6.20 \times 10^9}{2.81 \times 10^8} = \left(\dfrac{6.20}{2.81}\right)\left(\dfrac{10^9}{10^8}\right) \approx 2.21 \times 10 \approx 22.1$

The world is about 22.1 times greater than the U.S. population.

77. Minimum volume $= \left(100{,}000 \ \text{ft}^3 / \sec\right)\left(60 \ \sec / \min\right)\left(60 \ \min / \ \text{hr}\right)\left(24 \ \text{hrs}\right)$

$$= \left(1 \times 10^5\right)\left(6 \times 10^1\right)\left(6 \times 10^1\right)\left(2.4 \times 10^1\right)\text{ft}^3$$

$$= \left(1 \times 6 \times 6 \times 2.4\right)\left(10^5 \times 10^1 \times 10^1 \times 10^1\right)\text{ft}^3$$

$$= 86.4 \times 10^8 \text{ft}^3$$

$$= 8{,}640{,}000{,}000 \ \text{ft}^3$$

79. $\left(2 \times 10^{-6}\right) \times \left(8 \times 10^{12}\right) = \left(2 \times 8\right)\left(10^{-6} \times 10^{12}\right)$

$$= 16 \times 10^6$$

$$= 1.6 \times 10^7$$

It would take 1.6×10^7 seconds.

81. a. $18 \ \text{billion} = 18{,}000{,}000{,}000$

$$= 1.8 \times 10^{10}$$

    b. Distance to moon $= 2.38 \times 10^5$ miles
7 round trips is 14 one-way lengths.
$14\left(2.38 \times 10^5\right) = 33.32 \times 10^5$

$$= 3.332 \times 10^6$$

The length of the diapers placed end to end is 3.332×10^6 or 3,332,000 miles.

83. a. $\left(1.05 \times 10^5\right) - \left(2.23 \times 10^4\right) = \left(1.05 \times 10^5\right) - \left(.223 \times 10^5\right)$

$$= \left(1.05 - .223\right) \times 10^5$$

$$= .827 \times 10^5$$

$$= 82{,}700$$

The starting salary for an umpire was $82,700 more than for a referee.

    b. $\dfrac{1.05 \times 10^5}{2.23 \times 10^4} = \left(\dfrac{1.05}{2.23}\right)\left(\dfrac{10^5}{10^4}\right) = .471 \times 10^1 = 4.71$

         The starting salary for an umpire was 4.71 times greater than for a referee.

85. $\dfrac{9.3 \times 10^7}{1.86 \times 10^5} = \left(\dfrac{9.3}{1.86}\right)\left(\dfrac{10^7}{10^5}\right) = 5 \times 10^2 = 500$ seconds or 8.33 minutes

      It takes 500 seconds for light from the sun to reach Earth.

87. a. $2 \times \left(5.92 \times 10^9\right) = 11.84 \times 10^9$

                 $= 1.184 \times 10^{10}$

         The world's population in 2052 will be about 1.184×10^{10}.

    b.   (53 years)(365 days/year) = 19,345 days = 1.9345×10^4 days

         Increase of 5.92×10^9 people

         $\dfrac{5.92 \times 10^9}{1.9345 \times 10^4} \approx 3.06 \times 10^5 = 306,000$

         About 306,000 people are added per day.

89. a. $27,000,000 = 2.7 \times 10^7$ is the worldwide production of digital cameras in 2002.

    b.   22% of 10,342,000

         $\left(2.2 \times 10^{-1}\right)\left(1.0342 \times 10^7\right) = \left(2.2 \times 1.0342\right)\left(10^{-1} \times 10^7\right) = 2.27524 \times 10^6 = 2,275,240$

         Olympus produced 2,275,240 cameras in 2000.

91. a.   In decimal form, 6.02×10^{23} would contain 24 digits.

    b. $\dfrac{6.02 \times 10^{23}}{12} = \dfrac{6.02 \times 10^{23}}{1.2 \times 10^1}$

               $= \left(\dfrac{6.02}{1.2}\right)\left(\dfrac{10^{23}}{10^1}\right)$

               $\approx 5.02 \times 10^{22}$

93.   Answers will vary.

95.   1 nanosecond = 1×10^{-9} and 1 millisecond = 1×10^{-3}

      $\dfrac{1 \times 10^{-3}}{1 \times 10^{-9}} = 1 \times 10^{-3-(-9)} = 1 \times 10^6 = 1,000,000$ times smaller

98. $4x^2 + 3x + \dfrac{x}{2} = 4 \cdot 0^2 + 3 \cdot 0 + \dfrac{0}{2}$

                    $= 0 + 0 + 0$

                    $= 0$

99. a.   If $x = \dfrac{3}{2}$, $-x = -\dfrac{3}{2}$.

    b.   If $5x = 0$, then $x = 0$.

100. $2x - 3(x - 2) = x + 2$

        $2x - 3x + 6 = x + 2$

            $-x + 6 = x + 2$

                $4 = 2x$

                $2 = x$

101. $\left(-\dfrac{2x^5 y^7}{8x^8 y^3}\right)^3 = \left(\dfrac{-2}{8} \cdot \dfrac{x^5}{x^8} \cdot \dfrac{y^7}{y^3}\right)^3$

$\qquad\qquad = \left(\dfrac{-1}{4} \cdot \dfrac{1}{x^3} \cdot y^4\right)^3$

$\qquad\qquad = \left(-\dfrac{y^4}{4x^3}\right)^3$

$\qquad\qquad = \dfrac{(-1)^3 y^{4\cdot3}}{4^3 x^{3\cdot3}}$

$\qquad\qquad = -\dfrac{y^{12}}{64x^9}$

Exercise Set 4.4

1. A polynomial is an expression containing the sum of a finite number of terms of the form ax^n where a is a real number and n is a whole number.

3. **a.** The exponent on the variable is the degree of the term.

   b. The degree of the polynomial is the same as the degree of the highest degree term in the polynomial.

5. Add the exponents on the variable.

7. $(3x + 2) - (4x - 6) = 3x + 2 - 4x + 6 = -x + 8$

9. Because the exponent on the variable in a constant term is 0.

11. **a.** Answers will vary.

    b. $4x^3 + 5x - 7$ will be rewritten as $4x^3 + 0x^2 + 5x - 7$

13. No, it contains a fractional exponent.

15. Fifth

17. Fourth

19. Seventh

21. Third

23. Tenth

25. Twelfth

27. Binomial

29. Monomial

31. Binomial

33. Monomial

35. Not a polynomial

37. Polynomial

39. Trinomial

41. Polynomial

43. $5x + 4$, first

45. $x^2 - 2x - 4$, second

47. $3x^2 + x - 8$, second

49. Already in descending order, first

51. $2t^2$, second

53. $4x^3 - 3x^2 + x - 4$, third

55. $-2x^4 + 3x^2 + 5x - 6$, fourth

57. $(5x + 4) + (x - 5) = 5x + 4 + x - 5$
$\qquad\qquad\qquad\qquad = 5x + x + 4 - 5$
$\qquad\qquad\qquad\qquad = 6x - 1$

59. $(-4x + 8) + (2x + 3) = -4x + 8 + 2x + 3$
$\qquad\qquad\qquad\qquad\quad = -4x + 2x + 8 + 3$
$\qquad\qquad\qquad\qquad\quad = -2x + 11$

61. $(t + 7) + (-3t - 8) = t - 3t + 7 - 8$
$\qquad\qquad\qquad\qquad = -2t - 1$

63. $(x^2 + 2.6x - 3) + (4x + 3.8) = x^2 + 2.6x - 3 + 4x + 3.8$
$\qquad\qquad\qquad\qquad\qquad\quad = x^2 + 2.6x + 4x - 3 + 3.8$
$\qquad\qquad\qquad\qquad\qquad\quad = x^2 + 6.6x + 0.8$

65. $(4m - 3) + (5m^2 - 4m + 7) = 4m - 3 + 5m^2 - 4m + 7$
$$= 5m^2 + 4m - 4m - 3 + 7$$
$$= 5m^2 + 4$$

67. $(2x^2 - 3x + 5) + (-x^2 + 6x - 8) = 2x^2 - 3x + 5 - x^2 + 6x - 8$
$$= 2x^2 - x^2 + 6x - 3x + 5 - 8$$
$$= x^2 + 3x - 3$$

69. $\left(-x^2 - 4x + 8\right) + \left(5x - 2x^2 + \dfrac{1}{2}\right) = -x^2 - 4x + 8 + 5x - 2x^2 + \dfrac{1}{2}$
$$= -x^2 - 2x^2 - 4x + 5x + 8 + \dfrac{1}{2}$$
$$= -3x^2 + x + \dfrac{17}{2}$$

71. $(8x^2 + 4) + (-2.6x^2 - 5x - 2.3) = 8x^2 + 4 - 2.6x^2 - 5x - 2.3$
$$= 8x^2 - 2.6x^2 - 5x + 4 - 2.3$$
$$= 5.4x^2 - 5x + 1.7$$

73. $\left(-7x^3 - 3x^2 + 4\right) + \left(4x + 5x^3 - 7\right) = -7x^3 - 3x^2 + 4 + 4x + 5x^3 - 7$
$$= -7x^3 + 5x^3 - 3x^2 + 4x + 4 - 7$$
$$= -2x^3 - 3x^2 + 4x - 3$$

75. $\left(8x^2 + 2xy + 4\right) + \left(-x^2 - 3xy - 8\right) = 8x^2 + 2xy + 4 - x^2 - 3xy - 8$
$$= 8x^2 - x^2 + 2xy - 3xy + 4 - 8$$
$$= 7x^2 - xy - 4$$

77. $\left(2x^2 y + 2x - 3\right) + \left(3x^2 y - 5x + 5\right) = 2x^2 y + 2x - 3 + 3x^2 y - 5x + 5$
$$= 2x^2 y + 3x^2 y + 2x - 5x - 3 + 5$$
$$= 5x^2 y - 3x + 2$$

79. $\begin{array}{r} 3x - 6 \\ \underline{4x + 5} \\ 7x - 1 \end{array}$

81. $\begin{array}{r} 4y^2 - 2y + 4 \\ \underline{3y^2 \qquad +1} \\ 7y^2 - 2y + 5 \end{array}$

83. $\begin{array}{r} -x^2 - 3x + 3 \\ \underline{5x^2 + 5x - 7} \\ 4x^2 + 2x - 4 \end{array}$

85. $\begin{array}{r} 2x^3 + 3x^2 + 6x\ -9 \\ \underline{-4x^2 \qquad +7} \\ 2x^3 -\ x^2 + 6x\ -2 \end{array}$

87. $\begin{array}{r} 4n^3 - 5n^2 + n - 6 \\ \underline{-n^3 - 6n^2 - 2n + 8} \\ 3n^3 - 11n^2 - n + 2 \end{array}$

89. $(4x - 4) - (2x + 2) = 4x - 4 - 2x - 2$
$$= 4x - 2x - 4 - 2$$
$$= 2x - 6$$

91. $(-2x - 3) - (-5x - 7) = -2x - 3 + 5x + 7$
$$= -2x + 5x - 3 + 7$$
$$= 3x + 4$$

93. $(-r + 5) - (2r + 5) = -r + 5 - 2r - 5$
$$= -r - 2r + 5 - 5$$
$$= -3r$$

95. $\left(9x^2 + 7x - 5\right) - \left(3x^2 + 3.5\right)$
$$= 9x^2 + 7x - 5 - 3x^2 - 3.5$$
$$= 9x^2 - 3x^2 + 7x - 5 - 3.5$$
$$= 6x^2 + 7x - 8.5$$

97. $\left(5x^2 - x - 1\right) - \left(-3x^2 - 2x - 5\right)$
$$= 5x^2 - x - 1 + 3x^2 + 2x + 5$$
$$= 5x^2 + 3x^2 - x + 2x - 1 + 5$$
$$= 8x^2 + x + 4$$

99. $\left(-6m^2 - 2m\right) - \left(3m^2 - 7m + 6\right)$
$$= -6m^2 - 3m^2 - 2m + 7m - 6$$
$$= -9m^2 + 5m - 6$$

101. $\left(8x^3 - 2x^2 - 4x + 5\right) - \left(5x^2 + 8\right) = 8x^3 - 2x^2 - 4x + 5 - 5x^2 - 8$
$$= 8x^3 - 2x^2 - 5x^2 - 4x - 8 + 5$$
$$= 8x^3 - 7x^2 - 4x - 3$$

103. $\left(2x^3 - 4x^2 + 5x - 7\right) - \left(3x + \dfrac{3}{5}x^2 - 5\right) = 2x^3 - 4x^2 + 5x - 7 - 3x - \dfrac{3}{5}x^2 + 5$
$$= 2x^3 - 4x^2 - \dfrac{3}{5}x^2 + 5x - 3x - 7 + 5$$
$$= 2x^3 - \dfrac{23}{5}x^2 + 2x - 2$$

105. $(8x + 2) - (5x + 4) = 8x + 2 - 5x - 4$
$$= 8x - 5x + 2 - 4$$
$$= 3x - 2$$

107. $\left(2x^2 - 4x + 8\right) - (5x - 6) = 2x^2 - 4x + 8 - 5x + 6$
$$= 2x^2 - 4x - 5x + 8 + 6$$
$$= 2x^2 - 9x + 14$$

109. $\left(3x^3 + 5x^2 + 9x - 7\right) - \left(4x^3 - 6x^2\right) = 3x^3 + 5x^2 + 9x - 7 - 4x^3 + 6x^2$
$$= 3x^3 - 4x^3 + 5x^2 + 6x^2 + 9x - 7$$
$$= -x^3 + 11x^2 + 9x - 7$$

111. $\begin{array}{r} 6x + 5 \\ -(3x - 3) \\ \hline \end{array}$ or $\begin{array}{r} 6x + 5 \\ -3x + 3 \\ \hline 3x + 8 \end{array}$

113. $\begin{array}{r} -6d + 8 \\ -(-3d - 4) \\ \hline \end{array}$ or $\begin{array}{r} -6d + 8 \\ 3d + 4 \\ \hline -3d + 12 \end{array}$

115. $\begin{array}{r} 7x^2 - 3x - 4 \\ -(6x^2 \qquad - 1) \\ \hline \end{array}$ or $\begin{array}{r} 7x^2 - 3x - 4 \\ -6x^2 + 0x + 1 \\ \hline x^2 - 3x - 3 \end{array}$

117. $\begin{array}{r} m - 6 \\ -(-5m^2 + 6m) \\ \hline \end{array}$ or $\begin{array}{r} m - 6 \\ 5m^2 - 6m \\ \hline 5m^2 - 5m - 6 \end{array}$

119. $4x^3 - 6x^2 + 7x - 9$ $4x^3 - 6x^2 + 7x - 9$

$\underline{\quad - \left(x^2 + 6x - 7\right)}$ or $\dfrac{\quad -x^2 - 6x + 7\quad}{4x^3 - 7x^2 + x - 2}$

121. Answers will vary.

123. Answers will vary.

125. Sometimes

137. $\left(3x^2 - 6x + 3\right) - \left(2x^2 - x - 6\right) - \left(x^2 + 7x - 9\right) = 3x^2 - 6x + 3 - 2x^2 + x + 6 - x^2 - 7x + 9$

$$= \left(3x^2 - 2x^2 - x^2\right) + \left(-6x + x - 7x\right) + \left(3 + 6 + 9\right)$$
$$= -12x + 18$$

139. $4\left(x^2 + 2x - 3\right) - 6\left(2 - 4x - x^2\right) - 2x(x + 2) = 4x^2 + 8x - 12 - 12 + 24x + 6x^2 - 2x^2 - 4x$

$$= \left(4x^2 + 6x^2 - 2x^2\right) + \left(8x + 24x - 4x\right) + \left(-12 - 12\right)$$
$$= 8x^2 + 28x - 24$$

141. $\left|-9\right| > \left|-6\right|$ since $\left|-9\right| = 9$ and $\left|-6\right| = 6$.

142. True

143. True

144. False

145. False

146. $\left(\dfrac{4x^3 y^5}{12x^7 y^4}\right)^3 = \left(\dfrac{4}{12} \cdot \dfrac{x^3}{x^7} \cdot \dfrac{y^5}{y^4}\right)^3 = \left(\dfrac{1}{3} \cdot x^{3-7} \cdot y^{5-4}\right)^3$

$$= \left(\dfrac{1}{3} \cdot x^{-4} \cdot y\right)^3 = \left(\dfrac{y}{3x^4}\right)^3$$
$$= \dfrac{y^3}{3^3 x^{4 \cdot 3}}$$
$$= \dfrac{y^3}{27x^{12}}$$

Exercise Set 4.5

1. The distributive property is used when multiplying a monomial by a polynomial.

3. First, Outer, Inner, Last

127. Sometimes

129. Answers will vary; one example is: $x^5 + x^4 + x$

131. No, all three terms must have degree 5 or 0.

133. $a^2 + 2ab + b^2$

135. $x^2 + xz + yz$

5. Yes, FOIL is simply a way to remember the procedure.

7. $(a + b)^2 = a^2 + 2ab + b^2$
$(a - b)^2 = a^2 - 2ab + b^2$

9. No, $(x + 5)^2 = x^2 + 10x + 25$

11. Answers will vary.

13. Answers will vary.

15. $x^3 \cdot 2xy = 2x^{3+1}y = 2x^4 y$

17. $5x^3 y^5\left(4x^2 y\right) = (5 \cdot 4)x^{3+2} y^{5+1} = 20x^5 y^6$

19. $4x^4 y^6\left(-7x^2 y^9\right) = -28x^{4+2} y^{6+9}$
$$= -28x^6 y^{15}$$

21. $9xy^6 \cdot 6x^5 y^8 = 9 \cdot 6x^{1+5} y^{6+8}$
$$= 54x^6 y^{14}$$

23. $\left(6x^2 y\right)\left(\dfrac{1}{2} x^4\right) = 6 \cdot \dfrac{1}{2} x^{2+4} y$
$$= 3x^6 y$$

25. $\left(3.3x^4\right)\left(1.8x^4y^3\right) = (3.3 \cdot 1.8)x^{4+4}y^3$
$$= 5.94x^8y^3$$

27. $5(x+4) = 5 \cdot x + 5(4) = 5x + 20$

29. $-3x(2x-2) = -3x(2x) - 3x(-2) = -6x^2 + 6x$

31. $-2(8y+5) = (-2)8y + (-2)(5)$
$$= -16y - 10$$

33. $-2x\left(x^2 - 2x + 5\right) = (-2x)\left(x^2\right) + (-2x)(-2x) + (-2x)(5)$
$$= -2x^3 + 4x^2 - 10x$$

35. $5x\left(-4x^2 + 6x - 4\right) = 5x\left(-4x^2\right) + 5x(6x) + 5x(-4)$
$$= -20x^3 + 30x^2 - 20x$$

37. $0.5x^2\left(x^3 - 6x^2 - 1\right) = 0.5x^2(x^3) + 0.5x^2(-6x^2) + 0.5x^2(-1)$
$$= 0.5x^5 - 3x^4 - 0.5x^2$$

39. $0.3x(2xy + 5x - 6y) = (0.3x)(2xy) + (0.3x)(5x) + (0.3x)(-6y)$
$$= 0.6x^2y + 1.5x^2 - 1.8xy$$

41. $\left(x^2 - 4y^3 - 3\right)y^4 = x^2 \cdot y^4 + \left(-4y^3\right)y^4 + (-3)y^4$
$$= x^2y^4 - 4y^{3+4} - 3y^4$$
$$= x^2y^4 - 4y^7 - 3y^4$$

43. $(x+3)(x+4) = x \cdot x + x \cdot 4 + 3 \cdot x + 3 \cdot 4$
$$= x^2 + 4x + 3x + 12$$
$$= x^2 + 7x + 12$$

45. $(2x+5)(3x-6) = (2x)(3x) + 2x(-6) + 5 \cdot 3x + 5(-6)$
$$= 6x^2 - 12x + 15x - 30$$
$$= 6x^2 + 3x - 30$$

47. $(2x-4)(2x+4) = (2x)(2x) + (2x)(4) + (-4)(2x) + (-4)(4)$
$$= 4x^2 + 8x - 8x - 16$$
$$= 4x^2 - 16$$

49. $(5-3x)(6+2x) = 5 \cdot 6 + 5(2x) + (-3x)(6) + (-3x)(2x)$
$$= 30 + 10x - 18x - 6x^2$$
$$= 30 - 8x - 6x^2$$
$$= -6x^2 - 8x + 30$$

51. $(6x-1)(-2x+5) = 6x(-2x) + (6x)5 + (-1)(-2x) + (-1)5$
$$= -12x^2 + 30x + 2x - 5$$
$$= -12x^2 + 32x - 5$$

53. $(x-2)(4x-2) = 4x \cdot x - 2 \cdot x - 2 \cdot 4x + (-2)(-2)$

$$= 4x^2 - 2x - 8x + 4$$
$$= 4x^2 - 10x + 4$$

55. $(3k-6)(4k-2) = (3k)(4k) + (3k)(-2) + (-6)(4k) + (-6)(-2)$

$$= 12k^2 - 6k - 24k + 12$$
$$= 12k^2 - 30k + 12$$

57. $(x-2)(x+2) = x \cdot x + x \cdot 2 + (-2) \cdot x + (-2) \cdot 2$

$$= x^2 + 2x - 2x - 4$$
$$= x^2 - 4$$

59. $(2x-3)(2x-3) = 2x \cdot 2x - 3 \cdot 2x - 3 \cdot 2x + (-3)(-3)$

$$= 4x^2 - 6x - 6x + 9$$
$$= 4x^2 - 12x + 9$$

61. $(6z-4)(7-z) = 6z \cdot 7 - 6z \cdot z - 4 \cdot 7 - 4(-z)$

$$= 42z - 6z^2 - 28 + 4z$$
$$= -6z^2 + 46z - 28$$

63. $(2x+3)(4-2x) = (2x)4 + (2x)(-2x) + 3 \cdot 4 + 3(-2x)$

$$= 8x - 4x^2 + 12 - 6x$$
$$= -4x^2 + 2x + 12$$

65. $(x+y)(x-y) = x \cdot x + x(-y) + y \cdot x + y \cdot y$

$$= x^2 - xy + xy - y^2$$
$$= x^2 - y^2$$

67. $(2x-3y)(3x+2y) = (2x)(3x) + (2x)(2y) + (-3y)(3x) + (-3y)(2y)$

$$= 6x^2 + 4xy - 9xy - 6y^2$$
$$= 6x^2 - 5xy - 6y^2$$

69. $(3x+y)(2+2x) = 3x \cdot 2 + 2x \cdot 3x + 2 \cdot y + 2x \cdot y$

$$= 6x + 6x^2 + 2y + 2xy$$
$$= 6x^2 + 6x + 2xy + 2y$$

71. $(x+0.6)(x+0.3) = x \cdot x + x(0.3) + (0.6)x + (0.6)(0.3)$

$$= x^2 + 0.3x + 0.6x + 0.18$$
$$= x^2 + 0.9x + 0.18$$

73. $(2y-4)\left(\frac{1}{2}x-1\right) = 2y \cdot \left(\frac{1}{2}x\right) - 1 \cdot 2y - 4\left(\frac{1}{2}x\right) + (-4)(-1)$

$$= xy - 2y - 2x + 4$$
$$= xy - 2x - 2y + 4$$

75. $(x+6)(x-6) = x^2 - 6^2$
$$= x^2 - 36$$

77. $(3x-3)(3x+3) = (3x)^2 - 3^2 = 9x - 9$

79. $(x+y)^2 = (x)^2 + 2(x)(y) + (y)^2$
$$= x^2 + 2xy + y^2$$

81. $(x-0.2)^2 = (x)^2 - 2(x)(0.2) + (0.2)^2$
$$= x^2 - 0.4x + 0.04$$

83. $(4x+5)(4x+5) = (4x)^2 + 2(4x)(5) + (5)^2 = 16x^2 + 40x + 25$

85. $(0.4x+y)^2 = (0.4x)^2 + 2(0.4x)(y) + (y)^2$
$$= 0.16x^2 + 0.8xy + y^2$$

87. $(5a-7b)(5a+7b) = (5a)^2 - (7b)^2 = 25a^2 - 49b^2$

89. $(-2x+6)(-2x-6) = (-2x)^2 - 6^2 = 4x^2 - 36$

91. $(7a+2)^2 = (7a)^2 + 2(7a)(2) + 2^2 = 49a^2 + 28a + 4$

93. $(x+4)(3x^2 + 4x - 1) = x(3x^2 + 4x - 1) + 4(3x^2 + 4x - 1)$
$$= 3x^3 + 4x^2 - x + 12x^2 + 16x - 4$$
$$= 3x^3 + 16x^2 + 15x - 4$$

95. $(3x+2)(4x^2 - x + 5) = (3x)(4x^2 - x + 5) + 2(4x^2 - x + 5)$
$$= 12x^3 - 3x^2 + 15x + 8x^2 - 2x + 10$$
$$= 12x^3 + 5x^2 + 13x + 10$$

97. $(-2x^2 - 4x + 1)(7x - 3) = -2x^2(7x - 3) - 4x(7x - 3) + 1(7x - 3)$
$$= -14x^3 + 6x^2 - 28x^2 + 12x + 7x - 3$$
$$= -14x^3 - 22x^2 + 19x - 3$$

99. $(-3a+5)(2a^2 + 4a - 3) = -3a(2a^2 + 4a - 3) + 5(2a^2 + 4a - 3)$
$$= -6a^3 - 12a^2 + 9a + 10a^2 + 20a - 15$$
$$= -6a^3 - 2a^2 + 29a - 15$$

101. $(3x^2 - 2x + 4)(2x^2 + 3x + 1) = 3x^2(2x^2 + 3x + 1) - 2x(2x^2 + 3x + 1) + 4(2x^2 + 3x + 1)$
$$= 6x^4 + 9x^3 + 3x^2 - 4x^3 - 6x^2 - 2x + 8x^2 + 12x + 4$$
$$= 6x^4 + 5x^3 + 5x^2 + 10x + 4$$

103. $\left(x^2 - x + 3\right)\left(x^2 - 2x\right) = x^2\left(x^2 - 2x\right) - x\left(x^2 - 2x\right) + 3\left(x^2 - 2x\right)$
$$= x^4 - 2x^3 - x^3 + 2x^2 + 3x^2 - 6x$$
$$= x^4 - 3x^3 + 5x^2 - 6x$$

105. $\left(a + b\right)\left(a^2 - ab + b^2\right) = a\left(a^2 - ab + b^2\right) + b\left(a^2 - ab + b^2\right)$
$$= a^3 - a^2b + ab^2 + a^2b - ab^2 + b^3$$
$$= a^3 + b^3$$

107. $\left(x + 2\right)^3 = \left(x + 2\right)\left(x + 2\right)^2$
$$= \left(x + 2\right)\left(x^2 + 4x + 4\right)$$
$$= x\left(x^2 + 4x + 4\right) + 2\left(x^2 + 4x + 4\right)$$
$$= x^3 + 4x^2 + 4x + 2x^2 + 8x + 8$$
$$= x^3 + 6x^2 + 12x + 8$$

109. $\left(3a - 5\right)^3 = \left(3a - 5\right)\left(3a - 5\right)^2$
$$= \left(3a - 5\right)\left(9a^2 - 30a + 25\right)$$
$$= 3a\left(9a^2 - 30a + 25\right) - 5\left(9a^2 - 30a + 25\right)$$
$$= 27a^3 - 90a^2 + 75a - 45a^2 + 150a - 125$$
$$= 27a^3 - 135a^2 + 225a - 125$$

111. No, it will always be a binomial.

113. No, it could have 2 or 4 terms.

115. The missing exponents are 6, 3, and 1 since
$$3x^2(2x^6 - 5x^3 + 3x^1) = 3x^2(2x^6) - 3x^2(5x^3) + 3x^2(3x^1)$$
$$= 6x^8 - 15x^5 + 9x^3$$

117. a. $A = \left(x + 2\right)\left(2x + 1\right)$
$$= x(2x) + x \cdot 1 + 2 \cdot 2x + 2 \cdot 1$$
$$= 2x^2 + x + 4x + 2$$
$$= 2x^2 + 5x + 2$$

b. If $x = 4$, $A = 2 \cdot 4^2 + 5 \cdot 4 + 2 = 54$.
The area is 54 square feet.

c. For the rectangle to be a square, all sides must have the same length. Thus,
$x + 2 = 2x + 1$.
$$x + 2 = 2x + 1$$
$$2 = x + 1$$
$$1 = x$$
The rectangle is a square when $x = 1$ foot.

119. a. $a + b$

b. $a + b$

c. Yes

d. $\left(a + b\right)^2$

e. Area of small square $= a \cdot a$
Area of larger square $= b \cdot b$
Area of each rectangle $= a \cdot b$
$\left(a + b\right)^2 = a \cdot a + b \cdot b + 2(a \cdot b)$
$$= a^2 + 2ab + b^2$$

121. $\left(2x^3 - 6x^2 + 5x - 3\right)\left(3x^3 - 6x + 4\right)$

$= 2x^3(3x^3 - 6x + 4) - 6x^2(3x^3 - 6x + 4) + 5x(3x^3 - 6x + 4) - 3(3x^3 - 6x + 4)$

$= 2x^3(3x^3) + 2x^3(-6x) + 2x^3(4) - 6x^2(3x^3) - 6x^2(-6x) - 6x^2(4) + 5x(3x^3) + 5x(-6x)$

$\quad + 5x(4) - 3(3x^3) - 3(-6x) - 3(4)$

$= 6x^6 - 12x^4 + 8x^3 - 18x^5 + 36x^3 - 24x^2 + 15x^4 - 30x^2 + 20x - 9x^3 + 18x - 12$

$= 6x^6 - 18x^5 + 3x^4 + 35x^3 - 54x^2 + 38x - 12$

123. $4(x + 2) - 3 = 4x + 5$

$\quad 4x + 8 - 3 = 4x + 5$

$\quad\quad 4x + 5 = 4x + 5$ True

Since this is true, the solution is all real numbers.

124. Let x equal the maximum distance. Then

$2 + 1.5(x - 1) = 20$

$2 + 1.5x - 1.5 = 20$

$\quad 1.5x + 0.5 = 20$

$\quad\quad 1.5x = 19.5$

$\quad\quad\quad x = \dfrac{19.5}{1.5} = 13$

Bill can go a maximum of 13 miles.

125. $\left(\dfrac{3xy^4}{6y^6}\right)^4 = \left(\dfrac{3}{6} \cdot x \cdot \dfrac{y^4}{y^6}\right)^4$

$\quad = \left(\dfrac{1}{2} \cdot x \cdot \dfrac{1}{y^2}\right)^4$

$\quad = \left(\dfrac{x}{2y^2}\right)^4$

$\quad = \dfrac{x^4}{2^4 y^{2 \cdot 4}}$

$\quad = \dfrac{x^4}{16y^8}$

126. a. $-6^3 = -\left(6^3\right) = -216$

b. $6^{-3} = \dfrac{1}{6^3} = \dfrac{1}{216}$

127. $\left(-x^2 - 6x + 5\right) - \left(5x^2 - 4x - 3\right)$

$= -x^2 - 6x + 5 - 5x^2 + 4x + 3$

$= -x^2 - 5x^2 - 6x + 4x + 5 + 3$

$= -6x^2 - 2x + 8$

Exercise Set 4.6

1. To divide a polynomial by a monomial, divide each term in the polynomial by the monomial.

3. $\dfrac{y + 5}{y} = \dfrac{y}{y} + \dfrac{5}{y} = 1 + \dfrac{5}{y}$

5. Terms should be listed in descending order.

7. $\dfrac{x^3 - 14x + 15}{x - 3} = \dfrac{x^3 + 0x^2 - 14x + 15}{x - 3}$

9. $(x + 5)(x - 3) - 2 = x^2 + 2x - 15 - 2$

$\quad\quad\quad\quad\quad\quad\quad\quad = x^2 + 2x - 17$

11. $\dfrac{x^2 + x - 20}{x - 4} = x + 5$ or $\dfrac{x^2 + x - 20}{x + 5} = x - 4$

13. $\dfrac{2x^2 + 5x + 3}{2x + 3} = x + 1$ or $\dfrac{2x^2 + 5x + 3}{x + 1} = 2x + 3$

15. $\dfrac{4x^2 - 9}{2x + 3} = 2x - 3$ or $\dfrac{4x^2 - 9}{2x - 3} = 2x + 3$

17. $\dfrac{3x + 6}{3} = \dfrac{3x}{3} + \dfrac{6}{3} = x + 2$

19. $\dfrac{4n + 10}{2} = \dfrac{4n}{2} + \dfrac{10}{2} = 2n + 5$

21. $\dfrac{3x + 8}{2} = \dfrac{3x}{2} + \dfrac{8}{2} = \dfrac{3}{2}x + 4$

23. $\dfrac{-6x+4}{2} = \dfrac{-6x}{2} + \dfrac{4}{2} = -3x+2$

25. $\dfrac{-9x-3}{-3} = 3x+1$

27. $\dfrac{2x+16}{4} = \dfrac{2x}{4} + \dfrac{16}{4}$

             $= \dfrac{x}{2} + 4$

29. $\dfrac{4-10w}{-4} = \dfrac{(-1)(4-10w)}{(-1)(-4)}$

             $= \dfrac{-4+10w}{4}$

             $= -\dfrac{4}{4} + \dfrac{10w}{4}$

             $= -1 + \dfrac{5}{2}w$

31. $(3x^2+6x-9) \div 3x^2 = \dfrac{3x^2+6x-9}{3x^2}$

                        $= \dfrac{3x^2}{3x^2} + \dfrac{6x}{3x^2} + \dfrac{-9}{3x^2}$

                        $= 1 + \dfrac{2}{x} - \dfrac{3}{x^2}$

33. $\dfrac{-4x^5+6x+8}{2x^2} = \dfrac{-4x^5}{2x^2} + \dfrac{6x}{2x^2} + \dfrac{8}{2x^2}$

                  $= -2x^3 + \dfrac{3}{x} + \dfrac{4}{x^2}$

35. $(x^5+3x^4-3) \div x^3 = \dfrac{x^5+3x^4-3}{x^3}$

                    $= \dfrac{x^5}{x^3} + \dfrac{3x^4}{x^3} + \dfrac{-3}{x^3}$

                    $= x^2 + 3x - \dfrac{3}{x^3}$

37. $\dfrac{6x^5-4x^4+12x^3-5x^2}{2x^3} = \dfrac{6x^5}{2x^3} - \dfrac{4x^4}{2x^3} + \dfrac{12x^3}{2x^3} - \dfrac{5x^2}{2x^3}$

                                 $= 3x^2 - 2x + 6 - \dfrac{5}{2x}$

39. $\dfrac{8k^3+6k^2-8}{-4k} = \dfrac{(-1)\left(8k^3+6k^2-8\right)}{(-1)(-4k)}$

           $= \dfrac{-8k^3-6k^2+8}{4k}$

           $= \dfrac{-8k^3}{4k} - \dfrac{6k^2}{4k} + \dfrac{8}{4k}$

           $= -2k^2 - \dfrac{3}{2}k + \dfrac{2}{k}$

41. $\dfrac{12x^5+3x^4-10x^2-9}{-3x^2}$

       $= \dfrac{12x^5}{-3x^2} + \dfrac{3x^4}{-3x^2} - \dfrac{10x^2}{-3x^2} - \dfrac{9}{-3x^2}$

       $= -4x^3 - x^2 + \dfrac{10}{3} + \dfrac{3}{x^2}$

43.
$$
\begin{array}{r}
x+3 \\
x+1 \overline{)\, x^2+4x+3 } \\
\underline{x^2+\ x} \\
3x+3 \\
\underline{3x+3} \\
0
\end{array}
$$

      $\dfrac{x^2+4x+3}{x+1} = x+3$

45.
$$
\begin{array}{r}
2x+\ 3 \\
x-6 \overline{)\, 2x^2-9x-18 } \\
\underline{2x^2-12x} \\
3x-18 \\
\underline{3x-18} \\
0
\end{array}
$$

      $\dfrac{2x^2-9x-18}{x-6} = 2x+3$

47.
$$
\begin{array}{r}
2x+4 \\
3x+2 \overline{)\, 6x^2+16x+8 } \\
\underline{6x^2+\ 4x} \\
12x+8 \\
\underline{12x+8} \\
0
\end{array}
$$

      $\dfrac{6x^2+16x+8}{3x+2} = 2x+4$

49. $\dfrac{x^2-16}{-4+x} = \dfrac{x^2+0x-16}{x-4}$

$$
\begin{array}{r}
x+4 \\
x-4\,\overline{)\,x^2+0x-16} \\
\underline{x^2-4x} \\
4x-16 \\
\underline{4x-16} \\
0
\end{array}
$$

$\dfrac{x^2-16}{-4+x} = x+4$

51.
$$
\begin{array}{r}
x+5 \\
2x-3\,\overline{)\,2x^2+7x-18} \\
\underline{2x^2-3x} \\
10x-18 \\
\underline{10x-15} \\
-3
\end{array}
$$

$(2x^2+7x-18)\div(2x-3) = x+5-\dfrac{3}{2x-3}$

53. $(4a^2-25)\div(2a-5) = (4a^2+0a-25)\div(2a-5)$

$$
\begin{array}{r}
2a+5 \\
2a-5\,\overline{)\,4a^2+0a-25} \\
\underline{4a^2-10a} \\
10a-25 \\
\underline{10a-25} \\
0
\end{array}
$$

$\dfrac{4a^2-25}{2a-5} = 2a+5$

55. $\dfrac{6x+8x^2-25}{4x+9} = \dfrac{8x^2+6x-25}{4x+9}$

$$
\begin{array}{r}
2x-3 \\
4x+9\,\overline{)\,8x^2+6x-25} \\
\underline{8x^2+18x} \\
-12x-25 \\
\underline{-12x-27} \\
2
\end{array}
$$

$\dfrac{6x+8x^2-25}{4x+9} = 2x-3+\dfrac{2}{4x+9}$

57. $\dfrac{6x+8x^2-12}{2x+3} = \dfrac{8x^2+6x-12}{2x+3}$

$$
\begin{array}{r}
4x-3 \\
2x+3\,\overline{)\,8x^2+6x-12} \\
\underline{8x^2+12x} \\
-6x-12 \\
\underline{-6x-9} \\
-3
\end{array}
$$

$\dfrac{6x+8x^2-12}{2x+3} = 4x-3-\dfrac{3}{2x+3}$

59.
$$
\begin{array}{r}
3x^2-5 \\
x+6\,\overline{)\,3x^3+18x^2-5x-30} \\
\underline{3x^3+18x^2} \\
-5x-30 \\
\underline{-5x-30} \\
0
\end{array}
$$

$\dfrac{3x^3+18x^2-5x-30}{x+6} = 3x^2-5$

61. $\dfrac{2x^3-4x^2+12}{x-2} = \dfrac{2x^3-4x^2+0x+12}{x-2}$

$$
\begin{array}{r}
2x \\
x-2\,\overline{)\,2x^3-4x^2+0x+12} \\
\underline{2x^3-4x^2} \\
12
\end{array}
$$

$\dfrac{2x^3-4x^2+12}{x-2} = 2x^2+\dfrac{12}{x-2}$

63. $\left(w^3-8\right)\div\left(w-3\right) = (w^3+0w^2+0w-8)\div(w-3)$

$$
\begin{array}{r}
w^2+3w+9 \\
w-3\,\overline{)\,w^3+0w^2+0w-8} \\
\underline{w^3-3w^2} \\
3w^2+0w \\
\underline{3w^2-9w} \\
9w-8 \\
\underline{9w-27} \\
19
\end{array}
$$

$(w^3-8)\div(w-3) = w^2+3w+9+\dfrac{19}{w-3}$

65. $\dfrac{x^3 - 27}{x - 3} = \dfrac{x^3 + 0x^2 + 0x - 27}{x - 3}$

$$
\begin{array}{r}
x^2 + 3x + 9 \\
x-3{\overline{\smash{\big)}\,x^3 + 0x^2 + 0x - 27}} \\
\underline{x^3 - 3x^2} \\
3x^2 + 0x \\
\underline{3x^2 - 9x} \\
9x - 27 \\
\underline{9x - 27} \\
0
\end{array}
$$

$\dfrac{x^3 - 27}{x - 3} = x^2 + 3x + 9$

67. $\dfrac{4x^3 - 5x}{2x - 1} = \dfrac{4x^3 + 0x^2 - 5x + 0}{2x - 1}$

$$
\begin{array}{r}
2x^2 + x - 2 \\
2x-1{\overline{\smash{\big)}\,4x^3 + 0x^2 - 5x + 0}} \\
\underline{4x^3 - 2x^2} \\
2x^2 - 5x \\
\underline{2x^2 - \ x} \\
-4x + 0 \\
\underline{4x + 2} \\
-2
\end{array}
$$

$\dfrac{4x^3 - 5x}{2x - 1} = 2x^2 + x - 2 - \dfrac{2}{2x - 1}$

69.

$$
\begin{array}{r}
-m^2 - 7m - 5 \\
m-1{\overline{\smash{\big)}\,-m^3 - 6m^2 + 2m - 3}} \\
\underline{-m^3 + \ m^2} \\
-7m^2 + 2m \\
\underline{-7m^2 + 7m} \\
-5m - 3 \\
\underline{-5m + 5} \\
-8
\end{array}
$$

$\dfrac{-m^3 - 6m^2 + 2m - 3}{m - 1} = -m^2 - 7m - 5 - \dfrac{8}{m - 1}$

71. $\dfrac{9n^3 - 6n + 4}{3n - 3} = \dfrac{9n^3 + 0n^2 - 6n + 4}{3n - 3}$

$$
\begin{array}{r}
3n^2 + 3n + 1 \\
3n-3{\overline{\smash{\big)}\,9n^3 + 0n^2 - 6n + 4}} \\
\underline{9n^3 - 9n^2} \\
9n^2 - 6n \\
\underline{9n^2 - 9n} \\
3n + 4 \\
\underline{3n - 3} \\
7
\end{array}
$$

$\dfrac{9n^3 - 6n + 4}{3n - 3} = 3n^2 + 3n + 1 + \dfrac{7}{3n - 3}$

73. No, $\dfrac{2x + 1}{x^2} = \dfrac{2x}{x^2} + \dfrac{1}{x^2} = \dfrac{2}{x} + \dfrac{1}{x^2}$

75. $(x + 4)(2x + 3) + 4 = 2x^2 + 3x + 8x + 12 + 4$
$ = 2x^2 + 11x + 16$

77. First Degree

79. It has to be $4x$ since that is what must be multiplied with $4x^3$ in the quotient to get $16x^4$ in the dividend.

81. When dividing by $2x^2$, each exponent will decrease by two. So, the shaded areas must be 5, 3, 2, 1, respectively.

83. $\dfrac{4x^3 - 4x + 6}{2x + 3} = \dfrac{4x^3 + 0x^2 - 4x + 6}{2x + 3}$

$$
\begin{array}{r}
2x^2 - 3x + \dfrac{5}{2} \\
2x+3{\overline{\smash{\big)}\,4x^3 + 0x^2 - 4x + 6}} \\
\underline{4x^3 + 6x^2} \\
-6x^2 - 4x \\
\underline{-6x^2 - 9x} \\
5x + 6 \\
\underline{5x + \dfrac{15}{2}} \\
-\dfrac{3}{2}
\end{array}
$$

$\dfrac{4x^3 - 4x + 6}{2x + 3} = 2x^2 - 3x + \dfrac{5}{2} - \dfrac{3}{2(2x + 3)}$

85.

$$-x-3\overline{\smash{\big)}\,3x^2+6x-10}$$
$$\underline{3x^2+9x}$$
$$-3x-10$$
$$\underline{-3x-9}$$
$$-1$$

$$\frac{3x^2+6x-10}{-x-3}=-3x+3+\frac{1}{x+3}$$

88. a. 2 is a natural number.

b. 2 and 0 are whole numbers.

c. $2, -5, 0, \frac{2}{5}, -6.3,$ and $-\frac{23}{34}$ are rational numbers.

d. $\sqrt{7}$ and $\sqrt{3}$ are irrational numbers.

e. All of the numbers are real numbers.

89. a. $\frac{0}{1}=0$

b. $\frac{1}{0}$ is undefined

90. Evaluate expressions in parentheses first, then exponents, followed by multiplications and divisions from left to right, and finally additions and subtractions from left to right.

91. $2(x+3)+2x=x+4$
$2x+6+2x=x+4$
$4x+6=x+4$
$4x=x-2$
$3x=-2$
$x=-\frac{2}{3}$

92. Substitute 6 for r.
$$V=\frac{4}{3}\pi r^3$$
$$V=\frac{4}{3}\pi(6)^3$$
$$V=\frac{4}{3}\pi(216)$$
$$V\approx 904.78$$

93. $\dfrac{x^7}{x^{-3}}=x^{7-(-3)}=x^{7+3}=x^{10}$

Review Exercises

1. $x^5\cdot x^2=x^{5+2}=x^7$

2. $x^2\cdot x^4=x^{2+4}=x^6$

3. $3^2\cdot 3^3=3^{2+3}=3^5=243$

4. $2^4\cdot 2=2^{4+1}=2^5=32$

5. $\dfrac{x^4}{x}=x^{4-1}=x^3$

6. $\dfrac{a^5}{a^5}=a^{5-5}=a^0=1$

7. $\dfrac{5^5}{5^3}=5^{5-3}=5^2=25$

8. $\dfrac{2^5}{2}=2^{5-1}=2^4=16$

9. $\dfrac{x^6}{x^8}=\dfrac{1}{x^{8-6}}=\dfrac{1}{x^2}$

10. $\dfrac{y^4}{y}=y^{4-1}=y^3$

11. $x^0=1$

12. $4x^0=4\cdot 1=4$

13. $(3x)^0=1$

14. $6^0=1$

15. $(5x)^2=5^2x^2=25x^2$

16. $(3a)^3=3^3a^3=27a^3$

17. $(6s)^3=6^3s^3=216s^3$

18. $(-3x)^3=(-3)^3x^3=-27x^3$

19. $\left(2x^2\right)^4=2^4x^{2\cdot4}=16x^8$

20. $\left(-x^4\right)^6=(-1)^6x^{4\cdot6}=x^{24}$

21. $\left(-m^4\right)^5=(-1)^5m^{4\cdot5}=-m^{20}$

22. $\left(\dfrac{2x^3}{y}\right)^2 = \dfrac{2^2 x^{3\cdot2}}{y^2} = \dfrac{4x^6}{y^2}$

23. $\left(\dfrac{5y^2}{2b}\right)^2 = \dfrac{5^2 y^{2\cdot2}}{2^2 b^2}$

$\qquad = \dfrac{25y^4}{4b^2}$

24. $6x^2 \cdot 4x^3 = 6\cdot4x^{2+3}$

$\qquad = 24x^5$

25. $\dfrac{16x^2 y}{4xy^2} = \dfrac{16}{4}\cdot\dfrac{x^2}{x}\cdot\dfrac{y}{y^2}$

$\qquad = 4x\dfrac{1}{y}$

$\qquad = \dfrac{4x}{y}$

26. $2x(3xy^3)^2 = 2x(3^2 x^2 y^{3\cdot2})$

$\qquad = 2x(9x^2 y^6)$

$\qquad = 2\cdot9x^{1+2}y^6$

$\qquad = 18x^3 y^6$

27. $\left(\dfrac{9x^2 y}{3xy}\right)^2 = \left(\dfrac{9}{3}\cdot\dfrac{x^2}{x}\cdot\dfrac{y}{y}\right)^2$

$\qquad = (3x)^2$

$\qquad = 3^2 x^2$

$\qquad = 9x^2$

28. $(2x^2 y)^3(3xy^4) = (2^3 x^{2\cdot3} y^3)(3xy^4)$

$\qquad = (8x^6 y^3)(3xy^4)$

$\qquad = 8\cdot3x^{6+1}y^{3+4}$

$\qquad = 24x^7 y^7$

29. $4x^2 y^3\left(2x^3 y^4\right)^2 = 4x^2 y^3\left(2^2 x^{3\cdot2} y^{4\cdot2}\right)$

$\qquad = 4x^2 y^3\left(4x^6 y^8\right)$

$\qquad = 4\cdot4x^{2+6}y^{3+8}$

$\qquad = 16x^8 y^{11}$

30. $3c^2(2c^4 d^3) = 3\cdot2\cdot c^{2+4}\cdot d^3 = 6c^6 d^3$

31. $\left(\dfrac{8x^4 y^3}{2xy^5}\right)^2 = \left(\dfrac{8}{2}\cdot\dfrac{x^4}{x}\cdot\dfrac{y^3}{y^5}\right)^2$

$\qquad = \left(4x^3\cdot\dfrac{1}{y^2}\right)^2$

$\qquad = \left(\dfrac{4x^3}{y^2}\right)^2$

$\qquad = \dfrac{4^2 x^{3\cdot2}}{y^{2\cdot2}}$

$\qquad = \dfrac{16x^6}{y^4}$

32. $\left(\dfrac{21x^4 y^3}{7y^2}\right)^3 = \left(\dfrac{21}{7}\cdot x^4\cdot\dfrac{y^3}{y^2}\right)^3 = \left(3x^4 y\right)^3$

$\qquad = 3^3 x^{4\cdot3} y^3$

$\qquad = 27x^{12} y^3$

33. $x^{-4} = \dfrac{1}{x^4}$

34. $3^{-3} = \dfrac{1}{3^3} = \dfrac{1}{27}$

35. $5^{-2} = \dfrac{1}{5^2} = \dfrac{1}{25}$

36. $\dfrac{1}{z^{-2}} = z^2$

37. $\dfrac{1}{x^{-7}} = x^7$

38. $\dfrac{1}{3^{-2}} = 3^2 = 9$

39. $y^5\cdot y^{-8} = y^{5-8} = y^{-3} = \dfrac{1}{y^3}$

40. $x^{-2}\cdot x^{-3} = x^{-2-3} = x^{-5} = \dfrac{1}{x^5}$

41. $p^{-6}\cdot p^4 = p^{-6+4} = p^{-2} = \dfrac{1}{p^2}$

42. $a^{-2}\cdot a^{-3} = a^{-2+(-3)} = a^{-5} = \dfrac{1}{a^5}$

43. $\dfrac{x^3}{x^{-3}} = x^{3-(-3)} = x^6$

44. $\dfrac{x^5}{x^{-2}} = x^{5-(-2)} = x^7$

45. $\dfrac{x^{-3}}{x^3} = \dfrac{1}{x^{3+3}} = \dfrac{1}{x^6}$

46. $(3x^4)^{-2} = 3^{-2}x^{4(-2)}$

$\qquad = 3^{-2}x^{-8}$

$\qquad = \dfrac{1}{3^2 x^8}$

$\qquad = \dfrac{1}{9x^8}$

47. $(4x^{-3}y)^{-3} = 4^{-3}x^{(-3)(-3)}y^{-3}$

$\qquad = 4^{-3}x^9 y^{-3}$

$\qquad = \dfrac{x^9}{4^3 y^3}$

$\qquad = \dfrac{x^9}{64 y^3}$

48. $(-2m^{-3}n)^2 = (-2)^2 m^{-3\cdot 2}n^{1\cdot 2}$

$\qquad = 4m^{-6}n^2$

$\qquad = \dfrac{4n^2}{m^6}$

49. $6y^{-2}\cdot 2y^4 = 6\cdot 2y^{-2+4} = 12y^2$

50. $(5y^{-3}z)^3 = 5^3 y^{(-3)3}z^3$

$\qquad = 125 y^{-9}z^3$

$\qquad = \dfrac{125z^3}{y^9}$

51. $(4x^{-2}y^3)^{-2} = 4^{-2}x^{(-2)(-2)}y^{3(-2)}$

$\qquad = 4^{-2}x^4 y^{-6}$

$\qquad = \dfrac{x^4}{4^2 y^6}$

$\qquad = \dfrac{x^4}{16 y^6}$

52. $2x(3x^{-2}) = 2\cdot 3x^{1-2} = 6x^{-1} = \dfrac{6}{x}$

53. $(5x^{-2}y)(2x^4 y) = 5\cdot 2x^{-2+4}y^{1+1} = 10x^2 y^2$

54. $4x^5(6x^{-7}y^2) = 4\cdot 6x^{5-7}y^2$

$\qquad = 24x^{-2}y^2$

$\qquad = \dfrac{24y^2}{x^2}$

55. $4y^{-2}(3x^2 y) = 4\cdot 3x^2 y^{-2+1}$

$\qquad = 12x^2 y^{-1}$

$\qquad = \dfrac{12x^2}{y}$

56. $\dfrac{6xy^4}{2xy^{-1}} = \dfrac{6}{2}\cdot \dfrac{x}{x}\cdot \dfrac{y^4}{y^{-1}} = 3y^5$

57. $\dfrac{12x^{-2}y^3}{3xy^2} = \dfrac{12}{3}\cdot \dfrac{x^{-2}}{x}\cdot \dfrac{y^3}{y^2}$

$\qquad = 4\cdot \dfrac{1}{x^3}\cdot y$

$\qquad = \dfrac{4y}{x^3}$

58. $\dfrac{49x^2 y^{-3}}{7x^{-3}y} = \dfrac{49}{7}\cdot \dfrac{x^2}{x^{-3}}\cdot \dfrac{y^{-3}}{y}$

$\qquad = \left(\dfrac{49}{7}\right)x^{2-(-3)}y^{-3-1}$

$\qquad = 7x^5 y^{-4}$

$\qquad = \dfrac{7x^5}{y^4}$

59. $\dfrac{36x^4 y^7}{9x^5 y^{-3}} = \dfrac{36}{9}\cdot \dfrac{x^4}{x^5}\cdot \dfrac{y^7}{y^{-3}}$

$\qquad = 4\cdot \dfrac{1}{x}\cdot y^{10}$

$\qquad = \dfrac{4y^{10}}{x}$

60. $\dfrac{4x^8 y^{-2}}{8x^7 y^3} = \dfrac{4}{8}\cdot \dfrac{x^8}{x^7}\cdot \dfrac{y^{-2}}{y^3}$

$\qquad = \dfrac{1}{2}\cdot x\cdot \dfrac{1}{y^5}$

$\qquad = \dfrac{x}{2y^5}$

61. $1{,}720{,}000 = 1.72\times 10^6$

62. $0.153 = 1.53\times 10^{-1}$

63. $0.00763 = 7.63 \times 10^{-3}$

64. $47,000 = 4.7 \times 10^4$

65. $4,820 = 4.82 \times 10^3$

66. $0.000314 = 3.14 \times 10^{-4}$

67. $8.4 \times 10^{-3} = 0.0084$

68. $6.52 \times 10^{-4} = 0.000652$

69. $9.7 \times 10^5 = 970,000$

70. $4.38 \times 10^{-6} = 0.00000438$

71. $3.14 \times 10^{-5} = 0.0000314$

72. $1.103 \times 10^7 = 11,030,000$

73. 6 gigameters $= 6 \times 10^9 = 6,000,000,000$ meters

74. 92 milliliters $= 92 \times 10^{-3} = 0.092$ liters

75. 19.2 kilograms $= 19.2 \times 10^3 = 19,200$ grams

76. 12.8 micrograms $= 12.8 \times 10^{-6}$
$$= 0.0000128 \text{ grams}$$

77. $\left(2.5 \times 10^2\right)\left(3.4 \times 10^{-4}\right) = (2.5 \times 3.4)\left(10^2 \times 10^{-4}\right)$
$$= 8.5 \times 10^{-2}$$
$$= 0.085$$

78. $\left(4.2 \times 10^{-3}\right)\left(3 \times 10^5\right) = (4.2 \times 3)\left(10^{-3} \times 10^5\right)$
$$= 12.6 \times 10^2$$
$$= 1260$$

79. $\left(3.5 \times 10^{-2}\right)\left(7.0 \times 10^3\right) = (3.5 \times 7.0)\left(10^{-2} \times 10^3\right)$
$$= 24.5 \times 10^1$$
$$= 245$$

80. $\dfrac{7.94 \times 10^6}{2 \times 10^{-2}} = \left(\dfrac{7.94}{2}\right)\left(\dfrac{10^6}{10^{-2}}\right)$
$$= 3.97 \times 10^8$$
$$= 397,000,000$$

81. $\dfrac{6.5 \times 10^4}{2.0 \times 10^6} = \left(\dfrac{6.5}{2.0}\right)\left(\dfrac{10^4}{10^6}\right)$
$$= 3.25 \times 10^{-2}$$
$$= 0.0325$$

82. $\dfrac{15 \times 10^{-3}}{5 \times 10^2} = \left(\dfrac{15}{5}\right)\left(\dfrac{10^{-3}}{10^2}\right)$
$$= 3 \times 10^{-5}$$
$$= 0.00003$$

83. $(14,000)(260,000) = \left(1.4 \times 10^4\right)\left(2.6 \times 10^5\right)$
$$= (1.4 \times 2.6)\left(10^4 \times 10^5\right)$$
$$= 3.64 \times 10^9$$

84. $(12,500)(400,000) = \left(1.25 \times 10^4\right)\left(4.0 \times 10^5\right)$
$$= (1.25 \times 4.0) \times \left(10^4 \times 10^5\right)$$
$$= 5.0 \times 10^9$$

85. $(0.00053)(40,000) = \left(5.3 \times 10^{-4}\right)\left(4 \times 10^4\right)$
$$= (5.3 \times 4)\left(10^{-4} \times 10^4\right)$$
$$= 21.2 \times 10^0$$
$$= 2.12 \times 10^1$$

86. $\dfrac{250}{500,000} = \dfrac{2.5 \times 10^2}{5.0 \times 10^5}$
$$= \left(\dfrac{2.5}{5.0}\right)\left(\dfrac{10^2}{10^5}\right)$$
$$= 0.5 \times 10^{-3}$$
$$= 5.0 \times 10^{-4}$$

87. $\dfrac{0.000068}{0.02} = \dfrac{6.8 \times 10^{-5}}{2 \times 10^{-2}}$
$$= \left(\dfrac{6.8}{2}\right)\left(\dfrac{10^{-5}}{10^{-2}}\right)$$
$$= 3.4 \times 10^{-3}$$

88. $\dfrac{850,000}{0.025} = \dfrac{8.5 \times 10^5}{2.5 \times 10^{-2}}$
$$= \left(\dfrac{8.50}{2.50}\right)\left(\dfrac{10^5}{10^{-2}}\right)$$
$$= 3.40 \times 10^7$$

89. $\dfrac{6.4 \times 10^6}{1.28 \times 10^2} = \left(\dfrac{6.4}{1.28}\right)\left(\dfrac{10^6}{10^2}\right)$

$\qquad = 5 \times 10^4$

$\qquad = 50{,}000 \ \ \text{gallons}$

The milk tank holds 50,000 gallons.

90. a. $\left(1.38 \times 10^{10}\right) - \left(8.54 \times 10^9\right)$

$\qquad = \left(13.8 \times 10^9\right) - \left(8.54 \times 10^9\right)$

$\qquad = \left(13.8 - 8.54\right) \times 10^9$

$\qquad = 5.26 \times 10^9$

$\qquad = 5{,}260{,}000{,}000$

There was $\$5{,}260{,}000{,}000$ more in

circulation of the $10 bills than in $5 bills.

b. $\dfrac{1.38 \times 10^{10}}{8.54 \times 10^9} = \left(\dfrac{1.38}{8.54}\right)\left(\dfrac{10^{10}}{10^9}\right)$

$\qquad = .162 \times 10^1$

$\qquad = 1.62$

The amount of $10 bills in circulation is

1.62 times greater than in $5 bills.

91. Not a polynomial

92. Monomial, zero degree

93. $x^2 + 3x - 4$, trinomial, second degree

94. $4x^2 - x - 3$, trinomial, second degree

95. $13x^3 - 4$, Binomial, third degree

96. Not a polynomial

97. $-4x^2 + x$, binomial, second degree

98. Not a polynomial

99. $2x^3 + 4x^2 - 3x - 7$, polynomial, third degree

100. $(x - 5) + (2x + 4) = x - 5 + 2x + 4$

$\qquad\qquad\qquad\qquad = x + 2x - 5 + 4$

$\qquad\qquad\qquad\qquad = 3x - 1$

101. $(2d - 3) + (5d + 7) = 2d - 3 + 5d + 7$

$\qquad\qquad\qquad\qquad\ = 2d + 5d - 3 + 7$

$\qquad\qquad\qquad\qquad\ = 7d + 4$

102. $(-x - 10) + (-2x + 5) = -x - 10 - 2x + 5$

$\qquad\qquad\qquad\qquad\quad = -x - 2x - 10 + 5$

$\qquad\qquad\qquad\qquad\quad = -3x - 5$

103. $\left(-x^2 + 6x - 7\right) + \left(-2x^2 + 4x - 8\right) = -x^2 + 6x - 7 - 2x^2 + 4x - 8$

$\qquad\qquad\qquad\qquad\qquad\qquad\qquad\quad = -x^2 - 2x^2 + 6x + 4x - 7 - 8$

$\qquad\qquad\qquad\qquad\qquad\qquad\qquad\quad = -3x^2 + 10x - 15$

104. $\left(-m^2 + 5m - 8\right) + \left(6m^2 - 5m - 2\right)$

$\qquad = -m^2 + 6m^2 + 5m - 5m - 8 - 2$

$\qquad = 5m^2 - 10$

105. $(6.2p - 4.3) + (1.9p + 7.1)$

$\qquad = 6.2p + 1.9p - 4.3 + 7.1$

$\qquad = 8.1p + 2.8$

106. $(-4x + 8) - (-2x + 6) = -4x + 8 + 2x - 6$

$\qquad\qquad\qquad\qquad\ = -4x + 2x + 8 - 6$

$\qquad\qquad\qquad\qquad\ = -2x + 2$

107. $\left(4x^2 - 9x\right) - (3x + 15) = 4x^2 - 9x - 3x - 15$
$$= 4x^2 - 12x - 15$$

108. $\left(5a^2 - 6a - 9\right) - \left(2a^2 - a + 12\right)$
$$= 5a^2 - 6a - 9 - 2a^2 + a - 12$$
$$= 5a^2 - 2a^2 - 6a + a - 9 - 12$$
$$= 3a^2 - 5a - 21$$

109. $\left(-2x^2 + 8x - 7\right) - \left(3x^2 + 12\right) = -2x^2 + 8x - 7 - 3x^2 - 12$
$$= -2x^2 - 3x^2 + 8x - 7 - 12$$
$$= -5x^2 + 8x - 19$$

110. $\left(x^2 + 7x - 3\right) - \left(x^2 + 3x - 5\right) = x^2 + 7x - 3 - x^2 - 3x + 5$
$$= x^2 - x^2 + 7x - 3x - 3 + 5$$
$$= 4x + 2$$

111. $\dfrac{1}{7}x(21x + 21) = \dfrac{1}{7}x(21x) + \dfrac{1}{7}x(21)$
$$= \frac{21}{7}x^2 + \frac{21}{7}x$$
$$= 3x^2 + 3x$$

112. $-3x(5x + 4) = -3x \cdot 5x + (-3x)4$
$$= -15x^2 - 12x$$

113. $3x\left(2x^2 - 4x + 7\right) = 3x\left(2x^2\right) + 3x(-4x) + 3x(7)$
$$= 6x^3 - 12x^2 + 21x$$

114. $-c\left(2c^2 - 3c + 5\right) = (-c)\left(2c^2\right) + (-c)(-3c) + (-c)(5)$
$$= -2c^3 + 3c^2 - 5c$$

115. $-4z\left(-3z^2 - 2z - 8\right) = (-4z)(-3z^2) + (-4z)(-2z) + (-4z)(-8)$
$$= 12z^3 + 8z^2 + 32z$$

116. $(x + 4)(x + 5) = x \cdot x + x \cdot 5 + 4 \cdot x + 4 \cdot 5$
$$= x^2 + 5x + 4x + 20$$
$$= x^2 + 9x + 20$$

117. $(3x + 6)(-4x + 1) = 3x(-4x) + 3x(1) + 6(-4x) + 6(1)$
$$= -12x^2 + 3x - 24x + 6$$
$$= -12x^2 - 21x + 6$$

118. $(-2x + 6)^2 = (-2x)^2 + 2(-2x)(6) + (6)^2$
$$= 4x^2 - 24x + 36$$

119. $(6 - 2x)(2 + 3x) = 6 \cdot 2 + 6 \cdot 3x + (-2x)(2) + (-2x)(3x)$
$$= 12 + 18x - 4x - 6x^2$$
$$= 12 + 14x - 6x^2$$
$$= -6x^2 + 14x + 12$$

120. $(r + 5)(r - 5) = (r)^2 - (5)^2$
$$= r^2 - 25$$

121. $(3x + 1)(x^2 + 2x + 4) = 3x(x^2 + 2x + 4) + 1(x^2 + 2x + 4)$
$$= 3x^3 + 6x^2 + 12x + x^2 + 2x + 4$$
$$= 3x^3 + 7x^2 + 14x + 4$$

122. $(x - 1)(3x^2 + 4x - 6) = x(3x^2 + 4x - 6) - 1(3x^2 + 4x - 6)$
$$= 3x^3 + 4x^2 - 6x - 3x^2 - 4x + 6$$
$$= 3x^3 + x^2 - 10x + 6$$

123. $(-4x + 2)(3x^2 - x + 7) = -4x(3x^2 - x + 7) + 2(3x^2 - x + 7)$
$$= -12x^3 + 4x^2 - 28x + 6x^2 - 2x + 14$$
$$= -12x^3 + 10x^2 - 30x + 14$$

124. $\dfrac{2x + 4}{2} = \dfrac{2x}{2} + \dfrac{4}{2}$
$$= x + 2$$

125. $\dfrac{10x + 12}{2} = \dfrac{10x}{2} + \dfrac{12}{2}$
$$= 5x + 6$$

126. $\dfrac{8x^2 + 4x}{x} = \dfrac{8x^2}{x} + \dfrac{4x}{x}$
$$= 8x + 4$$

127. $\dfrac{6x^2 + 9x - 4}{3} = \dfrac{6x^2}{3} + \dfrac{9x}{3} - \dfrac{4}{3}$
$$= 2x^2 + 3x - \dfrac{4}{3}$$

128. $\dfrac{6w^2 - 5w + 3}{3w} = \dfrac{6w^2}{3w} - \dfrac{5w}{3w} - \dfrac{3}{3w}$
$$= 2w - \dfrac{5}{3} - \dfrac{1}{w}$$

129. $\dfrac{8x^5 - 4x^4 + 3x^2 - 2}{2x} = \dfrac{8x^5}{2x} - \dfrac{4x^4}{2x} + \dfrac{3x^2}{2x} - \dfrac{2}{2x}$
$$= 4x^4 - 2x^3 + \dfrac{3}{2}x - \dfrac{1}{x}$$

130. $\dfrac{8m - 4}{-2} = \dfrac{(-1)(8m - 4)}{(-1)(-2)}$
$$= \dfrac{-8m + 4}{2}$$
$$= \dfrac{-8m}{2} + \dfrac{4}{2}$$
$$= -4m + 2$$

131. $\dfrac{5x^2 - 6x + 15}{3x} = \dfrac{5x^2}{3x} - \dfrac{6x}{3x} + \dfrac{15}{3x}$
$$= \dfrac{5x}{3} - 2 + \dfrac{5}{x}$$

132. $\dfrac{5x^3 + 10x + 2}{2x^2} = \dfrac{5x^3}{2x^2} + \dfrac{10x}{2x^2} + \dfrac{2}{2x^2}$
$$= \dfrac{5x}{2} + \dfrac{5}{x} + \dfrac{1}{x^2}$$

133.
$$
\begin{array}{r}
x + 4 \\
x - 3 \overline{)\ x^2 + x - 12} \\
\underline{x^2 - 3x} \\
4x - 12 \\
\underline{4x - 12} \\
0
\end{array}
$$

$$\frac{x^2 + x - 12}{x - 3} = x + 4$$

134.
$$
\begin{array}{r}
n + 3 \\
6n + 1 \overline{)\ 6n^2 + 19n + 3} \\
\underline{6n^2 + \ n} \\
18n + 3 \\
\underline{18n + 3} \\
0
\end{array}
$$

$$\frac{6n^2 + 19n + 3}{6n + 1} = n + 3$$

135.
$$
\begin{array}{r}
5x - 2 \\
x + 6 \overline{)\ 5x^2 + 28x - 10} \\
\underline{5x^2 + 30x} \\
-2x - 10 \\
\underline{-2x - 12} \\
2
\end{array}
$$

$$\frac{5x^2 + 28x - 10}{x + 6} = 5x - 2 + \frac{2}{x + 6}$$

136.
$$
\begin{array}{r}
2x^2 + 3x - \ 4 \\
2x + 3 \overline{)\ 4x^3 + 12x^2 + x - 12} \\
\underline{4x^3 + \ 6x^2} \\
6x^2 + x \\
\underline{6x^2 + 9x} \\
-8x - 12 \\
\underline{-8x - 12} \\
0
\end{array}
$$

$$\frac{4x^3 + 12x^2 + x - 12}{2x + 3} = 2x^2 + 3x - 4$$

137.
$$
\begin{array}{r}
2x - 3 \\
2x - 3 \overline{)\ 4x^2 - 12x + 9} \\
\underline{4x^2 - \ 6x} \\
-6x + 9 \\
\underline{-6x + 9} \\
0
\end{array}
$$

$$\frac{4x^2 - 12x + 9}{2x - 3} = 2x - 3$$

Practice Test

1. $5x^4 \cdot 3x^2 = 5 \cdot 3x^{4+2}$
$$= 15x^6$$

2. $\left(3xy^2\right)^3 = 3^3 x^3 y^{2 \cdot 3}$
$$= 27x^3 y^6$$

3. $\dfrac{12d^5}{4d} = \dfrac{12}{4} d^{5-1}$
$$= 3d^4$$

4. $\left(\dfrac{3x^2 y}{6xy^3}\right)^3 = \left(\dfrac{3}{6} \cdot \dfrac{x^2}{x} \cdot \dfrac{y}{y^3}\right)^3$
$$= \left(\dfrac{1}{2} \cdot x \cdot \dfrac{1}{y^2}\right)^3$$
$$= \left(\dfrac{x}{2y^2}\right)^3$$
$$= \dfrac{x^3}{2^3 y^{2 \cdot 3}}$$
$$= \dfrac{x^3}{8y^6}$$

5. $\left(2x^3 y^{-2}\right)^{-2} = 2^{-2} x^{3(-2)} y^{(-2)(-2)}$
$$= 2^{-2} x^{-6} y^4$$
$$= \dfrac{y^4}{2^2 x^6}$$
$$= \dfrac{y^4}{4x^6}$$

6. $\dfrac{30x^6y^2}{45x^{-1}y} = \dfrac{30}{45}x^{6-(-1)}y^{2-1}$

$\qquad\qquad = \dfrac{2}{3}x^7y$

$\qquad\qquad = \dfrac{2x^7y}{3}$

7. $\left(4x^0\right)\left(3x^2\right)^0 = (4\cdot1)\cdot1$

$\qquad\qquad\qquad = 4$

8. $(175{,}000)(30{,}000) = \left(1.75\times10^5\right)\left(3.0\times10^4\right)$

$\qquad\qquad\qquad = (1.75\times3.0)\left(10^5\times10^4\right)$

$\qquad\qquad\qquad = 5.25\times10^9$

9. $\dfrac{0.0008}{4000} = \dfrac{8.0\times10^{-4}}{4.0\times10^3}$

$\qquad = \left(\dfrac{8.0}{4.0}\right)\left(\dfrac{10^{-4}}{10^3}\right)$

$\qquad = 2.0\times10^{-7}$

10. $4x$ is a monomial

11. $3b+2$, binomial

12. $x^{-2}+4$, not a polynomial

13. $-5+6x^3-2x^2+5x = 6x^3-2x^2+5x-5$, third degree

14. $\left(6x-4\right)+\left(2x^2-5x-3\right) = 6x-4+2x^2-5x-3$

$\qquad\qquad\qquad\qquad\qquad = 2x^2+6x-5x-4-3$

$\qquad\qquad\qquad\qquad\qquad = 2x^2+x-7$

15. $\left(x^2-4x+7\right)-\left(3x^2-8x+7\right)$

$\qquad = x^2-4x+7-3x^2+8x-7$

$\qquad = x^2-3x^2-4x+8x+7-7$

$\qquad = -2x^2+4x$

16. $\left(4x^2-5\right)-\left(x^2+x-8\right) = 4x^2-5-x^2-x+8$

$\qquad\qquad\qquad\qquad\qquad = 4x^2-x^2-x-5+8$

$\qquad\qquad\qquad\qquad\qquad = 3x^2-x+3$

17. $-5d(-3d+8) = -5d(-3d)-5d(8)$

$\qquad\qquad\qquad = 15d^2-40d$

18. $(4x+7)(2x-3)$

$\qquad = (4x)(2x)+(4x)(-3)+7(2x)+7(-3)$

$\qquad = 8x^2-12x+14x-21$

$\qquad = 8x^2+2x-21$

19. $(9-4c)(5+3c)$

$\qquad = 9\cdot5+9(3c)+(-4c)\cdot5+(-4c)(3c)$

$\qquad = 45+27c-20c-12c^2$

$\qquad = -12c^2+7c+45$

20. $(3x-5)\left(2x^2+4x-5\right)$

$\qquad = 3x\left(2x^2+4x-5\right)-5\left(2x^2+4x-5\right)$

$\qquad = 3x\cdot2x^2+3x\cdot4x-3x\cdot5-5\cdot2x^2-5\cdot4x-5(-5)$

$\qquad = 6x^3+12x^2-15x-10x^2-20x+25$

$\qquad = 6x^3+2x^2-35x+25$

21. $\dfrac{16x^2+8x-4}{4} = \dfrac{16x^2}{4}+\dfrac{8x}{4}-\dfrac{4}{4}$

$\qquad\qquad\qquad = 4x^2+2x-1$

22. $\dfrac{-12x^2 - 6x + 5}{-3x} = \dfrac{(-1)(-12x^2 - 6x + 5)}{(-1)(-3x)}$

$\qquad\qquad = \dfrac{12x^2 + 6x - 5}{3x}$

$\qquad\qquad = \dfrac{12x^2}{3x} + \dfrac{6x}{3x} - \dfrac{5}{3x}$

$\qquad\qquad = 4x + 2 - \dfrac{5}{3x}$

23.
$$\begin{array}{r} 4x + 5 \\ 2x - 3 \overline{\smash{)}\, 8x^2 - 2x - 15} \\ \underline{8x^2 - 12x} \\ 10x - 15 \\ \underline{10x - 15} \\ 0 \end{array}$$

$\dfrac{8x^2 - 2x - 15}{2x - 3} = 4x + 5$

24.
$$\begin{array}{r} 3x - 2 \\ 4x + 5 \overline{\smash{)}\, 12x^2 + 7x - 12} \\ \underline{12x^2 + 15x} \\ -8x - 12 \\ \underline{-8x - 10} \\ -2 \end{array}$$

$\dfrac{12x^2 + 7x - 12}{4x + 5} = 3x - 2 - \dfrac{2}{4x + 5}$

25. a. $5730 = 5.73 \times 10^3$

b. $\dfrac{4.46 \times 10^9}{5.73 \times 10^3} = \left(\dfrac{4.46}{5.73}\right)\left(\dfrac{10^9}{10^3}\right)$

$\qquad\qquad \approx 0.778 \times 10^6$

$\qquad\qquad \approx 7.78 \times 10^5$

Cumulative Review Test

1. $12 + 8 \div 2^2 + 3 = 12 + 8 \div 4 + 3$

$\qquad\qquad\qquad = 12 + 2 + 3$

$\qquad\qquad\qquad = 17$

2. $7 - (2x - 3) + 2x - 8(1 - x)$

$\quad = 7 - 2x + 3 + 2x - 8 + 8x$

$\quad = 7 + 3 - 8 - 2x + 2x + 8x$

$\quad = 2 + 8x$

$\quad = 8x + 2$

3. $-4x^2 + x - 7 = -4(-2)^2 + (-2) - 7$

$\qquad\qquad\qquad = -4(4) - 2 - 7$

$\qquad\qquad\qquad = -16 - 2 - 7$

$\qquad\qquad\qquad = -18 - 7$

$\qquad\qquad\qquad = -25$

4. a. Associative property of addition

b. Commutative property of multiplication

c. Commutative property of multiplication

5. $3x + 5 = 4(x - 2)$

$\quad 3x + 5 = 4x - 8$

$\qquad\quad 13 = x$

6. $3(x + 2) + 3x - 5 = 4x + 1$

$\quad 3x + 6 + 3x - 5 = 4x + 1$

$\qquad\qquad 6x + 1 = 4x + 1$

$\qquad\qquad\quad 2x = 0$

$\qquad\qquad\quad\, x = 0$

7. $3x - 11 < 5x - 2$

$\quad -11 + 2 < 5x - 3x$

$\qquad\quad -9 < 2x$

$\qquad\quad -\dfrac{9}{2} < x$

$\quad x > -\dfrac{9}{2}$

8. $3x - 2 = y - 7$

$y - 7 = 3x - 2$

$y = 3x - 2 + 7$

$y = 3x + 5$

9. $7x - 3y = 21$

$7x - 3y - 7x = -7x + 21$

$-3y = -7x + 21$

$y = \dfrac{-7x + 21}{-3}$

$y = \dfrac{7x - 21}{3}$

Substitute 6 for x.

$y = \dfrac{7(6) - 21}{3} = \dfrac{42 - 21}{3} = \dfrac{21}{3} = 7$

10. $\left(2x^4 y^3\right)^3 \left(5x^2 y\right) = \left(2^3 x^{4\cdot3} y^{3\cdot3}\right)\left(5x^2 y\right)$

$= \left(8x^{12} y^9\right)\left(5x^2 y\right)$

$= 8 \cdot 5 x^{12+2} y^{9+1}$

$= 40 x^{14} y^{10}$

11. $-5x + 2 - 7x^2 = -7x^2 - 5x + 2$

second degree

12. $\left(x^2 + 4x - 3\right) + \left(2x^2 + 5x + 1\right) = x^2 + 4x - 3 + 2x^2 + 5x + 1$

$= x^2 + 2x^2 + 4x + 5x - 3 + 1$

$= 3x^2 + 9x - 2$

13. $\left(6a^2 + 3a + 2\right) - \left(a^2 - 3a - 3\right) = 6a^2 + 3a + 2 - a^2 + 3a + 3$

$= 6a^2 - a^2 + 3a + 3a + 2 + 3$

$= 5a^2 + 6a + 5$

14. $(3y - 5)(2y + 3) = 3y \cdot 2y + 3 \cdot 3y - 5 \cdot 2y - 5 \cdot 3$

$= 6y^2 + 9y - 10y - 15$

$= 6y^2 - y - 15$

15. $(2x - 1)\left(3x^2 - 5x + 2\right) = 2x\left(3x^2 - 5x + 2\right) - 1\left(3x^2 - 5x + 2\right)$

$= 6x^3 - 10x^2 + 4x - 3x^2 + 5x - 2$

$= 6x^3 - 13x^2 + 9x - 2$

16. $\dfrac{10d^2 + 12d - 8}{4d} = \dfrac{10d^2}{4d} + \dfrac{12d}{4d} - \dfrac{8}{4d}$

$= \dfrac{5}{2} d + 3 - \dfrac{2}{d}$

17.

$$
\begin{array}{r}
2x + 5 \\
3x - 2 \overline{)\,6x^2 + 11x - 10} \\
\underline{6x^2 - 4x} \\
15x - 10 \\
\underline{15x - 10} \\
0
\end{array}
$$

$\dfrac{6x^2 + 11x - 10}{3x - 2} = 2x + 5$

18. $\dfrac{x}{8} = \dfrac{1.25}{3}$

$3x = 8(1.25)$

$3x = 10$

$x = \dfrac{10}{3} \approx 3.33$

Eight cans of soup cost $3.33.

19. Let x = the width of the rectangle. Then $3x - 2$ = the length of the rectangle.

$P = 2l + 2w$

$28 = 2(3x - 2) + 2x$

$28 = 6x - 4 + 2x$

$32 = 8x$

$4 = x$

The width of the rectangle is 4 feet and the length is $3(4) - 2 = 10$ feet.

20. Let b = Bob's average speed.

Then $b + 7$ = Nick's average speed.

$d = r \cdot t$. Both Bob and Nick drove for 0.5 hour and the total distance they covered was 60 miles.

$0.5b + 0.5(b + 7) = 60$

$0.5b + 0.5b + 3.5 = 60$

$b = 56.5$

Bob's average speed was 56.5 miles per hour and Nick's average speed was $56.5 + 7 = 63.5$ miles per hour.

Chapter 5

1. A prime number is an integer greater than 1 that has exactly two factors, itself and 1.

3. To factor an expression means to write the expression as the product of factors.

5. The greatest common factor of two or more numbers is the greatest number that divides into all the numbers.

7. A factoring problem may be checked by multiplying the factors.

9. $56 = 8 \cdot 7$
$= 2 \cdot 4 \cdot 7$
$= 2 \cdot 2 \cdot 2 \cdot 7$
$= 2^3 \cdot 7$

11. $90 = 9 \cdot 10$
$= 3 \cdot 3 \cdot 2 \cdot 5$
$= 2 \cdot 3^2 \cdot 5$

13. $196 = 4 \cdot 49$
$= 2 \cdot 2 \cdot 7 \cdot 7$
$= 2^2 \cdot 7^2$

15. $20 = 2^2 \cdot 5$, $24 = 2^3 \cdot 3$, so the greatest common factor is 2^2 or 4.

17. $70 = 2 \cdot 5 \cdot 7$, $98 = 2 \cdot 7^2$, so the greatest common factor is $2 \cdot 7$ or 14.

19. $80 = 2^4 \cdot 5$, $126 = 2 \cdot 3^2 \cdot 7$ so the greatest common factor is 2.

21. The greatest common factor is x.

23. The greatest common factor is $3x$.

25. The greatest common factor is 1.

27. The greatest common factor is mn.

29. The greatest common factor is $x^3 y^5$.

31. The greatest common factor is 5.

33. The greatest common factor is $x^2 y^2$.

35. The greatest common factor is x.

37. The greatest common factor is $x + 3$.

39. The greatest common factor is $2x - 3$.

41. The greatest common factor is $3w + 5$.

43. The greatest common factor is $x - 4$.

45. The greatest common factor is $x - 1$.

47. The greatest common factor is $x + 3$.

49. The greatest common factor is 4.
$4x - 8 = 4 \cdot x - 4 \cdot 2$
$= 4(x - 2)$

51. The greatest common factor is 5.
$15x - 5 = 5 \cdot 3x - 5 \cdot 1$
$= 5(3x - 1)$

53. The greatest common factor is 6.
$6p + 12 = 6 \cdot p + 6 \cdot 2$
$= 6(p + 2)$

55. The greatest common factor is $3x$.
$9x^2 - 12x = 3x \cdot 3x - 3x \cdot 4$
$= 3x(3x - 4)$

57. The greatest common factor is $2p$.
$26p^2 - 8p = 2p \cdot 13p - 2p \cdot 4$
$= 2p(13p - 4)$

59. The greatest common factor is $3x^2$.
$3x^5 - 12x^2 = 3x^2 \cdot x^3 - 3x^2 \cdot 4$
$= 3x^2(x^3 - 4)$

61. The greatest common factor is $12x^8$.
$36x^{12} + 24x^8 = 12x^8 \cdot 3x^4 + 12x^8 \cdot 2$
$= 12x^8(3x^4 + 2)$

63. The greatest common factor is $9y^3$.
$27y^{15} - 9y^3 = 9y^3 \cdot 3y^{12} - 9y^3 \cdot 1$
$= 9y^3(3y^{12} - 1)$

65. The greatest common factor is x.
$x + 3xy^2 = x \cdot 1 + x \cdot 3y^2$
$= x(1 + 3y^2)$

67. The greatest common factor is a^2.
$$7a^4 + 3a^2 = a^2 \cdot 7a^2 + a^2 \cdot 3$$
$$= a^2(7a^2 + 3)$$

69. The greatest common factor is $4xy$.
$$16xy^2z + 4x^3y = 4xy \cdot 4yz + 4xy \cdot x^2$$
$$= 4xy(4yz + x^2)$$

71. The greatest common factor is $16mn^2$.
$$48m^4n^2 - 16mn^2 = 16mn^2 \cdot 3m^3 - 16mn^2 \cdot 1$$
$$= 16mn^2(3m^3 - 1)$$

73. The greatest common factor is $25x^2yz$.
$$25x^2yz^3 + 25x^3yz = 25x^2yz \cdot z^2 + 25x^2yz \cdot x$$
$$= 25x^2yz(z^2 + x)$$

75. The greatest common factor is y^2z^3.
$$13y^5z^3 - 11xy^2z^5 = y^2z^3 \cdot 13y^3 - y^2z^3 \cdot 11xz^2$$
$$= y^2z^3(13y^3 - 11xz^2)$$

77. The greatest common factor is 4.
$$8c^2 - 4c - 32 = 4 \cdot 2c^2 - 4 \cdot c - 4 \cdot 8$$
$$= 4(2c^2 - c - 8)$$

79. The greatest common factor is 3.
$$9x^2 + 18x + 3 = 3 \cdot 3x^2 + 3 \cdot 6x + 3 \cdot 1$$
$$= 3(3x^2 + 6x + 1)$$

81. The greatest common factor is $4x$.
$$4x^3 - 8x^2 + 12x = 4x \cdot x^2 - 4x \cdot 2x + 4x \cdot 3$$
$$= 4x(x^2 - 2x + 3)$$

83. The greatest common factor is 5.
$$35x^2 - 15y + 10 = 5 \cdot 7x^2 - 5 \cdot 3y + 5 \cdot 2$$
$$= 5(7x^2 - 3y + 2)$$

85. The greatest common factor is 3.
$$15p^2 - 6p + 9 = 3 \cdot 5p^2 - 3 \cdot 2p + 3 \cdot 3$$
$$= 3(5p^2 - 2p + 3)$$

87. The greatest common factor is $3a$.
$$9a^4 - 6a^3 + 3ab = 3a \cdot 3a^3 - 3a \cdot 2a^2 + 3a \cdot b$$
$$= 3a(3a^3 - 2a^2 + b)$$

89. The greatest common factor is xy.
$$8x^2y + 12xy^2 + 5xy = xy \cdot 8x + xy \cdot 12y + xy \cdot 5$$
$$= xy(8x + 12y + 5)$$

91. The greatest common factor is $x + 4$.
$$x(x + 4) + 3(x + 4) = (x + 4)(x + 3)$$

93. The greatest common factor is $a - 2$.
$$3b(a - 2) - 4(a - 2) = (a - 2)(3b - 4)$$

95. The greatest common factor is $2x + 1$.
$$4x(2x + 1) + 1(2x + 1) = (2x + 1)(4x + 1)$$

97. The greatest common factor is $2x + 1$.
$$5x(2x + 1) + 2x + 1 = 5x(2x + 1) + 1(2x + 1)$$
$$= (2x + 1)(5x + 1)$$

99. The greatest common factor is $2z + 3$.
$$4z(2z + 3) - 3(2z + 3) = (2z + 3)(4z - 3)$$

101. $3\bigstar + 6 = 3\bigstar \cdot + 3 \cdot 2 = 3(\bigstar + 2)$

103. $35\Delta^3 - 7\Delta^2 + 14\Delta = 7\Delta \cdot 5\Delta^2 - 7\Delta \cdot \Delta + 7\Delta \cdot 2$
$$= 7\Delta(5\Delta^2 - \Delta + 2)$$

105. The greatest common factor is $2(x-3)$.

$$4x^2(x-3)^3 - 6x(x-3)^2 + 4(x-3) = 2(x-3) \cdot 2x^2(x-3)^2 - 2(x-3) \cdot 3x(x-3) - 2(x-3) \cdot 2$$
$$= 2(x-3)\left[2x^2(x-3)^2 - 3x(x-3) + 2\right]$$

107. First factor $x^{1/3}$ from terms.
$$x^{7/3} + 5x^{4/3} + 2x^{1/3} = x^{1/3}\left(x^2 + 5x + 2\right)$$

109. $x^2 + 2x + 3x + 6 = x \cdot x + x \cdot 2 + 3 \cdot x + 3 \cdot 2$
$$= x(x+2) + 3(x+2)$$
$$= (x+2)(x+3)$$

110. $2x - (x-5) + 4(3-x) = 2x - x + 5 + 12 - 4x$
$$= x - 4x + 17$$
$$= -3x + 17$$

111. $4 + 3(x-8) = x - 4(x+2)$
$$4 + 3x - 24 = x - 4x - 8$$
$$3x - 20 = -3x - 8$$
$$6x = 12$$
$$x = 2$$

112. $4x - 5y = 20$
$$-5y = -4x + 20$$
$$y = -\frac{-4x+20}{-5}$$
$$y = \frac{4}{5}x - 4$$

113. $V = \frac{1}{3}\pi r^2 h$
$$= \frac{1}{3}\pi(4)^2(12)$$
$$= \frac{1}{3}\pi(16)(12)$$
$$= 64\pi \text{ in.}^3 \text{ or } 201.06 \text{ in.}^3$$

114. Let x = smaller number, then $2x - 1$ = the larger number.
$$x + 2x - 1 = 41$$
$$3x - 1 = 41$$
$$3x = 42$$
$$x = 14$$
$$2x - 1 = 2(14) - 1 = 28 - 1 = 27$$
The numbers are 14 and 27.

115 $\left(\dfrac{3x^2 y^3}{2x^5 y^2}\right)^2 = \left(\dfrac{3y}{2x^3}\right)^2 = \dfrac{(3y)^2}{(2x^3)^2} = \dfrac{3^2 y^2}{2^2(x^3)^2} = \dfrac{9y^2}{4x^6}$

Exercise Set 5.2

1. The first step in any factoring by grouping problem is to factor out a common factor, if one exists.

3. If you multiply $(x-2)(x+4)$ by the FOIL method, you get the polynomial $x^2 + 4x - 2x - 8$

5. Answers will vary.

7. $x^2 + 3x + 2x + 6 = x(x+3) + 2(x+3)$
$$= (x+3)(x+2)$$

9. $x^2 + 5x + 4x + 20 = x(x+5) + 4(x+5)$
$$= (x+5)(x+4)$$

11. $x^2 + 2x + 5x + 10 = x(x+2) + 5(x+2)$
$$= (x+2)(x+5)$$

13. $x^2 + 3x - 5x - 15 = x(x+3) - 5(x+3)$
$$= (x+3)(x-5)$$

15. $4b^2 - 10b + 10b - 25 = 2b(2b-5) + 5(2b-5)$
$$= (2b-5)(2b+5)$$

17. $3x^2 + 9x + x + 3 = 3x(x+3) + 1(x+3)$
$$= (x+3)(3x+1)$$

19. $6x^2 + 3x - 2x - 1 = 3x(2x+1) - 1(2x+1)$
$$= (2x+1)(3x-1)$$

21. $8x^2 + 32x + x + 4 = 8x(x+4) + 1(x+4)$
$$= (x+4)(8x+1)$$

23. $12t^2 - 8t - 3t + 2 = 4t(3t - 2) - 1(3t - 2)$
$$= (3t - 2)(4t - 1)$$

25. $2x^2 - 4x - 3x + 6 = 2x(x - 2) - 3(x - 2)$
$$= (x - 2)(2x - 3)$$

27. $6p^2 + 15p - 4p - 10 = 3p(2p + 5) - 2(2p + 5)$
$$= (2p + 5)(3p - 2)$$

33. $10x^2 - 12xy - 25xy + 30y^2 = 2x(5x - 6y) - 5y(5x - 6y)$
$$= (5x - 6y)(2x - 5y)$$

35. $x^2 + bx + ax + ab = x(x + b) + a(x + b)$
$$= (x + b)(x + a)$$

37. $xy + 5x - 3y - 15 = x(y + 5) - 3(y + 5)$
$$= (y + 5)(x - 3)$$

39. $a^2 + 3a + ab + 3b = a(a + 3) + b(a + 3)$
$$= (a + 3)(a + b)$$

41. $xy - x + 5y - 5 = x(y - 1) + 5(y - 1)$
$$= (x + 5)(y - 1)$$

43. $12 + 8y - 3x - 2xy = 4(3 + 2y) - x(3 + 2y)$
$$= (4 - x)(3 + 2y)$$

45. $z^3 + 3z^2 + z + 3 = z^2(z + 3) + 1(z + 3)$
$$= (z^2 + 1)(z + 3)$$

47. $x^3 + 4x^2 - 3x - 12 = x^2(x + 4) - 3(x + 4)$
$$= (x^2 - 3)(x + 4)$$

49. $2x^2 - 12x + 8x - 48$
$$= 2 \cdot x^2 - 2 \cdot 6x + 2 \cdot 4x - 2 \cdot 24$$
$$= 2(x^2 - 6x + 4x - 24)$$
$$= 2[x(x - 6) + 4(x - 6)]$$
$$= 2(x - 6)(x + 4)$$

29. $x^2 + 2xy - 3xy - 6y^2 = x(x + 2y) - 3y(x + 2y)$
$$= (x + 2y)(x - 3y)$$

31. $3x^2 + 2xy - 9xy - 6y^2 = x(3x + 2y) - 3y(3x + 2y)$
$$= (3x + 2y)(x - 3y)$$

51. $4x^2 + 8x + 8x + 16 = 4 \cdot x^2 + 4 \cdot 2x + 4 \cdot 2x + 4 \cdot 4$
$$= 4(x^2 + 2x + 2x + 4)$$
$$= 4[x(x + 2) + 2(x + 2)]$$
$$= 4(x + 2)(x + 2)$$
$$= 4(x + 2)^2$$

53. $6x^3 + 9x^2 - 2x^2 - 3x$
$$= x \cdot 6x^2 + x \cdot 9x - x \cdot 2x - x \cdot 3$$
$$= x(6x^2 + 9x - 2x - 3)$$
$$= x[3x(2x + 3) - 1(2x + 3)]$$
$$= x(2x + 3)(3x - 1)$$

55. $x^3 + 3x^2y - 2x^2y - 6xy^2$
$$= x \cdot x^2 + x \cdot 3xy - x \cdot 2xy - x \cdot 6y^2$$
$$= x(x^2 + 3xy - 2xy - 6y^2)$$
$$= x[x(x + 3y) - 2y(x + 3y)]$$
$$= x(x + 3y)(x - 2y)$$

57. $5x + 3y + xy + 15 = xy + 5x + 3y + 15$
$$= x(y + 5) + 3(y + 5)$$
$$= (y + 5)(x + 3)$$

59. $6x + 5y + xy + 30 = 6x + xy + 5y + 30$
$$= x(6 + y) + 5(y + 6)$$
$$= (x + 5)(y + 6)$$

61. $ax + by + ay + bx = ax + ay + bx + by$
$$= a(x + y) + b(x + y)$$
$$= (a + b)(x + y)$$

63. $cd - 12 - 4d + 3c = cd - 4d + 3c - 12$
$$= d(c - 4) + 3(c - 4)$$
$$= (d + 3)(c - 4)$$

65. $ac - bd - ad + bc = ac - ad + bc - bd$
$$= a(c - d) + b(c - d)$$
$$= (a + b)(c - d)$$

67. Not *any* arrangement of the terms of a polynomial is factorable by grouping. $xy + 2x + 5y + 10$ is factorable but $xy + 10 + 2x + 5y$ is not factorable in this arrangement.

69. $\odot^2 + 3\odot - 5\odot - 15 = \odot(\odot + 3) - 5(\odot + 3)$
$$= (\odot + 3)(\odot - 5)$$

71. a. $3x^2 + 10x + 8 = 3x^2 + 6x + 4x + 8$

     b. $3x^2 + 6x + 4x + 8 = 3x(x + 2) + 4(x + 2)$
$$= (x + 2)(3x + 4)$$

73. a. $2x^2 - 11x + 15 = 2x^2 - 6x - 5x + 15$

     b. $2x^2 - 6x - 5x + 15 = 2x(x - 3) - 5(x - 3)$
$$= (x - 3)(2x - 5)$$

75. a. $4x^2 - 17x - 15 = 4x^2 - 20x + 3x - 15$

     b. $4x^2 - 20x + 3x - 15 = 4x(x - 5) + 3(x - 5)$
$$= (4x + 3)(x - 5)$$

77. $\star\odot + 3\star + 2\odot + 6 = \star(\odot + 3) + 2(\odot + 3)$
$$= (\odot + 3)(\star + 2)$$

79. $5 - 3(2x - 7) = 4(x + 5) - 6$
$$5 - 6x + 21 = 4x + 20 - 6$$
$$-6x + 26 = 4x + 14$$
$$12 = 10x$$
$$\frac{12}{10} = x$$
$$\frac{5}{6} = x$$

80. Let w = the number of pounds of chocolate wafers
p = the number of pounds of peppermint candies
$$w + p = 50$$
$$6.25w + 2.50p = 4.75(50)$$
or

$$w + p = 50$$
$$6.25w + 2.50p = 237.50$$

Multiply the first equation by –2.5 and then add.
$$-2.5[w + p = 50]$$
gives
$$-2.5w - 2.5p = -125$$
$$\underline{6.25w + 2.5p = 237.5}$$
$$3.75w \qquad = 112.5$$
$$w = 30$$
$$w + p = 50$$
$$30 + p = 50$$
$$p = 20$$

They should mix 30 pounds of chocolate wafers with 20 pounds of peppermint hard candies.

81. $\dfrac{15x^3 - 6x^2 - 9x + 5}{3x} = \dfrac{15x^3}{3x} - \dfrac{6x^2}{3x} - \dfrac{9x}{3x} + \dfrac{5}{3x}$
$$= 5x^2 - 2x - 3 + \frac{5}{3x}$$

82.
$$\begin{array}{r} x + 3 \\ x - 3 \overline{\smash{)}\, x^2 \qquad\; -9} \\ \underline{x^2 - 3x} \\ 3x - 9 \\ \underline{3x - 9} \\ 0 \end{array}$$

$$\frac{x^2 - 9}{x - 3} = x + 3$$

Exercise Set 5.3

1. Since 8000 is positive, both signs will be the same. Since 180 is positive, both signs will be positive.

3. Since –8000 is negative, one sign will be positive, the other will be negative.

5. Since 8000 is positive, both signs will be the same. Since –240 is negative, both signs will be negative.

7. The trinomial $x^2 + 4xy - 12y^2$ is obtained by multiplying the factors using the FOIL method.

9. The trinomial $4a^2 - 4b^2$ is obtained by multiplying all the factors and combing like terms.

11. The answer is not fully factored. A 2 can be factored from $(2x - 4)$.

13. To determine the factors when factoring a trinomial of the form $x^2 + bx + c$. First, find two numbers whose product is c, and whose sum is b. The factors are $(x + \text{first number})$ and $(x + \text{second number})$.

15. $x^2 - 7x + 10 = (x - 5)(x - 2)$

17. $x^2 + 6x + 8 = (x + 4)(x + 2)$

19. $x^2 + 7x + 12 = (x + 4)(x + 3)$

21. $x^2 + 4x - 6$ is prime.

23. $y^2 - 13y + 12 = (y - 12)(y - 1)$

25. $a^2 - 2a - 8 = (a - 4)(x + 2)$

27. $r^2 - 2r - 15 = (r - 5)(r + 3)$

29. $b^2 - 11b + 18 = (b - 9)(b - 2)$

31. $x^2 - 8x - 15$ is prime.

33. $a^2 + 12a + 11 = (a + 1)(a + 11)$

35. $x^2 - 7x - 30 = (x - 10)(x + 3)$

37. $x^2 + 4x + 4 = (x + 2)(x + 2)$
$\qquad = (x + 2)^2$

39. $p^2 + 6p + 9 = (p + 3)(p + 3)$
$\qquad = (p + 3)^2$

41. $p^2 - 12p + 36 = (p - 6)(p - 6)$
$\qquad = (p - 6)^2$

43. $w^2 - 18w + 45 = (w - 15)(w - 3)$

45. $x^2 + 10x - 39 = (x + 13)(x - 3)$

47. $x^2 - x - 20 = (x - 5)(x + 4)$

49. $y^2 + 9y + 14 = (y + 7)(y + 2)$

51. $x^2 + 12x - 64 = (x + 16)(x - 4)$

53. $s^2 + 14s - 24$ is prime.

55. $x^2 - 20x + 64 = (x - 16)(x - 4)$

57. $b^2 - 18b + 65 = (b - 5)(b - 13)$

59. $x^2 + 2 + 3x = x^2 + 3x + 2 = (x + 2)(x + 1)$

61. $7w - 18 + w^2 = w^2 + 7w - 18 = (w + 9)(w - 2)$

63. $x^2 - 8xy + 15y^2 = (x - 3y)(x - 5y)$

65. $m^2 - 6mn + 9n^2 = (m - 3n)(m - 3n)$
$\qquad = (m - 3n)^2$

67. $x^2 + 8xy + 15y^2 = (x + 3y)(x + 5y)$

69. $m^2 - 5mn - 24n^2 = (m + 3n)(m - 8n)$

71. $6x^2 - 30x + 24 = 6(x^2 - 5x + 4)$
$\qquad = 6(x - 4)(x - 1)$

73. $5x^2 + 20x + 15 = 5(x^2 + 4x + 3)$
$\qquad = 5(x + 1)(x + 3)$

75. $2x^2 - 14x + 24 = 2(x^2 - 7x + 12)$
$\qquad = 2(x - 4)(x - 3)$

77. $b^3 - 7b^2 + 10b = b(b^2 - 7b + 10)$
$\qquad = b(b - 5)(b - 2)$

79. $3z^3 - 21z^2 - 54z = 3z(z^2 - 7z - 18)$
$\qquad = 3z(z - 9)(z + 2)$

81. $x^3 + 8x^2 + 16x = x(x^2 + 8x + 16)$
$\qquad = x(x + 4)(x + 4)$
$\qquad = x(x + 4)^2$

83. $4a^2 - 24ab + 32b^2 = 4(a^2 - 6b + 8b^2)$
$\qquad = 4(a - 4b)(a - 2b)$

85. $r^2s + 7rs^2 + 12s^3 = s(r^2 + 7rs + 12s^2)$
$\qquad = s(r + 3s)(r + 4s)$

87. $x^4 - 4x^3 - 21x^2 = x^2(x^2 - 4x - 21)$
$\qquad = x^2(x - 7)(x + 3)$

89.

Sign of Coefficient of x-term	Sign of Constant of Trinomial	Signs of Constant Terms in the Binomial Factors
–	+	both negative
–	–	one positive and one negative
+	–	one positive and one negative
+	+	both positive

91. $x^2 + 5x + 4 = (x+1)(x+4)$

93. $x^2 + 12x + 32 = (x+8)(x+4)$

95. $x^2 + 0.6x + 0.08 = (x+0.4)(x+0.2)$

97. $x^2 + \dfrac{2}{5}x + \dfrac{1}{25} = \left(x+\dfrac{1}{5}\right)\left(x+\dfrac{1}{5}\right)$
$= \left(x+\dfrac{1}{5}\right)^2$

99. $x^2 + 5x - 300 = (x+20)(x-15)$

101.
$$4(2x-4) = 5x + 11$$
$$8x - 16 = 5x + 11$$
$$8x - 5x - 16 = 5x - 5x + 11$$
$$3x - 16 = 11$$
$$3x - 16 + 16 = 11 + 16$$
$$3x = 27$$
$$x = 9$$

102. Let x be the percent of acid in the mixture.

Solution	Strength	Liters	Amount
18%	0.18	4	0.72
26%	0.26	1	0.26
Mixture	$\dfrac{x}{100}$	5	$\dfrac{5x}{100}$

$$0.72 + 0.26 = \dfrac{5x}{100}$$
$$0.98 = \dfrac{x}{20}$$
$$19.6 = x$$

The mixture is a 19.6% acid solution.

103. $(2x^2 + 5x - 6)(x-2) = 2x^2(x-2) + 5x(x-2) - 6(x-2)$
$= 2x^3 - 4x^2 + 5x^2 - 10x - 6x + 12$
$= 2x^3 + x^2 - 16x + 12$

104.

$$\begin{array}{r} 3x+2 \\ x-4\overline{)\,3x^2-10x-10} \\ \underline{3x^2-12x} \\ 2x-10 \\ \underline{2x-8} \\ -2 \end{array}$$

$$\dfrac{3x^2 - 10x - 10}{x-4} = 3x + 2 - \dfrac{2}{x-4}$$

105. $3x^2 + 5x - 6x - 10 = x(3x + 5) - 2(3x + 5)$
$$= (3x + 5)(x - 2)$$

Exercise Set 5.4

1. Factoring trinomials is the reverse process of multiplying binomials.

3. When factoring` a trinomial of the form $ax^2 + bx + c$, the product of the constants in the binomial factors must equal the constant, c, of the trinomial.

5. $2x^2 + 11x + 5 = (2x + 1)(x + 5)$

7. $3x^2 + 14x + 8 = (3x + 2)(x + 4)$

9. $5x^2 - 9x - 2 = (5x + 1)(x - 2)$

11. $3r^2 + 13r - 10 = (3r - 2)(r + 5)$

13. $4z^2 - 12z + 9 = (2z - 3)(2z - 3)$
$$= (2z - 3)^2$$

15. $5y^2 - y - 4 = (5y + 4)(y - 1)$

17. $5a^2 - 12a + 6$ is prime.

19. $6z^2 + z - 12 = (2z + 3)(3z - 4)$

21. $3x^2 + 11x + 4$ is prime.

23. $5y^2 - 16y + 3 = (5y - 1)(y - 3)$

25. $7x^2 + 43x + 6 = (7x + 1)(x + 6)$

27. $7x^2 - 8x + 1 = (7x - 1)(x - 1)$

29. $5b^2 - 23b + 12 = (5b - 3)(b - 4)$

31. $5z^2 - 6z - 8 = (5z + 4)(z - 2)$

33. $4y^2 + 5y - 6 = (4y - 3)(y + 2)$

35. $10x^2 - 27x + 5 = (5x - 1)(2x - 5)$

37. $10d^2 - 7d - 12 = (5d + 4)(2d - 3)$

39. $6x^2 - 22x - 8 = 2 \cdot 3x^2 - 2 \cdot 11x - 2 \cdot 4$
$$= 2(3x^2 - 11x - 4)$$
$$= 2(3x + 1)(x - 4)$$

41. $10t + 3 + 7t^2 = 7t^2 + 10t + 3$
$$= (7t + 3)(t + 1)$$

43. $6x^2 + 16x + 10 = 2 \cdot 3x^2 + 2 \cdot 8x + 2 \cdot 5$
$$= 2(3x^2 + 8x + 5)$$
$$= 2(3x + 5)(x + 1)$$

45. $6x^3 - 5x^2 - 4x = x \cdot 6x^2 - x \cdot 5x - x \cdot 4$
$$= x(6x^2 - 5x - 4)$$
$$= x(2x + 1)(3x - 4)$$

47. $12x^3 + 28x^2 + 8x = 4x \cdot 3x^2 + 4x \cdot 7x + 4x \cdot 2$
$$= 4x(3x^2 + 7x + 2)$$
$$= 4x(3x + 1)(x + 2)$$

49. $4x^3 - 2x^2 - 12x = 2x \cdot 2x^2 - 2x \cdot x - 2x \cdot 6$
$$= 2x(2x^2 - x - 6)$$
$$= 2x(2x + 3)(x - 2)$$

51. $36z^2 + 6z - 6 = 6 \cdot 6z^2 + 6 \cdot z - 6 \cdot 1$
$$= 6(6z^2 + z - 1)$$
$$= 6(3z - 1)(2z + 1)$$

53. $72 + 3r^2 - 30r = 3r^2 - 30r + 72$
$$= 3 \cdot r^2 - 3 \cdot 10r + 3 \cdot 24$$
$$= 3(r^2 - 10r + 24)$$
$$= 3(r - 4)(r - 6)$$

55. $2x^2 + 5xy + 2y^2 = (2x + y)(x + 2y)$

57. $2x^2 - 7xy + 3y^2 = (2x - y)(x - 3y)$

59. $12x^2 + 10xy - 8y^2 = 2 \cdot 6x^2 + 2 \cdot 5xy - 2 \cdot 4y^2$
$$= 2(6x^2 + 5xy - 4y^2)$$
$$= 2(2x - y)(3x + 4y)$$

61. $6x^2 - 9xy - 27y^2 = 3 \cdot 2x^2 - 3 \cdot 3xy - 3 \cdot 9y^2$

$\qquad\qquad\qquad\quad = 3\left(2x^2 - 3xy - 9y^2\right)$

$\qquad\qquad\qquad\quad = 3(x - 3y)(2x + 3y)$

63. $6m^2 - mn - 2n^2 = (3m - 2n)(2m + n)$

65. $8x^3 + 10x^2y + 3xy^2 = x \cdot 8x^2 + x \cdot 10xy + x \cdot 3y^2$

$\qquad\qquad\qquad\qquad = x(8x^2 + 10xy + 3y^2)$

$\qquad\qquad\qquad\qquad = x(4x + 3y)(2x + y)$

67. $4x^4 + 8x^3y + 3x^2y^2 = x^2 \cdot 4x^2 + x^2 \cdot 8xy + x^2 \cdot 3y^2$

$\qquad\qquad\qquad\qquad = x^2(4x^2 + 8xy + 3y^2)$

$\qquad\qquad\qquad\qquad = x^2(2x + y)(2x + 3y)$

69. $3x^2 - 20x - 7$. This polynomial was obtained by multiplying the factors.

71. $10x^2 + 35x + 15$. This polynomial was obtained by multiplying the factors.

73. $2x^4 - x^3 - 3x^2$. This polynomial was obtained by multiplying the factors.

75. a. The second factor can be found by dividing the trinomial by the binomial.

   b.
$$
\begin{array}{r}
6x + 11 \\
3x + 10 \overline{) \; 18x^2 + 93x + 110} \\
\underline{18x^2 + 60x} \\
33x + 110 \\
\underline{33x + 110} \\
0
\end{array}
$$
The other factor is $6x + 11$.

77. $18x^2 + 9x - 20 = \left(6x - 5\right)\left(3x + 4\right)$

79. $15x^2 - 124x + 160 = \left(5x - 8\right)\left(3x - 20\right)$

81. $72x^2 - 180x - 200 = 4 \cdot 18x^2 - 4 \cdot 45x - 4 \cdot 50$

$\qquad\qquad\qquad\qquad = 4\left(18x^2 - 45x - 50\right)$

$\qquad\qquad\qquad\qquad = 4\left(6x + 5\right)\left(3x - 10\right)$

83. The other factor is $2x + 45$. The product of the three first terms must equal $6x^3$, and the product of the constants must equal $2250x$.

85. $-x^2 - 4(y + 3) + 2y^2$

$\qquad = -(-3)^2 - 4(-5 + 3) + 2(-5)^2$

$\qquad = -9 - 4(-2) + 2(25)$

$\qquad = -9 + 8 + 50$

$\qquad = 49$

86. $\dfrac{500}{3.82} \approx 130.89$

His average speed was about 130.89 miles per hour.

87. $36x^4y^3 - 12xy^2 + 24x^5y^6 = 12xy^2 \cdot 3x^3y - 12xy^2 \cdot 1 + 12xy^2 \cdot 2x^4y^4$
$$= 12xy^2\left(3x^3y - 1 + 2x^4y^4\right)$$

88. $x^2 - 15x + 54 = (x - 9)(x - 6)$

Exercise Set 5.5

1. a. $a^2 - b^2 = (a + b)(a - b)$

   b. Answers will vary.

3. a. $a^3 - b^3 = (a - b)\left(a^2 + ab + b^2\right)$

   b. Answers will vary.

5. No, there is no special formula for factoring the sum of two squares.

8. $4y^2 + 1$ is prime.

9. $4a^2 + 16 = 4\left(a^2 + 4\right)$

11. $16m^2 + 36n^2 = 4\left(4m^2 + 9n^2\right)$

13. $y^2 - 25 = y^2 - 5^2 = (y + 5)(y - 5)$

15. $z^2 - 81 = z^2 - 9^2$
$$= (z + 9)(z - 9)$$

17. $x^2 - 49 = x^2 - 7^2$
$$= (x + 7)(x - 7)$$

19. $x^2 - y^2 = (x + y)(x - y)$

21. $9y^2 - 25z^2 = (3y)^2 - (5z)^2$
$$= (3y + 5z)(3y - 5z)$$

23. $64a^2 - 36b^2 = 4\left(16a^2 - 9b^2\right)$
$$= 4\left[(4a)^2 - (3b)^2\right]$$
$$= 4(4a + 3b)(4a - 3b)$$

25. $49x^2 - 36 = (7x)^2 - 6^2$
$$= (7x + 6)(7x - 6)$$

27. $z^4 - 81x^2 = \left(z^2\right)^2 - (9x)^2$
$$= \left(z^2 + 9x\right)\left(z^2 - 9x\right)$$

29. $9x^4 - 81y^2 = 9\left(x^4 - 9y^2\right)$
$$= 9\left[\left(x^2\right)^2 - (3y)^2\right]$$
$$= 9\left(x^2 + 3y\right)\left(x^2 - 3y\right)$$

31. $36m^4 - 49n^2 = \left(6m^2\right)^2 - (7n)^2$
$$= \left(6m^2 + 7n\right)\left(6m^2 - 7n\right)$$

33. $10x^2 - 160 = 10\left(x^2 - 16\right)$
$$= 10\left(x^2 - 4^2\right)$$
$$= 10(x + 4)(x - 4)$$

35. $16x^2 - 100y^4 = 4\left(4x^2 - 25y^4\right)$
$$= 4\left[(2x)^2 - \left(5y^2\right)^2\right]$$
$$= 4\left(2x + 5y^2\right)\left(2x - 5y^2\right)$$

37. $x^3 + y^3 = (x + y)\left(x^2 - xy + y^2\right)$

39. $a^3 - b^3 = (a - b)\left(a^2 + ab + b^2\right)$

41. $x^3 + 8 = x^3 + 2^3$
$$= (x + 2)\left(x^2 - 2x + 4\right)$$

43. $x^3 - 27 = x^3 - 3^3$
$$= (x - 3)\left(x^2 + 3x + 9\right)$$

45. $a^3 + 1 = a^3 + 1^3$
$$= (a + 1)\left(a^2 - a + 1\right)$$

47. $27x^3 - 1 = (3x)^3 - 1^3$
$$= (3x - 1)\left(9x^2 + 3x + 1\right)$$

48. $27y^3 + 8 = (3y)^3 + 2^3$
$$= (3y + 2)\left(9y^2 - 6y + 4\right)$$

49. $27a^3 - 125 = (3a)^3 - 5^3$
$$= (3a - 5)(9a^2 + 15a + 25)$$

51. $27 - 8y^3 = 3^3 - (2y)^3$
$$= (3 - 2y)(9 + 6y + 4y^2)$$

53. $64m^3 + 27n^3 = (4m)^3 + (3n)^3$
$$= (4m + 3n)(16m^2 - 12mn + 9n^2)$$

55. $8a^3 - 27b^3 = (2a)^3 - (3b)^3$
$$= (2a - 3b)(4a^2 + 6ab + 9b^2)$$

57. $2x^2 + 8x + 8 = 2(x^2 + 4x + 4)$
$$= 2(x + 2)^2$$

59. $a^2 b - 25b = b(a^2 - 25)$
$$= b(a^2 - 5^2)$$
$$= b(a + 5)(a - 5)$$

61. $3c^2 - 18c + 27 = 3(c^2 - 6c + 9)$
$$= 3(c - 3)^2$$

63. $5x^2 - 10x - 15 = 5(x^2 - 2x - 3)$
$$= 5(x - 3)(x + 1)$$

65. $3xy - 6x + 9y - 18 = 3(xy - 2x + 3y - 6)$
$$= 3[x(y - 2) + 3(y - 2)]$$
$$= 3(x + 3)(y - 2)$$

67. $2x^2 - 50 = 2(x^2 - 25)$
$$= 2(x^2 - 5^2)$$
$$= 2(x + 5)(x - 5)$$

69. $3x^2 y - 27y = 3y(x^2 - 9)$
$$= 3y(x^2 - 3^2)$$
$$= 3y(x + 3)(x - 3)$$

71. $3x^3 y^2 + 3y^2 = 3y^2(x^3 + 1)$
$$= 3y^2(x^3 + 1^3)$$
$$= 3y^2(x + 1)(x^2 - x + 1)$$

73. $2x^3 - 16 = 2(x^3 - 8)$
$$= 2(x^3 - 2^3)$$
$$= 2(x - 2)(x^2 + 2x + 4)$$

75. $18x^2 - 50 = 2(9x^2 - 25)$
$$= 2((3x)^2 - 5^2)$$
$$= 2(3x + 5)(3x - 5)$$

77. $12x^2 + 36x + 27 = 3(4x^2 + 12x + 9)$
$$= 3(2x + 3)(2x + 3)$$
$$= 3(2x + 3)^2$$

78. $12n^2 + 4n - 16 = 4(3n^2 + n - 4)$
$$= 4(3n + 4)(n - 1)$$

79. $6x^2 - 4x + 24x - 16 = 2(3x^2 - 2x + 12x - 8)$
$$= 2[x(3x - 2) + 4(3x - 2)]$$
$$= 2(3x - 2)(x + 4)$$

81. $2rs^2 - 10rs - 48r = 2r(s^2 - 5s - 24)$
$$= 2r(s + 3)(s - 8)$$

82. $4x^4 - 26x^3 + 30x^2 = 2x^2(2x^2 - 13x + 15)$
$$= 2x^2(2x - 3)(x - 5)$$

83. $4x^2 + 5x - 6 = (x + 2)(4x - 3)$

85. $25b^2 - 100 = 25(b^2 - 4)$
$$= 25(b^2 - 2^2)$$
$$= 25(b + 2)(b - 2)$$

87. $a^5 b^2 - 4a^3 b^4 = a^3 b^2(a^2 - 4b^2)$
$$= a^3 b^2[a^2 - (2b)^2]$$
$$= a^3 b^2(a + 2b)(a - 2b)$$

89. $3x^4 - 18x^3 + 27x^2 = 3x^2(x^2 - 6x + 9)$
$$= 3x^2(x - 3)(x - 3)$$
$$= 3x^2(x - 3)^2$$

91. $x^3 + 25x = x\left(x^2 + 25\right)$

93. $y^4 - 16 = \left(y^2\right)^2 - 4^2$
$$= \left(y^2 + 4\right)\left(y^2 - 4\right)$$
$$= \left(y^2 + 4\right)\left(y^2 - 2^2\right)$$
$$= \left(y^2 + 4\right)(y + 2)(y - 2)$$

95. $36a^2 - 15ab - 6b^2 = 3\left(12a^2 - 5ab - 2b^2\right)$
$$= 3(3a - 2b)(4a + b)$$

97. $2ab - 3b + 4a - 6 = b(2a - 3) + 2(2a - 3)$
$$= (2a - 3)(b + 2)$$

99. $9 - 9y^4 = 9\left(1 - y^4\right)$
$$= 9\left[1^2 - \left(y^2\right)^2\right]$$
$$= 9\left(1 + y^2\right)\left(1 - y^2\right)$$
$$= 9\left(1 + y^2\right)\left(1^2 - y^2\right)$$
$$= 9\left(1 + y^2\right)(1 + y)(1 - y)$$

101. You cannot divide both sides of the equation by $(a - b)$, because it equals 0.

103. $2\blacklozenge^6 + 4\blacklozenge^4\maltese^2$
$$= 2\blacklozenge^4\left(\blacklozenge^2 + 2\maltese^2\right)$$

105. $x^6 + 1 = \left(x^2\right)^3 + 1^3$
$$= \left(x^2 + 1\right)\left(x^4 - x^2 + 1\right)$$

107. $x^2 - 6x + 9 - 4y^2 = (x - 3)^2 - (2y)^2$
$$= (x - 3 + 2y)(x - 3 - 2y)$$

109. $x^6 - y^6 = \left(x^3\right)^2 - \left(y^3\right)^2$
$$= \left(x^3 + y^3\right)\left(x^3 - y^3\right)$$
$$= \left[(x + y)\left(x^2 - xy + y^2\right)\right]\!\left[(x - y)\left(x^2 + xy + y^2\right)\right]$$
$$= (x + y)(x - y)\left(x^2 - xy + y^2\right)\left(x^2 + xy + y^2\right)$$

110. $3x - 2(x + 4) \geq 2x - 9$
$$3x - 2x - 8 \geq 2x - 9$$
$$x - 8 \geq 2x - 9$$
$$1 \geq x$$

111. Substitute 36 for A, 6 for b, and 12 for d.

$$A = \frac{1}{2}h(b + d)$$
$$36 = \frac{1}{2}h(6 + 12)$$
$$36 = \frac{1}{2}h(18)$$
$$36 = 9h$$
$$4 = h$$

The height is 4 inches.

112. $x + (5 - 2x) = 2$
The sum of a number, and 5 decreased by twice the number is 2.

113. $\left(\dfrac{4x^4y}{6xy^5}\right)^3 = \left(\dfrac{4}{6} \cdot \dfrac{x^4}{x} \cdot \dfrac{y}{y^5}\right)^3$

$\qquad = \left(\dfrac{2}{3} \cdot x^3 \cdot \dfrac{1}{y^4}\right)^3$

$\qquad = \left(\dfrac{2x^3}{3y^4}\right)^3$

$\qquad = \dfrac{2^3 x^{3 \cdot 3}}{3^3 y^{4 \cdot 3}}$

$\qquad = \dfrac{8x^9}{27y^{12}}$

114. $x^{-2}x^{-3} = x^{-2-3}$

$\qquad = x^{-5}$

$\qquad = \dfrac{1}{x^5}$

Exercise Set 5.6

1. Answers will vary.

3. The standard form of a quadratic equation is $ax^2 + bx + c = 0$.

5. a. The zero-factor property may only be used when one side of the equation is equal to 0.

   b. $(x+1)(x-2) = 4$

$\qquad x^2 - 2x + x - 2 = 4$

$\qquad\quad x^2 - x - 6 = 0$

$\qquad\quad (x-3)(x+2) = 0$

$\qquad x - 3 = 0 \quad$ or $\quad x + 2 = 0$

$\qquad\quad x = 3 \qquad\qquad x = -2$

7. $x(x+2) = 0$

$\quad x = 0 \quad$ or $\quad x + 2 = 0$

$\quad x = 0 \qquad\qquad x = -2$

9. $7x(x-8) = 0$

$\quad x = 0 \quad$ or $\quad x - 8 = 0$

$\qquad\qquad\qquad\quad x = 8$

11. $(2x+5)(x-3) = 0$

$\quad 2x + 5 = 0 \quad$ or $\quad x - 3 = 0$

$\qquad 2x = -5 \qquad\qquad x = 3$

$\qquad\quad x = -\dfrac{5}{2}$

13. $\qquad x^2 - 9 = 0$

$\qquad (x+3)(x-3) = 0$

$\qquad x + 3 = 0 \quad$ or $\quad x - 3 = 0$

$\qquad\quad x = -3 \qquad\qquad x = 3$

15. $x^2 - 12x = 0$

$\quad x(x-12) = 0$

$\quad x = 0 \quad$ or $\quad x - 12 = 0$

$\qquad\qquad\qquad\qquad x = 12$

17. $9x^2 + 27x = 0$

$\quad 9x(x+3) = 0$

$\quad x = 0 \quad$ or $\quad x + 3 = 0$

$\qquad\qquad\qquad\qquad x = -3$

19. $\quad x^2 - 8x + 16 = 0$

$\qquad (x-4)(x-4) = 0$

$\qquad\quad x - 4 = 0$

$\qquad\qquad x = 4$

21. $\qquad x^2 + 12x = -20$

$\qquad x^2 + 12x + 20 = 0$

$\qquad (x+10)(x+2) = 0$

$\qquad x + 10 = 0 \quad$ or $\quad x + 2 = 0$

$\qquad\quad x = -10 \qquad\qquad x = -2$

23. $\qquad z^2 + 3z = 18$

$\qquad z^2 + 3z - 18 = 0$

$\qquad (z+6)(z-3) = 0$

$\qquad z + 6 = 0 \quad$ or $\quad z - 3 = 0$

$\qquad\quad z = -6 \qquad\qquad z = 3$

25. $4a^2 - 4a - 48 = 0$

$\quad 4\left(a^2 - a - 12\right) = 0$

$\quad 4(a-4)(a+3) = 0$

$\quad a - 4 = 0 \quad$ or $\quad a + 3 = 0$

$\qquad a = 4 \qquad\qquad a = -3$

27. $\qquad 23p - 24 = -p^2$

$\qquad p^2 + 23p - 24 = 0$

$\qquad (p+24)(p-1) = 0$

$\qquad p + 24 = 0 \quad$ or $\quad p - 1 = 0$

$\qquad\quad p = -24 \qquad\qquad p = 1$

29.
$$33w + 90 = -3w^2$$
$$3w^2 + 33w + 90 = 0$$
$$3\left(w^2 + 11w + 30\right) = 0$$
$$3(w + 5)(w + 6) = 0$$
$$w + 5 = 0 \quad \text{or} \quad w + 6 = 0$$
$$w = -5 \qquad\qquad w = -6$$

31.
$$-2x - 15 = -x^2$$
$$x^2 - 2x - 15 = 0$$
$$(x - 5)(x + 3) = 0$$
$$x - 5 = 0 \quad \text{or} \quad x + 3 = 0$$
$$x = 5 \qquad\qquad x = -3$$

33.
$$-x^2 + 29x + 30 = 0$$
$$x^2 - 29x - 30 = 0$$
$$(x - 30)(x + 1) = 0$$
$$x - 30 = 0 \quad \text{or} \quad x + 1 = 0$$
$$x = 30 \qquad\qquad x = -1$$

35.
$$12 = 3n^2 + 16n$$
$$3n^2 + 16n - 12 = 0$$
$$(n + 6)(3n - 2) = 0$$
$$n + 6 = 0 \quad \text{or} \quad 3n - 2 = 0$$
$$n = 6 \qquad\qquad 3n = 2$$
$$n = \frac{2}{3}$$

37.
$$9p^2 = -21p - 6$$
$$9p^2 + 21p + 6 = 0$$
$$3\left(3p^2 + 7p + 2\right) = 0$$
$$3(3p + 1)(p + 2) = 0$$
$$3p + 1 = 0 \quad \text{or} \quad p + 2 = 0$$
$$3p = -1 \qquad\qquad p = -2$$
$$p = -\frac{1}{3}$$

39.
$$3r^2 + 13r = 10$$
$$3r^2 + 13r - 10 = 0$$
$$(3r - 2)(r + 5) = 0$$
$$3r - 2 = 0 \quad \text{or} \quad r + 5 = 0$$
$$3r = 2 \qquad\qquad r = -5$$
$$r = \frac{2}{3}$$

41.
$$4x^2 + 4x - 48 = 0$$
$$4\left(x^2 + x - 12\right) = 0$$
$$4(x + 4)(x - 3) = 0$$
$$x + 4 = 0 \quad \text{or} \quad x - 3 = 0$$
$$x = -4 \qquad\qquad x = 3$$

43.
$$8x^2 + 2x = 3$$
$$8x^2 + 2x - 3 = 0$$
$$(4x + 3)(2x - 1) = 0$$
$$4x + 3 = 0 \quad \text{or} \quad 2x - 1 = 0$$
$$4x = -3 \qquad\qquad 2x = 1$$
$$x = -\frac{3}{4} \qquad\qquad x = \frac{1}{2}$$

45.
$$2n^2 + 36 = -18n$$
$$2n^2 + 18n + 36 = 0$$
$$2\left(n^2 + 9n + 18\right) = 0$$
$$2(n + 6)(n + 3) = 0$$
$$n + 6 = 0 \quad \text{or} \quad n + 3 = 0$$
$$n = -6 \qquad\qquad n = -3$$

47.
$$2x^2 = 50x$$
$$2x^2 - 50x = 0$$
$$2x(x - 25) = 0$$
$$2x = 0 \quad \text{or} \quad x - 25 = 0$$
$$x = 0 \qquad\qquad x = 25$$

49.
$$x^2 = 100$$
$$x^2 - 100 = 0$$
$$x^2 - 10^2 = 0$$
$$(x + 10)(x - 10) = 0$$
$$x + 10 = 0 \quad \text{or} \quad x - 10 = 0$$
$$x = -10 \qquad\qquad x = 10$$

51.
$$(x - 2)(x - 1) = 12$$
$$x^2 - 3x + 2 = 12$$
$$x^2 - 3x - 10 = 0$$
$$(x + 2)(x - 5) = 0$$
$$x + 2 = 0 \quad \text{or} \quad x - 5 = 0$$
$$x = -2 \qquad\qquad x = 5$$

53. $(x-1)(2x-5) = 9$

$\qquad 2x^2 - 7x + 5 = 9$

$\qquad 2x^2 - 7x - 4 = 0$

$\qquad (2x+1)(x-4) = 0$

$\qquad 2x+1 = 0 \quad$ or $\quad x - 4 = 0$

$\qquad\qquad x = -\frac{1}{2} \qquad\qquad x = 4$

55. $\qquad x(x+5) = 6$

$\qquad\quad x^2 + 5x = 6$

$\qquad x^2 + 5x - 6 = 0$

$\qquad (x+6)(x-1) = 0$

$\qquad x + 6 = 0 \quad$ or $\quad x - 1 = 0$

$\qquad\quad x = -6 \qquad\qquad x = 1$

57. The solutions are 4 and –2, so the factors are $x - 4$ and $x + 2$.

$\qquad (x-4)(x+2) = x^2 - 2x - 8$

The equation is $x^2 - 2x - 8 = 0$.

59. The solutions are 6 and 0, so the factors are $x - 0$ and $x - 6$.

$\qquad (x-0)(x-6) = x(x-6)$

$\qquad\qquad\qquad\quad = x^2 - 6x$

The equation is $x^2 - 6x = 0$.

61. a. The solutions are

$\qquad x = \frac{1}{2} \quad$ or $\quad x = -\frac{1}{3}$

$\qquad 2x = 1 \qquad\qquad 3x = -1$

$\qquad 2x - 1 = 0 \qquad 3x + 1 = 0$

Thus the factors are:

$(2x - 1)$ and $(3x + 1)$.

b. The equation is $(2x - 1)(3x + 1)$

$\qquad = 6x^2 - x - 1 = 0$

63. $(x-3)(x-2) = (x+5)(2x-3) + 21$

$\qquad x^2 - 5x + 6 = 2x^2 + 7x - 15 + 21$

$\qquad x^2 - 5x + 6 = 2x^2 + 7x + 6$

$\qquad\qquad\quad 0 = x^2 + 12x$

$\qquad\qquad\quad 0 = x(x+12)$

$\qquad x = 0 \quad$ or $\quad x + 12 = 0$

$\qquad\qquad\qquad\qquad x = -12$

65. $x(x-3)(x+2) = 0$

$\qquad x = 0 \quad$ or $\quad x - 3 = 0 \quad$ or $\quad x + 2 = 0$

$\qquad\qquad\qquad x = 3 \qquad\qquad x = -2$

67. $\dfrac{3}{5} - \dfrac{4}{7} = \dfrac{21}{35} - \dfrac{20}{35} = \dfrac{21-20}{35} = \dfrac{1}{35}$

68. a. Identity

b. Contradiction

69. Let x be the number of people admitted in 60 minutes.

$\qquad \dfrac{160 \text{ people}}{13 \text{ minutes}} = \dfrac{x}{60 \text{ minutes}}$

$\qquad\qquad 13x = 160(60)$

$\qquad\qquad 13x = 9600$

$\qquad\qquad\quad x \approx 738$

About 738 people were admitted in 60 minutes.

70. $\left(\dfrac{2x^4 y^5}{x^5 y^7} \right)^3 = \left(2 \cdot x^{4-5} \cdot y^{5-7} \right)^3$

$\qquad\qquad\qquad = \left(2x^{-1} y^{-2} \right)^3$

$\qquad\qquad\qquad = \left(\dfrac{2}{xy^2} \right)^3$

$\qquad\qquad\qquad = \dfrac{2^3}{x^3 y^{2 \cdot 3}}$

$\qquad\qquad\qquad = \dfrac{8}{x^3 y^6}$

71. monomial

72. binomial

73. not a polynomial

74. trinomial

Exercise Set 5.7

1. A right triangle is a triangle with a 90° angle.

3. The Pythagorean Theorem is $a^2 + b^2 = c^2$.

5. $a^2 + b^2 = c^2$

$\qquad ?^2 + 4^2 = 5^2$

$\qquad ?^2 + 16 = 25$

$\qquad\qquad ?^2 = 9$

$\qquad\qquad\; ? = 3$

7. $a^2 + b^2 = c^2$

$8^2 + 15^2 = ?^2$

$64 + 225 = ?^2$

$289 = ?^2$

$17 = ?$

9. $a^2 + b^2 = c^2$

$3^2 + ?^2 = 5^2$

$9 + ?^2 = 25$

$?^2 = 16$

$? = 4$

11. $a^2 + b^2 = c^2$

$15^2 + 36^2 = ?^2$

$225 + 1296 = ?^2$

$1521 = ?^2$

$39 = ?$

13. Let x be the smaller of the two positive integers. Then $x + 4$ is the other integer.

$x(x + 4) = 117$

$x^2 + 4x + 117 = 0$

$(x - 9)(x + 13) = 0$

$x - 9 = 0$ or $x + 13 = 0$

$x = 9$　　　　$x = -13$

Since x must be positive, the two integers are 9 and $9 + 4 = 13$.

15. Let x = first positive number. Then $2x + 2$ is the other number.

$x(2x + 2) = 84$

$2x^2 + 2x = 84$

$2x^2 + 2x - 84 = 0$

$2(x^2 + x - 42) = 0$

$2(x + 7)(x - 6) = 0$

$x + 7 = 0$ 　or　 $x - 6 = 0$

$x = -7$　　　　$x = 6$

The numbers have to be positive. Thus the numbers are 6 and $2x + 2 = 14$.

17. Let x be the smaller of the two consecutive positive odd integers. Then $x + 2$ is the other integer.

$x(x + 2) = 63$

$x^2 + 2x - 63 = 0$

$(x + 9)(x - 7) = 0$

$x - 9 = 0$　　or　$x - 7 = 0$

$x = -9$　　　　$x = 7$

Since x must be positive, the two integers are 7 and $7 + 2 = 9$.

19. Let w = width. Then length = $4w$.

$A = lw$

$36 = (4w)(w)$

$36 = 4w^2$

$0 = 4w^2 - 36$

$0 = 4(w^2 - 9)$

$0 = 4(w + 3)(w - 3)$

$w + 3 = 0$ 　or　 $w - 3 = 0$

$w = -3$　　　　$w = 3$

Since dimensions must be positive, the width is 3 feet and the length is $4(3) = 12$ feet.

21. Let w = width of the garden, l = length of the garden.

$$w = \frac{2}{3}l$$

$$lw = 150$$

$$l\left(\frac{2}{3}l\right) = 150$$

$$\frac{2l^2}{3} = 450$$

$$2l^2 - 450 = 0$$

$$2\left(l^2 - 225\right) = 0$$

$$2\left(l^2 - 15^2\right) = 0$$

$$2(l + 15)(l - 15) = 0$$

$l + 15 = 0$ 　or　 $l - 15 = 0$

$l = -15$　　　　$l = 15$

Since dimensions must be positive, the length is 15 feet and the width is $\frac{2}{3}(15) = $ 10 feet.

23. Let a = length of a side of the original square. Then $a + 4$ is the length of the new side.

$(a + 4)(a + 4) = 49$

$a^2 + 8a + 16 = 49$

$a^2 + 8a - 33 = 0$

$(a - 3)(a + 11) = 0$

$a - 3 = 0$ 　or　 $a + 11 = 0$

$a = 3$ 　or　　　$a = -11$

Since length must be positive, the original square had sides of length 3 meters.

25. $d = 16t^2$

$$256 = 16t^2$$

$$\frac{256}{16} = t^2$$

$$16 = t^2$$

$$0 = t^2 - 16$$

$$0 = (t+4)(t-4)$$

$$t + 4 = 0 \quad \text{or} \quad t - 4 = 0$$

$$t = -4 \qquad\qquad t = 4$$

Since time must be positive, it would take the egg 4 seconds to hit the ground.

27. $a^2 + b^2 = c^2$

$$7^2 + 24^2 = 25^2$$

$$49 + 576 = 625$$

$$625 = 625 \ \text{True}$$

Since these values are true for the Pythagorean Theorem, a right triangle can exist.

29. $a^2 + b^2 = c^2$

$$9^2 + 40^2 = 41^2$$

$$81 + 1600 = 1681$$

$$1681 = 1681 \ \text{True}$$

Since these values are true for the Pythagorean Theorem, a right triangle can exist.

31. $a^2 + b^2 = c^2$

$$30^2 + ?^2 = 34^2$$

$$900 + ?^2 = 1156$$

$$?^2 = 256$$

$$? = 16 \text{ feet}$$

33. $a^2 + b^2 = c^2$

$$?^2 + 24^2 = 26^2$$

$$?^2 + 576 = 676$$

$$?^2 = 100$$

$$? = 10 \text{ inches}$$

35. Let x be the length of one leg of the triangle. Then $x + 2$ is the length of the other leg.

$$a^2 + b^2 = c^2$$

$$x^2 + (x+2)^2 = 10^2$$

$$x^2 + x^2 + 4x + 4 = 100$$

$$2x^2 + 4x + 4 = 100$$

$$2x^2 + 4x - 96 = 0$$

$$2\left(x^2 + 2x - 48\right) = 0$$

$$2(x+8)(x-6) = 0$$

$$x + 8 = 0 \quad \text{or} \quad x - 6 = 0$$

$$x = -8 \qquad\qquad x = 6$$

Since length is positive, the lengths are 6 ft, 8ft and 10ft.

37. Let d be the distance traveled by Bob. Then $3d - 3$ is the distance traveled by Alice and $2d + 3$ is the distance between Bob and Alice.

$$a^2 + b^2 = c^2$$

$$d^2 + (3d - 3)^2 = (2d + 3)^2$$

$$d^2 + 9d^2 - 18d + 9 = 4d^2 + 12d + 9$$

$$10d^2 - 18d + 9 = 4d^2 + 12d + 9$$

$$6d^2 - 30d = 0$$

$$6d(d - 5) = 0$$

$$6d = 0 \quad \text{or} \quad d - 5 = 0$$

$$d = 0 \qquad\qquad d = 5$$

Since distance is positive, the distance between Bob and Alice is $2d + 3 = 2(5) + 3 = 13$ miles.

39. Let w be the width of the rectangle. Then $3w + 3$ is the length and $3w + 4$ is the length of the diagonal.

$$a^2 + b^2 = c^2$$

$$w^2 + (3w + 3)^2 = (3w + 4)^2$$

$$w^2 + 9w^2 + 18w + 9 = 9w^2 + 24w + 16$$

$$10w^2 + 18w + 9 = 9w^2 + 24w + 16$$

$$w^2 - 6w - 7 = 0$$

$$(w - 7)(w + 1) = 0$$

$$w - 7 = 0 \quad \text{or} \quad w + 1 = 0$$

$$w = 7 \qquad\qquad w = -1$$

Since length is positive, the dimensions of the garden are 7 ft. for the width and $3w + 3 = 3(7) + 3 = 24$ ft. for the length.

41.
$$P = x^2 - 15x - 50$$
$$x^2 - 15x - 50 = 400$$
$$x^2 - 15 - 450 = 0$$
$$(x - 30)(x + 15) = 0$$
$$x - 30 = 0 \quad \text{or} \quad x + 15 = 0$$
$$x = 30 \qquad\qquad x = -15$$

Since x must be positive, she must sell 30 videos for a profit of $400.

43. a.
$$n^2 + n = 20$$
$$n^2 + n - 20 = 0$$
$$(n - 4)(n + 5) = 0$$
$$n - 4 = 0 \quad \text{or} \quad n + 5 = 0$$
$$n = 4 \qquad\qquad n = -5$$

Since n must be positive, $n = 4$.

45. Before area can be determined, the length of the rectangle must be found first. Let x be the length of the rectangle.
$$a^2 + b^2 = c^2$$
$$x^2 + 18^2 = 30^2$$
$$x^2 + 324 = 900$$
$$x^2 = 576$$
$$x = 24$$

Area of a rectangle can be found by multiplying the length and width.
$$A = lw$$
$$= 24 \cdot 18$$
$$= 432$$

The area of the rectangle is 432 square feet.

b.
$$n^2 + n = 90$$
$$n^2 + n - 90 = 0$$
$$(n - 9)(n + 10) = 0$$
$$n - 9 = 0 \quad \text{or} \quad n + 10 = 0$$
$$n = 9 \qquad\qquad n = -10$$

Since n must be positive, $n = 9$.

47.
$$x^3 + 3x^2 - 10x = 0$$
$$x(x^2 + 3x - 10) = 0$$
$$x(x + 5)(x - 2) = 0$$
$$x = 0 \quad \text{or} \quad x + 5 = 0 \quad \text{or} \quad x - 2 = 0$$
$$x = -5 \qquad\qquad x = 2$$

49. The numbers are the constants in the binomials that are factors of $x^2 + 3x - 40$.
$$x + 3x - 40 = (x - 5)(x + 8)$$
The numbers are –5 and 8.

53. "Five less than twice a number" is $2x - 5$.

54.
$$(3x + 2) - \left(x^2 - 4x + 6\right) = 3x + 2 - x^2 + 4x - 6$$
$$= -x^2 + 3x + 4x + 2 - 6$$
$$= -x^2 + 7x - 4$$

55.
$$\left(3x^2 + 2x - 4\right)(2x - 1) = 3x^2(2x - 1) + 2x(2x - 1) - 4(2x - 1)$$
$$= 6x^3 - 3x^2 + 4x^2 - 2x - 8x + 4$$
$$= 6x^3 + x^2 - 10x + 4$$

56.
$$\begin{array}{r}
2x - 3 \\
3x - 5 \overline{\smash{)}\ 6x^2 - 19x + 15} \\
\underline{6x^2 - 10x} \\
-9x + 15 \\
\underline{-9x + 15} \\
0
\end{array}$$

$$\frac{6x^2 - 19x + 15}{3x - 5} = 2x - 3$$

57.
$$\frac{6x^2 - 19x + 15}{3x - 5} = \frac{(3x - 5)(2x - 3)}{3x - 5}$$
$$= 2x - 3$$

Review Exercises

1. The greatest common factor is y^3.

2. The greatest common factor is $3p$.

3. The greatest common factor is $5a^2$.

4. The greatest common factor is $5x^2y^2$.

5. The greatest common factor is 1.

6. The greatest common factor is 1.

7. The greatest common factor is $x - 5$.

8. The greatest common factor is $x + 5$.

9. $4x - 12 = 4(x - 3)$

10. $35x - 5 = 5(7x - 1)$

11. $24y^2 - 4y = 4y(6y - 1)$

12. $55p^3 - 20p^2 = 5p^2(11p - 4)$

13. $60a^2b - 36ab^2 = 12ab(5a - 3b)$

14. $6xy - 12x^2y = 6xy(1 - 2x)$

15. $20x^3y^2 + 8x^9y^3 - 16x^5y^2$
    $= 4x^3y^2(5 + 2x^6y - 4x^2)$

16. $24x^2 - 13y^2 + 6xy$ is prime.

17. $14a^2b - 7b - a^3$ is prime.

18. $x(5x + 3) - 2(5x + 3) = (5x + 3)(x - 2)$

19. $5x(x + 2) - 2(x + 2) = (x + 2)(5x - 2)$

20. $2x(4x - 3) + 4x - 3 = 2x(4x - 3) + 1(4x - 3)$
    $= (4x - 3)(2x + 1)$

21. $x^2 + 6x + 2x + 12 = x(x + 6) + 2(x + 6)$
    $= (x + 6)(x + 2)$

22. $x^2 - 5x + 4x - 20 = x(x - 5) + 4(x - 5)$
    $= (x - 5)(x + 4)$

23. $y^2 - 9y - 9y + 81 = y(y - 9) - 9(y - 9)$
    $= (y - 9)(y - 9)$
    $= (y - 9)^2$

24. $4a^2 - 4ab - a + b = 4a(a - b) - 1(a - b)$
    $= (a - b)(4a - 1)$

25. $3xy + 3x + 2y + 2 = 3x(y + 1) + 2(y + 1)$
    $= (y + 1)(3x + 2)$

26. $x^2 + 3x - 2xy - 6y = x(x + 3) - 2y(x + 3)$
    $= (x + 3)(x - 2y)$

27. $2x^2 + 12x - x - 6 = 2x(x + 6) - 1(x + 6)$
    $= (x + 6)(2x - 1)$

28. $5x^2 - xy + 20xy - 4y^2 = x(5x - y) + 4y(5x - y)$
    $= (5x - y)(x + 4y)$

29. $4x^2 + 12xy - 5xy - 15y^2 = 4x(x + 3y) - 5y(x + 3y)$
    $= (x + 3y)(4x - 5y)$

30. $6a^2 - 10ab - 3ab + 5b^2 = 2a(3a - 5b) - b(3a - 5b)$
    $= (3a - 5b)(2a - b)$

31. $ab - a + b - 1 = a(b - 1) + 1(b - 1)$
    $= (b - 1)(a + 1)$

32. $3x^2 - 9xy + 2xy - 6y^2 = 3x(x - 3y) + 2y(x - 3y)$
    $= (x - 3y)(3x + 2y)$

33. $7a^2 + 14ab - ab - 2b^2 = 7a(a + 2b) - b(a + 2b)$
    $= (a + 2b)(7a - b)$

34. $6x^2 + 9x - 2x - 3 = 3x(2x + 3) - 1(2x + 3)$
    $= (2x + 3)(3x - 1)$

35. $x^2 - x - 6 = (x + 2)(x - 3)$

36. $x^2 + 4x - 15$ is prime.

151

37. $x^2 - 13x + 42 = (x - 6)(x - 7)$

38. $b^2 + b - 20 = (b - 4)(b + 5)$

39. $n^2 + 3n - 40 = (n + 8)(n - 5)$

40. $x^2 - 15x + 56 = (x - 8)(x - 7)$

41. $c^2 - 10c - 20$ is prime.

42. $x^2 + 11x - 24$ is prime.

43. $x^3 - 17x^2 + 72x = x(x^2 - 17x + 72)$
$= x(x - 9)(x - 8)$

44. $x^3 - 3x^2 - 40x = x(x^2 - 3x - 40)$
$= x(x - 8)(x + 5)$

45. $x^2 - 2xy - 15y^2 = (x - 5y)(x + 3y)$

46. $4x^3 + 32x^2 y + 60xy^2 = 4x(x^2 + 8xy + 15y^2)$
$= 4x(x + 3y)(x + 5y)$

47. $2x^2 - x - 15 = (2x + 5)(x - 3)$

48. $3x^2 - 13x + 4 = (3x - 1)(x - 4)$

49. $4x^2 - 9x + 5 = (4x - 5)(x - 1)$

50. $5m^2 - 14m + 8 = (5n - 4)(m - 2)$

51. $9x^2 + 3x - 2 = (3x - 1)(3x + 2)$

52. $5x^2 - 32x + 12 = (5x - 2)(x - 6)$

53. $2t^2 + 14t + 9$ is prime.

54. $6s^2 + 13s + 5 = (2s + 1)(3s + 5)$

55. $5x^2 + 37x - 24 = (5x - 3)(x + 8)$

56. $6x^2 + 11x - 10 = (3x - 2)(2x + 5)$

57. $12x^2 + 2x - 4 = 2(6x^2 + x - 2)$
$= 2(3x + 2)(2x - 1)$

58. $9x^2 - 6x + 1 = (3x - 1)(3x - 1)$
$= (3x - 1)^2$

59. $9x^3 - 12x^2 + 4x = x(9x^2 - 12x + 4)$
$= x(3x - 2)(3x - 2)$
$= x(3x - 2)^2$

60. $18x^3 + 12x^2 - 16x = 2x(9x^2 + 6x - 8)$
$= 2x(3x + 4)(3x - 2)$

61. $16a^2 - 22ab - 3b^2 = (8a + b)(2a - 3b)$

62. $4a^2 - 16ab + 15b^2 = (2a - 3b)(2a - 5b)$

63. $x^2 - 36 = x^2 - 6^2$
$= (x + 6)(x - 6)$

64. $x^2 - 100 = x^2 - 10^2$
$= (x + 10)(x - 10)$

65. $4x^2 - 16 = 4(x^2 - 4)$
$= 4(x^2 - 2^2)$
$= 4(x + 2)(x - 2)$

66. $81x^2 - 9y^2 = 9(9x^2 - y^2)$
$= 9[(3x)^2 - y^2]$
$= 9(3x + y)(3x - y)$

67. $81 - a^2 = 9^2 - a^2$
$= (9 + a)(9 - a)$

68. $64 - x^2 = 8^2 - x^2$
$= (8 + x)(8 - x)$

69. $16x^4 - 49y^2 = (4x^2)^2 - (7y)^2$
$= (4x^2 + 7y)(4x^2 - 7y)$

70. $100x^4 - 121y^4 = (10x^2)^2 - (11y^2)^2$
$= (10x^2 + 11y^2)(10x^2 - 11y^2)$

71. $x^3 - y^3 = (x - y)(x^2 + xy + y^2)$

72. $x^3 + y^3 = (x + y)(x^2 - xy + y^2)$

73. $x^3 - 1 = (x-1)(x^2 + x + 1)$

74. $x^3 + 8 = x^3 + 2^3$
$$= (x+2)(x^2 - 2x + 4)$$

75. $a^3 + 27 = a^3 + 3^3$
$$= (a+3)(a^2 - 3a + 9)$$

76. $b^3 - 64 = b^3 - 4^3$
$$= (b-4)(b^2 + 4b + 16)$$

77. $125a^3 + b^3 = (5a)^3 + b^3$
$$= (5a + b)(25a^2 - 5ab + b^2)$$

78. $27 - 8y^3 = 3^3 - (2y)^3$
$$= (3 - 2y)(9 + 6y + 4y^2)$$

79. $27x^4 - 75y^2 = 3\left(9x^4 - 25y^2\right)$
$$= 3\left[\left(3x^2\right)^2 - (5y)^2\right]$$
$$= 3\left(3x^2 + 5y\right)\left(3x^2 - 5y\right)$$

80. $3x^3 - 192y^3 = 3\left(x^3 - 64y^3\right)$
$$= 3\left[x^3 - (4y)^3\right]$$
$$= 3(x - 4y)\left(x^2 + 4xy + 16y^2\right)$$

81. $x^2 - 14x + 48 = (x - 6)(x - 8)$

82. $3x^2 - 18x + 27 = 3\left(x^2 - 6x + 9\right)$
$$= 3(x - 3)^2$$

83. $4a^2 - 64 = 4\left(a^2 - 16\right)$
$$= 4\left(a^2 - 4^2\right)$$
$$= 4(a + 4)(a - 4)$$

84. $4y^2 - 36 = 4\left(y^2 - 9\right)$
$$= 4\left(y^2 - 3^2\right)$$
$$= 4(y + 3)(y - 3)$$

85. $8x^2 + 16x - 24 = 8\left(x^2 + 2x - 3\right)$
$$= 8(x + 3)(x - 1)$$

86. $x^2 - 6x - 27 = (x - 9)(x + 3)$

87. $9x^2 - 6x + 1 = (3x - 1)(3x - 1)$
$$= (3x - 1)^2$$

88. $4x^2 + 7x - 2 = (4x - 1)(x + 2)$

89. $6x^3 - 6 = 6\left(x^3 - 1\right)$
$$= 6\left(x^3 - 1^3\right)$$
$$= 6(x - 1)\left(x^2 + x + 1\right)$$

90. $x^3y - 27y = y\left(x^3 - 27\right)$
$$= y\left(x^3 - 3^3\right)$$
$$= y(x - 3)\left(x^2 + 3x + 9\right)$$

91. $a^2b - 2ab - 15b = b\left(a^2 - 2a - 15\right)$
$$= b(a + 3)(a - 5)$$

92. $6x^3 + 30x^2 + 9x^2 + 45x = 3x\left(2x^2 + 10x + 3x + 15\right)$
$$= 3x\left[2x(x + 5) + 3(x + 5)\right]$$
$$= 3x(2x + 3)(x + 5)$$

93. $x^2 - 4xy + 3y^2 = (x - 3y)(x - y)$

94. $3m^2 + 2mn - 8n^2 = (3m - 4n)(m + 2n)$

95. $4x^2 - 20xy + 25y^2 = (2x - 5y)(2x - 5y)$
$$= (2x - 5y)^2$$

96. $25a^2 - 49b^2 = (5a)^2 - (7b)^2$
$$= (5a + 7b)(5a - 7b)$$

97. $xy - 7x + 2y - 14 = x(y - 7) + 2(y - 7)$
$$= (x + 2)(y - 7)$$

98. $16y^5 - 25y^7 = y^5\left(16 - 25y^2\right)$
$$= y^5\left[4^2 - (5y)^2\right]$$
$$= y^5(4 + 5y)(4 - 5y)$$

99. $4x^3 + 18x^2y + 20xy^2 = 2x\left(2x^2 + 9xy + 10y^2\right)$
$$= 2x(2x + 5y)(x + 2y)$$

100. $6x^2 + 5xy - 21y^2 = (2x - 3y)(3x + 7y)$

101. $16x^4 - 8x^3 - 3x^2 = x^2(16x^2 - 8x - 3)$
$$= x^2(4x + 1)(4x - 3)$$

102. $a^4 - 1 = (a^2)^2 - 1^2$
$$= (a^2 + 1)(a^2 - 1)$$
$$= (a^2 + 1)(a + 1)(a - 1)$$

103. $x(x - 5) = 0$
$x = 0$ or $x - 5 = 0$
$x = 5$

104. $(a - 2)(a + 6) = 0$
$a - 2 = 0$ or $a + 6 = 0$
$a = 2$ $a = -6$

105. $(x + 5)(4x - 3) = 0$
$x + 5 = 0$ or $4x - 3 = 0$
$x = -5$ $4x = 3$
$x = \dfrac{3}{4}$

106. $x^2 - 3x = 0$
$x(x - 3) = 0$
$x = 0$ or $x - 3 = 0$
$x = 3$

107. $5x^2 + 20x = 0$
$5x(x + 4) = 0$
$x = 0$ or $x + 4 = 0$
$x = -4$

108. $6x^2 + 18x = 0$
$6x(x + 3) = 0$
$x = 0$ or $x + 3 = 0$
$x = -3$

109. $r^2 + 9r + 18 = 0$
$(r + 3)(r + 6) = 0$
$r + 3 = 0$ or $r + 6 = 0$
$r = -3$ $r = -6$

110. $x^2 - 12 = -x$
$x^2 + x - 12 = 0$
$(x + 4)(x - 3) = 0$
$x + 4 = 0$ or $x - 3 = 0$
$x = -4$ $x = 3$

111. $x^2 - 3x = -2$
$x^2 - 3x + 2 = 0$
$(x - 1)(x - 2) = 0$
$x - 1 = 0$ or $x - 2 = 0$
$x = 1$ $x = 2$

112. $15x + 12 = -3x^2$
$3x^2 + 15x + 12 = 0$
$3(x^2 + 5x + 4) = 0$
$3(x + 1)(x + 4) = 0$
$x + 1 = 0$ or $x + 4 = 0$
$x = -1$ $x = -4$

113. $x^2 - 6x + 8 = 0$
$(x - 4)(x - 2) = 0$
$x - 4 = 0$ or $x - 2 = 0$
$x = 4$ $x = 2$

114. $3p^2 + 6p = 45$
$3p^2 + 6p - 45 = 0$
$3(p^2 + 2p - 15) = 0$
$3(x - 3)(x + 5) = 0$
$x - 3 = 0$ or $x + 5 = 0$
$x = 3$ $x = -5$

115. $8x^2 - 3 = -10x$
$8x^2 + 10x - 3 = 0$
$(4x - 1)(2x + 3) = 0$
$4x - 1 = 0$ or $2x + 3 = 0$
$4x = 1$ $2x = -3$
$x = \dfrac{1}{4}$ $x = -\dfrac{3}{2}$

116. $2x^2 + 15x = 8$
$2x^2 + 15x - 8 = 0$
$(2x - 1)(x + 8) = 0$
$2x - 1 = 0$ or $x + 8 = 0$
$2x = 1$ $x = -8$
$x = \dfrac{1}{2}$

117.
$$4x^2 - 16 = 0$$
$$4\left(x^2 - 4\right) = 0$$
$$4\left(x^2 - 2^2\right) = 0$$
$$4(x + 2)(x - 2) = 0$$
$$x + 2 = 0 \quad \text{or} \quad x - 2 = 0$$
$$x = -2 \qquad x = 2$$

118.
$$49x^2 - 100 = 0$$
$$(7x)^2 - 10^2 = 0$$
$$(7x + 10)(7x - 10) = 0$$
$$7x + 10 = 0 \qquad \text{or} \quad 7x - 10 = 0$$
$$7x = -10 \qquad\qquad 7x = 10$$
$$x = -\frac{10}{7} \qquad\qquad x = \frac{10}{7}$$

119.
$$8x^2 - 14x + 3 = 0$$
$$(2x - 3)(4x - 1) = 0$$
$$2x - 3 = 0 \quad \text{or} \quad 4x - 1 = 0$$
$$2x = 3 \qquad\qquad 4x = 1$$
$$x = \frac{3}{2} \qquad\qquad x = \frac{1}{4}$$

120.
$$-48x = -12x^2 - 45$$
$$12x^2 - 48x + 45 = 0$$
$$3\left(4x^2 - 16x + 15\right) = 0$$
$$3(2x - 3)(2x - 5) = 0$$
$$2x - 3 = 0 \quad \text{or} \quad 2x - 5 = 0$$
$$2x = 3 \qquad\qquad 2x = 5$$
$$x = \frac{3}{2} \qquad\qquad x = \frac{5}{2}$$

121. $a^2 + b^2 = c^2$

122. hypotenuse

123.
$$a^2 + b^2 = c^2$$
$$?^2 + 5^2 = 13^2$$
$$?^2 + 25 = 169$$
$$?^2 = 144$$
$$? = 12$$

124.
$$a^2 + b^2 = c^2$$
$$6^2 + 8^2 = ?^2$$
$$36 + 64 = ?^2$$
$$100 = ?^2$$
$$10 = ?$$

125. Let x be the smaller integer. The larger is $x + 2$.
$$x(x + 2) = 48$$
$$x^2 + 2x = 48$$
$$x^2 + 2x - 48 = 0$$
$$(x + 8)(x - 6) = 0$$
$$x + 8 = 0 \quad \text{or} \quad x - 6 = 0$$
$$x = -8 \qquad\qquad x = 6$$
Since the integers must be positive, they are 6 and 8.

126. Let x be the smaller integer. Then the larger is $2x + 6$.
$$x(2x + 6) = 56$$
$$2x^2 + 6x = 56$$
$$2x^2 + 6x - 56 = 0$$
$$2\left(x^2 + 3x - 28\right) = 0$$
$$(x + 7)(x - 4) = 0$$
$$x + 7 = 0 \quad \text{or} \quad x - 4 = 0$$
$$x = -7 \qquad\qquad x = 4$$
Since the integers must be positive, they are 4 and 14.

127. Let w be the width of the rectangle. Then the length is $w + 2$.
$$w(w + 2) = 63$$
$$w^2 + 2w = 63$$
$$w^2 + 2w - 63 = 0$$
$$(w + 9)(w - 7) = 0$$
$$w + 9 = 0 \quad \text{or} \quad w - 7 = 0$$
$$w = -9 \qquad\qquad w = 7$$
Since the width must be positive, it is 7 feet, and the length is 9 feet.

128. Let x be the length of a side of the original square. Then $x - 4$ is the length of a side of the smaller square.
$$(x - 4)^2 = 25$$
$$x^2 - 8x + 16 = 25$$
$$x^2 - 8x + 16 - 25 = 0$$
$$x^2 - 8x - 9 = 0$$
$$(x - 9)(x + 1) = 0$$
$$x - 9 = 0 \quad \text{or} \quad x + 1 = 0$$
$$x = 9 \qquad\qquad x = -1$$
Since lengths must be positive, the length of a side of the original square is 9 inches.

129. Let x be the length of one leg of the triangle. Then $x + 7$ is the length of the other leg and $x + 9$ is the length of the hypotenuse.

$$a^2 + b^2 = c^2$$
$$x^2 + (x + 7)^2 = (x + 9)^2$$
$$x^2 + x^2 + 14x + 49 = x^2 + 18x + 81$$
$$2x^2 + 14x + 49 = x^2 + 18x + 81$$
$$x^2 - 4x - 32 = 0$$
$$(x - 8)(x + 4) = 0$$
$$x - 8 = 0 \quad \text{or} \quad x + 4 = 0$$
$$x = 8 \qquad\qquad x = -4$$

Since lengths must be positive, the lengths of the three sides are 8ft, 15ft, and 17ft.

130. Let w be the width of the pool. Then the length is $w + 2$ and the diagonal is $w + 4$.

$$a^2 + b^2 = c^2$$
$$w^2 + (w + 2)^2 = (w + 4)^2$$
$$w^2 + w^2 + 4x + 4 = w^2 + 8x + 16$$
$$2w^2 + 4x + 4 = w^2 + 8x + 16$$
$$w^2 - 4w - 12 = 0$$
$$(w - 6)(w + 2) = 0$$
$$w - 6 = 0 \quad \text{or} \quad w + 2 = 0$$
$$w = 6 \qquad\qquad w = -2$$

Since lengths must be positive, the diagonal is $w + 4 = 6 + 4 = 10$ ft.

131. $d = 16t^2$
$$16 = 16t^2$$
$$1 = t^2$$
$$1 = t$$

It will take 1 second for the apple to hit the ground.

132. $C = x^2 - 79x + 20$
$$100 = x^2 - 79x + 20$$
$$0 = x^2 - 79x - 80$$
$$0 = (x - 80)(x + 1)$$
$$x - 80 = 0 \quad \text{or} \quad x + 1 = 0$$
$$x = 80 \qquad\qquad x = -1$$

Since only a positive number of dozens of cookies can be made, the association can make 80 dozen cookies.

Practice Test

1. The greatest common factor is $3y^3$.

2. The greatest common factor is $3xy^2$.

3. $5x^2y^3 - 15x^5y^2 = 5x^2y^2\left(y - 3x^3\right)$

4. $8a^3b - 12a^2b^2 + 28a^2b = 4a^2b(2a - 3b + 7)$

5. $5x^2 - 15x + 2x - 6 = 5x(x - 3) + 2(x - 3)$
$$= (x - 3)(5x + 2)$$

6. $a^2 - 4ab - 5ab + 20b^2 = a(a - 4b) - 5b(a - 4b)$
$$= (a - 4b)(a - 5b)$$

7. $r^2 + 5r - 24 = (r + 8)(r - 3)$

8. $25a^2 - 5ab - 6b^2 = (5a - 3b)(5a + 2b)$

9. $4x^2 - 16x - 48 = 4\left(x^2 - 4x - 12\right)$
$$= 4(x + 2)(x - 6)$$

10. $2x^3 - 3x^2 + x = x\left(2x^2 - 3x + 1\right)$
$$= x(2x - 1)(x - 1)$$

11. $12x^2 - xy - 6y^2 = (3x + 2y)(4x - 3y)$

12. $x^2 - 9y^2 = x^2 - (3y)^2$
$$= (x + 3y)(x - 3y)$$

13. $x^3 + 27 = x^3 + 3^3$
$$= (x + 3)\left(x^2 - 3x + 9\right)$$

14. $(5x - 3)(x - 1) = 0$
$$5x - 3 = 0 \quad \text{or} \quad x - 1 = 0$$
$$5x = 3 \qquad\qquad x = 1$$
$$x = \frac{3}{5}$$

15. $x^2 - 6x = 0$
$$x(x - 6) = 0$$
$$x = 0 \quad \text{or} \quad x - 6 = 0$$
$$x = 6$$

16.
$$x^2 = 64$$
$$x^2 - 64 = 0$$
$$x^2 - 8^2 = 0$$
$$(x + 8)(x - 8) = 0$$
$$x + 8 = 0 \quad \text{or} \quad x - 8 = 0$$
$$x = -8 \qquad x = 8$$

17.
$$x^2 - 14x + 49 = 0$$
$$(x - 7)^2 = 0$$
$$x - 7 = 0$$
$$x = 7$$

18.
$$x^2 + 6 = -5x$$
$$x^2 + 5x + 6 = 0$$
$$(x + 2)(x + 3) = 0$$
$$x - 2 = 0 \quad \text{or} \quad x + 3 = 0$$
$$x = -2 \qquad x = -3$$

19.
$$x^2 - 7x + 12 = 0$$
$$(x - 3)(x - 4) = 0$$
$$x - 3 = 0 \quad \text{or} \quad x - 4 = 0$$
$$x = 3 \qquad x = 4$$

20. Use Pythagorean Theorem.
$$a^2 + b^2 = c^2$$
$$?^2 + 10^2 = 26^2$$
$$?^2 + 100 = 676$$
$$?^2 = 576$$
$$? = 24 \text{ in.}$$

21. Let x be the length of one leg. Then $2x - 2$ is the length of the other leg and $2x + 2$ is the length of the hypotenuse.
$$x^2 + (2x - 2)^2 = (2x + 2)^2$$
$$x^2 + 4x^2 - 8x + 4 = 4x^2 + 8x + 4$$
$$5x^2 - 8x + 4 = 4x^2 + 8x + 4$$
$$x^2 - 16x = 0$$
$$x(x - 16) = 0$$
$$x = 0 \quad \text{or} \quad x - 16 = 0$$
$$x = 16$$

Since length has to be positive, the hypotenuse is $2x + 2 = 2(16) + 2 = 32 + 2 = 34$ ft.

22. Let x be the smaller of the two integers. Then $2x + 1$ is the larger.
$$x(2x + 1) = 36$$
$$2x^2 + x - 36 = 0$$
$$(x - 4)(2x + 9) = 0$$
$$x - 4 = 0 \quad \text{or} \quad 2x + 9 = 0$$
$$x = 4 \qquad 2x = -9$$
$$x = -\frac{9}{2}$$

Since x must be positive and an integer, the smaller integer is 4 and the larger is $2 \cdot 4 + 1 = 9$.

23. Let x be the smaller of the two consecutive odd integers. Then $x + 2$ is the larger.
$$x(x + 2) = 99$$
$$x^2 + 2x - 99 = 0$$
$$(x - 9)(x + 11) = 0$$
$$x - 9 = 0 \quad \text{or} \quad x + 11 = 0$$
$$x = 9 \qquad x = -11$$

Since x must be positive, then the smaller integer is 9 and the larger is 11.

24. Let w be the width of the rectangle. Then the length is $w + 2$.
$$w(w + 2) = 24$$
$$w^2 + 2w = 24$$
$$w^2 + 2w - 24 = 0$$
$$(w + 6)(w - 4) = 0$$
$$w + 6 = 0 \quad \text{or} \quad w - 4 = 0$$
$$w = -6 \qquad w = 4$$

Since the width is positive, it is 4 meters, and the length is 6 meters.

25. $d = 16t^2$

$$1600 = 16t^2$$
$$16t^2 - 1600 = 0$$
$$16\left(t^2 - 100\right) = 0$$
$$16\left(t^2 - 10^2\right) = 0$$
$$16(t + 10)(t - 10) = 0$$
$$t + 10 = 0 \quad \text{or} \quad t - 10 = 0$$
$$t = -10 \qquad\qquad t = 10$$

Since time must be positive, then it would take the object 10 seconds to fall 1600 feet to the ground..

Cumulative Review Test

1. $4 - 5(2x + 4x^2 - 21) = 4 - 5[\,2(-3) + 4(-3)^2 - 21]$

$$= 4 - 5[\,-6 + 4(9) - 21]$$
$$= 4 - 5(-6 + 36 - 21)$$
$$= 4 - 5(9)$$
$$= 4 - 45$$
$$= -41$$

2. $5x^2 - 3y + 7(2 + y^2 - 4x) = 5(3)^2 - 3(-2) + 7[2 + (-2)^2 - 4(3)]$

$$= 5(9) + 6 + 7(2 + 4 - 12)$$
$$= 45 + 6 + 7(-6)$$
$$= 51 - 42$$
$$= 9$$

3. Let $x =$ the cost of the room before tax.
$$x + (.15x) = 103.50$$
$$1.15x = 103.50$$
$$x = 90$$
The hotel room costs $90 before taxes.

4. a. 7 is a natural number

b. $-6,\ -0.2,\ \dfrac{3}{5},\ 7,\ 0,\ -\dfrac{5}{9}$, and 1.34 are rational numbers.

c. $\sqrt{7}$ and $-\sqrt{2}$ are irrational numbers.

d. All of the numbers are real numbers.

5. $|-4|$ is greater than $-|2|$ since $-|2| = -(2) = -2$.

6. $4x - 2 = 4(x - 7) + 2x$
$$4x - 2 = 4x - 28 + 2x$$
$$4x - 2 = 6x - 28$$
$$26 = 2x$$
$$13 = x$$

7. $\dfrac{5}{12} = \dfrac{8}{x}$
$$5x = 8(12)$$
$$5x = 96$$
$$x = \dfrac{96}{5} = 19.2$$

8. $3x - 5 \geq 10(6 - x)$
$$3x - 5 \geq 60 - 10x$$
$$13x \geq 65$$
$$x \geq 5$$

9. $5x - 2y = 6$

$$-2y = -5x + 6$$

$$y = \frac{-5x + 6}{-2}$$

$$y = \frac{5}{2}x - 3$$

10. Let t = the number of hours that Brooke has been skiing. Then Bob has been skiing for $\left(t + \frac{1}{4}\right)$ hours.

	rate	time	distance
Brooke	8 kph	t	$8t$
Bob	4 kph	$t + \frac{1}{4}$	$4\left(t + \frac{1}{4}\right)$

Brooke catches Bob when they have both gone the same distance.

$$8t = 4\left(t + \frac{1}{4}\right)$$

$$8t = 4t + 1$$

$$4t = 1$$

$$t = \frac{1}{4}$$

It will take Brooke $\frac{1}{4}$ hour to catch Bob.

11. Let x be the amount of 10% acid solution needed.

$$0.10x + 0.04(3) = 0.08(x + 3)$$

$$0.10x + 0.12 = 0.08x + 0.24$$

$$0.02x + 0.12 = 0.24$$

$$0.02x = 0.12$$

$$x = 6$$

Six liters of the 10% solution is needed.

12. Let x be the first of two consecutive odd integers. Then the other odd integer is $x + 2$.

$$x + x + 2 = 96$$

$$2x + 2 = 96$$

$$2x = 94$$

$$x = 47$$

The two integers are 47 and 49.

13. $\left(\dfrac{3x}{5y^2}\right)^3 = \dfrac{3^3 x^3}{5^3 y^{2 \cdot 3}} = \dfrac{27x^3}{125 y^6}$

14. $(2x^{-3})^{-2}(4x^{-3}y^2)^3 = 2^{-2}x^{-3(-2)}4^3 x^{-3(3)}y^{2(3)}$

$$= 2^{-2}x^6 4^3 x^{-9} y^6$$

$$= 2^{-2} \cdot 4^3 x^{-3} y^6$$

$$= \frac{4^3 y^6}{2^2 x^3}$$

$$= \frac{64 y^6}{4x^3}$$

$$= \frac{16 y^6}{x^3}$$

15. $(x^3 - x^2 + 6x - 5) - (4x^3 - 3x^2 + 7)$

$$= x^3 - x^2 + 6x - 5 - 4x^3 + 3x^2 - 7$$

$$= x^3 - 4x^3 - x^2 + 3x^2 + 6x - 5 - 7$$

$$= -3x^3 + 2x^2 + 6x - 12$$

16. $(3x - 2)(x^2 + 5x - 6)$

$$= 3x(x^2) - 2(x^2) + 3x(5x) - 2(5x) + 3x(-6) - 2(-6)$$

$$= 3x^3 - 2x^2 + 15x^2 - 10x - 18x + 12$$

$$= 3x^3 + 13x^2 - 28x + 12$$

17.
$$\begin{array}{r} x - 5 \\ x+3 \overline{)\, x^2 - 2x + 6} \\ \underline{x^2 + 3x} \\ -5x + 6 \\ \underline{-5x - 15} \\ 21 \end{array}$$

$$\frac{x^2 - 2x + 6}{x + 3} = x - 5 + \frac{21}{x + 3}$$

18. $ab + 3b - 6a - 18 = b(a + 3) - 6(a + 3)$

$$= (a + 3)(b - 6)$$

19. $x^2 - 2x - 63 = (x - 9)(x + 7)$

20. $5x^3 - 125x = 5x(x^2 - 25)$

$$= 5x(x^2 - 5^2)$$

$$= 5x(x + 5)(x - 5)$$

Chapter 6

Exercise Set 6.1

1. Answers will vary.

3. The value of the variable does not make the denominator equal to 0.

5. There is no factor common to both the numerator and denominator of $\dfrac{2+3x}{4}$.

7. The denominator cannot be 0.

9. $x - 2 = 0$
$x \neq 2$

11. $-\dfrac{x+5}{5-x} = \dfrac{x+5}{-(5-x)}$
$= \dfrac{x+5}{-5+x}$
$= \dfrac{x+5}{x-5}$

$\dfrac{x+5}{x-5} \quad -1$
No

13. The expression is defined for all real numbers except $x = 0$.

15. $4n - 12 = 0$
$4n = 12$
$n = 3$
The expression is defined for all real numbers except $n = 3$.

17. $x^2 - 4 = 0$
$(x-2)(x+2) = 0$
The expression is defined for all real numbers except $x = 2$, $x = -2$.

19. $2x^2 - 9x + 9 = 0$
$(2x-3)(x-3) = 0$
The expression is defined for all real numbers except $x = \dfrac{3}{2}$, $x = 3$.

21. All real numbers because $x^2 + 16 \neq 0$.

23. $4p^2 - 25 = 0$
$4p^2 = 25$
$p^2 = \dfrac{25}{4}$
$p = \pm\dfrac{5}{2}$
The expression is defined for all real numbers except $p = \pm\dfrac{5}{2}$.

25. $\dfrac{7x^3y}{21x^2y^5} = \dfrac{7}{21} \cdot x^{3-2} \cdot y^{1-5}$
$= \dfrac{1}{3}xy^{-4}$
$= \dfrac{x}{3y^4}$

27. $\dfrac{\left(2a^4b^5\right)^3}{2a^{12}b^{20}} = \dfrac{2^3 \cdot a^{4(3)} \cdot b^{5(3)}}{2a^{12}b^{20}}$
$= \dfrac{8a^{12}b^{15}}{2a^{12}b^{20}}$
$= 4a^{12-12}b^{15-20}$
$= 4a^0b^{-5}$
$= \dfrac{4}{b^5}$

29. $\dfrac{x}{x+xy} = \dfrac{x}{x(1+y)}$
$= \dfrac{1}{1+y}$

31. $\dfrac{5x+15}{x+3} = \dfrac{5(x+3)}{x+3}$
$= 5$

33. $\dfrac{x^3+6x^2+3x}{2x} = \dfrac{x\left(x^2+6x+3\right)}{2x}$
$= \dfrac{x^2+6x+3}{2}$

35. $\dfrac{r^2-r-2}{r+1} = \dfrac{(r-2)(r+1)}{r+1}$
$= r-2$

160

37. $\dfrac{x^2+2x}{x^2+4x+4}=\dfrac{x(x+2)}{(x+2)^2}$

$\qquad\qquad =\dfrac{x}{x+2}$

39. $\dfrac{k^2-6k+9}{k^2-9}=\dfrac{(k-3)(k-3)}{(k-3)(k+3)}$

$\qquad\qquad =\dfrac{k-3}{k+3}$

41. $\dfrac{x^2-2x-3}{x^2-x-6}=\dfrac{(x+1)(x-3)}{(x+2)(x-3)}$

$\qquad\qquad =\dfrac{x+1}{x+2}$

43. $\dfrac{2x-3}{3-2x}=\dfrac{2x-3}{-(2x-3)}$

$\qquad\qquad =-1$

45. $\dfrac{x^2-2x-8}{4-x}=\dfrac{(x-4)(x+2)}{-(x-4)}$

$\qquad\qquad =-(x+2)$

47. $\dfrac{x^2+3x-18}{-2x^2+6x}=\dfrac{(x+6)(x-3)}{-2x(x-3)}$

$\qquad\qquad =-\dfrac{x+6}{2x}$

49. $\dfrac{2x^2+5x-3}{1-2x}=\dfrac{(2x-1)(x+3)}{-(2x-1)}$

$\qquad\qquad =-(x+3)$

51. $\dfrac{m-2}{4m^2-13m+10}=\dfrac{m-2}{(4m-5)(m-2)}=\dfrac{1}{4m-5}$

53. $\dfrac{x^2-25}{(x+5)^2}=\dfrac{(x-5)(x+5)}{(x+5)^2}$

$\qquad\qquad =\dfrac{x-5}{x+5}$

55. $\dfrac{6x^2-13x+6}{3x-2}=\dfrac{(3x-2)(2x-3)}{3x-2}$

$\qquad\qquad =2x-3$

57. $\dfrac{x^2-3x+4x-12}{x-3}=\dfrac{x(x-3)+4(x-3)}{x-3}$

$\qquad\qquad =\dfrac{(x+4)(x-3)}{x-3}$

$\qquad\qquad =x+4$

59. $\dfrac{2x^2-8x+3x-12}{2x^2+8x+3x+12}=\dfrac{2x(x-4)+3(x-4)}{2x(x+4)+3(x+4)}$

$\qquad\qquad =\dfrac{(x-4)(2x+3)}{(x+4)(2x+3)}$

$\qquad\qquad =\dfrac{x-4}{x+4}$

61. $\dfrac{a^3-8}{a-2}=\dfrac{(a-2)(a^2+2a+4)}{a-2}$

$\qquad\qquad =a^2+2a+4$

63. $\dfrac{9s^2-16t^2}{3s-4t}=\dfrac{(3s+4t)(3s-4t)}{3s-4t}=3s+4t$

65. $\dfrac{4x+6y}{2x^2+xy-3y^2}=\dfrac{2(2x+3y)}{(2x+3y)(x-y)}=\dfrac{2}{x-y}$

67. $\dfrac{3\odot}{12}=\dfrac{3\odot}{3\cdot4}=\dfrac{\odot}{4}$

69. $\dfrac{7\Delta}{14\Delta+21}=\dfrac{7\Delta}{7(2\Delta+3)}=\dfrac{\Delta}{2\Delta+3}$

71. $\dfrac{3\Delta-2}{2-3\Delta}=\dfrac{-(2-3\Delta)}{(2-3\Delta)}=-1$

73. $x^2-x-6=(x-3)(x+2)$
Denominator $=x+2$

75. $(x+3)(x+4)=x^2+7x+12$
Numerator $=x^2+7x+12$

77. a. $\dfrac{x+3}{x^2-2x+3x-6}=\dfrac{x+3}{x(x-2)+3(x-2)}$

$\qquad\qquad =\dfrac{x+3}{(x+3)(x-2)}$

$\qquad x\neq-3, x\neq2$

b. $\dfrac{x+3}{(x+3)(x-2)}=\dfrac{1}{x-2}$

79. a. $\dfrac{x+5}{2x^3+7x^2-15x} = \dfrac{x+5}{x\left(2x^2+7x-15\right)}$

$$= \dfrac{x+5}{x(2x-3)(x+5)}$$

$$x \neq 0,\ x \neq \dfrac{3}{2},\ x \neq -5$$

b. $\dfrac{x+5}{x(2x-3)(x+5)} = \dfrac{1}{x(2x-3)}$

81. $\dfrac{\frac{1}{5}x^5-\frac{2}{3}x^4}{\frac{1}{5}x^5-\frac{2}{3}x^4} = 1$

84. $\quad z = \dfrac{x-y}{2}$

$$2z = x-y$$

$$2z - x = -y$$

$$y = x - 2z$$

85. Let x = measure of the smallest angle. Then the second angle = $x + 30$ and third angle = $3x + 10$.
angle 1 + angle 2 + angle 3 = $180°$
$$x + (x+30) + (3x+10) = 180$$
$$5x + 40 = 180$$
$$5x = 140$$
$$x = 28$$
$$x + 30 = 28 + 30 = 58$$
$3x + 10 = 3(28) + 10 = 84 + 10 = 94$. The three angles are $28°$, $58°$, and $94°$.

86. $\left(\dfrac{4x^2y^2}{9x^4y^3}\right)^2 = \left(\dfrac{4}{9x^2y}\right)^2$

$$= \dfrac{16}{81x^4y^2}$$

87. $3x^2 - 4x - 8 - \left(-3x^2 + 6x + 9\right)$

$$= 3x^2 - 4x - 8 + 3x^2 - 6x - 9$$

$$= 6x^2 - 10x - 17$$

88. $3a^2 - 30a + 72 = 3(a^2 - 10a + 24)$

$$= 3(a-4)(a-6)$$

89. $a^2 + b^2 = c^2$

$$5^2 + 12^2 = c^2$$

$$25 + 144 = c^2$$

$$169 = c^2$$

$$\sqrt{169} = \sqrt{c^2}$$

$$13 = c$$

The hypotenuse is 13 inches long.

Exercise Set 6.2

1. Answers will vary.

3. $\dfrac{x+3}{x-4} \cdot \dfrac{\Box}{x+3} = x+2$

Numerator must be $(x+2)(x-4) = x^2 - 2x - 8$

5. $\dfrac{x-4}{x+5} \cdot \dfrac{x+5}{\Box} = \dfrac{1}{x+3}$

Denominator must be
$(x+3)(x-4) = x^2 - x - 12$

7. $\dfrac{5x}{4y} \cdot \dfrac{y^2}{10} = \dfrac{5x}{4y} \cdot \dfrac{y^2}{5 \cdot 2}$

$$= \dfrac{xy}{8}$$

9. $\dfrac{16x^2}{y^4} \cdot \dfrac{5x^2}{y^2} = \dfrac{80x^4}{y^6}$

11. $\dfrac{6x^5y^3}{5z^3} \cdot \dfrac{6x^4}{5yz^4} = \dfrac{36x^9y^2}{25z^7}$

13. $\dfrac{3x-2}{3x+2} \cdot \dfrac{4x-1}{1-4x} = \dfrac{3x-2}{3x+2} \cdot \dfrac{4x-1}{-(4x-1)}$

$$= \dfrac{-3x+2}{3x+2}$$

15. $\dfrac{x^2 + 7x + 12}{x + 4} \cdot \dfrac{1}{x + 3} = \dfrac{(x+4)(x+3)}{(x+4)(x+3)}$

$\qquad\qquad\qquad\qquad = 1$

17. $\dfrac{a}{a^2 - b^2} \cdot \dfrac{a + b}{a^2 + ab} = \dfrac{a(a+b)}{(a+b)(a-b) \cdot a(a+b)}$

$\qquad\qquad\qquad\quad = \dfrac{1}{(a-b)(a+b)}$

$\qquad\qquad\qquad\quad = \dfrac{1}{a^2 - b^2}$

19. $\dfrac{6x^2 - 14x - 12}{6x + 4} \cdot \dfrac{x + 3}{2x^2 - 2x - 12} = \dfrac{2(3x^2 - 7x - 6)}{2(3x + 2)} \cdot \dfrac{x + 3}{2(x^2 - x - 6)}$

$\qquad\qquad\qquad\qquad\qquad\qquad = \dfrac{2(3x + 2)(x - 3)(x + 3)}{2(3x + 2) \cdot 2(x - 3)(x + 2)}$

$\qquad\qquad\qquad\qquad\qquad\qquad = \dfrac{x + 3}{2(x + 2)}$

21. $\dfrac{3x^2 - 13x - 10}{x^2 - 2x - 15} \cdot \dfrac{x^2 + x - 2}{3x^2 - x - 2} = \dfrac{(3x + 2)(x - 5)}{(x + 3)(x - 5)} \cdot \dfrac{(x + 2)(x - 1)}{(3x + 2)(x - 1)}$

$\qquad\qquad\qquad\qquad\qquad\qquad = \dfrac{x + 2}{x + 3}$

23. $\dfrac{x + 3}{x - 3} \cdot \dfrac{x^3 - 27}{x^2 + 3x + 9} = \dfrac{(x + 3)(x - 3)(x^2 + 3x + 9)}{(x - 3)(x^2 + 3x + 9)}$

$\qquad\qquad\qquad\qquad = x + 3$

25. $\dfrac{9x^3}{y^2} \div \dfrac{3x}{y^3} = \dfrac{9x^3}{y^2} \cdot \dfrac{y^3}{3x}$

$\qquad\qquad\quad = \dfrac{3 \cdot 3x^3}{y^2} \cdot \dfrac{y^3}{3x}$

$\qquad\qquad\quad = 3x^2 y$

27. $\dfrac{15xy^2}{4z} \div \dfrac{5x^2 y^2}{12z^2} = \dfrac{3 \cdot 5xy^2}{4z} \cdot \dfrac{12z^2}{5x^2 y^2}$

$\qquad\qquad\qquad\quad = \dfrac{3 \cdot 5xy^2}{4z} \cdot \dfrac{3 \cdot 4z^2}{5x^2 y^2}$

$\qquad\qquad\qquad\quad = \dfrac{9z}{x}$

29. $\dfrac{5xy}{7ab^2} \div \dfrac{6xy}{7} = \dfrac{5xy}{7ab^2} \cdot \dfrac{7}{6xy}$

$\qquad\qquad\qquad\ = \dfrac{5}{6ab^2}$

31. $\dfrac{10r + 5}{r} \div \dfrac{2r + 1}{r^2} = \dfrac{5(2r + 1)}{r} \cdot \dfrac{r^2}{2r + 1}$

$\qquad\qquad\qquad\ = 5r$

33. $\dfrac{x^2 + 5x - 14}{x} \div \dfrac{x - 2}{x} = \dfrac{(x - 2)(x + 7)}{x} \cdot \dfrac{x}{(x - 2)}$

$\qquad\qquad\qquad\qquad = x + 7$

35. $\dfrac{x^2-12x+32}{x^2-6x-16} \div \dfrac{x^2-x-12}{x^2-5x-24} = \dfrac{x^2-12x+32}{x^2-6x-16} \cdot \dfrac{x^2-5x-24}{x^2-x-12}$

$\qquad\qquad = \dfrac{(x-8)(x-4)}{(x-8)(x+2)} \cdot \dfrac{(x-8)(x+3)}{(x-4)(x+3)}$

$\qquad\qquad = \dfrac{x-8}{x+2}$

37. $\dfrac{2x^2+9x+4}{x^2+7x+12} \div \dfrac{2x^2-x-1}{(x+3)^2} = \dfrac{(2x+1)(x+4)}{(x+3)(x+4)} \cdot \dfrac{(x+3)^2}{(2x+1)(x-1)}$

$\qquad\qquad = \dfrac{x+3}{x-1}$

39. $\dfrac{x^2-y^2}{x^2-2xy+y^2} \div \dfrac{x+y}{y-x} = \dfrac{(x-y)(x+y)}{(x-y)^2} \cdot \dfrac{-(x-y)}{x+y}$

$\qquad\qquad = -1$

41. $\dfrac{5x^2-4x-1}{5x^2+6x+1} \div \dfrac{x^2-5x+4}{x^2+2x+1} = \dfrac{(5x+1)(x-1)}{(5x+1)(x+1)} \cdot \dfrac{(x+1)(x+1)}{(x-4)(x-1)}$

$\qquad\qquad = \dfrac{x+1}{x-4}$

43. $\dfrac{9x}{6y^2} \cdot \dfrac{24x^2y^4}{9x} = 4x^2y^2$

45. $\dfrac{63a^2b^3}{16c^3} \cdot \dfrac{4c^4}{9a^3b^5} = \dfrac{4\cdot7\cdot9a^2b^3c^4}{9\cdot4\cdot4a^3b^5c^3} = \dfrac{7c}{4ab^2}$

47. $\dfrac{-xy}{a} \div \dfrac{-2ax}{6y} = \dfrac{-xy}{a} \cdot \dfrac{6y}{-2ax}$

$\qquad\qquad = \dfrac{3y^2}{a^2}$

49. $\dfrac{100m^6}{21x^5y^7} \cdot \dfrac{14x^{12}y^5}{25m^5} = \dfrac{5\cdot5\cdot4m^6}{3\cdot7x^5y^7} \cdot \dfrac{2\cdot7x^{12}y^5}{5\cdot5m^5}$

$\qquad\qquad = \dfrac{8mx^7}{3y^2}$

51. $(3x+5) \cdot \dfrac{1}{6x+10} = (3x+5) \cdot \dfrac{1}{2(3x+5)}$

$\qquad\qquad = \dfrac{1}{2}$

53. $\dfrac{1}{4x^2y^2} \div \dfrac{1}{28x^3y} = \dfrac{1}{4x^2y^2} \cdot \dfrac{4\cdot7x^3y}{1}$

$\qquad\qquad = \dfrac{7x}{y}$

55. $\dfrac{(4m)^2}{8n^3} \div \dfrac{m^6n^8}{4} = \dfrac{16m^2}{8n^3} \cdot \dfrac{4}{m^6n^8}$

$\qquad\qquad = \dfrac{8\cdot2m^2}{8n^3} \cdot \dfrac{4}{m^6n^8}$

$\qquad\qquad = \dfrac{8}{m^4n^{11}}$

57. $\dfrac{r^2+5r+6}{r^2+9r+18} \cdot \dfrac{r^2+4r-12}{r^2-5r+6} = \dfrac{(r+2)(r+3)}{(r+6)(r+3)} \cdot \dfrac{(r+6)(r-2)}{(r-3)(r-2)} = \dfrac{r+2}{r-3}$

59. $\dfrac{x^2-10x+24}{x^2-8x+12} \div \dfrac{x^2-7x+12}{x^2-6x+8} = \dfrac{x^2-10x+24}{x^2-8x+12} \cdot \dfrac{x^2-6x+8}{x^2-7x+12}$

$\qquad\qquad\qquad = \dfrac{(x-6)(x-4)}{(x-6)(x-2)} \cdot \dfrac{(x-4)(x-2)}{(x-4)(x-3)}$

$\qquad\qquad\qquad = \dfrac{x-4}{x-3}$

61. $\dfrac{3z^2-4z-4}{z^2-4} \cdot \dfrac{2z^2+5z+2}{2z^2-3z-2} = \dfrac{(3z+2)(z-2)}{(z+2)(z-2)} \cdot \dfrac{(2z+1)(z+2)}{(2z+1)(z-2)} = \dfrac{3z+2}{z-2}$

63. $\dfrac{2x^2-19x+24}{x^2-12x+32} \div \dfrac{2x^2+x-6}{x^2+7x+10} = \dfrac{2x^2-19x+24}{x^2-12x+32} \cdot \dfrac{x^2+7x+10}{2x^2+x-6} = \dfrac{(2x-3)(x-8)}{(x-4)(x-8)} \cdot \dfrac{(x+5)(x+2)}{(2x-3)(x+2)} = \dfrac{x+5}{x-4}$

65. $\dfrac{4n^2-9}{9n^2-1} \cdot \dfrac{3n^2-2n-1}{2n^2-5n+3} = \dfrac{(2n+3)(2n-3)}{(3n+1)(3n-1)} \cdot \dfrac{(3n+1)(n-1)}{(2n-3)(n-1)} = \dfrac{2n+3}{3n-1}$

67. $\dfrac{6\Delta^2}{12} \cdot \dfrac{12}{36\Delta^5} = \dfrac{6\Delta^2}{12} \cdot \dfrac{12}{6\cdot 6\Delta^5} = \dfrac{1}{6\Delta^3}$

71. $(x+2)(x+1) = x^2+x+2x+2$

$\qquad\qquad\qquad = x^2+3x+2$

Numerator is x^2+3x+2.

73. $(x-5)(x+2) = x^2+2x-5x-10$

$\qquad\qquad\qquad = x^2-3x-10$

Numerator is $x^2-3x-10$.

75. $(x^2-4)(x-1) \div (x+2)$

$(x-2)(x+2)(x-1)\cdot \dfrac{1}{x+2} = x^2-x-2x+2$

$\qquad\qquad\qquad\qquad = x^2-3x+2$

Numerator is x^2-3x+2.

77. $\left(\dfrac{x+2}{x^2-4x-12} \cdot \dfrac{x^2-9x+18}{x-2} \right) \div \dfrac{x^2+5x+6}{x^2-4} = \dfrac{x+2}{(x-6)(x+2)} \cdot \dfrac{(x-3)(x-6)}{x-2} \cdot \dfrac{(x+2)(x-2)}{(x+2)(x+3)}$

$\qquad\qquad\qquad\qquad\qquad\qquad = \dfrac{x-3}{x+3}$

79. $\left(\dfrac{x^2+4x+3}{x^2-6x-16} \right) \div \left(\dfrac{x^2+5x+6}{x^2-9x+8} \cdot \dfrac{x^2-1}{x^2+4x+4} \right) = \dfrac{x^2+4x+3^2}{x^2-6x-16} \cdot \dfrac{x^2-9x+8}{x^2+5x+6} \cdot \dfrac{x^2+4x+4}{x^2-1}$

$\qquad\qquad\qquad\qquad\qquad\qquad = \dfrac{(x+1)(x+3)}{(x-8)(x+2)} \cdot \dfrac{(x-8)(x-1)}{(x+2)(x+3)} \cdot \dfrac{(x+2)^2}{(x-1)(x+1)}$

$\qquad\qquad\qquad\qquad\qquad\qquad = 1$

81. $\dfrac{(x-3)(x-2)}{(x+4)(x-5)} \cdot \dfrac{(x+4)(x-1)}{(x-3)(x-1)} = \dfrac{x-2}{x-5}$

The numerator is $(x-3)(x-2) = x^2 - 5x + 6$.

The denominator is $(x+4)(x-5) = x^2 - x - 20$.

84. Let $x =$ the time it takes the tug boat to reach the barge.
Then $x + 2 =$ the time it takes the tug boat to return to the dock.

	Rate	Time	Distance
Trip Out	15	x	$15(x)$
Return Trip	5	$x+2$	$5(x+2)$

Distance to barge = Distance back to dock
$15(x) = 5(x+2)$
$15x = 5x + 10$
$10x = 10$
$\;\;\;x = 1$
It took 1 hour for the tug boat to reach the barge.

85. $\left(4x^3y^2z^4\right)\left(5xy^3z^7\right) = 4 \cdot 5 \cdot x^3xy^2y^3z^4z^7$
$\qquad\qquad\qquad = 20x^4y^5z^{11}$

86.

$$2x-1 \overline{\smash{\big)}\,4x^3 + 0x^2 - 5x + 0}$$

$\qquad\qquad\quad 2x^2 + x - 2$

$\qquad\quad \underline{4x^3 - 2x^2}$
$\qquad\qquad\quad 2x^2 - 5x$
$\qquad\qquad\quad \underline{2x^2 - x}$
$\qquad\qquad\qquad\; -4x + 0$
$\qquad\qquad\qquad\; \underline{-4x + 2}$
$\qquad\qquad\qquad\qquad -2$

$\dfrac{4x^3 - 5x}{2x-1} = 2x^2 + x - 2 - \dfrac{2}{2x-1}$

87. $3x^2 - 9x - 30 = 3\left(x^2 - 3x - 10\right)$
$\qquad\qquad\qquad = 3(x-5)(x+2)$

88. $3x^2 - 9x - 30 = 0$
$\quad 3\left(x^2 - 3x - 10\right) = 0$
$\quad 3(x-5)(x+2) = 0$
$\quad x - 5 = 0 \;\;$ or $\;\; x + 2 = 0$
$\qquad x = 5 \qquad\qquad x = -2$

Exercise Set 6.3

1. Answers will vary.

3. Answers will vary.

5. $\dfrac{5}{x+6} - \dfrac{2}{x}$
The only factor (other than 1) of the first denominator is $x + 6$. The only factor (other than 1) of the second denominator is x. The LCD is therefore $x(x+6)$.

7. $\dfrac{2}{x+3} + \dfrac{1}{x} + \dfrac{1}{3}$
The only factor (other than 1) of the first denominator is $x + 3$. The only factor (other than 1) of the second denominator is x. The only factor (other than 1) of the third denominator is 3. The LCD is therefore $3x(x+3)$.

9. a. The negative sign in $-(2x-7)$ was not distributed.

   b. $\dfrac{4x-3}{5x+4} - \dfrac{2x-7}{5x+4} = \dfrac{4x-3-(2x-7)}{5x+4}$
   $\qquad\qquad\qquad\qquad\quad = \dfrac{4x-3-2x+7}{5x+4}$
   $\qquad\qquad\qquad\qquad\qquad\; \dfrac{4x-3-2x-7}{5x+4}$

10. a. The negative sign in $-(-3x-7)$ was not distributed.

b. $\dfrac{5x}{2x-3} - \dfrac{-3x-7}{2x-3} = \dfrac{5x-(-3x-7)}{2x-3}$

$= \dfrac{5x+3x+7}{2x-3}$

$\dfrac{5x+3x-7}{2x-3}$

11. a. The negative sign in $-\left(3x^2-4x+5\right)$ was not distributed.

b. $\dfrac{6x-2}{x^2-4x+3} - \dfrac{3x^2-4x+5}{x^2-4x+3} = \dfrac{6x-2-\left(3x^2-4x+5\right)}{x^2-4x+3}$

$= \dfrac{6x-2-3x^2+4x-5}{x^2-4x+3}$

$\dfrac{6x-2-3x^2-4x+5}{x^2-4x+3}$

13. $\dfrac{x-2}{7} + \dfrac{2x}{7} = \dfrac{x-2+2x}{7}$

$= \dfrac{3x-2}{7}$

15. $\dfrac{3r+2}{4} - \dfrac{3}{4} = \dfrac{3r+2-3}{4}$

$= \dfrac{3r-1}{4}$

17. $\dfrac{2}{x} + \dfrac{x+4}{x} = \dfrac{2+x+4}{x}$

$= \dfrac{x+6}{x}$

19. $\dfrac{n-5}{n} - \dfrac{n+7}{n} = \dfrac{n-5-n-7}{n}$

$= -\dfrac{12}{n}$

21. $\dfrac{x}{x-1} + \dfrac{4x+7}{x-1} = \dfrac{x+4x+7}{x-1}$

$= \dfrac{5x+7}{x-1}$

23. $\dfrac{4t+7}{5t^2} - \dfrac{3t+4}{5t^2} = \dfrac{4t+7-(3t+4)}{5t^2}$

$= \dfrac{4t+7-3t-4}{5t^2}$

$= \dfrac{t+3}{5t^2}$

25. $\dfrac{5x+4}{x^2-x-12} + \dfrac{-4x-1}{x^2-x-12} = \dfrac{5x+4-4x-1}{x^2-x-12}$

$= \dfrac{x+3}{(x+3)(x-4)}$

$= \dfrac{1}{x-4}$

27. $\dfrac{x+4}{3x+2} - \dfrac{x+4}{3x+2} = \dfrac{x+4-(x+4)}{3x+2}$

$= 0$

29. $\dfrac{2p-5}{p-5} - \dfrac{p+5}{p-5} = \dfrac{2p-5-(p+5)}{p-5}$

$= \dfrac{2p-5-p-5}{p-5}$

$= \dfrac{p-10}{p-5}$

31. $\dfrac{x^2+4x+3}{x+2} - \dfrac{5x+9}{x+2} = \dfrac{x^2+4x+3-(5x+9)}{x+2}$

$= \dfrac{x^2+4x+3-5x-9}{x+2}$

$= \dfrac{x^2-x-6}{x+2}$

$= \dfrac{(x-3)(x+2)}{x+2}$

$= x-3$

33. $\dfrac{3x+11}{2x+10} - \dfrac{2(x+3)}{2x+10} = \dfrac{3x+11-2(x+3)}{2x+10}$

$\qquad\qquad\qquad\qquad = \dfrac{3x+11-2x-6}{2x+10}$

$\qquad\qquad\qquad\qquad = \dfrac{x+5}{2(x+5)}$

$\qquad\qquad\qquad\qquad = \dfrac{1}{2}$

35. $\dfrac{b^2-2b-3}{b^2-b-6} + \dfrac{b-3}{b^2-b-6} = \dfrac{b^2-2b-3+b-3}{b^2-b-6}$

$\qquad\qquad\qquad\qquad\qquad = \dfrac{b^2-b-6}{b^2-b-6}$

$\qquad\qquad\qquad\qquad\qquad = 1$

37. $\dfrac{t-3}{t+3} - \dfrac{-3t-15}{t+3} = \dfrac{t-3-(-3t-15)}{t+3}$

$\qquad\qquad\qquad\qquad = \dfrac{t-3+3t+15}{t+3}$

$\qquad\qquad\qquad\qquad = \dfrac{4t+12}{t+3}$

$\qquad\qquad\qquad\qquad = \dfrac{4(t+3)}{t+3}$

$\qquad\qquad\qquad\qquad = 4$

43. $\dfrac{3x^2-4x+4}{3x^2+7x+2} - \dfrac{10x+9}{3x^2+7x+2} = \dfrac{3x^2-4x+4-(10x+9)}{3x^2+7x+2}$

$\qquad\qquad\qquad\qquad\qquad\qquad = \dfrac{3x^2-4x+4-10x-9}{3x^2+7x+2}$

$\qquad\qquad\qquad\qquad\qquad\qquad = \dfrac{3x^2-14x-5}{3x^2+7x+2}$

$\qquad\qquad\qquad\qquad\qquad\qquad = \dfrac{(3x+1)(x-5)}{(3x+1)(x+2)}$

$\qquad\qquad\qquad\qquad\qquad\qquad = \dfrac{x-5}{x+2}$

45. $\dfrac{x^2+3x-6}{x^2-5x+4} - \dfrac{-2x^2+4x-4}{x^2-5x+4} = \dfrac{x^2+3x-6-(-2x^2+4x-4)}{x^2-5x+4}$

$\qquad\qquad\qquad\qquad\qquad\qquad = \dfrac{x^2+3x-6+2x^2-4x+4}{x^2-5x+4}$

$\qquad\qquad\qquad\qquad\qquad\qquad = \dfrac{3x^2-x-2}{x^2-5x+4}$

$\qquad\qquad\qquad\qquad\qquad\qquad = \dfrac{(3x+2)(x-1)}{(x-4)(x-1)}$

$\qquad\qquad\qquad\qquad\qquad\qquad = \dfrac{3x+2}{x-4}$

39. $\dfrac{x^2+2x}{(x+6)(x-3)} - \dfrac{15}{(x+6)(x-3)} = \dfrac{x^2+2x-15}{(x+6)(x-3)}$

$\qquad\qquad\qquad\qquad\qquad\qquad = \dfrac{(x+5)(x-3)}{(x+6)(x-3)}$

$\qquad\qquad\qquad\qquad\qquad\qquad = \dfrac{x+5}{x+6}$

41. $\dfrac{3x^2-7x}{4x^2-8x} + \dfrac{x}{4x^2-8x} = \dfrac{3x^2-7x+x}{4x^2-8x}$

$\qquad\qquad\qquad\qquad\qquad = \dfrac{3x^2-6x}{4x^2-8x}$

$\qquad\qquad\qquad\qquad\qquad = \dfrac{3x(x-2)}{4x(x-2)}$

$\qquad\qquad\qquad\qquad\qquad = \dfrac{3}{4}$

47. $\dfrac{5x^2 + 40x + 8}{x^2 - 64} + \dfrac{x^2 + 9x}{x^2 - 64} = \dfrac{5x^2 + 40x + 8 + x^2 + 9x}{x^2 - 64}$

$$= \dfrac{6x^2 + 49x + 8}{x^2 - 64}$$

$$= \dfrac{(6x + 1)(x + 8)}{(x - 8)(x + 8)}$$

$$= \dfrac{6x + 1}{x - 8}$$

49. $\dfrac{x}{5} + \dfrac{x + 4}{5}$

Least common denominator = 5

51. $\dfrac{1}{n} + \dfrac{1}{5n}$

Least common denominator = $5n$

53. $\dfrac{3}{5x} + \dfrac{7}{4}$

Least common denominator = $5x \cdot 4 = 20x$

55. $\dfrac{6}{p} + \dfrac{3}{p^3}$

Least common denominator = p^3

57. $\dfrac{m + 3}{3m - 4} + m = \dfrac{m + 3}{3m - 4} + \dfrac{m}{1}$

Least common denominator = $3m - 4$

59. $\dfrac{x}{2x + 3} + \dfrac{4}{x^2}$

Least common denominator = $x^2(2x + 3)$

61. $\dfrac{x + 1}{12x^2 y} - \dfrac{7}{9x^3} = \dfrac{x + 1}{3 \cdot 4x^2 y} - \dfrac{7}{3^2 x^3}$

Least common denominator

$= 4 \cdot 3^2 \cdot x^3 \cdot y = 36x^3 y$

63. $\dfrac{4}{2r^4 s^5} - \dfrac{5}{9r^3 s^7} = \dfrac{4}{2r^4 s^5} - \dfrac{5}{3 \cdot 3r^3 s^7}$

Least common denominator =

$2 \cdot 3 \cdot 3r^4 s^7 = 18r^4 s^7$

65. $\dfrac{x^2 - 7}{24x} - \dfrac{x + 3}{9(x + 5)} = \dfrac{x^2 - 7}{3 \cdot 8x} - \dfrac{x + 3}{3^2(x + 5)}$

Least common denominator

$= 8 \cdot 3^2 x(x + 5) = 72x(x + 5)$

67. $\dfrac{5x - 2}{x^2 + x} - \dfrac{x^2}{x} = \dfrac{5x - 2}{x(x + 1)} - \dfrac{x^2}{x}$

Least common denominator = $x(x + 1)$

69. $\dfrac{n}{4n - 1} + \dfrac{n - 2}{1 - 4n} = \dfrac{n}{4n - 1} + \dfrac{(-1)(n - 2)}{(-1)(1 - 4n)}$

$$= \dfrac{n}{4n - 1} + \dfrac{-n + 2}{4n - 1}$$

Least common denominator = $4n - 1$

71. $\dfrac{6}{4k - 5r} - \dfrac{5}{-4k + 5r} = \dfrac{6}{4k - 5r} - \dfrac{(-1)5}{(-1)(-4k + 5r)}$

$$= \dfrac{6}{4k - 5r} - \dfrac{-5}{4k - 5r}$$

Least common denominator = $4k - 5r$

73. $\dfrac{5}{2q^2 + 2q} - \dfrac{5}{3q} = \dfrac{5}{2q(q + 1)} - \dfrac{5}{3q}$

Least common denominator = $2 \cdot 3q(q + 1)$

$$= 6q(q + 1)$$

75. $\dfrac{21}{24x^2 y} + \dfrac{x + 4}{15xy^3} = \dfrac{21}{3 \cdot 8x^2 y} + \dfrac{x + 4}{3 \cdot 5xy^3}$

Least common denominator

$= 8 \cdot 3 \cdot 5x^2 y^3 = 120x^2 y^3$

77. $\dfrac{3}{3x + 12} + \dfrac{3x + 6}{2x + 4} = \dfrac{3}{3(x + 4)} + \dfrac{3x + 6}{2(x + 2)}$

Least common denominator

$= 3 \cdot 2(x + 4)(x + 2) = 6(x + 4)(x + 2)$

79. $\dfrac{9x + 4}{x + 6} - \dfrac{3x - 6}{x + 5}$

Least common denominator = $(x + 6)(x + 5)$

81. $\dfrac{x-2}{x^2-5x-24}+\dfrac{3}{x^2+11x+24}$

$=\dfrac{x-2}{(x-8)(x+3)}+\dfrac{3}{(x+8)(x+3)}$

Least common denominator
$=(x-8)(x+3)(x+8)$

83. $\dfrac{7}{(a-4)^2}-\dfrac{a+2}{a^2-7a+12}$

$=\dfrac{7}{(a-4)^2}-\dfrac{a+2}{(a-4)(a-3)}$

Least common denominator
$=(a-4)^2(a-3)$

85. $\dfrac{2x}{x^2+6x+5}-\dfrac{5x^2}{x^2+4x+3}$

$=\dfrac{2x}{(x+5)(x+1)}-\dfrac{5x^2}{(x+3)(x+1)}$

Least common denominator
$=(x+5)(x+1)(x+3)$

87. $\dfrac{3x-5}{x^2-6x+9}+\dfrac{3}{x-3}$

$=\dfrac{3x+5}{(x-3)^2}+\dfrac{3}{x-3}$

Least common denominator $=(x-3)^2$

89. $\dfrac{8x^2}{x^2-7x+6}+x-3$

$=\dfrac{8x^2}{(x-6)(x-1)}+\dfrac{x-3}{1}$

Least common denominator $=(x-6)(x-1)$

91. $\dfrac{t-1}{3t^2+10t-8}-\dfrac{6}{3t^2+11t-4}$

$=\dfrac{t-1}{(3t-2)(t+4)}-\dfrac{6}{(3t-1)(t+4)}$

Least common denominator
$=(3t-2)(t+4)(3t-1)$

93. $\dfrac{2x-3}{4x^2+4x+1}+\dfrac{x^2-4}{8x^2+10x+3}$

$=\dfrac{2x-3}{(2x+1)^2}+\dfrac{x^2-4}{(2x+1)(4x+3)}$

Least common denominator
$=(2x+1)^2(4x+3)$

95. $x^2-6x+3+\square=2x^2-5x-6$

$\square=2x^2-5x-6-(x^2-6x+3)$

$=2x^2-5x-6-x^2+6x-3$

$=x^2+x-9$

Sum of numerators must be $2x^2-5x-6$

97. $-x^2-4x+3+\square=5x-7$

$\square=5x-7-(-x^2-4x+3)$

$=5x-7+x^2+4x-3$

$=x^2+9x-10$

Sum of numerator must be $5x-7$

98. $-3x^2-9-\square=x^2+3x$

$\square=-3x^2-9-(x^2+3x)$

$=-3x^2-9-x^2-3x$

$=-4x^2-3x-9$

Difference of numerators must be x^2+3x

99. $\dfrac{3}{☺}+\dfrac{4}{5☺}$

Least common denominator $=5☺$

101. $\dfrac{8}{\Delta^2-9}-\dfrac{2}{\Delta+3}=\dfrac{8}{(\Delta+3)(\Delta-3)}-\dfrac{2}{\Delta+3}$

Least common denominator $=(\Delta+3)(\Delta-3)$

103. $\dfrac{4x-1}{x^2-25}-\dfrac{3x^2-8}{x^2-25}+\dfrac{8x-3}{x^2-25}=\dfrac{4x-1-(3x^2-8)+(8x-3)}{x^2-25}$

$=\dfrac{4x-1-3x^2+8+8x-3}{x^2-25}$

$=\dfrac{-3x^2+12x+4}{x^2-25}$

105. $\dfrac{7}{6x^5y^9} - \dfrac{9}{2x^3y} + \dfrac{4}{5x^{12}y^2} = \dfrac{7}{2\cdot 3\cdot x^5y^9} - \dfrac{9}{2x^3y} + \dfrac{4}{5x^{12}y^2}$

Least common denominator $= 2\cdot 3\cdot 5x^{12}y^9 = 30x^{12}y^9$

107. $\dfrac{4}{x^2-x-12} + \dfrac{3}{x^2-6x+8} + \dfrac{5}{x^2+x-6} = \dfrac{4}{(x-4)(x+3)} + \dfrac{3}{(x-4)(x-2)} + \dfrac{5}{(x+3)(x-2)}$

Least common denominator $= (x-4)(x+3)(x-2)$

109. $4\dfrac{3}{5} - 2\dfrac{5}{9} = \dfrac{23}{5} - \dfrac{23}{9}$

$= \dfrac{207}{45} - \dfrac{115}{45}$

$= \dfrac{92}{45}$

$= 2\dfrac{2}{45}$

110. $6x + 4 = -(x+2) - 3x + 4$

$6x + 4 = -x - 2 - 3x + 4$

$6x + 4 = -4x + 2$

$6x + 4x = 2 - 4$

$10x = -2$

$x = \dfrac{-2}{10} = -\dfrac{1}{5}$

111. $\dfrac{6}{128} = \dfrac{x}{48}$

$128x = 6\cdot 48$

$128x = 288$

$x = \dfrac{288}{128}$

$x = \dfrac{9}{4} = 2\dfrac{1}{4}$

You should use 2.25 ounces of concentrate.

112. Let $h =$ the number of hours played.
The cost under Plan 1 is $C = 125 + 2.5h$ while the cost under Plan 2 is $C = 300$.

Set the two costs equal
$125 + 2.5h = 300$

$2.5h = 175$

$h = 70$

If Malcolm plays 70 hours in a year, the cost of the two plans is equal.

113. $\dfrac{4.2\times 10^8}{2.1\times 10^{-3}} = 2.0\times 10^{8-(-3)} = 2.0\times 10^{11}$

114. $2x^2 - 3 = x$

$2x^2 - x - 3 = 0$

$(2x-3)(x+1) = 0$

$2x - 3 = 0$ or $x + 1 = 0$

$2x = 3$ $x = -1$

$x = \dfrac{3}{2}$

Exercise Set 6.4

1. For each fraction, divide the LCD by the denominator.

3. a. Answers will vary.

    b. $\dfrac{x}{x^2-x-6} + \dfrac{3}{x^2-4}$

$= \dfrac{x}{(x-3)(x+2)} + \dfrac{3}{(x-2)(x+2)}$

$= \dfrac{x(x-2)}{(x-3)(x+2)(x-2)} + \dfrac{3(x-3)}{(x-2)(x+2)(x-3)}$

$= \dfrac{x^2 - 2x + 3x - 9}{(x-3)(x+2)(x-2)}$

$= \dfrac{x^2 + x - 9}{(x-3)(x+2)(x-2)}$

5. a. $\dfrac{y}{4z} + \dfrac{5}{6z^2}$

$4z = 2\cdot 2\cdot z$

$6z^2 = 2\cdot 3\cdot z^2$

Least common denominator

$2\cdot 2\cdot 3\cdot z^2 = 12z^2$

    b. $\dfrac{y}{4z} + \dfrac{5}{6z^2} = \dfrac{y}{4z}\cdot\dfrac{3z}{3z} + \dfrac{5}{6z^2}\cdot\dfrac{2}{2}$

$= \dfrac{3yz}{12z^2} + \dfrac{10}{12z^2}$

$= \dfrac{3yz + 10}{12z^2}$

c. Yes. After factoring out the common factors, the reduced form would be the same.

7. $\dfrac{1}{4x} + \dfrac{3}{x} = \dfrac{1}{4x} + \dfrac{3 \cdot 4}{4x}$

$\qquad = \dfrac{1 + 12}{4x}$

$\qquad = \dfrac{13}{4x}$

9. $\dfrac{5}{x^2} + \dfrac{3}{2x} = \dfrac{5 \cdot 2}{2x^2} + \dfrac{3x}{2x^2}$

$\qquad = \dfrac{3x + 10}{2x^2}$

11. $3 + \dfrac{5}{x} = \dfrac{3x}{x} + \dfrac{5}{x} = \dfrac{3x + 5}{x}$

13. $\dfrac{2}{x^2} + \dfrac{3}{5x} = \dfrac{2 \cdot 5}{5x^2} + \dfrac{3x}{5x^2} = \dfrac{3x + 10}{5x^2}$

15. $\dfrac{7}{4x^2 y} + \dfrac{3}{5xy^2} = \dfrac{7 \cdot 5y}{4x^2 y \cdot 5y} + \dfrac{3 \cdot 4x}{5xy^2 \cdot 4x}$

$\qquad = \dfrac{35y}{20x^2 y^2} + \dfrac{12x}{20x^2 y^2}$

$\qquad = \dfrac{35y + 12x}{20x^2 y^2}$

17. $3y + \dfrac{x}{y} = \dfrac{3y \cdot y}{y} + \dfrac{x}{y} = \dfrac{3y^2 + x}{y}$

19. $\dfrac{3a - 1}{2a} + \dfrac{2}{3a} = \dfrac{(3a - 1)3}{2a \cdot 3} + \dfrac{2 \cdot 2}{3a \cdot 2}$

$\qquad = \dfrac{9a - 3 + 4}{6a}$

$\qquad = \dfrac{9a + 1}{6a}$

21. $\dfrac{4x}{y} + \dfrac{2y}{xy} = \dfrac{4x \cdot x}{xy} + \dfrac{2y}{xy}$

$\qquad = \dfrac{4x^2 + 2y}{xy}$

23. $\dfrac{4}{b} - \dfrac{4}{5a^2} = \dfrac{4 \cdot 5a^2}{b \cdot 5a^2} - \dfrac{4 \cdot b}{5a^2 \cdot b}$

$\qquad = \dfrac{20a^2 - 4b}{5a^2 b}$

25. $\dfrac{4}{x} + \dfrac{7}{x - 3} = \dfrac{4 \cdot (x - 3)}{x \cdot (x - 3)} + \dfrac{7 \cdot x}{(x - 3) \cdot x}$

$\qquad = \dfrac{4x - 12 + 7x}{x(x - 3)}$

$\qquad = \dfrac{11x - 12}{x(x - 3)}$

27. $\dfrac{9}{p + 3} + \dfrac{2}{p} = \dfrac{9p}{p(p + 3)} + \dfrac{2(p + 3)}{p(p + 3)}$

$\qquad = \dfrac{9p + 2p + 6}{p(p + 3)}$

$\qquad = \dfrac{11p + 6}{p(p + 3)}$

29. $\dfrac{5}{6d} - \dfrac{d}{3d + 5} = \dfrac{5 \cdot (3d + 5)}{6d \cdot (3d + 5)} - \dfrac{d \cdot (6d)}{(3d + 5) \cdot (6d)}$

$\qquad = \dfrac{15d + 25 - 6d^2}{6d(3d + 5)}$

$\qquad = \dfrac{-6d^2 + 15d + 25}{6d(3d + 5)}$

31. $\dfrac{4}{p - 3} + \dfrac{2}{3 - p} = \dfrac{4}{p - 3} - \dfrac{2}{p - 3}$

$\qquad = \dfrac{2}{p - 3}$

33. $\dfrac{9}{x + 7} - \dfrac{5}{-x - 7} = \dfrac{9}{x + 7} + \dfrac{5}{x + 7}$

$\qquad = \dfrac{14}{x + 7}$

35. $\dfrac{6}{a - 2} + \dfrac{a}{2a - 4} = \dfrac{6 \cdot 2}{(a - 2) \cdot 2} + \dfrac{a}{2(a - 2)}$

$\qquad = \dfrac{a + 12}{2(a - 2)}$

37. $\dfrac{x + 5}{x - 5} - \dfrac{x - 5}{x + 5} = \dfrac{(x + 5)^2}{(x - 5)(x + 5)} - \dfrac{(x - 5)^2}{(x - 5)(x + 5)}$

$\qquad = \dfrac{x^2 + 10x + 25 - (x^2 - 10x + 25)}{(x - 5)(x + 5)}$

$\qquad = \dfrac{x^2 + 10x + 25 - x^2 + 10x - 25}{(x - 5)(x + 5)}$

$\qquad = \dfrac{20x}{(x - 5)(x + 5)}$

39.
$$\frac{5}{6n+3}-\frac{4}{n}=\frac{5}{3(2n+1)}-\frac{4}{n}$$
$$=\frac{5\cdot n}{3(2n+1)\cdot n}-\frac{4\cdot3(2n+1)}{n\cdot3(2n+1)}$$
$$=\frac{5n-24n-12}{3n(2n+1)}$$
$$=\frac{-19n-12}{3n(2n+1)}$$

41.
$$\frac{3}{2w+10}+\frac{5}{w+2}=\frac{3}{2(w+5)}+\frac{5}{w+2}$$
$$=\frac{3\cdot(w+2)}{2(w+5)\cdot(w+2)}+\frac{5\cdot2(w+5)}{(w+2)\cdot2(w+5)}$$
$$=\frac{3w+6+10w+50}{2(w+5)(w+2)}$$
$$=\frac{13w+56}{2(w+5)(w+2)}$$

43.
$$\frac{z}{z^2-16}+\frac{4}{z+4}=\frac{z}{(z+4)(z-4)}+\frac{4\cdot(z-4)}{(z+4)\cdot(z-4)}$$
$$=\frac{z+4z-16}{(z+4)(z-4)}$$
$$=\frac{5z-16}{(z+4)(z-4)}$$

45.
$$\frac{x+2}{x^2-4}-\frac{2}{x+2}=\frac{x+2}{(x+2)(x-2)}-\frac{2(x-2)}{(x+2)(x-2)}$$
$$=\frac{x+2-(2x-4)}{(x+2)(x-2)}$$
$$=\frac{x+2-2x+4}{(x+2)(x-2)}$$
$$=\frac{-x+6}{(x+2)(x-2)}$$

47.
$$\frac{3r+2}{r^2-10r+24}-\frac{2}{r-6}=\frac{3r+2}{(r-6)(r-4)}-\frac{2\cdot(r-4)}{(r-6)\cdot(r-4)}$$
$$=\frac{3r+2-(2r-4)}{(r-6)(r-4)}$$
$$=\frac{3r+2-2r+8}{(r-6)(r-4)}$$
$$=\frac{r+10}{(r-6)(r-4)}$$

49.
$$\frac{x^2}{x^2+2x-8}-\frac{x-4}{x+4}=\frac{x^2}{(x+4)(x-2)}-\frac{(x-4)(x-2)}{(x+4)(x-2)}$$
$$=\frac{x^2-\left(x^2-6x+8\right)}{(x+4)(x-2)}$$
$$=\frac{x^2-x^2+6x-8}{(x+4)(x-2)}$$
$$=\frac{6x-8}{(x+4)(x-2)}$$

51. $\dfrac{x-3}{x^2+10x+25} + \dfrac{x-3}{x+5} = \dfrac{x-3}{(x+5)^2} + \dfrac{(x-3)(x+5)}{(x+5)^2}$

$$= \dfrac{x-3+x^2+2x-15}{(x+5)^2}$$

$$= \dfrac{x^2+3x-18}{(x+5)^2}$$

53. $\dfrac{5}{a^2-9a+8} - \dfrac{3}{a^2-6a-16} = \dfrac{5}{(a-8)(a-1)} - \dfrac{3}{(a-8)(a+2)}$

$$= \dfrac{5(a+2)}{(a-8)(a-1)(a+2)} - \dfrac{3(a-1)}{(a-8)(a-1)(a+2)}$$

$$= \dfrac{5a+10-(3a-3)}{(a-8)(a-1)(a+2)}$$

$$= \dfrac{5a+10-3a+3}{(a-8)(a-1)(a+2)}$$

$$= \dfrac{2a+13}{(a-8)(a-1)(a+2)}$$

55. $\dfrac{2}{x^2+6x+9} + \dfrac{3}{x^2+x-6} = \dfrac{2}{(x+3)(x+3)} + \dfrac{3}{(x+3)(x-2)}$

$$= \dfrac{2(x-2)}{(x+3)(x+3)(x-2)} + \dfrac{3(x+3)}{(x+3)(x+3)(x-2)}$$

$$= \dfrac{2x-4+3x+9}{(x+3)(x+3)(x-2)}$$

$$= \dfrac{5x+5}{(x+3)^2(x-2)}$$

57. $\dfrac{x}{2x^2+7x+3} - \dfrac{3}{3x^2+7x-6} = \dfrac{x}{(2x+1)(x+3)} - \dfrac{3}{(3x-2)(x+3)}$

$$= \dfrac{x(3x-2)}{(2x+1)(3x-2)(x+3)} - \dfrac{3(2x+1)}{(2x+1)(3x-2)(x+3)}$$

$$= \dfrac{3x^2-2x-(6x+3)}{(2x+1)(3x-2)(x+3)}$$

$$= \dfrac{3x^2-2x-6x-3}{(2x+1)(3x-2)(x+3)}$$

$$= \dfrac{3x^2-8x-3}{(2x+1)(3x-2)(x+3)}$$

59.
$$\frac{x}{4x^2 + 11x + 6} - \frac{2}{8x^2 + 2x - 3} = \frac{x}{(4x+3)(x+2)} - \frac{2}{(4x+3)(2x-1)}$$
$$= \frac{x(2x-1)}{(4x+3)(x+2)(2x-1)} - \frac{2(x+2)}{(4x+3)(x+2)(2x-1)}$$
$$= \frac{2x^2 - x - (2x+4)}{(4x+3)(x+2)(2x-1)}$$
$$= \frac{2x^2 - x - 2x - 4}{(4x+3)(x+2)(2x-1)}$$
$$= \frac{2x^2 - 3x - 4}{(4x+3)(x+2)(2x-1)}$$

61.
$$\frac{3w+12}{w^2 + w - 12} - \frac{2}{w-3} = \frac{3(w+4)}{(w-3)(w+4)} - \frac{2}{w-3}$$
$$= \frac{3}{w-3} - \frac{2}{w-3}$$
$$= \frac{3-2}{w-3}$$
$$= \frac{1}{w-3}$$

63.
$$\frac{3r}{2r^2 - 10r + 12} + \frac{3}{r-2} = \frac{3r}{2(r^2 - 5r + 6)} + \frac{3}{r-2}$$
$$= \frac{3r}{2(r-3)(r-2)} + \frac{3}{r-2}$$
$$= \frac{3r}{2(r-3)(r-2)} + \frac{3 \cdot 2(r-3)}{(r-2) \cdot 2(r-3)}$$
$$= \frac{3r + 6r - 18}{2(r-3)(r-2)}$$
$$= \frac{9r - 18}{2(r-3)(r-2)}$$
$$= \frac{9(r-2)}{2(r-3)(r-2)}$$
$$= \frac{9}{2(r-3)}$$

65. $\dfrac{2}{x} + 6$ is defined for all real numbers except $x = 0$.

67. $\dfrac{5}{x-4} + \dfrac{7}{x+6}$ is defined for all real numbers except $x = 4$ and $x = -6$.

69.
$$\frac{3}{\Delta - 2} - \frac{1}{2 - \Delta} = \frac{3}{\Delta - 2} + \frac{1}{\Delta - 2}$$
$$= \frac{3+1}{\Delta - 2}$$
$$= \frac{4}{\Delta - 2}$$

71. $\dfrac{5}{a+b} + \dfrac{3}{a}$

$a + b = 0$ when $a = -b$. The expression is defined for all real numbers except $a = 0$ and $a = -b$.

73.
$$\frac{x}{x^2-9}+\frac{3x}{x+3}+\frac{3x^2-8x}{9-x^2}=\frac{x}{(x+3)(x-3)}+\frac{3x(x-3)}{(x+3)(x-3)}-\frac{3x^2-8x}{(x+3)(x-3)}$$
$$=\frac{x+3x^2-9x-(3x^2-8x)}{(x+3)(x-3)}$$
$$=\frac{x+3x^2-9x-3x^2+8x}{(x+3)(x-3)}$$
$$=\frac{0}{(x+3)(x-3)}$$
$$=0$$

77.
$$\frac{2}{x^2-x-6}+\frac{3}{x^2-2x-3}+\frac{1}{x^2+3x+2}=\frac{2}{(x+2)(x-3)}+\frac{3}{(x-3)(x+1)}+\frac{1}{(x+2)(x+1)}$$
$$=\frac{2(x+1)}{(x+2)(x-3)(x+1)}+\frac{3(x+2)}{(x+2)(x-3)(x+1)}+\frac{x-3}{(x+2)(x-3)(x+1)}$$
$$=\frac{2x+2+3x+6+x-3}{(x+2)(x-3)(x+1)}$$
$$=\frac{6x+5}{(x+2)(x-3)(x+1)}$$

80. Let x = the number of hours it takes the train to travel 42 miles.
$$\frac{22\text{ miles}}{0.8\text{ hours}}=\frac{42\text{ miles}}{x\text{ hours}}$$
$$22x=0.8(42)$$
$$22x=33.6$$
$$x\approx1.53$$
It takes about 1.53 hours for the train to travel 42 miles.

81. $3(x-2)+2<4(x+1)$
$$3x-6+2<4x+4$$
$$3x-4<4x+4$$
$$-8<x$$
$$x>-8$$

82.
$$\begin{array}{r}4x-3\\2x+3\overline{)\,8x^2+6x-13}\\\underline{8x^2+12x}\\-6x-13\\\underline{-6x-\;\,9}\\-4\end{array}$$
$$(8x^2+6x-13)\div(2x+3)=4x-3-\frac{4}{2x+3}$$

83.
$$\frac{x^2+xy-6y^2}{x^2-xy-2y^2}\cdot\frac{y^2-x^2}{x^2+2xy-3y^2}=\frac{(x+3y)(x-2y)}{(x+y)(x-2y)}\cdot\frac{-1(x-y)(x+y)}{(x+3y)(x-y)}$$
$$=-1$$

Exercise Set 6.5

1. A complex fraction is a fraction whose numerator or denominator (or both) contains a fraction.

3. a.

$$\dfrac{\dfrac{x+3}{4}}{\dfrac{7}{x^2+5x+6}}$$

Numerator: $\dfrac{x+3}{4}$

Denominator: $\dfrac{7}{x^2+5x+6}$

b.

$$\dfrac{\dfrac{1}{2y}+x}{\dfrac{3}{y}+x}$$

Numerator, $\dfrac{1}{2y}+x$

Denominator, $\dfrac{3}{y}+x$

5. $\dfrac{4+\frac{2}{3}}{2+\frac{1}{3}}=\dfrac{\left(4+\frac{2}{3}\right)3}{\left(2+\frac{1}{3}\right)3}$

$=\dfrac{12+2}{6+1}$

$=\dfrac{14}{7}$

$=2$

7. $\dfrac{2+\frac{3}{8}}{1+\frac{1}{3}}=\dfrac{\left(2+\frac{3}{8}\right)8\cdot3}{\left(1+\frac{1}{3}\right)8\cdot3}$

$=\dfrac{2\cdot8\cdot3+3\cdot3}{8\cdot3+8}$

$=\dfrac{48+9}{24+8}$

$=\dfrac{57}{32}$

9. $\dfrac{\frac{2}{7}-\frac{1}{4}}{6-\frac{2}{3}}=\dfrac{\left(\frac{2}{7}-\frac{1}{4}\right)3\cdot4\cdot7}{\left(6-\frac{2}{3}\right)3\cdot4\cdot7}$

$=\dfrac{2\cdot3\cdot4-1\cdot3\cdot7}{6\cdot3\cdot4\cdot7-2\cdot4\cdot7}$

$=\dfrac{24-21}{504-56}$

$=\dfrac{3}{448}$

10. $\dfrac{1-\frac{x}{y}}{x}=\dfrac{\left(1-\frac{x}{y}\right)y}{(x)y}$

$=\dfrac{y-x}{xy}$

11. $\dfrac{\frac{xy^2}{9}}{\frac{3}{x^2}}=\dfrac{xy^2}{9}\cdot\dfrac{x^2}{3}$

$=\dfrac{x^3y^2}{27}$

13. $\dfrac{\frac{6a^2b}{5}}{\frac{9ac^2}{b^2}}=\dfrac{6a^2b}{5}\cdot\dfrac{b^2}{9ac^2}$

$=\dfrac{6a^2b^3}{45ac^2}$

$=\dfrac{2ab^3}{15c^2}$

15. $\dfrac{a-\frac{a}{b}}{\frac{1+a}{b}}=\dfrac{\left(a-\frac{a}{b}\right)b}{\left(\frac{1+a}{b}\right)b}$

$=\dfrac{ab-a}{1+a}$

17. $\dfrac{\frac{9}{x}+\frac{3}{x^2}}{3+\frac{1}{x}}=\dfrac{\left(\frac{9}{x}+\frac{3}{x^2}\right)x^2}{\left(3+\frac{1}{x}\right)x^2}$

$=\dfrac{9x+3}{3x^2+x}$

$=\dfrac{3(3x+1)}{x(3x+1)}$

$=\dfrac{3}{x}$

19. $\dfrac{5-\frac{1}{x}}{4-\frac{1}{x}}=\dfrac{\left(5-\frac{1}{x}\right)x}{\left(4-\frac{1}{x}\right)x}$

$=\dfrac{5x-1}{4x-1}$

177

21. $\dfrac{\frac{m}{n}-\frac{n}{m}}{\frac{m+n}{n}} = \dfrac{\left(\frac{m}{n}-\frac{n}{m}\right)mn}{\left(\frac{m+n}{n}\right)mn}$

$\qquad = \dfrac{m^2 - n^2}{m(m+n)}$

$\qquad = \dfrac{(m+n)(m-n)}{m(m+n)}$

$\qquad = \dfrac{m-n}{m}$

23. $\dfrac{\frac{a^2}{b}-b}{\frac{b^2}{a}-a} = \dfrac{\left(\frac{a^2}{b}-b\right)ab}{\left(\frac{b^2}{a}-a\right)ab}$

$\qquad = \dfrac{\left(a^2-b^2\right)a}{\left(b^2-a^2\right)b}$

$\qquad = -\dfrac{a}{b}$

25. $\dfrac{5-\frac{a}{b}}{\frac{a}{b}-5} = \dfrac{\left(5-\frac{a}{b}\right)b}{\left(\frac{a}{b}-5\right)b}$

$\qquad = \dfrac{5b-a}{a-5b}$

$\qquad = \dfrac{-1(-5b+a)}{a-5b}$

$\qquad = \dfrac{-1(a-5b)}{(a-5b)}$

$\qquad = -1$

27. $\dfrac{\frac{a^2-b^2}{a}}{\frac{a+b}{a^3}} = \dfrac{a^2-b^2}{a} \cdot \dfrac{a^3}{a+b}$

$\qquad = \dfrac{(a+b)(a-b)}{a} \cdot \dfrac{a^3}{a+b}$

$\qquad = a^2(a-b)$

29. $\dfrac{\frac{1}{a}-\frac{1}{b}}{\frac{1}{ab}} = \dfrac{\left(\frac{1}{a}-\frac{1}{b}\right)ab}{\left(\frac{1}{ab}\right)ab}$

$\qquad = \dfrac{b-a}{1}$

$\qquad = b-a$

31. $\dfrac{\frac{a}{b}+\frac{1}{a}}{\frac{b}{a}+\frac{1}{a}} = \dfrac{\left(\frac{a}{b}+\frac{1}{a}\right)ab}{\left(\frac{b}{a}+\frac{1}{a}\right)ab}$

$\qquad = \dfrac{a^2+b}{b^2+b}$

$\qquad = \dfrac{a^2+b}{b(b+1)}$

33. $\dfrac{\frac{1}{xy}}{\frac{1}{x}-\frac{1}{y}} = \dfrac{\left(\frac{1}{xy}\right)xy}{\left(\frac{1}{x}-\frac{1}{y}\right)xy}$

$\qquad = \dfrac{1}{y-x}$

35. $\dfrac{\frac{3}{a}+\frac{3}{a^2}}{\frac{3}{b}+\frac{3}{b^2}} = \dfrac{\left(\frac{3}{a}+\frac{3}{a^2}\right)a^2b^2}{\left(\frac{3}{b}+\frac{3}{b^2}\right)a^2b^2}$

$\qquad = \dfrac{3ab^2+3b^2}{3a^2b+3a^2}$

$\qquad = \dfrac{3b^2(a+1)}{3a^2(b+1)}$

$\qquad = \dfrac{ab^2+b^2}{a^2(b+1)}$

37. a. Answers will vary.

b. c. $\dfrac{5+\frac{3}{5}}{\frac{1}{8}-4} = \dfrac{\frac{25}{5}+\frac{3}{5}}{\frac{1}{8}-\frac{32}{8}}$

$\qquad = \dfrac{\frac{28}{5}}{-\frac{31}{8}}$

$\qquad = \dfrac{28}{5} \cdot \left(-\dfrac{8}{31}\right)$

$\qquad = -\dfrac{224}{155}$

$\dfrac{5+\frac{3}{5}}{\frac{1}{8}-4} = \dfrac{\left(5+\frac{3}{5}\right)5\cdot8}{\left(\frac{1}{8}-4\right)5\cdot8}$

$\qquad = \dfrac{5\cdot5\cdot8+3\cdot8}{5-4\cdot5\cdot8}$

$\qquad = \dfrac{200+24}{5-160}$

$\qquad = -\dfrac{224}{155}$

39.a. Answers will vary.

b. c. $\dfrac{\frac{x-y}{x+y}+\frac{3}{x+y}}{2-\frac{7}{x+y}}=\dfrac{\frac{x-y+3}{x+y}}{\frac{2(x+y)}{x+y}-\frac{7}{x+y}}$

$=\dfrac{\frac{x-y+3}{x+y}}{\frac{2x+2y-7}{x+y}}$

$=\dfrac{x-y+3}{x+y}\cdot\dfrac{x+y}{2x+2y-7}$

$=\dfrac{x-y+3}{2x+2y-7}$

$\dfrac{\frac{x-y}{x+y}+\frac{3}{x+y}}{2-\frac{7}{x+y}}=\dfrac{\frac{x-y+3}{x+y}}{2-\frac{7}{x+y}}$

$=\dfrac{\left(\frac{x-y+3}{x+y}\right)(x+y)}{\left(2-\frac{7}{x+y}\right)(x+y)}$

$=\dfrac{x-y+3}{2(x+y)-7}$

$=\dfrac{x-y+3}{2x+2y-7}$

41. a. $\dfrac{\frac{5}{12x}}{\frac{8}{x^2}-\frac{4}{3x}}$

b. $\dfrac{\frac{5}{12x}}{\frac{8}{x^2}-\frac{4}{3x}}=\dfrac{\frac{5}{12x}}{\frac{24-4x}{3x^2}}=\dfrac{5}{12x}\cdot\dfrac{3x^2}{(24-4x)}$

$=\dfrac{5x}{4(24-4x)}$

$=\dfrac{5x}{96-16x}$

43. $\dfrac{x^{-1}+y^{-1}}{2}=\dfrac{\frac{1}{x}+\frac{1}{y}}{2}$

$=\dfrac{\left(\frac{1}{x}+\frac{1}{y}\right)xy}{2xy}$

$=\dfrac{y+x}{2xy}$

45. $\dfrac{x^{-1}+y^{-1}}{x^{-1}y^{-1}}=\dfrac{\frac{1}{x}+\frac{1}{y}}{\frac{1}{xy}}$

$=\dfrac{\left(\frac{1}{x}+\frac{1}{y}\right)xy}{\left(\frac{1}{xy}\right)xy}$

$=\dfrac{y+x}{1}$

$=x+y$

47. a. $E=\dfrac{\frac{1}{2}\left(\frac{2}{3}\right)}{\frac{2}{3}+\frac{1}{2}}$

$=\dfrac{\frac{2}{6}}{\frac{4+3}{6}}$

$=\dfrac{2}{6}\cdot\dfrac{6}{7}$

$=\dfrac{2}{7}$

b. $E=\dfrac{\frac{1}{2}\left(\frac{4}{5}\right)}{\frac{4}{5}+\frac{1}{2}}$

$=\dfrac{\frac{4}{10}}{\frac{8+5}{10}}$

$=\dfrac{4}{10}\cdot\dfrac{10}{13}$

$=\dfrac{4}{13}$

49. $\dfrac{\frac{a}{b}+b-\frac{1}{a}}{\frac{a}{b^2}-\frac{b}{a}+\frac{1}{a^2}}=\dfrac{\frac{a^2+b^2a-b}{ba}}{\frac{a^3-ab^3+b^2}{a^2b^2}}$

$=\dfrac{a^2+b^2a-b}{ba}\cdot\dfrac{a^2b^2}{a^3-ab^3+b^2}$

$=\dfrac{(a^2+b^2a-b)ab}{a^3-ab^3+b^2}$

$=\dfrac{a^3b+a^2b^3-ab^2}{a^3-ab^3+b^2}$

51. $2x-8(5-x)=9x-3(x+2)$

$2x-40+8x=9x-3x-6$

$10x-40=6x-6$

$4x=34$

$x=\dfrac{34}{4}=\dfrac{17}{2}$

52. A polynomial is a sum of terms of the form ax^n where a is a real number and n is a whole number.

53. $x^2 - 13x + 42 = (x - 6)(x - 7)$

54. $\dfrac{x}{3x^2 + 17x - 6} - \dfrac{2}{x^2 + 3x - 18} = \dfrac{x}{(3x-1)(x+6)} - \dfrac{2}{(x+6)(x-3)}$

$$= \dfrac{x(x-3)}{(3x+1)(x+6)(x-3)} - \dfrac{2(3x-1)}{(3x-1)(x+6)(x-3)}$$

$$= \dfrac{x^2 - 3x - (6x - 2)}{(3x-1)(x+6)(x-3)}$$

$$= \dfrac{x^2 - 3x - 6x + 2}{(3x-1)(x+6)(x-3)}$$

$$= \dfrac{x^2 - 9x + 2}{(3x-1)(x+6)(x-3)}$$

Exercise Set 6.6

1. a.   Answers will vary.

b. $\dfrac{1}{x-1} - \dfrac{1}{x+1} = \dfrac{3x}{x^2 - 1}$

$\dfrac{1}{x-1} - \dfrac{1}{x+1} = \dfrac{3x}{(x-1)(x+1)}$

Multiply both sides of the equation by the least common denominator, $(x-1)(x+1)$.

$$(x-1)(x+1)\left(\dfrac{1}{x-1} - \dfrac{1}{x+1}\right) = \left(\dfrac{3x}{(x-1)(x+1)}\right)(x-1)(x+1)$$

$$(x-1)(x+1)\left(\dfrac{1}{x-1}\right) - (x-1)(x+1)\left(\dfrac{1}{x+1}\right) = 3x$$

$$x + 1 - (x - 1) = 3x$$

$$x + 1 - x + 1 = 3x$$

$$2 = 3x$$

$$\dfrac{2}{3} = x$$

3. a.   The problem on the left is an expression to be simplified while the problem on the right is an equation to be solved.

b.   Left: Write the fractions with the LCD, $12(x - 1)$, then combine numerators.
Right: Multiply both sides of the equation by the LCD, $12(x - 1)$, then solve.

c.   Left: $\dfrac{x}{3} - \dfrac{x}{4} + \dfrac{1}{x-1} = \dfrac{x \cdot 4(x-1)}{3 \cdot 4(x-1)} - \dfrac{x \cdot 3(x-1)}{4 \cdot 3(x-1)} + \dfrac{1 \cdot 3 \cdot 4}{(x-1)3 \cdot 4}$

$$= \dfrac{4x(x-1) - 3x(x-1) + 12}{3 \cdot 4(x-1)}$$

$$= \dfrac{4x^2 - 4x - 3x^2 + 3x + 12}{12(x-1)}$$

$$= \dfrac{x^2 - x + 12}{12(x-1)}$$

Right:

$$\frac{x}{3} - \frac{x}{4} = \frac{1}{x-1}$$

$$12(x-1)\left(\frac{x}{3} - \frac{x}{4}\right) = \left(\frac{1}{x-1}\right)12(x-1)$$

$$12(x-1)\left(\frac{x}{3}\right) - 12(x-1)\left(\frac{x}{4}\right) = 12$$

$$4x(x-1) - 3x(x-1) = 12$$

$$4x^2 - 4x - 3x^2 + 3x = 12$$

$$x^2 - x - 12 = 0$$

$$(x-4)(x+3) = 0$$

$$x - 4 = 0 \quad \text{or} \quad x + 3 = 0$$

$$x = 4 \qquad\qquad x = -3$$

5. You must check for extraneous when there is a variable in the denominator.

7. 2 cannot be a solution because it makes the denominator zero in the first term.

9. No, because there are no variables in the denominator.

11. Yes, because there is a variable in the denominator.

13. $\dfrac{x}{3} - \dfrac{x}{4} = 1$

$$12\left(\frac{x}{3} - \frac{x}{4}\right) = 12(1)$$

$$4x - 3x = 12$$

$$x = 12$$

15. $\dfrac{r}{3} = \dfrac{r}{4} + \dfrac{1}{6}$

$$12\left(\frac{r}{3}\right) = 12\left(\frac{r}{4} + \frac{1}{6}\right)$$

$$4r = 3r + 2$$

$$r = 2$$

17. $\dfrac{z}{2} + 3 = \dfrac{z}{5}$

$$10\left(\frac{z}{2} + 3\right) = 10\left(\frac{z}{5}\right)$$

$$5z + 30 = 2z$$

$$3z = -30$$

$$z = -10$$

19. $\dfrac{z}{6} + \dfrac{1}{3} = \dfrac{z}{5} - \dfrac{2}{3}$

$$30\left(\frac{z}{6} + \frac{1}{3}\right) = 30\left(\frac{z}{5} - \frac{2}{3}\right)$$

$$5z + 10 = 6z - 20$$

$$-z = -30$$

$$z = 30$$

21. $d + 1 = \dfrac{3}{2}d - 1$

$$2(d+1) = 2\left(\frac{3}{2}d - 1\right)$$

$$2d + 2 = 3d - 2$$

$$-d = -4$$

$$d = 4$$

23. $k + \dfrac{1}{6} = 2k - 4$

$$6\left(k + \frac{1}{6}\right) = 6(2k - 4)$$

$$6k + 1 = 12k - 24$$

$$-6k = -25$$

$$k = \frac{25}{6}$$

25. $\dfrac{(n+6)}{3} = \dfrac{2(n-8)}{4}$

$$4(n+6) = 3 \cdot 2(n-8)$$

$$4n + 24 = 6n - 48$$

$$-2n = -72$$

$$n = 36$$

27. $\dfrac{x-5}{15} = \dfrac{3}{5} - \dfrac{x-4}{10}$

$30\left(\dfrac{x-5}{15}\right) = 30\left(\dfrac{3}{5} - \dfrac{x-4}{10}\right)$

$2(x-5) = 6(3) - 3(x-4)$

$2x - 10 = 18 - 3x + 12$

$2x - 10 = 30 - 3x$

$5x = 40$

$x = 8$

29. $\dfrac{-p+1}{4} + \dfrac{13}{20} = \dfrac{p}{5} - \dfrac{p-1}{2}$

$20\left(\dfrac{-p+1}{4} + \dfrac{13}{20}\right) = 20\left(\dfrac{p}{5} - \dfrac{p-1}{2}\right)$

$5(-p+1) + 13 = 4p - 10(p-1)$

$-5p + 5 + 13 = 4p - 10p + 10$

$-5p + 18 = -6p + 10$

$p = -8$

31. $\dfrac{d-3}{4} + \dfrac{1}{5} = \dfrac{2d+1}{3} - \dfrac{32}{15}$

$60\left(\dfrac{d-3}{4} + \dfrac{1}{5}\right) = 60\left(\dfrac{2d+1}{3} - \dfrac{32}{15}\right)$

$15(d-3) + 12 = 20(2d+1) - 4(32)$

$15d - 45 + 12 = 40d + 20 - 128$

$15d - 33 = 40d - 108$

$-25d = -75$

$d = 3$

33. $2 + \dfrac{3}{x} = \dfrac{11}{4}$

$4x\left(2 + \dfrac{3}{x}\right) = 4x\left(\dfrac{11}{4}\right)$

$8x + 12 = 44$

$8x = 32$

$x = 4$

Check: $2 + \dfrac{3}{4} = \dfrac{11}{4}$

$\dfrac{8}{4} + \dfrac{3}{4} = \dfrac{11}{4}$

$\dfrac{11}{4} = \dfrac{11}{4}$ True

35. $6 - \dfrac{3}{x} = \dfrac{9}{2}$

$2x\left(6 - \dfrac{3}{x}\right) = 2x\left(\dfrac{9}{2}\right)$

$12x - 6 = 9x$

$3x = 6$

$x = 2$

Check: $6 - \dfrac{3}{2} = \dfrac{9}{2}$

$\dfrac{12}{2} - \dfrac{3}{2} = \dfrac{9}{2}$

$\dfrac{9}{2} = \dfrac{9}{2}$ True

37. $\dfrac{4}{n} - \dfrac{3}{2n} = \dfrac{1}{2}$

$2n\left(\dfrac{4}{n} - \dfrac{3}{2n}\right) = 2n\left(\dfrac{1}{2}\right)$

$8 - 3 = n$

$5 = n$

Check: $\dfrac{4}{5} - \dfrac{3}{10} = \dfrac{1}{2}$

$\dfrac{8}{10} - \dfrac{3}{10} = \dfrac{1}{2}$

$\dfrac{5}{10} = \dfrac{1}{2}$

$\dfrac{1}{2} = \dfrac{1}{2}$ True

39. $\dfrac{x-1}{x-5} = \dfrac{4}{x-5}$

$(x-5)\left(\dfrac{x-1}{x-5}\right) = \left(\dfrac{4}{x-5}\right)(x-5)$

$x - 1 = 4$

$x = 5$

Check: $\dfrac{x-1}{x-5} = \dfrac{4}{x-5}$

$\dfrac{5-1}{5-5} = \dfrac{4}{5-5}$

$\dfrac{4}{0} = \dfrac{4}{0}$

Since $\dfrac{4}{0}$ is not a real number, 5 is an extraneous solution. This equation has no solution.

41. $\dfrac{3-5y}{4} = \dfrac{2-4y}{3}$

$3(3-5y) = 4(2-4y)$

$9-15y = 8-16y$

$y = -1$

Check: $\dfrac{3-5y}{4} = \dfrac{2-4y}{3}$

$\dfrac{3-5(-1)}{4} = \dfrac{2-4(-1)}{3}$

$\dfrac{3+5}{4} = \dfrac{2+4}{3}$

$\dfrac{8}{4} = \dfrac{6}{3}$ True

43. $\dfrac{4}{y-3} = \dfrac{6}{y+3}$

$4(y+3) = 6(y-3)$

$4y+12 = 6y-18$

$30 = 2y$

$15 = y$

Check: $\dfrac{4}{y-3} = \dfrac{6}{y+3}$

$\dfrac{4}{15-3} = \dfrac{6}{15+3}$

$\dfrac{4}{12} = \dfrac{6}{18}$

$\dfrac{1}{3} = \dfrac{1}{3}$ True

45. $\dfrac{2x-3}{x-4} = \dfrac{5}{x-4}$

$(x-4)\left(\dfrac{2x-3}{x-4}\right) = \left(\dfrac{5}{x-4}\right)(x-4)$

$2x-3 = 5$

$2x = 8$

$x = 4$

Check: $\dfrac{2x-3}{x-4} = \dfrac{5}{x-4}$

$\dfrac{2(4)-3}{4-4} = \dfrac{5}{4-4}$

$\dfrac{5}{0} = \dfrac{5}{0}$

Since $\dfrac{5}{0}$ is not a real number, 4 is an extraneous

solution. This equation has no solution.

47. $\dfrac{x^2}{x-4} = \dfrac{16}{x-4}$

$(x-4)\left(\dfrac{x^2}{x-4}\right) = (x-4)\left(\dfrac{16}{x-4}\right)$

$x^2 = 16$

$x^2 - 16 = 0$

$(x+4)(x-4) = 0$

$x+4 = 0 \ \text{ or } \ x-4 = 0$

$x = -4 \qquad\qquad x = 4$

Check: $\dfrac{(-4)^2}{-4-4} = \dfrac{16}{-4-4} \qquad \dfrac{(4)^2}{4-4} = \dfrac{16}{4-4}$

$\dfrac{16}{-8} = \dfrac{16}{-8} \qquad\qquad \dfrac{16}{0} = \dfrac{16}{0}$

$-2 = -2$ True

Since $\dfrac{16}{0}$ is not a real number, 4 is an extraneous

solution. The solution is $x = -4$.

49. $\dfrac{n+10}{n+2} = \dfrac{n+4}{n-3}$

$(n+10)(n-3) = (n+2)(n+4)$

$n^2 + 7n - 30 = n^2 + 6n + 8$

$n = 38$

Check: $\dfrac{38+10}{38+2} = \dfrac{38+4}{38-3}$

$\dfrac{48}{40} = \dfrac{42}{35}$

$\dfrac{6}{5} = \dfrac{6}{5}$ True

51. $\dfrac{1}{3r} = \dfrac{r}{8r+3}$

$1(8r+3) = 3r^2$

$0 = 3r^2 - 8r - 3$

$0 = (3r+1)(r-3)$

$3r+1 = 0$ or $r-3 = 0$

$3r = -1$ $\qquad r = 3$

$r = -\dfrac{1}{3}$

Check: $\dfrac{1}{3\left(-\dfrac{1}{3}\right)} = \dfrac{-\dfrac{1}{3}}{8\left(\dfrac{-1}{3}\right)+3}$ $\qquad \dfrac{1}{3(3)} = \dfrac{3}{8(3)+3}$

$\dfrac{1}{-1} = \dfrac{-\dfrac{1}{3}}{\dfrac{-8}{3}+\dfrac{9}{3}}$ $\qquad \dfrac{1}{9} = \dfrac{3}{27}$

$-1 = \dfrac{-\dfrac{1}{3}}{\dfrac{1}{3}}$ $\qquad\qquad \dfrac{1}{9} = \dfrac{1}{9}$ True

$-1 = -1$ True

53. $\dfrac{k}{k+2} = \dfrac{3}{k-2}$

$k(k-2) = 3(k+2)$

$k^2 - 2k = 3k+6$

$k^2 - 5k - 6 = 0$

$(k-6)(k+1) = 0$

$k-6 = 0$ or $k+1 = 0$

$k = 6$ $\qquad k = -1$

Check: $\dfrac{6}{6+2} = \dfrac{3}{6-2}$ $\qquad \dfrac{-1}{-1+2} = \dfrac{3}{-1-2}$

$\dfrac{6}{8} = \dfrac{3}{4}$ $\qquad\qquad \dfrac{-1}{1} = \dfrac{3}{-3}$

$\dfrac{3}{4} = \dfrac{3}{4}$ True $\qquad\quad -1 = -1$ True

55. $\dfrac{3}{r} + r = \dfrac{19}{r}$

$r\left(\dfrac{3}{r} + r\right) = r\left(\dfrac{19}{r}\right)$

$3 + r^2 = 19$

$r^2 - 16 = 0$

$(r+4)(r-4) = 0$

$r+4 = 0$ or $r-4 = 0$

$r = -4$ $\qquad r = 4$

Check: $\dfrac{3}{4} + 4 = \dfrac{19}{4}$ $\qquad \dfrac{3}{-4} - 4 = \dfrac{19}{-4}$

$\dfrac{3}{4} + \dfrac{16}{4} = \dfrac{19}{4}$ $\qquad \dfrac{3}{-4} - \dfrac{16}{4} = \dfrac{19}{-4}$

$\dfrac{19}{4} = \dfrac{19}{4}$ True $\qquad -\dfrac{19}{4} = -\dfrac{19}{4}$ True

57. $x + \dfrac{20}{x} = -9$

$x\left(x + \dfrac{20}{x}\right) = -9x$

$x^2 + 20 = -9x$

$x^2 + 9x + 20 = 0$

$(x+4)(x+5) = 0$

$x+4 = 0$ or $x+5 = 0$

$x = -4$ $\qquad x = -5$

Check $x = -4$: $\quad x + \dfrac{20}{x} = -9$

$-4 + \dfrac{20}{-4} = -9$

$-4 + (-5) = -9$ True

Check $x = -5$: $\quad x + \dfrac{20}{x} = -9$

$-5 + \dfrac{20}{-5} = -9$

$5 + (-4) = -9$ True

59.

$$\frac{3y-2}{y+1} = 4 - \frac{y+2}{y-1}$$

$$(y+1)(y-1)\left(\frac{3y-2}{y+1}\right) = \left(4 - \frac{y+2}{y-1}\right)(y+1)(y-1)$$

$$(y-1)(3y-2) = 4(y+1)(y-1) - \left(\frac{y+2}{y-1}\right)(y+1)(y-1)$$

$$3y^2 - 5y + 2 = 4\left(y^2 - 1\right) - (y+2)(y+1)$$

$$3y^2 - 5y + 2 = 4y^2 - 4 - (y^2 + 3y + 2)$$

$$3y^2 - 5y + 2 = 3y^2 - 3y - 6$$

$$-5y + 2 = -3y - 6$$

$$8 = 2y$$

$$4 = y$$

Check: $\dfrac{3y-2}{y+1} = 4 - \dfrac{y+2}{y-1}$

$$\frac{3(4)-2}{4+1} = 4 - \frac{4+2}{4-1}$$

$$\frac{12-2}{5} = 4 - \frac{6}{3}$$

$$\frac{10}{5} = 4 - 2$$

$$2 = 2 \text{ True}$$

61.

$$\frac{1}{x+3} + \frac{1}{x-3} = \frac{-5}{x^2-9}$$

$$\frac{1}{x+3} + \frac{1}{x-3} = \frac{-5}{(x-3)(x+3)}$$

$$(x-3)(x+3)\left[\frac{1}{x+3} + \frac{1}{x-3}\right] = \left[\frac{-5}{(x-3)(x+3)}\right](x-3)(x+3)$$

$$(x-3)(x+3)\left(\frac{1}{x+3}\right) + (x-3)(x+3)\left(\frac{1}{x-3}\right) = -5$$

$$x - 3 + x + 3 = -5$$

$$2x = -5$$

$$x = -\frac{5}{2}$$

Check: $\dfrac{1}{x+3} + \dfrac{1}{x-3} = \dfrac{-5}{x^2-9}$

$$\frac{1}{-\frac{5}{2}+3} + \frac{1}{-\frac{5}{2}-3} = \frac{-5}{\left(-\frac{5}{2}\right)^2 - 9}$$

$$\frac{1}{\frac{1}{2}} - \frac{1}{-\frac{11}{2}} = \frac{-5}{\frac{25}{4} - 9}$$

$$2 - \frac{2}{11} = \frac{-5}{-\frac{11}{4}}$$

$$\frac{20}{11} = \frac{20}{11} \text{ True}$$

63.

$$\frac{x}{x-3}+\frac{3}{2}=\frac{3}{x-3}$$

$$2(x-3)\left(\frac{x}{x-3}+\frac{3}{2}\right)=2(x-3)\left(\frac{3}{x-3}\right)$$

$$2x+3(x-3)=2(3)$$

$$2x+3x-9=6$$

$$5x=15$$

$$x=3$$

Check: $\dfrac{x}{x-3}+\dfrac{3}{2}=\dfrac{3}{x-3}$

$$\frac{3}{3-3}+\frac{3}{2}=\frac{3}{3-3}$$

$$\frac{3}{0}+\frac{3}{2}=\frac{3}{0}$$

Since $\dfrac{3}{0}$ is not a real number, 3 is an extraneous solution. This equation has no solution.

65.

$$\frac{3}{x-5}-\frac{4}{x+5}=\frac{11}{x^2-25}$$

$$\frac{3}{x-5}-\frac{4}{x+5}=\frac{11}{(x-5)(x+5)}$$

$$(x-5)(x+5)\left[\frac{3}{x-5}-\frac{4}{x+5}\right]=\left[\frac{11}{(x-5)(x+5)}\right](x-5)(x+5)$$

$$(x-5)(x+5)\left(\frac{3}{x-5}\right)-(x-5)(x+5)\left(\frac{4}{x+5}\right)=11$$

$$3(x+5)-4(x-5)=11$$

$$3x+15-4x+20=11$$

$$-x+35=11$$

$$24=x$$

Check: $\dfrac{3}{x-5}-\dfrac{4}{x+5}=\dfrac{11}{x^2-25}$

$$\frac{3}{24-5}-\frac{4}{24+5}=\frac{11}{24^2-25}$$

$$\frac{3}{19}-\frac{4}{29}=\frac{11}{576-25}$$

$$\frac{87}{551}-\frac{76}{551}=\frac{11}{551}$$

$$\frac{11}{551}=\frac{11}{551}\ \ \text{True}$$

67.

$$\frac{y}{2y+2}+\frac{2y-16}{4y+4}=\frac{y-3}{y+1}$$

$$\frac{y}{2(y+1)}+\frac{2y-16}{4(y+1)}=\frac{y-3}{y+1}$$

$$4(y+1)\left[\frac{y}{2(y+1)}+\frac{2y-16}{4(y+1)}\right]=\left[\frac{y-3}{y+1}\right]4(y+1)$$

$$4(y+1)\left[\frac{y}{2(y+1)}\right]+4(y+1)\left[\frac{2y-16}{4(y+1)}\right]=4(y-3)$$

$$2y+2y-16=4y-12$$

$$4y-16=4y-12$$

$$-16=-12 \qquad \text{False}$$

Since this is a false statement, the equation has no solution.

69.

$$\frac{1}{y-1}+\frac{1}{2}=\frac{2}{y^2-1}$$

$$\frac{1}{y-1}+\frac{1}{2}=\frac{2}{(y+1)(y-1)}$$

$$2(y+1)(y-1)\left[\frac{1}{y-1}+\frac{1}{2}\right]=2(y+1)(y-1)\left[\frac{2}{(y+1)(y-1)}\right]$$

$$2(y+1)(y-1)\left(\frac{1}{y-1}\right)+2(y+1)(y-1)\left(\frac{1}{2}\right)=2(2)$$

$$2(y+1)+(y+1)(y-1)=4$$

$$2y+2+y^2-1=4$$

$$y^2+2y-3=0$$

$$(y+3)(y-1)=0$$

$$y+3=0 \quad \text{or} \quad y-1=0$$
$$y=-3 \qquad\qquad y=1$$

Check: $y=-3$

$$\frac{1}{y-1}+\frac{1}{2}=\frac{2}{y^2-1}$$

$$\frac{1}{-3-1}+\frac{1}{2}=\frac{2}{(-3)^2-1}$$

$$\frac{1}{-4}+\frac{1}{2}=\frac{2}{8}$$

$$\frac{1}{4}=\frac{1}{4} \qquad \text{True}$$

Check: $y=1$

$$\frac{1}{y-1}+\frac{1}{2}=\frac{2}{y^2-1}$$

$$\frac{1}{1-1}+\frac{1}{2}=\frac{2}{1^2-1}$$

$$\frac{1}{0}+\frac{1}{2}=\frac{2}{0}$$

The solution to the equation is -3. Since $\frac{1}{0}$ and $\frac{2}{0}$ are not real numbers, 1 is an extraneous solution.

71.

$$\frac{2t}{4t+4} + \frac{t}{2t+2} = \frac{2t-3}{t+1}$$

$$\frac{2t}{4(t+1)} + \frac{t}{2(t+1)} = \frac{2t-3}{t+1}$$

$$4(t+1)\left[\frac{2t}{4(t+1)} + \frac{t}{2(t+1)}\right] = 4(t+1)\left(\frac{2t-3}{t+1}\right)$$

$$2t + 2t = 4(2t-3)$$

$$4t = 8t - 12$$

$$-4t = -12$$

$$t = 3$$

Check:
$$\frac{2(3)}{4(3)+4} + \frac{3}{2(3)+2} = \frac{2(3)-3}{3+1}$$

$$\frac{6}{12+4} + \frac{3}{6+2} = \frac{6-3}{4}$$

$$\frac{6}{16} + \frac{3}{8} = \frac{3}{4}$$

$$\frac{3}{8} + \frac{3}{8} = \frac{3}{4}$$

$$\frac{6}{8} = \frac{3}{4}$$

$$\frac{3}{4} = \frac{3}{4} \text{ True}$$

73. The solution is 5. Since $3 = x - 2$, $x = 5$.

75. The solution is 0.
Since $x + x = 0$, $x = 0$.

81.

$$\frac{x-4}{x^2-2x} = \frac{-4}{x^2-4}$$

$$\frac{x-4}{x(x-2)} = \frac{-4}{(x+2)(x-2)}$$

$$x(x+2)(x-2)\left(\frac{x-4}{x(x-2)}\right) = x(x+2)(x-2)\left(\frac{-4}{(x+2)(x-2)}\right)$$

$$(x+2)(x-4) = -4x$$

$$x^2 - 2x - 8 = -4x$$

$$x^2 + 2x - 8 = 0$$

$$(x+4)(x-2) = 0$$

$$x + 4 = 0 \text{ or } x - 2 = 0$$

$$x = -4 \qquad x = 2$$

Since $\frac{-4}{0}$ and $\frac{-2}{0}$ is not a real number, 2 is an extraneous solution.

The solution to the equation is –4.

77. x can be any real number.
$x - 2 + x - 2 = 2x - 4$.

79.

$$\frac{1}{p} + \frac{1}{q} = \frac{1}{f}$$

$$\frac{1}{30} + \frac{1}{q} = \frac{1}{10}$$

$$\frac{1}{q} = \frac{1}{10} - \frac{1}{30}$$

$$\frac{1}{q} = \frac{2}{30}$$

$$2q = 30$$

$$q = 15$$

The image will appear 15 cm from the mirror.

83. No, it is impossible for both sides of the equation
to be equal.

85. Let x be the number of minutes of internet access over 5 hours.

Plan 1: $7.95 + 0.15x$

Plan 2: 19.95

$$7.95 + 0.15x = 19.95$$
$$0.15x = 12$$
$$x = 80$$

80 minutes $= \dfrac{80}{60}$ hours $= 1\dfrac{1}{3}$ hours

Jake would have to use the internet more than

$5 + 1\dfrac{1}{3} = 6\dfrac{1}{3}$ hours.

86. Let x = measure of larger angle

y = measure of smaller angle

$$x + y = 180$$

$$\frac{1}{2}x - 30 = y$$

Substitute $\frac{1}{2}x - 30$ for y in the first equation.

$$x + \frac{1}{2}x - 30 = 180$$
$$\frac{3}{2}x = 210$$
$$x = 140$$

$$y = \frac{1}{2}x - 30$$
$$y = \frac{1}{2}(140) - 30$$
$$y = 70 - 30$$
$$y = 40$$

The angles measure $40°$ and $140°$.

87. $\dfrac{600 \text{ gallons}}{8 \text{ gallons / minute}} = 75$ minutes

88. $(3.4 \times 10^{-5})(2 \times 10^{7}) = (3.4)(2) \times (10^{-5})(10^{7})$
$$= 6.8 \times 10^{-5+7}$$
$$= 6.8 \times 10^{2}$$

Exercise Set 6.7

1. Some examples are:

$A = \dfrac{1}{2}bh$, $A = \dfrac{1}{2}h(b_1 + b_2)$, $V = \dfrac{1}{3}\pi r^2 h$, and

$V = \dfrac{4}{3}\pi r^3$

3. It represents 1 complete task.

5. Let w = width, then

$\dfrac{2}{3}w + 4 =$ length

area = width $\cdot$ length

$$90 = w\left(\frac{2}{3}w + 4\right)$$

$$90 = \frac{2w^2}{3} + 4w$$

$$3(90) = 3\left(\frac{2w^2}{3} + 4w\right)$$

$$270 = 2w^2 + 12w$$

$$2w^2 + 12w - 270 = 0$$
$$w^2 + 6w - 135 = 0$$
$$(w + 15)(w - 9) = 0$$
$$w + 15 = 0 \quad \text{or} \quad w - 9 = 0$$
$$w = -15 \qquad\quad w = 9$$

Since the width cannot be negative, $w = 9$

$$l = \frac{2}{3}w + 4$$
$$l = \frac{2}{3}(9) + 4$$
$$l = 6 + 4 = 10$$

The length = 10 inches and the width = 9 inches.

7. Let x = height, then $x + 5$ = base

area $= \dfrac{1}{2} \cdot$ height $\cdot$ base

$$42 = \frac{1}{2}x(x + 5)$$

$$2(42) = 2\left[\frac{1}{2}x(x + 5)\right]$$

$$84 = x(x + 5)$$

$$84 = x^2 + 5x$$

$$0 = x^2 + 5x - 84$$

$$0 = (x - 7)(x + 12)$$

$$x - 7 = 0 \quad \text{or} \quad x + 12 = 0$$

$$x = 7 \qquad\qquad x = -12$$

Since the height cannot be negative, $x = 7$.

base $= x + 5 = 7 + 15 = 12$

The base is 12 cm and the height is 7 cm.

9. Let b = the base of the triangle, then $\left(\dfrac{1}{2}b - 1\right)$ is the height.

$$A = \frac{1}{2}bh$$

$$12 = \frac{1}{2}b\left(\frac{1}{2}b - 1\right)$$

$$12 = \frac{1}{4}b^2 - \frac{1}{2}b$$

$$4(12) = 4\left(\frac{1}{4}b^2 - \frac{1}{2}b\right)$$

$$48 = b^2 - 2b$$

$$0 = b^2 - 2b - 48$$

$$0 = (b - 8)(b + 6)$$

$$b - 8 = 0 \quad \text{or} \quad b + 6 = 0$$

$$b = 8 \quad \text{or} \qquad b = -6$$

Since a length cannot be negative, the base is 8 feet.

11. Let one number be x, then the other number is $10x$.

$$\frac{1}{x} - \frac{1}{10x} = 3$$

$$10x\left(\frac{1}{x} - \frac{1}{10x}\right) = 10x(3)$$

$$10 - 1 = 30x$$

$$9 = 30x$$

$$\frac{9}{30} = x$$

$$\frac{3}{10} = x$$

$$3 = 10x$$

The numbers are $\dfrac{3}{10}$ and 3.

13. Let x = amount by which the numerator was increased.

$$\frac{3 + x}{4} = \frac{5}{2}$$

$$4\left(\frac{3 + x}{4}\right) = \left(\frac{5}{2}\right)4$$

$$3 + x = 10$$

$$x = 7$$

The numerator was increased by 7.

15. Let r = speed of Creole Queen paddle boat.

$$t = \frac{d}{r}$$

Time upstream = time downstream

$$\frac{4}{r - 2} = \frac{6}{r + 2}$$

$$4(r + 2) = 6(r - 2)$$

$$4r + 8 = 6r - 12$$

$$20 = 2r$$

$$10 = r$$

The boat's speed in still water is 10 mph.

17. Let d = distance and $t = \dfrac{d}{r}$.

Time going + Time returning = $\dfrac{5}{2}$.

$$\frac{d}{15} + \frac{d}{15} = \frac{5}{2}$$

$$\frac{2d}{15} = \frac{5}{2}$$

$$4d = 75$$

$$d = \frac{75}{4} = 18.75$$

The trolley traveled 18.75 miles in one direction.

19. Let r be the speed of the propeller plane, then $4r$ is the speed of the jet.

$$\frac{d}{r} = t$$

time by jet + time by propeller plane = 6 hr

$$\frac{1600}{4r} + \frac{500}{r} = 6$$

$$\frac{400}{r} + \frac{300}{r} = 6$$

$$\frac{900}{r} = 6$$

$$r = \frac{900}{6} = 150$$

The speed of the propeller plane is 150 mph and the speed of the jet is 600 mph.

21. Let d = distance traveled by car, then $200 - d$ = distance traveled by train.

$$t = \frac{d}{r}$$

time traveled by car + time traveled by train = total time

$$\frac{d}{40} + \frac{200 - d}{120} = 2.2$$

$$120\left(\frac{d}{40} + \frac{200 - d}{120}\right) = 2.2(120)$$

$$3d + 200 - d = 264$$

$$2d = 64$$

$$d = 32$$

$$200 - 32 = 168$$

She travels 32 miles by car and 168 miles by train.

23. Let d = the distance flown with the wind, then $2800 - d$ = the time flown against the wind.

time with wind = $\dfrac{d}{600}$

time against wind = $\dfrac{2800 - d}{500}$

$$\dfrac{d}{600} + \dfrac{2800 - d}{500} = 5$$

$$3000\left(\dfrac{d}{600} + \dfrac{2800 - d}{500}\right) = 5(3000)$$

$$5d + 16,800 - 6d = 15,000$$

$$d = 1800$$

time with wind = $\dfrac{1800}{600} = 3$

time against wind = $\dfrac{1000}{500} = 2$

It flew 3 hours at 600 mph and 2 hours at 500 mph.

25. time at 30 ft/s = $\dfrac{d}{30}$

time at 20 ft/s = $\dfrac{d}{20}$

$$\dfrac{d}{20} = \dfrac{d}{30} + 15$$

$$60\left(\dfrac{d}{20}\right) = \left(\dfrac{d}{30} + 15\right)60$$

$$3d = 2d + 900$$

$$d = 900$$

The boat traveled 900 feet in one direction.

27. Felicia's rate = $\dfrac{1}{6}$

Reynaldo's rate = $\dfrac{1}{8}$

$$\dfrac{t}{6} + \dfrac{t}{8} = 1$$

$$48\left(\dfrac{t}{6} + \dfrac{t}{8}\right) = 48(1)$$

$$8t + 6t = 48$$

$$14t = 48$$

$$t = 3\dfrac{3}{7}$$

It will take them $3\dfrac{3}{7}$ hours.

29. input rate = $\dfrac{1}{2}$

output rate = $\dfrac{1}{3}$

$$\dfrac{t}{2} - \dfrac{t}{3} = 1$$

$$6\left(\dfrac{t}{2} - \dfrac{t}{3}\right) = 6(1)$$

$$3t - 2t = 6$$

$$t = 6$$

It will take 6 hours.

31. Input rate for small hose = $\dfrac{1}{5}$

Input rat for larger hose = $\dfrac{1}{t}$

In 2 hours, the smaller hose does $\dfrac{2}{5}$ of the filling and the larger hose does $\dfrac{2}{t}$.

$$\dfrac{2}{5} + \dfrac{2}{t} = 1$$

$$5t\left(\dfrac{2}{5} + \dfrac{2}{t}\right) = 5t$$

$$2t + 10 = 5t$$

$$10 = 3t$$

$$t = \dfrac{10}{3} = 3\dfrac{1}{3}$$

It would take the larger hose $3\dfrac{1}{3}$ hours

33. Rate for first backhoe = $\dfrac{1}{12}$

Rate for second backhoe = $\dfrac{1}{15}$

Work done by first = $\dfrac{1}{12} \cdot 5 = \dfrac{5}{12}$

Work done by second = $\dfrac{1}{15} \cdot t = \dfrac{t}{15}$

$$\dfrac{5}{12} + \dfrac{t}{15} = 1$$

$$60\left(\dfrac{5}{12} + \dfrac{t}{15}\right) = 1 \cdot 60$$

$$25 + 4t = 60$$

$$4t = 35$$

$$t = \dfrac{35}{4} = 8\dfrac{3}{4}$$

It takes the smaller backhoe $8\dfrac{3}{4}$ days to finish the trench.

35. Ken's rate $= \dfrac{1}{4}$

Bettina's rate $= \dfrac{1}{6}$

$$\frac{t}{6} + \frac{t+3}{4} = 1$$

$$12\left(\frac{t}{6} + \frac{t+3}{4}\right) = 12$$

$$2t + 3(t+3) = 12$$

$$2t + 3t + 9 = 12$$

$$5t = 3$$

$$t = \frac{3}{5}$$

It will take them $\dfrac{3}{5}$ hour or 36 minutes longer.

37. Rate of first skimmer $= \dfrac{1}{60}$

Rate of second skimmer $= \dfrac{1}{50}$

Rate of transfer $= \dfrac{1}{30}$

$$\frac{t}{60} + \frac{t}{50} - \frac{t}{30} = 1$$

$$300\left(\frac{t}{60} + \frac{t}{50} - \frac{t}{30}\right) = 300$$

$$5t + 6t - 10t = 300$$

$$t = 300$$

It will take 300 hours to fill the tank.

39. Let x be the number.

$$\frac{4}{x} + 5x = 12$$

$$x\left(\frac{4}{x} + 5x\right) = 12x$$

$$4 + 5x^2 = 12x$$

$$5x^2 - 12x + 4 = 0$$

$$(5x - 2)(x - 2) = 0$$

$$5x - 2 = 0 \quad \text{or} \quad x - 2 = 0$$

$$x = \frac{2}{5} \qquad\qquad x = 2$$

The numbers are 2 or $\dfrac{2}{5}$

41. Ed's rate $= \dfrac{1}{8}$

Samantha's rate $= \dfrac{1}{4}$

$$\frac{p}{4} - 1 = \frac{p}{8}$$

$$8\left(\frac{p}{4} - 1\right) = 8\left(\frac{p}{8}\right)$$

$$2p - 8 = p$$

$$p = 8$$

Each must pick 8 pints.

43. $\dfrac{1}{2}(x+3) - (2x+6) = \dfrac{1}{2}x + \dfrac{3}{2} - 2x - 6$

$$= \frac{x}{2} - \frac{4x}{2} + \frac{3}{2} - \frac{12}{2}$$

$$= -\frac{3x}{2} - \frac{9}{2}$$

44. $y^2 + 5y - y - 5 = y(y+5) - 1(y+5)$

$$= (y-1)(y+5)$$

45. $\dfrac{x^2 - 14x + 48}{x^2 - 5x - 24} \div \dfrac{2x^2 - 13x + 6}{2x^2 + 5x - 3} = \dfrac{x^2 - 14x + 48}{x^2 - 5x - 24} \cdot \dfrac{2x^2 + 5x - 3}{2x^2 - 13x + 6}$

$$= \frac{(x-6)(x-8)}{(x+3)(x-8)} \cdot \frac{(2x-1)(x+3)}{(2x-1)(x-6)}$$

$$= 1$$

46. $\dfrac{x}{6x^2 - x - 15} - \dfrac{5}{9x^2 - 12x - 5} = \dfrac{x}{(2x+3)(3x-5)} - \dfrac{5}{(3x+1)(3x-5)}$

$$= \dfrac{x(3x+1)}{(2x+3)(3x-5)(3x+1)} - \dfrac{5(2x+3)}{(2x+3)(3x-5)(3x+1)}$$

$$= \dfrac{3x^2 + x - (10x + 15)}{(2x+3)(3x-5)(3x+1)}$$

$$= \dfrac{3x^2 + x - 10x - 15}{(2x+3)(3x-5)(3x+1)}$$

$$= \dfrac{3x^2 - 9x - 15}{(2x+3)(3x-5)(3x+1)}$$

Exercise Set 6.8

1. 40

3. $y = kx$

5. direct; The diameter of the hose varies directly as the water coming out of the hose.

7. inverse; The speed of the turtle varies inversely as the length of time it takes the turtle to cross the road.

9. inverse; The temperature of the water varies inversely as the time it tales for an ice cube placed in the water to melt.

11. direct: The length of a roll of scotch tape varies directly with the number of two inch strips that can be obtained from the roll.

13. direct: The cubic inch displacement varies directly as the horsepower of the engine.

15. a. $x = kz$

    b. $x = 3(11) = 33$

17. a. $x = \dfrac{k}{y}$

    b. $x = \dfrac{5}{25} = \dfrac{1}{5}$

19. a. $C = kZ^2$

    b. $C = 2(5)^2 = 2(25) = 50$

21. a. $y = \dfrac{k}{x^2}$

    b. $y = \dfrac{320}{10^2} = \dfrac{320}{100} = 3.2$

23. a. $x = ky$

    b. k must be determined first; $x = ky$

$$9 = k(18)$$

$$\frac{1}{2} = k$$

    Now substitute 36 for y and $\dfrac{1}{2}$ for k.

$$x = ky = \frac{1}{2}(36) = 18$$

25. a. $C = \dfrac{k}{J}$

    b. k must be determined first; $C = \dfrac{k}{J}$

$$7 = \frac{k}{1}$$

$$7 = k$$

    Now substitute 2 for J and 7 for k.

$$C = \frac{k}{J} = \frac{7}{2} = 3.5$$

27. a. $y = kR^2$

    b. k must be determined first; $y = kR^2$

$$4 = k(4)^2$$

$$4 = 16k$$

$$.25 = k$$

    Now substitute 8 for R and .25 for k.

$$y = kR^2 = .25(8)^2 = .25(64) = 16$$

29. a. $L = \dfrac{k}{P^2}$

b. k must be determined first;

$$L = \dfrac{k}{P^2}$$

$$270 = \dfrac{k}{10^2}$$

$$270 = \dfrac{k}{100}$$

$$27000 = k$$

Now substitute 30 for P and 27000 for k.

$$L = \dfrac{k}{P^2} = \dfrac{27000}{30^2} = \dfrac{27000}{900} = 30$$

31. $a = kb = k(2b) = 2kb$ If b is doubled, then a is also doubled.

33. $y = \dfrac{k}{x} = \dfrac{k}{2x} = \dfrac{1}{2} \cdot \dfrac{k}{x}$ If x is doubled, then y is halved.

35. a. $d = ks$

b. Substitute 2 for k and 40 for s.
$d = ks = 2(40) = 80$
The distance traveled was 80 miles.

37. a. $t = \dfrac{k}{s}$

b. $t = \dfrac{k}{s} = \dfrac{100}{50} = 2$
It will take 2 hours to reach the destination.

39. a. $d = ks$

b. k must be determined first;

$$d = ks$$
$$300 = k(120)$$
$$2.5 = k$$

Now substitute 150 for s and 2.5 for k.
$d = ks = 2.5(150) = 375$
The distance traveled is 375 feet,

41. a. $t = \dfrac{k}{n}$

b. k must be determined first;

$$t = \dfrac{k}{n}$$
$$200 = \dfrac{k}{10}$$
$$2000 = k$$

Now substitute 15 for n and 2000 for k.

$$t = \dfrac{k}{n}$$
$$= \dfrac{2000}{15}$$
$$\approx 133.33$$

It will take them about 133.33 hours to put up the fence.

43. a. $r = kn$

b. k must be determined first;

$$r = kn$$
$$12000 = k(800)$$
$$15 = k$$

Now substitute 15000 for r and 15 for k.

$$r = kn$$
$$15000 = 15n$$
$$1000 = n$$

The number of people that attended the game was 1,000.

45. a. $c = kn$

b. k must be determined first;

$$c = kn$$
$$4000 = k(80)$$
$$50 = k$$

Now substitute 3000 for c and 50 for k.

$$c = kn$$
$$3000 = 50n$$
$$60 = n$$

The number of people attending the wedding was 60.

47. a. $A = kr^2$

b. k must be determined first;

$$A = kr^2$$
$$78.5 = k(5)^2$$
$$78.5 = k(25)$$
$$3.14 = k$$

Now substitute 12 for r and 3.14 for k.

$$A = kr^2$$
$$= 3.14(12)^2$$
$$= 3.14(144)$$
$$= 452.16$$

The area of the circle is 452.16 square inches.

49 a. $r = \dfrac{k}{c^2}$

b. k must be determined first;

$$r = \frac{k}{c^2}$$

$$100 = \frac{k}{0.4^2}$$

$$100 = \frac{k}{.16}$$

$$16 = k$$

Now substitute 0.6 for c and 16 for k.

$$r = \frac{k}{c^2}$$

$$= \frac{16}{0.6^2}$$

$$= \frac{16}{.36}$$

$$\approx 44.44$$

The resistance is about 44.44 ohms.

51. a. $I = kr$

b. k must be determined first; $I = kr$

$$40 = k(0.04)$$

$$1000 = k$$

Now substitute 0.06 for r and 1000 for k.

$I = kr = 1000(0.06) = 60$

The amount of interest earned was $60.

53. a. $V = \dfrac{k}{P}$

b. k must be determined first; $V = \dfrac{k}{P}$

$$800 = \frac{k}{200}$$

$$160,000 = k$$

Now substitute 25 for P and 160,000 for k.

$$V = \frac{k}{P}$$

$$= \frac{160,000}{25}$$

$$= 6400$$

The volume is 6400 cubic centimeters.

55. a. $x = kyz$

b. k must be determined first; $x = kyz$

$$72 = k(18)(2)$$

$$72 = k(36)$$

$$2 = k$$

Now substitute 36 for y, 3 for z and 2 for k.

$x = kyz = 2(36)(3) = 216$

Thus, $x = 216$.

57.

$$4x + 9 \overline{\smash{\big)}\, 8x^2 + 6x - 25} \quad \overset{\displaystyle 2x - 3}{}$$

$$\underline{8x^2 + 18x}$$

$$-12x - 25$$

$$\underline{-12x - 27}$$

$$2$$

$$\frac{8x^2 + 6x - 25}{4x + 9} = 2x - 3 + \frac{2}{4x + 9}$$

58. $\dfrac{y(z-2) + 3(z-2)}{(z-2)(y+3)}$

59.

$$3x^2 - 24 = -6x$$

$$3x^2 + 6x - 24 = 0$$

$$3\left(x^2 + 2x - 8\right) = 0$$

$$3(x+4)(x-2) = 0$$

$$x + 4 = 0 \quad \text{or} \quad x - 2 = 0$$

$$x = -4 \qquad\qquad x = 2$$

60. $\dfrac{x+3}{x-3} \cdot \dfrac{x^3 - 27}{x^2 + 3x + 9} = \dfrac{x+3}{x-3} \cdot \dfrac{(x-3)\left(x^2 + 3x + 9\right)}{x^2 + 3x + 9}$

$$= x + 3$$

Review Exercises

1. $\dfrac{5}{2x - 12}$

$$2x - 12 = 0$$

$$2(x - 6) = 0$$

$$x - 6 = 0$$

The expression is defined for all real numbers except $x = 6$.

2. $\dfrac{2}{x^2 - 8x + 15}$

$x^2 - 8x + 15 = 0$

$(x - 3)(x - 5) = 0$

$x - 3 = 0, x - 5 = 0$

The expression is defined for all real numbers except $x = 3, x = 5$.

3. $\dfrac{2}{5x^2 + 4x - 1}$

$5x^2 + 4x - 1 = 0$

$(5x - 1)(x + 1) = 0$

$5x - 1 = 0, x + 1 = 0$

The expression is defined for all real numbers except $x = \dfrac{1}{5}, x = -1$.

4. $\dfrac{y}{xy - 3y} = \dfrac{y}{y(x - 3)}$

$= \dfrac{1}{x - 3}$

5. $\dfrac{x^3 + 4x^2 + 12x}{x} = \dfrac{x\left(x^2 + 4x + 12\right)}{x}$

$= x^2 + 4x + 12$

6. $\dfrac{9x^2 + 6xy}{3x} = \dfrac{3x(3x + 2y)}{3x}$

$= 3x + 2y$

7. $\dfrac{x^2 + 2x - 8}{x - 2} = \dfrac{(x - 2)(x + 4)}{x - 2}$

$= x + 4$

8. $\dfrac{a^2 - 36}{a - 6} = \dfrac{(a - 6)(a + 6)}{a - 6}$

$= a + 6$

9. $\dfrac{-2x^2 + 7x + 4}{x - 4} = \dfrac{-1\left(2x^2 + 7x + 4\right)}{(x - 4)}$

$= \dfrac{-1(2x + 1)(x - 4)}{(x - 4)}$

$= -(2x + 1)$

10. $\dfrac{b^2 - 8b + 15}{b^2 - 3b - 10} = \dfrac{(b - 5)(b - 3)}{(b - 5)(b + 2)}$

$= \dfrac{b - 3}{b + 2}$

11. $\dfrac{4x^2 - 11x - 3}{4x^2 - 7x - 2} = \dfrac{(4x + 1)(x - 3)}{(4x + 1)(x - 2)}$

$= \dfrac{x - 3}{x - 2}$

12. $\dfrac{2x^2 - 21x + 40}{4x^2 - 4x - 15} = \dfrac{(x - 8)(2x - 5)}{(2x + 3)(2x - 5)}$

$= \dfrac{x - 8}{2x + 3}$

13. $\dfrac{5a^2}{6b} \cdot \dfrac{2}{4a^2b} = \dfrac{5 \cdot 2}{6 \cdot 4} \cdot \dfrac{a^2}{a^2} \cdot \dfrac{1}{b \cdot b}$

$= \dfrac{10}{24b^2}$

$= \dfrac{5}{12b^2}$

14. $\dfrac{15x^2y^3}{3z} \cdot \dfrac{6z^3}{5xy^3} = \dfrac{15 \cdot 6}{15}\left(\dfrac{x^2}{x}\right)\left(\dfrac{y^3}{y^3}\right)\left(\dfrac{z^3}{z}\right)$

$= 6xz^2$

15. $\dfrac{40a^3b^4}{7c^3} \cdot \dfrac{14c^5}{5a^5b} = \dfrac{40}{5} \cdot \dfrac{14}{7} \cdot \dfrac{a^3}{a^5} \cdot \dfrac{b^4}{b} \cdot \dfrac{c^5}{c^3}$

$= 16\dfrac{1}{a^2}b^3c^2$

$= \dfrac{16b^3c^2}{a^2}$

16. $\dfrac{1}{x - 4} \cdot \dfrac{4 - x}{3} = \dfrac{1}{x - 4} \cdot \dfrac{-1(x - 4)}{3}$

$= -\dfrac{1}{3}$

17. $\dfrac{-m + 4}{15m} \cdot \dfrac{10m}{m - 4} = \dfrac{-1(m - 4)}{3 \cdot 5m} \cdot \dfrac{2 \cdot 5m}{m - 4}$

$= \dfrac{-2}{3}$

18. $\dfrac{a - 2}{a + 3} \cdot \dfrac{a^2 + 4a + 3}{a^2 - a - 2} = \dfrac{(a - 2)(a + 3)(a + 1)}{(a + 3)(a - 2)(a + 1)}$

$= 1$

19.
$$\frac{16x^6}{y^2} \div \frac{x^4}{4y} = \frac{16x^6}{y^2} \cdot \frac{4y}{x^4}$$
$$= \frac{64x^6 y}{x^4 y^2}$$
$$= \frac{64x^2}{y}$$

20.
$$\frac{8xy^2}{z} \div \frac{x^4 y^2}{4z^2} = \frac{8xy^2}{z} \cdot \frac{4z^2}{x^4 y^2}$$
$$= \frac{32z}{x^3}$$

21.
$$\frac{5a+5b}{a^2} \div \frac{a^2-b^2}{a^2} = \frac{5(a+b)}{a^2} \cdot \frac{a^2}{(a+b)(a-b)}$$
$$= \frac{5}{a-b}$$

22.
$$\frac{1}{a^2+8a+15} \div \frac{3}{a+5} = \frac{1}{(a+5)(a+3)} \cdot \frac{a+5}{3}$$
$$= \frac{1}{3(a+3)}$$

23.
$$(t+8) \div \frac{t^2+5t-24}{t-3} = (t+8) \cdot \frac{t-3}{(t-3)(t+8)}$$
$$= 1$$

24.
$$\frac{x^2+xy-2y^2}{4y} \div \frac{x+2y}{12y^2} = \frac{(x-y)(x+2y)}{4y} \cdot \frac{12y^2}{x+2y}$$
$$= 3y(x-y)$$

25.
$$\frac{n}{n+5} - \frac{5}{n+5} = \frac{n-5}{n+5}$$

26.
$$\frac{3x}{x+7} + \frac{21}{x+7} = \frac{3x+21}{x+7}$$
$$= \frac{3(x+7)}{x+7}$$
$$= 3$$

27.
$$\frac{9x-4}{x+8} + \frac{76}{x+8} = \frac{9x-4+76}{x+8}$$
$$= \frac{9x+72}{x+8}$$
$$= \frac{9(x+8)}{x+8}$$
$$= 9$$

28.
$$\frac{7x-3}{x^2+7x-30} - \frac{3x+9}{x^2+7x-30} = \frac{7x-3-(3x+9)}{x^2+7x-30}$$
$$= \frac{7x-3-3x-9}{x^2+7x-30}$$
$$= \frac{4x-12}{x^2+7x-30}$$
$$= \frac{4(x-3)}{(x+10)(x-3)}$$
$$= \frac{4}{x+10}$$

29.
$$\frac{5h^2+12h-1}{h+5} - \frac{h^2-5h+14}{h+5} = \frac{5h^2+12h-1-\left(h^2-5h+14\right)}{h+5}$$
$$= \frac{5h^2+12h-1-h^2+5h-14}{h+5}$$
$$= \frac{4h^2+17h-15}{h+5}$$
$$\frac{(4h-3)(h+5)}{h+5}$$
$$= 4h-3$$

30.

$$\frac{6x^2 - 4x}{2x - 3} - \frac{-3x + 12}{2x - 3} = \frac{6x^2 + 4x - (-3x + 12)}{2x - 3}$$

$$= \frac{6x^2 - 4x + 3x - 12}{2x - 3}$$

$$= \frac{6x^2 - x - 12}{2x - 3}$$

$$= \frac{(3x + 4)(2x - 3)}{2x - 3}$$

$$= 3x + 4$$

31. $\dfrac{a}{10} + \dfrac{4a}{3}$

Least common denominator $= 2(5)(3) = 30$

32. $\dfrac{8}{x + 3} + \dfrac{4}{x + 3}$

Least common denominator $= x + 3$

33. $\dfrac{5}{4xy^3} - \dfrac{7}{10x^2 y}$

Least common denominator $= 20x^2 y^3$

34. $\dfrac{6}{x + 1} - \dfrac{3x}{x}$

Least common denominator $= x(x + 1)$

35. $\dfrac{4}{n - 5} + \dfrac{2n - 3}{n - 4}$

Least common denominator $= (n - 5)(n - 4)$

36. $\dfrac{7x - 12}{x^2 + x} - \dfrac{4}{x + 1} = \dfrac{7x - 12}{x(x + 1)} - \dfrac{4}{x + 1}$

Least common denominator $= x(x + 1)$

37. $\dfrac{2r - 9}{r - s} - \dfrac{6}{r^2 - s^2} = \dfrac{2r - 9}{r - s} - \dfrac{6}{(r + s)(r - s)}$

Least common denominator $= (r + s)(r - s)$

38. $\dfrac{4x^2}{x - 7} + 8x^2 = \dfrac{4x^2}{x - y} + \dfrac{8x^2}{1}$

Least common denominator $= x - 7$

39. $\dfrac{19x - 5}{x^2 + 2x - 35} + \dfrac{3x - 2}{x^2 + 9x + 14}$

$$= \dfrac{19x - 5}{(x + 7)(x - 5)} + \dfrac{3x - 2}{(x + 7)(x + 2)}$$

Least common denominator
$= (x + 7)(x - 5)(x + 2)$

40.

$$\frac{4}{3y^2} + \frac{y}{2y} = \frac{4}{3y^2} + \frac{1}{2}$$

$$= \frac{4}{3y^2} \cdot \frac{2}{2} + \frac{1}{2} \cdot \frac{3y^2}{3y^2}$$

$$= \frac{8}{6y^2} + \frac{3y^2}{6y^2}$$

$$= \frac{8 + 3y^2}{6y^2}$$

$$= \frac{3y^2 + 8}{6y^2}$$

41.

$$\frac{2x}{xy} + \frac{1}{5x} = \frac{2x}{xy} \cdot \frac{5}{5} + \frac{1}{5x} \cdot \frac{y}{y}$$

$$= \frac{10x}{5xy} + \frac{y}{5xy}$$

$$= \frac{10x + y}{5xy}$$

42.

$$\frac{5x}{3xy} - \frac{4}{x^2} = \frac{5x}{3xy} \cdot \frac{x}{x} - \frac{4}{x^2} \cdot \frac{3y}{3y}$$

$$= \frac{5x^2}{3x^2 y} - \frac{12y}{3x^2 y}$$

$$= \frac{5x^2 - 12y}{3x^2 y}$$

43.

$$6 - \frac{2}{x + 2} = 6\left(\frac{x + 2}{x + 2}\right) - \frac{2}{x + 2}$$

$$= \frac{6x + 12 - 2}{x + 2}$$

$$= \frac{6x + 10}{x + 2}$$

44. $\dfrac{x-y}{y} - \dfrac{x+y}{x} = \dfrac{x-y}{y} \cdot \dfrac{x}{x} - \dfrac{x+y}{x} \cdot \dfrac{y}{y}$

$\qquad = \dfrac{x(x-y)}{xy} - \dfrac{y(x+y)}{xy}$

$\qquad = \dfrac{x^2 - xy - xy - y^2}{xy}$

$\qquad = \dfrac{x^2 - 2xy - y^2}{xy}$

45. $\dfrac{7}{x+4} + \dfrac{4}{x} = \dfrac{7}{x+4} \cdot \dfrac{x}{x} + \dfrac{4}{x} \cdot \dfrac{x+4}{x+4}$

$\qquad = \dfrac{7x}{x(x+4)} + \dfrac{4(x+4)}{x(x+4)}$

$\qquad = \dfrac{7x + 4x + 16}{x(x+4)}$

$\qquad = \dfrac{11x + 16}{x(x+4)}$

46. $\dfrac{2}{3x} - \dfrac{3}{3x-6} = \dfrac{2}{3x} - \dfrac{3}{3(x-2)}$

$\qquad = \dfrac{2}{3x} \cdot \dfrac{x-2}{x-2} - \dfrac{3}{3(x-2)} \cdot \dfrac{x}{x}$

$\qquad = \dfrac{2(x-2)}{3x(x-2)} - \dfrac{3x}{3x(x-2)}$

$\qquad = \dfrac{2x - 4 - 3x}{3x(x-2)}$

$\qquad = \dfrac{-x-4}{3x(x-2)}$

47. $\dfrac{3}{z+5} + \dfrac{7}{(z+5)^2} = \dfrac{3}{z+5} \cdot \dfrac{z+5}{z+5} + \dfrac{7}{(z+5)^2}$

$\qquad = \dfrac{3(z+5)}{(z+5)^2} + \dfrac{7}{(z+5)^2}$

$\qquad = \dfrac{3z + 15 + 7}{(z+5)^2}$

$\qquad = \dfrac{3z + 22}{(z+5)^2}$

48. $\dfrac{x+2}{x^2-x-6} + \dfrac{x-3}{x^2-8x+15} = \dfrac{x+2}{(x-3)(x+2)} + \dfrac{x-3}{(x-3)(x-5)}$

$\qquad = \dfrac{1}{x-3} + \dfrac{1}{x-5}$

$\qquad = \dfrac{1}{x-3} \cdot \dfrac{x-5}{x-5} + \dfrac{1}{x-5} \cdot \dfrac{x-3}{x-3}$

$\qquad = \dfrac{x-5}{(x-3)(x-5)} + \dfrac{x-3}{(x-5)(x-3)}$

$\qquad = \dfrac{x-5 + x-3}{(x-5)(x-3)}$

$\qquad = \dfrac{2x-8}{(x-5)(x-3)}$

49. $\dfrac{x+4}{x+6} - \dfrac{x-5}{x+2} = \dfrac{(x+4)(x+2)}{(x+6)(x+2)} - \dfrac{(x-5)(x+6)}{(x+2)(x+6)}$

$$= \dfrac{x^2 + 6x + 8 - (x^2 + x - 30)}{(x+6)(x+2)}$$

$$= \dfrac{x^2 + 6x + 8 - x^2 + x + 30}{(x+6)(x+2)}$$

$$= \dfrac{5x + 38}{(x+6)(x+2)}$$

50. $3 + \dfrac{x}{x-4} = \dfrac{3(x-4)}{x-4} + \dfrac{x}{x-4}$

$$= \dfrac{3x - 12 + x}{x-4}$$

$$= \dfrac{4x - 12}{x-4}$$

51. $\dfrac{a+2}{b} \div \dfrac{a-2}{4b^2} = \dfrac{a+2}{b} \cdot \dfrac{4b^2}{a-2}$

$$= \dfrac{4b(a+2)}{a-2}$$

$$= \dfrac{4ab + 8b}{a-2}$$

52. $\dfrac{x+3}{x^2-9} + \dfrac{2}{x+3} = \dfrac{x+3}{(x-3)(x+3)} + \dfrac{2}{x+3}$

$$= \dfrac{x+3}{(x-3)(x+3)} + \dfrac{2(x-3)}{(x-3)(x+3)}$$

$$= \dfrac{x+3+2x-6}{(x-3)(x+3)}$$

$$= \dfrac{3x-3}{(x-3)(x+3)}$$

53. $\dfrac{5p+10q}{p^2 q} \cdot \dfrac{p^4}{p+2q} = \dfrac{5(p+2q)p^4}{(p+2q)p^2 q}$

$$= \dfrac{5p^2}{q}$$

54. $\dfrac{4}{(x+2)(x-3)} - \dfrac{4}{(x-2)(x+2)} = \dfrac{4(x-2)}{(x+2)(x-3)(x-2)} - \dfrac{4(x-3)}{(x+2)(x-3)(x-2)}$

$$= \dfrac{4(x-2) - 4(x-3)}{(x+2)(x-3)(x-2)}$$

$$= \dfrac{4x - 8 - 4x + 12}{(x+2)(x-3)(x-2)}$$

$$= \dfrac{4}{(x+2)(x-3)(x-2)}$$

55. $\dfrac{x+7}{x^2+9x+14} - \dfrac{x-10}{x^2-49} = \dfrac{x+7}{(x+7)(x+2)} - \dfrac{x-10}{(x+7)(x-7)}$

$$= \dfrac{x+7}{(x+7)(x+2)} \cdot \dfrac{(x-7)}{(x-7)} - \dfrac{x-10}{(x+7)(x-7)} \cdot \dfrac{(x+2)}{(x+2)}$$

$$= \dfrac{x^2-49-\left(x^2-8x-20\right)}{(x+7)(x-7)(x+2)}$$

$$= \dfrac{8x-29}{(x+7)(x-7)(x+2)}$$

56. $\dfrac{x-y}{x+y} \cdot \dfrac{xy+x^2}{x^2-y^2} = \dfrac{x-y}{x+y} \cdot \dfrac{x(y+x)}{(x+y)(x-y)}$

$$= \dfrac{x}{x+y}$$

57. $\dfrac{3x^2-27y^2}{20} \div \dfrac{(x-3y)^2}{4} = \dfrac{3\left(x^2-9y^2\right)}{20} \cdot \dfrac{4}{(x-3y)^2}$

$$= \dfrac{3(x-3y)(x+3y)}{4 \cdot 5} \cdot \dfrac{4}{(x-3y)^2}$$

$$= \dfrac{3(x+3y)}{5(x-3y)}$$

58. $\dfrac{a^2-9a+20}{a-4} \cdot \dfrac{a^2-8a+15}{a^2-10a+25} = \dfrac{(a-4)(a-5)}{a-4} \cdot \dfrac{(a-5)(a-3)}{(a-5)^2}$

$$= a-3$$

59. $\dfrac{a}{a^2-1} - \dfrac{2}{3a^2-2a-5} = \dfrac{a}{(a-1)(a+1)} - \dfrac{2}{(3a-5)(a+1)}$

$$= \dfrac{a(3a-5)}{(a-1)(a+1)(3a-5)} - \dfrac{2(a-1)}{(a-1)(a+1)(3a-5)}$$

$$= \dfrac{a(3a-5)-2(a-1)}{(a-1)(a+1)(3a-5)}$$

$$= \dfrac{3a^2-5a-2a+2}{(a-1)(a+1)(3a-5)}$$

$$= \dfrac{3a^2-7a+2}{(a-1)(a+1)(3a-5)}$$

60. $\dfrac{2x^2+6x-20}{x^2-2x} \div \dfrac{x^2+7x+10}{4x^2-16} = \dfrac{2\left(x^2+3x-10\right)}{x(x-2)} \cdot \dfrac{4\left(x^2-4\right)}{(x+5)(x+2)}$

$$= \dfrac{2(x+5)(x-2)}{x(x-2)} \cdot \dfrac{4(x+2)(x-2)}{(x+5)(x+2)}$$

$$= \dfrac{8(x-2)}{x}$$

$$= \dfrac{8x-16}{x}$$

61. $\dfrac{3+\frac{2}{3}}{\frac{3}{5}} = \dfrac{15\left(3+\frac{2}{3}\right)}{15\left(\frac{3}{5}\right)}$

$\qquad = \dfrac{45+10}{9}$

$\qquad = \dfrac{55}{9}$

62. $\dfrac{1+\frac{5}{8}}{4-\frac{9}{16}} = \dfrac{16\left(1+\frac{5}{8}\right)}{16\left(4-\frac{9}{16}\right)}$

$\qquad = \dfrac{16+10}{64-9}$

$\qquad = \dfrac{26}{55}$

63. $\dfrac{\frac{12ab}{9c}}{\frac{4a}{c^2}} = \dfrac{12ab}{9c}\cdot\dfrac{c^2}{4a}$

$\qquad = \dfrac{bc}{3}$

64. $\dfrac{36x^4y^2}{\frac{9xy^5}{4z^2}} = \dfrac{36x^4y^2\cdot 4z^2}{\frac{9xy^5}{4z^2}\cdot 4z^2}$

$\qquad = \dfrac{144x^4y^2z^2}{9xy^5}$

$\qquad = \dfrac{16x^3z^2}{y^3}$

65. $\dfrac{a-\frac{a}{b}}{\frac{1+a}{b}} = \dfrac{\left(a-\frac{a}{b}\right)b}{\left(\frac{1+a}{b}\right)b} = \dfrac{ab-a}{1+a}$

66. $\dfrac{r^2+\frac{1}{s}}{s^2} = \dfrac{\left(r^2+\frac{1}{s}\right)s}{\left(s^2\right)s}$

$\qquad = \dfrac{r^2s+1}{s^3}$

67. $\dfrac{\frac{4}{x}+\frac{2}{x^2}}{6-\frac{1}{x}} = \dfrac{\left(\frac{4}{x}+\frac{2}{x^2}\right)x^2}{\left(6-\frac{1}{x}\right)x^2}$

$\qquad = \dfrac{4x+2}{6x^2-x}$

$\qquad = \dfrac{4x+2}{x(6x-1)}$

68. $\dfrac{\frac{x}{x+y}}{\frac{x^2}{2x+2y}} = \dfrac{x}{x+y}\cdot\dfrac{2x+2y}{x^2}$

$\qquad = \dfrac{1}{x+y}\cdot\dfrac{2(x+y)}{x}$

$\qquad = \dfrac{2}{x}$

69. $\dfrac{\frac{3}{x}}{\frac{3}{x^2}} = \dfrac{3}{x}\cdot\dfrac{x^2}{3} = x$

70. $\dfrac{\frac{1}{a}+2}{\frac{1}{a}+\frac{1}{a}} = \dfrac{\frac{1}{a}+2}{\frac{2}{a}}$

$\qquad = \dfrac{\left(\frac{1}{a}+2\right)a}{\left(\frac{2}{a}\right)a}$

$\qquad = \dfrac{1+2a}{2}$

71. $\dfrac{\frac{1}{x^2}-\frac{1}{x}}{\frac{1}{x^2}+\frac{1}{x}} = \dfrac{x^2\left(\frac{1}{x^2}-\frac{1}{x}\right)}{x^2\left(\frac{1}{x^2}+\frac{1}{x}\right)}$

$\qquad = \dfrac{1-x}{1+x}$

$\qquad = \dfrac{-x+1}{x+1}$

72. $\dfrac{\frac{3x}{y}-x}{\frac{y}{x}-1} = \dfrac{\left(\frac{3x}{y}-x\right)xy}{\left(\frac{y}{x}-1\right)xy}$

$\qquad = \dfrac{3x^2-x^2y}{y^2-xy}$

$\qquad = \dfrac{3x^2-x^2y}{y(y-x)}$

73. $\dfrac{5}{9} = \dfrac{5}{x+3}$

$\qquad 5(x+3) = 5(9)$

$\qquad 5x+15 = 45$

$\qquad\qquad 5x = 30$

$\qquad\qquad\ \ x = 6$

74. $\dfrac{x}{6} = \dfrac{x-4}{2}$

$2x = 6(x-4)$

$2x = 6x - 24$

$24 = 4x$

$6 = x$

75. $\dfrac{n}{5} + 12 = \dfrac{n}{2}$

$10\left(\dfrac{n}{5} + 12\right) = 10\left(\dfrac{n}{2}\right)$

$2n + 120 = 5n$

$120 = 3n$

$40 = n$

76. $\dfrac{3}{x} - \dfrac{1}{6} = \dfrac{1}{x}$

$6x\left(\dfrac{3}{x} - \dfrac{1}{6}\right) = 6x\left(\dfrac{1}{x}\right)$

$18 - x = 6$

$-x = -12$

$x = 12$

77. $\dfrac{-4}{d} = \dfrac{3}{2} + \dfrac{4-d}{d}$

$2d\left(\dfrac{-4}{d}\right) = 2d\left(\dfrac{3}{2} + \dfrac{4-d}{d}\right)$

$-8 = 3d + 8 - 2d$

$-8 = d + 8$

$-16 = d$

78. $\dfrac{1}{x-7} + \dfrac{1}{x+7} = \dfrac{1}{x^2-49}$

$\dfrac{1}{x-7} + \dfrac{1}{x+7} = \dfrac{1}{(x-7)(x+7)}$

$(x-7)(x+7)\left[\dfrac{1}{x-7} + \dfrac{1}{x+7}\right] = \left[\dfrac{1}{(x-7)(x+7)}\right](x-7)(x+7)$

$x + 7 + x - 7 = 1$

$2x = 1$

$x = \dfrac{1}{2}$

79.

$$\frac{x-3}{x-2} + \frac{x+1}{x+3} = \frac{2x^2+x+1}{x^2+x-6}$$

$$\frac{x-3}{x-2} + \frac{x+1}{x+3} = \frac{2x^2+x+1}{(x-2)(x+3)}$$

$$(x-2)(x+3)\left(\frac{x-3}{x-2} + \frac{x+1}{x+3}\right) = (x-2)(x+3)\left[\frac{2x^2+x+1}{(x-2)(x+3)}\right]$$

$$(x+3)(x-3) + (x-2)(x+1) = 2x^2+x+1$$

$$x^2-9+x^2-x-2 = 2x^2+x+1$$

$$2x^2-x-11 = 2x^2+x+1$$

$$-12 = 2x$$

$$-6 = x$$

80.

$$\frac{a}{a^2-64} + \frac{4}{a+8} = \frac{3}{a-8}$$

$$\frac{a}{(a+8)(a-8)} + \frac{4}{a+8} = \frac{3}{a-8}$$

$$(a+8)(a-8)\left[\frac{a}{(a+8)(a-8)} + \frac{4}{a+8}\right] = (a+8)(a-8)\left(\frac{3}{a-8}\right)$$

$$a+4(a-8) = 3(a+8)$$

$$a+4a-32 = 3a+24$$

$$5a-32 = 3a+24$$

$$2a = 56$$

$$a = 28$$

81.

$$\frac{d}{d-2} - 2 = \frac{2}{d-2}$$

$$(d-2)\left(\frac{d}{d-2} - 2\right) = (d-2)\left(\frac{2}{d-2}\right)$$

$$d-2(d-2) = 2$$

$$d-2d+4 = 2$$

$$-d+4 = 2$$

$$-d = -2$$

$$d = 2$$

Since $\frac{2}{0}$ is not a real number, there is no solution.

82. John and Amy rate $= \frac{1}{6}$

Paul and Cindy rate $= \frac{1}{5}$

$$\frac{t}{6} + \frac{t}{5} = 1$$

$$30\left(\frac{t}{6} + \frac{t}{5}\right) = 30(1)$$

$$5t+6t = 30$$

$$11t = 30$$

$$t = \frac{30}{11} = 2\frac{8}{11}$$

It will take the 4 people $2\frac{8}{11}$ hours.

83. $\frac{3}{4}$-inch hose's rate $= \frac{1}{7}$

$\frac{5}{16}$-inch hose's rate $= \frac{1}{12}$

$$\frac{t}{7} - \frac{t}{12} = 1$$

$$\frac{12t-7t}{84} = 1$$

$$5t = 84$$

$$t = \frac{84}{5} = 16\frac{4}{5}$$

It will take $16\frac{4}{5}$ hours to fill the pool.

84. Let x be one number then, $5x$ is the other number.

$$\frac{1}{x} + \frac{1}{5x} = 6$$

$$5x\left(\frac{1}{x} + \frac{1}{5x}\right) = 5x(6)$$

$$5 + 1 = 30x$$

$$6 = 30x$$

$$\frac{6}{30} = x$$

$$\frac{1}{5} = x$$

$$5x = 5\left(\frac{1}{5}\right) = 1$$

The numbers are $\frac{1}{5}$ and 1.

85. Let x = Robert's speed, then
$3.5 + x$ = Tran's speed

$$t = \frac{d}{r}$$

Robert's time = Tran's time

$$\frac{3}{x} = \frac{8}{3.5 + x}$$

$$3(3.5 + x) = 8x$$

$$10.5 + 3x = 8x$$

$$10.5 = 5x$$

$$2.1 = x$$

$$x + 3.5 = 2.1 + 3.5 = 5.6$$

Robert's speed is 2.1 mph and Tran's speed is 5.6 mph.

86.　　$d = kw$

$$2376 = k \cdot 132$$

$$2376 = 132k$$

$$18 = k$$

Now we have to substitute 172 for w and 18 for k to find the recommended dosage for Bill.

$$d = kw$$

$$d = 18 \cdot 172$$

$$d = 3096$$

Thus, 3096 mg is needed for Bill.

87.　　$t = \dfrac{k}{s}$

$$1.4 = \frac{k}{6}$$

$$8.4 = k$$

Now we have to substitute 5 for s and 8.4 for k to find Leif's time.

$$t = \frac{k}{s}$$

$$t = \frac{8.4}{5}$$

$$t = 1.68$$

Thus, it will take Leif 1.68 hours.

Practice Test

1. $\dfrac{-6 + x}{x - 6} = \dfrac{x - 6}{x - 6} = 1$

2. $\dfrac{x^3 - 1}{x^2 - 1} = \dfrac{(x - 1)(x^2 + x + 1)}{(x - 1)(x + 1)}$

$$= \frac{x^2 + x + 1}{x + 1}$$

3. $\dfrac{15x^2 y^3}{4z^2} \cdot \dfrac{8xz^3}{5xy^4} = \dfrac{3 \cdot 5x^2 y^3}{4z^2} \cdot \dfrac{2 \cdot 4xz^3}{5xy^4}$

$$= \frac{6x^3 y^3 z^3}{xy^4 z^2}$$

$$= \frac{6x^2 z}{y}$$

4. $\dfrac{a^2 - 9a + 14}{a - 2} \cdot \dfrac{a^2 - 4a - 21}{(a-7)^2} = \dfrac{(a-7)(a-2)}{a-2} \cdot \dfrac{(a-7)(a+3)}{(a-7)^2}$

$$= a + 3$$

5. $\dfrac{x^2 - x - 6}{x^2 - 9} \cdot \dfrac{x^2 - 6x + 9}{x^2 + 4x + 4} = \dfrac{(x-3)(x+2)}{(x-3)(x+3)} \cdot \dfrac{(x-3)(x-3)}{(x+2)(x+2)}$

$$= \dfrac{(x-3)^2}{(x+3)(x+2)}$$

$$= \dfrac{x^2 - 6x + 9}{(x+3)(x+2)}$$

6. $\dfrac{x^2 - 1}{x + 2} \cdot \dfrac{2x + 4}{2 - 2x^2} = \dfrac{(x-1)(x+1)}{x+2} \cdot \dfrac{2(x+2)}{-2(x-1)(x+1)}$

$$= -1$$

7. $\dfrac{x^2 - 4y^2}{3x + 12y} \div \dfrac{x + 2y}{x + 4y} = \dfrac{(x-2y)(x+2y)}{3(x+4y)} \cdot \dfrac{x + 4y}{x + 2y}$

$$= \dfrac{x - 2y}{3}$$

8. $\dfrac{15}{y^2 + 2y - 15} \div \dfrac{3}{y - 3} = \dfrac{15}{(y-3)(y+5)} \cdot \dfrac{y - 3}{3}$

$$= \dfrac{5}{y + 5}$$

9. $\dfrac{m^2 + 3m - 18}{m - 3} \div \dfrac{m^2 - 8m + 15}{3 - m} = \dfrac{(m+6)(m-3)}{m-3} \cdot \dfrac{-1(m-3)}{(m-5)(m-3)}$

$$= \dfrac{-(m+6)}{m-5}$$

$$= -\dfrac{m+6}{m-5}$$

10. $\dfrac{4x + 3}{2y} + \dfrac{2x - 5}{2y} = \dfrac{4x + 3 + 2x - 5}{2y}$

$$= \dfrac{6x - 2}{2y}$$

$$= \dfrac{2(3x - 1)}{2y}$$

$$= \dfrac{3x - 1}{y}$$

11. $\dfrac{7x^2 - 4}{x + 3} - \dfrac{6x + 7}{x + 3} = \dfrac{7x^2 - 4 - (6x + 7)}{x + 3}$

$$= \dfrac{7x^2 - 4 - 6x - 7}{x + 3}$$

$$= \dfrac{7x^2 - 6x - 11}{x + 3}$$

12.
$$\frac{4}{xy} - \frac{3}{xy^3} = \frac{4}{xy} \cdot \frac{y^2}{y^2} - \frac{3}{xy^3}$$
$$= \frac{4y^2}{xy^3} - \frac{3}{xy^3}$$
$$= \frac{4y^2 - 3}{xy^3}$$

13.
$$4 - \frac{5z}{z-5} = 4\left(\frac{z-5}{z-5}\right) - \frac{5z}{z-5}$$
$$= \frac{4z - 20}{z-5} - \frac{5z}{z-5}$$
$$= \frac{4z - 20 - 5z}{z-5}$$
$$= \frac{-z - 20}{z-5}$$
$$= \frac{-1(z + 20)}{z-5}$$
$$= -\frac{z + 20}{z-5}$$

14.
$$\frac{x-5}{x^2-16} - \frac{x-2}{x^2+2x-8} = \frac{x-5}{(x-4)(x+4)} - \frac{x-2}{(x-2)(x+4)}$$
$$= \frac{x-5}{(x-4)(x+4)} - \frac{1}{x+4}$$
$$= \frac{x-5}{(x-4)(x+4)} - \frac{1}{x+4} \cdot \frac{x-4}{x-4}$$
$$= \frac{x-5-(x-4)}{(x-4)(x+4)}$$
$$= \frac{x-5-x+4}{(x-4)(x+4)}$$
$$= \frac{-1}{(x-4)(x+4)}$$

15.
$$\frac{5 + \frac{1}{2}}{3 - \frac{1}{5}} = \frac{10\left(5 + \frac{1}{2}\right)}{10\left(3 - \frac{1}{5}\right)}$$
$$= \frac{50 + 5}{30 - 2}$$
$$= \frac{55}{28}$$

16.
$$\frac{x + \frac{x}{y}}{\frac{1}{x}} = \left(x + \frac{x}{y}\right)\frac{x}{1}$$
$$= \left(\frac{xy + x}{y}\right)\left(\frac{x}{1}\right)$$
$$= \frac{yx^2 + x^2}{y}$$

17.
$$\frac{2 + \frac{3}{x}}{\frac{2}{x} - 5} = \frac{x\left(2 + \frac{3}{x}\right)}{x\left(\frac{2}{x} - 5\right)}$$
$$= \frac{2x + 3}{2 - 5x}$$

18.
$$6 + \frac{2}{x} = 7$$
$$x\left(6 + \frac{2}{x}\right) = 7x$$
$$6x + 2 = 7x$$
$$2 = x$$

19.
$$\frac{2x}{3} - \frac{x}{4} = x + 1$$
$$12\left(\frac{2x}{3} - \frac{x}{4}\right) = 12(x+1)$$
$$8x - 3x = 12x + 12$$
$$5x = 12x + 12$$
$$-7x = 12$$
$$x = -\frac{12}{7}$$

20.
$$\frac{x}{x-8} + \frac{6}{x-2} = \frac{x^2}{x^2 - 10x + 16}$$
$$\frac{x}{x-8} + \frac{6}{x-2} = \frac{x^2}{(x-8)(x-2)}$$
$$(x-8)(x-2)\left(\frac{x}{x-8} + \frac{6}{x-2}\right) = (x-8)(x-2)\left[\frac{x^2}{(x-8)(x-2)}\right]$$
$$x(x-2) + 6(x-8) = x^2$$
$$x^2 - 2x + 6x - 48 = x^2$$
$$4x - 48 = 0$$
$$4x = 48$$
$$x = 12$$

21.
$$\frac{t}{8} + \frac{t}{5} = 1$$
$$\frac{5t + 8t}{40} = 1$$
$$13t = 40$$
$$t = \frac{40}{13} = 3\frac{1}{13}$$

It will take them $3\frac{1}{13}$ hours to level one acre together.

22. Let x be the number.
$$x + \frac{1}{x} = 2$$
$$x\left(x + \frac{1}{x}\right) = x(2)$$
$$x^2 + 1 = 2x$$
$$x^2 - 2x + 1 = 0$$
$$(x-1)(x-1) = 0$$
$$x - 1 = 0$$
$$x = 1$$
The number is 1.

23. Let x = base, then $2x - 3$ = height.
$$\text{area} = \frac{1}{2} \cdot \text{base} \cdot \text{height}$$

$$27 = \frac{1}{2}x(2x-3)$$
$$2(27) = 2\left[\frac{1}{2}x(2x-3)\right]$$
$$54 = x(2x-3)$$
$$54 = 2x^2 - 3x$$
$$0 = 2x^2 - 3x - 54$$
$$0 = (2x+9)(x-6)$$
$$2x + 9 = 0 \quad \text{or} \quad x - 6 = 0$$
$$x = -\frac{9}{2} \qquad\qquad x = 6$$

Since the base cannot be negative, the base is 6 inches and the height is $2(6) - 3 = 9$ inches.

24. Let d = the distance she rollerblades, then $12 - d$ is the distance she bicycles.
$$t = \frac{d}{r}$$
$$\frac{d}{4} + \frac{12-d}{10} = 1.5$$
$$20\left(\frac{d}{4} + \frac{12-d}{10}\right) = 20(1.5)$$
$$5d + 2(12-d) = 30$$
$$5d + 24 - 2d = 30$$
$$3d = 6$$
$$d = 2$$
She rollerblades for 2 miles.

25. $w = \dfrac{k}{f}$

   $4.3 = \dfrac{k}{263}$

   $1130.9 = k$

Now substitute 1000 for f and 1130.9 for k.

$w = \dfrac{k}{f}$

$w = \dfrac{1130.9}{1000}$

$w = 1.1309$

The wavelength would be about 1.13 feet.

Cumulative Review Test

1. $3x^2 - 5xy^2 + 3 = 3(-4)^2 - 5(-4)(-2)^2 + 3$

   $= 3(16) - 5(-4)(4) + 3$

   $= 48 + 80 + 3$

   $= 131$

2. $5z + 4 = -3(z - 7)$

   $5z + 4 = -3z + 21$

   $5z + 3z = 21 - 4$

   $8z = 17$

   $z = \dfrac{17}{8}$

3. $\left(\dfrac{8x^6 y^3}{2x^5 y^5} \right)^3 = \left(\dfrac{4x}{y^2} \right)^3$

   $= \dfrac{64x^3}{y^6}$

4. $P = 2E + 3R$

   $P - 2E = 3R$

   $R = \dfrac{P - 2E}{3}$

5. $\left(6x^2 - 3x - 5\right) - \left(-2x^2 - 8x - 9\right) = 6x^2 - 3x - 5 + 2x^2 + 8x + 9$

   $= 6x^2 + 2x^2 - 3x + 8x - 5 + 9$

   $= 8x^2 + 5x + 4$

6. $\left(3n^2 - 4n + 3\right)(2n - 5) = 3n^2(2n - 5) - 4n(2n - 5) + 3(2n - 5)$

   $= 6n^3 - 15n^2 - 8n^2 + 20n + 6n - 15$

   $= 6n^3 - 23n^2 + 26n - 15$

7. $6a^2 - 6a - 5a + 5 = 6a(a - 1) - 5(a - 1)$

   $= (6a - 5)(a - 1)$

8. $13x^2 + 26x - 39 = 13(x^2 + 2x - 3)$
$= 13(x+3)(x-1)$

9. $[7 - [3(8 \div 4)]^2 + 9 \cdot 4]^2 = [7 - [3(2)]^2 + 9 \cdot 4]^2$
$= [7 - (6)^2 + 9 \cdot 4]^2$
$= [7 - 36 + 9 \cdot 4]^2$
$= [7 - 36 + 36]^2$
$= [7]^2$
$= 49$

10. $2(x+3) \le -(x+5) - 1$
$2x + 6 \le -x - 5 - 1$
$2x + 6 \le -x - 6$
$3x \le -12$
$x \le -4$

-4

11. $\dfrac{4x-34}{8} = \dfrac{4x}{8} - \dfrac{34}{8} = \dfrac{1}{2}x - \dfrac{17}{4}$

12. $2x^2 = 11x - 12$
$2x^2 - 11x + 12 = 0$
$(x-4)(2x-3) = 0$
$x - 4 = 0 \quad \text{or} \quad 2x - 3 = 0$
$x = 4 \qquad\qquad x = \frac{3}{2}$

13. $\dfrac{x^2-9}{x^2-x-6} \cdot \dfrac{x^2-2x-8}{2x^2-7x-4} = \dfrac{(x-3)(x+3)}{(x-3)(x+2)} \cdot \dfrac{(x-4)(x+2)}{(2x+1)(x-4)}$
$= \dfrac{x+3}{2x+1}$

14. $\dfrac{r}{r+2} - \dfrac{6}{r-5} = \dfrac{r}{r+2} \cdot \dfrac{r-5}{r-5} - \dfrac{6}{r-5} \cdot \dfrac{r+2}{r+2}$
$= \dfrac{r(r-5)}{(r+2)(r-5)} - \dfrac{6(r+2)}{(r+2)(r-5)}$
$= \dfrac{r^2 - 5r - (6r+12)}{(r+2)(r-5)}$
$= \dfrac{r^2 - 5r - 6r - 12}{(r+2)(r-5)}$
$= \dfrac{r^2 - 11r - 12}{(r+2)(r-5)}$

15. $\dfrac{4}{x^2-3x-10} + \dfrac{2}{x^2+5x+6} = \dfrac{4}{(x-5)(x+2)} + \dfrac{2}{(x+2)(x+3)}$
$= \dfrac{4(x+3)}{(x-5)(x+2)(x+3)} + \dfrac{2(x-5)}{(x-5)(x+2)(x+3)}$
$= \dfrac{4(x+3) + 2(x-5)}{(x-5)(x+2)(x+3)}$
$= \dfrac{4x + 12 + 2x - 10}{(x-5)(x+2)(x+3)}$
$= \dfrac{6x+2}{(x-5)(x+2)(x+3)}$

16.

$$\frac{x}{9} - \frac{x}{6} = \frac{1}{12}$$

$$36\left(\frac{x}{9} - \frac{x}{6}\right) = 36\left(\frac{1}{12}\right)$$

$$4x - 6x = 3$$

$$-2x = 3$$

$$x = -\frac{3}{2}$$

17.

$$\frac{7}{x+3} + \frac{5}{x+2} = \frac{5}{x^2 + 5x + 6}$$

$$\frac{7}{x+3} + \frac{5}{x+2} = \frac{5}{(x+3)(x+2)}$$

$$(x+3)(x+2)\left(\frac{7}{x+3} + \frac{5}{x+2}\right) = (x+3)(x+2)\left[\frac{5}{(x+3)(x+2)}\right]$$

$$7(x+2) + 5(x+3) = 5$$

$$7x + 14 + 5x + 15 = 5$$

$$12x + 29 = 5$$

$$12x = -24$$

$$x = -2$$

Check:

$$\frac{7}{x+3} + \frac{5}{x+2} = \frac{5}{x^2 + 5x + 6}$$

$$\frac{7}{-2+3} + \frac{5}{-2+2} = \frac{5}{(-2)^2 + 5(-2) + 6}$$

$$\frac{7}{1} + \frac{5}{0} = \frac{5}{0}$$

Since $\dfrac{5}{0}$ is not a real number, there is no solution.

18. Let x = the total medical bills. The cost under plan 1 is $0.10x$, while the cost under plan 2 is $100 + 0.05x$.

$$0.10x = 100 + 0.05x$$

$$0.05x = 100$$

$$x = 2000$$

The cost under both plans is the same for $2000 in total medical bills.

19. Let x = pounds of sunflower seed and
y = pounds of premixed assorted seed mix

$$x + y = 50$$

$$0.50x + 0.15y = 14.50$$

Solve the first equation for y.

$$y = 50 - x$$

Substitute $50 - x$ for y in the second equation.

$$0.50x + 0.15(50 - x) = 14.50$$

$$0.50x + 7.5 - 0.15x = 14.50$$

$$0.35x = 7$$

$$x = 20$$

$$y = 50 - x = 50 - 20 = 30$$

He will have to use 20 pounds of sunflower seed and 30 pounds of premixed assorted seed mix.

20. Let d = distance on first leg, then the distance on the second leg is $12.75 - d$.

$$t = \frac{d}{r}$$

Time for first leg + time for second leg = total time

$$\frac{d}{6.5} + \frac{12.75 - d}{9.5} = 1.5$$

$$(9.5)(6.5)\left[\frac{d}{6.5} + \frac{12.75 - d}{9.5}\right] = (9.5)(6.5)(1.5)$$

$$9.5d + 6.5(12.75 - d) = 92.625$$

$$9.5d + 82.875 - 6.5d = 92.625$$

$$3d = 9.75$$

$$d = 3.25$$

$$12.75 - d = 12.75 - 3.25 = 9.5$$

The distance traveled during the first leg of the race was 3.25 miles and the distance traveled in the second leg of the race was 9.5 miles.

Chapter 7

Exercise Set 7.1

1. The *x*-coordinate is always listed first.

3. a. The horizontal axis is the *x*-axis.

   b. The vertical axis is the *y*-axis.

5. Axis is singular, while axes is plural.

7. The graph of a linear equation is an illustration of the set of points whose coordinates satisfy the equation.

9. a. Two points are needed to graph a linear equation.

   b. It is a good idea to use three or more points when graphing a linear equation to catch errors.

11. $ax + by = c$

13.

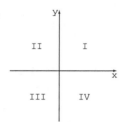

15. II

17. IV

19. II

21. III

23. III

25. II

27. $A(3, 1)$; $B(-3, 0)$; $C(1, -3)$; $D(-2, -3)$; $E(0, 3)$; $F\left(\dfrac{3}{2}, -1\right)$

29.

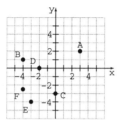

31.

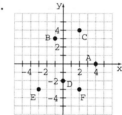

33.

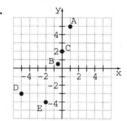

The points are collinear.

35.

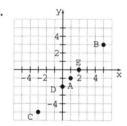

The points are not collinear since $(-5, -3)$ is not on the line.

37. a.

$y = x + 2$	$y = x + 2$
$4 = 2 + 2$	$0 = -2 + 2$
$4 = 4$ True	$0 = 0$ True

$y = x + 2$	$y = x + 2$
$3 = 2 + 2$	$2 = 0 + 2$
$3 = 4$ False	$2 = 2$ True

Point c) does not satisfy the equation.

b.

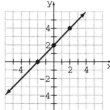

39. a.

$$3x - 2y = 6 \qquad\qquad 3x - 2y = 6$$
$$3(4) - 2(0) = 6 \qquad\qquad 3(2) - 2(0) = 6$$
$$12 = 6 \quad \text{False} \qquad\qquad 6 = 6 \quad \text{True}$$
$$3x - 2y = 6 \qquad\qquad 3x - 2y = 6$$
$$3\left(\frac{2}{3}\right) - 2(-2) = 6 \qquad 3\left(\frac{4}{3}\right) - 2(-1) = 6$$
$$2 + 4 = 6 \qquad\qquad 4 + 2 = 6$$
$$6 = 6 \quad \text{True} \qquad\qquad 6 = 6 \quad \text{True}$$

Point a) does not satisfy the equation.

b.

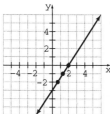

41. a.

$$\frac{1}{2}x + 4y = 4 \qquad\qquad \frac{1}{2}x + 4y = 4$$
$$\frac{1}{2}(2) + 4(-1) = 4 \qquad \frac{1}{2}(2) + 4\left(\frac{3}{4}\right) = 4$$
$$1 - 4 = 4 \qquad\qquad 1 + 3 = 4$$
$$-3 = 4 \quad \text{False} \qquad\qquad 4 = 4 \quad \text{True}$$

$$\frac{1}{2}x + 4y = 4 \qquad\qquad \frac{1}{2}x + 4y = 4$$
$$\frac{1}{2}(0) + 4(1) = 4 \qquad \frac{1}{2}(-4) + 4\left(\frac{3}{2}\right) = 4$$
$$0 + 4 = 4 \qquad\qquad -2 + 6 = 4$$
$$4 = 4 \quad \text{True} \qquad\qquad 4 = 4 \quad \text{True}$$

Point a) does not satisfy the equation.

b.

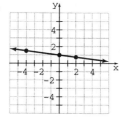

43. $y = 3x - 4$

$y = 3(2) - 4$

$y = 6 - 4$

$y = 2$

45. $y = 3x - 4$

$y = 3(0) - 4$

$y = 0 - 4$

$y = -4$

47. $2x + 3y = 12$

$2(3) + 3y = 12$

$6 + 3y = 12$

$3y = 6$

$y = 2$

49. $2x + 3y = 12$

$2\left(\dfrac{1}{2}\right) + 3y = 12$

$1 + 3y = 12$

$3y = 11$

$y = \dfrac{11}{3}$

51. The value of y is 0 when a straight line crosses the x-axis, because any point on the x-axis is neither above or below the origin.

53. **a.** Latitude: 16°N   Longitude: 56°W
b. Latitude: 29°N   Longitude: 90.5°W
c. Latitude: 26°N   Longitude: 80.5°W
d. Answers will vary.

57. $\dfrac{1}{2}(x - 3) = \dfrac{1}{3}x + 2$

$\dfrac{1}{2}x - \dfrac{3}{2} = \dfrac{1}{3}x + 2$

$6\left(\dfrac{1}{2}x - \dfrac{3}{2}\right) = 6\left(\dfrac{1}{3}x + 2\right)$

$3x - 9 = 2x + 12$

$x = 21$

58. $2x - 5y = 6$

$2x - 2x - 5y = 6 - 2x$

$-5y = 6 - 2x$

$\dfrac{-5y}{-5} = \dfrac{6 - 2x}{-5}$

$y = \dfrac{6 - 2x}{-5}$

$y = \dfrac{2x - 6}{5}$

$y = \dfrac{2}{5}x - \dfrac{6}{5}$

59. $(2x^4)^3 = 2^3(x^4)^3 = 8x^{4 \cdot 3} = 8x^{12}$

60. $x^2 - 6x - 27 = (x + 3)(x - 9)$

61. $y(y - 8) = 0$

$y = 0$ or $y - 8 = 0$

$y = 8$

The solutions are 0 and 8.

62. $\dfrac{4}{x^2} + \dfrac{7}{3x} = \dfrac{4}{x^2} \cdot \dfrac{3}{3} + \dfrac{7}{3x} \cdot \dfrac{x}{x}$

$= \dfrac{12}{3x^2} + \dfrac{7x}{3x^2}$

$= \dfrac{12 + 7x}{3x^2}$

$= \dfrac{7x + 12}{3x^2}$

Exercise Set 7.2

1. To find the x-intercept, substitute 0 for y and find the corresponding value of x. To find the y-intercept, substitute 0 for x and find the corresponding value of y.

3. The graph of $y = b$ is a horizontal line.

5. You may not be able to read exact answers from a graph.

7. Yes. The equation goes through the origin because the point $(0, 0)$ satisfies the equation.

9. $3x + y = 9$

$3(3) + y = 9$

$9 + y = 9$

$y = 0$

11.
$$3x + y = 9$$
$$3x + (-6) = 9$$
$$3x - 6 = 9$$
$$3x = 15$$
$$x = 5$$

13.
$$3x + y = 9$$
$$3x + 0 = 9$$
$$3x = 9$$
$$x = 3$$

15.
$$3x - 2y = 8$$
$$3 \cdot 4 - 2y = 8$$
$$12 - 2y = 8$$
$$-2y = -4$$
$$y = 2$$

17.
$$3x - 2y = 8$$
$$3x - 2(0) = 8$$
$$3x = 8$$
$$x = \frac{8}{3}$$

19.
$$3x - 2y = 8$$
$$3(-4) - 2y = 8$$
$$-12 - 2y = 8$$
$$-2y = 20$$
$$y = -10$$

21. An equation of the form $x = c$ is a vertical line with x-intercept at $(c, 0)$.

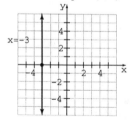

23. An equation of the form $y = c$ is a horizontal line with y-intercept at $(0, c)$.

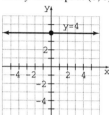

25. Let $x = 0$, $y = 3(0) - 1 = -1$, $(0, -1)$
Let $x = 1$, $y = 3(1) - 1 = 2$, $(1, 2)$
Let $x = 2$, $y = 3(2) - 1 = 5$, $(2, 5)$

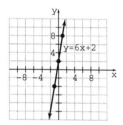

27. Let $x = -1$, $y = 6(-1) + 2 = -4$, $(-1, -4)$
Let $x = 0$, $y = 6(0) + 2 = 2$, $(0, 2)$
Let $x = 1$, $y = 6(1) + 2 = 8$, $(1, 8)$, $(1, 8)$

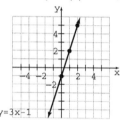

29. Let $x = 0$, $y = -\frac{1}{2}(0) + 3 = 3$, $(0, 3)$
Let $x = 2$, $y = -\frac{1}{2}(2) + 3 = 2$, $(2, 2)$
Let $x = 4$, $y = -\frac{1}{2}(4) + 3 = 1$, $(4, 1)$

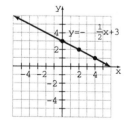

31. $2x - 4y = 4$
$$-4y = -2x + 4$$
$$y = \frac{1}{2}x - 1$$

Let $x = 0,\ y = \frac{1}{2}(0) - 1 = -1,\ (0, -1)$

Let $x = 2,\ y = \frac{1}{2}(2) - 1 = 0,\ (2, 0)$

Let $x = 4,\ y = \frac{1}{2}(4) - 1 = 1,\ (4, 1)$

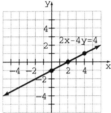

33. $5x - 2y = 8$
$$-2y = -5x + 8$$
$$y = \frac{5}{2}x - 4$$

Let $x = 0,\ y = \frac{5}{2}(0) - 4 = -4,\ (0, -4)$

Let $x = 2,\ y = \frac{5}{2}(2) - 4 = 1,\ (2, 1)$

Let $x = 4,\ y = \frac{5}{2}(4) - 4 = 6,\ (4, 6)$

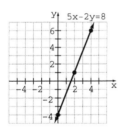

35. $6x + 5y = 30$
$$5y = -6x + 30$$
$$y = -\frac{6}{5}x + 6$$

Let $x = 0,\ y = -\frac{6}{5}(0) + 6 = 6,\ (0, 6)$

Let $x = 5,\ y = -\frac{6}{5}(5) + 6 = 0,\ (5, 0)$

Let $x = 10,\ y = -\frac{6}{5}(10) + 6 = -6,\ (10, -6)$

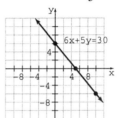

37. $-4x + 5y = 0$
$$5y = 4x$$
$$y = \frac{4}{5}x$$

Let $x = -5,\ y = \frac{4}{5}(-5) = -4,\ (-5, -4)$

Let $x = 0,\ y = \frac{4}{5}(0) = 0,\ (0, 0)$

Let $x = 5,\ y = \frac{4}{5}(5) = 4,\ (5, 4)$

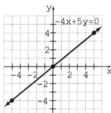

39. Let $x = 0,\ y = -20(0) + 60 = 60,\ (0, 60)$
Let $x = 2,\ y = -20(2) + 60 = 20,\ (2, 20)$
Let $x = 4,\ y = -20(4) + 60 = -20,\ (4, -20)$

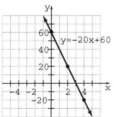

41. Let $x = -3,\ y = \frac{4}{3}(-3) = -4,\ (-3, -4)$

Let $x = 0,\ y = \frac{4}{3}(0) = 0,\ (0, 0)$

Let $x = 3$, $y = \dfrac{4}{3}(3) = 4$, $(3, 4)$

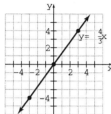

43. Let $x = 0$, $y = \dfrac{1}{2}(0) + 4 = 4$, $(0, 4)$

Let $x = 2$, $y = \dfrac{1}{2}(2) + 4 = 5$, $(2, 5)$

Let $x = 4$, $y = \dfrac{1}{2}(4) + 4 = 6$, $(4, 6)$

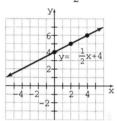

45. Let $x = 0$ Let $y = 0$

$\quad y = 3x + 3 \qquad\qquad y = 3x + 3$

$\quad y = 3(0) + 3 \qquad\quad 0 = 3x + 3$

$\quad y = 3 \qquad\qquad\qquad -3x = 3$

$\qquad\qquad\qquad\qquad\qquad x = -1$

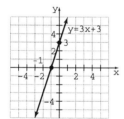

47. Let $x = 0$ Let $y = 0$

$\quad y = -4x + 2 \qquad\qquad y = -4x + 2$

$\quad y = -4(0) + 2 \qquad\quad 0 = -4x + 2$

$\quad y = 2 \qquad\qquad\qquad -2 = -4x$

$\qquad\qquad\qquad\qquad\qquad x = \dfrac{1}{2}$

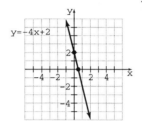

49. Let $x = 0$ Let $y = 0$

$\quad y = -5x + 4 \qquad\qquad y = -5x + 4$

$\quad y = -5(0) + 4 \qquad\quad 0 = -5x + 4$

$\quad y = 4 \qquad\qquad\qquad -4 = -5x$

$\qquad\qquad\qquad\qquad\qquad x = \dfrac{4}{5}$

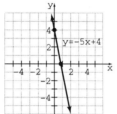

51. $4y + 6x = 24$

$\qquad 4y = -6x + 24$

$\qquad\; y = -\dfrac{3}{2}x + 6$

Let $x = 0$ Let $y = 0$

$y = -\dfrac{3}{2}(0) + 6 \qquad 0 = -\dfrac{3}{2}x + 6$

$y = 6 \qquad\qquad\qquad \dfrac{3}{2}x = 6$

$\qquad\qquad\qquad\qquad\quad x = 4$

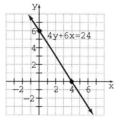

53. Let $x = 0$　　Let $y = 0$

$$\frac{1}{2}x + 2y = 4 \qquad \frac{1}{2}x + 2y = 4$$

$$\frac{1}{2}(0) + 2y = 4 \qquad \frac{1}{2}x + 0 = 4$$

$$2y = 4 \qquad \frac{1}{2}x = 4$$

$$y = 2 \qquad x = 8$$

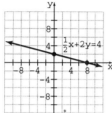

55. Let $x = 0$　　　　Let $y = 0$

$$6x - 12y = 24 \qquad 6x - 12y = 24$$

$$6(0) - 12y = 24 \qquad 6x - 12(0) = 24$$

$$-12y = 24 \qquad 6x = 24$$

$$y = -2 \qquad x = 4$$

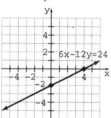

57. Let $x = 0$　　　Let $y = 0$

$$8y = 6x - 12 \qquad 8y = 6x - 12$$

$$8y = 6(0) - 12 \qquad 8(0) = 6x - 12$$

$$8y = -12 \qquad 0 = 6x - 12$$

$$y = -\frac{3}{2} \qquad -6x = -12$$

$$x = 2$$

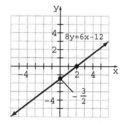

58. Let $x = 0$　　　　Let $y = 0$

$$-3y - 2x = -6 \qquad -3y - 2x = -6$$

$$-3y - 2(0) = -6 \qquad -3(0) - 2x = -6$$

$$-3y = -6 \qquad -2x = -6$$

$$y = 2 \qquad x = 3$$

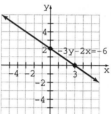

59. Let $x = 0$　　　　Let $y = 0$

$$-20y - 30x = 40 \qquad -20y - 30x = 40$$

$$-20y - 30(0) = 40 \qquad -20(0) - 30x = 40$$

$$-20y = 40 \qquad -30x = 40$$

$$y = -2 \qquad x = -\frac{4}{3}$$

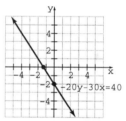

61. Let $x = 0$　　　　Let $y = 0$

$$\frac{1}{3}x + \frac{1}{4}y = 12 \qquad \frac{1}{3}x + \frac{1}{4}y = 12$$

$$\frac{1}{3}(0) + \frac{1}{4}y = 12 \qquad \frac{1}{3}x + \frac{1}{4}(0) = 12$$

$$\frac{1}{4}y = 12 \qquad \frac{1}{3}x = 12$$

$$y = 48 \qquad x = 36$$

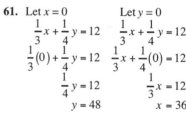

63. Let $x = 0$　　Let $y = 0$

$$\frac{1}{2}x = \frac{2}{5}y - 80 \qquad \frac{1}{2}x = \frac{2}{5}y - 80$$

$$\frac{1}{2}(0) = \frac{2}{5}y - 80 \qquad \frac{1}{2}x = \frac{2}{5}(0) - 80$$

$$0 = \frac{2}{5}y - 80 \qquad \frac{1}{2}x = -80$$

$$-\frac{2}{5}y = -80 \qquad x = -160$$

$$y = 200$$

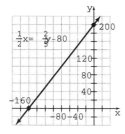

65. $x = -2$

67. $y = 6$

69.
$$ax + 4y = 8$$
$$a(2) + 4(0) = 8$$
$$2a + 0 = 8$$
$$2a = 8$$
$$a = 4$$

71.
$$3x + by = 10$$
$$3(0) + b(5) = 10$$
$$0 + 5b = 10$$
$$5b = 10$$
$$b = 2$$

73. Yes. For each 15 minutes of time, the number of calories burned increases by 200 calories.

75. a. $C = 2n + 30$

b.

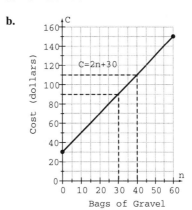

c. $90

d. 40 bags

77. a. $C = m + 40$

b.

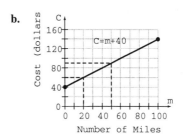

c. $90

d. 20 miles

79. a.

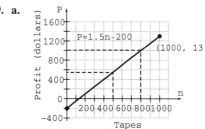

b. $550

c. 800 tapes

81. Since each shaded area multiplied by the corresponding intercept must equal 20, the coefficients are 5 and 4 respectively.

83. Since the first shaded area multiplied by the *x*-intercept must equal –12, the coefficient of *x* is 6. Since the opposite of the second shaded area multiplied by the *y*-intercept must equal –12, the coefficient of *y* is 4.

88.
$$2\big[6-(4-5)\big] \div 2 - 5^2 = 2\big[6-(-1)\big] \div 2 - 25$$
$$= 2[7] \div 2 - 25$$
$$= 14 \div 2 - 25$$
$$= 7 - 25$$
$$= -18$$

89.
$$\frac{8 \text{ ounces}}{3 \text{ gallons}} = \frac{x \text{ ounces}}{2.5 \text{ gallons}}$$
$$\frac{8}{3} = \frac{x}{2.5}$$
$$20 = 3x$$
$$6.67 \approx x$$
You should use 6.67 ounces of cleaner.

90. Let *x* = smaller integer. Then 3*x* + 1 = larger integer.
$$x + (3x + 1) = 37$$
$$4x + 1 = 37$$
$$4x = 36$$
$$x = 9$$
The smaller integer is 9.
The larger is $3(9) + 1 = 27 + 1 = 28$.

91.
$$\frac{10xy^3}{z} \div \frac{x^2 y^2}{5z^2} = \frac{10xy^3}{z} \cdot \frac{5z^2}{x^2 y^2}$$
$$= \frac{50yz}{x}$$

92.
$$\frac{3}{x-2} + \frac{4}{x-3} + 3$$
$$= \frac{3(x-3)}{(x-2)(x-3)} + \frac{4(x-2)}{(x-2)(x-3)} + \frac{3(x-2)(x-3)}{(x-2)(x-3)}$$
$$= \frac{3x-9}{(x-2)(x-3)} + \frac{4x-8}{(x-2)(x-3)} + \frac{3x^2-15x+18}{(x-2)(x-3)}$$
$$= \frac{3x-9+4x-8+3x^2-15x+18}{(x-2)(x-3)}$$
$$= \frac{3x^2-8x+1}{(x-2)(x-3)}$$

93.
$$\frac{3}{x-2} + \frac{4}{x-3} = 3$$
$$(x-2)(x-3) \cdot \frac{3}{x-2} + (x-2)(x-3) \cdot \frac{4}{x-3} = 3(x-2)(x-3)$$
$$3(x-3) + 4(x-2) = 3(x-2)(x-3)$$
$$3x-9+4x-8 = 3x^2-15x+18$$
$$7x-17 = 3x^2-15x+18$$
$$0 = 3x^2-22x+35$$
$$0 = (3x-7)(x-5)$$
$$3x-7 = 0 \quad \text{or} \quad x-5 = 0$$
$$3x = 7 \qquad\qquad x = 5$$
$$x = \frac{7}{3}$$

Exercise Set 7.3

1. The slope of a line is the ratio of the vertical change to the horizontal change between any two points on the line.

3. A line with a positive slope rises from left to right.

5. Lines that rise from the left to right have a positive slope. Lines that fall from left to right have a negative slope.

7. No, since we cannot divide by 0, the slope is undefined.

9. Their slopes are the same.

11. $m = \dfrac{5-1}{7-5}$
$$= \frac{4}{2}$$
$$= 2$$

13. $m = \dfrac{-2-0}{5-9}$
$$= \frac{-2}{-4}$$
$$= \frac{1}{2}$$

15. $m = \dfrac{\frac{1}{2} - \frac{1}{2}}{-3-3}$
$$= \frac{0}{-6}$$
$$= 0$$

17. $m = \dfrac{6-6}{-2-(-7)}$

$= \dfrac{0}{5}$

$= 0$

19. $m = \dfrac{-2-4}{6-6}$

$= \dfrac{-6}{0}$ undefined

21. $m = \dfrac{3-0}{-2-6}$

$= \dfrac{3}{-8}$

$= -\dfrac{3}{8}$

23. $m = \dfrac{1-\frac{3}{2}}{-\frac{3}{4}-0}$

$= \dfrac{-\frac{1}{2}}{-\frac{3}{4}}$

$= \dfrac{-1}{2} \cdot \dfrac{4}{-3}$

$= \dfrac{-4}{-6}$

$= \dfrac{2}{3}$

25. $m = \dfrac{6}{3}$

$= 2$

27. $m = \dfrac{6}{-3}$

$= -2$

29. $m = \dfrac{4}{-7}$

$= -\dfrac{4}{7}$

31. $m = \dfrac{7}{4}$

33. $m = \dfrac{0}{3}$

$= 0$

35. Vertical line, slope is undefined.

37. Horizontal line, slope is 0.

39.
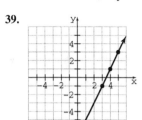

41.
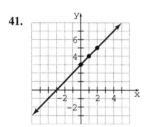

43.
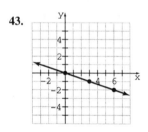

45.
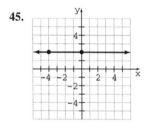

47.
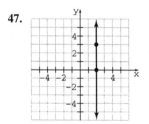

49. The lines are parallel because the slopes are the same.

51. The lines are perpendicular because the slopes are negative reciprocals.

53. The lines are perpendicular because the slopes are negative reciprocals.

55. The lines are neither parallel or perpendicular.

57. The lines are neither parallel or perpendicular.

59. The lines are parallel because the slopes are the same.

61. The lines are parallel because the slopes are the same.

63. The lines are perpendicular because if the slope is 0, the line is horizontal and if the slope is undefined the line is vertical.

65. Its slope would be 2.

67. Its slope would be $\dfrac{1}{4}$.

69. The first graph appears to pass through the points $(-1, 0)$ and $(0, 6)$. It's slope is
$m = \dfrac{6-0}{0-(-1)} = \dfrac{6}{1} = 6$. The second graph appears
to pass through the points $(-4, 0)$ and $(0, 6)$. It's
slope is $m = \dfrac{6-0}{0-(-4)} = \dfrac{6}{4} = \dfrac{6}{4} = \dfrac{3}{2}$. The first
graph has the greater slope.

71. a. $m = \dfrac{45-22}{1957-1961} = \dfrac{23}{-4} = -\dfrac{23}{4}$

   b. $m = \dfrac{51-7}{1989-1985} = \dfrac{44}{4} = 11$

73. $m = \dfrac{-2-6}{3-1} = \dfrac{-8}{2} = -4$

A line parallel to the given line would
have a slope of -4.

75. $m = \dfrac{5-(-3)}{2-1} = \dfrac{5+3}{1} = 8$

A line perpendicular to the given line
would have a slope of $-\dfrac{1}{8}$.

77.
$$m = \dfrac{-\frac{7}{2} - \left(-\frac{3}{8}\right)}{-\frac{4}{9} - \frac{1}{2}}$$
$$= \dfrac{-\frac{28}{8} + \frac{3}{8}}{-\frac{8}{18} - \frac{9}{18}}$$
$$= \dfrac{-\frac{25}{8}}{-\frac{17}{18}}$$
$$= \left(-\dfrac{25}{8}\right)\left(-\dfrac{18}{17}\right)$$
$$= \dfrac{(-25)(-9)}{(4)(17)}$$
$$= \dfrac{225}{68}$$

79. a.

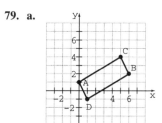

   b. $AC; m = \dfrac{4-1}{5-0} = \dfrac{3}{5}$

       $CB; m = \dfrac{4-2}{5-6} = \dfrac{2}{-1} = -2$

       $DB; m = \dfrac{2-(-1)}{6-1} = \dfrac{3}{5}$

       $AD; m = \dfrac{-1-1}{1-0} = \dfrac{-2}{1} = -2$

   c.   Yes; opposite sides are parallel.

83. $4x^2 + 3x + \dfrac{x}{2} = 4(0)^2 + 3(0) + \dfrac{0}{2}$
$$= 0 + 0 + 0$$
$$= 0$$

84. a. $-x = -\dfrac{3}{2}$

$$(-1)(-x) = (-1)\left(-\dfrac{3}{2}\right)$$
$$x = \dfrac{3}{2}$$

   b. $5x = 0$
$$\dfrac{5x}{5} = \dfrac{0}{5}$$
$$x = 0$$

85. $(4x + 7) - (2x - 8) = 4x + 7 - 2x + 8$
$$= 4x - 2x + 7 + 8$$
$$= 2x + 15$$

86.
$$\frac{2x}{x-3} = 2 + \frac{3}{x}$$
$$x(x-3)\left(\frac{2x}{x-3}\right) = x(x-3)\left[2 + \frac{3}{x}\right]$$
$$x \cdot 2x = x(x-3) \cdot 2 + (x-3)3$$
$$2x^2 = 2x^2 - 6x + 3x - 9$$
$$9 = -3x$$
$$-3 = x$$

87. $5x - 3y = 15$

$x = 0$	$y = 0$
$5(0) - 3y = 15$	$5x - 3(0) = 15$
$-3y = 15$	$5x = 15$
$y = -5$	$x = 5$
$(0, -5)$	$(5, 0)$

Exercise Set 7.4

1. $y = mx + b$

3. $y = 3x - 5$

5. Compare their slopes: If slopes are the same and their y-intercepts are different, the lines are parallel.

7. $y - y_1 = m(x - x_1)$

9. $m = 4$; y-intercept: $(0, -6)$

11. $m = \frac{4}{3}$; y-intercept: $(0, -5)$

13. $m = 1$; y-intercept: $(0, -3)$

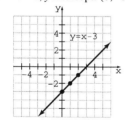

15. $m = 3$; y-intercept: $(0, 2)$

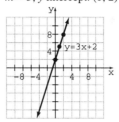

17. $m = -4$; y-intercept: $(0, 0)$

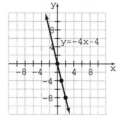

19. $-2x + y = -3$
$$y = 2x - 3$$
$m = 2$; y-intercept: $(0, -3)$

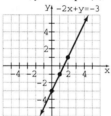

21. $5x - 2y = 10$
$$-2y = -5x + 10$$
$$y = \frac{5}{2}x - 5$$
$m = \frac{5}{2}$; y-intercept: $(0, -5)$

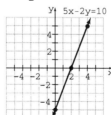

23. $6x + 12y = 18$

$$12y = -6x + 18$$

$$y = -\frac{1}{2}x + \frac{3}{2}$$

$m = -\frac{1}{2}$; y-intercept: $\left(0, \frac{3}{2}\right)$

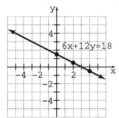

25. $-6x + 2y - 8 = 0$

$$2y = 6x + 8$$

$$y = 3x + 4$$

$m = 3$; y-intercept: $(0, 4)$

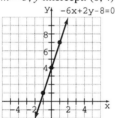

27. $3x = 2y - 4$

$$-2y = -3x - 4$$

$$y = \frac{3}{2}x + 2$$

$m = \frac{3}{2}$; y-intercept: $(0, 2)$

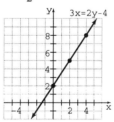

29. $m = \frac{4}{4} = 1$, $b = -2$

$$y = x - 2$$

31. $m = \frac{-2}{6} = -\frac{1}{3}$, $b = 2$

$$y = -\frac{1}{3}x + 2$$

33. $m = \frac{10}{30} = \frac{1}{3}$, $b = 5$

$$y = \frac{1}{3}x + 5$$

35. $m = \frac{-3}{1} = -3$, $b = 4$

$$y = -3x + 4$$

37. Since the slopes of the lines are the same and y-intercepts are different, the lines are parallel.

38. $2x + 3y = 8$ $y = -\frac{2}{3}x + 5$

$$3y = -2x + 8$$

$$y = -\frac{2}{3}x + \frac{8}{3}$$

Since the slopes of the lines are the same and y-intercepts are different, the lines are parallel.

39. $4x + 2y = 9$ $4x = 8y + 4$

$$2y = -4x + 9 \quad -8y = -4x + 4$$

$$y = -2x + \frac{9}{2} \quad y = \frac{1}{2}x - \frac{1}{2}$$

Since the slopes of the lines are opposite reciprocals, the lines are perpendicular.

41. $3x + 5y = 9$ $6x = -10y + 9$

$$5y = -3x + 9 \quad 10y = -6x + 9$$

$$y = -\frac{3}{5}x + \frac{9}{5} \quad y = \frac{-6}{10}x + \frac{9}{10}$$

$$y = -\frac{3}{5}x + \frac{9}{10}$$

Since the slopes of the lines are the same and y-intercepts are different, the lines are parallel.

43. $y = \frac{1}{2}x - 4$ $2y = 6x + 9$

$$y = 3x + \frac{9}{2}$$

Since the slopes of the lines are not equal and are not opposite reciprocals, the lines are neither parallel nor perpendicular.

45. $5y = 2x + 3$ $-10x = 4y + 8$

$\quad\quad y = \dfrac{2}{5}x + \dfrac{3}{5}$ $-4y = 10x + 8$

$\quad\quad\quad\quad\quad\quad\quad y = -\dfrac{5}{2}x - 2$

Since the slopes of the lines are opposite reciprocals, the lines are perpendicular.

47. $3x + 7y = 8$ or $7x + 3y = 8$

$\quad\quad 7y = -3x + 8$ $3y = -7x + 8$

$\quad\quad y = -\dfrac{3}{7}x + \dfrac{8}{7}$ $y = -\dfrac{7}{3}x + \dfrac{8}{3}$

Since the slopes of the lines are not equal and are not opposite reciprocals, the lines are neither parallel or perpendicular.

49. $y - 2 = 3(x - 0)$

$\quad\quad y = 3x + 2$

51. $y - 5 = -3[x - (-4)]$

$\quad\quad y - 5 = -3(x + 4)$

$\quad\quad y - 5 = -3x - 12$

$\quad\quad y = -3x - 7$

53. $y - (-5) = \dfrac{1}{2}[x - (-1)]$

$\quad\quad y + 5 = \dfrac{1}{2}(x + 1)$

$\quad\quad y + 5 = \dfrac{1}{2}x + \dfrac{1}{2}$

$\quad\quad y = \dfrac{1}{2}x - \dfrac{9}{2}$

55. $y - 6 = \dfrac{2}{5}(x - 0)$

$\quad\quad y - 6 = \dfrac{2}{5}x$

$\quad\quad y = \dfrac{2}{5}x + 6$

57. $m = \dfrac{4 - (-2)}{-2 - (-4)} = \dfrac{6}{2} = 3$

$\quad\quad y - (-2) = 3[x - (-4)]$

$\quad\quad y + 2 = 3(x + 4)$

$\quad\quad y + 2 = 3x + 12$

$\quad\quad y = 3x + 10$

59. $m = \dfrac{-9 - 9}{6 - (-6)} = \dfrac{-18}{12} = -\dfrac{3}{2}$

$\quad\quad y - 9 = -\dfrac{3}{2}(x - (-6))$

$\quad\quad y - 9 = -\dfrac{3}{2}(x + 6)$

$\quad\quad y - 9 = -\dfrac{3}{2}x - 9$

$\quad\quad y = -\dfrac{3}{2}x$

61. $m = \dfrac{-2 - 3}{0 - 10} = \dfrac{-5}{-10} = \dfrac{1}{2}$

$\quad\quad y - 3 = \dfrac{1}{2}(x - 10)$

$\quad\quad y - 3 = \dfrac{1}{2}x - 5$

$\quad\quad y = \dfrac{1}{2}x - 2$

63. $y - (-4.5) = 6.3(x - 0)$

$\quad\quad y + 4.5 = 6.3x$

$\quad\quad y = 6.3x - 4.5$

65. a. $y = 5x + 60$

    b. $y = 5(30) + 60 = 150 + 60 = \$210$

67. a. Use the slope-intercept form.

    b. Use the point-slope form.

    c. Use the point-slope form but first find the slope.

69. a. No. The equations will look different because different points are used.

    b. $y - (-4) = 2[x - (-5)]$

$\quad\quad\quad y + 4 = 2(x + 5)$

    c. $y - 10 = 2(x - 2)$

    d. $y + 4 = 2(x + 5)$

$\quad\quad\quad y + 4 = 2x + 10$

$\quad\quad\quad\quad y = 2x + 6$

    e. $y - 10 = 2(x - 2)$

$\quad\quad\quad y - 10 = 2x - 4$

$\quad\quad\quad\quad y = 2x + 6$

    f. Yes

71. a. Use the points $(0,0)$ and $(200,293)$ and substitute into the slope formula.

$$m = \frac{293 - 0}{200 - 0} = \frac{293}{200} \approx 1.465$$

b. Using the point-slope formula, the equation of the line is:

$$y - y_1 = m(x - x_1)$$
$$f - 0 = 1.465(m - 0)$$
$$f = 1.465m$$

c. $f = 1.465m$

$$f = 1.465(130.81)$$
$$f \approx 191.64$$

The speed was 191.64 feet per second.

d. It is about 150 feet per second.

e. It is about 55 miles per hour.

73. First, find the slope of the line $2x + y = 6$.

$$2x + y = 6$$
$$y = -2x + 6$$
$$m = -2$$

Use $m = -2$ and $b = 4$ in the slope-intercept equation.

$$y = -2x + 4$$

75. $3x - 4y = 6$

$$4y = 3x - 6$$
$$y = \frac{3}{4}x - \frac{3}{2}$$
$$m = \frac{3}{4}$$
$$y - (-1) = \frac{3}{4}[x - (-4)]$$
$$y + 1 = \frac{3}{4}(x + 4)$$
$$y + 1 = \frac{3}{4}x + 3$$
$$y = \frac{3}{4}x + 2$$

78. $|-4| < |-6|$ because $4 < 6$.

79. $2(x - 3) \geq 5x + 6$

$$2x - 6 \geq 5x + 6$$
$$-6 \geq 3x + 6$$
$$-12 \geq 3x$$
$$-4 \geq x$$
$$x \leq -4$$

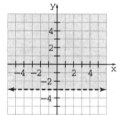

80. $i = prt$

$$\frac{i}{pt} = \frac{prt}{pt}$$
$$\frac{i}{pt} = r$$

81. $x^2 - 2xy + 3xy - 6y^2 = x(x - 2y) + 3y(x - 2y)$

$$= (x - 2y)(x + 3y)$$

82. $\dfrac{x}{3} - \dfrac{3x + 2}{6} = \dfrac{1}{2}$

$$6\left(\frac{x}{3} - \frac{3x + 2}{6}\right) = 6\left(\frac{1}{2}\right)$$
$$6\left(\frac{x}{3}\right) - 6\left(\frac{3x + 2}{6}\right) = 3$$
$$2x - (3x + 2) = 3$$
$$2x - 3x - 2 = 3$$
$$-x = 5$$
$$x = -5$$

Exercise Set 7.5

1. Points on the line satisfy the = part of the inequality.

3. The shadings are on opposite sides of the line.

5.

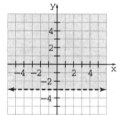

Check $(0, 0)$: $0 > -3$ True

7.

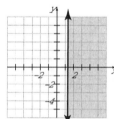

Check $(0, 0)$: $x \geq \dfrac{3}{2}$

$$0 \geq \frac{3}{2} \qquad \text{False}$$

9.

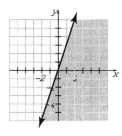

Check $(1, 0)$: $y \leq 3x$
$$0 \leq 3(1)$$
$$0 \leq 3 \qquad \text{True}$$

11.

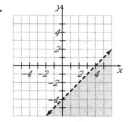

Check $(0, 0)$: $y < x - 4$
$$0 < 0 - 4$$
$$0 < -4 \qquad \text{False}$$

13.

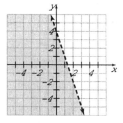

Check $(0, 0)$: $y < -3x + 4$
$$0 < -3 \cdot 0 + 4$$
$$0 < 4 \qquad \text{True}$$

15.

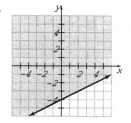

Check $(0, 0)$: $y \geq \dfrac{1}{2}x - 4$
$$0 \geq \dfrac{1}{2} \cdot 0 - 4$$
$$0 \geq -4 \qquad \text{True}$$

17.

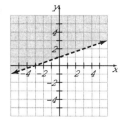

Check $(0, 0)$: $y > \dfrac{1}{3}x + 1$
$$0 > \dfrac{1}{3} \cdot 0 + 1$$
$$0 > 1 \qquad \text{False}$$

19.

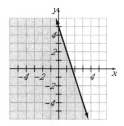

Check $(0, 0)$: $3x + y \leq 5$
$$3 \cdot 0 + 0 \leq 5$$
$$0 \leq 5 \text{ True}$$

21.

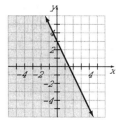

Check $(0, 0)$: $2x + y \leq 3$
$$2 \cdot 0 + 0 \leq 3$$
$$0 \leq 3 \text{ True}$$

23.

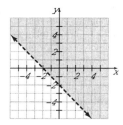

Check $(0, 0)$: $y + 2 > -x$

$$0 + 2 > -0$$

$$2 > 0 \quad \text{True}$$

25. a. $2(4) + 4(2) < 16$

$$8 + 8 < 16$$

$$16 < 16$$

No

b. $2(4) + 4(2) > 16$

$$16 > 16$$

No

c. $2(4) + 4(2) \geq 16$

$$16 \geq 16$$

Yes

d. $2(4) + 4(2) \leq 16$

$$16 \leq 16$$

Yes

27. No, the ordered pair could be a solution to $ax + by = c$.

29. No. If an ordered pair satisfies $ax + by > c$, it means the ordered pair lies on one side of the line $ax + by = c$. The ordered pair cannot lie on the other side of the line or on the line itself.

31. a. less than or equal to

b. greater than or equal to

c. less than or equal to

d. greater than or equal to

33. a. $2x - y > 4$

$$-y > -2x + 4$$

$$y < 2x - 4$$

b. $-2x + y < -4$

$$y < 2x - 4$$

c. $y < 2x - 4$

d. $-2y + 4x < -8$

$$-2y < -4x - 8$$

$$y > 2x + 4$$

After solving each inequality for y, compare the inequalities. Only (a), (b), and (c) will have the same graphs.

34. a. 2

b. 2, 0

c. $2, -5, 0, \dfrac{2}{5}, -6.3, -\dfrac{23}{34}$

d. $\sqrt{7}, \sqrt{3}$

e. $2, -5, 0, \sqrt{7}, \dfrac{2}{5}, -6.3, \sqrt{3}, -\dfrac{23}{34}$

35. $2(x + 3) + 2x = x + 4$

$$2x + 6 + 2x = x + 4$$

$$4x + 6 = x + 4$$

$$3x = -2$$

$$x = -\dfrac{2}{3}$$

36. $\dfrac{10x^2 - 15x + 30}{5x} = \dfrac{10x^2}{5x} - \dfrac{15x}{5x} + \dfrac{30}{5x}$

$$= 2x - 3 + \dfrac{6}{x}$$

37. $\dfrac{2x}{2x^2 + 4xy} = \dfrac{2x}{2x(x + 2y)} = \dfrac{1}{x + 2y}$

Exercise Set 7.6

1. A relation is any set of ordered pairs.

3. A function is a set of ordered pairs in which each first component corresponds to exactly one second component.

5. a. The domain is the set of first components in the set of ordered pairs.

b. The range is the set of second components in the set of ordered pairs.

7. No, each x must have a unique y for it to be a function.

9. Function
Domain $\{1, 2, 3, 4, 5\}$
Range $\{1, 2, 3, 4, 5\}$

11. Relation
Domain $\{1, 2, 3, 5, 7\}$
Range $\{-2, 0, 2, 4, 5\}$

13. Relation
Domain $\{0, 1, 3, 4, 5\}$
Range $\{-4, -1, 0, 1, 2\}$

15. Relation
Domain $\{0, 1, 3\}$
Range $\{-3, 0, 2, 5\}$

17. Function
Domain $\{0, 1, 2, 3, 4\}$
Range $\{3\}$

19. a. $\{(1, 4), (2, 5), (3, 5), (4, 7)\}$

    b. The relation is a function; every element of the domain corresponds to exactly one element of the range.

21. a. $\{(-5, 4), (0, 7), (6, 9), (6, 3)\}$
The relation is not a function; 6, a first component, is paired with more than 1 value.

23. Function

25. Not a function

27. Function

29. Function

31. Since a vertical line drawn at $x > -1$ will intersect the graph at more than one point, the relation is not a function.

33. Function

35. a. $f(3) = 4 \cdot 3 + 2 = 14$

    b. $f(-1) = 4(-1) + 2 = -2$

37. a. $f(6) = 6^2 - 5 = 31$

    b. $f(-2) = (-2)^2 - 5 = -1$

39. a. $f(0) = 3 \cdot 0^2 - 0 + 4 = 4$

    b. $f(2) = 3 \cdot 2^2 - 2 + 4 = 14$

41. a. $f(2) = \dfrac{2 + 4}{2} = \dfrac{6}{2} = 3$

    b. $f(6) = \dfrac{6 + 4}{2} = \dfrac{10}{2} = 5$

43. Let $x = 0$, $y = f(0) = 0 + 3 = 3$, $(0, 3)$
Let $x = 1$, $y = f(1) = 1 + 3 = 4$, $(1, 4)$
Let $x = 2$, $y = f(2) = 2 + 3 = 5$, $(2, 5)$

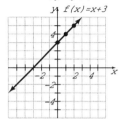

45. Let $x = -2$, $y = f(-2) = 2(-2) - 1 = -5$, $(-2, -5)$
Let $x = 0$, $y = f(0) = 2 \cdot 0 - 1 = -1$, $(0, -1)$
Let $x = 2$, $y = f(2) = 2 \cdot 2 - 1 = 3$, $(2, 3)$

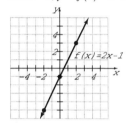

47. Let $x = 0$, $y = f(0) = -2 \cdot 0 + 4 = 4$, $(0, 4)$
Let $x = 1$, $y = f(1) = -2 \cdot 1 + 4 = 2$, $(1, 2)$
Let $x = 2$, $y = f(2) = -2 \cdot 2 + 4 = 0$, $(2, 0)$

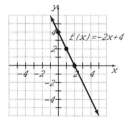

49. Let $x = 0$, $y = f(0) = -\dfrac{1}{2}(0) + 2 = 2$, $(0, 2)$

Let $x = 2$, $y = f(2) = -\dfrac{1}{2}(2) + 2 = 1$, $(2, 1)$

Let $x = 4$, $y = f(4) = -\dfrac{1}{2}(4) + 2 = 0$, $(4, 0)$

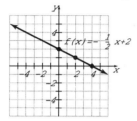

51. No, each x cannot have a unique y.

53. Yes, each year has only one value for the miles per gallon.

55. a.

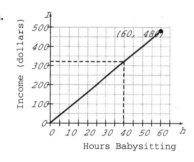

b. $320

57. a.

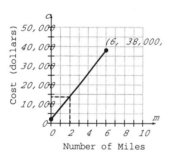

b. $14,000

59. a.

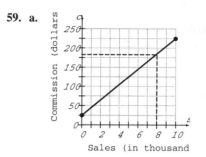

b. $185

61. a.

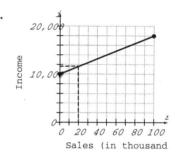

b. $11,600

63. Yes.

65. No. At $x = 1$, there are two y values: $y = 1$ and $y = 2$.

67. a. $f\left(\dfrac{1}{2}\right) = \dfrac{1}{2}\left(\dfrac{1}{2}\right)^2 - 3\left(\dfrac{1}{2}\right) + 5$

$= \dfrac{1}{8} - \dfrac{3}{2} + 5$

$= \dfrac{1}{8} - \dfrac{12}{8} + \dfrac{40}{8}$

$= \dfrac{29}{8}$

b. $f\left(\dfrac{2}{3}\right) = \dfrac{1}{2}\left(\dfrac{2}{3}\right)^2 - 3\left(\dfrac{2}{3}\right) + 5$

$= \dfrac{4}{18} - 2 + 5$

$= \dfrac{2}{9} + 3$

$= \dfrac{2}{9} + \dfrac{27}{9}$

$= \dfrac{29}{9}$

c. $f(0.2) = \frac{1}{2}(0.2)^2 - 3(0.2) + 5$
$= 0.02 - 0.6 + 5$
$= 4.42$

71. $\frac{5}{9} - \frac{3}{7} = \frac{35}{63} - \frac{27}{63} = \frac{8}{63}$

72. $2x - 3(x+2) = 8$
$2x - 3x - 6 = 8$
$-x - 6 = 8$
$-x = 14$
$x = -14$

73. Let x = the number of additional miles.
Then
Cost $= \$2.00 + \$1.50x$
$20.00 = 2.00 + 1.50x$
$20 = 2 + 1.5x$
$18 = 1.5x$
$12 = x$
Andrew can travel 12 additional miles for a total of 13 miles.

74. $25x^2 - 121y^2 = (5x)^2 - (11y)^2$
$= (5x + 11y)(5x - 11y)$

75. $\frac{\frac{21x}{y^2}}{\frac{7}{xy}} = \frac{21x}{y^2} \div \frac{7}{xy} = \frac{21x}{y^2} \cdot \frac{xy}{7} = \frac{3x^2}{y}$

76. A graph is an illustration of a set of points whose coordinates satisfy an equation.

Review Exercises

1.

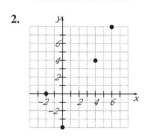

2.

The points are not collinear.

3. a. $2x + 3y = 9$
$2 \cdot 5 + 3 \cdot \left(-\frac{1}{3}\right) = 9$
$10 - 1 = 9$
$9 = 9$ True

b. $2x + 3y = 9$
$2 \cdot 0 + 3 \cdot 3 = 9$
$9 = 9$ True

c. $2x + 3y = 9$
$2(-1) + 3 \cdot 4 = 9$
$-2 + 12 = 9$
$10 = 9$ False

d. $2x + 3y = 9$
$2 \cdot 2 + 3\left(\frac{5}{3}\right) = 9$
$4 + 5 = 9$
$9 = 9$ True

4. a. $3x - 2y = 8$
$3 \cdot 4 - 2y = 8$
$12 - 2y = 8$
$-2y = -4$
$y = 2$

b. $3x - 2y = 8$
$3 \cdot 0 - 2y = 8$
$-2y = 8$
$y = -4$

c. $3x - 2y = 8$
$3x - 2 \cdot 4 = 8$
$3x - 8 = 8$
$3x = 16$
$x = \frac{16}{3}$

d. $3x - 2y = 8$
$3x - 2 \cdot 0 = 8$
$3x = 8$
$x = \frac{8}{3}$

5. $y = 4$ is a horizontal line with
　　y-intercept $= (0, 4)$.

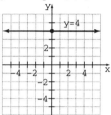

6. $x = 2$ is a vertical line with x-intercept $= (2, 0)$.

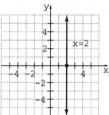

7. Let $x = -1$, $y = 3(-1) = -3$, $(-1, -3)$
　　Let $x = 0$, $y = 3 \cdot 0 = 0$, $(0, 0)$
　　Let $x = 1$, $y = 3 \cdot 1 = 3$, $(1, 3)$

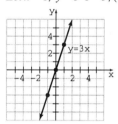

8. Let $x = 0$, $y = 2 \cdot 0 - 1 = -1$, $(0, -1)$
　　Let $x = 1$, $y = 2 \cdot 1 - 1 = 1$, $(1, 1)$
　　Let $x = 2$, $y = 2 \cdot 2 - 1 = 3$, $(2, 3)$

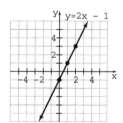

9. Let $x = 0$, $y = -2 \cdot 0 + 5 = 5$, $(0, 5)$
　　Let $x = 1$, $y = -2 \cdot 1 + 5 = 3$, $(1, 3)$
　　Let $x = 2$, $y = -2 \cdot 2 + 5 = 1$, $(2, 1)$

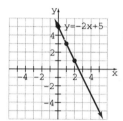

10. Let $x = 0$, $y = -\dfrac{1}{2}(0) + 4 = 4$, $(0, 4)$

　　Let $x = 2$, $y = -\dfrac{1}{2}(2) + 4 = 3$, $(2, 3)$

　　Let $x = 4$, $y = -\dfrac{1}{2}(4) + 4 = 2$, $(4, 2)$

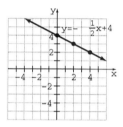

11. Let $x = 0$　　　Let $y = 0$
　　$-2x + 3y = 6$　　$-2x + 3y = 6$
　　$-2 \cdot 0 + 3y = 6$　　$-2x + 3 \cdot 0 = 6$
　　　　$3y = 6$　　　　$-2x = 6$
　　　　$y = 2$　　　　$x = -3$

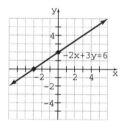

12. Let $x = 0$　　　　Let $y = 0$
　　$-5x - 2y = 10$　　$-5x - 2y = 10$
　　$-5 \cdot 0 - 2y = 10$　　$-5x - 2 \cdot 0 = 10$
　　　　$-2y = 10$　　　　$-5x = 10$
　　　　$y = -5$　　　　$x = -2$

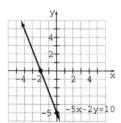

13. Let $x = 0$ Let $y = 0$
$$25x + 50y = 100 \qquad 25x + 50y = 100$$
$$25 \cdot 0 + 50y = 100 \qquad 25x + 50 \cdot 0 = 100$$
$$50y = 100 \qquad\qquad 25x = 100$$
$$y = 2 \qquad\qquad\qquad x = 4$$

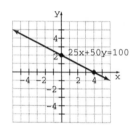

14. Let $x = 0$ Let $y = 0$
$$\frac{2}{3}x = \frac{1}{4}y + 20 \qquad \frac{2}{3}x = \frac{1}{4}y + 20$$
$$\frac{2}{3} \cdot 0 = \frac{1}{4}y + 20 \qquad \frac{2}{3}x = \frac{1}{4} \cdot 0 + 20$$
$$0 = \frac{1}{4}y + 20 \qquad \frac{2}{3}x = 20$$
$$-\frac{1}{4}y = 20 \qquad\qquad x = 30$$
$$y = -80$$

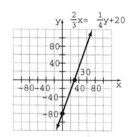

15. $m = \dfrac{5 - (-4)}{-2 - 3}$

$\quad = \dfrac{9}{-5}$

$\quad = -\dfrac{9}{5}$

16. $m = \dfrac{-3 - (-2)}{8 - (-4)}$

$\quad = \dfrac{-1}{12}$

$\quad = -\dfrac{1}{12}$

17. $m = \dfrac{3 - (-1)}{-4 - (-2)}$

$\quad = \dfrac{4}{-2}$

$\quad = -2$

18. The slope of a horizontal line is 0.

19. The slope of a vertical line is undefined.

20. The slope of a straight line is the ratio of the vertical change to the horizontal change between any two points on the line.

21. $m = \dfrac{-6}{3}$

$\quad = -2$

22. $m = \dfrac{2}{8}$

$\quad = \dfrac{1}{4}$

23. Neither. For the lines to be parallel the slopes have to be the same. For the lines to be perpendicular the slopes have to be opposite reciprocals.

24. Perpendicular, because the slopes are opposite reciprocals.

25. a. $m = \dfrac{201 - 145}{1995 - 1993}$

$\qquad = \dfrac{56}{2}$

$\qquad = 28$

b. $m = \dfrac{415 - 268}{1996 - 1999}$

$\qquad = \dfrac{147}{-3}$

$\qquad = -49$

26. $6x + 7y = 14$
$7y = -6x + 14$

$y = -\dfrac{6}{7}x + \dfrac{14}{7}$

$y = -\dfrac{6}{7}x + 2$

$m = -\dfrac{6}{7}, b = 2$

The slope is $-\dfrac{6}{7}$; the y-intercept is $(0, 2)$.

27. $2x + 5 = 0$
$2x = -5$

$x = -\dfrac{5}{2}$

This is a vertical line, so the slope is undefined and there is no y-intercept.

28. $3y + 9 = 0$
$3y = -9$
$y = -3$

This is a horizontal line, so the slope is 0 and the y-intercept is $(0, -3)$.

29. $m = \dfrac{3}{1} = 3, b = -3$
$y = 3x - 3$

30. $m = \dfrac{-2}{4} = -\dfrac{1}{2}, b = 2$
$y = -\dfrac{1}{2}x + 2$

31. $y = 2x - 6 \quad 6y = 12x + 6$
$\qquad\qquad y = 2x + 1$

Since the slopes are the same and the y-intercepts are different, the lines are parallel.

32. $2x - 3y = 9 \qquad\qquad 3x + 2y = 6$
$-3y = -2x + 9 \qquad +2y = -3x + 6$

$y = \dfrac{2}{3}x - 3 \qquad\quad y = -\dfrac{3}{2}x + 3$

Since the slopes are opposite reciprocals, the lines are perpendicular.

33. $y - 4 = 3(x - 2)$
$y - 4 = 3x - 6$
$y = 3x - 2$

34. $y - 2 = -\dfrac{2}{3}(x - 3)$

$y - 2 = -\dfrac{2}{3}x + 2$

$y = -\dfrac{2}{3}x + 4$

35. $y - 2 = 0(x - 4)$
$y - 2 = 0$
$y = 2$

36. Lines with undefined slopes are vertical and have the form $x = c$ where c is the value of x for any point on the line.
$x = 4$

37. $m = \dfrac{-4 - 3}{0 - (-2)} = \dfrac{-7}{2} = -\dfrac{7}{2}$

$y - 3 = -\dfrac{7}{2}[x - (-2)]$

$y - 3 = -\dfrac{7}{2}(x + 2)$

$y - 3 = -\dfrac{7}{2}x - 7$

$y = -\dfrac{7}{2}x - 4$

38. $m = \dfrac{3 - (-2)}{-4 - (-4)} = \dfrac{5}{0} =$ undefined

Lines with undefined slopes are vertical and have the form $x = c$ where c is the value of x for any point on the line.
$x = -4$

39.

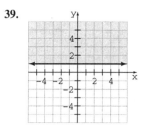

Check $(0, 0)$: $y \geq 1$
$\qquad\qquad\quad 0 \geq 1 \qquad$ False

40.

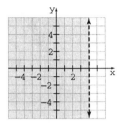

Check $(0, 0)$: $x < 4$

$0 < 4$ True

41.

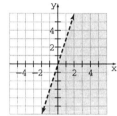

Check $(1, -1)$: $y < 3x$

$-1 < 3 \cdot 1$

$-1 < 3$ True

42.

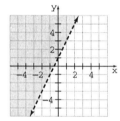

Check $(0, 0)$: $y > 2x + 1$

$0 > 2 \cdot 0 + 1$

$0 > 1$ False

43.

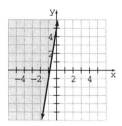

Check $(0, 0)$: $-6x + y \geq 5$

$-6 \cdot 0 + 0 \geq 5$

$0 \geq 5$ False

44.

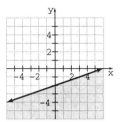

45. Function
     Domain $\{0, 1, 2, 4, 6\}$
     Range $\{-3, -1, 2, 4, 5\}$

46. Not a function
     Domain $\{3, 4, 6, 7\}$
     Range $\{0, 1, 2, 5\}$

47. Not a function
     Domain $\{3, 4, 5, 6\}$
     Range $\{-3, 1, 2\}$

48. Function
     Domain $\{-2, 3, 4, 5, 9\}$
     Range $\{-2\}$

49. a. $\{(1, 3), (4, 5), (7, 2), (9, 2)\}$

     b. The relation is a function; every element of the domain corresponds to exactly one element of the range.

50. a. $\{(4, 1), (6, 3), (6, 5), (8, 7)\}$

     b. The relation is not a function; 6 is paired with more than 1 value.

51. a. Domain: {Mary, Pete, George, Carlos}
        Range: {Apple, Orange, Grape}

     b. Not a function.

52. a. Domain: {Sarah, Jacob, Kristen, Erin}
        Range: {Seat 1, Seat 2, Seat 3, Seat 4}

     b. Not a function.

53. a. Domain: {Blue, Green , Yellow}
        Range: {Paul, Maria, Lalo, Duc}

     b. Function

54. a. Domain: $\{1, 2, 3, 4, 5\}$
        Range: {A, B, C}

     b. Function

55. Function

56. Since a vertical line at $x = 0$ will intersect the graph more than once, the graph is not a function.

57. Function

58. Function

59. a. $f(1) = 6 \cdot 1 - 4 = 6 - 4 = 2$

   b. $f(-5) = 6 \cdot (-5) - 4 = -30 - 4 = -34$

60. a. $f(-4) = -4(-4) - 5 = 11$

   b. $f(8) = -4 \cdot 8 - 5 = -37$

61. a. $f(3) = \frac{1}{3}(3) - 5 = -4$

   b. $f(-9) = \frac{1}{3}(-9) - 5 = -8$

62. a. $f(3) = 2 \cdot 3^2 - 4 \cdot 3 + 6 = 12$

   b. $f(-5) = 2(-5)^2 - 4(-5) + 6 = 76$

63. Yes, it is a function since it passes the vertical line test.

64. Yes, it is a function since it passes the vertical line test.

65. Let $x = 0$, $y = f(0) = 3 \cdot 0 - 5 = -5$, $(0, -5)$
   Let $x = 1$, $y = f(1) = 3 \cdot 1 - 5 = -2$, $(1, -2)$
   Let $x = 2$, $y = f(2) = 3 \cdot 2 - 5 = 1$, $(2, 1)$

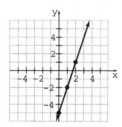

66. Let $x = 0$, $y = f(0) = -2 \cdot 0 + 3 = 3$, $(0, 3)$
   Let $x = 1$, $y = f(1) = -2 \cdot 1 + 3 = 1$, $(1, 1)$
   Let $x = 2$, $y = f(2) = -2 \cdot 2 + 3 = -1$, $(2, -1)$

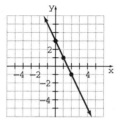

67. a.

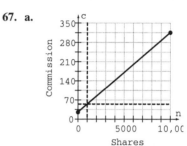

   b. $55

68. a.

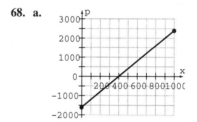

   b. $0

   Check $(0, 0)$: $3y + 6 \leq x$
   $\qquad\qquad 3 \cdot 0 + 6 \leq 0$
   $\qquad\qquad\qquad 6 \leq 0 \qquad$ False

Practice Test

1. A graph is an illustration of the set of points that satisfy an equation.

2. a. IV

   b. III

3. a. $ax + by = c$

   b. $y = mx + b$

   c. $y - y_1 = m(x - x_1)$

4. a. $3y = 5x - 9$
$3 \cdot 2 = 5 \cdot 4 - 9$
$6 = 20 - 9$
$6 = 11$ False

b. $3y = 5x - 9$
$3 \cdot 0 = 5 \cdot \dfrac{9}{5} - 9$
$0 = 9 - 9$
$0 = 0$ True

c. $3y = 5x - 9$
$3(-6) = 5(-2) - 9$
$-18 = -10 - 9$
$-18 = -19$ False

d. $3y = 5x - 9$
$3 \cdot (-3) = 5 \cdot 0 - 9$
$-9 = -9$ True

$\left(\dfrac{9}{5},\ 0\right)$ and (0, -3) satisfy the equation.

5. $m = \dfrac{3 - (-5)}{-4 - 2} = \dfrac{8}{-6} = -\dfrac{4}{3}$

6. $4x - 9y = 15$
$-9y = -4x + 15$
$y = \dfrac{4}{9}x - \dfrac{5}{3}$
$m = \dfrac{4}{9},\ b = -\dfrac{5}{3}$
The slope is $\dfrac{4}{9}$; the y-intercept is $\left(0,\ -\dfrac{5}{3}\right)$.

7. $m = \dfrac{-1}{1} = -1,\ b = -1$
$y = -x - 1$

8. $x = -3$ is a vertical line with x-intercept = (−3, 0).

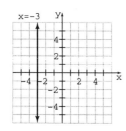

9. $y = 2$ is a horizontal line with y-intercept = (0, 2).

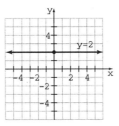

10. Let $x = 0$, $y = 3 \cdot 0 - 2 = -2$, (0, −2)
Let $x = 1$, $y = 3 \cdot 1 - 2 = 1$, (1, 1)
Let $x = 2$, $y = 3 \cdot 2 - 2 = 4$, (2, 4)

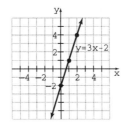

11. a. $2x - 4y = 8$
$-4y = -2x + 8$
$y = \dfrac{1}{2}x - 2$

b. Let $x = 0$, $y = \dfrac{1}{2}(0) - 2 = -2$, (0, −2)
Let $x = 2$, $y = \dfrac{1}{2}(2) - 2 = -1$, (2, −1)
Let $x = 4$, $y = \dfrac{1}{2}(4) - 2 = 0$, (4, 0)

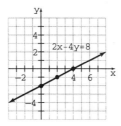

12. $3x + 5y = 15$
Let $x = 0$ Let $y = 0$

$$3(0) + 5y = 15 \quad 3x + 5(0) = 15$$
$$5y = 15 \qquad 3x = 15$$
$$y = 3 \qquad x = 5$$

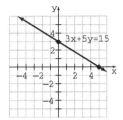

13. $y - (-5) = 4(x - 2)$
$$y + 5 = 4x - 8$$
$$y = 4x - 13$$

14. $m = \dfrac{2 - (-1)}{-4 - 3} = \dfrac{3}{-7} = -\dfrac{3}{7}$
$$y - (-1) = -\dfrac{3}{7}(x - 3)$$
$$y + 1 = -\dfrac{3}{7}x + \dfrac{9}{7}$$
$$y = -\dfrac{3}{7}x + \dfrac{2}{7}$$

15. $2y = 3x - 6 \quad y - \dfrac{3}{2}x = -5$
$$y = \dfrac{3}{2}x - 3 \qquad y = \dfrac{3}{2}x - 5$$

The lines are parallel since they have the same slope but different y-intercepts.

16. slope = 3, y intercept is $(0, -4)$.

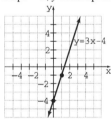

17. $4x - 2y = 6$
$$-2y = -4x + 6$$
$$y = 2x - 3$$
Slope = 2, y intercept is $(0, -3)$.

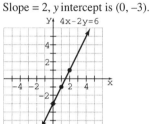

18. A function is a set of ordered pairs in which each first component corresponds to exactly one second component.

19. a. The relation is not a function; 1, a first component, is paired with more than 1 value.

   b. Domain $\{1, 3, 5, 6\}$
   Range $\{-4, 0, 2, 3, 5\}$

20. a. The graph is a function because it passes the vertical line test.

   b. The graph is not a function because a vertical line can be drawn that intersects the graph at more than one point.

21. a. $f(2) = 2(2)^2 + 3(2)$
   $$= 8 + 6$$
   $$= 14$$

   b. $f(-3) = 2(-3)^2 + 3(-3)$
   $$= 18 - 9$$
   $$= 9$$

22. Let $x = 0$, $y = f(0) = 2 \cdot 0 - 4 = -4$, $(0, -4)$
Let $x = 1$, $y = f(1) = 2 \cdot 1 - 4 = -2$, $(1, -2)$
Let $x = 2$, $y = f(2) = 2 \cdot 2 - 4 = 0$, $(2, 0)$

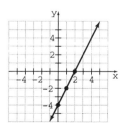

23.

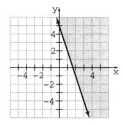

Check $(0, 0)$: $y \geq -3x + 5$
$0 \geq -3 \cdot 0 + 5$
$0 \geq 5$ False

24.

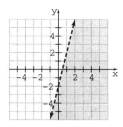

Check $(0, 0)$: $y < 4x - 2$
$0 < 4 \cdot 0 - 2$
$0 < -2$ False

25. a.

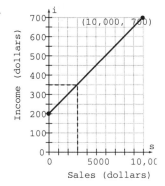

b. $350

Cumulative Review Test

1. a. $\{1, 2, 3, \ldots\}$

b. $\{0, 1, 2, 3, \ldots\}$

2. a. Distributive Property

b. Commutative Property of Addition

3. $2x + 5 = 3(x - 5)$
$2x + 5 = 3x - 15$
$-x + 5 = -15$
$-x = -20$
$x = 20$

4. $3(x - 2) - (x + 4) = 2x - 10$
$3x - 6 - x - 4 = 2x - 10$
$2x - 10 = 2x - 10$
$0 = 0$
All real numbers are solutions.

5. $2x - 14 > 5x + 1$
$-3x > 15$
$x < -5$

```
◄——————○—+—+—+—+—+—+—►
   -8  -7  -6  -5  -4  -3  -2  -1   0
```

6. $\dfrac{3 \text{ cans}}{\$1.50} = \dfrac{8 \text{ cans}}{x \text{ dollars}}$

$\dfrac{3}{1.50} = \dfrac{8}{x}$

$3x = 12$

$x = \dfrac{12}{3} = 4$

8 cans sell for $4.00.

7. Let x = width of rectangle.
Then $2x + 4$ = length of rectangle.
$P = 2l + 2w$
$26 = 2(2x + 4) + 2x$
$26 = 4x + 8 + 2x$
$26 = 6x + 8$
$18 = 6x$
$3 = x$
The width is 3 feet and the length is
$2(3) + 4 = 10$ feet. The dimensions are 3' x 10'.

8. Let x = number of hours until the runners are
28 miles apart.

Runner	Rate	Time	Distance
First	6 mph	x	$6x$
Second	8 mph	x	$8x$

(Distance run by first runner) + (Distance run by
second runner) = 28 miles
$6x + 8x = 28$
$14x = 28$
$x = 2$
It will take 2 hours.

9. $\dfrac{x^{-4}}{x^{11}} = \dfrac{1}{x^{11-(-4)}} = \dfrac{1}{x^{11+4}} = \dfrac{1}{x^{15}}$

10. $652.3 = 6.523 \times 10^2$

11. $2x^2 - 12x + 10 = 2(x^2 - 6x + 5)$
$$= 2(x - 5)(x - 1)$$

12. $4a^2 + 4a - 35 = (2a - 5)(2a + 7)$

13. $\qquad 3x^2 = 18x$
$3x^2 - 18x = 0$
$3x(x - 6) = 0$
$3x = 0$ or $x - 6 = 0$
$\quad x = 0$ or $\qquad x = 6$

14. $\dfrac{2r - 7}{14 - 4r} = \dfrac{2r - 7}{-2(2r - 7)} = -\dfrac{1}{2}$

15. $\dfrac{x - 2}{3x + 7} \cdot \dfrac{3x}{x - 2} = \dfrac{3x}{3x + 7}$

16. $\qquad \dfrac{y^2}{y - 5} = \dfrac{25}{y - 5}$
$$(y - 5)\left(\dfrac{y^2}{y - 5}\right) = \left(\dfrac{25}{y - 5}\right)(y - 5)$$
$$y^2 = 25$$
$$y^2 - 25 = 0$$
$$(y + 5)(y - 5) = 0$$
$y + 5 = 0$ or $y - 5 = 0$
$\quad y = -5 \qquad\quad y = 5$

$y = 5$ is an extraneous solution since $\dfrac{y}{y - 5}$ and

$\dfrac{25}{y - 5}$ are undefined when $y = 5$. The only

solution is $y = -5$.

17. $6x - 3y = -12$
Let $x = 0$ $\qquad$ Let $y = 0$
$6(0) - 3y = -12$ $\quad$ $6x - 3(0) = -12$
$\qquad -3y = -12$ $\qquad$ $6x = -12$
$\qquad\quad y = 4$ $\qquad\qquad x = -2$

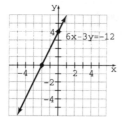

18. Slope $= \dfrac{2}{3}$, y intercept is $(0, -3)$

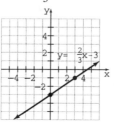

19. $y - 2 = 3(x - 5)$

20. a. The relation is not a function; it does not pass the vertical line test.

b. The relation is a function; each first component corresponds to exactly one second component.

Chapter 8

1. The solution to a system of equations represents the ordered pairs that satisfy all the equations in the system.

3. Write the equations in slope-intercept form and compare their slopes and y-intercepts.

5. The point of intersection can only be estimated.

7. **a.** $y = 4x - 6$ $y = -2x$
   $-10 = 4(-1) - 6$ $-10 = -2(-1)$
   $-10 = -4 - 6$ $-10 = 2$ False
   $-10 = -10$ True
   Since $(-1, -10)$ does not satisfy both equations, it is not a solution to the system of equations.

   b. $y = 4x - 6$
   $0 = 4(3) - 6$
   $0 = 6$ False

   Since $(3, 0)$ does not satisfy the first equation, it is not a solution to the system of equations.

   c. $y = 4x - 6$ $y = -2x$
   $-2 = 4(1) - 6$ $-2 = -2(1)$
   $-2 = -2$ True $-2 = -2$ True
   Since $(1, -2)$ satisfies both equations, it is a solution to the system of linear equations.

9. **a.** $y = 2x - 3$ $y = x + 5$
   $13 = 2(8) - 3$ $13 = 8 + 5$
   $13 = 13$ True $13 = 13$ True

   Since $(8, 13)$ satisfies both equations, it is a solution to the system.

   b. $y = 2x - 3$ $y = x + 5$
   $5 = 2(4) - 3$ $5 = 4 + 5$
   $5 = 5$ True $5 = 9$ False

   Since $(4, 5)$ does not satisfy both equations, it is not a solution to the system.

   c. $y = 2x - 3$
   $9 = 2(4) - 3$
   $9 = 5$ False
   Since $(4, 9)$ does not satisfy the first equation, it is not a solution to the system.

---

b. $x + 2y = 4$ $y = 3x + 3$
$-2 + 2(3) = 4$ $3 = 3(-2) + 3$
$4 = 4$ True $3 = -3$ False
Since $(-2, 3)$ does not satisfy both equations, it is not a solution to the system.

c. $x + 2y = 4$
$4 + 2(15) = 4$
$34 = 4$ False
Since $(4, 15)$ does not satisfy the first equation, it is not a solution to the system.

11. **a.** $2x + y = 9$ $5x + y = 10$
   $2(3) + 3 = 9$ $5(3) + 3 = 10$
   $9 = 9$ True $18 = 10$ False

   Since $(3, 3)$ does not satisfy both equations, it is not a solution to the system.

   b. $2x + y = 9$
   $2(2) + (0) = 9$
   $4 = 9$ False
   Since $(2, 0)$ does not satisfy the first equation, it is not a solution to the system.

   c. $2x + y = 9$ $5x + y = 10$
   $2(4) + 1 = 6$ $5(4) + 1 = 10$
   $9 = 9$ True $21 = 10$ False
   Since $(4, 1)$ does not satisfy both equations, it is not a solution to the system.

13. Solve the first equation for y.
   $2x - 3y = 6$
   $-3y = -2x + 6$
   $y = \dfrac{2}{3}x - 2$

   Notice that it is the same as the second equation. If the ordered pair satisfies the first equation, then it also satisfies the second equation.

   a. $2x - 3y = 6$
   $2(3) - 3(0) = 6$
   $6 = 6$ True
   Since $(3, 0)$ satisfies both equations, it is a solution to the system.

b.
$$2x - 3y = 6$$
$$2(3) - 3(-2) = 6$$
$$12 = 6 \text{ False}$$

Since $(3, -2)$ does not satisfy the first equation, it is not a solution to the system.

c.
$$2x - 3y = 6$$
$$2(6) - 3(2) = 6$$
$$6 = 6 \quad \text{True}$$

Since $(6, 2)$ satisfies both equations, it is a solution to the system.

15. a.
$$3x - 4y = 8$$
$$3(0) - 4(-2) = 8$$
$$8 = 8 \quad \text{True}$$

$$2y = \frac{2}{3}x - 4$$
$$2(-2) = \frac{2}{3}(0) - 4$$
$$-4 = -4 \quad \text{True}$$

Since $(0, -2)$ satisfies both equations, it is a solution to the system.

b.
$$3x - 4y = 8$$
$$3(1) - 4(-6) = 8$$
$$27 = 8 \text{ False}$$

Since $(1, -6)$ does not satisfy the first equation, it is not a solution to the system.

c.
$$3x - 4y = 8$$
$$3\left(-\frac{1}{3}\right) - 4\left(-\frac{9}{4}\right) = 8$$
$$8 = 8 \text{ True}$$

$$2y = \frac{2}{3}x - 4$$
$$2\left(-\frac{9}{4}\right) = \frac{2}{3}\left(-\frac{1}{3}\right) - 4$$
$$-\frac{9}{2} = -\frac{38}{9} \text{ False}$$

Since $\left(-\frac{1}{3}, -\frac{9}{4}\right)$ does not satisfy both equations, it is not a solution to the system.

17. consistent—one solution

19. dependent—infinite number of solutions

21. consistent—one solution

23. inconsistent—no solution

25. Write each equation in slope-intercept form.
$$3y = 4x - 6$$
$$y = \frac{4}{3}x - 2$$

Since the slopes of the lines are not the same, the lines intersect to produce one solution. This is a consistent system.

27. Write each equation in slope-intercept form.
$$2y = 3x + 3 \qquad y = \frac{3}{2}x - 2$$
$$y = \frac{3}{2}x + \frac{3}{2}$$

Since the lines have the same slope, $\frac{3}{2}$, and different y-intercepts, the lines are parallel. There is no solution. This is an inconsistent system.

29. Write each equation in slope-intercept form.
$$4x = 4y + 5$$
$$2x = y - 6 \qquad 4y = 4x - 5$$
$$y = 2x + 6 \qquad y = x - \frac{5}{4}$$

Since the slopes of the lines are not the same, the lines intersect to produce one solution. This is a consistent system.

31. Write each equation in slope-intercept form.
$$3x + 5y = -7 \qquad\qquad -3x - 5y = -7$$
$$5y = -3x - 7 \qquad\qquad -5y = 3x - 7$$
$$y = -\frac{3}{5}x - \frac{7}{5} \qquad\qquad y = -\frac{3}{5}x + \frac{7}{5}$$

Since the lines have the same slope and different y-intercepts, the lines are parallel. There is no solution. This is an inconsistent system.

33. Write each equation in slope-intercept form.
$$x = 3y + 4 \qquad\qquad 2x - 6y = 8$$
$$x - 4 = 3y \qquad\qquad -6y = -2x + 8$$
$$\frac{1}{3}x - \frac{4}{3} = y \qquad\qquad y = \frac{1}{3}x - \frac{4}{3}$$

Since both equations are identical, the line is the same for both of them. There are an infinite number of solutions. This is a dependent system.

35. Write each equation in slope-intercept form.
$$y = \frac{3}{2}x + \frac{1}{2} \qquad\qquad 3x - 2y = -\frac{1}{2}$$
$$-2y = -3x - \frac{1}{2}$$
$$y = \frac{3}{2}x + \frac{1}{4}$$

Since the lines have the same slope and different y-intercepts, the lines are parallel. There is no solution. This is an inconsistent system.

37. Graph the equations $y = x + 3$ and $y = -x + 3$.

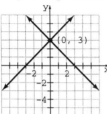

The lines intersect and the point of intersection is $(0, 3)$. This is a consistent system.

39. Graph the equations $y = 3x - 6$ and $y = -x + 6$.

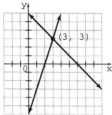

The lines intersect and the point of intersection is $(3, 3)$. This is a consistent system.

41. Graph the equations $2x = 4$ or $x = 2$ and $y = -3$.

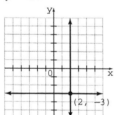

The lines intersect and the point of intersection is $(2, -3)$. This is a consistent system.

43. Graph the equations $y = -x + 5$ and $-x + y = 1$ or $y = x + 1$.

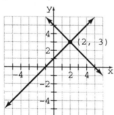

The lines intersect and the point of intersection is $(2, 3)$. This is a consistent system.

45. Graph the equations $y = -\dfrac{1}{2}x + 4$ and

$x + 2y = 6$ or $y = -\dfrac{1}{2}x + 3$.

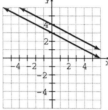

The lines are parallel. The system is inconsistent and there is no solution.

47. Graph the equations $x + 2y = 8$ or $y = -\dfrac{1}{2}x + 4$

and $5x + 2y = 0$ or $y = -\dfrac{5}{2}x$.

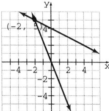

The lines intersect and the point of intersection is $(-2, 5)$. This is a consistent system.

49. Graph the equations $2x + 3y = 6$ or $y = -\dfrac{2}{3}x + 2$

and $4x = -6y + 12$ or $y = -\dfrac{2}{3}x + 2$.

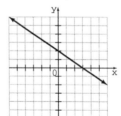

The lines are identical. There are an infinite number of solutions. This is a dependent system.

51. Graph the equations $y = 3$ and $y = 2x - 3$.

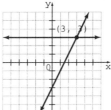

The lines intersect and the point of intersection is (3, 3). This is a consistent system.

53. Graph the equations $x - 2y = 4$ or $y = \frac{1}{2}x - 2$

and $2x - 4y = 8$ or $y = \frac{1}{2}x - 2$.

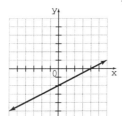

The lines are identical. There are an infinite number of solutions. This is a dependent system.

55. Graph the equations $2x + y = -2$ or $y = -2x - 2$ and $6x + 3y = 6$ or $y = -2x + 2$.

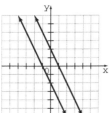

The lines are parallel. The system is inconsistent and there is no solution.

57. Graph the equations $4x - 3y = 6$ or $y = \frac{4}{3}x - 2$

and $2x + 4y = 14$ or $y = -\frac{1}{2}x + \frac{7}{2}$.

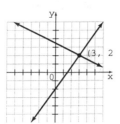

The lines intersect and the point of intersection is (3, 2). This is a consistent system.

59. Graph the equations $2x - 3y = 0$ or $y = \frac{2}{3}x$ and

$x + 2y = 0$ or $y = -\frac{1}{2}x$.

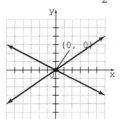

The lines intersect and the point of intersection is (0, 0). This is a consistent system.

61. Write each equation in slope-intercept form.

$$6x - 4y = 12 \qquad\qquad 12y = 18x - 24$$
$$-4y = -6x + 12$$
$$y = \frac{3}{2}x - 3 \qquad\qquad y = \frac{3}{2}x - 2$$

The lines are parallel because they have the same slope, $\frac{3}{2}$, and different y-intercepts.

63. The system has an infinite number of solutions. If the two lines have two points in common then they must be the same line.

65. The system has no solutions. Distinct parallel lines do not intersect.

67. $x = 5, y = 3$ has one solution, (5, 3).

69. (repair) $c = 600 + 650n$
(replacement) $c = 1800 + 450n$
Graph the equations and determine the intersection.

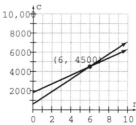

The solution is (6, 4500). Therefore, the total cost of repair equals the total cost of replacement at 6 years.

71. $c = 25h$

$c = 22h + 18$
Graph the equations and determine the intersection.

The solution (6, 150). Therefore, the boats must be rented for 6 hours for the cost to be the same.

79. $3x - (x - 6) + 4(3 - x) = 3x - x + 6 + 12 - 4x$
$$= 3x - x - 4x + 6 + 12$$
$$= -2x + 18$$

80. $2(x + 3) - x = 5x + 2$
$$2x + 6 - x = 5x + 2$$
$$x + 6 = 5x + 2$$
$$-4x = -4$$
$$x = 1$$

81. $\dfrac{x^2 - 9x + 14}{2 - x} = \dfrac{(x - 7)(x - 2)}{-(x - 2)} = -(x - 7)$

82. $\dfrac{4}{b} + 2b = \dfrac{38}{3}$

$$3b\left(\dfrac{4}{b} + 2b\right) = 3b\left(\dfrac{38}{3}\right)$$

$$12 + 6b^2 = 38b$$

$$6b^2 - 38b + 12 = 0$$

$$2\left(3b^2 - 19b + 6\right) = 0$$

$$2(3b - 1)(b - 6) = 0$$

$3b - 1 = 0$ or $b - 6 = 0$

$b = \dfrac{1}{3}$ $b = 6$

83. a. For the x-intercept, set $y = 0$.
$$2x + 3y = 12$$
$$2x + 3(0) = 12$$
$$2x = 12$$
$$x = 6$$
The x-intercept is $(6, 0)$.
For the y-intercept, set $x = 0$.
$$2x + 3y = 12$$
$$2(0) + 3y = 12$$
$$3y = 12$$
$$y = 4$$
The y-intercept is $(0, 4)$.

b.

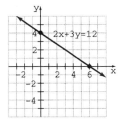

Exercise Set 8.2

1. The x in the first equation, since both 6 and 12 are divisible by 3.

3. You will obtain a false statement, such as $3 = 0$.

5. $x + 2y = 6$

$2x - 3y = 5$
Solve the first equation for x, $x = 6 - 2y$.
Substitute $6 - 2y$ for x in the second equation.
$$2(6 - 2y) - 3y = 5$$
$$12 - 4y - 3y = 5$$
$$-7y = -7$$
$$y = 1$$
Substitute 1 for y in the equation $x = 6 - 2y$.
$$x = 6 - 2(1)$$
$$x = 4$$
The solution is $(4, 1)$.

7. $x + y = -2$
$x - y = 0$
Solve the first equation for y, $y = -2 - x$.
Substitute $-2 - x$ for y in the second equation.
$$x - (-2 - x) = 0$$
$$x + 2 + x = 0$$
$$2x = -2$$
$$x = -1$$
Substitute -1 for x in the equation $y = -2 - x$.
$$y = -2 - (-1)$$
$$y = -2 + 1$$
$$y = -1$$
The solution is $(-1, -1)$.

9. $3x + y = 3$
$3x + y + 5 = 0$
Solve the first equation for y, $y = -3x + 3$.
Substitute $-3x + 3$ for y in the second equation.
$$3x + y + 5 = 0$$
$$3x - 3x + 3 + 5 = 0$$
$$8 = 0 \text{ False}$$
There is no solution.

11. $x = 3$

$x + y + 5 = 0$

Substitute 3 for x in the second equation.

$x + y + 5 = 0$

$3 + y + 5 = 0$

$y = -8$

The solution is $(3, -8)$.

13. $x - \dfrac{1}{2}y = 6$

$y = 2x - 12$

Substitute $2x - 12$ for y in the first equation.

$$x - \frac{1}{2}y = 6$$

$$x - \frac{1}{2}(2x - 12) = 6$$

$$x - x + 6 = 6$$

$$6 = 6$$

Since this is a true statement, there are an infinite number of solutions. This is a dependent system.

15. $2x + y = 9$

$y = 4x - 3$

Substitute $4x - 3$ for y in the first equation.

$2x + y = 9$

$2x + 4x - 3 = 9$

$6x = 12$

$x = 2$

Now substitute 2 for x in the second equation.

$y = 4x - 3$

$y = 4(2) - 3$

$y = 8 - 3$

$y = 5$

The solution is $(2, 5)$.

17. $y = \dfrac{1}{3}x - 2$

$x - 3y = 6$

Substitute $\dfrac{1}{3}x - 2$ for y in the second equation.

$$x - 3y = 6$$

$$x - 3\left(\frac{1}{3}x - 2\right) = 6$$

$$x - x + 6 = 6$$

$$6 = 6$$

Since this is a true statement, there are an infinite number of solutions. This is a dependent system.

19. $2x + 3y = 7$

$6x - 2y = 10$

First solve the second equation for y.

$$\frac{1}{2}(6x - 2y) = \frac{1}{2}(10)$$

$$3x - y = 5$$

$$y = 3x - 5$$

Now substitute $3x - 5$ for y in the first equation.

$2x + 3y = 7$

$2x + 3(3x - 5) = 7$

$2x + 9x - 15 = 7$

$11x = 22$

$x = 2$

Finally substitute 2 for x in the equation

$y = 3x - 5$.

$y = 3(2) - 5$

$y = 6 - 5$

$y = 1$

The solution is $(2, 1)$.

21. $3x - y = 14$

$6x - 2y = 10$

First solve the first equation for y.

$3x - y = 14$

$y = 3x - 14$

Now substitute $3x - 14$ for y in the second equation.

$6x - 2y = 10$

$6x - 2(3x - 14) = 10$

$6x - 6x + 28 = 10$

$28 = 10$ False

There is no solution.

23. $4x - 5y = -4$

$3x = 2y - 3$

First solve the second equation for x.

$$\frac{1}{3}(3x) = \frac{1}{3}(2y - 3)$$

$$x = \frac{2}{3}y - 1$$

Now substitute $\dfrac{2}{3}y - 1$ for x in the first equation.

$$4x - 5y = -4$$

$$4\left(\frac{2}{3}y - 1\right) - 5y = -4$$

$$\frac{8}{3}y - 4 - 5y = -4$$

$$\frac{8}{3}y - \frac{15}{3}y = 0$$

$$-\frac{7}{3}y = 0$$

$$y = 0$$

Finally substitute 0 for y in the equation

$x = \dfrac{2}{3}y - 1$.

$x = \dfrac{2}{3}(0) - 1$

$x = -1$

The solution is $(-1, 0)$.

25. $4x + 5y = -6$

$x - \dfrac{5}{3}y = -2$

First solve the second equation for x,

$x = \dfrac{5}{3}y - 2$. Now substitute $\dfrac{5}{3}y - 2$ for x in the

first equation.

$$5x + 4y = -7$$

$$4\left(\dfrac{5}{3}y - 2\right) + 5y = -6$$

$$\dfrac{20}{3}y - 8 + 5y = -6$$

$$\dfrac{20}{3}y + \dfrac{15}{3}y = 8 - 6$$

$$\dfrac{35}{3}y = 2$$

$$y = \dfrac{6}{35}$$

Finally, substitute $\dfrac{9}{37}$ for y in the equation

$x = \dfrac{5}{3}y - 2$.

$$x = \dfrac{5}{3}\left(\dfrac{6}{35}\right) - 2$$

$$x = \dfrac{2}{7} - \dfrac{14}{7}$$

$$x = -\dfrac{12}{7}$$

The solution is $\left(-\dfrac{12}{7}, \dfrac{6}{35}\right)$.

27. Let x = the smaller number,
then y = the larger number.
$x + y = 79$
$x + 7 = y$

Substitute $x + 7$ for y in the first equation.

$$x + y = 79$$

$$x + (x + 7) = 79$$

$$2x + 7 = 79$$

$$2x = 72$$

$$x = 36$$

Now substitute 36 for x in the second equation:

$x + 7 = y$
$36 + 7 = y$
$43 = y$
The two integers are 36 and 43.

29. Let l = the length of the rectangle,
then w = the width.
$2l + 2w = 40$
$l = 4 + w$

Substitute $4 + w$ for l in the first equation and
solve for w.

$$2l + 2w = 40$$

$$2(4 + w) + 2w = 40$$

$$8 + 2w + 2w = 40$$

$$4w = 32$$

$$w = 8$$

Now substitute 8 for w in the second equation
to find l.

$l = 4 + w$

$l = 4 + 8$

$l = 12$

The length of the rectangle is 12 feet and the
width is 8 feet.

31. Let b = the amount of money Billy had
and j = the amount of money Jean had.

$b + j = 726$
$j = 134 + b$

Substitute $134 + b$ for j in the first equation.

$$b + j = 726$$

$$b + (134 + b) = 726$$

$$2b + 134 = 726$$

$$2b = 592$$

$$b = 296$$

Now substitute 296 for b in the first equation and
solve for j.

$b + j = 726$

$296 + j = 726$

$j = 430$

Billy had \$296 and Jean had \$430.

33. Let c = the client's portion of the award
and a = the attorneys portion.

$c + a = 20{,}000$
$c = 3a$

Now solve the first equation for a and substitute it for a in the second equation.

$c + a = 20000$

$a = 20000 - c$

$c = 3a$

$c = 3(20000 - c)$

$c = 60000 - 3c$

$4c = 60000$

$c = 15000$

The client received $15,000.

35. $c = 1280 + 794n$

$c = 874n$

a. Substitute $874n$ for c in the first equation.
$874n = 1280 + 794n$

$80n = 1280$

$n = 16$

The mortgage plans will have the same total cost at 16 months.

b. $12 \text{ years} \cdot \left(\dfrac{12 \text{ months}}{1 \text{ year}} \right) = 144 \text{ months}$

$c = 1280 + 794(144) = 115,616$

$c = 874(144) = 125,856$

Yes, since $115,616 is less than $125,856, she should refinance.

37. a. Substitute $65 + 72t$ for m in the

first equation and solve for t.

$65 + 72t = 80 + 60t$

$12t = 15$

$t = \dfrac{15}{12} = 1.25$

It will take Roberta 1.25 hours

to catch up to Jean.

b. Now substitute 1.25 for t

in one of the original equtions.

$m = 80 + 60(1.25)$

$m = 80 + 75$

$m = 155$

They will be at mile marker 155 when they meet.

39. a. $T = 180 - 10t$

b. $T = 20 + 6t$

c. $T = 180 - 10t$

$T = 20 + 6t$

Substitute $20 + 6t$ for T in the first equation.
$20 + 6t = 180 - 10t$

$16t = 160$

$t = 10$

It will take 10 minutes for the ball and oil to reach the same temperature.

d. Substitute 10 for t in one of the original equations.
$T = 180 - 10t$

$T = 180 - 10(10)$

$T = 180 - 100$

$T = 80$

The temperature will be 80°F.

41. $\dfrac{25}{3.5} \approx 7.14$

The willow tree is about 7.14 years old.

42. $(6x + 7)(3x - 2) = 18x^2 - 12x + 21x - 14$

$\qquad\qquad\qquad\quad = 18x^2 + 9x - 14$

43. $4x - 8y = 16$

Let $x = 0$ and solve for y.
$4(0) - 8y = 16$

$y = -2$

Let $y = 0$ and solve for x.
$4x - 8(0) = 16$

$x = 4$

The intercepts are $(0, -2)$ and $(4, 0)$.

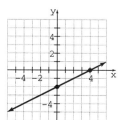

44. $3x - 5y = 8$

Write in slope-intercept form.
$-5y = -3x + 8$

$y = \dfrac{3}{5}x - \dfrac{8}{5}$

The slope is $\dfrac{3}{5}$ and the y intercept is $\left(0, -\dfrac{8}{5} \right)$.

45. Find the slope of the line using points (-2, 0) and (0, 4).

$$m = \frac{4-0}{0-(-2)} = \frac{4}{2} = 2$$

The y-intercept is 4, therefore $b = 4$.

$y = mx + b$

$y = 2x + 4$ is the equation of the line

Exercise Set 8.3

1. Multiply the top equation by 2.
Now the top equation contains a $-2x$ and the bottom equation contains a $2x$. When the equations are added together, the variable x will be eliminated.

3. You will obtain a false statement, such as $0 = 6$

5.
$$x + y = 6$$
$$\underline{x - y = 4}$$
Add: $2x \quad = 10$
$$x = 5$$
Substitute 5 for x in the first equation.
$x + y = 6$
$5 + y = 6$
$y = 1$
The solution is (5, 1).

7.
$$x + y = 5$$
$$\underline{-x + y = 1}$$
Add: $\quad 2y = 6$
$$y = 3$$
Substitute 3 for y in the first equation.
$x + y = 5$
$x + 3 = 5$
$x = 2$
The solution is (2, 3).

9.
$$x + 2y = 15$$
$$\underline{x - 2y = -7}$$
Add: $2x \quad = 8$
$$x = 4$$
Substitute 4 for x in the first equation.
$x + 2y = 15$
$4 + 2y = 15$
$2y = 11$
$$y = \frac{11}{2}$$
The solution is $\left(4, \frac{11}{2}\right)$.

11.
$$4x + y = 6$$
$$-8x - 2y = 20$$
Multiply the first equation by 2, then add to the

second equation.
$2[4x + y = 6]$
gives
$$8x + 2y = 12$$
$$\underline{-8x - 2y = 20}$$
$$0 = 32 \quad \text{False}$$
There is no solution.

13. $-5x + y = 14$
$-3x + y = -2$
To eliminate y, multiply the first equation by -1 and then add.
$-1[-5x + y = 14]$
gives
$$5x - y = -14$$
$$\underline{-3x + y = -2}$$
$$2x \quad = -16$$
$$x = -8$$
Substitute -8 for x in the first equation.
$-5x + y = 14$
$-5(-8) + y = 14$
$40 + y = 14$
$y = -26$
The solution is $(-8, -26)$.

15. $2x + y = -6$
$2x - 2y = 3$
To eliminate y, multiply the first equation by 2 and then add.
$2[2x + y = -6]$
gives
$$4x + 2y = -12$$
$$\underline{2x - 2y = 3}$$
$$6x \quad = -9$$
$$x = -\frac{3}{2}$$
Substitute $-\frac{3}{2}$ for x in the first equation.
$$2x + y = -6$$
$$2\left(-\frac{3}{2}\right) + y = -6$$
$$-3 + y = -6$$
$$y = -3$$
The solution is $\left(-\frac{3}{2}, -3\right)$.

17. $2y = 6x + 16$
$y = -3x - 4$
Rewrite the equations to align the variables on the left hand side of the equal sign.

$-6x + 2y = 16$

$3x + y = -4$

To eliminate x, multiply the second equation by 2, then add.

$2[3x + y = -4]$

gives

$-6x + 2y = 16$

$\underline{6x + 2y = -8}$

$4y = 8$

$y = 2$

Substitute 2 for y in the second equation.

$3x + y = -4$

$3x + 2 = -4$

$3x = -6$

$x = -2$

The solution is (-2, 2).

19. $5x + 3y = 12$

$2x - 4y = 10$

To eliminate y, multiply the first equation by 4 and the second equation by 3 and then add.

$4[5x + 3y = 12]$

$3[2x - 4y = 10]$

gives

$20x + 12y = 48$

$\underline{6x - 12y = 30}$

$26x \qquad = 78$

$x = 3$

Substitute 3 for x in the first equation.

$5x + 3y = 12$

$5(3) + 3y = 12$

$15 + 3y = 12$

$3y = -3$

$y = -1$

The solution is (3, −1).

21. $4x - 2y = 6$

$y = 2x - 3$

Align x- and y-terms on the left side.

$4x - 2y = 6$

$-2x + y = -3$

To eliminate x, multiply the second equation by 2 and then add.

$2[-2x + y = -3]$

gives

$4x - 2y = 6$

$\underline{-4x + 2y = -6}$

$0 = 0$

Since this is a true statement, there are an infinite number of solutions. This is a dependent system.

23. $5x - 4y = -3$

$5y = 2x + 8$

Align x- and y-terms on the left side.

$5x - 4y = -3$

$-2x + 5y = 8$

To eliminate x, multiply the first equation by 2 and the second equation by 5 and then add.

$2[5x - 4y = -3]$

$5[-2x + 5y = 8]$

gives

$10x - 8y = -6$

$\underline{-10x + 25y = 40}$

$17y = 34$

$y = 2$

Substitute 2 for y in the first equation.

$5x - 4y = -3$

$5x - 4(2) = -3$

$5x - 8 = -3$

$5x = 5$

$x = 1$

The solution is (1, 2).

25. $5x - 4y = 1$

$-10x + 8y = -4$

Multiply the first equation by 2, then add.

$2[5x - 4y = 1]$

gives

$10x - 8y = 1$

$\underline{-10x + 8y = -4}$

$0 = -3$ False

There is no solution.

27. $3x - 5y = 0$

$2x + 3y = 0$

To eliminate y, multiply the first equation by 3 and the second equation by 5 and then add.

$3[3x - 5y = 0]$

$5[2x + 3y = 0]$

gives

$9x - 15y = 0$

$\underline{10x + 15y = 0}$

$19x \qquad = 0$

$x = 0$

Substitute 0 for x in the second equation.

$2x + 3y = 0$

$2(0) + 3y = 0$

$3y = 0$

$y = 0$

The solution is (0, 0).

29. $-5x + 4y = -20$
$3x - 2y = 15$
To eliminate y, multiply the second equation by 2, then add.
$2[3x - 2y = 15]$
gives
$-5x + 4y = -20$
$\underline{6x - 4y = 30}$
$x = 10$
Substitute 10 for x in the first equation.
$-5x + 4y = -20$
$-5(10) + 4y = -20$
$-50 + 4y = -20$
$4y = 30$
$y = \dfrac{15}{2}$
The solution is $\left(10, \dfrac{15}{2}\right)$.

31. $6x = 4y + 12$
$-3y = -5x + 6$
Align the x- and y-terms on the left side.
$6x - 4y = 12$
$5x - 3y = 6$
To eliminate x, multiply the first equation by 5 and the second equation by -6 and then add.
$5(6x - 4y = 12)$
$-6(5x - 3y = 6)$
gives
$30x - 20y = 60$
$\underline{-30x + 18y = -36}$
$-2y = 24$
$y = -12$
Substitute -12 for y in the first equation.
$6x - 4y = 12$
$6x - 4(-12) = 12$
$6x + 48 = 12$
$6x = -36$
$x = -6$
The solution is $(-6, -12)$.

33. $4x + 5y = 0$
$3x = 6y + 4$
Align the x- and y-terms on the left side.
$4x + 5y = 0$
$3x - 6y = 4$
To eliminate y, multiply the first equation by 6 and the second equation by 5 and then add.
$6[4x + 5y = 0]$
$5[3x - 6y = 4]$
gives

$24x + 30y = 0$
$\underline{15x - 30y = 20}$
$39x = 20$
$x = \dfrac{20}{39}$
Substitute $\dfrac{20}{39}$ for x in the first equation.
$4x + 5y = 0$
$4\left(\dfrac{20}{39}\right) + 5y = 0$
$5y = -\dfrac{80}{39}$
$y = -\dfrac{16}{39}$
The solution is $\left(\dfrac{20}{39}, -\dfrac{16}{39}\right)$.

35. $x - \dfrac{1}{2}y = 4$
$3x + y = 6$
To eliminate y, multiply the first equation by 2 and then add.
$2\left[x - \dfrac{1}{2}y = 4\right]$
gives
$2x - y = 8$
$\underline{3x + y = 6}$
$5x = 14$
$x = \dfrac{14}{5}$
Substitute $\dfrac{14}{5}$ for x in the second equation.
$3x + y = 6$
$3\left(\dfrac{14}{5}\right) + y = 6$
$\dfrac{42}{5} + y = 6$
$y = 6 - \dfrac{42}{5}$
$y = \dfrac{30}{5} - \dfrac{42}{5}$
$y = -\dfrac{12}{5}$
The solution is $\left(\dfrac{14}{5}, -\dfrac{12}{5}\right)$.

37. $3x - y = 4$

$2x - \dfrac{2}{3}y = 6$

To eliminate y, multiply the first equation by

$-\dfrac{2}{3}$ and then add.

$-\dfrac{2}{3}\left[3x - y = 4\right]$

gives

$-2x + \dfrac{2}{3}y = \dfrac{8}{3}$

$\underline{2x - \dfrac{2}{3}y = 6}$

$0 = \dfrac{26}{3}$ False

There is no solution.

39. $x + y = 16$

$\underline{x - y = 8}$

$2x = 24$

$x = 12$

Substitute 12 for x in the first equation to find the second number.

$x + y = 16$

$12 + y = 16$

$y = 4$

The numbers are 12 and 4.

41. $x + 2y = 14$

$\underline{x - y = 2}$

To eliminate y, multiply the second equation by 2 and then add.

$2\left[x - y = 2\right]$

gives

$x + 2y = 14$

$\underline{2x - 2y = 4}$

$3x = 18$

$x = 6$

Substitute 6 for x in the second equation to find the other number.

$x - y = 2$

$6 - y = 2$

$y = 4$

The numbers are 6 and 4.

43. Let x be the length of the rectangle and y be the width.

$2x + 2y = 18$

$\underline{x = 2y}$

Align the x and y variables on the left hand side of the equal sign.

$2x + 2y = 18$

$\underline{x - 2y = 0}$

Now add the equations to eliminate the y.

$3x = 18$

$x = 6$

Substitute 6 for x in the second equation and solve for y.

$x = 2y$

$6 = 2y$

$3 = y$

The width is 3 inches and the length is 6 inches.

45. Let l = the length and w = the width of the photograph.

$2l + 2w = 36$

$l - w = 2$

Multiply the second equation by 2

$2[l - w = 2]$

gives

$2l + 2w = 36$

$\underline{2l - 2w = 4}$

$4l = 40$

$l = 10$

$10 - w = 2$

$w = 8$

The length is 10 inches and the width is 8 inches.

47. Answers will vary.

49. a. $4x + 2y = 1000$

$2x + 4y = 800$

To eliminate x, multiply the first equation by –2.

$-2[4x + 2y = 1000]$

gives

$-8x - 4y = -2000$

$\underline{2x + 4y = 800}$

$-6x = -1200$

$x = 200$

Substitute 200 for x in the first equation.

$$4x + 2y = 1000$$
$$4(200) + 2y = 1000$$
$$800 + 2y = 1000$$
$$2y = 200$$
$$y = 100$$

The solution is (200, 100).

b. They will have the same solution. Dividing an equation by a nonzero number does not change the solutions.
$$2x + y = 500$$
$$2x + 4y = 800$$

To eliminate x, multiply the first equation by -1 and then add.
$$-1[2x + y = 500]$$
gives
$$-2x - y = -500$$
$$\underline{2x + 4y = 800}$$
$$3y = 300$$
$$y = 100$$

Substitute 100 for y in the first equation.
$$2x + y = 500$$
$$2x + 100 = 500$$
$$2x = 400$$
$$x = 200$$
The solution is (200, 100).

51. $\dfrac{x+2}{2} - \dfrac{y+4}{3} = 4$

$\dfrac{x+y}{2} = \dfrac{1}{2} + \dfrac{x-y}{3}$

Start by writing each equation in standard form after clearing fractions.
For the first equation:
$$6\left[\frac{x+2}{2} - \frac{y+4}{3} = 4\right]$$
$$3(x + 2) - 2(y + 4) = 24$$
$$3x + 6 - 2y - 8 = 24$$
$$3x - 2y - 2 = 24$$
$$3x - 2y = 26$$

For the second equation:
$$6\left[\frac{x+y}{2} = \frac{1}{2} + \frac{x-y}{3}\right]$$
$$3(x + y) = 3 + 2(x - y)$$
$$3x + 3y = 3 + 2x - 2y$$
$$x + 5y = 3$$

The new system is:
$$3x - 2y = 26$$
$$x + 5y = 3$$

To eliminate x, multiply the second equation by -3 and then add.
$$-3[x + 5y = 3]$$
gives

$$3x - 2y = 26$$
$$\underline{-3x - 15y = -9}$$
$$-17y = 17$$
$$y = -1$$

Now, substitute -1 for y in the equation $x + 5y = 3$.
$$x + 5(-1) = 3$$
$$x - 5 = 3$$
$$x = 8$$
The solution is (8, -1).

$$-23x - 2y = 48$$
$$-23\left(-\frac{105}{41}\right) - 2y = 48$$
$$\frac{2415}{41} - 2y = 48$$
$$-2y = \frac{1968}{41} - \frac{2415}{41}$$
$$-2y = -\frac{447}{41}$$
$$y = \frac{447}{82}$$

The solution is $\left(-\dfrac{105}{41}, \dfrac{447}{82}\right)$.

53. $x + 2y - z = 2$

$2x - y + z = 3$

$2x + y + z = 7$

Add the second and third equations to eliminate y.
$$2x - y + z = 3$$
$$\underline{2x + y + z = 7}$$
$$4x + 2z = 10$$
Multiply the second equation by 2 and then add the third equation to eliminate y.
$$2[2x - y + z = 3]$$
gives
$$4x - 2y + 2z = 6$$
$$\underline{x + 2y - z = 2}$$
$$5x + z = 8$$
Now we have two equations with two unknowns.
$$4x + 2z = 10$$
$$5x + z = 8$$
To eliminate z, multiply the second equation by -2 and then add.
$$-2[5x + z = 8]$$
gives
$$4x + 2z = 10$$
$$\underline{-10x - 2z = -16}$$
$$-6x = -6$$
$$x = 1$$

Substitute1 for x in the second equation and solve for z

$$5x + z = 8$$
$$5(1) + z = 8$$
$$5 + z = 8$$
$$z = 3$$

Now go back to one of the original equations and substitute 1 for x and 3 for z and then find y. The third equation is used below.

$$2x + y + z = 7$$
$$2(1) + y + 3 = 7$$
$$2 + y + 3 = 7$$
$$y + 5 = 7$$
$$y = 2$$

The solution to the system is (1, 2, 3).

55. $5^3 = 5 \cdot 5 \cdot 5 = 125$

56. $2(2x - 3) = 2x + 8$
$$4x - 6 = 2x + 8$$
$$4x - 2x = 8 + 6$$
$$2x = 14$$
$$x = 7$$

57. $\left(4x^2y - 3xy + y\right) - \left(2x^2y + 6xy - 3y\right)$
$$= 4x^2y - 3xy + y - 2x^2y - 6xy + 3y$$
$$= 4x^2y - 2x^2y - 3xy - 6xy + y + 3y$$
$$= 2x^2y - 9xy + 4y$$

58. $\left(8a^4b^2c\right)\left(4a^2b^7c^4\right)$
$$= 8 \cdot 4 \cdot a^4 \cdot a^2 \cdot b^2 \cdot b^7 \cdot c \cdot c^4$$
$$= 32a^{4+2}b^{2+7}c^{1+4}$$
$$= 32a^6b^9c^5$$

59. $xy + xc - ay - ac$
$$= x(y + c) - a(y + c)$$
$$= (y + c)(x - a)$$

60. $f(x) = 2x^2 - 4$
$$f(3) = 2(3)^2 - 4$$
$$= 2(9) - 4$$
$$= 18 - 4$$
$$= 14$$
$$f(3) = 14$$

Exercise Set 8.4

1. Let x and y be the integers, with x the larger integer.
$$x + y = 41$$
$$x = y + 7$$
Substitute $y + 7$ for x in the first equation.
$$(y + 7) + y = 41$$
$$2y + 7 = 41$$
$$2y = 34$$
$$y = \frac{34}{2} = 17$$
$$x = y + 7$$
$$x = 17 + 7$$
$$x = 24$$
The integers are 17 and 24.

3. $A + B = 90$
$$B = A + 18$$
Substitute $A + 18$ for B in the first equation.
$$A + (A + 18) = 90$$
$$2A + 18 = 90$$
$$2A = 72$$
$$A = \frac{72}{2} = 36$$
$$B = A + 18$$
$$B = 36 + 18$$
$$B = 54$$
The angles are $A = 36°$ and $B = 54°$.

5. $A + B = 180$
$$A = B + 24$$
Substitute $B + 24$ for A in the first equation.
$$(B + 24) + B = 180$$
$$2B + 24 = 180$$
$$2B = 156$$
$$B = \frac{156}{2} = 78$$
$$A = B + 48$$
$$A = 78 + 24$$
$$A = 102$$
The angles are $A = 102°$ and $B = 78°$.

7. Let w = the width of the flag
　　　l = the length of the flag
The formula for the perimeter of the flag is $P = 2w + 2l$.
$$2w + 2l = 2260$$
$$l = w + 350$$
Substitute $w + 350$ for l in the first equation.

$$2w + 2l = 2260$$
$$2w + 2(w + 350) = 2260$$
$$2w + 2w + 700 = 2260$$
$$4w = 1560$$
$$w = 390$$
$$l = w + 350$$
$$l = 390 + 350$$
$$l = 740$$

The width of the flag is 390 feet and the length is 740 feet.

9. Let c = number of acres of corn
   w = number of acres of wheat
   $$c + w = 100$$
   $$450c + 430w = 44,400$$
   Solve the first equation for w.
   $$w = 100 - c$$
   Substitute $100 - c$ for w in the second equation.
   $$450c + 430(100 - c) = 44,400$$
   $$450c + 43,000 - 430c = 44,400$$
   $$20c + 43,000 = 44,400$$
   $$20c = 1400$$
   $$c = \frac{1400}{20} = 70$$
   $$w = 100 - c$$
   $$w = 100 - 70$$
   $$w = 30$$
   She planted 70 acres of corn and 30 acres of wheat.

11. Let k = the speed of the kayak
    c = the speed of the current
    $$k + c = 4.7$$
    $$\underline{k - c = 3.4}$$
    $$2k \quad\;\; = 8.1$$
    $$k = 4.05$$
    $$k + c = 4.7$$
    $$4.05 + c = 4.7$$
    $$c = 0.65$$
    The speed of the kayak in still water is 4.05 miles per hour and the speed of the current is 0.65 miles per hour.

13. Let p = the population
    y = the number of years that have passed
    For Green Mountain, $p = 40,000 + 800y$, while for Pleasant View Valley, $p = 66,000 - 500y$. Set the two populations equal.
    $$40,000 + 800y = 66,000 - 500y$$
    $$1300y = 26,000$$
    $$y = 20$$
    The populations of both areas will be the same after 20 years.

15. Let a = the number of adult tickets purchased
    c = the number of children's tickets purchased
    $$a + c = 27$$
    $$40a + 30c = 930$$
    Solve the first equation for c.
    $$c = 27 - a$$
    Substitute it in for c in the second equation.
    $$40a + 30(27 - a) = 930$$
    $$40a + 810 - 30a = 930$$
    $$10a + 810 = 930$$
    $$10a = 120$$
    $$a = 12$$
    $$a + c = 27$$
    $$12 + c = 27$$
    $$c = 15$$
    There were 12 adult tickets and 15 children's tickets purchased.

17. a. Let n = the number of copies
       c = the monthly cost
       With the Kate Spence Company,
       $c = 18 + 0.02n$, while with Office Depot,
       $c = 25 + 0.015n$. Set the monthly costs equal
       $$18 + 0.02n = 25 + 0.015n$$
       $$0.005n = 7$$
       $$n = 1400$$
       When 1400 copies are made, the monthly costs of both plans are the same.

    b. With Kate Spence Company:
       $$c = 18 + 0.02(2500)$$
       $$c = 18 + 50$$
       $$c = 68$$
       With Office Depot:
       $$c = 25 + 0.015(2500)$$
       $$c = 25 + 37.5$$
       $$c = 62.5$$
       When 2500 copies are made, it is less expensive to get the service contract from Office Depot.

19. Let x = the amount giving 10% interest
    y = the amount giving 8% interest
    $$x + y = 8000$$
    $$0.10x + 0.08y = 750$$
    Eliminate the decimal numbers.
    $$x + y = 8000$$
    $$10x + 8y = 75,000$$
    Multiply the first equation by -8.
    $$-8[x + y = 8000]$$
    $$10x + 8y = 75,000$$
    gives

$$-8x - 8y = -64,000$$
$$\underline{10x + 8y = 75,000}$$
$$2x = 11,000$$
$$x = 5500$$
$$x + y = 8000$$
$$5500 + y = 8000$$
$$y = 2500$$

They invested \$5500 at 10%, and \$2500 at 8%.

21. **a.** Let $y =$ the number of yards of carpet
$c =$ the total cost of the carpet
At Carpet U.S.A., $c = 200 + 20y$, while at Tom Taylor's National Carpet Stores,
$c = 260 + 16y$. Set the two costs equal.
$$200 + 20y = 260 + 16y$$
$$4y = 60$$
$$y = 15$$

The total cost of the carpet is the same at both stores when 15 square yards are purchased.

b. Carpet U.S.A.:
$$c = 200 + 20(25)$$
$$= 200 + 500$$
$$= 700$$
Tom Taylor's:
$$c = 260 + 16(25)$$
$$= 260 + 400$$
$$= 660$$
The total cost of 25 square yards of carpet is less at Tom Taylor's National Carpet Stores.

23. Let $d =$ Dave's speed
$a =$ Alice's speed
The distance that Dave has traveled after 7 hours is $7d$ and the distance that Alice has traveled is $7a$. These distances add up to 903 miles.
$$7d + 7a = 903$$
$$a = d + 15$$
Substitute $d + 15$ for a in the first equation.
$$7d + 7(d + 15) = 903$$
$$7d + 7d + 105 = 903$$
$$14d = 798$$
$$d = 57$$
$$a = d + 15$$
$$a = 57 + 15$$
$$a = 72$$
Dave's speed is 57 miles per hour and Alice's speed is 72 miles per hour.

25. Let $e =$ the speed of Elizabeth's boat and
$m =$ the speed of Melissa's boat
If d is the distance that both boats travel, then
$d = 3e$ and $d = 3.2m$.

$$e = m + 4$$
$$3e = 3.2m$$
Multiply the first equation by –3.
$$-3[e = m + 4]$$
$$3e = 3.2m$$
gives
$$-3e = -3m - 12$$
$$\underline{3e = 3.2m}$$
$$0 = 0.2m - 12$$
$$12 = 0.2m$$
$$60 = m$$
$$e = m + 4$$
$$e = 60 + 4$$
$$e = 64$$
The speed of Elizabeth's boat is 64 miles per hour and the speed of Melissa's boat is 60 miles per hour.

27. Let $a =$ time that Amanda jogs
$d =$ time that Dolores jogs
The distance that Amanda jogs is $5a$ and the distance that Dolores jogs is $8d$.
$$5a = 8d$$
$$a = d + 0.3$$
Substitute $d + 0.3$ for a in the first equation.
$$5(d + 0.3) = 8d$$
$$5d + 1.5 = 8d$$
$$1.5 = 3d$$
$$0.5 = d$$
Dolores will catch up to Amanda when Dolores has been jogging for 0.5 hour.

29. Let $t =$ the amount of time it took Randy to catch up to Terri
$r =$ the distance that Terri and Randy traveled

Traveler	Rate	Time	Distance
Terri	5	$0.75 + t$	r
Randy	10.5	t	r

$$5(0.75 + t) = r$$
$$10.5t = r$$
Substitute 10.5 for r in the first equation.
$$5(0.75 + t) = 10.5t$$
$$3.75 + 5t = 10.5t$$
$$3.75 = 5.5t$$
$$.68 \approx t$$
They met after about 0.68 hours.

31. Let x = amount of 15% solution
     y = amount of 40% solution

Solution	Number of Liters	Concentration	Acid Content
15% solution	x	0.15	$0.15x$
40% solution	y	0.40	$0.40y$
Mixture	10	0.30	$0.30(10)$

$$x + y = 10$$
$$0.15x + 0.40y = 3$$
Solve the first equation for x.
$$x = 10 - y$$
Substitute $10 - y$ for x in the second equation.
$$0.15(10 - y) + 0.40y = 3$$
$$1.5 - 0.15y + 0.40y = 3$$
$$0.25y = 1.5$$
$$y = 6$$
$$x = 10 - y$$
$$x = 10 - 6$$
$$x = 4$$
She must use 4 liters of the 15% solution and 6 liters of the 40% solution.

33. Let x = the number of \$3 tiles
     y = the number of \$5 tiles
$$x + y = 380$$
$$3x + 5y = 1500$$
Solve the first equation for x.
$$x = 380 - y$$
Substitute $380 - y$ for x in the second equation.
$$3(380 - y) + 5y = 1500$$
$$1140 - 3y + 5y = 1500$$
$$2y = 360$$
$$y = 180$$
She can purchase at most 180 of the \$5 tiles.

35. Let x = the amount of 5% butterfat milk
     y = the amount of skim milk

Milk	Number of Gallons	Percentage butterfat	Butterfat Content
5% butterfat	x	0.05	$0.05x$
skim	y	0	0
Mixture	100	0.035	$0.035(100)$

$$x + y = 100$$
$$0.05x = 3.5$$

From the second equation, $x = 70$.

$$x + y = 100$$
$$70 + y = 100$$
$$y = 30$$

Wayne must use 70 gallons of 5% butterfat milk and 30 gallons of skim milk.

37. Let x = the amount of apple juice
    y = the amount of apple drink

Liquid	Number of ounces	Cost per ounce	Total cost
Apple juice	x	12	$12x$
Apple drink	y	6	$6y$
Mixture	8	10	$10(8)$

$$x + y = 8$$
$$12x + 6y = 80$$

Solve the first equation for y.
$$y = 8 - x$$

Substitute $8 - x$ for y in the second equation.
$$12x + 6(8 - x) = 80$$
$$12x + 48 - 6x = 80$$
$$6x = 32$$
$$x = \frac{32}{6} = 5\frac{1}{3}$$
$$y = 8 - x$$
$$y = 8 - 5\frac{1}{3}$$
$$y = \frac{24}{3} - \frac{16}{3}$$
$$y = \frac{8}{3} = 2\frac{2}{3}$$

The cans should contain $5\frac{1}{3}$ ounces apple juice and $2\frac{2}{3}$ ounces apple drink.

39. Let $p = e$.
$$p = -1.6x + 108$$
$$e = 3.6x + 5$$
$$p = e$$
$$-1.6x + 108 = 3.6x + 5$$
$$103 = 5.2x$$
$$19.8 \approx x$$

In about 19.8 years, the number of tax returns filed electronically will be the same as the number of paper returns.

41. Let t = the amount of time they jog
    d = the distance to the school
The distance that Sean jogs is $9t$, while the distance that Meghan jogs is $5t$.
$$9t = d$$
$$5t = d - 0.5$$

Substitute $9t$ for d in the second equation.
$$5t = 9t - 0.5$$
$$0.5 = 4t$$
$$0.125 = t$$
$$d = 9t$$
$$d = 9(0.125)$$
$$d = 1.125$$

The school is 1.125 miles from their house.

43. Let x = number of minutes
    a = pressure in tank one and
    b = pressure in tank two

$a = 200 - 2x$

$b = 20 + 2x$

Let $a = b$

$200 - 2x = 20 + 2x$

$180 = 4x$

$45 = x$

It will take 45 minutes for the pressure in the tanks to be equal.

45. a. $x + 4 = 4 + x$ illustrates the commutative property of addition.

b. $(3x)y = 3(xy)$ illustrates the associative property of multiplication.

c. $4(x + 2) = 4x + 8$ illustrates the distributive property.

46. Let $l =$ the length of the rectangle

$w =$ the width of the rectangle

$l = 2w + 2$

The formula for the perimeter of a rectangle is

$P = 2l + 2w$.

$22 = 2l + 2w$

$22 = 2(2w + 2) + 2w$

$22 = 4w + 4 + 2w$

$18 = 6w$

$3 = w$

$l = 2w + 2$

$l = 2(3) + 2$

$l = 8$

The length of the rectangle is 8 feet and the width is 3 feet.

47. $x + \dfrac{2}{x} = \dfrac{6}{x}$

$x\left(x + \dfrac{2}{x}\right) = x\left(\dfrac{6}{x}\right)$

$x^2 + \dfrac{2x}{x} = \dfrac{6x}{x}$

$x^2 + 2 = 6$

$x^2 = 4$

$x = \pm 2$

48. A graph is an illustration of the set of points that satisfy an equation.

Exercise Set 8.5

1. Yes, the solution to a system of linear inequalities contains all of the ordered pairs which satisfy both inequalities.

3. Yes, when the lines are parallel. One possible system is $x + y > 2$, $x + y < 1$.

5.

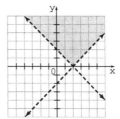

7.

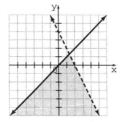

9.

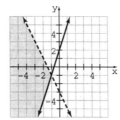

11.

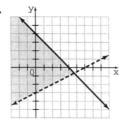

13.

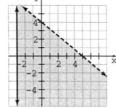

15.

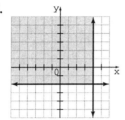

17.

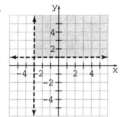

19.

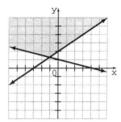

21.

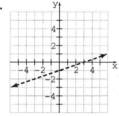

23.

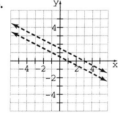

25. No, the system can have no solutions or infinitely many solutions. If the lines involved are parallel, the system will have no solutions or infinitely many solutions. If the lines intersect, they will divide the plane into 4 regions, each

containing infinitely many points. One of these regions will be the solution to the system.

29. $6(x - 2) < 4x - 3 + 2x$
$6x - 12 < 6x - 3$
$-12 < -3$
Since this is a true statement, the solution is all real numbers.

30. $2x - 5y = 6$
$2x = 5y + 6$
$2x - 6 = 5y$
$\dfrac{2x - 6}{5} = y$
$y = \dfrac{2}{5}x - \dfrac{6}{5}$

31. $4x^2 - 11x - 3 = 0$
$(4x + 1)(x - 3) = 0$
$4x + 1 = 0 \qquad x - 3 = 0$
$4x = -1 \qquad x - 3 = 0$
$x = -\dfrac{1}{4} \qquad x = 3$

32. $\dfrac{x^{-6}y^2}{x^3y^{-4}} = \dfrac{y^2 y^4}{x^3 x^6}$
$= \dfrac{y^{2+4}}{x^{3+6}}$
$= \dfrac{y^6}{x^9}$

Review Exercises

1. a. $y = 4x - 2 \qquad 2x + 3y = 8$
$-2 = 4(0) - 2 \qquad 2(0) + 3(-2) = 8$
$-2 = -2$ True $\qquad -6 = 8$ False
Since $(0, -2)$ does not satisfy both equations, it is not a solution to the system.

b. $y = 4x - 2$
$4 = 4(-2) - 2$
$4 = -10$ False
Since $(-2, 4)$ does not satisfy the first equation, it is not a solution to the system.

c. $y = 4x - 2 \qquad 2x + 3y = 8$
$2 = 4(1) - 2 \qquad 2(1) + 3(2) = 8$
$2 = 2$ True $\qquad 8 = 8$ True
Since $(1, 2)$ satisfies both equations, it is a solution to the system.

2. a. $y = -x + 4$

$$\frac{3}{2} = -\frac{5}{2} + 4$$

$$\frac{3}{2} = \frac{3}{2} \text{ True}$$

$$3x + 5y = 15$$

$$3\left(\frac{5}{2}\right) + 5\left(\frac{3}{2}\right) = 15$$

$$15 = 15 \text{ True}$$

Since $\left(\frac{5}{2}, \frac{3}{2}\right)$ satisfies both equations, it is a solution to the system.

b. $y = -x + 4$

$$4 = -0 + 4$$

$$4 = 4 \text{ True}$$

$$3x + 5y = 15$$

$$3(0) + 5(4) = 15$$

$$20 = 15 \text{ False}$$

Since $(0, 4)$ does not satisfy both equations, it is not a solution to the system.

c. $y = -x + 4$

$$\frac{3}{5} = -\frac{1}{2} + 4$$

$$\frac{3}{5} = \frac{7}{2} \text{ False}$$

Since $\left(\frac{1}{2}, \frac{3}{5}\right)$ does not satisfy the first equation, it is not a solution to the system.

3. consistent, one solution

4. inconsistent, no solutions

5. dependent, infinite number of solutions

6. consistent, one solution

7. Write each equation in slope-intercept form.

$$x + 2y = 10 \qquad\qquad 3x = -6y + 12$$

$$2y = -x + 10 \qquad\qquad 6y = -3x + 12$$

$$y = -\frac{1}{2}x + 5 \qquad\qquad y = -\frac{1}{2}x + 2$$

Since the slope of each line is $-\frac{1}{2}$ but the y-intercepts are different, the two lines are parallel. There is no solution. This is an inconsistent system.

8. Write each equation in slope-intercept form.
$y = -3x - 6$ is already in this form.

$$2x + 5y = 8$$

$$5y = -2x + 8$$

$$y = -\frac{2}{5}x + \frac{8}{5}$$

Since the slopes of the lines are different, the lines intersect to produce one solution. This is a consistent system.

9. Write each equation in slope-intercept form.

$y = \frac{1}{2}x - 4$ is already in this form.

$$x - 2y = 8$$

$$-2y = -x + 8$$

$$y = \frac{1}{2}x - 4$$

Since both equations are identical, the line is the same for both of them. There are an infinite number of solutions. This is a dependent system.

10. Write each equation in slope-intercept form.

$$6x = 4y - 8 \qquad\qquad 4x = 6y + 8$$

$$6x + 8 = 4y \qquad\qquad 4x - 8 = 6y$$

$$\frac{6x + 8}{4} = y \qquad\qquad \frac{4x - 8}{6} = y$$

$$\frac{3}{2}x + 2 = y \qquad\qquad \frac{2}{3}x - \frac{4}{3} = y$$

Since the slopes of the lines are different, the lines intersect to produce one solution. This is a consistent system.

11. Graph $y = x - 4$ and $y = 2x - 7$.

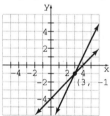

The lines intersect and the point of intersection is $(3, -1)$. This is a consistent system.

12. Graph $x = -2$ and $y = 3$.

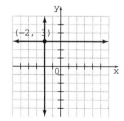

The lines intersect and the point of intersection is (–2, 3). This is a consistent system.

13. Graph $y = 3$ and $y = -2x + 5$.

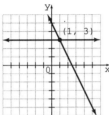

The lines intersect and the point of intersection is (1, 3). This is a consistent system.

14. Graph $x + 3y = 6$ and $y = 2$.

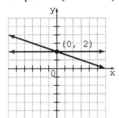

The lines intersect and the point of intersection is (0, 2). This is a consistent system.

15. Graph the equations $x + 2y = 8$ and $2x - y = -4$.

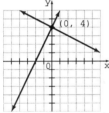

The lines intersect and the point of intersection is (0, 4). This is a consistent system.

16. Graph the equations $y = x - 3$ and $2x - 2y = 6$.

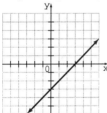

Both equations produce the same line. This is a dependent system. There are an infinite number of solutions.

17. Graph $3x + y = 0$ and $3x - 3y = 12$.

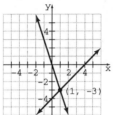

The lines intersect and the point of intersection is (1, –3). This is a consistent system.

18. Graph $x + 2y = 4$ and $\dfrac{1}{2}x + y = -2$.

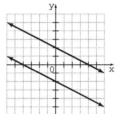

The lines are parallel and do not intersect. The system is inconsistent and there is no solution.

19. $y = 3x - 13$

$2x - 5y = 0$

Substitute $3x - 13$ for y in the second equation.
$$2x - 5y = 0$$
$$2x - 5(3x - 13) = 0$$
$$2x - 15x + 65 = 0$$
$$-13x + 65 = 0$$
$$-13x = -65$$
$$x = 5$$

Now, substitute 5 for x in the first equation.
$$y = 3x - 13$$
$$y = 3(5) - 13$$
$$y = 15 - 3$$
$$y = 2$$

The solution is (5, 2).

20. $x = 3y - 9$

$x + 2y = 1$

Substitute $3y - 9$ for x in the second equation.
$$x + 2y = 1$$
$$3y - 9 + 2y = 1$$
$$5y - 9 = 1$$
$$5y = 10$$
$$y = 2$$

Now substitute 2 for y in the first equation.

$x = 3y - 9$
$x = 3(2) - 9$
$x = 6 - 9$
$x = -3$
The solution is $(-3, 2)$.

21. $2x - y = 6$
$x + 2y = 13$
Solve the second equation for x, $x = 13 - 2y$.
Substitute $13 - 2y$ for x in the first equation.
$$2x - y = 6$$
$$2(13 - 2y) - y = 6$$
$$26 - 4y - y = 6$$
$$-5y = -20$$
$$y = 4$$
Substitute 4 for y in the equation $x = 13 - 2y$.
$x = 13 - 2(4)$
$x = 13 - 8$
$x = 5$
The solution is $(5, 4)$.

22. $x = -3y$
$x + 4y = 6$
Substitute $-3y$ for x in the second equation.
$$x + 4y = 6$$
$$-3y + 4y = 6$$
$$y = 6$$
Substitute 6 for y in the first equation.
$x = -3y$
$x = -3(6)$
$x = -18$
The solution is $(-18, 6)$.

23. $4x - 2y = 10$
$y = 2x + 3$
Substitute $2x + 3$ for y in the first equation.
$$4x - 2y = 10$$
$$4x - 2(2x + 3) = 10$$
$$4x - 4x - 6 = 10$$
$$-6 = 10 \text{ False}$$
There is no solution.

24. $2x + 4y = 8$
$4x + 8y = 16$
Solve the first equation for x.
$$\frac{1}{2}(2x + 4y) = \frac{1}{2}(8)$$
$$x + 2y = 4$$
$$x = 4 - 2y$$
Substitute $4 - 2y$ for x in the second equation.

$4x + 8y = 16$
$4(4 - 2y) + 8y = 16$
$16 - 8y + 8y = 16$
$16 = 16 \text{ True}$
There are an infinite number of solutions.

25. $2x - 3y = 8$
$6x + 5y = 10$
Solve the first equation for x.
$$\frac{1}{2}(2x - 3y) = \frac{1}{2}(8)$$
$$x - \frac{3}{2}y = 4$$
$$x = \frac{3}{2}y + 4$$
Substitute $\frac{3}{2}y + 4$ for x in the second equation.
$$6x + 5y = 10$$
$$6\left(\frac{3}{2}y + 4\right) + 5y = 10$$
$$9y + 24 + 5y = 10$$
$$14y = -14$$
$$y = -1$$
Substitute -1 for y in the equation $x = \frac{3}{2}y + 4$.
$$x = \frac{3}{2}(-1) + 4$$
$$x = -\frac{3}{2} + \frac{8}{2}$$
$$x = \frac{5}{2}$$
The solution is $\left(\frac{5}{2}, -1\right)$.

26. $3x - y = -5$
$x + 2y = 8$
Solve the second equation for x, $x = 8 - 2y$.
Substitute $8 - 2y$ for x in the first equation.
$$3x - y = -5$$
$$3(8 - 2y) - y = -5$$
$$24 - 6y - y = -5$$
$$-7y = -29$$
$$y = \frac{29}{7}$$
Substitute $\frac{29}{7}$ for y in the equation $x = 8 - 2y$.

$$x = 8 - 2\left(\frac{29}{7}\right)$$

$$x = \frac{56}{7} - \frac{58}{7}$$

$$x = -\frac{2}{7}$$

The solution is $\left(-\frac{2}{7}, \frac{29}{7}\right)$.

27.
$$-x - y = 6$$
$$\underline{-x + y = 10}$$
$$-2x \quad\quad = 16$$
$$x = -8$$
$$x = \frac{16}{2} = -8$$
Substitute -8 for x in the first equation.
$$-x - y = 6$$
$$-(-8) - y = 6$$
$$8 - y = 6$$
$$-y = -2$$
$$y = 2$$
The solution is (-8, 2).

28.
$$x + 2y = -3$$
$$\underline{2x - 2y = 6}$$
$$3x \quad\quad = 3$$
$$x = 1$$
Substitute 1 for x in the first equation.
$$x + 2y = -3$$
$$1 + 2y = -3$$
$$2y = -4$$
$$y = -2$$
The solution is (1, –2).

29.
$$x + y = 12$$
$$2x + y = 5$$
To eliminate y, multiply the first equation by –1 and then add.
$$-1[x + y = 12]$$
gives
$$-x - y = -12$$
$$\underline{2x + y = 5}$$
$$x \quad\quad = -7$$
Substitute –7 for x in the first equation.
$$x + y = 12$$
$$-7 + y = 12$$
$$y = 19$$
The solution is (–7, 19).

30.
$$4x - 3y = 8$$
$$2x + 5y = 8$$
To eliminate x, multiply the second equation by –2 and then add.
$$-2[2x + 5y = 8]$$
gives
$$4x - 3y = 8$$
$$\underline{-4x - 10y = -16}$$
$$-13y = -8$$
$$y = \frac{8}{13}$$
Substitute $\frac{8}{13}$ for y in the first equation.
$$4x - 3y = 8$$
$$4x - 3\left(\frac{8}{13}\right) = 8$$
$$4x - \frac{24}{13} = 8$$
$$4x = \frac{104}{13} + \frac{24}{13}$$
$$4x = \frac{128}{13}$$
$$x = \frac{32}{13}$$
The solution is $\left(\frac{32}{13}, \frac{8}{13}\right)$.

31.
$$-2x + 3y = 15$$
$$3x + 3y = 10$$
To eliminate y, multiply the second equation by –1 and then add.
$$-1[3x + 3y = 10]$$
gives
$$-2x + 3y = 15$$
$$\underline{-3x - 3y = -10}$$
$$-5x \quad\quad = 5$$
$$x = -1$$
Substitute –1 for x in the second equation.
$$3x + 3y = 10$$
$$3(-1) + 3y = 10$$
$$-3 + 3y = 10$$
$$3y = 13$$
$$y = \frac{13}{3}$$
The solution is $\left(-1, \frac{13}{3}\right)$.

32.
$$2x + y = 9$$
$$-4x - 2y = 4$$
Multiply the first equation by 2, and then add.
$$2[2x + y = 9]$$
gives

$$4x + 2y = 18$$
$$\underline{-4x - 2y = \ 4}$$
$$0 = 22 \ \text{False}$$
There is no solution.

33. $3x = -4y + 10$

$8y = -6x + 20$

Align the x and y terms.

$$3x + 4y = 10$$
$$-6x - 8y = -20$$

To eliminate x, multiply the first equation by 2, and then add.
$2[3x + 4y = 10]$
gives
$$6x + 8y = 20$$
$$\underline{-6x - 8y = -20}$$
$$0 = 0 \quad \text{True}$$
There are an infinite number of solutions.

34. $2x - 5y = 12$
$3x - 4y = -6$

To eliminate x, multiply the first equation by -3 and the second equation by 2 and then add.
$-3[2x - 5y = 12]$
$2[3x - 4y = -6]$

gives
$$-6x + 15y = -36$$
$$\underline{6x - 8y = -12}$$
$$7y = -48$$
$$y = -\frac{48}{7}$$

Now, substitute $-\frac{48}{7}$ for y in the first equation.
$$2x - 5y = 12$$
$$2x - 5\left(-\frac{48}{7}\right) = 12$$
$$2x + \frac{240}{7} = 12$$
$$2x = \frac{84}{7} - \frac{240}{7}$$
$$2x = -\frac{156}{7}$$
$$x = -\frac{78}{7}$$

The solution is $\left(-\dfrac{78}{7}, -\dfrac{48}{7}\right)$.

35. Let x be the larger number and y be the smaller number.
$x + y = 49$

$x = 2y - 8$
Substitute $2y - 8$ for x in the first equation.

$$x + y = 49$$
$$2y - 8 + y = 49$$
$$3y = 57$$
$$y = 19$$
Substitute 19 for y in the second equation.
$x = 2y - 8$

$x = 2(19) - 8$

$x = 30$
The numbers are 19 and 30.

36. Let x be the speed of the plane in still air and y be the speed of the wind.
$$x + y = \ \ 600$$
$$\underline{x - y = \ \ 530}$$
$$\text{Add: } 2x \quad \ \ = 1130$$
$$x = 565$$
Substitute 565 for x in the first equation.
$x + y = 600$

$565 + y = 600$

$y = 35$
The speed of the plane is 565 miles per hour and the speed of the wind is 35 miles per hour.

37. Let x be the number of miles traveled and c be the cost.
$c = 30 + 0.5x$

$c = 40 + 0.4x$
Substitute $30 + 0.5x$ for c in the second equation.
$$30 + 0.5x = 40 + 0.4x$$
$$0.1x = 10$$
$$x = 100$$
The cost is the same for 100 miles of travel.

38. Let x be the amount invested at 4% and y be the amount invested at 6%.
$x + y = 16,000$
$0.04x + 0.06y = 760$
Solve the first equation for x, $x = 16,000 - y$.
Substitute $16,000 - y$ for x in the second equation.
$$0.04(16,000 - y) + 0.06y = 760$$
$$640 - 0.04y + 0.06y = 760$$
$$0.02y = 120$$
$$y = 6000$$
Substitute 6000 for y in the equation
$x = 16,000 - y$.
$x = 16,000 - 6000$
$x = 10,000$
She invested \$10,000 at 4% and \$6000 at 6%.

39. Let l be Liz's speed and m be Mary's speed. The distance that Liz traveled is $5l$ and the distance

that Mary traveled is $5m$.
$m = l + 6$
$5l + 5m = 600$
Substitute $l + 6$ for m in the second equation.
$5l + 5(l + 6) = 600$
$5l + 5l + 30 = 600$
$10l = 570$
$l = 57$
Substitute 57 for l in the first equation.
$m = 57 + 6$
$m = 63$
Liz's speed was 57 miles per hour and Mary's speed was 63 miles per hour.

40. Let g be the pounds of Green Turf's grass seed and a be the pounds of Agway's grass seed.
$0.6g + 0.45a = 20.25$
$g + a = 40$
Solve the second equation for a, $a = 40 - g$.
Substitute $40 - g$ for a in the first equation.
$0.6g + 0.45(40 - g) = 20.25$
$0.6g + 18 - 0.45g = 20.25$
$0.15g = 2.25$
$g = 15$
Substitute 15 for g in the equation $a = 40 - g$.
$a = 40 - 15$
$a = 25$
There were 15 pounds of Green Turf's grass seed and 25 pounds of Agway's grass seed.

41. Let x be the amount of 30% acid solution and y be the amount of 50% acid solution.
$x + y = 6$
$0.3x + 0.5y = 0.4(6)$
To clear decimals, multiply the second equation by 10.
$x + y = 6$
$3x + 5y = 24$
Solve the first equation for y, $y = -x + 6$.
Substitute $-x + 6$ for y in the second equation.
$3x + 5y = 24$
$3x + 5(-x + 6) = 24$
$3x - 5x + 30 = 24$
$-2x = -6$
$x = 3$
Finally, substitute 3 for x in the equation $y = -x + 6$.
$y = -x + 6$
$y = -3 + 6$
$y = 3$
The chemist should combine 3 liters of each solution to produce the desired result.

42. $2x + y > 2$
$2x - y \le 4$

43. $2x - 3y \le 6$
$x + 4y > 4$

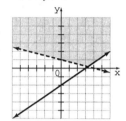

44. $2x - 6y > 6$
$x > -2$

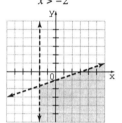

45. $x < 2$
$y \ge -3$

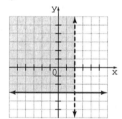

Practice Test

1. a. $\quad x + 2y = -6$
$\quad 0 + 2(-6) = -6$
$\quad -12 = -6 \quad$ False
Since $(0, 6)$ does not satisfy the first equation, it is not a solution to the system.

b. $\quad x + 2y = -6$
$\quad -3 + 2\left(-\dfrac{3}{2}\right) = -6$
$\quad -6 = -6 \quad$ True

$$3x + 2y = -12$$

$$3(-3) + 2\left(-\frac{3}{2}\right) = -12$$

$$-12 = -12 \text{ True}$$

$\left(-3, -\frac{3}{2}\right)$ is a solution to the system.

c.　　$x + 2y = -6$

$$2 + 2(-4) = -6$$

$$-6 = -6 \text{ True}$$

$$3x + 2y = -12$$

$$3(2) + 2(-4) = -12$$

$$-2 = -12 \text{ False}$$

Since $(2, -4)$ does not satisfy both equations, it is not a solution to the system.

2. The system is inconsistent, it has no solution.

3. The system is consistent; it has exactly one solution.

4. The system is dependent; it has an infinite number of solutions.

5. 　$-3y = 6x - 9$　　　　　$2x + y = 6$

　　$y = -2x + 3$　　　　　$y = -2x + 6$

The lines have the same slope, but different *y*-intercepts, so they are parallel. Thus, the system of equations is inconsistent and has no solution.

6. $3x + 2y = 10$　　　　$3x - 2y = 10$

　　$2y = -3x + 10$　　　$-2y = -3x + 10$

　　$y = -\frac{3}{2}x + 5$　　　$y = \frac{3}{2}x - 5$

The slopes of the lines are different. Thus, the system of equations is consistent and has one solution.

7. $4x = 6y - 12$　　　　$2x - 3y = -6$

　　$6y = 4x + 12$　　　　$-3y = -2x - 6$

　　$y = \frac{2}{3}x + 2$　　　　$y = \frac{2}{3}x + 2$

The lines are the same. Thus, the system of equations is consistent and dependent, and it has infinite number of solutions.

8. a.　You will obtain a false statement, such as $6 = 0$.

　　b.　You will obtain a true statement, such as $0 = 0$.

9. $y = 2x - 4$　　　$y = -2x + 8$

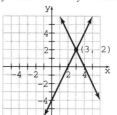

It appears that $(3, 2)$ is the solution to the system.

$y = 2x - 4$　　　　　$y = -2x + 8$

$2 = 2(3) - 4$　　　　$2 = -2(3) + 8$

$4 = 4$ True　　　　　$2 = 2$ True

$(3, 2)$ is the solution to the system.

10. $3x - 2y = -3$　　　　$3x + y = 6$

　　$-2y = -3x - 3$　　　$y = -3x + 6$

　　$y = \frac{3}{2}x + \frac{3}{2}$

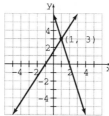

It appears that $(1, 3)$ is the solution to the system

$3x - 2y = -3$　　　　$3x + y = 6$

$3(1) - 2(3) = -3$　　$3(1) + 3 = 6$

$-3 = -3$ True　　　　$6 = 6$ True

$(1, 3)$ is the solution to the system.

11. $y = 2x + 4$　　　　$4x - 2y = 6$

　　　　　　　　　　　$-2y = -4x + 6$

　　　　　　　　　　　$y = 2x - 3$

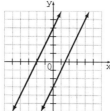

The lines are parallel, so the system has no solution.

12. $3x + y = 8$

　　$x - y = 6$

Solve the first equation for *y*,

$y = 8 - 3x$.

Substitute $8 - 3x$ for *y* in the second equation.

$x - (8 - 3x) = 6$

$x - 8 + 3x = 6$

$4x = 14$

$x = \dfrac{14}{4} = \dfrac{7}{2}$

Substitute $\dfrac{7}{2}$ for x in the equation $y = 8 - 3x$.

$y = 8 - 3x$

$y = 8 - 3\left(\dfrac{7}{2}\right)$

$y = \dfrac{16}{2} - \dfrac{21}{2}$

$y = -\dfrac{5}{2}$

The solution to the system is $\left(\dfrac{7}{2}, -\dfrac{5}{2}\right)$.

13. $3x - 4y = 8$

$4x + 2y = 18$

Solve the second equation for y since all the numbers are divisible by 2.

$4x + 2y = 18$

$2y = -4x + 18$

$y = -2x + 9$

Substitute $-2x + 9$ for y in the first equation.

$3x - 4(-2x + 9) = 8$

$3x + 8x - 36 = 8$

$11x = 44$

$x = 4$

Substitute 4 for x in the equation $y = -2x + 9$.

$y = -2x + 9$

$y = -2(4) + 9$

$y = 1$

The solution to the system is (4, 1).

14. $y = 5x - 7$

$y = 3x + 5$

Both equations are solved for y. Substitute $5x - 7$ for y in the second equation.

$5x - 7 = 3x + 5$

$2x = 12$

$x = 6$

Substitute 6 for x in the first equation.

$y = 5x - 7$

$y = 5(6) - 7$

$y = 23$

The solution to the system is (6, 23).

15. $4x + y = -6$

$x + 3y = 4$

To eliminate x, multiply the second equation by -4.

$-4[x + 3y = 4]$

gives

$\begin{array}{r} 4x\ \ + y = -6 \\ -4x - 12y = -16 \\ \hline -11y = -22 \end{array}$

$y = 2$

Substitute 2 for y in the first equation.

$4x + y = -6$

$4x + 2 = -6$

$4x = -8$

$x = -2$

The solution to the system is (−2, 2).

16. $3x + 2y = 12$

$-2x + 5y = 8$

To eliminate x, multiply the first equation by 2 and the second equation by 3.

$2[3x + 2y = 12]$

$3[-2x + 5y = 8]$

gives

$\begin{array}{r} 6x + 4y = 24 \\ -6x + 15y = 24 \\ \hline 19y = 48 \end{array}$

$y = \dfrac{48}{19}$

To eliminate y, multiply the first equation by 5 and the second equation by −2.

$5[3x + 2y = 12]$

$-2[-2x + 5y = 8]$

gives

$\begin{array}{r} 15x + 10y = 60 \\ 4x - 10y = -16 \\ \hline 19x = 44 \end{array}$

$x = \dfrac{44}{19}$

The solution to the system is $\left(\dfrac{44}{19}, \dfrac{48}{19}\right)$.

17. $5x - 10y = 20$

$x = 2y + 4$

Align the x- and y-terms on the left side of each equation.

$5x - 10y = 20$

$x - 2y = 4$

Multiply the second equation by −5.

$-5[x - 2y = 4]$

gives

$\begin{array}{r} 5x - 10y = 20 \\ -5x + 10y = -20 \\ \hline 0 = 0 \ \ \text{True} \end{array}$

This is a true statement for all values of x and y. Thus, the system is dependent and has an infinite number of solutions.

18. $y = 3x - 7$
    $y = -2x + 8$
    Substitute $3x - 7$ for y in the second equation.
    $3x - 7 = -2x + 8$
    $$5x = 15$$
    $$x = 3$$
    Substitute 3 for x in the first equation.
    $y = 3x - 7$
    $y = 3(3) - 7$
    $y = 2$
    The solution to the system is (3, 2).

19. $3x + 5y = 20$
    $6x + 3y = -12$
    To eliminate x, multiply the first equation by -2.
    $-2[3x + 5y = 20]$
    gives
    $-6x - 10y = -40$
    $\underline{6x + 3y = -12}$
    $\qquad -7y = -52$
    $$y = \frac{52}{7}$$
    To eliminate y, multiply the first equation by -3 and the second equation by 5.
    $-3[3x + 5y = 20]$
    $5[6x + 3y = -12]$
    gives
    $-9x - 15y = -60$
    $\underline{30x + 15y = -60}$
    $21x \qquad\quad = -120$
    $$x = -\frac{120}{21} = -\frac{40}{7}$$
    The solution to the system is $\left(-\dfrac{40}{7}, \dfrac{52}{7}\right)$.

20. $4x - 6y = 8$
    $3x + 5y = 10$
    To eliminate x, multiply the first equation by -3 and the second equation by 4.
    $-3[4x - 6y = 8]$
    $4[3x + 5y = 10]$
    gives
    $-12x + 18y = -24$
    $\underline{12x + 20y = 40}$
    $\qquad\quad 38y = 16$
    $$y = \frac{16}{38} = \frac{8}{19}$$
    To eliminate y, multiply the first equation by 5 and the second equation by 6.
    $5[4x - 6y = 8]$
    $6[3x + 5y = 10]$
    gives
    $20x - 30y = 40$
    $\underline{18x + 30y = 60}$
    $38x \qquad\quad = 100$
    $$x = \frac{100}{38} = \frac{50}{19}$$
    The solution to the system is $\left(\dfrac{50}{19}, \dfrac{8}{19}\right)$.

21. Let m = the number of miles driven
    c = the total cost per day
    With Charley's Rent A Truck,
    $c = 54 + 0.08m$, while with Hugh's Rent a Truck, $c = 40 + 0.15m$. Set the two costs equal.
    $54 + 0.08m = 40 + 0.15m$
    $$14 = 0.07m$$
    $$200 = m$$

    The cars cost an equal amount when they are driven 200 miles per day.

22. Let l = amount of lemon candies
    b = amount of butterscotch candies

Candy	Number of pounds	Cost per pound	Total cost
lemon	l	6	$6l$
butterscotch	b	4.5	$4.5b$
Mixture	20	5	$5(20)$

$l + b = 20$
$6l + 4.5b = 100$
Solve the first equation for b.
$l + b = 20$
$b = 20 - l$
Substitute $20 - l$ for b in the second equation.
$6l + 4.5(20 - l) = 100$
$6l + 90 - 4.5l = 100$
$1.5l = 10$
$l = \dfrac{10}{1.5} = 6\dfrac{2}{3}$

$b = 20 - l$
$b = 20 - 6\dfrac{2}{3}$
$b = 13\dfrac{1}{3}$

The mixture must contain $6\dfrac{2}{3}$ pounds of lemon candies and $13\dfrac{1}{3}$ pounds of butterscotch candies.

23. Let h = the speed of Dante Hull's boat
    r = the speed of Deja Rocket's boat
In 3 hours, Dante's boat travels $3h$ miles, while in 3.2 hours, Deja's boat travels $3.2r$ miles. The distance that the two boats travel are the same.
$3h = 3.2r$
$h = r + 4$
Substitute $r + 4$ for h in the first equation.
$3(r + 4) = 3.2r$
$3r + 12 = 3.2r$
$12 = 0.2r$
$60 = r$
Substitute 60 for r in the second equation.
$h = r + 4$
$h = 60 + 4$
$h = 64$
The speed of Dante Hull's boat is 64 miles per hour and the speed of Deja Rocket's boat is 60 miles per hour.

24. $2x + 4y < 8$
    $x - 3y \geq 6$

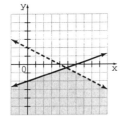

25. $x + 3y \geq 6$
    $y < 3$

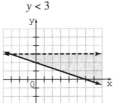

Cumulative Review Test

1. a. Air Force and Army

b. Air Force, Army and Navy

2. a. 7

b. $-5, -0.6, \dfrac{3}{5}, 7, 0, -\dfrac{5}{9}, 1.34$

c. $\sqrt{7}, -\sqrt{2}$

d. $-5, -0.6, \dfrac{3}{5}, \sqrt{7}, -\sqrt{2}, 7, 0, -\dfrac{5}{9}, 1.34$

3. $-237 + 63 + (-192) = -174 + (-192) = -366$

4. $8 - (3a - 2) + 4(a + 3) = 8 - 3a + 2 + 4a + 12$
$$= (-3a + 4a) + (8 + 2 + 12)$$
$$= a + 22$$

5. $2(x - 4) + 2 = 3x - 4$
$$2x - 8 + 2 = 3x - 4$$
$$2x - 6 = 3x - 4$$
$$-2 = x$$

6. $3x - 4 \le x + 6$
$$2x \le 10$$
$$x \le 5$$

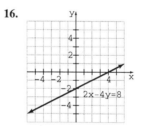

7. $P = 2l + 2w$
$$P - 2l = 2w$$
$$\frac{P - 2l}{2} = \frac{2w}{2}$$
$$w = \frac{P - 2l}{2}$$

8. Let s = Maria's weekly sales
w = Maria's weekly salary
Under plan A, $w = 0.12s$, while under plan B,
$w = 350 + 0.06s$. Set the two salaries equal.
$$0.12s = 350 + 0.06s$$
$$0.06s = 350$$
$$s = \frac{350}{0.06} \approx 5833.33$$
Maria's weekly sales must be $5833.33 for both
plans to pay the same amount.

9. Let x = the measure of the smallest angle
Then the other angles measure $x + 20$ and $6x$.
The sum of the measures of the angles in any
triangle is 180°.
$$x + (x + 20) + 6x = 180$$
$$8x + 20 = 180$$
$$8x = 160$$
$$x = 20$$
$$x + 20 = 20 + 20 = 40$$
$$6x = 6(20) = 120$$
The angles of the triangle measure 20°, 40°, and
120°.

10. $(5x^3y^2)^3(x^2y) = (5^3x^9y^6)(x^2y)$
$$= 125x^{9+2}y^{6+1}$$
$$= 125x^{11}y^7$$

11. $(x - 2y)^2 = (x - 2y)(x - 2y)$
$$= x^2 - 2xy - 2xy + 4y^2$$
$$= x^2 - 4xy + 4y^2$$

12. $2n^2 - 5n - 12 = (2n + 3)(n - 4)$

13. $x^2 - 3x - 40 = 0$
$$(x + 5)(x - 8) = 0$$
$$x + 5 = 0 \quad x - 8 = 0$$
$$x = -5 \quad\quad x = 8$$

14. $\dfrac{x^2 - 4x - 12}{3x} \cdot \dfrac{x^2 - x}{x^2 - 7x + 6}$
$$= \frac{(x - 6)(x + 2)}{3x} \cdot \frac{x(x - 1)}{(x - 1)(x - 6)}$$
$$= \frac{(x - 6)(x + 2) \cdot x(x - 1)}{3x \cdot (x - 1)(x - 6)}$$
$$= \frac{x + 2}{3}$$

15. $\dfrac{2x + 3}{3} = \dfrac{x - 2}{2}$
$$2(2x + 3) = 3(x - 2)$$
$$4x + 6 = 3x - 6$$
$$x = -12$$

16.

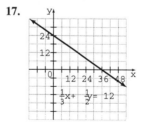

17.

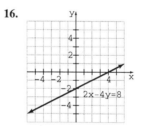

18. $3x - y = 6$ $\qquad\qquad \dfrac{3}{2}x - 3 = \dfrac{1}{2}y$
$\quad -y = -3x + 6 \qquad\qquad \dfrac{1}{2}y = \dfrac{3}{2}x - 3$
$\quad\quad y = 3x - 6 \qquad\qquad\qquad y = 3x - 6$
The lines are the same, so the system has an
infinite number of solutions.

19. Graph $2x + y = 5$ and $x - 2y = 0$.

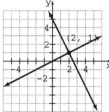

The solution is (2, 1).

20. $3x - 2y = 8$
$-6x + 3y = 2$

To eliminate x, multiply the first equation by 2.
$2[3x - 2y = 8]$
gives
$$\begin{array}{r} 6x - 4y = 16 \\ \underline{-6x + 3y = 2} \\ -y = 18 \\ y = -18 \end{array}$$

To eliminate y, multiply the first equation by 3 and the second equation by 2.
$3[3x - 2y = 8]$
$2[-6x + 3y = 2]$
gives
$$\begin{array}{r} 9x - 6y = 24 \\ \underline{-12x + 6y = 4} \\ -3x \quad\quad = 28 \\ x = -\dfrac{28}{3} \end{array}$$

The solution to the system is $\left(-\dfrac{28}{3}, -18 \right)$.

Chapter 9

Exercise Set 9.1

1. The principal square root of a positive real number x is a positive number whose square equals x.

3. Answers will vary.

5. Answers will vary.

7. Yes, since $5^2 = 25$.

9. No, because the square root of a negative number is not a real number.

11. Yes, since $\sqrt{\dfrac{16}{25}} = \dfrac{4}{5}$ which is a rational number.

13. $\sqrt{0} = 0$ since $(0)^2 = 0$

15. $\sqrt{1} = 1$ since $1^2 = 1$

17. $\sqrt{49} = 7$ since $(7)^2 = 49$
    Take the opposite of both sides to get
    $-\sqrt{49} = -7$

19. $\sqrt{400} = 20$ since $20^2 = 400$

21. $\sqrt{16} = 4$ since $(4)^2 = 16$
    Take the opposite of both sides to get
    $-\sqrt{16} = -4$

23. $\sqrt{144} = 12$ since $(12)^2 = 144$

25. $\sqrt{169} = 13$ since $(13)^2 = 169$

27. $\sqrt{1} = 1$ since $(1)^2 = 1$
    Take the opposite of both sides to get $-\sqrt{1} = -1$

29. $\sqrt{81} = 9$ since $9^2 = 81$

31. $\sqrt{121} = 11$ since $(11)^2 = 121$
    Take the opposite of both sides to get
    $-\sqrt{121} = -11$

33. $\sqrt{\dfrac{1}{4}} = \dfrac{1}{2}$ since $\left(\dfrac{1}{2}\right)^2 = \dfrac{1}{4}$

35. $\sqrt{\dfrac{36}{49}} = \dfrac{6}{7}$ since $\left(\dfrac{6}{7}\right)^2 = \dfrac{36}{49}$

37. $\sqrt{\dfrac{25}{30}} = \dfrac{5}{6}$ since $\left(\dfrac{5}{6}\right)^2 = \dfrac{25}{36}$
    Take the opposite of both sides to get
    $-\sqrt{\dfrac{25}{30}} = -\dfrac{5}{6}$

39. $\sqrt{\dfrac{36}{49}} = \dfrac{6}{7}$ since $\left(\dfrac{6}{7}\right)^2 = \dfrac{36}{49}$

41. $\sqrt{12} \approx 3.4641016$

43. $\sqrt{15} \approx 3.8729833$

45. $\sqrt{80} \approx 8.9442719$

47. $\sqrt{324} = 18$

49. $\sqrt{97} \approx 9.8488578$

51. $\sqrt{3} \approx 1.7320508$

53. False; since 18 is not a perfect square, $\sqrt{18}$ is an irrational number.

55. True; since 25 is a perfect square, $\sqrt{25}$ is a rational number

57. False; since 4 is a perfect square, $\sqrt{4}$ is a rational number

59. True; $\sqrt{\dfrac{9}{16}} = \dfrac{3}{4}$ which is a rational number

61. True; since 125 is not a perfect square, $\sqrt{125}$ is an irrational number

63. True; $\sqrt{(15)^2} = \sqrt{225} = 15$ which is an integer

65. $\sqrt{7} = 7^{1/2}$

67. $\sqrt{17} = (17)^{1/2}$

69. $\sqrt{8x} = (8x)^{1/2}$

71. $\sqrt{12x^2} = \left(12x^2\right)^{1/2}$

73. $\sqrt{15ab^2} = (15ab^2)^{1/2}$

75. $\sqrt{62n^3} = (62n^3)^{1/2}$

77. Rational:

$5,\ 9.83,\ \dfrac{3}{7}, \dfrac{3}{5},\ 0.333...,\ \sqrt{\dfrac{4}{49}},\ -\sqrt{9}$

Irrational: $\sqrt{\dfrac{5}{16}}$

Imaginary: $\sqrt{-4},\ -\sqrt{-16}$

79. 6 and 7 since $6^2 = 36,\ 7^2 = 49$, and $36 < 47 < 49$

81. a. Square 4.6 and compare it with 20.

   b. $(4.6)^2 = 21.16 > 20$, so 4.6 is greater.

83. $-\sqrt{9},\ -\sqrt{7},\ -\dfrac{1}{2},\ 2.5,\ \sqrt{16},\ 4.01, 5,\ 12$

85.
$\sqrt{4} = 2$
$6^{1/2} \approx 2.45$
$-\sqrt{9} = -3$
$-(25)^{1/2} = -5$
$(30)^{1/2} \approx 5.48$
$(-4)^{1/2}$, imaginary number

87. $\sqrt{0} = 0$ which is neither a positive nor negative number.
0 is a perfect square since $0^2 = 0$

   a. Yes

   b. No

   c. No

   d. Yes

   e. No

89. a. Yes, $\sqrt{2^2} = \sqrt{4} = 2.$

   b. Yes, $\sqrt{5^2} = \sqrt{25} = 5.$

   c. $\sqrt{a^2} = a,\ a \ge 0$

91. $(x^3)^{1/2} = x^{3 \cdot (1/2)} = x^{3/2}$

93. $x^{1/2} x^{5/2} = x^{(1/2) + (5/2)} = x^{6/2} = x^3$

95. Let $j =$ the number of jumps the mother did, then $2j =$ the number of jumps Allison did.
$j + 2j = 78$
$3j = 78$
$j = 26$
Thus Allison made $2j = 2(26) = 52$ jumps.

96.

$$\dfrac{2x}{x^2 - 4} + \dfrac{1}{x - 2} = \dfrac{2}{x + 2}$$

$$\dfrac{2x}{(x-2)(x+2)} + \dfrac{1}{x - 2} = \dfrac{2}{x + 2}$$

$$(x-2)(x+2)\left[\dfrac{2x}{(x-2)(x+2)} + \dfrac{1}{(x-2)}\right] = \dfrac{2}{x+2} \cdot (x-2)(x+2)$$

$$2x + (x + 2) = 2(x - 2)$$
$$2x + x + 2 = 2x - 4$$
$$3x + 2 = 2x - 4$$
$$3x = 2x - 6$$
$$x = -6$$

97. $\dfrac{4x}{x^2+6x+9} - \dfrac{2x}{x+3} = \dfrac{x+1}{x+3}$

$$\dfrac{4x}{(x+3)^2} - \dfrac{2x}{x+3} = \dfrac{x+1}{x+3}$$

$$(x+3)^2 \left[\dfrac{4x}{(x+3)^2} - \dfrac{2x}{x+3} \right] = \dfrac{x+1}{x+3} \cdot (x+3)^2$$

$$4x - 2x(x+3) = (x+1)(x+3)$$
$$4x - 2x^2 - 6x = x^2 + 4x + 3$$
$$0 = 3x^2 + 6x + 3$$
$$0 = 3(x^2 + 2x + 1)$$
$$0 = 3(x+1)^2$$
$$0 = x+1$$
$$x = -1$$

98. $m = \dfrac{7-3}{6-(-5)} = \dfrac{4}{11}$

99. $f(x) = x^2 - 4x - 5$
$$f(-3) = (-3)^2 - 4(-3) - 5$$
$$= 9 + 12 - 5$$
$$= 16$$

Exercise Set 9.2

1. Answers will vary.

    b. $\sqrt{20} = \sqrt{4 \cdot 5} = \sqrt{4}\sqrt{5} = 2\sqrt{5}$

3. The product rule cannot be used when radicands are negative.

5. a. Answers will vary.

    b. $\sqrt{x^{13}} = \sqrt{x^{12} \cdot x} = \sqrt{x^{12}}\sqrt{x} = x^6\sqrt{x}$

    b. $\sqrt{32x^3} = \sqrt{16x^2} \cdot \sqrt{2x} = 4x\sqrt{2x}$

7. a. There can be no perfect square factors or any exponents greater than 1 in the radicand.

    b. $\sqrt{75x^5} = \sqrt{25x^4} \cdot \sqrt{3x} = 5x^2\sqrt{3x}$

9. Yes; since $\sqrt{75} = \sqrt{25 \cdot 3} = \sqrt{25}\sqrt{3} = 5\sqrt{3}$

11. No; $\sqrt{32} = \sqrt{16 \cdot 2} = \sqrt{16}\sqrt{2} = 4\sqrt{2}$

13. $\sqrt{12} = \sqrt{4 \cdot 3} = \sqrt{4} \cdot \sqrt{3} = 2\sqrt{3}$

15. $\sqrt{8} = \sqrt{4 \cdot 2}$
$$= \sqrt{4} \cdot \sqrt{2}$$
$$= 2\sqrt{2}$$

17. $\sqrt{96} = \sqrt{16 \cdot 6}$
$$= \sqrt{16} \cdot \sqrt{6}$$
$$= 4\sqrt{6}$$

19. $\sqrt{32} = \sqrt{16 \cdot 2}$
$$= \sqrt{16} \cdot \sqrt{2}$$
$$= 4\sqrt{2}$$

21. $\sqrt{160} = \sqrt{16 \cdot 10}$
$$= \sqrt{16} \cdot \sqrt{10}$$
$$= 4\sqrt{10}$$

23. $\sqrt{80} = \sqrt{16 \cdot 5}$
$$= \sqrt{16} \cdot \sqrt{5}$$
$$= 4\sqrt{5}$$

25. $\sqrt{72} = \sqrt{36 \cdot 2}$
$$= \sqrt{36} \cdot \sqrt{2}$$
$$= 6\sqrt{2}$$

27. $\sqrt{140} = \sqrt{4 \cdot 35}$
$$= \sqrt{4} \cdot \sqrt{35}$$
$$= 2\sqrt{35}$$

29. $\sqrt{243} = \sqrt{81 \cdot 3}$
$\qquad = \sqrt{81} \cdot \sqrt{3}$
$\qquad = 9\sqrt{3}$

31. $\sqrt{150} = \sqrt{25 \cdot 6}$
$\qquad = \sqrt{25} \cdot \sqrt{6}$
$\qquad = 5\sqrt{6}$

33. $\sqrt{x^6} = x^3$ since $(x^3)^2 = x^6$

35. $\sqrt{x^2 y^4} = \sqrt{x^2} \sqrt{y^4} = xy^2$

37. $\sqrt{a^{12} b^9} = \sqrt{a^{12} b^8} \sqrt{b} = a^6 b^4 \sqrt{b}$

39. $\sqrt{a^2 b^4 c} = \sqrt{a^2 b^4} \cdot \sqrt{c} = ab^2 \sqrt{c}$

41. $\sqrt{3n^3} = \sqrt{n^2} \sqrt{3n} = n\sqrt{3n}$

43. $\sqrt{75 a^3 b^2} = \sqrt{25 a^2 b^2} \sqrt{3a} = 5ab\sqrt{3a}$

45. $\sqrt{300 a^5 b^{11}} = \sqrt{100 a^4 b^{10}} \sqrt{3ab} = 10 a^2 b^5 \sqrt{3ab}$

47. $\sqrt{243 x^3 y^4} = \sqrt{81 x^2 y^4} \sqrt{3x} = 9xy^2 \sqrt{3x}$

49. $\sqrt{108 a^2 b^7 c} = \sqrt{36 a^2 b^6} \sqrt{3bc} = 6ab^3 \sqrt{3bc}$

51. $\sqrt{180 r^3 s^4 t^5} = \sqrt{36 r^2 s^4 t^4} \cdot \sqrt{5rt} = 6rs^2 t^2 \sqrt{5rt}$

53. $\sqrt{5} \cdot \sqrt{5} = \sqrt{5 \cdot 5} = \sqrt{25} = 5$

55. $\sqrt{24} \cdot \sqrt{5} = \sqrt{120} = \sqrt{4} \cdot \sqrt{30} = 2\sqrt{30}$

57. $\sqrt{48} \cdot \sqrt{15} = \sqrt{720}$
$\qquad = \sqrt{144} \cdot \sqrt{5}$
$\qquad = 12\sqrt{5}$

59. $\sqrt{3x} \sqrt{7x} = \sqrt{21 x^2} = \sqrt{21} \sqrt{x^2} = x\sqrt{21}$

61. $\sqrt{4a^2} \sqrt{12 ab^2} = \sqrt{48 a^3 b^2}$
$\qquad = \sqrt{16 a^2 b^2} \sqrt{3a}$
$\qquad = 4ab\sqrt{3a}$

63. $\sqrt{6xy^3} \sqrt{12 x^2 y} = \sqrt{72 x^3 y^4}$
$\qquad = \sqrt{36 x^2 y^4} \sqrt{2x}$
$\qquad = 6xy^2 \sqrt{2x}$

65. $\sqrt{3 r^4 s^7} \sqrt{21 r^6 s^5} = \sqrt{63 r^{10} s^{12}}$
$\qquad = \sqrt{9 r^{10} s^{12}} \sqrt{7}$
$\qquad = 3 r^5 s^6 \sqrt{7}$

67. $\sqrt{15 xy^6} \sqrt{6xyz} = \sqrt{90 x^2 y^7 z}$
$\qquad = \sqrt{9 x^2 y^6} \sqrt{10 yz}$
$\qquad = 3xy^3 \sqrt{10 yz}$

69. $\sqrt{6 a^2 b^4} \sqrt{9 a^4 b^6} = \sqrt{54 a^6 b^{10}}$
$\qquad = \sqrt{9 a^6 b^{10}} \sqrt{6}$
$\qquad = 3 a^3 b^5 \sqrt{6}$

71. $\left(\sqrt{2x}\right)^2 = (2x)^{(1/2) \cdot 2}$
$\qquad = (2x)^1$
$\qquad = 2x$

73. $\left(\sqrt{13 x^4 y^6}\right)^2 = (13 x^4 y^6)^{(1/2) \cdot 2}$
$\qquad = (13 x^4 y^6)^1$
$\qquad = 13 x^4 y^6$

75. $\left(\sqrt{5a}\right)^2 \left(\sqrt{3a}\right)^2 = (5a)^{(1/2) \cdot 2} (3a)^{(1/2) \cdot 2}$
$\qquad = (5a)^1 (3a)^1$
$\qquad = 5a \cdot 3a$
$\qquad = 15 a^2$

77. Coefficient is 5 because $\sqrt{25} = 5$.
Exponent on x is 4 because $\sqrt{x^4} = x^2$.

79. Exponent on x is 6 because $\sqrt{x^6} = x^3$; exponent on y is 5 because $\sqrt{y^5} = \sqrt{y^4} \sqrt{y} = y^2 \sqrt{y}$.

81. Coefficient is 8 because $\sqrt{2} \cdot \sqrt{8} = \sqrt{16} = 4$.
Exponent on x is 12 because $\sqrt{x^{12}} \cdot \sqrt{x^3} = \sqrt{x^{15}} = x^7 \sqrt{x}$.
Exponent on y is 7 because $\sqrt{y^5} \cdot \sqrt{y^7} = \sqrt{y^{12}} = y^6$.

83. a. $\left(\sqrt{13x^3}\right)^2 = \left(13x^3\right)^{(1/2)\cdot 2} = \left(13x^3\right)^1 = 13x^3$

   b. $\sqrt{\left(13x^3\right)^2} = \left(13x^3\right)^{2\cdot(1/2)} = \left(13x^3\right)^1 = 13x^3$

   c. Yes

85. $\sqrt{200\odot^{11}} = \sqrt{100\odot^{10}}\sqrt{2\odot} = 10\odot^5\sqrt{2\odot}$

87. $\sqrt{5\odot^{100}}\cdot\sqrt{5\otimes^{36}} = \sqrt{25\odot^{100}\otimes^{36}}$
$$= 5\odot^{50}\otimes^{18}$$

89. $\sqrt{x^{2/6}} = \left(x^{2/6}\right)^{1/2} = x^{(2/6)(1/2)} = x^{1/6}$

91. $\sqrt{4x^{4/5}} = \sqrt{4}\sqrt{x^{4/5}}$
$$= 2\left(x^{4/5}\right)^{1/2}$$
$$= 2x^{(4/5)(1/2)}$$
$$= 2x^{2/5}$$

93. It is rational since $\sqrt{6.25} = 2.5$ and 2.5 is a terminating decimal number.

95. a. $\sqrt{16} = 4$
     The side has length 4 feet.

   b. No, it is increased $\sqrt{2}$ or ≈ 1.414 times.

   c. 4 times

97. a. Yes; a rational number is one that can be written in the form $\dfrac{a}{b}$ where a and b are integers and $b \neq 0$.
    Let x and y be 2 rational numbers
$$x = \frac{a}{b},\ a, b,\ \text{integers } b \neq 0$$
$$y = \frac{c}{d},\ c, d\ \text{integers } d \neq 0$$
$$xy = \frac{a}{b}\cdot\frac{c}{d} = \frac{ac}{bd},\ ac \text{ and } bd \text{ are integers and}$$
$bd \neq 0$, hence xy is rational.

   b. No, for example $\sqrt{2}\cdot\sqrt{2} = 2$

102. Substitute 15 for b and 18 for d.
$$A = \frac{1}{2}h(b + d)$$
$$= \frac{1}{2}(9)(15 + 8)$$
$$= \frac{1}{2}(9)(23)$$
$$= (4.5)(23)$$
$$= 148$$
The area of the trapezoid is 148.5 square inches.

103. Substitute 2 for r and 6 for h.
$$V = \frac{1}{3}\pi r^2 h$$
$$= \frac{1}{3}\pi(2)^2(6)$$
$$= \frac{1}{3}\pi(4)(6)$$
$$= 8\pi$$
$$\approx 25.13$$
The volume of the cone is about 25.13 cubic feet.

104.
$$\frac{3x^2 - 16x - 12}{3x^2 - 10x - 8} \div \frac{x^2 - 7x + 6}{3x^2 - 11x - 4}$$
$$= \frac{3x^2 - 16x - 12}{3x^2 - 10x - 8} \cdot \frac{3x^2 - 11x - 4}{x^2 - 7x + 6}$$
$$= \frac{(3x + 2)(x - 6)}{(3x + 2)(x - 4)} \cdot \frac{(3x + 1)(x - 4)}{(x - 6)(x - 1)}$$
$$= \frac{3x + 1}{x - 1}$$

105. $3x + 6y = 9$
$$6y = -3x + 9$$
$$\frac{6y}{6} = \frac{-3x + 9}{6}$$
$$y = -\frac{1}{2}x + \frac{3}{2}$$
$$m = -\frac{1}{2},\ \left(0, \frac{3}{2}\right)$$

106. Graph the line $6x - 5y = 30$.
Since the inequality symbol is $\geq$, draw a solid line.

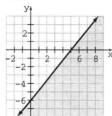

Check $(0, 0)$:　　$6x - 5y \geq 30$
　　　　　　　$6(0) - 5(0) \geq 30$
　　　　　　　　$0 - 0 \geq 30$
　　　　　　　　　$0 \geq 30$　False
Since $(0, 0)$ does not satisfy the inequality, shade the region that does not include $(0, 0)$.

107. $3x - 4y = 6$
$5x - 3y = 5$
Multiply the first equation by 5 and the second equation by -3.
$5[3x - 4y = 6]$
$-3[5x - 3y = 5]$
gives
$15x - 20y = 30$
$-15x + 9y = -15$
　　$-11y = 15$
　　　　$y = -\dfrac{15}{11}$

Substitute $-\dfrac{15}{11}$ for y in the first equation.
$3x - 4y = 6$
$3x - 4\left(-\dfrac{15}{11}\right) = 6$
$3x + \dfrac{60}{11} = 6$
$3x = \dfrac{6}{11}$
$x = \dfrac{2}{11}$

The solution is $\left(\dfrac{2}{11},\ -\dfrac{15}{11}\right)$.

Exercise Set 9.3

1. Like square roots are square roots having the same radicand. One example is $\sqrt{3},\ 5\sqrt{3}$.

3. Only like square roots can be added or subtracted.

5. $6\sqrt{5} - 4\sqrt{5} = (6 - 4)\sqrt{5} = 2\sqrt{5}$

7. $7\sqrt{5} - 11\sqrt{5} = (7 - 11)\sqrt{5} = -4\sqrt{5}$

9. $\sqrt{7} + 4\sqrt{7} - 3\sqrt{7} + 6 = (1 + 4 - 3)\sqrt{7} + 6$
　　　　　　　　　　　$= 2\sqrt{7} + 6$

11. $5\sqrt{x} + \sqrt{x} = (5 + 1)\sqrt{x} = 6\sqrt{x}$

13. $-\sqrt{y} + 3\sqrt{y} - 5\sqrt{y} = (-1 + 3 - 5)\sqrt{y} = -3\sqrt{y}$

15. $-6\sqrt{t} + 2\sqrt{t} - 6 = (-6 + 2)\sqrt{t} - 6 = -4\sqrt{t} - 6$

17. $\sqrt{x} + \sqrt{y} + x + 3\sqrt{y} = \sqrt{x} + (1 + 3)\sqrt{y} + x$
　　　　　　　　　　　$= \sqrt{x} + 4\sqrt{y} + x$

19. $4 + 4\sqrt{m} - 6\sqrt{m} + 5m - 2$
　$= 5m + (4 - 6)\sqrt{m} + (4 - 2)$
　$= 5m - 2\sqrt{m} + 2$

21. $-3\sqrt{7} + \sqrt{7} - 2\sqrt{x} - 7\sqrt{x}$
　$= (-3 + 1)\sqrt{7} + (-2 - 7)\sqrt{x}$
　$= -2\sqrt{7} - 9\sqrt{x}$

23. $\sqrt{20} + \sqrt{18} = \sqrt{4 \cdot 5} + \sqrt{9 \cdot 2}$
　　　　　　　$= \sqrt{4}\sqrt{5} + \sqrt{9}\sqrt{2}$
　　　　　　　$= 2\sqrt{5} + 3\sqrt{2}$

25. $\sqrt{300} - \sqrt{27} = \sqrt{100 \cdot 3} - \sqrt{9 \cdot 3}$
　　　　　　　$= \sqrt{100}\sqrt{3} - \sqrt{9}\sqrt{3}$
　　　　　　　$= 10\sqrt{3} - 3\sqrt{3}$
　　　　　　　$= 7\sqrt{3}$

27. $\sqrt{75} + \sqrt{108} = \sqrt{25 \cdot 3} + \sqrt{36 \cdot 3}$
　　　　　　　$= \sqrt{25}\sqrt{3} + \sqrt{36}\sqrt{3}$
　　　　　　　$= 5\sqrt{3} + 6\sqrt{3}$
　　　　　　　$= 11\sqrt{3}$

29. $4\sqrt{50} - \sqrt{72} + \sqrt{8} = 4\sqrt{25 \cdot 2} - \sqrt{36 \cdot 2} + \sqrt{4 \cdot 2}$
　　　　　　　　　$= 4\sqrt{25}\sqrt{2} - \sqrt{36}\sqrt{2} + \sqrt{4}\sqrt{2}$
　　　　　　　　　$= 4 \cdot 5\sqrt{2} - 6\sqrt{2} + 2\sqrt{2}$
　　　　　　　　　$= 20\sqrt{2} - 6\sqrt{2} + 2\sqrt{2}$
　　　　　　　　　$= 16\sqrt{2}$

31. $-3\sqrt{125} + 7\sqrt{75} = -3\sqrt{25 \cdot 5} + 7\sqrt{25 \cdot 3}$
　　　　　　　　　$= -3\sqrt{25}\sqrt{5} + 7\sqrt{25}\sqrt{3}$
　　　　　　　　　$= -3 \cdot 5\sqrt{5} + 7 \cdot 5\sqrt{3}$
　　　　　　　　　$= -15\sqrt{5} + 35\sqrt{3}$

33. $2\sqrt{360} + 4\sqrt{160} = 2\sqrt{36 \cdot 10} + 4\sqrt{16 \cdot 10}$
　　　　　　　　　$= 2\sqrt{36}\sqrt{10} + 4\sqrt{16}\sqrt{10}$
　　　　　　　　　$= 2 \cdot 6\sqrt{10} + 4 \cdot 4\sqrt{10}$
　　　　　　　　　$= 12\sqrt{10} + 16\sqrt{10}$
　　　　　　　　　$= (12 + 16)\sqrt{10}$
　　　　　　　　　$= 28\sqrt{10}$

35. $4\sqrt{16} - \sqrt{48} = 4 \cdot 4 - \sqrt{16 \cdot 3}$
$$= 16 - \sqrt{16}\sqrt{3}$$
$$= 16 - 4\sqrt{3}$$

37. $\sqrt{3}\left(4 + \sqrt{3}\right) = \sqrt{3} \cdot 4 + \sqrt{3} \cdot \sqrt{3}$
$$= 4\sqrt{3} + \sqrt{9}$$
$$= 4\sqrt{3} + 3$$

39. $4\left(\sqrt{x} - \sqrt{2}\right) = 4 \cdot \sqrt{x} - 4 \cdot \sqrt{2}$
$$= 4\sqrt{x} - 4\sqrt{2}$$

41. $y\left(\sqrt{y} + y\right) = y \cdot \sqrt{y} + y \cdot y$
$$= y\sqrt{y} + y^2$$

43. $\sqrt{5}\left(\sqrt{8} - 2\right) = \sqrt{5} \cdot \sqrt{8} - \sqrt{5} \cdot 2$
$$= \sqrt{40} - 2\sqrt{5}$$
$$= \sqrt{4 \cdot 10} - 2\sqrt{5}$$
$$= \sqrt{4} \cdot \sqrt{10} - 2\sqrt{5}$$
$$= 2\sqrt{10} - 2\sqrt{5}$$

45. $\sqrt{x}\left(\sqrt{x} + \sqrt{3}\right) = \sqrt{x} \cdot \sqrt{x} + \sqrt{x} \cdot \sqrt{3}$
$$= \sqrt{x^2} + \sqrt{x \cdot 3}$$
$$= x + \sqrt{3x}$$

47. $\sqrt{a}\left(6 - \sqrt{2a}\right) = \sqrt{a} \cdot 6 - \sqrt{a} \cdot \sqrt{2a}$
$$= 6\sqrt{a} - \sqrt{2a^2}$$
$$= 6\sqrt{a} - a\sqrt{2}$$

49. $x\left(x + 4\sqrt{y}\right) = x \cdot x + x \cdot 4\sqrt{y}$
$$= x^2 + 4x\sqrt{y}$$

51. $3x\left(4x - 3\sqrt{x}\right) = 3x \cdot 4x + 3x \cdot -3\sqrt{x}$
$$= (3 \cdot 4)x^2 + (3 \cdot -3)x\sqrt{x}$$
$$= 12x^2 - 9x\sqrt{x}$$

53.
$\left(6 + \sqrt{3}\right)\left(4 - \sqrt{2}\right) = 6(4) + 6\left(-\sqrt{2}\right) + \sqrt{3}(4) + \sqrt{3}\left(-\sqrt{2}\right)$
$$= 24 - 6\sqrt{2} + 4\sqrt{3} - \sqrt{3 \cdot 2}$$
$$= 24 - 6\sqrt{2} + 4\sqrt{3} - \sqrt{6}$$

55.
$\left(\sqrt{5} - 2\right)\left(\sqrt{6} + 3\right) = \sqrt{5}\left(\sqrt{6}\right) + \sqrt{5}(3) + (-2)\left(\sqrt{6}\right) + (-2)(3)$
$$= \sqrt{5 \cdot 6} + 3\sqrt{5} - 2\sqrt{6} - 6$$
$$= \sqrt{30} + 3\sqrt{5} - 2\sqrt{6} - 6$$

57. $\left(6 - 2\sqrt{7}\right)\left(8 - 2\sqrt{7}\right) = 6(8) + 6\left(-2\sqrt{7}\right) + \left(-2\sqrt{7}\right)(8) + \left(-2\sqrt{7}\right)\left(-2\sqrt{7}\right)$
$$= 48 - 12\sqrt{7} - 16\sqrt{7} + 4\sqrt{49}$$
$$= 48 - 12\sqrt{7} - 16\sqrt{7} + 4(7)$$
$$= 48 - 12\sqrt{7} - 16\sqrt{7} + 28$$
$$= (48 + 28) + (-12 - 16)\sqrt{7}$$
$$= 76 - 28\sqrt{7}$$

59. $\left(4 - \sqrt{x}\right)\left(4 - \sqrt{x}\right) = 4(4) + 4\left(-\sqrt{x}\right) + \left(-\sqrt{x}\right)(4) + \left(-\sqrt{x}\right)\left(-\sqrt{x}\right)$
$$= 16 - 4\sqrt{x} - 4\sqrt{x} + \sqrt{x^2}$$
$$= 16 - 4\sqrt{x} - 4\sqrt{x} + x$$
$$= 16 + (-4 - 4)\sqrt{x} + x$$
$$= 16 - 8\sqrt{x} + x$$

61. $\left(\sqrt{3z}-4\right)\left(\sqrt{5z}+2\right)=\left(\sqrt{3z}\right)\left(\sqrt{5z}\right)+\left(\sqrt{3z}\right)(2)+(-4)\left(\sqrt{5z}\right)+(-4)(2)$

$$=\sqrt{3\cdot 5z^2}+2\sqrt{3z}-4\sqrt{5z}-8$$
$$=\sqrt{15z^2}+2\sqrt{3z}-4\sqrt{5z}-8$$
$$=z\sqrt{15}+2\sqrt{3z}-4\sqrt{5z}-8$$

63. $\left(r+2\sqrt{s}\right)\left(2r-3\sqrt{s}\right)=r(2r)+r\left(-3\sqrt{s}\right)+\left(2\sqrt{s}\right)(2r)+\left(2\sqrt{s}\right)\left(-3\sqrt{s}\right)$

$$=2r^2-3r\sqrt{s}+4r\sqrt{s}-6\sqrt{s^2}$$
$$=2r^2-3r\sqrt{s}+4r\sqrt{s}-6s$$
$$=2r^2+\left(-3r+4r\right)\sqrt{s}-6s$$
$$=2r^2+r\sqrt{s}-6s$$

65. $\left(x-\sqrt{2y}\right)\left(2x-2\sqrt{2y}\right)=x(2x)+x\left(-2\sqrt{2y}\right)+\left(-\sqrt{2y}\right)(2x)+\left(-\sqrt{2y}\right)\left(-2\sqrt{2y}\right)$

$$=2x^2-2x\sqrt{2y}-2x\sqrt{2y}+2\sqrt{2y\cdot 2y}$$
$$=2x^2-2x\sqrt{2y}-2x\sqrt{2y}+2\sqrt{4y^2}$$
$$=2x^2-2x\sqrt{2y}-2x\sqrt{2y}+2(2y)$$
$$=2x^2-2x\sqrt{2y}-2x\sqrt{2y}+4y$$
$$=2x^2+\left(-2x-2x\right)\sqrt{2y}+4y$$
$$=2x^2-4x\sqrt{2y}+4y$$

67. $\left(4p-2\sqrt{3q}\right)\left(p+2\sqrt{3q}\right)=4p(p)+4p\left(2\sqrt{3q}\right)+\left(-2\sqrt{3q}\right)(p)+\left(-2\sqrt{3q}\right)\left(2\sqrt{3q}\right)$

$$=4p^2+8p\sqrt{3q}-2p\sqrt{3q}-4\sqrt{3q\cdot 3q}$$
$$=4p^2+8p\sqrt{3q}-2p\sqrt{3q}-4\sqrt{9q^2}$$
$$=4p^2+8p\sqrt{3q}-2p\sqrt{3q}-4(3q)$$
$$=4p^2+\left(8p-2p\right)\sqrt{3q}-12q$$
$$=4p^2+6p\sqrt{3q}-12q$$

69. $(1 + \sqrt{3})(1 - \sqrt{3})$
$$= 1(1) + 1(-\sqrt{3}) + 1(\sqrt{3}) + \sqrt{3}(-\sqrt{3})$$
$$= 1 - \sqrt{3} + \sqrt{3} - \sqrt{9}$$
$$= 1 - 3$$
$$= -2$$

71. $(4 - \sqrt{2})(4 + \sqrt{2})$
$$= 4(4) + 4(\sqrt{2}) + 4(-\sqrt{2}) + \sqrt{2}(-\sqrt{2})$$
$$= 16 + 4\sqrt{2} - 4\sqrt{2} - 2$$
$$= 16 - 2$$
$$= 14$$

73. $(\sqrt{x} + 3)(\sqrt{x} - 3)$
$$= \sqrt{x}(\sqrt{x}) + \sqrt{x}(-3) + 3\sqrt{x} + 3(-3)$$
$$= x - 3\sqrt{x} + 3\sqrt{x} - 9$$
$$= x - 9$$

79. $(2\sqrt{x} + 3\sqrt{y})(2\sqrt{x} - 3\sqrt{y}) = (2\sqrt{x})(2\sqrt{x}) + (2\sqrt{x})(-3\sqrt{y}) + (3\sqrt{y})(2\sqrt{x}) + (3\sqrt{y})(-3\sqrt{y})$
$$= 4x - 6\sqrt{xy} + 6\sqrt{xy} - 9y$$
$$= 4x - 9y$$

81. a. No

    b. $2 \cdot \sqrt{5} = 2\sqrt{5}$ is twice as large as $\sqrt{5}$.

83. $x + 2$

85. Yes

87. The missing expression is 343 since
$$\sqrt{343} - \sqrt{63} = \sqrt{49 \cdot 7} - \sqrt{9 \cdot 7}$$
$$= 7\sqrt{7} - 3\sqrt{7}$$
$$= 4\sqrt{7}$$

89. Perimeter:
$$(\sqrt{2} + \sqrt{3}) + (\sqrt{2} + \sqrt{3}) + (\sqrt{2} + \sqrt{3}) + (\sqrt{2} + \sqrt{3})$$
$$= 4(\sqrt{2} + \sqrt{3}) \text{ units}$$
Area:
$$(\sqrt{2} + \sqrt{3})(\sqrt{2} + \sqrt{3})$$
$$= (\sqrt{2})^2 + 2\sqrt{2}\sqrt{3} + (\sqrt{3})^2$$
$$= 2 + 2\sqrt{2}\sqrt{3} + 3$$
$$= 5 + 2\sqrt{6} \text{ square units}$$

91. Perimeter:
$$\sqrt{7} + \sqrt{15} + \sqrt{22} \text{ units}$$

Area:
$$= \frac{1}{2}bh$$
$$= \frac{1}{2}\left(\sqrt{7}\right)\left(\sqrt{15}\right)$$
$$= \frac{1}{2}\left(\sqrt{7 \cdot 15}\right)$$
$$= \frac{1}{2}\sqrt{105} \text{ square units}$$

93. $\sqrt{(3^2) - 4 \cdot 1 \cdot 2} = \sqrt{9 - 8} = \sqrt{1} = 1$

95. $\sqrt{(-14)^2 - 4 \cdot 1 \cdot (-5)} = \sqrt{196 + 20}$
$$= \sqrt{216}$$
$$= \sqrt{36 \cdot 6}$$
$$= 6\sqrt{6}$$

97. $\sqrt{(4)^2 - 4 \cdot (-2)(7)} = \sqrt{16 + 56}$
$$= \sqrt{72}$$
$$= \sqrt{36 \cdot 2}$$
$$= 6\sqrt{2}$$

99. The missing expression is 48 since

$$-5\sqrt{48} + 2\sqrt{3} + 3\sqrt{27}$$
$$= -5\sqrt{16 \cdot 3} + 2\sqrt{3} + 3\sqrt{9 \cdot 3}$$
$$= -5 \cdot 4\sqrt{3} + 2\sqrt{3} + 3 \cdot 3\sqrt{3}$$
$$= -20\sqrt{3} + 2\sqrt{3} + 9\sqrt{3}$$
$$= (-20 + 2 + 9)\sqrt{3}$$
$$= -9\sqrt{3}$$

101. Let x = the amount of time he spent riding the sled downhill.

	Rate	Time	Distance
Riding	10	x	$10x$
Walking	2	$x + 0.2$	$2(x + 0.2)$

$10x = 2x + 0.4$
$8x = 0.4$
$\quad x = 0.05$ hours or $(0.05 \times 60) = 3$ minutes
Jason's sleigh ride took 3 minutes.

102. $3x^2 - 12x - 96 = 3(x^2 - 4x - 32)$
$$= 3(x + 4)(x - 8)$$

103. $\dfrac{x-1}{x^2 - 1} = \dfrac{x-1}{(x+1)(x-1)} = \dfrac{1}{x+1}$

104.
$$x + \frac{24}{x} = 10$$
$$x\left(x + \frac{24}{x}\right) = 10 \cdot x$$
$$x^2 + 24 = 10x$$
$$x^2 - 10x + 24 = 0$$
$$(x - 6)(x - 4) = 0$$
$$x - 6 = 0 \text{ or } x - 4 = 0$$
$$x = 6 \qquad x = 4$$

105.

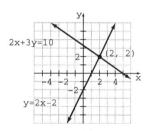

The solution is (2, 2).

Exercise Set 9.4

1. Cannot be simplified: the radicand does not have a factor that is a perfect square, the radicand does not contain a fraction, and the denominator does not contain a square root.

3. The numerator and denominator have a common factor.
$$\frac{x^2\sqrt{2}}{x} = x\sqrt{2}$$

5. Cannot be simplified: the radicand does not have a factor that is a perfect square, the radicand does not contain a fraction, and the denominator does not contain a square root.

7. 1. No perfect square factors in any radicand.
2. No radicand contains a fraction.
3. No square roots in any denominator.

9. a. The radicand contains a perfect square factor.
$$\sqrt{27} = \sqrt{9 \cdot 3} = \sqrt{9} \cdot \sqrt{3} = 3\sqrt{3}$$

b. The radicand contains a fraction.
$$\sqrt{\frac{1}{2}} = \frac{\sqrt{1}}{\sqrt{2}} = \frac{1}{\sqrt{2}} = \frac{1}{\sqrt{2}} \cdot \frac{\sqrt{2}}{\sqrt{2}} = \frac{\sqrt{2}}{2}$$

c. The denominator contains a square root.

$$\frac{3}{\sqrt{5}} = \frac{3}{\sqrt{5}} \cdot \frac{\sqrt{5}}{\sqrt{5}} = \frac{3\sqrt{5}}{5}$$

11. $\sqrt{\dfrac{27}{3}} = \sqrt{9} = 3$

13. $\sqrt{\dfrac{63}{7}} = \sqrt{9} = 3$

15. $\dfrac{\sqrt{18}}{\sqrt{2}} = \sqrt{\dfrac{18}{2}} = \sqrt{9} = 3$

17. $\sqrt{\dfrac{1}{49}} = \dfrac{\sqrt{1}}{\sqrt{49}} = \dfrac{1}{7}$

19. $\sqrt{\dfrac{81}{144}} = \dfrac{\sqrt{81}}{\sqrt{144}} = \dfrac{9}{12} = \dfrac{3}{4}$

21. $\dfrac{\sqrt{10}}{\sqrt{1000}} = \sqrt{\dfrac{10}{1000}} = \sqrt{\dfrac{1}{100}} = \dfrac{\sqrt{1}}{\sqrt{100}} = \dfrac{1}{10}$

23. $\sqrt{\dfrac{48x^3}{2x}} = \sqrt{24x^2} = \sqrt{4x^2} \cdot \sqrt{6} = 2x\sqrt{6}$

25. $\sqrt{\dfrac{45x^2}{16x^2y^4}} = \sqrt{\dfrac{45}{16y^4}} = \dfrac{\sqrt{45}}{\sqrt{16y^4}} = \dfrac{\sqrt{9 \cdot 5}}{4y^2} = \dfrac{3\sqrt{5}}{4y^2}$

27. $\sqrt{\dfrac{16x^5y^3}{100x^7y}} = \sqrt{\dfrac{4y^2}{25x^2}} = \dfrac{\sqrt{4y^2}}{\sqrt{25x^2}} = \dfrac{2y}{5x}$

29. $\sqrt{\dfrac{24ab}{24a^5b^3}} = \sqrt{\dfrac{1}{a^4b^2}} = \dfrac{\sqrt{1}}{\sqrt{a^4b^2}} = \dfrac{1}{a^2b}$

31. $\dfrac{\sqrt{32n^5}}{\sqrt{8n}} = \sqrt{\dfrac{32n^5}{8n}} = \sqrt{4n^4} = 2n^2$

33. $\dfrac{\sqrt{81w^5z}}{\sqrt{144wz^3}} = \sqrt{\dfrac{81w^5z}{144wz^3}}$

$$= \sqrt{\dfrac{81w^4}{144z^2}}$$

$$= \dfrac{\sqrt{81w^4}}{\sqrt{144z^2}}$$

$$= \dfrac{9w^2}{12z}$$

35. $\dfrac{\sqrt{45ab^6}}{\sqrt{9ab^4c^2}} = \sqrt{\dfrac{45ab^6}{9ab^4c^2}} = \sqrt{\dfrac{5b^2}{c^2}} = \dfrac{\sqrt{5b^2}}{\sqrt{c^2}} = \dfrac{b\sqrt{5}}{c}$

37. $\dfrac{\sqrt{125a^6b^8}}{\sqrt{5a^2b^2}} = \sqrt{\dfrac{125a^6b^8}{5a^2b^2}} = \sqrt{25a^4b^6} = 5a^2b^3$

39. $\dfrac{1}{\sqrt{5}} = \dfrac{1}{\sqrt{5}} \cdot \dfrac{\sqrt{5}}{\sqrt{5}} = \dfrac{\sqrt{5}}{\sqrt{25}} = \dfrac{\sqrt{5}}{5}$

41. $\dfrac{4}{\sqrt{8}} = \dfrac{4}{\sqrt{4}\sqrt{2}}$

$$= \dfrac{4}{2\sqrt{2}}$$

$$= \dfrac{2}{\sqrt{2}}$$

$$= \dfrac{2}{\sqrt{2}} \cdot \dfrac{\sqrt{2}}{\sqrt{2}}$$

$$= \dfrac{2\sqrt{2}}{2}$$

$$= \sqrt{2}$$

43. $\dfrac{6}{\sqrt{12}} = \dfrac{6}{\sqrt{4 \cdot 3}}$

$$= \dfrac{6}{2\sqrt{3}}$$

$$= \dfrac{3}{\sqrt{3}}$$

$$= \dfrac{3}{\sqrt{3}} \cdot \dfrac{\sqrt{3}}{\sqrt{3}}$$

$$= \dfrac{3\sqrt{3}}{\sqrt{9}}$$

$$= \dfrac{3\sqrt{3}}{3}$$

$$= \sqrt{3}$$

45. $\sqrt{\dfrac{1}{5}} = \dfrac{\sqrt{1}}{\sqrt{5}} = \dfrac{\sqrt{1}}{\sqrt{5}} \cdot \dfrac{\sqrt{5}}{\sqrt{5}} = \dfrac{\sqrt{5}}{\sqrt{25}} = \dfrac{\sqrt{5}}{5}$

47. $\sqrt{\dfrac{2}{3}} = \dfrac{\sqrt{2}}{\sqrt{3}} = \dfrac{\sqrt{2}}{\sqrt{3}} \cdot \dfrac{\sqrt{3}}{\sqrt{3}} = \dfrac{\sqrt{6}}{\sqrt{9}} = \dfrac{\sqrt{6}}{3}$

49. $\sqrt{\dfrac{5}{15}} = \sqrt{\dfrac{1}{3}} = \dfrac{\sqrt{1}}{\sqrt{3}} = \dfrac{1}{\sqrt{3}} = \dfrac{1}{\sqrt{3}} \cdot \dfrac{\sqrt{3}}{\sqrt{3}} = \dfrac{\sqrt{3}}{\sqrt{9}} = \dfrac{\sqrt{3}}{3}$

51. $\sqrt{\dfrac{3}{8}} = \dfrac{\sqrt{3}}{\sqrt{8}} = \dfrac{\sqrt{3}}{\sqrt{4}\sqrt{2}}$

$\qquad = \dfrac{\sqrt{3}}{2\sqrt{2}}$

$\qquad = \dfrac{\sqrt{3}}{2\sqrt{2}} \cdot \dfrac{\sqrt{2}}{\sqrt{2}}$

$\qquad = \dfrac{\sqrt{6}}{2 \cdot 2}$

$\qquad = \dfrac{\sqrt{6}}{4}$

53. $\sqrt{\dfrac{3}{x}} = \dfrac{\sqrt{3}}{\sqrt{x}} = \dfrac{\sqrt{3}}{\sqrt{x}} \cdot \dfrac{\sqrt{x}}{\sqrt{x}} = \dfrac{\sqrt{3x}}{\sqrt{x^2}} = \dfrac{\sqrt{3x}}{x}$

55. $\sqrt{\dfrac{a}{b}} = \dfrac{\sqrt{a}}{\sqrt{b}} = \dfrac{\sqrt{a}}{\sqrt{b}} \cdot \dfrac{\sqrt{b}}{\sqrt{b}} = \dfrac{\sqrt{ab}}{b}$

57. $\sqrt{\dfrac{c}{d}} = \dfrac{\sqrt{c}}{\sqrt{d}} = \dfrac{\sqrt{c}}{\sqrt{d}} \cdot \dfrac{\sqrt{d}}{\sqrt{d}} = \dfrac{\sqrt{cd}}{d}$

59. $\sqrt{\dfrac{3x}{5}} = \dfrac{\sqrt{3x}}{\sqrt{5}} = \dfrac{\sqrt{3x}}{\sqrt{5}} \cdot \dfrac{\sqrt{5}}{\sqrt{5}} = \dfrac{\sqrt{15x}}{5}$

61. $\sqrt{\dfrac{x^2}{2}} = \dfrac{\sqrt{x^2}}{\sqrt{2}} = \dfrac{x}{\sqrt{2}} = \dfrac{x}{\sqrt{2}} \cdot \dfrac{\sqrt{2}}{\sqrt{2}} = \dfrac{x\sqrt{2}}{2}$

63. $\sqrt{\dfrac{a^2}{8}} = \dfrac{\sqrt{a^2}}{\sqrt{8}}$

$\qquad = \dfrac{a}{\sqrt{8}}$

$\qquad = \dfrac{a}{\sqrt{4 \cdot 2}}$

$\qquad = \dfrac{a}{2\sqrt{2}}$

$\qquad = \dfrac{a}{2\sqrt{2}} \cdot \dfrac{\sqrt{2}}{\sqrt{2}}$

$\qquad = \dfrac{a\sqrt{2}}{2 \cdot 2}$

$\qquad = \dfrac{a\sqrt{2}}{4}$

65. $\sqrt{\dfrac{t^5}{5}} = \dfrac{\sqrt{t^5}}{\sqrt{5}} = \dfrac{\sqrt{t^4}\sqrt{t}}{\sqrt{5}} = \dfrac{t^2\sqrt{t}}{\sqrt{5}} \cdot \dfrac{\sqrt{5}}{\sqrt{5}} = \dfrac{t^2\sqrt{5t}}{5}$

67. $\sqrt{\dfrac{a^8}{14b}} = \dfrac{\sqrt{a^8}}{\sqrt{14b}}$

$\qquad = \dfrac{a^4}{\sqrt{14b}}$

$\qquad = \dfrac{a^4}{\sqrt{14b}} \cdot \dfrac{\sqrt{14b}}{\sqrt{14b}}$

$\qquad = \dfrac{a^4\sqrt{14b}}{\sqrt{196b^2}}$

$\qquad = \dfrac{a^4\sqrt{14b}}{14b}$

69. $\sqrt{\dfrac{6c^2d^4}{30c^2d^5}} = \sqrt{\dfrac{1}{5d}}$

$\qquad = \dfrac{\sqrt{1}}{\sqrt{5d}}$

$\qquad = \dfrac{1}{\sqrt{5d}} \cdot \dfrac{\sqrt{5d}}{\sqrt{5d}}$

$\qquad = \dfrac{\sqrt{5d}}{5d}$

71. $\sqrt{\dfrac{50yz}{24x^4y^5z^3}} = \sqrt{\dfrac{25}{12x^4y^4z^2}}$

$\qquad = \dfrac{\sqrt{25}}{\sqrt{12x^4y^4z^2}}$

$\qquad = \dfrac{5}{2x^2y^2z\sqrt{3}}$

$\qquad = \dfrac{5}{2x^2y^2z\sqrt{3}} \cdot \dfrac{\sqrt{3}}{\sqrt{3}}$

$\qquad = \dfrac{5\sqrt{3}}{6x^2y^2z}$

73. $\dfrac{\sqrt{90x^4y}}{\sqrt{2x^5y^5}} = \sqrt{\dfrac{90x^4y}{2x^5y^5}}$

$= \sqrt{\dfrac{45}{xy^4}}$

$= \dfrac{\sqrt{45}}{\sqrt{xy^4}}$

$= \dfrac{\sqrt{9}\sqrt{5}}{\sqrt{y^4}\sqrt{x}}$

$= \dfrac{3\sqrt{5}}{y^2\sqrt{x}}$

$= \dfrac{3\sqrt{5}}{y^2\sqrt{x}} \cdot \dfrac{\sqrt{x}}{\sqrt{x}}$

$= \dfrac{3\sqrt{5x}}{xy^2}$

75. $\left(5+\sqrt{3}\right)\left(5-\sqrt{3}\right)$

$= 5(5) + 5\left(-\sqrt{3}\right) + \sqrt{3}(5) + \sqrt{3}\left(-\sqrt{3}\right)$

$= 25 - 5\sqrt{3} + 5\sqrt{3} - 3$

$= 22$

77. $\left(\sqrt{3}-\sqrt{6}\right)\left(\sqrt{3}+\sqrt{6}\right)$

$= \sqrt{3}\left(\sqrt{3}\right) + \sqrt{3}\left(\sqrt{6}\right) + \left(-\sqrt{6}\right)\left(\sqrt{3}\right) + \left(-\sqrt{6}\right)\left(\sqrt{6}\right)$

$= 3 + \sqrt{18} - \sqrt{18} - 6$

$= -3$

79. $\left(\sqrt{x}-y\right)\left(\sqrt{x}+y\right)$

$= \sqrt{x}\cdot\sqrt{x} + y\sqrt{x} - y\sqrt{x} - y(y)$

$= x + y\sqrt{x} - y\sqrt{x} - y^2$

$= x - y^2$

81. $\left(\sqrt{a}+\sqrt{b}\right)\left(\sqrt{a}-\sqrt{b}\right)$

$= \sqrt{a}\sqrt{a} + \sqrt{a}\left(-\sqrt{b}\right) + \sqrt{b}\sqrt{a} + \sqrt{b}\left(-\sqrt{b}\right)$

$= a - \sqrt{a}\sqrt{b} + \sqrt{a}\sqrt{b} - b$

$= a - b$

83. $\dfrac{2}{\sqrt{5}+2} = \dfrac{2}{\sqrt{5}+2} \cdot \dfrac{\sqrt{5}-2}{\sqrt{5}-2}$

$= \dfrac{2\left(\sqrt{5}-2\right)}{5-4}$

$= \dfrac{2\sqrt{5}-4}{1}$

$= 2\sqrt{5} - 4$

85. $\dfrac{2}{\sqrt{6}-1} = \dfrac{2}{\sqrt{6}-1} \cdot \dfrac{\sqrt{6}+1}{\sqrt{6}+1}$

$= \dfrac{2\left(\sqrt{6}+1\right)}{6-1}$

$= \dfrac{2\sqrt{6}+2}{5}$

87. $\dfrac{6}{\sqrt{3}+\sqrt{5}} = \dfrac{6}{\sqrt{3}+\sqrt{5}} \cdot \dfrac{\sqrt{3}-\sqrt{5}}{\sqrt{3}-\sqrt{5}}$

$= \dfrac{6\left(\sqrt{3}-\sqrt{5}\right)}{3-5}$

$= \dfrac{6\left(\sqrt{3}-\sqrt{5}\right)}{-2}$

$= -3\left(\sqrt{3}-\sqrt{5}\right)$

$= -3\sqrt{3} + 3\sqrt{5}$

89. $\dfrac{8}{\sqrt{5}-\sqrt{8}} = \dfrac{8}{\sqrt{5}-\sqrt{8}} \cdot \dfrac{\sqrt{5}+\sqrt{8}}{\sqrt{5}+\sqrt{8}}$

$= \dfrac{8\left(\sqrt{5}+\sqrt{8}\right)}{5-8}$

$= \dfrac{8\sqrt{5}+8\sqrt{8}}{-3}$

$= \dfrac{8\sqrt{5}+8\sqrt{4}\sqrt{2}}{-3}$

$= \dfrac{8\sqrt{5}+8\cdot2\sqrt{2}}{-3}$

$= \dfrac{8\sqrt{5}+16\sqrt{2}}{-3}$

$= \dfrac{-8\sqrt{5}-16\sqrt{2}}{3}$

90.
$$\frac{1}{\sqrt{17}-\sqrt{8}} = \frac{1}{\sqrt{17}-\sqrt{8}} \cdot \frac{\sqrt{17}+\sqrt{8}}{\sqrt{17}+\sqrt{8}}$$
$$= \frac{\sqrt{17}+\sqrt{8}}{17-8}$$
$$= \frac{\sqrt{17}+\sqrt{4}\sqrt{2}}{9}$$
$$= \frac{\sqrt{17}+2\sqrt{2}}{9}$$

91.
$$\frac{2}{\sqrt{y}+3} = \frac{2}{\sqrt{y}+3} \cdot \frac{\sqrt{y}-3}{\sqrt{y}-3}$$
$$= \frac{2(\sqrt{y}-3)}{y-9}$$
$$= \frac{2\sqrt{y}-6}{y-9}$$

93.
$$\frac{6}{4-\sqrt{y}} = \frac{6}{4-\sqrt{y}} \cdot \frac{4+\sqrt{y}}{4+\sqrt{y}}$$
$$= \frac{6(4+\sqrt{y})}{16-y}$$
$$= \frac{24+6\sqrt{y}}{16-y}$$

95.
$$\frac{16}{\sqrt{y}+x} = \frac{16}{\sqrt{y}+x} \cdot \frac{\sqrt{y}-x}{\sqrt{y}-x}$$
$$= \frac{16(\sqrt{y}-x)}{y-x^2}$$
$$= \frac{16\sqrt{y}-16x}{y-x^2}$$

97.
$$\frac{x}{\sqrt{x}+\sqrt{y}} = \frac{x}{\sqrt{x}+\sqrt{y}} \cdot \frac{\sqrt{x}-\sqrt{y}}{\sqrt{x}-\sqrt{y}}$$
$$= \frac{x(\sqrt{x}-\sqrt{y})}{x-y}$$
$$= \frac{x\sqrt{x}-x\sqrt{y}}{x-y}$$

99.
$$\frac{\sqrt{3}}{\sqrt{3}-\sqrt{n}} = \frac{\sqrt{3}}{\sqrt{3}-\sqrt{n}} \cdot \frac{\sqrt{3}+\sqrt{n}}{\sqrt{3}+\sqrt{n}}$$
$$= \frac{\sqrt{3}(\sqrt{3}+\sqrt{n})}{3-n}$$
$$= \frac{3+\sqrt{3n}}{3-n}$$

101.
$$\frac{5\sqrt{x}}{6-\sqrt{x}} = \frac{5\sqrt{x}}{6-\sqrt{x}} \cdot \frac{6+\sqrt{x}}{6+\sqrt{x}}$$
$$= \frac{5\sqrt{x}(6+\sqrt{x})}{36-x}$$
$$= \frac{30\sqrt{x}+5x}{36-x}$$

103. Yes, $\frac{a}{b} \div \frac{c}{d} = \frac{a}{b} \cdot \frac{d}{c} = \frac{ad}{bc}$, which is a rational

number since b, c, and d cannot be zero $\left(\frac{a}{b}, \frac{c}{d}\right.$

both rational and $\left.\frac{c}{d} \neq 0\right)$.

105. $\sqrt{5}+\sqrt{10} \approx 2.236+3.162 \approx 5.398 \approx 5.40$

107. $\sqrt{5} / \sqrt{10} \approx (2.236) \div (3.162) \approx 0.71$

109. $\sqrt{7}+\sqrt{21} \approx 2.646+4.583 \approx 7.229 \approx 7.23$

111. $\sqrt{7} / \sqrt{21} \approx (2.646) \div (4.583) \approx 0.58$

113.
$$lw = A$$
$$\left(4+\sqrt{3}\right)w = 24$$
$$w = \frac{24}{4+\sqrt{3}}$$
$$= \frac{24}{4+\sqrt{3}} \cdot \frac{4-\sqrt{3}}{4-\sqrt{3}}$$
$$= \frac{24\left(4-\sqrt{3}\right)}{16-3}$$
$$= \frac{24\left(4-\sqrt{3}\right)}{13}$$

115. The missing expression is $64x^{10}$ since
$$\sqrt{\frac{64x^{10}}{4x^2}} = \sqrt{16x^8} = 4x^4.$$

117. The missing expression is 2 since
$$\frac{1}{\sqrt{2}} = \frac{1}{\sqrt{2}} \cdot \frac{\sqrt{2}}{\sqrt{2}} = \frac{\sqrt{2}}{2}.$$

119.
$$\frac{\sqrt{x}}{1-\sqrt{3}} = \frac{\sqrt{x}}{1-\sqrt{3}} \cdot \frac{1+\sqrt{3}}{1+\sqrt{3}}$$
$$= \frac{\sqrt{x}(1+\sqrt{3})}{1-3}$$
$$= \frac{\sqrt{x}(1+\sqrt{3})}{-2}$$
$$= \frac{-\sqrt{x}-\sqrt{3}}{2}$$

122.
$$
\begin{array}{r}
3x-8 \\
x+4\overline{)3x^2+4x-25} \\
\underline{3x^2+12x} \\
-8x-25 \\
\underline{-8x-32} \\
7
\end{array}
$$
$$\frac{3x^2+4x-25}{x+4} = 3x-8+\frac{7}{x+4}$$

123.
$$2x^2 - x - 36 = 0$$
$$(2x-9)(x+4) = 0$$
$$2x-9 = 0 \text{ or } x+4 = 0$$
$$x = \frac{9}{2} \qquad x = -4$$

124.
$$\frac{1}{x^2-4} - \frac{2}{x-2} = \frac{1}{(x-2)(x+2)} - \frac{2}{x-2}$$
$$= \frac{1}{(x-2)(x+2)} - \frac{2}{x-2}\cdot\frac{x+2}{x+2}$$
$$= \frac{1}{(x-2)(x+2)} - \frac{2x+4}{(x-2)(x+2)}$$
$$= \frac{1-(2x+4)}{(x-2)(x+2)}$$
$$= \frac{-2x-3}{(x-2)(x+2)}$$

125. Mark's rate: $\dfrac{1}{20}$, Terry's rate: $\dfrac{1}{t}$
$$\frac{12}{20} + \frac{12}{t} = 1$$
$$20t\left(\frac{12}{20} + \frac{12}{t}\right) = 20t$$
$$12t + 240 = 20t$$
$$240 = 8t$$
$$30 = t$$
It would take Mrs. DeGroat 30 minutes to stack the wood by herself.

Exercise Set 9.5

1. A radical equation is an equation that contains a variable in a radicand.

3. It is necessary to check solutions because they may be extraneous.

5. Yes

7. No; $-\sqrt{64} = -8$

9. Yes

11. No; $-2 \ne \sqrt{-4}$

13.
$$\sqrt{x} = 4$$
$$(\sqrt{x})^2 = (4)^2$$
$$x = 16$$

Check: $\sqrt{x} = 4$
$$\sqrt{16} = 4$$
$$4 = 4 \text{ True}$$

15. $\sqrt{x} = -5$
No solution.

17.
$$\sqrt{x+5} = 3$$
$$(\sqrt{x+5})^2 = 3^2$$
$$x+5 = 9$$
$$x+5-5 = 9-5$$
$$x = 4$$
Check: $\sqrt{x+5} = 3$
$$\sqrt{4+5} = 3$$
$$\sqrt{9} = 3$$
$$3 = 3 \text{ True}$$

19.
$$\sqrt{x} + 5 = -7$$
$$\sqrt{x} = -7-5$$
$$\sqrt{x} = -12$$
No solution.

21.
$$\sqrt{z} - 3 = 7$$
$$\sqrt{z} = 7+3$$
$$\sqrt{z} = 10$$
$$(\sqrt{z})^2 = 10^2$$
$$z = 100$$
Check: $\sqrt{z} - 3 = 7$
$$\sqrt{100} - 3 = 7$$
$$10 - 3 = 7$$
$$7 = 7 \text{ True}$$

23.
$$11 = 6 + \sqrt{x}$$
$$\sqrt{x} = 11 - 6$$
$$\sqrt{x} = 5$$
$$(\sqrt{x})^2 = 5^2$$
$$x = 25$$
Check: $11 = 6 + \sqrt{x}$
$$11 = 6 + \sqrt{25}$$
$$11 = 6 + 5$$
$$11 = 11 \text{ True}$$

25. $7 + \sqrt{n} = 3$
$$\sqrt{n} = 3 - 7$$
$$\sqrt{n} = -4$$
No solution.

27.
$$\sqrt{2x - 5} = x - 4$$
$$(\sqrt{2x - 5})^2 = (x - 4)^2$$
$$2x - 5 = x^2 - 8x + 16$$
$$0 = x^2 - 10x + 21$$
$$0 = (x - 3)(x - 7)$$
$$x - 3 = 0 \text{ or } x - 7 = 0$$
$$x = 3 \qquad x = 7$$
Check:
$x = 3$ | $x = 7$
$\sqrt{2x - 5} = x - 4$ | $\sqrt{2x - 5} = x - 4$
$\sqrt{2(3) - 5} = 3 - 4$ | $\sqrt{2(7) - 5} = 7 - 4$
$\sqrt{1} = -1$ | $\sqrt{9} = 3$
$1 = -1$ False | $3 = 3$ True

The solution is 7; 3 is not a solution.

29.
$$\sqrt{3r - 9} = \sqrt{r + 3}$$
$$(\sqrt{3r - 9})^2 = (\sqrt{r + 3})^2$$
$$3r - 9 = r + 3$$
$$3r - r = 3 + 9$$
$$2r = 12$$
$$r = 6$$
Check: $\sqrt{3r - 9} = \sqrt{r + 3}$
$$\sqrt{3(6) - 9} = \sqrt{6 + 3}$$
$$\sqrt{18 - 9} = \sqrt{9}$$
$$\sqrt{9} = \sqrt{9} \text{ True}$$

31.
$$\sqrt{4x + 4} = \sqrt{6x - 2}$$
$$(\sqrt{4x + 4})^2 = (\sqrt{6x - 2})^2$$
$$4x + 4 = 6x - 2$$
$$4 + 2 = 6x - 4x$$
$$6 = 2x$$
$$x = 3$$
Check: $\sqrt{4 \cdot 3 + 4} = \sqrt{6 \cdot 3 - 2}$
$$\sqrt{16} = \sqrt{16} \text{ True}$$

33.
$$\sqrt{x^2 + 3} = x + 1$$
$$\left(\sqrt{x^2 + 3}\right)^2 = (x + 1)^2$$
$$x^2 + 3 = x^2 + 2x + 1$$
$$2 = 2x$$
$$1 = x$$
Check: $\sqrt{x^2 + 3} = x + 1$
$$\sqrt{1^2 + 3} = 1 + 1$$
$$\sqrt{4} = 2$$
$$2 = 2 \text{ True}$$

35.
$$\sqrt{4x - 5} = \sqrt{x + 9}$$
$$(\sqrt{4x - 5})^2 = (\sqrt{x + 9})^2$$
$$4x - 5 = x + 9$$
$$3x - 5 = 9$$
$$3x = 14$$
$$x = \frac{14}{3}$$
Check: $\sqrt{4x - 5} = \sqrt{x + 9}$
$$\sqrt{4\left(\frac{14}{3}\right) - 5} = \sqrt{\frac{14}{3} + 9}$$
$$\sqrt{\frac{41}{3}} = \sqrt{\frac{41}{3}} \text{ True}$$

37.
$$3\sqrt{x} = \sqrt{x + 8}$$
$$(3\sqrt{x})^2 = (\sqrt{x + 8})^2$$
$$9x = x + 8$$
$$8x = 8$$
$$x = 1$$
Check: $3\sqrt{x} = \sqrt{x + 8}$
$$3\sqrt{1} = \sqrt{1 + 8}$$
$$3(1) = \sqrt{9}$$
$$3 = 3 \text{ True}$$

39.
$$4\sqrt{x} = x + 3$$
$$(4\sqrt{x})^2 = (x+3)^2$$
$$16x = x^2 + 6x + 9$$
$$0 = x^2 - 10x + 9$$
$$0 = (x-9)(x-1)$$
$$x - 9 = 0 \text{ or } x - 1 = 0$$
$$x = 9 \qquad x = 1$$
Check: $\quad x = 9 \qquad\qquad x = 1$
$$4\sqrt{x} = x+3 \qquad 4\sqrt{x} = x+3$$
$$4\sqrt{9} = 9+3 \qquad 4\sqrt{1} = 1+3$$
$$4\cdot3 = 12 \qquad\quad 4\cdot1 = 4$$
$$12 = 12 \text{ True} \qquad 4 = 4 \text{ True}$$

41.
$$\sqrt{3f-4} = 2\sqrt{3f-2}$$
$$(\sqrt{3f-4})^2 = (2\sqrt{3f-2})^2$$
$$3f - 4 = 4(3f-2)$$
$$3f - 4 = 12f - 8$$
$$-4 + 8 = 12f - 3f$$
$$4 = 9f$$
$$\frac{4}{9} = f$$

Check: $\quad \sqrt{3f-4} = 2\sqrt{3f-2}$
$$\sqrt{3\left(\frac{4}{9}\right)-4} = 2\sqrt{3\left(\frac{4}{9}\right)-2}$$
$$\sqrt{\frac{4}{3}-\frac{12}{3}} = 2\sqrt{\frac{4}{3}-\frac{6}{3}}$$
$$\sqrt{-\frac{8}{3}} = 2\sqrt{-\frac{2}{3}} \quad \text{False}$$

$\frac{4}{9}$ is an extraneous root. There is no solution.

43.
$$\sqrt{x^2-4} = x+2$$
$$\left(\sqrt{x^2-4}\right)^2 = (x+2)^2$$
$$x^2 - 4 = x^2 + 4x + 4$$
$$0 = x^2 + 4x + 4 - x^2 + 4$$
$$0 = 4x + 8$$
$$4x = -8$$
$$x = -2$$
Check: $\sqrt{(-2)^2-4} = -2+2$
$$\sqrt{4-4} = 0$$
$$0 = 0 \text{ True}$$

45.
$$3 + \sqrt{3x-5} = x$$
$$\sqrt{3x-5} = x - 3$$
$$(\sqrt{3x-5})^2 = (x-3)^2$$
$$3x - 5 = x^2 - 6x + 9$$
$$0 = x^2 - 6x + 9 - 3x + 5$$
$$0 = x^2 - 9x + 14$$
$$(x-7)(x-2) = 0$$
$$x - 7 = 0 \text{ or } x - 2 = 0$$
$$x = 7 \text{ or } x = 2$$
Check: $\qquad x = 7$
$$3 + \sqrt{3\cdot7-5} = 7$$
$$3 + \sqrt{16} = 7$$
$$3 + 4 = 7$$
$$7 = 7 \text{ True}$$
Check: $\qquad x = 2$
$$3 + \sqrt{3\cdot2-5} = 2$$
$$3 + \sqrt{1} = 2$$
$$4 = 2 \text{ False}$$
The solution is 7, 2 is an extraneous root.

47.
$$\sqrt{8-7x} = x - 2$$
$$(\sqrt{8-7x})^2 = (x-2)^2$$
$$8 - 7x = x^2 - 4x + 4$$
$$0 = x^2 + 3x - 4$$
$$0 = (x+4)(x-1)$$
$$x + 4 = 0 \text{ or } x - 1 = 0$$
$$x = -4 \text{ or } x = 1$$
Check: $\qquad x = -4$
$$\sqrt{8-7x} = x - 2$$
$$\sqrt{8-7(-4)} = -4-2$$
$$\sqrt{8+28} = -6$$
$$\sqrt{36} = -6$$
$$6 = -6 \text{ False}$$
Check: $\qquad x = 1$
$$\sqrt{8-7x} = x - 2$$
$$\sqrt{8-7(1)} = 1-2$$
$$\sqrt{8-7} = -1$$
$$\sqrt{1} = -1$$
$$1 = -1 \text{ False}$$
Both $x = -4$ and $x = -1$ are extraneous roots. There is no solution.

49. $2\sqrt{3b-5} = \sqrt{2b+10}$

$\left(2\sqrt{3b-5}\right)^2 = \left(\sqrt{2b+10}\right)^2$

$4(3b-5) = 2b+10$

$12b-20 = 2b+10$

$10b-20 = 10$

$10b = 30$

$b = 3$

Check: $2\sqrt{3b-5} = \sqrt{2b+10}$

$2\sqrt{3(3)-5} = \sqrt{2(3)+10}$

$2\sqrt{9-5} = \sqrt{6+10}$

$2\sqrt{4} = \sqrt{16}$

$2(2) = 4$

$4 = 4$ True

51. $3\sqrt{2w+3} = 3w$

$\dfrac{1}{3}\left(3\sqrt{2w+3}\right) = \dfrac{1}{3}(3w)$

$\sqrt{2w+3} = w$

$\left(\sqrt{2w+3}\right)^2 = w^2$

$2w+3 = w^2$

$0 = w^2 - 2w - 3$

$0 = (w-3)(w+1)$

$w - 3 = 0$ or $w + 1 = 0$

$w = 3$ $w = -1$

Check: $w = 3$

$3\sqrt{s+4} = s+6$

$3\sqrt{2w+3} = 3w$

$3\sqrt{2(3)+3} = 3(3)$

$3\sqrt{6+3} = 9$

$3\sqrt{9} = 9$

$3(3) = 9$

$9 = 9$ True

$w = -1$

$3\sqrt{2w+3} = 3w$

$3\sqrt{2(-1)+3} = 3(-1)$

$3\sqrt{-2+3} = -3$

$3\sqrt{1} = -3$

$3 = -3$ False

$w = 3$ is a solution and $w = -1$ is an extraneous solution

53. $lw = A$

$\sqrt{w+9}(6) = 24$

$\dfrac{1}{6}\left(6\sqrt{w+9}\right) = \dfrac{1}{6}(24)$

$\sqrt{w+9} = 4$

$\left(\sqrt{w+9}\right)^2 = 4^2$

$w+9 = 16$

$w = 7$

55. $lw = A$

$6.2\sqrt{3n+3} = 37.2$

$\dfrac{6.2\sqrt{3n+3}}{6.2} = \dfrac{37.2}{6.2}$

$\sqrt{3n+3} = 6$

$\left(\sqrt{3n+3}\right)^2 = 6^2$

$3n+3 = 36$

$3n = 33$

$n = 11$

57. $(x+3)^{1/2} = 7$

$\sqrt{x+3} = 7$

$(\sqrt{x+3})^2 = 7^2$

$x+3 = 49$

$x = 46$

Check: $\sqrt{46+3} = 7$

$\sqrt{49} = 7$

$7 = 7$ True

59. $(x-2)^{1/2} = (2x-9)^{1/2}$

$\sqrt{x-2} = \sqrt{2x-9}$

$(\sqrt{x-2})^2 = (\sqrt{2x-9})^2$

$x-2 = 2x-9$

$7 = x$

Check: $\sqrt{7-2} = \sqrt{2\cdot 7 - 9}$

$\sqrt{5} = \sqrt{14-9}$

$\sqrt{5} = \sqrt{5}$ True

61. a. $\left(\sqrt{x}-3\right)\left(\sqrt{x}+3\right) = 40$

$\left(\sqrt{x}\right)\left(\sqrt{x}\right) + 3\sqrt{x} - 3\sqrt{x} - 3(3) = 40$

$x - 9 = 40$

b. $x = 40 + 9$

$x = 49$

Check: $(\sqrt{49} - 3)(\sqrt{49} + 3) = 40$

$(7 - 3)(7 + 3) = 40$

$4 \cdot 10 = 40$

$40 = 40$ True

63. a. $(7 - \sqrt{x})(5 + \sqrt{x}) = 35$

$7 \cdot 5 + 7\sqrt{x} - 5\sqrt{x} + \left(-\sqrt{x}\right)\left(\sqrt{x}\right) = 35$

$35 + 7\sqrt{x} - 5\sqrt{x} - x = 35$

$35 + 2\sqrt{x} - x = 35$

b. $35 + 2\sqrt{x} - x = 35$

$2\sqrt{x} - x = 0$

$2\sqrt{x} = x$

$\left(2\sqrt{x}\right)^2 = x^2$

$4x = x^2$

$0 = x^2 - 4x$

$0 = x(x - 4)$

$x = 0$ or $x = 4$

Check $x = 0$:

$\left(7 - \sqrt{x}\right)\left(5 + \sqrt{x}\right) = 35$

$\left(7 - \sqrt{0}\right)\left(5 + \sqrt{0}\right) = 35$

$(7)(5) = 35$

$35 = 35$ True

Check $x = 4$:

$\left(7 - \sqrt{x}\right)\left(5 + \sqrt{x}\right) = 35$

$\left(7 - \sqrt{4}\right)\left(5 + \sqrt{4}\right) = 35$

$(7 - 2)(5 + 2) = 35$

$(5)(7) = 35$

$35 = 35$ True

65. $n + \sqrt{n} = 2$

$\sqrt{n} = 2 - n$

$\left(\sqrt{n}\right)^2 = (2 - n)^2$

$n^2 = 4 - 4n + n^2$

$4n = 4$

$n = 1$

Check: $1 + \sqrt{1} = 2$

$2 = 2$ True

67. $\sqrt{x} + 2 = \sqrt{x + 16}$

$\left(\sqrt{x} + 2\right)^2 = \left(\sqrt{x + 16}\right)^2$

$x + 4\sqrt{x} + 4 = x + 16$

$4\sqrt{x} = 12$

$\left(4\sqrt{x}\right)^2 = (12)^2$

$16x = 144$

$x = 9$

Check: $\sqrt{x} + 2 = \sqrt{x + 16}$

$\sqrt{9} + 2 = \sqrt{9 + 16}$

$3 + 2 = \sqrt{25}$

$5 = 5$ True

69. $\sqrt{x + 7} = 5 - \sqrt{x - 8}$

$\left(\sqrt{x + 7}\right)^2 = \left(5 - \sqrt{x - 8}\right)^2$

$x + 7 = 25 - 10\sqrt{x - 8} + x - 8$

$10\sqrt{x - 8} = 25 + x - 8 - x - 7$

$10\sqrt{x - 8} = 10$

$\sqrt{x - 8} = 1$

$\left(\sqrt{x - 8}\right)^2 = 1^2$

$x - 8 = 1$

$x = 9$

Check: $\sqrt{x + 7} = 5 - \sqrt{x - 8}$

$\sqrt{9 + 7} = 5 - \sqrt{9 - 8}$

$\sqrt{16} = 5 - \sqrt{1}$

$4 = 5 - 1$

$4 = 4$ True

73.

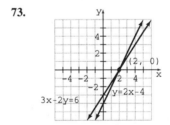

The solution is $(2, 0)$.

74. Substitute $2x - 4$ for y in the first equation.

$3x - 2y = 6$

$3x - 2(2x - 4) = 6$

$3x - 4x + 8 = 6$

$-x + 8 = 6$

$-x = -2$

$x = 2$

Substitute 2 for x in the second equation.

$y = 2x - 4$

$y = 2(2) - 4 = 4 - 4 = 0$

The solution is $(2, 0)$.

75. Align the x- and y-terms on the left side of the equation.
$$3x - 2y = 6$$
$$-2x + y = -4$$
Multiply the second equation by 2.
$$2[-2x + y = -4]$$
gives
$$\begin{aligned} 3x - 2y &= 6 \\ -4x + 2y &= -8 \\ \hline -x &= -2 \\ x &= 2 \end{aligned}$$
Substitute 2 for x in the second equation.
$$y = 2x - 4$$
$$y = 2(2) - 4 = 4 - 4 = 0$$
The solution is (2, 0).

76. Let b = the speed of the ferry in still water, c = speed of the current.
Speed of ferry with current = 18 mph.
Speed of ferry against current = 14 mph.
$$b + c = 18$$
$$\begin{aligned} b - c &= 14 \\ \hline 2b &= 32 \\ b &= 16 \end{aligned}$$
Substitute 16 for b in the first equation.
$$b + c = 18$$
$$16 + c = 18$$
$$c = 2$$
Speed of ferry in still water = 16 mph, speed of the current = 2 mph.

Exercise Set 9.6

1. A right triangle is a triangle that contains a 90° angle.

3. No; only with right triangles.

5. They represent the two points in the coordinate plane that you are trying to find the distance between.

7. $\sqrt{(0-0)^2 + [-10-(-4)]^2} = \sqrt{0 + (-6)^2}$
$$= \sqrt{36}$$
$$= 6$$

9. $a^2 + b^2 = c^2$
$$x^2 + 4^2 = 7^2$$
$$x^2 + 16 = 49$$
$$x^2 = 33$$
$$x = \sqrt{33} \approx 5.74$$

11. $a^2 + b^2 = c^2$
$$(11)^2 + 7^2 = x^2$$
$$121 + 49 = x^2$$
$$170 = x^2$$
$$x = \sqrt{170} \approx 13.04$$

13. $a^2 + b^2 = c^2$
$$12^2 + (\sqrt{5})^2 = y^2$$
$$144 + 5 = y^2$$
$$149 = y^2$$
$$y = \sqrt{149} \approx 12.21$$

15. $a^2 + b^2 = c^2$
$$8^2 + (\sqrt{3})^2 = x^2$$
$$64 + 3 = x^2$$
$$67 = x^2$$
$$x = \sqrt{67} \approx 8.19$$

17. $a^2 + b^2 = c^2$
$$(\sqrt{6})^2 + 14^2 = x^2$$
$$6 + 196 = x^2$$
$$202 = x^2$$
$$x = \sqrt{202} \approx 14.21$$

19. $a^2 + b^2 = c^2$
$$4^2 + x^2 = 14^2$$
$$16 + x^2 = 196$$
$$x^2 = 180$$
$$x = \sqrt{180} \approx 13.42$$

21. $d = \sqrt{(2-7)^2 + (9-6)^2}$
$$= \sqrt{25 + 9}$$
$$= \sqrt{34}$$
$$\approx 5.83$$

23. $d = \sqrt{[4-(-8)]^2 + (11-4)^2}$
$$= \sqrt{(12)^2 + 7^2}$$
$$= \sqrt{193}$$
$$\approx 13.89$$

25.
$$a^2 + b^2 = c^2$$
$$(120)^2 + (53.3)^2 = x^2$$
$$14,400 + 2840.89 = x^2$$
$$x^2 = 17,240.89$$
$$x = \sqrt{17,240.89}$$
The diagonal is $\sqrt{17,240.89} \approx 131.30$ yards.

27.
$$a^2 + b^2 = c^2$$
$$2^2 + x^2 = 8^2$$
$$4 + x^2 = 64$$
$$x^2 = 60$$
$$x = \sqrt{60}$$
The top of the ladder will be $\sqrt{60} \approx 7.75$ meters high.

29.
$$A = s^2$$
$$s^2 = 256$$
$$s^2 = (16)^2$$
$$(s^2)^{1/2} = [(16)^2]^{1/2}$$
$$s = 16$$
The sides are 16 feet long.

31.
$$A = \pi r^2$$
$$80 = (3.14)r^2$$
$$\frac{80}{3.14} = r^2$$
$$r^2 \approx 25.48$$
$$r \approx \sqrt{25.48}$$
The radius of the circle is about $\sqrt{25.48} \approx 5.05$ feet .

33.
$$a^2 + b^2 = c^2$$
$$(90)^2 + (90)^2 = c^2$$
$$8100 + 8100 = c^2$$
$$c^2 = 16,200$$
$$c = \sqrt{16,200}$$
The distance is $\sqrt{16,200} \approx 127.28$ feet.

35.
$$a^2 + b^2 = c^2$$
$$(24)^2 + (16)^2 = x^2$$
$$576 + 256 = x^2$$
$$x^2 = 832$$
$$x = \sqrt{832} \approx 28.84$$
The length of the diagonal is about 28.84 inches.

37.
$$T = 2\pi\sqrt{\frac{L}{32}}$$
$$43 \text{ in. } = \frac{43}{12}\text{ ft}$$
$$T = 2 \cdot 3.14\sqrt{\frac{(\frac{43}{12})}{32}}$$
$$\approx 6.28\sqrt{0.11}$$
$$\approx 2.08 \text{ sec}$$

39.
$$T = 2\pi\sqrt{\frac{L}{32}}$$
$$= 2 \cdot 3.14\sqrt{\frac{61.6}{32}}$$
$$= 6.28\sqrt{1.925}$$
$$\approx 8.71 \text{ sec}$$

41.
$$N = 0.2(\sqrt{R})^3$$
$$N = 0.2(\sqrt{149.4})^3 \approx 365 \text{ Earth days}$$

43.
$$v = \sqrt{2gR}$$
$$v = \sqrt{2 \cdot 9.75(6,370,000)} \approx 11,145.18 \text{ m / sec}$$

45.
$$R = \sqrt{F_1^2 + F_2^2}$$
$$R = \sqrt{(600)^2 + (800)^2}$$
$$R = \sqrt{360,000 + 640,000}$$
$$R = \sqrt{1,000,000} = 1000$$
The resulting force is 1000 pounds.

47. The gravity on the moon is
$$\frac{1}{6}g = \frac{32}{6}$$
$$v = \sqrt{2\left(\frac{32}{6}\right) \cdot 100}$$
$$\approx \sqrt{1066.666}$$
$$\approx 32.66 \text{ ft / sec}$$

49.
$$d = \sqrt{a^2 + b^2 + c^2}$$
$$= \sqrt{(24)^2 + (16)^2 + (10)^2}$$
$$= \sqrt{932}$$
$$\approx 30.53 \text{ in.}$$

50.
$$2(x + 3) < 4x - 6$$
$$2x + 6 < 4x - 6$$
$$6 + 6 < 4x - 2x$$
$$12 < 2x$$
$$6 < x$$
$$x > 6$$

51. $(4x^{-4}y^3)^{-1} = (4y^3)^{-1}(x^{-4})^{-1}$
$$= (4y^3)^{-1}x^4$$
$$= \frac{x^4}{4y^3}$$

52. $3x + 4y = 12$
$$\frac{1}{2}x - 2y = 8$$

Multiply the second equation by 2.
$$2\left[\frac{1}{2}x - 2y = 8\right]$$
gives
$$\begin{array}{r} 3x + 4y = 12 \\ + \quad x - 4y = 16 \\ \hline 4x \qquad = 28 \\ x = 7 \end{array}$$

Substitute 7 for x in the first equation.
$$3x + 4y = 12$$
$$3(7) + 4y = 12$$
$$21 + 4y = 12$$
$$4y = -9$$
$$y = -\frac{9}{4}$$

The solution is $\left(7, -\frac{9}{4}\right)$.

53. $5 + \dfrac{6}{x} = \dfrac{2}{3x}$
$$\frac{5x+6}{x} = \frac{2}{3x}$$
$$3x(5x+6) = 2x$$
$$15x^2 + 18x = 2x$$
$$15x^2 + 16x = 0$$
$$x(15x+16) = 0$$
$$x = 0 \text{ or } 15x + 16 = 0$$
$$x = -\frac{16}{15}$$

The solution is $x = -\dfrac{16}{15}$ since x cannot be 0.

Exercise Set 9.7

1. a.   The square root of 9

b.   The cube root of 9

c.   The fourth root of 9

3. Write the radicand as a product of a perfect cube and another number.

5. a.   Answers will vary.

b. $\sqrt[3]{y^7} = y^{7/3}$

7. Yes, because any real positive number raised to an odd power will be positive.

9. $\sqrt[3]{8} = 2$ since $2^3 = 8$

11. $\sqrt[3]{-27} = -3$ since $(-3)^3 = -27$

13. $\sqrt[4]{16} = 2$ since $2^4 = 16$

15. $\sqrt[4]{81} = 3$ since $3^4 = 81$

17. $\sqrt[3]{-1} = -1$ since $(-1)^3 = -1$

19. $\sqrt[3]{-1000} = -10$ since $(-10)^3 = -1000$

21. $\sqrt[3]{40} = \sqrt[3]{8 \cdot 5} = \sqrt[3]{8}\sqrt[3]{5} = 2\sqrt[3]{5}$

23. $\sqrt[3]{16} = \sqrt[3]{8 \cdot 2} = \sqrt[3]{8}\sqrt[3]{2} = 2\sqrt[3]{2}$

25. $\sqrt[3]{108} = \sqrt[3]{27 \cdot 4} = \sqrt[3]{27}\sqrt[3]{4} = 3\sqrt[3]{4}$

27. $\sqrt[4]{32} = \sqrt[4]{16 \cdot 2} = \sqrt[4]{16}\sqrt[4]{2} = 2\sqrt[4]{2}$

29. $\sqrt[4]{1250} = \sqrt[4]{625 \cdot 2} = \sqrt[4]{625}\sqrt[4]{2} = 5\sqrt[4]{2}$

31. $\sqrt[3]{x^7} = x^{7/3}$

33. $\sqrt[5]{a^2} = a^{2/5}$

35. $\sqrt[4]{y^{15}} = y^{15/4}$

37. $\sqrt[3]{y^8} = y^{8/3}$

39. $\sqrt[4]{x^4} = x^{4/4} = x$

41. $\sqrt[3]{y^{21}} = y^{21/3} = y^7$

43. $\sqrt[3]{m^{18}} = m^{18/3} = m^6$

45. $\sqrt[4]{a^{60}} = a^{60/4} = a^{15}$

47. $\sqrt[3]{x^{15}} = x^{15/3} = x^5$

49. $\sqrt[4]{m^2} = m^{2/4} = m^{1/2} = \sqrt{m}$

51. $\sqrt[6]{t^3} = t^{3/6} = t^{1/2} = \sqrt{t}$

53. $\sqrt[9]{x^3} = x^{3/9} = x^{1/2} = \sqrt{x}$

55. $\sqrt[8]{w^4} = w^{4/8} = w^{1/2} = \sqrt{w}$

57. $\sqrt[6]{x^4} = x^{4/6} = x^{2/3} = \sqrt[3]{x^2}$

59. $\sqrt[8]{z^6} = z^{6/8} = z^{3/4} = \sqrt[4]{z^3}$

61. $27^{2/3} = (\sqrt[3]{27})^2 = 3^2 = 9$

63. $216^{2/3} = (\sqrt[3]{216})^2 = 6^2 = 36$

65. $1^{2/3} = (\sqrt[3]{1})^2 = 1^2 = 1$

67. $9^{3/2} = (\sqrt[2]{9})^3 = 3^3 = 27$

69. $27^{4/3} = (\sqrt[3]{27})^4 = 3^4 = 81$

71. $256^{5/4} = (\sqrt[4]{256})^5 = 4^5 = 1024$

73. $8^{-1/3} = \dfrac{1}{8^{1/3}} = \dfrac{1}{\sqrt[3]{8}} = \dfrac{1}{2}$

75. $27^{-2/3} = \dfrac{1}{27^{2/3}} = \dfrac{1}{(\sqrt[3]{27})^2} = \dfrac{1}{3^2} = \dfrac{1}{9}$

77. $\sqrt[4]{4^2} = 4^{2/4} = 4^{1/2} = \sqrt{4} = 2$

79. $\sqrt[6]{9^3} = 9^{3/6} = 9^{1/2} = \sqrt{9} = 3$

81. $\sqrt[8]{36^4} = 36^{4/8} = 36^{1/2} = \sqrt{36} = 6$

83. $\sqrt[4]{5^8} = 5^{8/4} = 5^2 = 25$

85. $\sqrt[4]{2^{12}} = 2^{12/4} = 2^3 = 8$

87. $\sqrt[5]{4^{10}} = 4^{10/5} = 4^2 = 16$

89. $\sqrt[5]{6^{15}} = 6^{15/5} = 6^3 = 216$

91. $\sqrt[4]{t^2} \cdot \sqrt[4]{t^2} = t^{2/4} \cdot t^{2/4} = t^{1/2} \cdot t^{1/2} = t$

93. $(\sqrt[3]{r^4})^6 = (r^{4/3})^6 = r^{(4/3)\cdot 6} = r^{24/3} = r^8$

95. $\left(\sqrt[4]{a^2}\right)^4 = (a^{2/4})^4 = (a^{1/2})^4 = a^2$

97. For $x = 8$, $(\sqrt[3]{x})^2 = (\sqrt[3]{8})^2 = 2^2 = 4$

For $x = 8$, $\left(\sqrt[3]{x^2}\right) = \left(\sqrt[3]{8^2}\right) = \sqrt[3]{64} = 4$

99. $\sqrt[3]{5^2}$

101. $\sqrt[3]{6^2}$

103. $\sqrt[4]{5^3}$

105. The missing number is 3 since
$\sqrt[3]{5^2} \cdot \sqrt[3]{5} = \sqrt[3]{5^3} = 5$.

107. The missing number is 1 since
$\sqrt[3]{6^1} \cdot \sqrt[3]{6^2} = \sqrt[3]{6^3}$.

109. $\sqrt[3]{xy} \cdot \sqrt[3]{x^2 y^2} = \sqrt[3]{x^3 y^3} = xy$

111. $\sqrt[4]{32} - \sqrt[4]{2} = \sqrt[4]{16 \cdot 2} - \sqrt[4]{2}$
$= \sqrt[4]{16} \cdot \sqrt[4]{2} - \sqrt[4]{2}$
$= \sqrt[4]{2}(\sqrt[4]{16} - 1)$
$= \sqrt[4]{2}(2 - 1)$
$= \sqrt[4]{2}$

113. a. When multiplying $\sqrt[3]{2} \cdot \sqrt[3]{2^2}$, the radicand
becomes a perfect cube.
$\sqrt[3]{2} \cdot \sqrt[3]{2^2} = \sqrt[3]{2^3} = \sqrt[3]{8} = 2$

b. $\dfrac{1}{\sqrt[3]{2}} \cdot \dfrac{\sqrt[3]{2^2}}{\sqrt[3]{2^2}} = \dfrac{\sqrt[3]{2^2}}{\sqrt[3]{2^8}} = \dfrac{\sqrt[3]{2^2}}{\sqrt[3]{8}} = \dfrac{\sqrt[3]{4}}{2}$

114. $-x^2 + 4xy - 6 = (-2)^2 + 4(2)(-4) - 6$
$= -4 - 32 - 6$
$= -42$

115. $3x^2 - 28x + 32 = 3x^2 - 24x - 4x + 32$
$= 3x(x - 8) - 4(x - 8)$
$= (3x - 4)(x - 8)$

116. Put $2x - 3y = 4$ in slope–intercept form.
$2x - 3y = 4$
$-3y = -2x + 4$
$y = \dfrac{-2}{-3}x + \dfrac{4}{-3}$
$y = \dfrac{2}{3}x - \dfrac{4}{3}$

Thus, the slope is $\dfrac{2}{3}$ and the y-intercept is $-\dfrac{4}{3}$.

117. $\sqrt{\dfrac{64x^3y^7}{2x^4}} = \sqrt{\dfrac{32y^7}{x}}$

$\qquad = \dfrac{\sqrt{32y^7}}{\sqrt{x}}$

$\qquad = \dfrac{\sqrt{16y^6}\sqrt{2y}}{\sqrt{x}}$

$\qquad = \dfrac{4y^3\sqrt{2y}}{\sqrt{x}}$

$\qquad = \dfrac{4y^3\sqrt{2y}}{\sqrt{x}} \cdot \dfrac{\sqrt{x}}{\sqrt{x}}$

$\qquad = \dfrac{4y^3\sqrt{2xy}}{x}$

Review Exercises

1. $\sqrt{81} = 9$ since $9^2 = 81$

2. $\sqrt{49} = 7$ since $7^2 = 49$

3. $-\sqrt{64} = -8$ since $\sqrt{64} = 8 \;\; (8^2 = 64)$

4. $\sqrt{5} = 5^{1/2}$

5. $\sqrt{26x} = (26x)^{1/2}$

6. $\sqrt{13x^2y} = (13x^2y)^{1/2}$

7. $\sqrt{32} = \sqrt{16 \cdot 2} = \sqrt{16}\sqrt{2} = 4\sqrt{2}$

8. $\sqrt{44} = \sqrt{4 \cdot 11} = \sqrt{4}\sqrt{11} = 2\sqrt{11}$

9. $\sqrt{27x^7y^4} = \sqrt{9x^6y^4}\sqrt{3x} = 3x^3y^2\sqrt{3x}$

10. $\sqrt{125x^4y^6} = \sqrt{25x^4y^6}\sqrt{5} = 5x^2y^3\sqrt{5}$

11. $\sqrt{60ab^5c^4} = \sqrt{4b^4c^4}\sqrt{15ab} = 2b^2c^2\sqrt{15ab}$

12. $\sqrt{72a^2b^2c^7} = \sqrt{36a^2b^2c^6}\sqrt{2c} = 6abc^3\sqrt{2c}$

13. $\sqrt{72}\sqrt{20} = \sqrt{72 \cdot 20}$

$\qquad = \sqrt{1440}$

$\qquad = \sqrt{144 \cdot 10}$

$\qquad = 12\sqrt{10}$

14. $\sqrt{7y}\sqrt{7y} = \sqrt{49y^2} = 7y$

15. $\sqrt{18x} \cdot \sqrt{2xy} = \sqrt{36x^2y} = \sqrt{36x^2}\sqrt{y} = 6x\sqrt{y}$

16. $\sqrt{25x^2y} \cdot \sqrt{3y} = \sqrt{75x^2y^2}$

$\qquad = \sqrt{25x^2y^2}\sqrt{3}$

$\qquad = 5xy\sqrt{3}$

17. $\sqrt{12a^3b^4} \cdot \sqrt{3b^4} = \sqrt{36a^3b^8}$

$\qquad = \sqrt{36a^2b^8}\sqrt{a}$

$\qquad = 6ab^4\sqrt{a}$

18. $\sqrt{5ab^3} \cdot \sqrt{20ab^4} = \sqrt{100a^2b^7}$

$\qquad = \sqrt{100a^2b^6}\sqrt{b}$

$\qquad = 10ab^3\sqrt{b}$

19. $5\sqrt{3} - 4\sqrt{3} = (5-4)\sqrt{3} = \sqrt{3}$

20. $4\sqrt{5} - 7\sqrt{5} - 3\sqrt{5} = (4-7-3)\sqrt{5} = -6\sqrt{5}$

21. $3\sqrt{x} - 5\sqrt{x} = (3-5)\sqrt{x} = -2\sqrt{x}$

22. $\sqrt{k} + 3\sqrt{k} - 4\sqrt{k} = (1+3-4)\sqrt{k} = 0\sqrt{k} = 0$

23. $\sqrt{18} - \sqrt{27} = \sqrt{9 \cdot 2} - \sqrt{9 \cdot 3}$

$\qquad = \sqrt{9}\sqrt{2} - \sqrt{9}\sqrt{3}$

$\qquad = 3\sqrt{2} - 3\sqrt{3}$

24. $7\sqrt{40} - 2\sqrt{10} = 7\sqrt{4}\sqrt{10} - 2\sqrt{10}$

$\qquad = 7 \cdot 2\sqrt{10} - 2\sqrt{10}$

$\qquad = 14\sqrt{10} - 2\sqrt{10}$

$\qquad = (14-2)\sqrt{10}$

$\qquad = 12\sqrt{10}$

25. $2\sqrt{98} - 4\sqrt{72} = 2\sqrt{49}\sqrt{2} - 4\sqrt{36}\sqrt{2}$

$\qquad = 2 \cdot 7\sqrt{2} - 4 \cdot 6\sqrt{2}$

$\qquad = 14\sqrt{2} - 24\sqrt{2}$

$\qquad = (14-24)\sqrt{2}$

$\qquad = -10\sqrt{2}$

26. $7\sqrt{50} + 2\sqrt{18} - 4\sqrt{32}$

$\qquad = 7\sqrt{25}\sqrt{2} + 2\sqrt{9}\sqrt{2} - 4\sqrt{16}\sqrt{2}$

$\qquad = 7 \cdot 5\sqrt{2} + 2 \cdot 3\sqrt{2} - 4 \cdot 4\sqrt{2}$

$\qquad = (35+6-16)\sqrt{2}$

$\qquad = 25\sqrt{2}$

27. $\sqrt{5}\left(2+\sqrt{5}\right) = \sqrt{5}(2) + \sqrt{5}\left(\sqrt{5}\right)$

$$= 2\sqrt{5} + \sqrt{25}$$

$$= 2\sqrt{5} + 5$$

28. $\sqrt{2}\left(\sqrt{2}+3\right) = \sqrt{2}\left(\sqrt{2}\right) + \sqrt{2}(3)$

$$= \sqrt{4} + 3\sqrt{2}$$

$$= 2 + 3\sqrt{2}$$

29. $\sqrt{y}\left(x - 2\sqrt{y}\right) = \sqrt{y}(x) + \sqrt{y}\left(-2\sqrt{y}\right)$

$$= x\sqrt{y} - 2\sqrt{y^2}$$

$$= x\sqrt{y} - 2y$$

30. $5a\left(3a + \sqrt{2a}\right) = 5a(3a) + 5a\left(\sqrt{2a}\right)$

$$= 15a^2 + 5a\sqrt{2a}$$

31. $\left(\sqrt{3}-2\right)\left(\sqrt{3}+2\right) = \sqrt{3}\left(\sqrt{3}\right) + 2\sqrt{3} - 2\sqrt{3} - 2(2)$

$$= \sqrt{9} - 4$$

$$= 3 - 4$$

$$= -1$$

32. $\left(9-\sqrt{3}\right)\left(9+\sqrt{3}\right) = 9(9) + 9\sqrt{3} - 9\sqrt{3} - \sqrt{3}\left(\sqrt{3}\right)$

$$= 81 - \sqrt{9}$$

$$= 81 - 3$$

$$= 78$$

33. $\left(x - 2\sqrt{y}\right)\left(x + 2\sqrt{y}\right)$

$$= x(x) + x\left(2\sqrt{y}\right) - 2\sqrt{y}(x) - 2\sqrt{y}\left(2\sqrt{y}\right)$$

$$= x^2 - 4\sqrt{y^2}$$

$$= x^2 - 4y$$

34. $\left(\sqrt{c} - 2\sqrt{d}\right)\left(\sqrt{c} + 2\sqrt{d}\right)$

$$= \sqrt{c}\left(\sqrt{c}\right) + \sqrt{c}\left(2\sqrt{d}\right) - 2\sqrt{d}\left(\sqrt{c}\right) - 2\sqrt{d}\left(2\sqrt{d}\right)$$

$$= \sqrt{c^2} - 4\sqrt{d^2}$$

$$= c - 4d$$

35. $\left(m + 2\sqrt{r}\right)\left(m - 5\sqrt{r}\right)$

$$= m(m) + m\left(-5\sqrt{r}\right) + 2\sqrt{r}(m) + 2\sqrt{r}\left(-5\sqrt{r}\right)$$

$$= m^2 - 5m\sqrt{r} + 2m\sqrt{r} - 10\sqrt{r^2}$$

$$= m^2 + (-5 + 2)m\sqrt{r} - 10r$$

$$= m^2 - 3m\sqrt{r} - 10r$$

36. $\left(\sqrt{t} + 2s\right)\left(3\sqrt{t} - s\right)$

$$= \sqrt{t}\left(3\sqrt{t}\right) + \sqrt{t}(-s) + 2s\left(3\sqrt{t}\right) + 2s(-s)$$

$$= 3\sqrt{t^2} - s\sqrt{t} + 6s\sqrt{t} - 2s^2$$

$$= 3t + (-1 + 6)s\sqrt{t} - 2s^2$$

$$= 3t + 5s\sqrt{t} - 2s^2$$

37. $\left(\sqrt{5m} + 2\sqrt{n}\right)\left(3\sqrt{5m} - \sqrt{n}\right)$

$$= \sqrt{5m}\left(3\sqrt{5m}\right) + \sqrt{5m}\left(-\sqrt{n}\right) + 2\sqrt{n}\left(3\sqrt{5m}\right) + 2\sqrt{n}\left(-\sqrt{n}\right)$$

$$= 3\sqrt{25m^2} - \sqrt{5mn} + 6\sqrt{5mn} - 2\sqrt{n^2}$$

$$= 3(5m) + (-1 + 6)\sqrt{5mn} - 2n$$

$$= 15m + 5\sqrt{5mn} - 2n$$

38. $\left(\sqrt{7} - 3\sqrt{p}\right)\left(2\sqrt{7} - 3\sqrt{p}\right)$

$$= \sqrt{7}\left(2\sqrt{7}\right) + \sqrt{7}\left(-3\sqrt{p}\right) - 3\sqrt{p}\left(2\sqrt{7}\right) - 3\sqrt{p}\left(-3\sqrt{p}\right)$$

$$= 2\sqrt{49} - 3\sqrt{7p} - 6\sqrt{7p} + 9\sqrt{p^2}$$

$$= 2(7) + (-3 - 6)\sqrt{7p} + 9p$$

$$= 14 - 9\sqrt{7p} + 9p$$

39. $\dfrac{\sqrt{32}}{\sqrt{2}} = \sqrt{\dfrac{32}{2}} = \sqrt{16} = 4$

40. $\sqrt{\dfrac{10}{490}} = \sqrt{\dfrac{1}{49}} = \dfrac{\sqrt{1}}{\sqrt{49}} = \dfrac{1}{7}$

41. $\sqrt{\dfrac{7}{28}} = \sqrt{\dfrac{1}{4}} = \dfrac{\sqrt{1}}{\sqrt{4}} = \dfrac{1}{2}$

42. $\dfrac{3}{\sqrt{5}} = \dfrac{3}{\sqrt{5}} \cdot \dfrac{\sqrt{5}}{\sqrt{5}} = \dfrac{3\sqrt{5}}{5}$

43. $\sqrt{\dfrac{n}{7}} = \dfrac{\sqrt{n}}{\sqrt{7}} = \dfrac{\sqrt{n}}{\sqrt{7}} \cdot \dfrac{\sqrt{7}}{\sqrt{7}} = \dfrac{\sqrt{7n}}{7}$

44. $\sqrt{\dfrac{5a}{12}} = \dfrac{\sqrt{5a}}{\sqrt{12}}$

$\phantom{\sqrt{\dfrac{5a}{12}}} = \dfrac{\sqrt{5a}}{\sqrt{4}\sqrt{3}}$

$\phantom{\sqrt{\dfrac{5a}{12}}} = \dfrac{\sqrt{5a}}{2\sqrt{3}}$

$\phantom{\sqrt{\dfrac{5a}{12}}} = \dfrac{\sqrt{5a}}{2\sqrt{3}} \cdot \dfrac{\sqrt{3}}{\sqrt{3}}$

$\phantom{\sqrt{\dfrac{5a}{12}}} = \dfrac{\sqrt{15a}}{6}$

45. $\sqrt{\dfrac{x^2}{3}} = \dfrac{\sqrt{x^2}}{\sqrt{3}} = \dfrac{x}{\sqrt{3}} = \dfrac{x}{\sqrt{3}} \cdot \dfrac{\sqrt{3}}{\sqrt{3}} = \dfrac{x\sqrt{3}}{3}$

46. $\sqrt{\dfrac{z^4}{8}} = \dfrac{\sqrt{z^4}}{\sqrt{8}}$

$\phantom{\sqrt{\dfrac{z^4}{8}}} = \dfrac{z^2}{\sqrt{4}\sqrt{2}}$

$\phantom{\sqrt{\dfrac{z^4}{8}}} = \dfrac{z^2}{2\sqrt{2}}$

$\phantom{\sqrt{\dfrac{z^4}{8}}} = \dfrac{z^2}{2\sqrt{2}} \cdot \dfrac{\sqrt{2}}{\sqrt{2}}$

$\phantom{\sqrt{\dfrac{z^4}{8}}} = \dfrac{z^2\sqrt{2}}{4}$

47. $\sqrt{\dfrac{21x^3 y^7}{3x^3 y^3}} = \sqrt{7y^4} = \sqrt{7}\sqrt{y^4} = y^2\sqrt{7}$

48. $\sqrt{\dfrac{30x^4 y}{15x^2 y^4}} = \sqrt{\dfrac{2x^2}{y^3}}$

$\phantom{\sqrt{\dfrac{30x^4 y}{15x^2 y^4}}} = \dfrac{\sqrt{2x^2}}{\sqrt{y^3}}$

$\phantom{\sqrt{\dfrac{30x^4 y}{15x^2 y^4}}} = \dfrac{\sqrt{2}\sqrt{x^2}}{\sqrt{y^2}\sqrt{y}}$

$\phantom{\sqrt{\dfrac{30x^4 y}{15x^2 y^4}}} = \dfrac{x\sqrt{2}}{y\sqrt{y}}$

$\phantom{\sqrt{\dfrac{30x^4 y}{15x^2 y^4}}} = \dfrac{x\sqrt{2}}{y\sqrt{y}} \cdot \dfrac{\sqrt{y}}{\sqrt{y}}$

$\phantom{\sqrt{\dfrac{30x^4 y}{15x^2 y^4}}} = \dfrac{x\sqrt{2y}}{y^2}$

49. $\dfrac{\sqrt{60}}{\sqrt{27a^3 b^2}} = \sqrt{\dfrac{60}{27a^3 b^2}}$

$\phantom{\dfrac{\sqrt{60}}{\sqrt{27a^3 b^2}}} = \sqrt{\dfrac{20}{9a^3 b^2}}$

$\phantom{\dfrac{\sqrt{60}}{\sqrt{27a^3 b^2}}} = \dfrac{\sqrt{20}}{\sqrt{9a^3 b^2}}$

$\phantom{\dfrac{\sqrt{60}}{\sqrt{27a^3 b^2}}} = \dfrac{\sqrt{4}\sqrt{5}}{\sqrt{9a^2 b^2}\sqrt{a}}$

$\phantom{\dfrac{\sqrt{60}}{\sqrt{27a^3 b^2}}} = \dfrac{2\sqrt{5}}{3ab\sqrt{a}}$

$\phantom{\dfrac{\sqrt{60}}{\sqrt{27a^3 b^2}}} = \dfrac{2\sqrt{5}}{3ab\sqrt{a}} \cdot \dfrac{\sqrt{a}}{\sqrt{a}}$

$\phantom{\dfrac{\sqrt{60}}{\sqrt{27a^3 b^2}}} = \dfrac{2\sqrt{5a}}{3a^2 b}$

50. $\dfrac{\sqrt{2a^4 bc^4}}{\sqrt{7a^5 bc^2}} = \sqrt{\dfrac{2a^4 bc^4}{7a^5 bc^2}}$

$\phantom{\dfrac{\sqrt{2a^4 bc^4}}{\sqrt{7a^5 bc^2}}} = \sqrt{\dfrac{2c^2}{7a}}$

$\phantom{\dfrac{\sqrt{2a^4 bc^4}}{\sqrt{7a^5 bc^2}}} = \dfrac{\sqrt{2c^2}}{\sqrt{7a}}$

$\phantom{\dfrac{\sqrt{2a^4 bc^4}}{\sqrt{7a^5 bc^2}}} = \dfrac{c\sqrt{2}}{\sqrt{7a}}$

$\phantom{\dfrac{\sqrt{2a^4 bc^4}}{\sqrt{7a^5 bc^2}}} = \dfrac{c\sqrt{2}}{\sqrt{7a}} \cdot \dfrac{\sqrt{7a}}{\sqrt{7a}}$

$\phantom{\dfrac{\sqrt{2a^4 bc^4}}{\sqrt{7a^5 bc^2}}} = \dfrac{c\sqrt{14a}}{7a}$

51. $\dfrac{3}{1-\sqrt{6}} = \dfrac{3}{1-\sqrt{6}} \cdot \dfrac{1+\sqrt{6}}{1+\sqrt{6}}$

$\phantom{\dfrac{3}{1-\sqrt{6}}} = \dfrac{3(1+\sqrt{6})}{1-6}$

$\phantom{\dfrac{3}{1-\sqrt{6}}} = \dfrac{3(1+\sqrt{6})}{-5}$

$\phantom{\dfrac{3}{1-\sqrt{6}}} = \dfrac{3+3\sqrt{6}}{-5}$

$\phantom{\dfrac{3}{1-\sqrt{6}}} = \dfrac{(-1)\left(3+3\sqrt{6}\right)}{(-1)(-5)}$

$\phantom{\dfrac{3}{1-\sqrt{6}}} = \dfrac{-3-3\sqrt{6}}{5}$

52. $\dfrac{5}{3-\sqrt{6}} = \dfrac{5}{3-\sqrt{6}} \cdot \dfrac{3+\sqrt{6}}{3+\sqrt{6}}$

$\qquad = \dfrac{5(3+\sqrt{6})}{9-6}$

$\qquad = \dfrac{15+5\sqrt{6}}{3}$

53. $\dfrac{\sqrt{2}}{2+\sqrt{y}} = \dfrac{\sqrt{2}}{2+\sqrt{y}} \cdot \dfrac{2-\sqrt{y}}{2-\sqrt{y}}$

$\qquad = \dfrac{\sqrt{2}(2-\sqrt{y})}{4-y}$

$\qquad = \dfrac{2\sqrt{2}-\sqrt{2y}}{4-y}$

54. $\dfrac{2}{\sqrt{x}-5} = \dfrac{2}{\sqrt{x}-5} \cdot \dfrac{\sqrt{x}+5}{\sqrt{x}+5}$

$\qquad = \dfrac{2(\sqrt{x}+5)}{x-25}$

$\qquad = \dfrac{2\sqrt{x}+10}{x-25}$

55. $\dfrac{\sqrt{5}}{\sqrt{x}+\sqrt{3}} = \dfrac{\sqrt{5}}{\sqrt{x}+\sqrt{3}} \cdot \dfrac{\sqrt{x}-\sqrt{3}}{\sqrt{x}-\sqrt{3}}$

$\qquad = \dfrac{\sqrt{5}(\sqrt{x}-\sqrt{3})}{x-3}$

$\qquad = \dfrac{\sqrt{5x}-\sqrt{15}}{x-3}$

56. $\dfrac{\sqrt{7}}{\sqrt{5}-x} = \dfrac{\sqrt{7}}{\sqrt{5}-x} \cdot \dfrac{\sqrt{5}+x}{\sqrt{5}+x}$

$\qquad = \dfrac{\sqrt{7}\left(\sqrt{5}+x\right)}{5-x^2}$

$\qquad = \dfrac{\sqrt{35}+x\sqrt{7}}{5-x^2}$

57. $\sqrt{x} = 36$

$\qquad (\sqrt{x})^2 = 36^2$

$\qquad x = 1296$

$\quad$ Check: $\quad \sqrt{x} = 36$

$\qquad\qquad \sqrt{1296} = 36$

$\qquad\qquad\quad 36 = 36$ True

58. $\sqrt{g} = -5$

No solution

59. $\sqrt{h-5} = 3$

$\qquad (\sqrt{h-5})^2 = 3^2$

$\qquad\quad h-5 = 9$

$\qquad\qquad h = 14$

$\quad$ Check: $\sqrt{14-5} = 3$

$\qquad\qquad\quad \sqrt{9} = 3$

$\qquad\qquad\quad 3 = 3$ True

60. $\sqrt{3x+1} = 5$

$\qquad (\sqrt{3x+1})^2 = 5^2$

$\qquad\quad 3x+1 = 25$

$\qquad\qquad 3x = 24$

$\qquad\qquad x = 8$

$\quad$ Check: $\quad \sqrt{3x+1} = 5$

$\qquad\qquad \sqrt{3(8)+1} = 5$

$\qquad\qquad\quad \sqrt{25} = 5$

$\qquad\qquad\qquad 5 = 5$ True

61. $\sqrt{5x+6} = \sqrt{4x+8}$

$\qquad (\sqrt{5x+6})^2 = (\sqrt{4x+8})^2$

$\qquad\quad 5x+6 = 4x+8$

$\qquad\quad 5x-4x = 8-6$

$\qquad\qquad x = 2$

$\quad$ Check: $\quad \sqrt{5x+6} = \sqrt{4x+8}$

$\qquad\qquad \sqrt{5(2)+6} = \sqrt{4(2)+8}$

$\qquad\qquad\qquad \sqrt{16} = \sqrt{16}$ True

62. $4\sqrt{x}-x = 4$

$\qquad 4\sqrt{x} = x+4$

$\qquad (4\sqrt{x})^2 = (x+4)^2$

$\qquad\quad 16x = x^2+8x+16$

$\qquad\qquad 0 = x^2-8x+16$

$\qquad\qquad 0 = (x-4)^2$

$\qquad x-4 = 0$

$\qquad\qquad x = 4$

$\quad$ Check: $4\sqrt{x}-x = 4$

$\qquad\qquad 4\sqrt{4}-4 = 4$

$\qquad\qquad 4\cdot 2-4 = 4$

$\qquad\qquad\quad 4 = 4$ True

63. $\sqrt{x^2 - 3} = x - 1$

$\left(\sqrt{x^2 - 3}\right)^2 = (x-1)^2$

$x^2 - 3 = x^2 - 2x + 1$

$2x - 1 - 3 = 0$

$2x - 4 = 0$

$2x = 4$

$x = 2$

Check: $\sqrt{x^2 - 3} = x - 1$

$\sqrt{2^2 - 3} = 2 - 1$

$\sqrt{1} = 1$

$1 = 1$ True

64. $\sqrt{4x + 8} - \sqrt{7x - 13} = 0$

$\sqrt{4x + 8} = \sqrt{7x - 13}$

$(\sqrt{4x + 8})^2 = (\sqrt{7x - 13})^2$

$4x + 8 = 7x - 13$

$8 + 13 = 7x - 4x$

$21 = 3x$

$x = \dfrac{21}{3} = 7$

Check: $\sqrt{4x + 8} - \sqrt{7x - 13} = 0$

$\sqrt{4(7) + 8} - \sqrt{7(7) - 13} = 0$

$\sqrt{36} - \sqrt{36} = 0$

$0 = 0$ True

65. $\sqrt{4p + 1} = 2p - 1$

$\left(\sqrt{4p + 1}\right)^2 = (2p - 1)^2$

$4p + 1 = 4p^2 - 4p + 1$

$0 = 4p^2 - 8p$

$0 = 4p(p - 2)$

$4p = 0$ or $p - 2 = 0$

$p = 0$ $p = 2$

Check: p = 0   p = 2

$\sqrt{4(0) + 1} = 2(0) - 1$ $\sqrt{4(2) + 1} = 2(2) - 1$

$\sqrt{5} = -1$ False $\sqrt{9} = 4 - 1$

$3 = 3$ True

Thus, $p = 2$ is a solution and $p = 0$ is an extraneous solution.

66. $a^2 + b^2 = c^2$

$10^2 + 24^2 = x^2$

$100 + 576 = x^2$

$x^2 = 676$

$x = \sqrt{676} = 26$

67. $a^2 + b^2 = c^2$

$10^2 + x^2 = 15^2$

$100 + x^2 = 225$

$x^2 = 225 - 100$

$x^2 = 125$

$x = \sqrt{125} \approx 11.18$

68. $a^2 + b^2 = c^2$

$x^2 + (\sqrt{3})^2 = (\sqrt{15})^2$

$x^2 + 3 = 15$

$x^2 = 12$

$x = \sqrt{12} \approx 3.46$

69. $a^2 + b^2 = c^2$

$6^2 + 5^2 = x^2$

$36 + 25 = x^2$

$61 = x^2$

$x = \sqrt{61} \approx 7.81$

70. $a^2 + b^2 = c^2$

$h^2 + 3^2 = 12^2$

$h^2 + 9 = 144$

$h^2 = 135$

$h = \sqrt{135}$

The height of the ladder on the house is $\sqrt{135} \approx 11.62$ feet.

71. $a^2 + b^2 = c^2$

$15^2 + 6^2 = d^2$

$225 + 36 = d^2$

$261 = d^2$

$d = \sqrt{261}$

The length of the diagonal is $\sqrt{261} \approx 16.16$ inches.

72. $d = \sqrt{(x_2 - x_1)^2 + (y_2 - y_1)^2}$

$= \sqrt{(1 - 4)^2 + [7 - (-3)]^2}$

$= \sqrt{(-3)^2 + (10)^2}$

$= \sqrt{9 + 100}$

$= \sqrt{109}$

≈ 10.44

73. $d = \sqrt{(x_2 - x_1)^2 + (y_2 - y_1)^2}$

$= \sqrt{(-6 - 6)^2 + (8 - 5)^2}$

$= \sqrt{(-12)^2 + (3)^2}$

$= \sqrt{144 + 9}$

$= \sqrt{153}$

≈ 12.37

74. $A = \dfrac{s^2 \sqrt{3}}{4}$

$A = \dfrac{36^2 \sqrt{3}}{4}$

$= \dfrac{1296\sqrt{3}}{4}$

$= 324\sqrt{3}$

$\approx 324(1.732)$

≈ 561.18 square inches

75. $d = \sqrt{(3/2)h}$

$= \sqrt{(3/2)40}$

$= \sqrt{60}$

≈ 7.75

He can see about 7.75 miles.

76. $s = \sqrt{(3V)/h}$

$= \sqrt{3(48,686,866.67)/350}$

$= \sqrt{417,315.99}$

$= 646$

The sides are 755 feet long.

77. $\sqrt[3]{64} = 4$ since $4^3 = 64$

78. $\sqrt[3]{-64} = -4$ since $(-4)^3 = -64$

79. $\sqrt[4]{16} = 2$ since $2^4 = 16$

80. $\sqrt[4]{81} = 3$ since $3^4 = 81$

81. $\sqrt[3]{64} = 4$ since $4^3 = 64$

82. $\sqrt[3]{-8} = -2$ since $(-2)^3 = -8$

83. $\sqrt[4]{32} = \sqrt[4]{16 \cdot 2} = \sqrt[4]{16}\sqrt[4]{2} = 2\sqrt[4]{2}$

84. $\sqrt[3]{48} = \sqrt[3]{8 \cdot 6} = \sqrt[3]{8}\sqrt[3]{6} = 2\sqrt[3]{6}$

85. $\sqrt[3]{54} = \sqrt[3]{27 \cdot 2} = \sqrt[3]{27}\sqrt[3]{2} = 3\sqrt[3]{2}$

86. $\sqrt[4]{96} = \sqrt[4]{16 \cdot 6} = \sqrt[4]{16}\sqrt[4]{6} = 2\sqrt[4]{6}$

87. $\sqrt[3]{x^{21}} = x^{21/3} = x^7$

88. $\sqrt[3]{s^{30}} = s^{30/3} = s^{10}$

89. $27^{2/3} = \left(\sqrt[3]{27}\right)^2 = 3^2 = 9$

90. $25^{1/2} = \sqrt{25} = 5$

91. $27^{-2/3} = (\sqrt[3]{27})^{-2} = 3^{-2} = \dfrac{1}{3^2} = \dfrac{1}{9}$

92. $64^{2/3} = (\sqrt[3]{64})^2 = 4^2 = 16$

93. $125^{-4/3} = (\sqrt[3]{125})^{-4} = 5^{-4} = \dfrac{1}{5^4} = \dfrac{1}{625}$

94. $49^{3/2} = (\sqrt{49})^3 = 7^3 = 343$

95. $\sqrt[3]{z^{11}} = x^{11/3}$

96. $\sqrt[3]{x^8} = x^{8/3}$

97. $\sqrt[4]{y^9} = y^{9/4}$

98. $\sqrt{x^5} = x^{5/2}$

99. $\sqrt{y^3} = y^{3/2}$

100. $\sqrt[4]{m^6} = m^{6/4} = m^{3/2}$

101. $\sqrt[3]{x}\sqrt[3]{x^2} = x^{1/3}x^{2/3} = x^{1/3+2/3} = x^{3/3} = x$

102. $\sqrt[3]{x} \cdot \sqrt[3]{x} = x^{1/3} \cdot x^{1/3} = x^{1/3+1/3} = x^{2/3} = \sqrt[3]{x^2}$

103. $\sqrt[3]{a^5} \cdot \sqrt[3]{a^7} = a^{5/3} \cdot a^{7/3} = a^{5/3+7/3} = a^{12/3} = a^4$

104. $\sqrt[4]{x^2} \cdot \sqrt[4]{x^6} = x^{2/4} \cdot x^{6/4} = x^{2/4+6/4} = x^{8/4} = x^2$

105. $\left(\sqrt[3]{q^3}\right)^3 = (q^{3/3})^3 = q^3$

106. $\left(\sqrt[4]{d}\right)^4 = (d^{1/4})^4 = d$

107. $\left(\sqrt[4]{x^8}\right)^3 = (4^{8/4})^3 = (x^2)^3 = x^{3(2)} = x^6$

108. $\left(\sqrt[4]{x^3}\right)^8 = (x^{3/4})^8 = x^{(3/4)8} = x^6$

Practice Test

1. $\sqrt{3x} = (3x)^{1/2}$

2. $x^{2/3} = \sqrt[3]{x^2}$

3. $\sqrt{(y-4)^2} = y - 4$

4. $\sqrt{90} = \sqrt{9(10)} = \sqrt{9}\sqrt{10} = 3\sqrt{10}$

5. $\sqrt{12x^2} = \sqrt{4x^2}\sqrt{3} = 2x\sqrt{3}$

6. $\sqrt{50x^7y^3} = \sqrt{25x^6y^2}\sqrt{2xy} = 5x^3y\sqrt{2xy}$

7. $\sqrt{8x^2y} \cdot \sqrt{10xy} = \sqrt{80x^3y^2}$
   $= \sqrt{16x^2y^2}\sqrt{5x}$
   $= 4xy\sqrt{5x}$

8. $\sqrt{15xy^2} \cdot \sqrt{5x^3y^3} = \sqrt{75x^4y^5}$
   $= \sqrt{25x^4y^4}\sqrt{3y}$
   $= 5x^2y^2\sqrt{3y}$

9. $\sqrt{\dfrac{5}{125}} = \sqrt{\dfrac{1}{25}} = \dfrac{\sqrt{1}}{\sqrt{25}} = \dfrac{1}{5}$

10. $\dfrac{\sqrt{7c^4d}}{\sqrt{7d^3}} = \sqrt{\dfrac{7c^4d}{7d^3}} = \sqrt{\dfrac{c^4}{d^2}} = \dfrac{\sqrt{c^4}}{\sqrt{d^2}} = \dfrac{c^2}{d}$

11. $\dfrac{1}{\sqrt{6}} = \dfrac{1}{\sqrt{6}} \cdot \dfrac{\sqrt{6}}{\sqrt{6}} = \dfrac{\sqrt{6}}{6}$

12. $\sqrt{\dfrac{9r}{5}} = \dfrac{\sqrt{9r}}{\sqrt{5}}$
    $= \dfrac{\sqrt{9}\sqrt{r}}{\sqrt{5}}$
    $= \dfrac{3\sqrt{r}}{\sqrt{5}}$
    $= \dfrac{3\sqrt{r}}{\sqrt{5}} \cdot \dfrac{\sqrt{5}}{\sqrt{5}}$
    $= \dfrac{3\sqrt{5r}}{5}$

13. $\sqrt{\dfrac{40x^2y^5}{6x^3y^7}} = \sqrt{\dfrac{20}{3xy^2}}$
    $= \dfrac{\sqrt{20}}{\sqrt{3xy^2}}$
    $= \dfrac{\sqrt{4(5)}}{\sqrt{y^2}\sqrt{3x}}$
    $= \dfrac{\sqrt{4}\sqrt{5}}{y\sqrt{3x}}$
    $= \dfrac{2\sqrt{5}}{y\sqrt{3x}}$
    $= \dfrac{2\sqrt{5}}{y\sqrt{3x}} \cdot \dfrac{\sqrt{3x}}{\sqrt{3x}}$
    $= \dfrac{2\sqrt{15x}}{3xy}$

14. $\dfrac{3}{2-\sqrt{7}} = \dfrac{3}{2-\sqrt{7}} \cdot \dfrac{2+\sqrt{7}}{2+\sqrt{7}}$
    $= \dfrac{3(2+\sqrt{7})}{4-7}$
    $= \dfrac{3(2+\sqrt{7})}{-3}$
    $= -2 - \sqrt{7}$

15. $\dfrac{6}{\sqrt{x}-3} = \dfrac{6}{\sqrt{x}-3} \cdot \dfrac{\sqrt{x}+3}{\sqrt{x}+3}$
    $= \dfrac{6(\sqrt{x}+3)}{x-9}$
    $= \dfrac{6\sqrt{x}+18}{x-9}$

16. $\sqrt{48} + \sqrt{75} + 2\sqrt{3} = \sqrt{16\cdot3} + \sqrt{25\cdot3} + 2\sqrt{3}$
    $= 4\sqrt{3} + 5\sqrt{3} + 2\sqrt{3}$
    $= 11\sqrt{3}$

17. $7\sqrt{y} - 3\sqrt{y} - \sqrt{y} = (7-3-1)\sqrt{y} = 3\sqrt{y}$

18. $\sqrt{x-8} = 4$
    $(\sqrt{x-8})^2 = 4^2$
    $x - 8 = 16$
    $x = 24$
    Check: $\sqrt{24-8} = 4$
    $\sqrt{16} = 4$
    $4 = 4$ True

19.
$$2\sqrt{x-4}+4=x$$
$$2\sqrt{x-4}=x-4$$
$$(2\sqrt{x-4})^2=(x-4)^2$$
$$4(x-4)=x^2-8x+16$$
$$4x-16=x^2-8x+16$$
$$0=x^2-12x+32$$
$$0=(x-4)(x-8)$$
$$x-4=0 \text{ or } x-8=0$$
$$x=4 \text{ or } x=8$$

Check: $x=4$
$$2\sqrt{x-4}+4=x$$
$$2\sqrt{4-4}+4=4$$
$$2\sqrt{0}+4=4$$
$$4=4 \text{ True}$$

Check: $x=8$
$$2\sqrt{x-4}+4=x$$
$$2\sqrt{8-4}+4=8$$
$$2\sqrt{4}+4=8$$
$$2\cdot 2+4=8$$
$$8=8 \text{ True}$$

The solutions are 4 and 8.

20.
$$a^2+b^2=c^2$$
$$9^2+5^2=x^2$$
$$81+25=x^2$$
$$106=x^2$$
$$x=\sqrt{106}\approx 10.30$$

21.
$$\sqrt{(-4-3)^2+[-5-(-2)]^2}=\sqrt{(-7)^2+(-3)^2}$$
$$=\sqrt{49+9}$$
$$=\sqrt{58}$$
$$\approx 7.62$$

22. $27^{-4/3}=\dfrac{1}{27^{4/3}}=\dfrac{1}{(\sqrt[3]{27})^4}=\dfrac{1}{3^4}=\dfrac{1}{81}$

23.
$$\sqrt[4]{x^5}\cdot\sqrt[4]{x^7}=x^{5/4}x^{7/4}$$
$$=x^{(5/4)+(7/4)}$$
$$=x^{12/4}$$
$$=x^3$$

24.
$$s^2=121$$
$$s=\sqrt{121}=11$$
The side is 11 meters.

25. $v=\sqrt{2gh}=\sqrt{2(32)10}=\sqrt{640}\approx 25.30 \text{ ft / sec}$

Cumulative Review Test

1. a. $-5, 735,$ and 4 are integers.

    b. 4 and 735 are whole numbers.

    c. $-5, 735, 0.5, 4,$ and $\dfrac{1}{2}$ are rational numbers.

    d. $\sqrt{12}$ is an irrational number.

    e. All of the numbers are real numbers.

2.
$$7a^2-4b^2+2ab$$
$$=7(-3)^2-4(2)^2+2(-3)(2)$$
$$=7(9)-4(4)-12$$
$$=63-16-12$$
$$=35$$

3.
$$-7(3-x)=4(x+2)-3x$$
$$-21+7x=4x+8-3x$$
$$-21+7x=x+8$$
$$7x-x=8+21$$
$$6x=29$$
$$x=\dfrac{29}{6}$$

4.
$$3(x+2)>5-4(2x-7)$$
$$3x+6>5-8x+28$$
$$3x+8x>5+28-6$$
$$11x>27$$
$$x>\dfrac{27}{11}$$

5.
$$3x^3+x^2+6x+2=x^2(3x+1)+2(3x+1)$$
$$=(3x+1)(x^2+2)$$

6. $2x^2-17x+21=(2x-3)(x-7)$

7.
$$r^2-12r=0$$
$$r(r-12)=0$$
$$r=0 \text{ or } r-12=0$$
$$r=0 \text{ or } \quad r=12$$

8. $\dfrac{4a^3b^{-5}}{28a^8b} = \dfrac{1}{7a^5b^6}$

9.

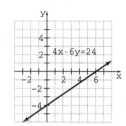

10. The y-intercept is $(0, -2)$ and the slope is
$m = \dfrac{1-(-2)}{1-0} = \dfrac{1+2}{1} = 3.$
$y = 3x - 2$

11. Use the slope-intercept form with $m = \dfrac{2}{5}$ and
$(x_1, y_1) = (-5, 2).$
$y - y_1 = m(x - x_1)$

$y - 2 = \dfrac{2}{5}\left[x - (-5)\right]$

$y - 2 = \dfrac{2}{5}(x + 5)$

$y - 2 = \dfrac{2}{5}x + 2$

$y = \dfrac{2}{5}x + 4$

12. $-2x + 3y = 6$
$4x - 2y = -4$
Solve the second equation for y.
$y = 2x + 2$
Substitute $2x + 2$ for y in the first equation.
$-2x + 3(2x + 2) = 6$
$-2x + 6x + 6 = 6$
$4x + 6 = 6$
$4x + 6 - 6 = 6 - 6$
$4x = 0$
$x = 0$
Substitute 0 for x in the equation $y = 2x + 2$.
$y = -2(0) + 2 = 0 + 2 = 2$
The solution is $(0, 2)$.

13. $\dfrac{y+5}{8} + \dfrac{2y-7}{8} = \dfrac{y+5+2y-7}{8} = \dfrac{3y-2}{8}$

14.. $\dfrac{1}{2} + \dfrac{1}{z} = 3$

$2z\left(\dfrac{1}{2}\right) + 2z\left(\dfrac{1}{z}\right) = 2z(3)$

$z + 2 = 6z$

$z - z + 2 = 6z - z$

$2 = 5z$

$\dfrac{2}{5} = z$

15. $3\sqrt{11} - 4\sqrt{11} = (3-4)\sqrt{11} = -\sqrt{11}$

16. $\sqrt{\dfrac{3z}{28y}} = \dfrac{\sqrt{3z}}{\sqrt{28y}} \cdot \dfrac{\sqrt{28y}}{\sqrt{28y}}$

$= \dfrac{\sqrt{84yz}}{28y}$

$= \dfrac{\sqrt{4}\sqrt{21yz}}{28y}$

$= \dfrac{2\sqrt{21yz}}{28y}$

$= \dfrac{\sqrt{21yz}}{14y}$

17. $\sqrt{x+5} = 6$
$(\sqrt{x+5})^2 = 6^2$
$x + 5 = 36$
$x = 36 - 5$
$x = 31$
Check: $\sqrt{31+5} = 6$
$\sqrt{36} = 6$
$6 = 6$ True

18. $\dfrac{3}{11} = \dfrac{x}{10}$
$11x = 3(10)$
$11x = 30$
$x = \dfrac{30}{11} = 2\dfrac{8}{11}$
She must use $2\dfrac{8}{11}$ cups of flour.

19. Let r = the Hyatt's regular room rate.
Regular room rate − 40% discount = Final cost
$$r - 0.40r = 69$$
$$0.6r = 69$$
$$r = \frac{69}{0.6} = 115$$
The regular room rate is $115.

20. Let x = the distance. Since $d = rt$, $t = \dfrac{d}{r}$.
$$\frac{x}{100} + \frac{x}{125} = 2$$
$$500\left(\frac{x}{100} + \frac{x}{125}\right) = 500(2)$$
$$5x + 4x = 1000$$
$$9x = 1000$$
$$x = \frac{1000}{9} \approx 111.1$$
The distance is about 111.1 miles.

Chapter 10

Exercise Set 10.1

1. If $x^2 = a$, then $x = \sqrt{a}$ or $x = -\sqrt{a}$.

3. In any golden rectangle, the length is about 1.62 times its width.

5. a. $x^2 = 9$ has 2 solutions

   b. $x^2 = 0$ has 1 solution

   c. $(x-2)^2 = 2$ has 2 solutions

   d. $(x-3)^2 = -2$ has no real solutions

7. $x^2 = 64$
$$x = \pm\sqrt{64}$$
$$x = 8, -8$$

9. $x^2 = 81$
$$x = \pm\sqrt{81}$$
$$x = 9, -9$$

11. $y^2 = 169$
$$y = \pm\sqrt{169}$$
$$y = 13, -13$$

13. $x^2 = 100$
$$x = \pm\sqrt{100}$$
$$x = 10, -10$$

15. $x^2 - 20 = 0$
$$x^2 = 20$$
$$x = \pm\sqrt{20}$$
$$x = 2\sqrt{5}, -2\sqrt{5}$$

17. $3x^2 = 12$
$$x^2 = 4$$
$$x = \pm\sqrt{4}$$
$$x = 2, -2$$

19. $2w^2 = 34$
$$w^2 = 17$$
$$w = \pm\sqrt{17}$$
$$w = \sqrt{17}, -\sqrt{17}$$

21. $3z^2 + 1 = 28$
$$3z^2 = 27$$
$$z^2 = 9$$
$$z = \pm\sqrt{9}$$
$$z = 3, -3$$

23. $9w^2 + 5 = 20$
$$9w^2 = 15$$
$$w^2 = \frac{15}{9}$$
$$w = \pm\sqrt{\frac{15}{9}}$$
$$w = \pm\frac{\sqrt{15}}{3}$$
$$w = \frac{\sqrt{15}}{3}, -\frac{\sqrt{15}}{3}$$

25. $16x^2 - 17 = 56$
$$16x^2 = 73$$
$$x^2 = \frac{73}{16}$$
$$x = \pm\sqrt{\frac{73}{16}}$$
$$x = \pm\frac{\sqrt{73}}{\sqrt{16}}$$
$$x = \pm\frac{\sqrt{73}}{4}$$
$$x = \frac{\sqrt{73}}{4}, -\frac{\sqrt{73}}{4}$$

27. $(x-4)^2 = 25$
$$x - 4 = \pm\sqrt{25}$$
$$x = 4 \pm 5$$
$$x = 4 + 5 \text{ or } x = 4 - 5$$
$$x = 9 \quad \text{ or } x = -1$$
The solutions are 9 and −1.

29. $(a + 3)^2 = 81$

$\quad a + 3 = \pm\sqrt{81}$

$\quad a + 3 = \pm 9$

$\quad\quad a = -3 \pm 9$

$\quad\quad a = -3 + 9 \text{ or } a = -3 - 9$

$\quad\quad a = 6 \quad\quad \text{ or } a = -12$

The solutions are 6 and –12.

31. $(x + 4)^2 = 64$

$\quad x + 4 = \pm\sqrt{64}$

$\quad x + 4 = \pm 8$

$\quad\quad x = -4 \pm 8$

$\quad\quad x = -4 + 8 \text{ or } x = -4 - 8$

$\quad\quad x = 4 \quad\quad \text{ or } x = -12$

The solutions are 4 and –12.

33. $(r + 6)^2 = 32$

$\quad r + 6 = \pm\sqrt{32}$

$\quad r + 6 = \pm\sqrt{16}\sqrt{2}$

$\quad r + 6 = \pm 4\sqrt{2}$

$\quad\quad r = -6 \pm 4\sqrt{2}$

The solutions are $-6 + 4\sqrt{2}$ and $-6 - 4\sqrt{2}$.

35. $(d + 6)^2 = 20$

$\quad d + 6 = \pm\sqrt{20}$

$\quad d + 6 = \pm\sqrt{4}\sqrt{5}$

$\quad d + 6 = \pm 2\sqrt{5}$

$\quad\quad d = -6 \pm 2\sqrt{5}$

The solutions are $-6 + 2\sqrt{5}$ and $-6 - 2\sqrt{5}$.

37. $(n - 3)^2 = 49$

$\quad n - 3 = \pm\sqrt{49}$

$\quad n - 3 = \pm 7$

$\quad\quad n = 3 \pm 7$

$\quad\quad n = 3 + 7 \text{ or } n = 3 - 7$

$\quad\quad n = 10 \quad\quad \text{ or } n = -4$

The solutions are 10 and –4.

39. $(x - 9)^2 = 100$

$\quad x - 9 = \pm\sqrt{100}$

$\quad x - 9 = \pm 10$

$\quad\quad x = 9 \pm 10$

$\quad\quad x = 9 + 10 \text{ or } x = 9 - 10$

$\quad\quad x = 19 \quad\quad \text{ or } x = -1$

The solutions are 19 and –1.

41. $(2x + 3)^2 = 18$

$\quad 2x + 3 = \pm\sqrt{18}$

$\quad 2x + 3 = \pm\sqrt{9}\sqrt{2}$

$\quad 2x + 3 = \pm 3\sqrt{2}$

$\quad\quad 2x = -3 \pm 3\sqrt{2}$

$\quad\quad x = \dfrac{-3 \pm 3\sqrt{2}}{2}$

The solutions are $\dfrac{-3 + 3\sqrt{2}}{2}$ and $\dfrac{-3 - 3\sqrt{2}}{2}$.

43. $(4x + 1)^2 - 2 = 18$

$\quad (4x + 1)^2 = 20$

$\quad 4x + 1 = \pm\sqrt{20}$

$\quad 4x + 1 = \pm\sqrt{4}\sqrt{5}$

$\quad 4x + 1 = \pm 2\sqrt{5}$

$\quad\quad 4x = -1 \pm 2\sqrt{5}$

$\quad\quad x = \dfrac{-1 \pm 2\sqrt{5}}{4}$

The solutions are $\dfrac{-1 + 2\sqrt{5}}{4}$ and $\dfrac{-1 - 2\sqrt{5}}{4}$.

45. $(2p - 7)^2 + 4 = 22$

$\quad (2p - 7)^2 = 18$

$\quad 2p - 7 = \pm\sqrt{18}$

$\quad 2p - 7 = \pm\sqrt{9}\sqrt{2}$

$\quad 2p - 7 = \pm 3\sqrt{2}$

$\quad\quad 2p = 7 \pm 3\sqrt{2}$

$\quad\quad p = \dfrac{7 \pm 3\sqrt{2}}{2}$

The solutions are $\dfrac{7 + 3\sqrt{2}}{2}$ and $\dfrac{7 - 3\sqrt{2}}{2}$.

47. $x = \pm 6$

$\quad x^2 = (\pm 6)^2$

$\quad x^2 = 36$

Other answers are possible.

49. $x^2 - 9 = 27$; need an equation equivalent to $x^2 = 36$.

51. a. $-3x^2 + 9x - 6 = 0$

Multiply both sides by –1

$\quad -1(-3x^2 + 9x - 6) = (-1)(0)$

$\quad\quad 3x^2 - 9x + 6 = 0$

b. $-3x^2 + 9x - 6 = 0$

Multiply both sides by $-\dfrac{1}{3}$

$$-\dfrac{1}{3}(3x^2 + 9x - 6) = \left(-\dfrac{1}{3}\right)(0)$$

$$x^2 - 3x + 2 = 0$$

53. Let $x =$ the smaller positive number,
then $4.25x =$ the larger number.
(smaller number)(larger number) = 68
$x(4.25x) = 68$

$$4.25x^2 = 68$$

$$x^2 = 16$$

$$x = \sqrt{16}$$

$$x = 4$$

$$4.25x = 4.25(4) = 17$$
The numbers are 4 and 7.

55. Let $x =$ width of newspaper,
then $1.21x =$ length of newspaper.
Area $=$ length $\cdot$ width
$631.92 = 1.21x(x)$

$631.92 = 1.21x^2$

$522.25 = x^2$

$\sqrt{522.25} = x$

$x \approx 22.85$

$1.21x \approx 1.21\sqrt{522.25} \approx 27.65$
The width is about 22.85 inches and
the length is about 27.65 inches.

57. Let $x =$ width of rectangle,
then $1.62x =$ length of rectangle.
Area $=$ length $\cdot$ width
$2000 = (1.62x)x$

$2000 = 1.62x^2$

$\dfrac{2000}{1.62} = x^2$

$x = \pm\sqrt{\dfrac{2000}{1.62}} \approx \pm35.14$

Since the width is positive $x \approx 35.14$ feet. The
length is $1.62 \cdot 35.14 \approx 56.93$ feet.

59. a. Left x^2, right $(x + 3)^2$

b. $x^2 = 36$

$x = \pm\sqrt{36}$.

$x = \pm6$

Since the length cannot be negative, the

length of each side of the square is
$= 6$ inches.

c. $x^2 = 50$

$x = \pm\sqrt{50}$

$x = \pm\sqrt{25}\sqrt{2}$

$x = \pm5\sqrt{2}$

Since the length cannot be negative, the
length of each side of the square is
$5\sqrt{2} \approx 7.07$ inches.

d. $(x + 3)^2 = 81$

$x + 3 = \pm\sqrt{81}$

$x + 3 = \pm9$

Since the length cannot be negative, the
length of each side of the square is
$= 9$ inches.

e. $(x + 3)^2 = 92$

$x + 3 = \pm\sqrt{92}$

Since the length cannot be negative, the
length of each side of the square is
$\sqrt{92} \approx 9.59$ inches.

61. $A = s^2$

$\sqrt{A} = \sqrt{s^2}$

$\sqrt{A} = s$

$s = \sqrt{A}$

63. $A = \pi r^2$

$\dfrac{A}{\pi} = r^2$

$\sqrt{\dfrac{A}{\pi}} = \sqrt{r^2}$

$\sqrt{\dfrac{A}{\pi}} = r$

$r = \sqrt{\dfrac{A}{\pi}}$

65.

$I = \dfrac{k}{d^2}$

$d^2 I = k$

$d^2 = \dfrac{k}{I}$

$\sqrt{d^2} = \sqrt{\dfrac{k}{I}}$

$d = \sqrt{\dfrac{k}{I}}$

67. $4x^2 - 10x - 24 = 2(2x^2 - 5x - 12)$
$$= 2(2x^2 - 8x + 3x - 12)$$
$$= 2[2x(x-4) + 3(x-4)]$$
$$= 2(2x+3)(x-4)$$

68. $\dfrac{3-\frac{1}{y}}{6-\frac{1}{y}} = \dfrac{\left(3-\frac{1}{y}\right)y}{\left(6-\frac{1}{y}\right)y} = \dfrac{3y-1}{6y-1}$

69. $m = \dfrac{y_2 - y_1}{x_2 - x_1} = \dfrac{3-(-1)}{1-0} = \dfrac{3+1}{1} = 4$

The y-intercept is $(0, -1)$. Thus, the equation of the line is $y = 4x - 1$.

70. $\dfrac{\sqrt{135a^4b}}{\sqrt{3a^5b^5}} = \sqrt{\dfrac{135a^4b}{3a^5b^5}}$

$$= \sqrt{\dfrac{45}{ab^4}}$$

$$= \dfrac{\sqrt{45}}{\sqrt{ab^4}}$$

$$= \dfrac{\sqrt{9}\sqrt{5}}{\sqrt{b^4}\sqrt{a}}$$

$$= \dfrac{3\sqrt{5}}{b^2\sqrt{a}}$$

$$= \dfrac{3\sqrt{5}}{b^2\sqrt{a}} \cdot \dfrac{\sqrt{a}}{\sqrt{a}}$$

$$= \dfrac{3\sqrt{5a}}{ab^2}$$

Exercise Set 10.2

1. a. A perfect square trinomial is a trinomial that can be expressed as the square of a binomial.

b. $x^2 + 8x + 16$; the constant is the square of half the coefficient of the x-term.

3. The constant is the square of half the coefficient of the x-term.

5. $\left(\dfrac{-12}{2}\right)^2 = (-6)^2 = 36$

7. $x^2 - 7x + 10 = 0$
$$x^2 - 7x = -10$$
$$x^2 - 7x + \dfrac{49}{4} = -10 + \dfrac{49}{4}$$
$$\left(x - \dfrac{7}{2}\right)^2 = -\dfrac{40}{4} + \dfrac{49}{4}$$
$$\left(x - \dfrac{7}{2}\right)^2 = \dfrac{9}{4}$$
$$x - \dfrac{7}{2} = \pm\sqrt{\dfrac{9}{4}}$$
$$x - \dfrac{7}{2} = \pm\dfrac{3}{2}$$
$$x = \dfrac{7}{2} \pm \dfrac{3}{2}$$
$$x = \dfrac{7}{2} + \dfrac{3}{2} \text{ or } x = \dfrac{7}{2} - \dfrac{3}{2}$$
$$x = 5 \qquad \text{or } x = 2$$

The solutions are 5 and 2.

9. $x^2 - 8x + 7 = 0$
$$x^2 - 8x = -7$$
$$x^2 - 8x + 16 = -7 + 16$$
$$(x - 4)^2 = 9$$
$$x - 4 = \pm\sqrt{9}$$
$$x - 4 = \pm 3$$
$$x = 4 \pm 3$$
$$x = 4 + 3 \text{ or } x = 4 - 3$$
$$x = 7 \qquad \text{or } x = 1$$
The solutions are 7 and 1.

11. $x^2 + 3x + 2 = 0$

$$x^2 + 3x = -2$$

$$x^2 + 3x + \frac{9}{4} = -2 + \frac{9}{4}$$

$$\left(x + \frac{3}{2}\right)^2 = -\frac{8}{4} + \frac{9}{4}$$

$$\left(x + \frac{3}{2}\right)^2 = \frac{1}{4}$$

$$x + \frac{3}{2} = \pm\sqrt{\frac{1}{4}}$$

$$x + \frac{3}{2} = \pm\frac{1}{2}$$

$$x = -\frac{3}{2} \pm \frac{1}{2}$$

$$x = -\frac{3}{2} + \frac{1}{2} \text{ or } x = -\frac{3}{2} - \frac{1}{2}$$

$$x = -1 \qquad \text{or } x = -2$$

The solutions are -1 and -2.

13. $z^2 - 2z - 8 = 0$

$$x^2 - 2z = 8$$

$$z^2 - 2z + 1 = 8 + 1$$

$$(z - 1)^2 = 9$$

$$z - 1 = \pm\sqrt{9}$$

$$z - 1 = \pm 3$$

$$z = 1 \pm 3$$

$$z = 1 + 3 \text{ or } z = 1 - 3$$

$$z = 4 \qquad \text{or } z = -2$$

The solutions are 4 and -2.

15. $n^2 = -6n - 9$

$$n^2 + 6n = -9$$

$$n^2 + 6n + 9 = -9 + 9$$

$$(n + 3)^2 = 0$$

$$n + 3 = \pm\sqrt{0}$$

$$n + 3 = \pm 0$$

$$n = -3 \pm 0$$

$$n = -3$$

The solution is -3.

17. $x^2 = 2x + 15$

$$x^2 - 2x = 15$$

$$x^2 - 2x + 1 = 15 + 1$$

$$(x - 1)^2 = 16$$

$$x - 1 = \pm\sqrt{16}$$

$$x - 1 = \pm 4$$

$$x = 1 \pm 4$$

$$x = 1 + 4 \text{ or } x = 1 - 4$$

$$x = 5 \qquad \text{or } x = -3$$

The solutions are 5 and -3.

19. $x^2 + 10x + 24 = 0$

$$x^2 + 10x = -24$$

$$x^2 + 10x + 25 = -24 + 25$$

$$(x + 5)^2 = 1$$

$$x + 5 = \pm\sqrt{1}$$

$$x + 5 = \pm 1$$

$$x = -5 \pm 1$$

$$x = -5 + 1 \text{ or } x = -5 - 1$$

$$x = -4 \qquad \text{or } x = -6$$

The solutions are -4 and -6.

21. $x^2 = 15x - 56$

$$x^2 - 15x = -56$$

$$x^2 - 15 + \frac{225}{4} = -56 + \frac{225}{4}$$

$$\left(x - \frac{15}{2}\right)^2 = -\frac{224}{4} + \frac{225}{4}$$

$$\left(x - \frac{15}{2}\right)^2 = \frac{1}{4}$$

$$x - \frac{15}{2} = \pm\sqrt{\frac{1}{4}}$$

$$x - \frac{15}{2} = \pm\frac{1}{2}$$

$$x = \frac{15}{2} \pm \frac{1}{2}$$

$$x = \frac{15}{2} + \frac{1}{2} \text{ or } x = \frac{15}{2} - \frac{1}{2}$$

$$x = 8 \qquad \text{or } x = 7$$

The solutions are 8 and 7.

23.
$$-32 = -p^2 + 4p$$
$$p^2 - 4p = 32$$
$$p^2 - 4p + 4 = 32 + 4$$
$$(p-2)^2 = 36$$
$$p - 2 = \pm\sqrt{36}$$
$$p - 2 = \pm 6$$
$$p = 2 \pm 6$$
$$p = 2 + 6 \text{ or } p = 2 - 6$$
$$p = 8 \quad \text{ or } p = -4$$
The solutions are 8 and –4.

25.
$$z^2 - 4z = -2$$
$$z^2 - 4z + 4 = -2 + 4$$
$$(z-2)^2 = 2$$
$$z - 2 = \pm\sqrt{2}$$
$$z = 2 \pm \sqrt{2}$$
The solutions are $2 + \sqrt{2}$ and $2 - \sqrt{2}$.

27.
$$6w + 4 = -w^2$$
$$w^2 + 6w + 4 = 0$$
$$w^2 + 6w = -4$$
$$w^2 + 6w + 9 = -4 + 9$$
$$(w+3)^2 = 5$$
$$w + 3 = \pm\sqrt{5}$$
$$w = -3 \pm \sqrt{5}$$
The solutions are $-3 + \sqrt{5}$ and $-3 - \sqrt{5}$.

29.
$$m^2 + 7m + 2 = 0$$
$$m^2 + 7m = -2$$
$$m^2 + 7m + \frac{49}{4} = -2 + \frac{49}{4}$$
$$\left(m + \frac{7}{2}\right)^2 = \frac{41}{4}$$
$$m + \frac{7}{2} = \pm\sqrt{\frac{41}{4}}$$
$$m + \frac{7}{2} = \pm\frac{\sqrt{41}}{2}$$
$$m = -\frac{7}{2} \pm \frac{\sqrt{41}}{2}$$
$$m = \frac{-7 \pm \sqrt{41}}{2}$$

The solutions are $\dfrac{-7 + \sqrt{41}}{2}$ and $\dfrac{-7 - \sqrt{41}}{2}$.

31.
$$2x^2 + 4x - 6 = 0$$
$$\frac{1}{2}(2x^2 + 4x - 6) = \frac{1}{2}(0)$$
$$x^2 + 2x - 3 = 0$$
$$x^2 + 2x = 3$$
$$x^2 + 2x + 1 = 3 + 1$$
$$(x+1)^2 = 4$$
$$x + 1 = \pm\sqrt{4}$$
$$x + 1 = \pm 2$$
$$x = -1 \pm 2$$

$$x = -1 + 2 \text{ or } x = -1 - 2$$
$$x = 1 \quad \text{ or } x = -3$$

The solutions are 1 and –3.

33.
$$2x^2 + 18x + 4 = 0$$
$$\frac{1}{2}(2x^2 + 18x + 4) = \frac{1}{2}(0)$$
$$x^2 + 9x + 2 = 0$$
$$x^2 + 9x = -2$$
$$x^2 + 9x + \frac{81}{4} = -2 + \frac{81}{4}$$
$$\left(x + \frac{9}{2}\right)^2 = \frac{73}{4}$$
$$x + \frac{9}{2} = \pm\sqrt{\frac{73}{4}}$$
$$x + \frac{9}{2} = \pm\frac{\sqrt{73}}{2}$$
$$x = -\frac{9}{2} \pm \frac{\sqrt{73}}{2}$$
$$x = \frac{-9 \pm \sqrt{73}}{2}$$

The solutions are $\dfrac{-9 + \sqrt{73}}{2}$ and $\dfrac{-9 - \sqrt{73}}{2}$.

35.
$$3h^2 - 15h = 18$$
$$\frac{1}{3}(3h^2 - 15h) = \frac{1}{3}(18)$$
$$h^2 - 5h = 6$$
$$h^2 - 5h + \frac{25}{4} = 6 + \frac{25}{4}$$
$$\left(h - \frac{5}{2}\right)^2 = \frac{24}{4} + \frac{25}{4}$$
$$\left(h - \frac{5}{2}\right)^2 = \frac{49}{4}$$
$$h - \frac{5}{2} = \pm\sqrt{\frac{49}{4}}$$
$$h - \frac{5}{2} = \pm\frac{7}{2}$$
$$h = \frac{5}{2} \pm \frac{7}{2}$$
$$x = \frac{5}{2} + \frac{7}{2} \text{ or } x = \frac{5}{2} - \frac{7}{2}$$
$$x = 6 \qquad \text{ or } x = -1$$

The solutions are 6 and –1.

37.
$$3x^2 - 11x - 4 = 0$$
$$\frac{1}{3}(3x^2 - 11x - 4) = \frac{1}{3}(0)$$
$$x^2 - \frac{11}{3}x - \frac{4}{3} = 0$$
$$x^2 - \frac{11}{3}x = \frac{4}{3}$$
$$x^2 - \frac{11}{3}x + \frac{121}{36} = \frac{4}{3} + \frac{121}{36}$$
$$\left(x - \frac{11}{6}\right)^2 = \frac{48}{36} + \frac{121}{36}$$
$$\left(x - \frac{11}{6}\right)^2 = \frac{169}{36}$$
$$x - \frac{11}{6} = \pm\sqrt{\frac{169}{36}}$$
$$x - \frac{11}{6} = \pm\frac{13}{6}$$
$$x = \frac{11}{6} \pm \frac{13}{6}$$
$$x = \frac{11}{6} + \frac{13}{6} \text{ or } x = \frac{11}{6} - \frac{13}{6}$$
$$x = 4 \qquad\qquad \text{ or } x = -\frac{1}{3}$$

The solutions are 4 and $-\dfrac{1}{3}$.

39.
$$9t^2 + 6t = 6$$
$$\frac{1}{9}(9t^2 + 6t) = \frac{1}{9}(6)$$
$$t^2 + \frac{6}{9}t = \frac{6}{9}$$
$$t^2 + \frac{6}{9}x + \frac{1}{9} = \frac{6}{9} + \frac{1}{9}$$
$$\left(t + \frac{1}{3}\right)^2 = \frac{7}{9}$$
$$t + \frac{1}{3} = \pm\sqrt{\frac{7}{9}}$$
$$t = -\frac{1}{3} \pm \frac{\sqrt{7}}{3}$$

The solutions are
$$t = \frac{-1 + \sqrt{7}}{3} \text{ and } t = \frac{-1 - \sqrt{7}}{3}.$$

41.

$$x^2 - 5x = 0$$

$$x^2 - 5x + \frac{25}{4} = 0 + \frac{25}{4}$$

$$\left(x - \frac{5}{2}\right)^2 = \frac{25}{4}$$

$$x - \frac{5}{2} = \pm\sqrt{\frac{25}{4}}$$

$$x - \frac{5}{2} = \pm\frac{5}{2}$$

$$x = \frac{5}{2} \pm \frac{5}{2}$$

$$x = \frac{5}{2} + \frac{5}{2} \text{ or } x = \frac{5}{2} - \frac{5}{2}$$

$$x = 5 \qquad \text{ or } x = 0$$

The solutions are 5 and 0.

43.

$$2x^2 = 12x$$

$$2x^2 - 12x = 0$$

$$\frac{1}{2}(2x^2 - 12x) = \frac{1}{2}(0)$$

$$x^2 - 6x = 0$$

$$x^2 - 6x + 9 = 0 + 9$$

$$(x - 3)^2 = 9$$

$$x - 3 = \pm\sqrt{9}$$

$$x - 3 = \pm 3$$

$$x = 3 \pm 3$$

$$x = 3 + 3 \text{ or } x = 3 - 3$$

$$x = 6 \quad \text{ or } x = 0$$

The solutions are 6 and 0.

45. a. $x^2 + 20x + 100$

    b. The constant is the square of half the coefficient of the *x*-term.

$$\left(\frac{20}{2}\right)^2 = 10^2 = 100$$

47. Let x be the number.

$$x^2 + 3x = 4$$

$$x^2 + 3x + \frac{9}{4} = 4 + \frac{9}{4}$$

$$\left(x + \frac{3}{2}\right)^2 = \frac{16}{4} + \frac{9}{4}$$

$$\left(x + \frac{3}{2}\right)^2 = \frac{25}{4}$$

$$x + \frac{3}{2} = \pm\sqrt{\frac{25}{4}}$$

$$x + \frac{3}{2} = \pm\frac{5}{2}$$

$$x = -\frac{3}{2} \pm \frac{5}{2}$$

$$x = -\frac{3}{2} + \frac{5}{2} \text{ or } x = -\frac{3}{2} - \frac{5}{2}$$

$$x = 1 \qquad \text{ or } x = -4$$

The numbers are 1 and –4.

49. Let x be the number.

$$(x + 3)^2 = 9$$

$$x + 3 = \pm\sqrt{9}$$

$$x + 3 = \pm 3$$

$$x = -3 \pm 3$$

$$x = -3 + 3 \text{ or } x = -3 - 3$$

$$x = 0 \qquad \text{ or } x = -6$$

The numbers are 0 and –6.

51. Let x and y be the numbers.

$$xy = 21$$

$$y = x + 4$$

Substitute $x + 4$ for y in the first equation.

$$xy = 21$$

$$x(x + 4) = 21$$

$$x^2 + 4x = 21$$

$$x^2 + 4x + 4 = 21 + 4$$

$$(x + 2)^2 = 25$$

$$x + 2 = \pm\sqrt{25}$$

$$x + 2 = \pm 5$$

$$x = -2 \pm 5$$

$$x = -2 + 5 \text{ or } x = -2 - 5$$

$$x = 3 \qquad \text{ or } x = -7$$

Since the numbers must be positive, $x = 3$; $y = 3 + 4 = 7$. The numbers are 3 and 7.

53. Use Pythagorean Theorem

$$a^2 + b^2 = c^2$$

$$a^2 + (a + 18)^2 = 30^2$$

$$a^2 + a^2 + 36a + 324 = 900$$

$$2a^2 + 36a = 576$$

$$\frac{1}{2}\left(2a^2 + 36a\right) = \frac{1}{2}(576)$$

$$a^2 + 18a = 288$$

$$a^2 + 18a + 81 = 288 + 81$$

$$(a + 9)^2 = 369$$

$$a + 9 = \pm\sqrt{369}$$

$$a = -9 \pm \sqrt{369}$$

Since a must be positive, $a = -9 + \sqrt{369} \approx 10.21$. The vertical distance is $a + 18 = 10.21 + 18 = 28.21$ feet.

55. Substitute 192 for s.

$$192 = -16t^2 + 128t$$

$$-\frac{1}{16}(192) = -\frac{1}{16}\left(-16t^2 + 128t\right)$$

$$-12 = t^2 - 8t$$

$$-12 + 16 = t^2 - 8t + 16$$

$$4 = (t - 4)^2$$

$$\pm\sqrt{4} = t - 4$$

$$4 \pm 2 = t$$

$t = 4 + 2 = 6$ and $t = 4 - 2 = 2$

It takes 2 and 6 seconds for the object to reach a height of 192 feet.

57. $+28x$ or $-28x$

The coefficient of the x-term is plus or minus twice the square root of the constant.

$$b = \pm 2\sqrt{c} = \pm 2\sqrt{196} = \pm 2(14) = \pm 28.$$

59. a.

$$x^2 - 14x - 1 = 0$$

$$x^2 - 14x = 1$$

$$x^2 - 14x + 49 = 1 + 49$$

$$(x - 7)^2 = 50$$

$$x - 7 = \pm\sqrt{50}$$

$$x - 7 = \pm 5\sqrt{2}$$

$$x = 7 \pm 5\sqrt{2}$$

b. $x = 7 + 5\sqrt{2}$

$$x^2 - 14x - 1 = 0$$

$$(7 + 5\sqrt{2})^2 - 14(7 + 5\sqrt{2}) - 1 = 0$$

$$49 + 70\sqrt{2} + 50 - 98 - 70\sqrt{2} - 1 = 0$$

$$49 + 50 - 98 - 1 + 70\sqrt{2} - 70\sqrt{2} = 0$$

$$0 = 0 \text{ True}$$

$x = 7 - 5\sqrt{2}$

$$x - 14x - 1 = 0$$

$$(7 - 5\sqrt{2})^2 - 14(7 - 5\sqrt{2}) - 1 = 0$$

$$49 - 70\sqrt{2} + 50 - 98 + 70\sqrt{2} - 1 = 0$$

$$49 + 50 - 98 - 1 - 70\sqrt{2} + 70\sqrt{2} = 0$$

$$0 = 0 \text{ True}$$

61.

$$x^2 + \frac{3}{5}x - \frac{1}{2} = 0$$

$$x^2 + \frac{3}{5}x = \frac{1}{2}$$

$$x^2 + \frac{3}{5}x + \frac{9}{100} = \frac{1}{2} + \frac{9}{100}$$

$$\left(x + \frac{3}{10}\right)^2 = \frac{59}{100}$$

$$x + \frac{3}{10} = \pm\sqrt{\frac{59}{100}}$$

$$x + \frac{3}{10} = \pm\frac{\sqrt{59}}{10}$$

$$x = \frac{-3 \pm \sqrt{59}}{10}$$

The solutions are: $\dfrac{-3 + \sqrt{59}}{10}$ and $\dfrac{-3 - \sqrt{59}}{10}$.

63.

$$3x^2 + \frac{1}{2}x = 4$$

$$x^2 + \frac{1}{6}x = \frac{4}{3}$$

$$x + \frac{1}{6}x + \frac{1}{144} = \frac{4}{3} + \frac{1}{144}$$

$$\left(x + \frac{1}{12}\right)^2 = \frac{194}{144}$$

$$x + \frac{1}{12} = \pm\sqrt{\frac{193}{144}}$$

$$x + \frac{1}{12} = \pm\frac{\sqrt{193}}{12}$$

$$x = -\frac{1}{12} \pm \frac{\sqrt{193}}{12}$$

$$x = \frac{-1 \pm \sqrt{193}}{12}$$

The solutions are:

$$\frac{-1+\sqrt{193}}{12} \text{ and } \frac{-1-\sqrt{193}}{12}.$$

65. $-5.26x^2 + 7.89x + 15.78 = 0$

$$x^2 - 1.5x - 3 = 0$$

$$x^2 - 1.5x = 3$$

$$x^2 - 1.5x + 0.5625 = 3 + 0.5625$$

$$(x - 0.75)^2 = 3.5625$$

$$x - 0.75 = \pm\sqrt{3.5625}$$

$$x = 0.75 \pm \sqrt{3.5625}$$

The solutions are:

$$0.75 + \sqrt{3.5625} \text{ and } 0.75 - \sqrt{3.5625}$$

66.

$$\frac{x^2}{x^2 - x - 6} - \frac{x-2}{x-3}$$

$$= \frac{x^2}{(x-3)(x+2)} - \frac{x-2}{x-3}$$

$$= \frac{x^2}{(x-3)(x+2)} - \frac{(x-2)}{(x-3)} \cdot \frac{(x+2)}{(x+2)}$$

$$= \frac{x^2}{(x-3)(x+2)} - \frac{x^2-4}{(x-3)(x+2)}$$

$$= \frac{x^2 - (x^2 - 4)}{(x-3)(x+2)}$$

$$= \frac{4}{(x-3)(x+2)}$$

67. If the slopes are the same and the y-intercepts are different, the equations represent parallel lines.

68. $3x - 4y = 6$

$2x + y = 8$

Multiply the second equation by 4.

$4[2x + y = 8]$

gives

$$\begin{array}{r} 3x - 4y = 6 \\ 8x + 4y = 32 \\ \hline 11x = 38 \\ x = \dfrac{38}{11} \end{array}$$

Substitute $\frac{38}{11}$ for x in the first equation.

$$3x - 4y = 6$$

$$3\left(\frac{38}{11}\right) - 4y = 6$$

$$\frac{114}{11} - 4y = 6$$

$$-4y = -\frac{48}{11}$$

$$y = \frac{12}{11}$$

The solution is $\left(\frac{38}{11}, \frac{12}{11}\right)$.

69.

$$\sqrt{2x+3} = 2x - 3$$

$$(\sqrt{2x+3})^2 = (2x - 3)^2$$

$$2x + 3 = 4x^2 - 12x + 9$$

$$0 = 4x^2 - 14x + 6$$

$$0 = 2(2x - 1)(x - 3)$$

$$2x - 1 = 0 \text{ or } x - 3 = 0$$

$$x = \frac{1}{2} \quad \text{ or } x = 3$$

Check: $x = \dfrac{1}{2}$

$$\sqrt{2x+3} = 2x - 3$$

$$\sqrt{2\left(\frac{1}{2}\right) + 3} = 2\left(\frac{1}{2}\right) - 3$$

$$\sqrt{4} = -2$$

$$2 = -2 \text{ False}$$

Check: $x = 3$

$$\sqrt{2x+3} = 2x - 3$$

$$\sqrt{2(3)+3} = 2(3) - 3$$

$$\sqrt{9} = 3$$

$$3 = 3 \text{ True}$$

$\frac{1}{2}$ is an extraneous root. The solution is 3.

Exercise Set 10.3

1. a. $b^2 - 4ac$

b. If the discriminant is:
greater than 0 there are two solutions;
equal to 0 there is one solution;
less than 0 there is no real solution.

3. $x = \dfrac{-b \pm \sqrt{b^2 - 4ac}}{2a}$

5. The first step to take when solving a quadratic equation is to write the equation in standard form.

7. The values used for b and c are incorrect because the equation was not first put in standard form.

9. $b^2 - 4ac = (5)^2 - 4(1)(-9) = 25 + 36 = 61$
Since the discriminant is positive, this equation has two distinct real number solutions.

11. $b^2 - 4ac = (1)^2 - 4(2)(1) = 1 - 8 = -7$
Since the discriminant is negative, this equation has no real number solution.

13. $b^2 - 4ac = (3)^2 - 4(6)(-7) = 9 + 168 = 177$
Since the discriminant is positive, this equation has two distinct real number solutions.

15. $\qquad 2x^2 = 16x - 32$
$2x^2 - 16x + 32 = 0$
$b^2 - 4ac = (-16)^2 - 4(2)(32) = 256 - 256 = 0$
Since the discriminant is zero, this equation has one real number solution.

17. $b^2 - 4ac = (-7)^2 - 4(2)(8) = 49 - 64 = -15$
Since the discriminant is negative, this equation has no real number solution.

19. $4x = 8 + x^2$
$0 = x^2 - 4x + 8$
$b^2 - 4ac = (-4)^2 - 4(1)(8) = 16 - 32 = -16$
Since the discriminant is negative, this equation has no real number solution.

21. $b^2 - 4ac = (7)^2 - 4(1)(-3) = 49 + 12 = 61$
Since the discriminant is positive, this equation has two distinct real number solutions.

23. $b^2 - 4ac = (-9)^2 - 4(3)(0) = 81 - 0 = 81$
Since the discriminant is positive, this equation has two distinct real number solutions.

25. $b^2 - 4ac = (-6)^2 - 4(1)(9) = 36 - 36 = 0$
Since the discriminant is zero, this equation has one real number solution.

27. $a = 1, b = -2, c = -8$
$$x = \frac{-b \pm \sqrt{b^2 - 4ac}}{2a}$$
$$= \frac{-(-2) \pm \sqrt{(-2)^2 - 4(1)(-8)}}{2(1)}$$
$$= \frac{2 \pm \sqrt{4 + 32}}{2}$$
$$= \frac{2 \pm \sqrt{36}}{2}$$
$$= \frac{2 \pm 6}{2}$$
$$x = \frac{2 + 6}{2} \text{ or } x = \frac{2 - 6}{2}$$
$$x = 4 \qquad \text{ or } x = -2$$

29. $a = 1, b = 9, c = 18$
$$x = \frac{-b \pm \sqrt{b^2 - 4ac}}{2a}$$
$$= \frac{-9 \pm \sqrt{(9)^2 - 4(1)(18)}}{2(1)}$$
$$= \frac{-9 \pm \sqrt{81 - 72}}{2}$$
$$= \frac{-9 \pm \sqrt{9}}{2}$$
$$= \frac{-9 \pm 3}{2}$$
$$x = \frac{-9 + 3}{2} \text{ or } x = \frac{-9 - 3}{2}$$
$$x = -3 \qquad \text{ or } x = -6$$

31. Write in standard form
$x^2 - 6x + 5 = 0$

$a = 1$, $b = -6$, $c = 5$

$$x = \frac{-b \pm \sqrt{b^2 - 4ac}}{2a}$$

$$= \frac{-(-6) \pm \sqrt{(-6)^2 - 4(1)(5)}}{2(1)}$$

$$= \frac{6 \pm \sqrt{36 - 20}}{2}$$

$$= \frac{6 \pm \sqrt{16}}{2}$$

$$= \frac{6 \pm 4}{2}$$

$$x = \frac{6 + 4}{2} \text{ or } x = \frac{6 - 4}{2}$$

$$x = 5 \qquad \text{or } x = 1$$

33. Write in standard form

$z^2 + 11z + 30 = 0$

$a = 1$, $b = 11$, $c = 30$

$$x = \frac{-b \pm \sqrt{b^2 - 4ac}}{2a}$$

$$= \frac{-(11) \pm \sqrt{(11)^2 - 4(1)(30)}}{2(1)}$$

$$= \frac{11 \pm \sqrt{121 - 120}}{2}$$

$$= \frac{11 \pm \sqrt{1}}{2}$$

$$= \frac{11 \pm 1}{2}$$

$$x = \frac{11 + 1}{2} \text{ or } x = \frac{11 - 1}{2}$$

$$x = 6 \qquad \text{or } x = 5$$

35. Write in standard form

$m^2 - 81 = 0$

$a = 1$, $b = 0$, $c = -81$

$$m = \frac{-b \pm \sqrt{b^2 - 4ac}}{2a}$$

$$= \frac{-0 \pm \sqrt{(0)^2 - 4(1)(-81)}}{2(1)}$$

$$= \frac{\pm\sqrt{324}}{2}$$

$$= \frac{\pm 18}{2}$$

$$= \pm 9$$

$m = 9$ or $m = -9$

37. $a = 1$, $b = -5$, $c = 0$

$$t = \frac{-b \pm \sqrt{b^2 - 4ac}}{2a}$$

$$= \frac{-(-5) \pm \sqrt{(-5)^2 - 4(1)(0)}}{2(1)}$$

$$= \frac{5 \pm \sqrt{25}}{2}$$

$$= \frac{5 \pm 5}{2}$$

$$t = \frac{5 + 5}{2} \text{ or } t = \frac{5 - 5}{2}$$

$$t = 5 \qquad \text{or } t = 0$$

39. $a = 2$, $b = -3$, $c = 2$

$$x = \frac{-b \pm \sqrt{b^2 - 4ac}}{2a}$$

$$= \frac{-(-3) \pm \sqrt{(-3)^2 - 4(2)(2)}}{2(2)}$$

$$= \frac{3 \pm \sqrt{9 - 16}}{4}$$

$$= \frac{3 \pm \sqrt{-7}}{4}$$

Since $\sqrt{-7}$ is not a real number, this equation has no real number solution.

41. $a = 2$, $b = -7$, $c = 4$

$$y = \frac{-b \pm \sqrt{b^2 - 4ac}}{2a}$$

$$= \frac{-(-7) \pm \sqrt{(-7)^2 - 4(2)(4)}}{2(2)}$$

$$= \frac{7 \pm \sqrt{49 - 32}}{4}$$

$$= \frac{7 \pm \sqrt{17}}{4}$$

$$x = \frac{7 + \sqrt{17}}{4} \text{ or } x = \frac{7 - \sqrt{17}}{4}$$

43. Write in standard form

$6x^2 + x - 1 = 0$

$a = 6, b = 1, c = -1$

$x = \dfrac{-b \pm \sqrt{b^2 - 4ac}}{2a}$

$= \dfrac{-1 \pm \sqrt{(1)^2 - 4(6)(-1)}}{2(6)}$

$= \dfrac{-1 \pm \sqrt{1 + 24}}{12}$

$= \dfrac{-1 \pm \sqrt{25}}{12}$

$= \dfrac{-1 \pm 5}{12}$

$x = \dfrac{-1 + 5}{12}$ or $x = \dfrac{-1 - 5}{12}$

$x = \dfrac{1}{3}$ or $x = -\dfrac{1}{2}$

45. Write in standard form

$2x^2 - 5x - 7 = 0$

$a = 2, b = -5, c = -7$

$x = \dfrac{-b \pm \sqrt{b^2 - 4ac}}{2a}$

$= \dfrac{-(-5) \pm \sqrt{(-5)^2 - 4(2)(-7)}}{2(2)}$

$= \dfrac{5 \pm \sqrt{25 + 56}}{4}$

$= \dfrac{5 \pm \sqrt{81}}{4}$

$= \dfrac{5 \pm 9}{4}$

$x = \dfrac{5 + 9}{4}$ or $x = \dfrac{5 - 9}{4}$

$x = \dfrac{7}{2}$ or $x = -1$

47. $a = 2, b = -4, c = 3$

$s = \dfrac{-b \pm \sqrt{b^2 - 4ac}}{2a}$

$= \dfrac{-(-4) \pm \sqrt{(-4)^2 - 4(2)(3)}}{2(2)}$

$= \dfrac{4 \pm \sqrt{16 - 24}}{4}$

$= \dfrac{4 \pm \sqrt{-8}}{4}$

Since $\sqrt{-8}$ is not a real number, this equation has no real number solution.

49. Write in standard form

$4x^2 - x - 5 = 0$

$a = 4, b = -1, c = -5$

$x = \dfrac{-b \pm \sqrt{b^2 - 4ac}}{2a}$

$= \dfrac{-(-1) \pm \sqrt{(-1)^2 - 4(4)(-5)}}{2(4)}$

$= \dfrac{1 \pm \sqrt{1 + 80}}{8}$

$= \dfrac{1 \pm \sqrt{81}}{8}$

$= \dfrac{1 \pm 9}{8}$

$x = \dfrac{1 + 9}{8}$ or $x = \dfrac{1 - 9}{8}$

$x = \dfrac{5}{4}$ or $x = -1$

51. Write in standard form

$2x^2 - 7x - 9 = 0$

$a = 2, b = -7, c = -9$

$x = \dfrac{-b \pm \sqrt{b^2 - 4ac}}{2a}$

$= \dfrac{-(-7) \pm \sqrt{(-7)^2 - 4(2)(-9)}}{2(2)}$

$= \dfrac{7 \pm \sqrt{49 + 72}}{4}$

$= \dfrac{7 \pm \sqrt{121}}{4}$

$= \dfrac{7 \pm 11}{4}$

$x = \dfrac{7 + 11}{4}$ or $x = \dfrac{7 - 11}{4}$

$x = \dfrac{9}{2}$ or $x = -1$

53. $a = -2, b = 11, c = -15$

$$x = \frac{-b \pm \sqrt{b^2 - 4ac}}{2a}$$

$$= \frac{-11 \pm \sqrt{(11)^2 - 4(-2)(-15)}}{2(-2)}$$

$$= \frac{-11 \pm \sqrt{121 - 120}}{-4}$$

$$= \frac{-11 \pm \sqrt{1}}{-4}$$

$$= \frac{-11 \pm 1}{-4}$$

$$x = \frac{-11 + 1}{-4} \text{ or } x = \frac{-11 - 1}{-4}$$

$$x = \frac{5}{2} \qquad \text{ or } x = 3$$

55. Factor out a 2.

$$2\left(t^2 + 2t - 15\right) = 0$$

Multiply both sides by $\frac{1}{2}$ and use

$$t^2 + 2t - 15 = 0$$

$$a = 1, \; b = 2, \; c = -15$$

$$t = \frac{-b \pm \sqrt{b^2 - 4ac}}{2a}$$

$$= \frac{-2 \pm \sqrt{(2)^2 - 4(1)(-15)}}{2(1)}$$

$$= \frac{-2 \pm \sqrt{4 + 60}}{2}$$

$$= \frac{-2 \pm \sqrt{64}}{2}$$

$$= \frac{-2 \pm 8}{2}$$

$$t = \frac{-2 + 8}{2} \text{ or } t = \frac{-2 - 8}{2}$$

$$t = 3 \qquad \text{ or } t = -5$$

57. Put in standard form and then factor out a 4.

$$4s^2 - 40s + 36 = 0$$

$$4\left(s^2 - 10s + 9\right) = 0$$

Multiply both sides by $\frac{1}{4}$ and use

$$s^2 - 10s + 9 = 0$$

$$a = 1, b = -10, c = 9$$

$$s = \frac{-b \pm \sqrt{b^2 - 4ac}}{2a}$$

$$= \frac{-(-10) \pm \sqrt{(10)^2 - 4(1)(9)}}{2(1)}$$

$$= \frac{10 \pm \sqrt{100 - 36}}{2}$$

$$= \frac{10 \pm \sqrt{64}}{2}$$

$$= \frac{10 \pm 8}{2}$$

$$s = \frac{10 + 8}{2} \text{ or } s = \frac{10 - 8}{2}$$

$$s = 9 \qquad \text{ or } s = 1$$

59. Let x = the smaller integer,
then $x + 1$ = the larger integer.

$$x(x + 1) = 42$$

$$x^2 + x = 42$$

$$x^2 + x - 42 = 0$$

$$a = 1, b = 1, c = -42$$

$$x = \frac{-b \pm \sqrt{b^2 - 4ac}}{2a}$$

$$= \frac{-1 \pm \sqrt{(1)^2 - 4(1)(-42)}}{2(1)}$$

$$= \frac{-1 \pm \sqrt{1 + 168}}{2}$$

$$= \frac{-1 \pm \sqrt{169}}{2}$$

$$= \frac{-1 \pm 13}{2}$$

$$x = \frac{-1 + 13}{2} \text{ or } x = \frac{-1 - 13}{2}$$

$$x = 6 \qquad \text{ or } x = -7$$

Since the numbers are positive, $x = 6$. The numbers are 6 and $6 + 1 = 7$.

61. Let w = width of rectangle,
then $2w - 3$ = length of rectangle.
Area = length $\cdot$ width
$$20 = (2w - 3)w$$
$$20 = 2w^2 - 3w$$
$$0 = 2w^2 - 3w - 20$$
$a = 2, b = -3, c = -20$
$$x = \frac{-b \pm \sqrt{b^2 - 4ac}}{2a}$$
$$= \frac{-(-3) \pm \sqrt{(-3)^2 - 4(2)(-20)}}{2(2)}$$
$$= \frac{3 \pm \sqrt{9 + 160}}{4}$$
$$= \frac{3 \pm \sqrt{169}}{4}$$
$$= \frac{3 \pm 13}{4}$$
$$x = \frac{3 + 13}{4} \text{ or } x = \frac{3 - 13}{4}$$
$$x = 4 \qquad \text{ or } x = -\frac{5}{2}$$
Since the width is positive, $w = 4$. The width is 4 feet and the length is $2(4) - 3 = 5$ feet.

63. Let x = the width of the tile border.
Area of the pool = $(30)(40) = 1200$ square feet
Area of the pool plus border = $(2x + 30)(2x + 40)$
$$= 4x^2 + 140x + 1200$$
Area of the border = $4x^2 + 140x + 1200 - 1200$
$$= 4x^2 + 140x$$
$$4x^2 + 140x = 296$$
$$4x^2 + 140x - 296 = 0$$
$$x^2 + 35x - 74 = 0$$
$a = 1, b = 35, c = -74$
$$x = \frac{-b \pm \sqrt{b^2 - 4ac}}{2a}$$
$$= \frac{-35 \pm \sqrt{(35)^2 - 4(1)(-74)}}{2(1)}$$
$$= \frac{-35 \pm \sqrt{1225 + 296}}{2}$$
$$= \frac{-35 \pm \sqrt{1521}}{2}$$
$$= \frac{-35 \pm 39}{2}$$
$$x = \frac{-35 + 39}{2} \text{ or } x = \frac{-35 - 39}{2}$$
$$x = 2 \qquad \text{ or } x = -37$$
Since the width must be positive, the border can be 2 feet wide.

65. Substitute 27 for d.
$$d = \frac{n^2 - 3n}{2}$$
$$27 = \frac{n^2 - 3n}{2}$$
$$54 = n^2 - 3n$$
$$0 = n^2 - 3n - 54$$
$a = 1, b = -3, c = -54$
$$n = \frac{-b \pm \sqrt{b^2 - 4ac}}{2a}$$
$$= \frac{-(-3) \pm \sqrt{(-3)^2 - 4(1)(-54)}}{2(1)}$$
$$= \frac{3 \pm \sqrt{9 + 216}}{2}$$
$$= \frac{3 \pm \sqrt{225}}{2}$$
$$= \frac{3 \pm 15}{2}$$
$$n = \frac{3 + 15}{2} \text{ or } n = \frac{3 - 15}{2}$$
$$n = 9 \qquad \text{ or } n = -6$$
Since the number of sides must be positive, the polygon has 9 sides.

67. Substitute 1000 for c.
$$c = x^2 - 16x + 40$$
$$1000 = x^2 - 16x + 40$$
$$0 = x^2 - 16x - 960$$
$a = 1, b = -16, c = -960$
$$x = \frac{-b \pm \sqrt{b^2 - 4ac}}{2a}$$
$$= \frac{-(-16) \pm \sqrt{(-16)^2 - 4(1)(-960)}}{2(1)}$$
$$= \frac{16 \pm \sqrt{256 + 3840}}{2}$$
$$= \frac{16 \pm \sqrt{4096}}{2}$$
$$= \frac{16 \pm 64}{2}$$
$$x = \frac{16 + 64}{2} \text{ or } x = \frac{16 - 64}{2}$$
$$x = 40 \qquad \text{ or } x = -24$$
x must be positive. Therefore, 40 chairs were manufactured.

69. Substitute 80 for *s*.

$$s = -16t^2 + 90t$$

$$80 = -16t^2 + 90t$$

$$16t^2 - 90t + 80 = 0$$

$$8t^2 - 45t + 40 = 0$$

$$a = 8,\ b = -45,\ c = 40$$

$$t = \frac{-b \pm \sqrt{b^2 - 4ac}}{2a}$$

$$= \frac{-(-45) \pm \sqrt{(-45)^2 - 4(8)(40)}}{2(8)}$$

$$= \frac{45 \pm \sqrt{2025 - 1280}}{16}$$

$$= \frac{45 \pm \sqrt{745}}{16}$$

$$= \frac{45 \pm 27.29}{16}$$

$$t = \frac{45 + 27.29}{16} \quad \text{or} \quad t = \frac{45 - 27.29}{16}$$

$$t \approx 4.52 \qquad \text{or} \quad t \approx 1.11$$

t must be positive. Therefore, it will take 1.11 and 4.52 seconds.

71. $x^2 + 6x + c = 0$

$a = 1, b = 6$

The discriminant is

$$b^2 - 4ac = 6^2 - 4(1)c = 36 - 4c = 4(9 - c)$$

a. The equation has two real number solutions
when $b^2 - 4ac > 0$.

$$4(9 - c) > 0$$

$$9 - c > 0$$

$$9 > c$$

$$c < 9$$

b. The equation has one real number solution
when $b^2 - 4ac = 0$.

$$4(9 - c) = 0$$

$$9 - c = 0$$

$$9 = c$$

$$c = 9$$

c. The equation has no real number solution
when $b^2 - 4ac < 0$.

$$4(9 - c) < 0$$

$$9 - c < 0$$

$$9 < c$$

$$c > 9$$

73. $-3x^2 + 6x + c = 0$

$a = -3, b = 6$

The discriminant is

$$b^2 - 4ac = 6^2 - 4(-3)c = 36 + 12c = 12(3 + c).$$

a. The equation has two real number solutions
when $b^2 - 4ac > 0$.

$$12(3 + c) > 0$$

$$3 + c > 0$$

$$c > -3$$

b. The equation has one real number solution
when $b^2 - 4ac = 0$.

$$12(3 + c) = 0$$

$$3 + c = 0$$

$$c = -3$$

c. The equation has no real number solution
when $b^2 - 4ac < 0$.

$$12(3 + c) < 0$$

$$3 + c < 0$$

$$c < -3$$

76. a. $x^2 - 13x + 42 = 0$

$$(x - 7)(x - 6) = 0$$

$$x - 7 = 0 \text{ or } x - 6 = 0$$

$$x = 7 \qquad \text{or } x = 6$$

b.

$$x^2 - 13x + 42 = 0$$

$$x^2 - 13x = -42$$

$$x^2 - 13x + \frac{169}{4} = -42 + \frac{169}{4}$$

$$\left(x - \frac{13}{2}\right)^2 = \frac{1}{4}$$

$$x - \frac{13}{2} = \pm\sqrt{\frac{1}{4}}$$

$$x - \frac{13}{2} = \pm\frac{1}{2}$$

$$x = \frac{13}{2} \pm \frac{1}{2}$$

$$x = \frac{13}{2} + \frac{1}{2} \text{ or } x = \frac{13}{2} - \frac{1}{2}$$

$$x = 7 \qquad \text{or } x = 6$$

c. $a = 1, b = -13, c = 42$

$$x = \frac{-b \pm \sqrt{b^2 - 4ac}}{2a}$$

$$= \frac{-(-13) \pm \sqrt{(-13)^2 - 4(1)(42)}}{2(1)}$$

$$= \frac{13 \pm \sqrt{169 - 168}}{2}$$

$$= \frac{13 \pm \sqrt{1}}{2}$$

$$= \frac{13 \pm 1}{2}$$

$$x = \frac{13 + 1}{2} \text{ or } x = \frac{13 - 1}{2}$$

$$x = 7 \qquad \text{ or } x = 6$$

77. a.

$$6x^2 + 11x - 35 = 0$$

$$6x^2 + 21x - 10x - 35 = 0$$

$$3x(2x + 7) - 5(2x + 7) = 0$$

$$(3x - 5)(2x + 7) = 0$$

$$3x - 5 = 0 \text{ or } 2x + 7 = 0$$

$$x = \frac{5}{3} \text{ or } \qquad x = -\frac{7}{2}$$

b.

$$6x^2 + 11x - 35 = 0$$

$$x^2 + \frac{11}{6}x - \frac{35}{6} = 0$$

$$x^2 + \frac{11}{6}x = \frac{35}{6}$$

$$x^2 + \frac{11}{6}x + \frac{121}{144} = \frac{35}{6} + \frac{121}{144}$$

$$\left(x + \frac{11}{12}\right)^2 = \frac{961}{144}$$

$$x + \frac{11}{12} = \pm\sqrt{\frac{961}{144}}$$

$$x + \frac{11}{12} = \pm\frac{31}{12}$$

$$x = -\frac{11}{12} \pm \frac{31}{12}$$

$$x = -\frac{11}{12} + \frac{31}{12} \text{ or } x = -\frac{11}{12} - \frac{31}{12}$$

$$x = \frac{20}{12} = \frac{5}{3} \qquad \text{ or } x = -\frac{42}{12} = -\frac{7}{2}$$

c. $a = 6, b = 11, c = -35$

$$x = \frac{-b \pm \sqrt{b^2 - 4ac}}{2a}$$

$$= \frac{-11 \pm \sqrt{11^2 - 4(6)(-35)}}{2(6)}$$

$$= \frac{-11 \pm \sqrt{121 + 840}}{12}$$

$$= \frac{-11 \pm \sqrt{961}}{12}$$

$$= \frac{-11 \pm 31}{12}$$

$$x = \frac{-11 + 31}{12} \text{ or } x = \frac{-11 - 31}{12}$$

$$x = \frac{20}{12} = \frac{5}{3} \qquad \text{ or } x = \frac{-42}{12} = -\frac{7}{2}$$

78. a. $2x^2 + 3x - 4 = 0$

Since there are no integers whose product is -8 and whose sum is 3, this equation cannot be solved by factoring.

b.

$$2x^2 + 3x - 4 = 0$$

$$x^2 + \frac{3}{2}x - 2 = 0$$

$$x^2 + \frac{3}{2}x = 2$$

$$x^2 + \frac{3}{2}x + \frac{9}{16} = 2 + \frac{9}{16}$$

$$\left(x + \frac{3}{4}\right)^2 = \frac{41}{16}$$

$$x + \frac{3}{4} = \pm\sqrt{\frac{41}{16}}$$

$$x + \frac{3}{4} = \pm\frac{\sqrt{41}}{4}$$

$$x = -\frac{3}{4} \pm \frac{\sqrt{41}}{4}$$

$$x = \frac{-3 \pm \sqrt{41}}{4}$$

$$x = \frac{-3 + \sqrt{41}}{4} \text{ or } x = \frac{-3 - \sqrt{41}}{4}$$

c. $a = 2, b = 3, c = -4$

$$x = \frac{-b \pm \sqrt{b^2 - 4ac}}{2(a)}$$

$$= \frac{-3 \pm \sqrt{3^2 - 4(2)(-4)}}{2(2)}$$

$$= \frac{-3 \pm \sqrt{9 + 32}}{4}$$

$$= \frac{-3 \pm \sqrt{41}}{4}$$

$$x = \frac{-3 + \sqrt{41}}{4} \text{ or } x = \frac{-3 - \sqrt{41}}{4}$$

79. a.
$$6x^2 = 54$$
$$6x^2 - 54 = 0$$
$$6(x^2 - 9) = 0$$
$$6(x - 3)(x + 3) = 0$$
$$x - 3 = 0 \text{ or } x + 3 = 0$$
$$x = 3 \text{ or } \qquad x = -3$$

b. $6x^2 = 54$
$$x^2 = 9$$
$$x = \pm\sqrt{9}$$
$$x = \pm 3$$
$$x = 3 \text{ or } x = -3$$

c. $6x^2 - 54 = 0$
$$a = 6, b = 0, c = -54$$
$$x = \frac{-b \pm \sqrt{b^2 - 4ac}}{2(a)}$$
$$= \frac{-0 \pm \sqrt{0^2 - 4(6)(-54)}}{2(6)}$$
$$= \frac{\pm\sqrt{1296}}{12}$$
$$= \frac{\pm 36}{12}$$
$$= \pm 3$$
$$x = 3 \text{ or } x = -3$$

80.
$$\frac{x}{2x^2 + 7x - 4} - \frac{2}{x^2 - x - 20}$$

$$= \frac{x}{(2x - 1)(x + 4)} - \frac{2}{(x - 5)(x + 4)}$$

LCD is $(2x - 1)(x + 4)(x - 5)$

$$= \frac{x - 5}{x - 5} \cdot \frac{x}{(2x - 1)(x + 4)} - \frac{2x - 1}{2x - 1} \cdot \frac{2}{(x - 5)(x + 4)}$$

$$= \frac{x^2 - 5x}{(2x - 1)(x + 4)(x - 5)} - \frac{4x - 2}{(2x - 1)(x + 4)(x - 5)}$$

$$= \frac{x^2 - 5x - 4x + 2}{(2x - 1)(x + 4)(x - 5)}$$

$$= \frac{x^2 - 9x + 2}{(2x - 1)(x + 4)(x - 5)}$$

Exercise Set 10.4

1. The graph of a quadratic equation of the form $y = ax^2 + bx + c, a \neq 0$ is called a parabola.

3. Answers will vary.

5. **a.**   Where the graph crosses the x-axis.

    b.   The x-intercepts are found by setting $y = 0$ and solving for x.

7. **a.** $x = -\dfrac{b}{2a}$

    b.   This line is called the axis of symmetry.

9. $a = 1, b = 4, c = -3$
$$x = -\frac{b}{2a} = -\frac{4}{2(1)} = -2$$
The axis of symmetry is $x = -2$.
Find the y-coordinate of the vertex:
$$y = x^2 + 4x - 3$$
$$y = (-2)^2 + 4(-2) - 3$$
$$= 4 - 8 - 3$$
$$= -7$$
The vertex is $(-2, -7)$
Since $a > 0$, the parabola opens upward.

11. $a = -1, b = 3, c = -4$
$$x = -\frac{b}{2a} = -\frac{3}{2(-1)} = \frac{3}{2}$$
The axis of symmetry is $x = \dfrac{3}{2}$
Find the y-coordinate of the vertex:

$y = -x^2 + 3x - 4$

$y = -\left(\dfrac{3}{2}\right)^2 + 3\left(\dfrac{3}{2}\right) - 4$

$= -\dfrac{9}{4} + \dfrac{9}{2} - 4$

$= -\dfrac{7}{4}$

The vertex is $\left(\dfrac{3}{2}, -\dfrac{7}{4}\right)$.

Since $a < 0$, the parabola opens downward.

13. $a = -3, b = 2, c = 8$

$x = -\dfrac{b}{2a} = -\dfrac{2}{2(-3)} = \dfrac{2}{6} = \dfrac{1}{3}$

The axis of symmetry is $x = \dfrac{1}{3}$

Find the y-coordinate of the vertex:

$y = -3x^2 + 2x + 8$

$y = -3\left(\dfrac{1}{3}\right)^2 + 2\left(\dfrac{1}{3}\right) + 8$

$= -\dfrac{1}{3} + \dfrac{2}{3} + 8$

$= \dfrac{25}{3}$

The vertex is $\left(\dfrac{1}{3}, \dfrac{25}{3}\right)$.

Since $a < 0$, the parabola opens downward.

15. $a = 4, b = 8, c = 3$

$x = -\dfrac{b}{2a} = -\dfrac{8}{2(4)} = -1$

The axis of symmetry is $x = -1$.
Find the y-coordinate of the vertex:

$y = 4x^2 + 8x + 3$

$y = 4(-1)^2 + 8(-1) + 3$

$= 4 - 8 + 3$

$= -1$

The vertex is $(-1, -1)$.
Since $a > 0$, the parabola opens upward.

17. $a = 2, b = 3, c = 8$

$x = -\dfrac{b}{2a} = -\dfrac{3}{2(2)} = -\dfrac{3}{4}$

The axis of symmetry is $x = -\dfrac{3}{4}$.

Find the y-coordinate of the vertex:

$y = 2x^2 + 3x + 5$

$y = 2\left(-\dfrac{3}{4}\right)^2 + 3\left(-\dfrac{3}{4}\right) + 5$

$= \dfrac{9}{8} - \dfrac{9}{4} + 5$

$= \dfrac{31}{8}$

The vertex is $\left(-\dfrac{3}{4}, \dfrac{31}{8}\right)$.

Since $a > 0$, the parabola opens upward.

19. $a = -5, b = 6, c = -1$

$x = -\dfrac{b}{2a} = -\dfrac{6}{2(-5)} = \dfrac{3}{5}$

The axis of symmetry is $x = \dfrac{3}{5}$.

Find the y-coordinate of the vertex:

$y = -5x^2 + 6x - 1$

$y = -5\left(\dfrac{3}{5}\right)^2 + 6\left(\dfrac{3}{5}\right) - 1$

$= -\dfrac{9}{5} + \dfrac{18}{5} - 1$

$= \dfrac{4}{5}$

The vertex is $\left(\dfrac{3}{5}, \dfrac{4}{5}\right)$.

Since $a < 0$, the parabola opens downward.

21. $a = 1, b = 0, c = -4$
Since $a > 0$, the parabola opens upward.

Axis of symmetry is $x = -\dfrac{b}{2a} = -\dfrac{0}{2(1)} = 0$.

y-coordinate of the vertex:

$y = x^2 - 4$

$y = 0^2 - 4 = -4$

The vertex is $(0, -4)$

$y = x^2 - 4$

Let $x = -2$ $\quad y = (-2)^2 - 4 = 0$

Let $x = 2$ $\quad y = 2^2 - 4 = 0$

x	y
-2	0
2	0

$0 = x^2 - 4$

$0 = (x + 2)(x - 2)$

$x = -2$ or $x = 2$

$3x^2 + 1 = 28$

$3x^2 = 27$

$x^2 = 9$

$x = \pm\sqrt{9}$

$x = 3, -3$

23. $a = -1, b = 0, c = 5$

Since $a < 0$, the parabola opens downward.

Axis of symmetry is $x = -\dfrac{b}{2a} = -\dfrac{0}{2(-1)} = 0$

y-coordinate of the vertex:

$y = -x^2 + 5$

$y = -0^2 + 5 = 5$

The vertex is (0, 5).

$$y = -x^2 + 5$$

Let $x = -1$ $y = -(-1)^2 + 5 = 4$

Let $x = 1$ $y = -(1)^2 + 5 = 4$

x	y
-1	4
1	4

$0 = -x^2 + 5$

$x^2 = 5$

$x = \pm\sqrt{5}$

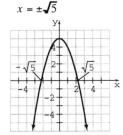

25. $a = 1, b = 4, c = 3$

Since $a > 0$, the parabola opens upward.

Axis of symmetry is $x = -\dfrac{b}{2a} = -\dfrac{4}{2(1)} = -2$

y-coordinate of the vertex:

$y = x^2 + 4x + 3$

$y = (-2)^2 + 4(-2) + 3 = 1$

The vertex is (−2, −1).

$$y = x^2 + 4x + 3$$

Let $x = -1$ $y = (-1)^2 + 4(-1) + 3 = 0$

Let $x = 0$ $y = 0^2 + 4(0) + 3 = 3$

x	y
-1	0
0	3

$0 = x^2 + 4x + 3$

$0 = (x + 3)(x + 1)$

$x = -3$ or $x = -1$

27. $a = 1, b = 4, c = 4$

Since $a > 0$, the parabola opens upward.

Axis of symmetry is $x = -\dfrac{b}{2a} = -\dfrac{4}{2(1)} = -2$

y-coordinate of the vertex:

$y = x^2 + 4x + 4$

$y = (-2)^2 + 4(-2) + 4 = 0$

The vertex is (−2, 0)

$$y = x^2 + 4x + 4$$

Let $x = -3$ $y = (-3)^2 + 4(-3) + 4 = 1$

Let $x = -1$ $y = (-1)^2 + 4(-1) + 4 = 1$

x	y
-3	1
-1	1

$0 = x^2 + 4x + 4$

$0 = (x + 2)^2$

$x = -2$

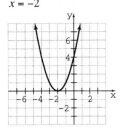

29. $a = -1, b = -5, c = -4$

Since $a < 0$, the parabola opens downward.

Axis of symmetry is $x = -\dfrac{b}{2a} = -\dfrac{-5}{2(-1)} = -\dfrac{5}{2}$

y-coordinate of the vertex:

$$y = -x^2 - 5x - 4$$

$$y = -\left(-\frac{5}{2}\right)^2 - 5\left(-\frac{5}{2}\right) - 4$$

$$= -\frac{25}{4} + \frac{25}{2} - 4$$

$$= \frac{9}{4}$$

The vertex is $\left(-\frac{5}{2}, \frac{9}{4}\right)$

$$y = -x^2 - 5x - 4$$

Let $x = -1$ $y = -(-1)^2 - 5(-1) - 4 = 0$

Let $x = -4$ $y = -(-4)^2 - 5(-4) - 4 = 0$

x	y
-4	0
-1	0

$$0 = -x^2 - 5x - 4$$

$$0 = x^2 + 5x + 4$$

$$0 = (x + 4)(x + 1)$$

$$x = -4 \text{ or } x = -1$$

31. $a = 1, b = 5, c = -6$

Since $a > 0$, the parabola opens upward.

Axis of symmetry is $x = -\dfrac{b}{2a} = -\dfrac{5}{2(1)} = -\dfrac{5}{2}$

y-coordinate of the vertex:

$$y = x^2 + 5x - 6$$

$$y = \left(-\frac{5}{2}\right)^2 + 5\left(-\frac{5}{2}\right) - 6 = -\frac{49}{4}$$

The vertex is $\left(-\dfrac{5}{2}, -\dfrac{49}{4}\right)$.

$$y = x^2 + 5x - 6$$

Let $x = -6$ $y = (-6)^2 + 5(-6) - 6 = 0$

Let $x = 1$ $y = 1^2 + 5(1) - 6 = 0$

x	y
-6	0
1	0

$$0 = x^2 + 5x - 6$$

$$0 = (x + 6)(x - 1)$$

$$x = -6 \text{ or } x = 1$$

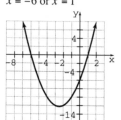

33. $a = 1, b = 5, c = -14$

Since $a > 0$, the parabola opens upward.

Axis of symmetry is $x = -\dfrac{b}{2a} = -\dfrac{5}{2(1)} = -\dfrac{5}{2}$

y-coordinate of the vertex:

$$y = x^2 + 5x - 14$$

$$y = \left(-\frac{5}{2}\right)^2 + 5\left(-\frac{5}{2}\right) - 14 = -\frac{81}{4}$$

The vertex is $\left(-\dfrac{5}{2}, -\dfrac{81}{4}\right)$

$$y = x^2 + 5x - 14$$

Let $x = -7$ $y = (-7)^2 + 5(-7) - 14 = 0$

Let $x = 2$ $y = 2^2 + 5(2) - 14 = 0$

x	y
-7	0
2	0

$$0 = x^2 + 5x - 14$$

$$0 = (x + 7)(x - 2)$$

$$x = -7 \text{ or } x = 2$$

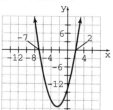

35. $a = 1, b = -6, c = 9$

Since $a > 0$, the parabola opens upward.

Axis of symmetry: $x = -\dfrac{b}{2a} = -\dfrac{-6}{2(1)} = 3$

y-coordinate of the vertex:

$$y = x^2 - 6x + 9$$

$$y = 3^2 - 6(3) + 9 = 0$$

The vertex is at $(3, 0)$

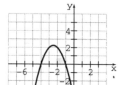

$$y = x^2 - 6x + 9$$

Let $x = 4$ $y = 4^2 - 6(4) + 9 = 1$

Let $x = 5$ $y = 5^2 - 6(5) + 9 = 4$

Let $x = 6$ $y = 6^2 - 6(6) + 9 = 9$

x	y
4	1
5	4
6	9

$$0 = x^2 - 6x + 9$$
$$0 = (x - 3)^2$$
$$x = 3$$

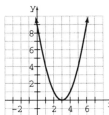

37. $a = 1, b = -6, c = 0$

Since $a > 0$, the parabola opens upward.

axis of symmetry is $x = -\dfrac{b}{2a} = -\dfrac{-6}{2(1)} = 3$

y-coordinate of the vertex:
$$y = x^2 - 6x$$
$$y = 3^2 - 6(3) = -9$$
The vertex is $(3, -9)$.

$$y = x^2 - 6x$$

Let $x = 0$ $y = 0^2 - 6(0) = 0$

Let $x = 6$ $y = 6^2 - 6(6) = 0$

x	y
0	0
6	0

$$0 = x^2 - 6x$$
$$0 = x(x - 6)$$
$$x = 0 \text{ or } x = 6$$

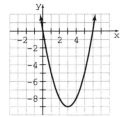

39. $a = 4, b = 12, c = 9$

Since $a > 0$, the parabola opens upward.

Axis of symmetry is $x = -\dfrac{b}{2a} = -\dfrac{12}{2(4)} = -\dfrac{3}{2}$

y-coordinate of the vertex:
$$y = 4x^2 + 12x + 9$$
$$y = 4\left(-\frac{3}{2}\right)^2 + 12\left(-\frac{3}{2}\right) + 9 = 0$$
The vertex is $\left(-\dfrac{3}{2}, 0\right)$.

$$y = 4x^2 + 12x + 9$$

Let $x = -1$ $y = 4(-1)^2 + 12(-1) + 9 = 1$

Let $x = 0$ $y = 4(0)^2 + 12(0) + 9 = 9$

x	y
-1	1
0	9

$$0 = 4x^2 + 12x + 9$$
$$0 = (2x + 3)^2$$
$$x = -\frac{3}{2}$$

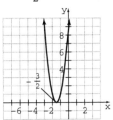

41. $a = -1, b = 7, c = -10$

Since $a < 0$, the parabola opens downward.

Axis of symmetry: $x = -\dfrac{b}{2a} = -\dfrac{7}{2(-1)} = \dfrac{7}{2}$

y-coordinate of the vertex:
$$y = -x^2 + 7x - 10$$
$$y = -\left(\frac{7}{2}\right)^2 + 7\left(\frac{7}{2}\right) - 10 = \frac{9}{4}$$
The vertex is at $\left(\dfrac{7}{2}, \dfrac{9}{4}\right)$.

$$y = -x^2 + 7x - 10$$

Let $x = 1$ $y = -1^2 + 7(1) - 10 = -4$

Let $x = 6$ $y = -6^2 + 7(6) - 10 = -4$

Let $x = 0$ $y = -0^2 + 7(0) - 10 = -10$

x	y
1	-4
6	-4
0	-10

$0 = -x^2 + 7x - 10$

$0 = x^2 - 7x + 10$

$0 = (x - 5)(x - 2)$

$x = 5 \text{ or } x = 2$

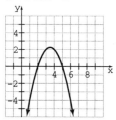

43. $a = 1, b = -2, c = -16$

Since $a > 0$, the parabola opens upward.

Axis of symmetry is $x = -\dfrac{b}{2a} = -\dfrac{-2}{2(1)} = 1$

y-coordinate of the vertex:

$y = x^2 - 2x - 16$

$y = 1^2 - 2(1) - 16 = -17$

The vertex is $(1, -17)$.

$$y = x^2 - 2x - 16$$

Let $x = -2$ $y = (-2)^2 - 2(-2) - 16 = -8$

Let $x = 0$ $y = 0^2 - 2(0) - 16 = -16$

x	y
-2	-8
0	-16

$0 = x^2 - 2x - 16$

$x = \dfrac{-(-2) \pm \sqrt{(-2)^2 - 4(1)(-16)}}{2(1)}$

$\quad = \dfrac{2 \pm \sqrt{68}}{2}$

$\quad = 1 \pm \sqrt{17}$

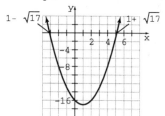

45. $a = -2, b = 3, c = -2$

Since $a < 0$, the parabola opens downward.

Axis of symmetry: $x = -\dfrac{b}{2a} = -\dfrac{3}{2(-2)} = \dfrac{3}{4}$

y-coordinate of the vertex:

$y = -2x^2 + 3x - 2$

$y = -2\left(\dfrac{3}{4}\right)^2 + 3\left(\dfrac{3}{4}\right) - 2 = -\dfrac{7}{8}$

The vertex is $\left(\dfrac{3}{4}, -\dfrac{7}{8}\right)$.

$$y = -2x^2 + 3x - 2$$

Let $x = -1$ $y = -2(-1)^2 + 3(-1) - 2 = -7$

Let $x = 0$ $y = -2(0)^2 + 3(0) - 2 = -2$

Let $x = 1$ $y = -2(1)^2 + 3(1) - 2 = -1$

Let $x = 2$ $y = -2(2)^2 + 3(2) - 2 = -4$

x	y
-1	-7
0	-2
1	-1
2	-4

$0 = -2x^2 + 3x - 2$

$x = \dfrac{-3 \pm \sqrt{3^2 - 4(-2)(-2)}}{2(-2)}$

$\quad = \dfrac{-3 \pm \sqrt{-7}}{-4}$

No real number solution

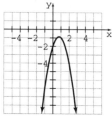

No x-intercepts

47. $a = 2, b = -1, c = -15$

Since $a > 0$, the parabola opens upward.

Axis of symmetry is $x = -\dfrac{b}{2a} = -\dfrac{-1}{2(2)} = \dfrac{1}{4}$

y-coordinate of the vertex:

$y = 2x^2 - x - 15$

$y = 2\left(\dfrac{1}{4}\right)^2 - \dfrac{1}{4} - 15 = -\dfrac{121}{8}$

The vertex is $\left(\dfrac{1}{4}, -\dfrac{121}{8}\right)$.

$$y = 2x^2 - x - 15$$

Let $x = -2$ $y = 2(-2)^2 - (-2) - 15 = -5$

Let $x = 2$ $y = 2(2)^2 - 2 - 15 = -9$

x	y
-2	-5
2	-9

$0 = 2x^2 - x - 15$
$0 = (2x + 5)(x - 3)$
$x = -\dfrac{5}{2}$ or $x = 3$

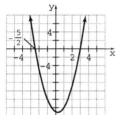

49. $b^2 - 4ac = (-2)^2 - 4(4)(-16)$
$\qquad = 4 + 256$
$\qquad = 260$
Since the discriminant is positive, there will be two x-intercepts.

51. $b^2 - 4ac = (-6)^2 - 4(4)(-7) = 36 + 112 = 148$
Since the discriminant is positive, there will be two x-intercepts.

53. $b^2 - 4ac = (-20)^2 - 4(1)(100) = 400 - 400 = 0$
Since the discriminant is zero, there will be one x-intercept.

55. $b^2 - 4ac = 2^2 - 4(1.6)(-3.9)$
$\qquad = 4 + 24.96$
$\qquad = 28.96$
Since the discriminant is positive, there will be two x-intercepts.

57. None; the vertex is below the x-axis and the parabola opens downward.

59. One; the vertex of the parabola is on the x-axis.

61. Yes; if y is set to 0, both equations have the same solutions, 5 and –3.

63. **a.** The maximum height is about 255 feet.

     b. It will take 4 seconds.

     c. It will strike the ground in 8 seconds.

     d. At 2 seconds it is about 190 feet high and about 240 feet high at 5 seconds.

65. **a.**

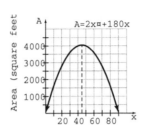

     b. The maximum area is when $x = 45$ feet.

     c. Substitute 45 for x.
$A = -2x^2 + 180x$
$\quad = -2(45)^2 + 180(45)$
$\quad = -4050 + 8100$
$\quad = 4050$
The maximum are is 4050 square feet.

67. **a.** $a = -1, b = 6, c = 0$
Since $a < 0$, the parabola opens downward.
Axis of symmetry is $x = -\dfrac{b}{2a} = -\dfrac{6}{2(-1)} = 3$

y-coordinate of the vertex:
$y = -x^2 + 6x$
$y = -(3)^2 + 6(3) = 9$
The vertex is (3, 9).
$$y = -x^2 + 6x$$
Let $x = 0$ $y = -(0)^2 + 6(0) = 0$
Let $x = 6$ $y = -(6)^2 + 6(6) = 6$

x	y
0	0
6	0

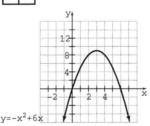

$y = -x^2 + 6x$

     b. For $y = x^2 - 2x$
$a = 1, b = -2, c = 0$
Since $a > 0$, the parabola opens upward.
Axis of symmetry is $x = -\dfrac{b}{2a} = -\dfrac{-2}{2(1)} = 1$

y-coordinate of the vertex:
$y = x^2 - 2x$
$y = (1)^2 - 2(1) = -1$

The vertex is $(1, -1)$.

$$y = x^2 - 2x$$

Let $x = 2$ $y = 2^2 - 2(2) = 0$

Let $x = -1$ $y = (-1)^2 - 2(-1) = 3$

x	y
2	0
-1	3

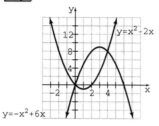

c. $(0, 0), (4, 8)$

69. $\dfrac{3}{x+3} - \dfrac{x-2}{x-4} = \dfrac{3}{x+3} \cdot \dfrac{x-4}{x-4} - \dfrac{x-2}{x-4} \cdot \dfrac{x+3}{x+3}$

$= \dfrac{3x-12}{(x+3)(x-4)} - \dfrac{x^2+x-6}{(x+3)(x-4)}$

$= \dfrac{3x-12-(x^2+x-6)}{(x+3)(x-4)}$

$= \dfrac{-x^2+2x-6}{(x+3)(x-4)}$

70. $\dfrac{1}{3}(x+6) = 3 - \dfrac{1}{4}(x-5)$

$12\left[\dfrac{1}{3}(x+6)\right] = 12\left[3 - \dfrac{1}{4}(x-5)\right]$

$4(x+6) = 36 - 3(x-5)$

$4x + 24 = 36 - 3x + 15$

$7x = 27$

$x = \dfrac{27}{7}$

71. $5x + 4y = 10$

$3x + 5y = -7$

Multiply the first equation by -3.

Multiply the second equation by 5.

$-15x - 12y = -30$

$\underline{15x + 25y = -35}$

$13y = -65$

$y = -5$

Substitute -5 for y in the first equation and solve for x.

$5x + 4(-5) = 10$

$5x - 20 = 10$

$5x = 30$

$x = 6$

The solution is $(6, -5)$.

72. $3\sqrt{2x} - 12 = 0$

$3\sqrt{2x} = 12$

$\sqrt{2x} = 4$

$\left(\sqrt{2x}\right)^2 = 4^2$

$2x = 16$

$x = 8$

Exercise Set 10.5

1. Yes, every real number is a complex number because it can be written in the form $a + bi$ where $b = 0$.

3. $i = \sqrt{-1}$

5. The general form of a complex number is $a + bi$.

7. $\sqrt{-4} = \sqrt{4}\sqrt{-1} = 2i$

9. $\sqrt{-100} = \sqrt{100}\sqrt{-1} = 10i$

11. $\sqrt{-15} = i\sqrt{15}$

13. $\sqrt{-23} = i\sqrt{23}$

15. $\sqrt{-!} = \sqrt{"}\sqrt{\#}\sqrt{-\$} = \#\sqrt{\#}i = \#i\sqrt{\#}$

17. $\sqrt{-20} = \sqrt{4}\sqrt{5}\sqrt{-1} = 2\sqrt{5}i = 2i\sqrt{5}$

19. $5 + \sqrt{-4} = 5 + i\sqrt{4} = 5 + 2i$

21. $-3 + \sqrt{-25} = -3 + i\sqrt{25} = -3 + 5i$

23. $-1-\sqrt{-9} = -1-i\sqrt{9} = -1-3i$

25. $-3-\sqrt{-15} = -3-i\sqrt{15}$

27. $5.2 + \sqrt{-50} = 5.2 + i\sqrt{50}$
$$= 5.2 + i\sqrt{25}\sqrt{2}$$
$$= 5.2 + 5i\sqrt{2}$$

29. $\dfrac{1}{2} + \sqrt{-75} = \dfrac{1}{2} + i\sqrt{75}$
$$= \dfrac{1}{2} + i\sqrt{25}\sqrt{3}$$
$$= \dfrac{1}{2} + 5i\sqrt{3}$$

31. $(2+3i)+5 = 2+5+3i = 7+3i$

33. $(4-3i)-8i = 4-3i-8i = 4-(3+8)i = 4-11i$

35. $(5+3i)+(6+2i) = 5+6+3i+2i$
$$= 11+(3+2)i$$
$$= 11+5i$$

37. $(4-3i)-(6+4i) = 4-3i-6-4i$
$$= 4-6-3i-4i$$
$$= -2-(3+4)i$$
$$= -2-7i$$

39. $(8-6i)-(8-6i) = 8-6i-8+6i$
$$= 8-8-6i+6i$$
$$= 0$$

41. $(45-3i)-(36+i) = 45-3i-36-i$
$$= 45-36-3i-i$$
$$= 9-(3+1)i$$
$$= 9-4i$$

43. $x^2 = -16$
$$x = \pm\sqrt{-16}$$
$$x = \pm\sqrt{16}\sqrt{-1}$$
$$x = \pm 4i$$
The solutions are $4i$ and $-4i$.

45. $2x^2 = -20$
$$x^2 = -10$$
$$x = \pm\sqrt{-10}$$
$$x = \pm\sqrt{-1}\sqrt{10}$$
$$x = \pm i\sqrt{10}$$
The solutions are $i\sqrt{10}$ and $-i\sqrt{10}$.

47. $x^2 - 4x + 5 = 0$
$$a = 1, b = -4, c = 5$$
$$x = \frac{-b \pm \sqrt{b^2 - 4ac}}{4ac}$$
$$x = \frac{-(-4) \pm \sqrt{(-4)^2 - 4(1)(5)}}{2(1)}$$
$$x = \frac{4 \pm \sqrt{16 - 20}}{2}$$
$$x = \frac{4 \pm \sqrt{-4}}{2}$$
$$x = \frac{4 \pm \sqrt{4}\sqrt{-1}}{2}$$
$$x = \frac{4 \pm 2i}{2} = 2 \pm i$$
The solutions are $2+i$ and $2-i$.

49. $2r^2 + 3r + 5 = 0$
$$a = 2, b = 3, c = 5$$
$$r = \frac{-b \pm \sqrt{b^2 - 4ac}}{2a}$$
$$r = \frac{-3 \pm \sqrt{3^2 - 4(2)(5)}}{2(2)}$$
$$r = \frac{-3 \pm \sqrt{9 - 40}}{4}$$
$$r = \frac{-3 \pm \sqrt{-31}}{4}$$
$$r = \frac{-3 \pm \sqrt{-1}\sqrt{31}}{4}$$
$$r = \frac{-3 \pm i\sqrt{31}}{4}$$
The solutions are $\dfrac{-3+i\sqrt{31}}{4}$ and $\dfrac{-3-i\sqrt{31}}{4}$.

51. $2p^2 + 4p + 9 = 0$

$a = 2, \ b = 4, \ c = 9$

$$p = \frac{-b \pm \sqrt{b^2 - 4ac}}{2a}$$

$$p = \frac{-4 \pm \sqrt{4^2 - 4(2)(9)}}{2(2)}$$

$$p = \frac{-4 \pm \sqrt{16 - 72}}{4}$$

$$p = \frac{-4 \pm \sqrt{-56}}{4}$$

$$p = \frac{-4 \pm \sqrt{-1}\sqrt{4}\sqrt{14}}{4}$$

$$p = \frac{-4 \pm 2i\sqrt{14}}{4} = \frac{-2 \pm i\sqrt{14}}{2}$$

The solutions are $\dfrac{-2 + i\sqrt{14}}{2}$ and $\dfrac{-2 - i\sqrt{14}}{2}$.

53. $-4w^2 + 5w - 9 = 0$

$a = -4, \ b = 5, \ c = -9$

$$w = \frac{-b \pm \sqrt{b^2 - 4ac}}{2a}$$

$$w = \frac{-5 \pm \sqrt{5^2 - 4(-4)(-9)}}{2(-4)}$$

$$w = \frac{5 \pm \sqrt{25 - 144}}{8}$$

$$w = \frac{5 \pm \sqrt{-119}}{8}$$

$$w = \frac{5 \pm \sqrt{-1}\sqrt{119}}{8}$$

$$w = \frac{5 \pm i\sqrt{119}}{8}$$

The solutions are $\dfrac{5 + i\sqrt{119}}{8}$ and $\dfrac{5 - i\sqrt{119}}{8}$.

55. The equation will have imaginary solutions when $c \le 0$.

57. The discriminant has to equal 0, that is when $b^2 - 4ac < 0$.

59. Substitute 6 for x.

$$-\left\{ \left[3(x - 4)^2 - 5\right] - 3x \right\}$$

$$= -\left\{ \left[3(6 - 4)^2 - 5\right] - 3(6) \right\}$$

$$= -\left\{ \left[3(4) - 5\right] - 18 \right\}$$

$$= -\left\{ \left[12 - 5\right] - 18 \right\}$$

$$= -\left\{ 7 - 18 \right\}$$

$$= -(-11)$$

$$= 11$$

60. $\dfrac{1}{2}x + \dfrac{3}{5}x = \dfrac{1}{2}(x - 2)$

$$\frac{1}{2}x + \frac{3}{5}x = \frac{1}{2}x - 1$$

$$10\left(\frac{1}{2}x + \frac{3}{5}x\right) = 10\left(\frac{1}{2}x - 1\right)$$

$$5x + 6x = 5x - 10$$

$$11x = 5x + 10$$

$$6x = -10$$

$$x = -\frac{10}{6} = -\frac{5}{3}$$

61.
$$\frac{w - 1}{w - 5} = \frac{3}{w - 5} + \frac{3}{4}$$

$$4(w - 5)\left(\frac{w - 1}{w - 5}\right) = 4(w - 5)\left(\frac{3}{w - 5} + \frac{3}{4}\right)$$

$$4w - 4 = 12 + 3w - 15$$

$$4w - 4 = 3w - 3$$

$$w - 4 = -3$$

$$w = 1$$

62. $2\sqrt{r - 4} + 3 = 9$

$$2\sqrt{r - 4} = 6$$

$$\sqrt{r - 4} = 3$$

$$\left(\sqrt{r - 4}\right)^2 = 3^2$$

$$r - 4 = 9$$

$$r = 13$$

Review Exercises

1. $x^2 = 64$

$$x = \pm\sqrt{64}$$

$$x = \pm 8$$

The solutions are 8 and –8.

2. $x^2 = 12$

$x = \pm\sqrt{12}$

$x = \pm 2\sqrt{3}$

The solutions are $2\sqrt{3}$ and $-2\sqrt{3}$.

3. $\quad 2x^2 = 12$

$\dfrac{1}{2}(2x^2) = \dfrac{1}{2}(12)$

$x^2 = 6$

$x = \pm\sqrt{6}$

The solutions are $\sqrt{6}$ and $-\sqrt{6}$.

4. $x^2 + 4 = 9$

$x^2 = 5$

$x = \pm\sqrt{5}$

The solutions are $\sqrt{5}$ and $-\sqrt{5}$.

5. $x^2 - 4 = 16$

$x^2 = 20$

$x = \pm\sqrt{20}$

$x = \pm 2\sqrt{5}$

The solutions are $2\sqrt{5}$ and $-2\sqrt{5}$.

6. $2x^2 - 4 = 10$

$2x^2 = 14$

$x^2 = 7$

$x = \pm\sqrt{7}$

The solutions are $\sqrt{7}$ and $-\sqrt{7}$.

7. $4x^2 - 30 = 2$

$4x^2 = 32$

$x^2 = 8$

$x = \pm\sqrt{8}$

$x = \pm 2\sqrt{2}$

The solutions are $2\sqrt{2}$ and $-2\sqrt{2}$.

8. $(r - 3)^2 = 20$

$r - 3 = \pm\sqrt{20}$

$r - 3 = \pm 2\sqrt{5}$

$x = 3 \pm 2\sqrt{5}$

The solutions are $3 + 2\sqrt{5}$ and $3 - 2\sqrt{5}$.

9. $(4t - 3)^2 = 50$

$4t - 3 = \pm\sqrt{50}$

$4t - 3 = \pm 5\sqrt{2}$

$4t = 3 \pm 5\sqrt{2}$

$t = \dfrac{3 \pm 5\sqrt{2}}{4}$

The solutions are $\dfrac{3 + 5\sqrt{2}}{4}$ and $\dfrac{3 - 5\sqrt{2}}{4}$.

10. $(2x + 4)^2 = 30$

$2x + 4 = \pm\sqrt{30}$

$2x = -4 \pm\sqrt{30}$

$x = \dfrac{-4 \pm\sqrt{30}}{2}$

The solutions are $\dfrac{-4 + \sqrt{30}}{2}$ and $\dfrac{-4 - \sqrt{30}}{2}$.

11. $\quad x^2 - 7x + 10 = 0$

$x^2 - 7x = -10$

$x^2 - 7x + \dfrac{49}{4} = -10 + \dfrac{49}{4}$

$\left(x - \dfrac{7}{2}\right)^2 = \dfrac{9}{4}$

$x - \dfrac{7}{2} = \pm\sqrt{\dfrac{9}{4}}$

$x - \dfrac{7}{2} = \pm\dfrac{3}{2}$

$x = \dfrac{7}{2} \pm \dfrac{3}{2}$

$x = \dfrac{7}{2} + \dfrac{3}{2} \text{ or } x = \dfrac{7}{2} - \dfrac{3}{2}$

$x = 5 \qquad \text{ or } x = 2$

The solutions are 5 and 2.

12.
$$x^2 - 11x + 28 = 0$$
$$x^2 - 11x = -28$$
$$x^2 - 11x + \frac{121}{4} = -28 + \frac{121}{4}$$
$$\left(x - \frac{11}{2}\right)^2 = \frac{9}{4}$$
$$x - \frac{11}{2} = \pm\sqrt{\frac{9}{4}}$$
$$x - \frac{11}{2} = \pm\frac{3}{2}$$
$$x = \frac{11}{2} \pm \frac{3}{2}$$
$$x = \frac{11}{2} + \frac{3}{2} \text{ or } x = \frac{11}{2} - \frac{3}{2}$$
$$x = 7 \qquad \text{ or } x = 4$$

The solutions are 7 and 4.

13.
$$x^2 - 18x + 17 = 0$$
$$x^2 - 18x = -17$$
$$x^2 - 18x + 81 = -17 + 81$$
$$(x - 9)^2 = 64$$
$$x - 9 = \pm\sqrt{64}$$
$$x - 9 = \pm 8$$
$$x = 9 \pm 8$$
$$x = 9 + 8 \text{ or } x = 9 - 8$$
$$x = 17 \qquad \text{ or } x = 1$$

The solutions are 17 and 1.

14.
$$x^2 + x - 6 = 0$$
$$x^2 + x = 6$$
$$x^2 + x + \frac{1}{4} = 6 + \frac{1}{4}$$
$$\left(x + \frac{1}{2}\right)^2 = \frac{25}{4}$$
$$x + \frac{1}{2} = \pm\sqrt{\frac{25}{4}}$$
$$x + \frac{1}{2} = \pm\frac{5}{2}$$
$$x = -\frac{1}{2} \pm \frac{5}{2}$$
$$x = -\frac{1}{2} + \frac{5}{2} \text{ or } x = -\frac{1}{2} - \frac{5}{2}$$
$$x = 2 \qquad \text{ or } x = -3$$

The solutions are 2 and –3.

15.
$$t^2 - 3x + \frac{9}{4} = 54 + \frac{9}{4}$$
$$\left(t - \frac{3}{2}\right)^2 = \frac{225}{4}$$
$$t - \frac{3}{2} = \pm\sqrt{\frac{225}{4}}$$
$$t - \frac{3}{2} = \pm\frac{15}{2}$$
$$t = \frac{3}{2} \pm \frac{15}{2}$$
$$t^2 - 3x - 54 = 0$$
$$t^2 - 3x = 54$$
$$t = \frac{3}{2} + \frac{15}{2} \text{ or } t = \frac{3}{2} - \frac{15}{2}$$
$$t = 9 \qquad \text{ or } t = -6$$

The solutions are 9 and –6.

16.
$$x^2 = -5x + 6$$
$$x^2 + 5x = 6$$
$$x^2 + 5x + \frac{25}{4} = 6 + \frac{25}{4}$$
$$\left(x + \frac{5}{2}\right)^2 = \frac{49}{4}$$
$$x + \frac{5}{2} = \pm\sqrt{\frac{49}{4}}$$
$$x + \frac{5}{2} = \pm\frac{7}{2}$$
$$x - = -\frac{5}{2} \pm \frac{7}{2}$$
$$x = -\frac{5}{2} + \frac{7}{2} \text{ or } x = -\frac{5}{2} - \frac{7}{2}$$
$$x = 1 \qquad \text{ or } x = -6$$

The solutions are 1 and –6.

17.

$$y^2 - 5y - 7 = 0$$

$$y^2 - 5y = 7$$

$$y^2 - 5y + \frac{25}{4} = 7 + \frac{25}{4}$$

$$\left(y - \frac{5}{2}\right)^2 = \frac{53}{4}$$

$$y - \frac{5}{2} = \pm\sqrt{\frac{53}{4}}$$

$$y - \frac{5}{2} = \pm\frac{\sqrt{53}}{2}$$

$$y = \frac{5}{2} \pm \frac{\sqrt{53}}{2}$$

$$y = \frac{5 \pm \sqrt{53}}{2}$$

$$y = \frac{5 + \sqrt{53}}{2} \text{ or } y = \frac{5 - \sqrt{53}}{2}$$

The solutions are $\dfrac{5 + \sqrt{53}}{2}$ and $\dfrac{5 - \sqrt{53}}{2}$.

18.

$$x^2 + 2x - 5 = 0$$

$$x^2 + 2x = 5$$

$$x^2 + 2x + 1 = 5 + 1$$

$$(x + 1)^2 = 6$$

$$x + 1 = \pm\sqrt{6}$$

$$x = -1 \pm \sqrt{6}$$

$$x = -1 + \sqrt{6} \text{ or } x = -1 - \sqrt{6}$$

The solutions are $-1 + \sqrt{6}$ and $-1 - \sqrt{6}$.

19.

$$2x^2 - 8x = 64$$

$$\frac{1}{2}(2x^2 - 8x) = \frac{1}{2}(64)$$

$$x^2 - 4x = 32$$

$$x^2 - 4x + 4 = 32 + 4$$

$$(x - 2)^2 = 36$$

$$x - 2 = \pm\sqrt{36}$$

$$x - 2 = \pm 6$$

$$x = 2 \pm 6$$

$$x = 2 + 6 \text{ or } x = 2 - 6$$

$$x = 8 \quad \text{ or } x = -4$$

The solutions are 8 and –4.

20.

$$30 = 2n^2 - 4n$$

$$2n^2 - 4n = 30$$

$$\frac{1}{2}(2n^2 - 4n) = \frac{1}{2}(30)$$

$$n^2 - 2n = 15$$

$$n^2 - 2n + 1 = 15 + 1$$

$$(n - 1)^2 = 16$$

$$n - 1 = \pm\sqrt{16}$$

$$n - 1 = \pm 4$$

$$n = 1 \pm 4$$

$$n = 1 + 4 \text{ or } n = 1 - 4$$

$$n = 5 \quad \text{ or } n = -3$$

The solutions are 5 and –3.

21.

$$3p^2 = -2p + 8$$

$$3p^2 + 2p - 8 = 0$$

$$\frac{1}{3}(3p^2 + 2p - 8) = \frac{1}{3}(0)$$

$$p^2 + \frac{2}{3}p - \frac{8}{3} = 0$$

$$p^2 + \frac{2}{3}p = \frac{8}{3}$$

$$p^2 + \frac{2}{3}p + \frac{1}{9} = \frac{8}{3} + \frac{1}{9}$$

$$\left(p + \frac{1}{3}\right)^2 = \frac{25}{9}$$

$$p + \frac{1}{3} = \pm\sqrt{\frac{25}{9}}$$

$$p + \frac{1}{3} = \pm\frac{5}{3}$$

$$p = -\frac{1}{3} \pm \frac{5}{3}$$

$$p = -\frac{1}{3} + \frac{5}{3} \text{ or } p = -\frac{1}{3} - \frac{5}{3}$$

$$p = \frac{4}{3} \quad \text{ or } p = -2$$

The solutions are $\dfrac{4}{3}$ and -2.

22.

$$6x^2 - 19x + 15 = 0$$

$$\frac{1}{6}(6x^2 - 19x + 15) = \frac{1}{6}(0)$$

$$x^2 - \frac{19}{6}x + \frac{5}{2} = 0$$

$$x^2 - \frac{19}{6}x = -\frac{5}{2}$$

$$x^2 - \frac{19}{6}x + \frac{361}{144} = -\frac{5}{2} + \frac{361}{144}$$

$$\left(x - \frac{19}{12}\right)^2 = \frac{1}{144}$$

$$x - \frac{19}{12} = \pm\sqrt{\frac{1}{144}}$$

$$x - \frac{19}{12} = \pm\frac{1}{12}$$

$$x = \frac{19}{12} \pm \frac{1}{12}$$

$$x = \frac{19}{12} + \frac{1}{12} \text{ or } x = \frac{19}{12} - \frac{1}{12}$$

$$x = \frac{5}{3} \qquad \text{or } x = \frac{3}{2}$$

The solutions are $\frac{5}{3}$ and $\frac{3}{2}$.

23. $b^2 - 4ac = 4^2 - 4(-4)(-6) = 16 - 96 = -80$
Since the discriminant is negative, there is no real number solution.

24. Write in standard form.
$-3x^2 + 4x - 9 = 0$
$b^2 - 4ac = (4)^2 - 4(-3)(-9) = 16 - 108 = -92$
Since the discriminant is negative, there is no real number solution.

25. $b^2 - 4ac = (-10)^2 - 4(1)(25) = 100 - 100 = 0$
Since the discriminant is zero, there is one real number solution.

26. $b^2 - 4ac = (2)^2 - 4(1)(-8) = 4 + 32 = 36$
Since the discriminant is positive, there are two real number solutions.

27. Write in standard form.
$4z^2 - 3z - 6 = 0$
$b^2 - 4ac = (-3)^2 - 4(4)(-6) = 9 + 96 = 102$
Since the discriminant is positive, there are two real number solutions.

28. $b^2 - 4ac = (-4)^2 - 4(3)(5) = 16 - 60 = -44$

Since the discriminant is negative, there is no real number solution.

29. $b^2 - 4ac = (-4)^2 - 4(-3)(8) = 16 + 96 = 112$
Since the discriminant is positive, there are two real number solutions.

30. $b^2 - 4ac = (-9)^2 - 4(1)(6) = 81 - 24 = 57$
Since the discriminant is positive, there are two real number solutions.

31. $a = 1, b = -10, c = 16$

$$x = \frac{-b \pm \sqrt{b^2 - 4ac}}{2a}$$

$$= \frac{-(-10) \pm \sqrt{(-10)^2 - 4(1)(16)}}{2(1)}$$

$$= \frac{10 \pm \sqrt{100 - 64}}{2}$$

$$= \frac{10 \pm \sqrt{36}}{2}$$

$$= \frac{10 \pm 6}{2}$$

$$x = \frac{10 + 6}{2} \text{ or } x = \frac{10 - 6}{2}$$

$$x = 8 \qquad \text{or } x = 2$$

The solutions are 8 and 2.

32. $a = 1, b = -7, c = -44$

$$x = \frac{-b \pm \sqrt{b^2 - 4ac}}{2a}$$

$$= \frac{-(-7) \pm \sqrt{(-7)^2 - 4(1)(-44)}}{2(1)}$$

$$= \frac{7 \pm \sqrt{49 + 176}}{2}$$

$$= \frac{7 \pm \sqrt{225}}{2}$$

$$= \frac{7 \pm 15}{2}$$

$$x = \frac{7 + 15}{2} \text{ or } x = \frac{7 - 15}{2}$$

$$x = 11 \qquad \text{or } x = -4$$

The solutions are 11 and –4.

33. Write in standard form.

$$x^2 - 10x + 9 = 0$$
$$a = 1, b = -10, c = 9$$
$$x = \frac{-b \pm \sqrt{b^2 - 4ac}}{2a}$$
$$= \frac{-(-10) \pm \sqrt{(-10)^2 - 4(1)(9)}}{2(1)}$$
$$= \frac{10 \pm \sqrt{100 - 36}}{2}$$
$$= \frac{10 \pm \sqrt{64}}{2}$$
$$= \frac{10 \pm 8}{2}$$
$$x = \frac{10 + 8}{2} \text{ or } x = \frac{10 - 8}{2}$$
$$x = 9 \qquad \text{or } x = 1$$

The solutions are 9 and 1.

34. Write in standard form.

$$5x^2 - 7x - 6 = 0$$
$$a = 5, b = -7, c = -6$$
$$x = \frac{-b \pm \sqrt{b^2 - 4ac}}{2a}$$
$$= \frac{-(-7) \pm \sqrt{(-7)^2 - 4(5)(-6)}}{2(5)}$$
$$= \frac{7 \pm \sqrt{49 + 120}}{10}$$
$$= \frac{7 \pm \sqrt{169}}{10}$$
$$= \frac{7 \pm 13}{10}$$
$$x = \frac{7 + 13}{10} \text{ or } x = \frac{7 - 13}{10}$$
$$x = 2 \qquad \text{or } x = -\frac{3}{5}$$

The solutions are 2 and $-\frac{3}{5}$.

35. Write in standard form.

$$r^2 + 4r - 21 = 0$$
$$a = 1, b = 4, c = -21$$
$$r = \frac{-b \pm \sqrt{b^2 - 4ac}}{2a}$$
$$= \frac{-4 \pm \sqrt{4^2 - 4(1)(-21)}}{2(1)}$$
$$= \frac{-4 \pm \sqrt{16 + 84}}{2}$$
$$= \frac{-4 \pm \sqrt{100}}{2}$$
$$= \frac{-4 \pm 10}{2}$$
$$r = \frac{-4 + 10}{2} \text{ or } r = \frac{-4 - 10}{2}$$
$$r = 3 \qquad \text{or } \quad r = -7$$

The solutions are 3 and –7.

36. $a = 1, b = -1, c = 12$

$$x = \frac{-b \pm \sqrt{b^2 - 4ac}}{2a}$$
$$= \frac{-(-1) \pm \sqrt{(-1)^2 - 4(1)(12)}}{2(1)}$$
$$= \frac{1 \pm \sqrt{1 - 48}}{2}$$
$$= \frac{1 \pm \sqrt{-47}}{2}$$

Since $\sqrt{-47}$ is not a real number, there is no real number solution.

37. $a = 6, b = 1, c = -15$

$$x = \frac{-b \pm \sqrt{b^2 - 4ac}}{2a}$$
$$= \frac{-1 \pm \sqrt{1^2 - 4(6)(-15)}}{2(6)}$$
$$= \frac{-1 \pm \sqrt{1 + 360}}{12}$$
$$= \frac{-1 \pm \sqrt{361}}{12}$$
$$= \frac{-1 \pm 19}{12}$$

$$x = \frac{-1+19}{12} \text{ or } x = \frac{-1-19}{12}$$

$$x = \frac{3}{2} \qquad \text{ or } x = -\frac{5}{3}$$

The solutions are $\frac{3}{2}$ and $-\frac{5}{3}$.

38. $a = -2, b = 3, c = 6$

$$x = \frac{-b \pm \sqrt{b^2 - 4ac}}{2a}$$

$$= \frac{-3 \pm \sqrt{3^2 - 4(-2)(6)}}{2(-2)}$$

$$= \frac{-3 \pm \sqrt{9 + 48}}{-4}$$

$$= \frac{-3 \pm \sqrt{57}}{-4}$$

$$= \frac{3 \pm \sqrt{57}}{4}$$

$$x = \frac{3 + \sqrt{57}}{4} \text{ or } x = \frac{3 - \sqrt{57}}{4}$$

The solutions are $\frac{3 + \sqrt{57}}{4}$ and $\frac{3 - \sqrt{57}}{4}$.

39. $a = 2, b = 4, c = -3$

$$x = \frac{-b \pm \sqrt{b^2 - 4ac}}{2a}$$

$$= \frac{-4 \pm \sqrt{4^2 - 4(2)(-3)}}{2(2)}$$

$$= \frac{-4 \pm \sqrt{16 + 24}}{4}$$

$$= \frac{-4 \pm \sqrt{40}}{4}$$

$$= \frac{-4 \pm 2\sqrt{10}}{4}$$

$$= \frac{2(-2 \pm \sqrt{10})}{4}$$

$$= \frac{-2 \pm \sqrt{10}}{2}$$

$$x = \frac{-2 + \sqrt{10}}{2} \text{ or } x = \frac{-2 - \sqrt{10}}{2}$$

The solutions are $\frac{-2 + \sqrt{10}}{2}$ and $\frac{-2 - \sqrt{10}}{2}$.

40. $a = 1, b = -6, c = 3$

$$y = \frac{-b \pm \sqrt{b^2 - 4ac}}{2a}$$

$$= \frac{-(-6) \pm \sqrt{(-6)^2 - 4(1)(3)}}{2(1)}$$

$$= \frac{6 \pm \sqrt{36 - 12}}{2}$$

$$= \frac{6 \pm \sqrt{24}}{2}$$

$$= \frac{6 \pm 2\sqrt{6}}{2}$$

$$= \frac{2(3 \pm \sqrt{6})}{2}$$

$$= 3 \pm \sqrt{6}$$

$y = 3 + \sqrt{6}$ or $y = 3 - \sqrt{6}$
The solutions are $3 + \sqrt{6}$ and $3 - \sqrt{6}$.

41. $a = 3, b = -4, c = 6$

$$x = \frac{-b \pm \sqrt{b^2 - 4ac}}{2a}$$

$$= \frac{-(-4) \pm \sqrt{(-4)^2 - 4(3)(6)}}{2(3)}$$

$$= \frac{4 \pm \sqrt{16 - 72}}{6}$$

$$= \frac{4 \pm \sqrt{-56}}{6}$$

Since $\sqrt{-56}$ is not a real number, there is no real number solution.

42. $a = 3, b = -6, c = -8$

$$x = \frac{-b \pm \sqrt{b^2 - 4ac}}{2a}$$

$$= \frac{-(-6) \pm \sqrt{(-6)^2 - 4(3)(-8)}}{2(3)}$$

$$= \frac{6 \pm \sqrt{36 + 96}}{6}$$

$$= \frac{6 \pm \sqrt{132}}{6}$$

$$= \frac{6 \pm 2\sqrt{33}}{6}$$

$$= \frac{2(3 \pm \sqrt{33})}{6}$$

$$= \frac{3 \pm \sqrt{33}}{3}$$

$$x = \frac{3 + \sqrt{33}}{3} \text{ or } x = \frac{3 - \sqrt{33}}{3}$$

The solutions are $\frac{3 + \sqrt{33}}{3}$ and $\frac{3 - \sqrt{33}}{3}$.

43. $a = 7, b = -3, c = 0$

$$x = \frac{-b \pm \sqrt{b^2 - 4ac}}{2a}$$

$$= \frac{-(-3) \pm \sqrt{(-3)^2 - 4(7)(0)}}{2(7)}$$

$$= \frac{3 \pm \sqrt{9}}{14}$$

$$= \frac{3 \pm 3}{14}$$

$$x = \frac{3 + 3}{14} \text{ or } x = \frac{3 - 3}{14}$$

$$x = \frac{3}{7} \quad \text{ or } x = 0$$

The solutions are $\frac{3}{7}$ and 0.

44. Write in standard form.

$2z^2 - 5z = 0$

$a = 2, b = -5, c = 0$

$$z = \frac{-b \pm \sqrt{b^2 - 4ac}}{2a}$$

$$= \frac{-(-5) \pm \sqrt{(-5)^2 - 4(2)(0)}}{2(2)}$$

$$= \frac{5 \pm \sqrt{25}}{4}$$

$$= \frac{5 \pm 5}{4}$$

$$z = \frac{5 + 5}{4} \text{ or } z = \frac{5 - 5}{4}$$

$$z = \frac{5}{2} \quad \text{ or } z = 0$$

The solutions are $\frac{5}{2}$ and 0.

45. $x^2 - 10x + 24 = 0$

$(x - 6)(x - 4) = 0$

$x - 6 = 0$ or $x - 4 = 0$

$x = 6$ or $\quad x = 4$

46. $x^2 + 15x + 56 = 0$

$(x + 7)(x + 8) = 0$

$x + 7 = 0$ or $x + 8 = 0$

$x = -7$ or $\quad x = -8$

47. $x^2 - 3x - 70 = 0$

$(x - 10)(x + 7) = 0$

$x - 10 = 0$ or $x + 7 = 0$

$x = 10$ or $\quad x = -7$

48. $\quad x^2 + 6x = 27$

$x^2 + 6x - 27 = 0$

$(x - 3)(x + 9) = 0$

$x - 3 = 0$ or $x + 9 = 0$

$x = 3$ or $\quad x = -9$

49. $x^2 - 4x - 60 = 0$

$(x + 6)(x - 10) = 0$

$x + 6 = 0$ or $x - 10 = 0$

$x = -6$ or $\quad x = 10$

50. $\quad x^2 - x - 42 = 0$

$(x - 7)(x + 6) = 0$

$x - 7 = 0$ or $x + 6 = 0$

$x = 7$ or $\quad x = -6$

51. $\quad y^2 + 9y - 22 = 0$

$(y + 11)(y - 2) = 0$

$y + 11 = 0$ or $y - 2 = 0$

$y = -11$ or $y = 2$

52. $\quad t^2 = 5t$

$t^2 - 5t = 0$

$t(t - 5) = 0$

$t = 0$ or $t - 5 = 0$

$t = 0$ or $\quad t = 5$

53. $x^2 = 81$

$x = \pm\sqrt{81}$

$x = \pm 9$

$x = 9$ or $x = -9$

54. $\quad 2x^2 + 5x = 3$

$2x^2 + 5x - 3 = 0$

$(2x - 1)(x + 3) = 0$

$2x - 1 = 0$ or $x + 3 = 0$

$x = \frac{1}{2}$ or $\quad x = -3$

55. $\quad 2x^2 = 9x - 10$

$2x^2 - 9x + 10 = 0$

$(2x - 5)(x - 2) = 0$

$2x - 5 = 0$ or $x - 2 = 0$

$x = \frac{5}{2}$ or $\quad x = 2$

56.
$$6x^2 + 5x = 6$$
$$6x^2 + 5x - 6 = 0$$
$$(2x + 3)(3x - 2) = 0$$
$$2x + 3 = 0 \text{ or } 3x - 2 = 0$$
$$x = -\frac{3}{2} \text{ or } \quad x = \frac{2}{3}$$

57. $a = -2, b = 6, c = 9$
$$x = \frac{-b \pm \sqrt{b^2 - 4ac}}{2a}$$
$$= \frac{-6 \pm \sqrt{6^2 - 4(-2)(9)}}{2(-2)}$$
$$= \frac{-6 \pm \sqrt{36 + 72}}{-4}$$
$$= \frac{-6 + \sqrt{108}}{-4}$$
$$= \frac{-6 \pm 6\sqrt{3}}{-4}$$
$$= \frac{-2(3 \pm 3\sqrt{2})}{-2(2)}$$
$$= \frac{3 \pm 3\sqrt{2}}{2}$$
$$x = \frac{3 + 3\sqrt{3}}{2} \text{ or } x = \frac{3 - 3\sqrt{3}}{2}$$

58. $3x^2 - 11x + 10 = 0$
$$(3x - 5)(x - 2) = 0$$
$$3x - 5 = 0 \text{ or } x - 2 = 0$$
$$x = \frac{5}{3} \text{ or } \quad x = 2$$

59.
$$-3x^2 - 5x + 8 = 0$$
$$-1(-3x^2 - 5x + 8) = (-1)(0)$$
$$3x^2 + 5x - 8 = 0$$
$$(3x + 8)(x - 1) = 0$$
$$3x + 8 = 0 \text{ or } x - 1 = 0$$
$$x = -\frac{8}{3} \text{ or } x = 1$$

60. Write in standard form.
$$x^2 + 3x - 6 = 0$$
$$a = 1, b = 3, c = -6$$
$$x = \frac{-b \pm \sqrt{b^2 - 4ac}}{2a}$$
$$= \frac{-3 \pm \sqrt{3^2 - 4(1)(-6)}}{2(1)}$$
$$= \frac{-3 \pm \sqrt{9 + 24}}{2}$$
$$= \frac{-3 \pm \sqrt{33}}{2}$$
$$x = \frac{-3 + \sqrt{33}}{2} \text{ or } x = \frac{-3 - \sqrt{33}}{2}$$

61. $a = 4, b = -9, c = 0$
$$x = \frac{-b \pm \sqrt{b^2 - 4ac}}{2a}$$
$$= \frac{-(-9) \pm \sqrt{(-9)^2 - 4(4)(0)}}{2(4)}$$
$$= \frac{9 \pm \sqrt{81}}{8}$$
$$= \frac{9 \pm 9}{8}$$
$$x = \frac{9 + 9}{8} \text{ or } x = \frac{9 - 9}{8}$$
$$x = \frac{9}{4} \quad \text{ or } x = 0$$

62. $3x^2 + 5x = 0$
$$x(3x + 5) = 0$$
$$x = 0 \text{ or } 3x + 5 = 0$$
$$x = 0 \text{ or } \quad x = -\frac{5}{3}$$

63. $a = 1, b = -6, c = -5$
$$x = -\frac{b}{2a} = -\frac{-6}{2(1)} = 3$$
The axis of symmetry is $x = 3$.
y-coordinate of the vertex:
$$y = x^2 - 6x - 5$$
$$y = (3)^2 - 6(3) - 5$$
$$= 9 - 18 - 5$$
$$= -14$$
The vertex is $(3, -14)$.
Since $a > 0$, the parabola opens upward.

64. $a = 1, b = -12, c = 6$

$$x = -\frac{b}{2a} = -\frac{-12}{2(1)} = 6$$

The axis of symmetry is $x = 6$

y-coordinate of the vertex:

$$y = x^2 - 12x + 6$$
$$y = 6^2 - 12(6) + 6$$
$$= 36 - 72 + 6$$
$$= -30$$

The vertex is $(6, -30)$

Since $a > 0$, the parabola opens upward.

65. $a = 1, b = -3, c = 7$

$$x = -\frac{b}{2a} = -\frac{-3}{2(1)} = \frac{3}{2}$$

The axis of symmetry is $x = \frac{3}{2}$.

y-coordinate of the vertex:

$$y = x^2 - 3x + 7$$
$$y = \left(\frac{3}{2}\right)^2 - 3\left(\frac{3}{2}\right) + 7$$
$$= \frac{9}{4} - \frac{9}{2} + 7$$
$$= \frac{19}{4}$$

The vertex is $\left(\frac{3}{2}, \frac{19}{4}\right)$.

Since $a > 0$, the parabola opens upward.

66. $a = -1, b = -2, c = 15$

$$x = -\frac{b}{2a} = -\frac{-2}{2(-1)} = -1$$

The axis of symmetry is $x = -1$.

y-coordinate of the vertex:

$$y = -x^2 - 2x + 15$$
$$y = -(-1)^2 - 2(-1) + 15$$
$$= -1 + 2 + 15$$
$$= 16$$

The vertex is $(-1, 16)$.

Since $a < 0$, the parabola opens downward.

67. $a = 3, b = 7, c = 3$

$$x = -\frac{b}{2a} = -\frac{7}{2(3)} = -\frac{7}{6}$$

The axis of symmetry is $x = -\frac{7}{6}$.

y-coordinate of the vertex:

$$y = 3x^2 + 7x + 3$$
$$y = 3\left(-\frac{7}{6}\right)^2 + 7\left(-\frac{7}{6}\right) + 3$$
$$= \frac{49}{12} - \frac{49}{6} + 3$$
$$= -\frac{13}{12}$$

The vertex is $\left(-\frac{7}{6}, -\frac{13}{12}\right)$.

Since $a > 0$, the parabola opens upward.

68. $a = -1, b = -5, c = 0$

$$x = -\frac{b}{2a} = -\frac{-5}{2(-1)} = -\frac{5}{2}$$

The axis of symmetry is $x = -\frac{5}{2}$.

y-coordinate of the vertex:

$$y = -x^2 - 5x$$
$$y = -\left(-\frac{5}{2}\right)^2 - 5\left(-\frac{5}{2}\right)$$
$$= -\frac{25}{4} + \frac{25}{2}$$
$$= \frac{25}{4}$$

The vertex is $\left(-\frac{5}{2}, \frac{25}{4}\right)$.

Since $a < 0$, the parabola opens downward.

69. $a = -1, b = 0, c = -8$

$$x = -\frac{b}{2a} = -\frac{0}{2(-1)} = 0$$

The axis of symmetry is $x = 0$.

y-coordinate of the vertex:

$$y = -x^2 - 8$$
$$y = -0^2 - 8 = -8$$

The vertex is $(0, -8)$.

Since $a < 0$, the parabola opens downward.

70. $a = -2, b = -1, c = 20$

$$x = -\frac{b}{2a} = -\frac{-1}{2(-2)} = -\frac{1}{4}$$

The axis of symmetry is $x = -\frac{1}{4}$.

y-coordinate of the vertex:

$$y = -2x^2 - x + 20$$

$$y = -2\left(-\frac{1}{4}\right)^2 - \left(-\frac{1}{4}\right) + 20$$

$$= -\frac{1}{8} + \frac{1}{4} + 20$$

$$= \frac{161}{8}$$

The vertex is $\left(-\frac{1}{4}, \frac{161}{8}\right)$.

Since $a < 0$, the parabola opens downward.

71. $a = -4, b = 8, c = 5$

$$x = -\frac{b}{2a} = -\frac{8}{2(-4)} = 1$$

The axis of symmetry is $x = 1$.

y-coordinate of the vertex:

$$y = -4x^2 + 8x + 5$$

$$y = -4(1)^2 + 8(1) + 5$$

$$= -4 + 8 + 5$$

$$= 9$$

The vertex is $(1, 9)$.

Since $a < 0$, the parabola opens downward.

72. $a = 3, b = 5, c = -8$

$$x = -\frac{b}{2a} = -\frac{5}{2(3)} = -\frac{5}{6}$$

The axis of symmetry is $x = -\frac{5}{6}$.

y-coordinate of the vertex:

$$y = 3x^2 + 5x - 8$$

$$y = 3\left(-\frac{5}{6}\right)^2 + 5\left(-\frac{5}{6}\right) - 8$$

$$= \frac{25}{12} - \frac{25}{6} - 8$$

$$= -\frac{121}{12}$$

The vertex is $\left(-\frac{5}{6}, -\frac{121}{12}\right)$.

Since $a > 0$, the parabola opens upward.

73. $a = 1, b = -2, c = 0$

Since $a > 0$, the parabola opens upward.

The axis of symmetry is

$$y = -\frac{b}{2a} = -\frac{-2}{2(1)} = 1$$

y-coordinate of the vertex:

$$y = x^2 - 2x$$

$$y = (1)^2 - 2(1) = -1$$

The vertex is $(1, -1)$.

$$y = x^2 - 2x$$

Let $x = 2$ $y = 2^2 - 2(2) = 0$

Let $x = 0$ $y = 0^2 - 2(0) = 0$

x	y
2	0
0	0

$$0 = x^2 - 2x$$

$$0 = x(x - 2)$$

$$x = 0 \text{ or } x = 2$$

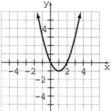

74. $a = -3, b = 0, c = 6$

Since $a < 0$, the parabola opens downward.

The axis of symmetry is

$$x = -\frac{b}{2a} = -\frac{0}{2(-3)} = 0$$

y-coordinate of the vertex:

$$y = -3x^2 + 6$$

$$y = -3(0)^2 + 6 = 6$$

The vertex is $(0, 6)$.

$$y = -3x^2 + 6$$

Let $x = -1$ $y = -3(-1)^2 + 6 = 3$

Let $x = 1$ $y = -3(1)^2 + 6 = 3$

x	y
-1	3
1	3

$$0 = -3x^2 + 6$$

$$3x^2 = 6$$

$$x^2 = 2$$

$$x = \pm\sqrt{2}$$

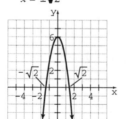

75. $a = 1, b = -2, c = -15$
Since $a > 0$, the parabola opens upward.
The axis of symmetry is
$$x = -\frac{b}{2a} = -\frac{-2}{2(1)} = 1$$
y-coordinate of the vertex:
$$y = x^2 - 2x - 15$$
$$y = (1)^2 - 2(1) - 15$$
$$= 1 - 2 - 15$$
$$= -16$$
The vertex is $(1, -16)$.
$$y = x^2 - 2x - 15$$
Let $x = -3$ $y = (-3)^2 - 2(-3) - 15 = 0$
Let $x = 5$ $y = (5)^2 - 2(5) - 15 = 0$

x	y
-3	0
5	0

$$0 = x^2 - 2x - 15$$
$$0 = (x + 3)(x - 5)$$
$$x = -3 \text{ or } x = 5$$

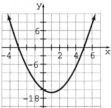

76. $a = -1, b = 5, c = -6$
Since $a < 0$, the parabola opens downward.
The axis of symmetry is
$$x = -\frac{b}{2a} = -\frac{5}{2(-1)} = \frac{5}{2}$$
y-coordinate of the vertex:
$$y = -x^2 + 5x - 6$$
$$y = -\left(\frac{5}{2}\right)^2 + 5\left(\frac{5}{2}\right) - 6$$
$$= -\frac{25}{4} + \frac{25}{2} - 6$$
$$= \frac{1}{4}$$
The vertex is $\left(\frac{5}{2}, \frac{1}{4}\right)$.
$$y = -x^2 + 5x - 6$$
Let $x = 0$ $y = -0^2 + 5(0) - 6 = -6$
Let $x = 3$ $y = -(3)^2 + 5(3) - 6 = 0$

x	y
0	-6
3	0

$$0 = -x^2 + 5x - 6$$
$$x^2 - 5x + 6 = 0$$
$$(x - 2)(x - 3) = 0$$
$$x = 2 \text{ or } x = 3$$

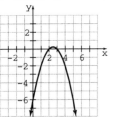

77. $a = 1, b = -1, c = 1$
Since $a > 0$, the parabola opens upward.
The axis of symmetry is
$$x = -\frac{b}{2a} = -\frac{-1}{2(1)} = \frac{1}{2}$$
y-coordinate of the vertex:
$$y = x^2 - x + 1$$
$$y = \left(\frac{1}{2}\right)^2 - \frac{1}{2} + 1 = \frac{3}{4}$$
The vertex is $\left(\frac{1}{2}, \frac{3}{4}\right)$.
$$y = x^2 - x + 1$$
Let $x = 0$ $y = 0^2 - 0 + 1 = 1$
Let $x = 2$ $y = 2^2 - (2) + 1 = 3$

x	y
0	1
2	3

$$0 = x^2 - x + 1$$
$$x = \frac{-(-1) \pm \sqrt{(-1)^2 - 4(1)(1)}}{2(1)}$$
$$= \frac{1 \pm \sqrt{-3}}{2}$$
No real number solution

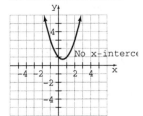

78. $a = 1, b = 5, c = 4$

Since $a > 0$, the parabola opens upward.

The axis of symmetry is

$$x = -\frac{b}{2a} = -\frac{5}{2(1)} = -\frac{5}{2}$$

y-coordinate of the vertex:

$y = x^2 + 5x + 4$

$y = \left(-\frac{5}{2}\right)^2 + 5\left(-\frac{5}{2}\right) + 4$

$= \frac{25}{4} - \frac{25}{2} + 4$

$= -\frac{9}{4}$

The vertex is $\left(-\frac{5}{2}, -\frac{9}{4}\right)$.

$$y = x^2 + 5x + 4$$

Let $x = -2$ $y = (-2)^2 + 5(-2) + 4 = -2$

Let $x = -1$ $y = (-1)^2 + 5(-1) + 4 = 0$

Let $x = 0$ $y = (0)^2 + 5(0) + 4 = 4$

x	y
-2	-2
-1	0
0	4

$0 = x^2 + 5x + 4$

$0 = (x + 1)(x + 4)$

$x + 1 = 0$ or $x + 4 = 0$

$\quad x = -1 \quad$ or $x = -4$

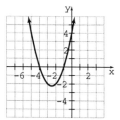

79. $a = -1, b = -6, c = 0$

Since $a < 0$, the parabola opens downward.

The axis of symmetry is

$$x = -\frac{b}{2a} = -\frac{-6}{2(-1)} = -3$$

y-coordinate of the vertex:

$y = -x^2 - 6x$

$y = -(-3)^2 - 6(-3) = -9 + 18 = 9$

The vertex is $(-3, 9)$.

$$y = -x^2 - 6x$$

Let $x = 0$ $y = -0^2 - 6(0) = 0$

Let $x = -6$ $y = -(-6)^2 - 6(-6) = -36 + 36 = 0$

x	y
0	0
-6	0

$0 = -x^2 - 6x$

$0 = -x(x + 6)$

$x = 0$ or $x = -6$

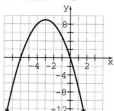

80. $a = 1, b = 4, c = 3$

Since $a > 0$, the parabola opens upward.

The axis of symmetry is $x = -\dfrac{b}{2a} = -\dfrac{4}{2(1)} = -2$

y-coordinate of the vertex:

$y = x^2 + 4x + 3$

$y = (-2)^2 + 4(-2) + 3$

$= 4 - 8 + 3$

$= -1$

The vertex is $(-2, -1)$.

$$y = x^2 + 4x + 3$$

Let $x = -1$ $y = (-1)^2 + 4(-1) + 3 = 0$

Let $x = 0$ $y = (0)^2 + 4(0) + 3 = 3$

x	y
-1	0
0	3

$0 = x^2 + 4x + 3$

$0 = (x + 1)(x + 3)$

$x + 1 = 0$ or $x + 3 = 0$

$\quad x = -1$ or $\quad x = -3$

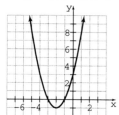

81. $a = -1, b = 2, c = -3$

Since $a < 0$, the parabola opens downward.

The axis of symmetry is $x = -\dfrac{b}{2a} = -\dfrac{2}{2(-1)} = 1$

y-coordinate of the vertex:

$y = -x^2 + 2x - 3$

$y = -(1)^2 + 2(1) - 3$

$\quad = -1 + 2 - 3$

$\quad = -2$

The vertex is (1, -2).

$\qquad\qquad y = -x^2 + 2x - 3$

Let $x = 0 \qquad y = -0^2 + 0 - 3 = -3$

Let $x = 2 \qquad y = -(2)^2 + 2(2) - 3 = -3$

x	y
0	-3
2	-3

$0 = -x^2 + 2x - 3$

$x = \dfrac{-2 \pm \sqrt{1^2 - 4(-1)(-3)}}{2(-1)}$

$\quad = \dfrac{-2 \pm \sqrt{-11}}{-2}$

No real number solution

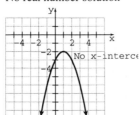

82. $a = 3, b = -4, c = -8$

Since $a > 0$, the parabola opens upward.

The axis of symmetry is

$x = -\dfrac{b}{2a} = -\dfrac{-4}{2(3)} = \dfrac{2}{3}$

y-coordinate of the vertex:

$y = 3x^2 - 4x - 8$

$y = 3\left(\dfrac{2}{3}\right)^2 - 4\left(\dfrac{2}{3}\right) - 8$

$\quad = \dfrac{4}{3} - \dfrac{8}{3} - 8$

$\quad = -\dfrac{28}{3}$

The vertex is $\left(\dfrac{2}{3}, -\dfrac{28}{3}\right)$.

$\qquad\qquad y = 3x^2 - 4x - 8$

Let $x = 0 \qquad y = 3(0)^2 - 4(0) - 8 = -8$

Let $x = 2 \qquad y = 3(2)^2 - 4(2) - 8 = -4$

x	y
0	-8
2	-4

$0 = 3x^2 - 4x - 8$

$x = \dfrac{-(-4) \pm \sqrt{(-4)^2 - 4(3)(-8)}}{2(3)}$

$\quad = \dfrac{4 \pm \sqrt{112}}{6}$

$\quad = \dfrac{2(2 \pm 2\sqrt{7})}{2(3)}$

$\quad = \dfrac{2 \pm 2\sqrt{7}}{3}$

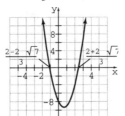

83. $a = -2, b = 7, c = -3$

Since $a < 0$, the parabola opens downward.

The axis of symmetry is

$x = -\dfrac{b}{2a} = -\dfrac{7}{2(-2)} = \dfrac{7}{4}$

y-coordinate of the vertex:

$y = -2x^2 + 7x - 3$

$y = -2\left(\dfrac{7}{4}\right)^2 + 7\left(\dfrac{7}{4}\right) - 3 = -\dfrac{49}{8} + \dfrac{49}{4} - 3 = \dfrac{25}{8}$

The vertex is $\left(\dfrac{7}{4}, \dfrac{25}{8}\right)$.

$\qquad\qquad y = -2x^2 + 7x - 3$

Let $x = 0 \qquad y = -2(0)^2 + 7(0) - 3 = -3$

Let $x = 3 \qquad y = -2(3)^2 + 7(3) - 3 = 0$

x	y
0	-3
3	0

$0 = -2x^2 + 7x - 3$

$0 = -(2x - 1)(x - 3)$

$x = \dfrac{1}{2}$ or $x = 3$

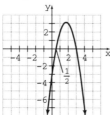

84. $a = 1$, $b = -5$, $c = 4$

Since $a > 0$, the parabola opens upward.

The axis of symmetry is $x = -\dfrac{b}{2a} = -\dfrac{-5}{2(1)} = \dfrac{5}{2}$

y-coordinate of the vertex:

$y = x^2 - 5x + 4$

$y = \left(\dfrac{5}{2}\right)^2 - 5\left(\dfrac{5}{2}\right) + 4 = \dfrac{25}{4} - \dfrac{25}{2} + 4 = -\dfrac{9}{4}$

The vertex is $\left(\dfrac{5}{2}, -\dfrac{9}{4}\right)$.

$\qquad\qquad y = x^2 - 5x + 4$

Let $x = 4$ $\qquad y = 4^2 - 5(4) + 4 = 0$

Let $x = 1$ $\qquad y = 1^2 - 5(1) + 4 = 0$

x	y
4	0
1	0

$0 = x^2 - 5x + 4$

$0 = (x - 1)(x - 4)$

$x = 1$ or $x = 4$

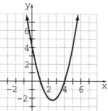

85. Let $x =$ the smaller integer,
then $x + 2 =$ the larger integer.

$x(x + 2) = 48$

$x^2 + 2x = 48$

$x^2 + 2x + 1 = 48 + 1$

$(x + 1)^2 = 49$

$x + 1 = \pm\sqrt{49}$

$x + 1 = \pm 7$

$x = -1 \pm 7$

$x = -1 + 7$ or $x = -1 - 7$

$x = 6$ $\qquad$ or $x = -8$

Since the numbers are positive,

$x = 6$ and $x + 2 = 6 + 2 = 8$.

86. Let $x =$ the smaller integer,
then $x + 3 =$ the larger integer.

$x(x + 3) = 88$

$x^2 + 3x = 88$

$x^2 + 3x + \dfrac{9}{4} = 88 + \dfrac{9}{4}$

$\left(x + \dfrac{3}{2}\right)^2 = \dfrac{361}{4}$

$x + \dfrac{3}{2} = \pm\sqrt{\dfrac{361}{4}}$

$x + \dfrac{3}{2} = \pm\dfrac{19}{2}$

$x = -\dfrac{3}{2} \pm \dfrac{19}{2}$

$x = -\dfrac{3}{2} + \dfrac{19}{2}$ or $x = -\dfrac{3}{2} - \dfrac{19}{2}$

$x = 8$ $\qquad$ or $x = -11$

Since the numbers are positive,

$x = 8$ and $x + 3 = 8 + 3 = 11$.

87. Let $w =$ width of table,
then $2w + 6 =$ length of table.

$\text{Area} = \text{length} \cdot \text{width}$

$920 = w(2w + 6)$

$2w^2 + 6w = 920$

$\dfrac{1}{2}(2w^2 + 6w) = \dfrac{1}{2}(920)$

$w^2 + 3w = 460$

$w^2 + 3w + \dfrac{9}{4} = 460 + \dfrac{9}{4}$

$\left(w + \dfrac{3}{2}\right)^2 = \dfrac{1849}{4}$

$w + \dfrac{3}{2} = \pm\sqrt{\dfrac{1849}{4}}$

$w + \dfrac{3}{2} = \pm\dfrac{43}{2}$

$w = -\dfrac{3}{2} \pm \dfrac{43}{2}$

$w = -\dfrac{3}{2} + \dfrac{43}{2}$ or $w = -\dfrac{3}{2} - \dfrac{43}{2}$

$w = 20$ $\qquad$ or $w = -23$

Since w is positive, the width is 20 inches and
the length is $2(20) + 6 = 46$ inches.

88. Let w = width of the desktop,
then $w + 20$ = length of the desktop.

$$\text{Area} = \text{length} \cdot \text{width}$$
$$1344 = w(w + 20)$$
$$1344 = w^2 + 20w$$
$$w^2 + 20w - 1344 = 0$$
$$(w - 28)(w + 48) = 0$$
$$w - 28 = 0 \text{ or } w + 48 = 0$$
$$w = 28 \text{ or } \quad w = -48$$

Since w is positive, the width is 28 inches and the length is $28 + 20 = 48$ inches.

89. $\sqrt{-4} = \sqrt{4}\sqrt{-1} = 2i$

90. $\sqrt{-30} = \sqrt{-1}\sqrt{30} = i\sqrt{30}$

91. $4 - \sqrt{-25} = 4 - \sqrt{25}\sqrt{-1} = 4 - 5i$

92. $5 - \sqrt{-60} = 5 - \sqrt{4}\sqrt{-1}\sqrt{15} = 5 - 2i\sqrt{15}$

93. $(4 - 6i) + (5 - 3i) = 4 + 5 - 6i - 3i$
$$= 9 - (6 + 3)i$$
$$= 9 - 9i$$

94. $(9 + 5i) - (6 - 3i) = 9 + 5i - 6 + 3i$
$$= 9 - 6 + 5i + 3i$$
$$= 3 + (5 + 3)i$$
$$= 3 + 8i$$

95. $3x^2 = -27$
$$x^2 = -9$$
$$x = \pm\sqrt{-9}$$
$$x = \pm 3i$$
The solutions are $3i$ and $-3i$.

96. $4p^2 = -20$
$$p^2 = -5$$
$$p = \pm\sqrt{-5}$$
$$p = \pm i\sqrt{5}$$
The solutions are $i\sqrt{5}$ and $-i\sqrt{5}$.

97. $2r^2 - 5r + 8 = 0$
$$a = 2, b = -5, c = 8$$
$$r = \frac{-b \pm \sqrt{b^2 - 4ac}}{2a}$$
$$= \frac{-(-5) \pm \sqrt{(-5)^2 - 4(2)(8)}}{2(2)}$$
$$= \frac{5 \pm \sqrt{25 - 64}}{4}$$
$$= \frac{5 \pm \sqrt{-39}}{4}$$
$$= \frac{5 \pm i\sqrt{39}}{4}$$

The solutions are $\dfrac{5 + i\sqrt{39}}{4}$ and $\dfrac{5 - i\sqrt{39}}{4}$.

98. $4w^2 - 8w + 9 = 0$
$$a = 4, b = -8, c = 9$$
$$w = \frac{-b \pm \sqrt{b^2 - 4ac}}{2a}$$
$$= \frac{-(-8) \pm \sqrt{(-8)^2 - 4(4)(9)}}{2(4)}$$
$$= \frac{8 \pm \sqrt{64 - 144}}{8}$$
$$= \frac{8 \pm \sqrt{-80}}{8}$$
$$= \frac{8 \pm 4i\sqrt{5}}{8}$$
$$= \frac{4(2 \pm i\sqrt{5})}{4(2)}$$
$$= \frac{2 \pm i\sqrt{5}}{2}$$

The solutions are $\dfrac{2 + i\sqrt{5}}{2}$ and $\dfrac{2 - i\sqrt{5}}{2}$.

Practice Test

1. $x^2 - 4 = 28$
$$x^2 = 32$$
$$x = \pm\sqrt{32}$$
$$x = \pm 4\sqrt{2}$$
The solutions are $4\sqrt{2}$ and $-4\sqrt{2}$.

2. $(2p-4)^2 = 17$

$$2p - 4 = \pm\sqrt{17}$$

$$2p = 4 \pm \sqrt{17}$$

$$p = \frac{4 \pm \sqrt{17}}{2}$$

The solutions are $\dfrac{4+\sqrt{17}}{2}$ and $\dfrac{4-\sqrt{17}}{2}$.

3. $x^2 - 6x = 40$

$$x^2 - 6x + 9 = 40 + 9$$

$$(x-3)^2 = 49$$

$$x - 3 = \pm\sqrt{49}$$

$$x - 3 = \pm 7$$

$$x = 3 \pm 7$$

$$x = 3 + 7 \text{ or } x = 3 - 7$$

$$x = 10 \quad \text{ or } x = -4$$

The solutions are 10 and –4.

4. $r^2 + 7r = 44$

$$r^2 + 7r + \frac{49}{4} = 44 + \frac{49}{4}$$

$$\left(r + \frac{7}{2}\right)^2 = \frac{225}{4}$$

$$r + \frac{7}{2} = \pm\sqrt{\frac{225}{4}}$$

$$r + \frac{7}{2} = \pm\frac{15}{2}$$

$$r = -\frac{7}{2} \pm \frac{15}{2}$$

$$r = -\frac{7}{2} + \frac{15}{2} \text{ or } r = -\frac{7}{2} - \frac{15}{2}$$

$$r = 4 \qquad \text{ or } r = -11$$

The solutions are 4 and –11.

5. Write in standard form.

$k^2 - 13k + 42 = 0$

$a = 1, b = -13, c = 42$

$$k = \frac{-b \pm \sqrt{b^2 - 4ac}}{2a}$$

$$= \frac{-(-13) \pm \sqrt{(-13)^2 - 4(1)(42)}}{2(1)}$$

$$= \frac{13 \pm \sqrt{169 - 168}}{2}$$

$$= \frac{13 \pm \sqrt{1}}{2}$$

$$= \frac{13 \pm 1}{2}$$

$$k = \frac{13 + 1}{2} \text{ or } k = \frac{13 - 1}{2}$$

$$k = 7 \qquad \text{ or } k = 6$$

The solutions are 7 and 6.

6. $2x^2 + 5 = -8x$

$$2x^2 + 8x + 5 = 0$$

$$a = 2, b = 8, c = 5$$

$$x = \frac{-b \pm \sqrt{b^2 - 4ac}}{2a}$$

$$= \frac{-8 \pm \sqrt{8^2 - 4(2)(5)}}{2(2)}$$

$$= \frac{-8 \pm \sqrt{64 - 40}}{4}$$

$$= \frac{-8 \pm \sqrt{24}}{4}$$

$$= \frac{-8 \pm 2\sqrt{6}}{4}$$

$$= \frac{-4 \pm \sqrt{6}}{2}$$

$$x = \frac{-4 + \sqrt{6}}{2} \text{ or } x = \frac{-4 - \sqrt{6}}{2}$$

The solutions are $\dfrac{-4+\sqrt{6}}{2}$ and $\dfrac{-4-\sqrt{6}}{2}$.

7. $16x^2 = 49$

$$x^2 = \frac{49}{16}$$

$$x = \pm\sqrt{\frac{49}{16}}$$

$$x = \pm\frac{7}{4}$$

The solutions are $\dfrac{7}{4}$ and $-\dfrac{7}{4}$.

8. $x = \dfrac{-b \pm \sqrt{b^2 - 4ac}}{2a}$

9. Answers will vary.

10. $b^2 - 4ac = (-4)^2 - 4(-2)(2) = 16 + 16 = 32$
Since the discriminant is positive, the equation has two distinct real solutions.

11. $b^2 - 4ac = (8)^2 - 4(1)(16) = 64 - 64 = 0$
Since the discriminant is zero, the equation has one real solution.

12. $a = -1, b = -6, c = 7$
Axis of symmetry: $x = -\dfrac{b}{2a} = -\dfrac{-6}{2(-1)} = -3$
The axis of symmetry is $x = -3$.

13. $a = 4, b = -16, c = 9$
Axis of symmetry: $x = -\dfrac{b}{2a} = -\dfrac{-16}{2(4)} = 2$
The axis of symmetry is $x = 2$.

14. $a = -1, b = -6, c = 7$
Since $a < 0$, the graph opens downward.

15. $a = 4, b = -8, c = 9$
Since $a > 0$, the graph opens upward.

16. The vertex of the graph of a parabola is the lowest point on a parabola that opens upward or the highest point on a parabola that opens downward.

17. $a = -1, b = -8, c = -12$
Axis of symmetry: $x = -\dfrac{b}{2a} = -\dfrac{-8}{2(-1)} = -4$
The axis of symmetry is $x = -4$.
y-coordinate of vertex:
$y = -x^2 - 8x - 12$
$y = -(-4)^2 - 8(-4) - 12$
$= -16 + 32 - 12$
$= 4$
The vertex is $(-4, 4)$.

18. $a = 3, b = -8, c = 9$
Axis of symmetry: $x = -\dfrac{b}{2a} = -\dfrac{-8}{2(3)} = \dfrac{4}{3}$
The axis of symmetry is $x = \dfrac{4}{3}$.
y-coordinate of vertex:

$y = 3x^2 - 8x + 9$
$y = 3\left(\dfrac{4}{3}\right)^2 - 8\left(\dfrac{4}{3}\right) + 9$
$= \dfrac{16}{3} - \dfrac{32}{3} + 9$
$= \dfrac{11}{3}$
The vertex is $\left(\dfrac{4}{3}, \dfrac{11}{3}\right)$.

19. $a = 1, b = 2, c = -8$
Since $a > 0$, the parabola opens upward.
Axis of symmetry: $x = -\dfrac{b}{2a} = -\dfrac{2}{2(1)} = -1$
y-coordinate of vertex:
$y = x^2 + 2x - 8$
$y = (-1)^2 + 2(-1) - 8 = 1 - 2 - 8 = -9$
The vertex is $(-1, -9)$
$\qquad\qquad y = x^2 + 2x - 8$
Let $x = 0 \qquad y = 0^2 + 2(0) - 8 = -8$
Let $x = 1 \qquad y = 1^2 + 2(1) - 8 = -5$
Let $x = 2 \qquad y = 2^2 + 2(2) - 8 = 0$
Let $x = 3 \qquad y = 3^2 + 2(3) - 8 = 7$

x	y
0	−8
1	−5
2	0
3	7

$0 = x^2 + 2x - 8$
$0 = (x + 4)(x - 2)$
$x = -4 \text{ or } x = 2$

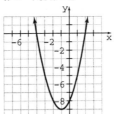

20. $a = -1, b = 6, c = -9$
Since $a < 0$, the parabola opens downward.
Axis of symmetry: $x = -\dfrac{b}{2a} = -\dfrac{6}{2(-1)} = 3$
y-coordinate of vertex:
$y = -x^2 + 6x - 9$
$y = -3^2 + 6(3) - 9 = -9 + 18 - 9 = 0$
The vertex is $(3, 0)$.

$$y = -x^2 + 6x - 9$$

Let $x = 0$ $y = -0^2 + 6(0) - 9 = -9$

Let $x = 1$ $y = -1^2 + 6(1) - 9 = -4$

Let $x = 2$ $y = -2^2 + 6(2) - 9 = -1$

x	y
0	-9
1	-4
2	-1

$$0 = -x^2 + 6x - 9$$
$$0 = -(x - 3)^2$$
$$x = 3$$

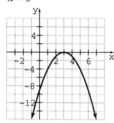

21. $a = 2$, $b = -6$, $c = 0$
Since $a > 0$, the parabola opens upward.

Axis of symmetry: $x = -\dfrac{b}{2a} = -\dfrac{-6}{2(2)} = \dfrac{3}{2}$

y-coordinate of vertex:
$$y = 2x^2 - 6x$$
$$y = 2\left(\frac{3}{2}\right)^2 - 6\left(\frac{3}{2}\right) = \frac{9}{2} - \frac{18}{2} = -\frac{9}{2}$$

The vertex is $\left(\dfrac{3}{2}, -\dfrac{9}{2}\right)$.

$$y = 2x^2 - 6x$$

Let $x = 1$ $y = 2(1)^2 - 6(1) = -4$

Let $x = 2$ $y = 2(2)^2 - 6(2) = -4$

x	y
1	-4
2	-4

$$0 = 2x^2 - 6x$$
$$0 = 2x(x - 3)$$
$$x = 0 \text{ or } x = 3$$

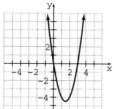

22. Let w = width of the mural,
then $3w + 1$ = length of the mural.
$$\text{Area} = \text{length} \cdot \text{width}$$
$$30 = (3w + 1)w$$
$$3w^2 + w = 30$$
$$3w^2 + w - 30 = 0$$
$$(3w + 10)(w - 3) = 0$$
$$3w + 10 = 0 \text{ or } w - 3 = 0$$
$$w = -\frac{10}{3} \text{ or } w = 3$$

Since w is positive, the width is 3 feet and the length is $3(3) + 1 = 10$ feet.

23. Let x = the larger integer,
then $x - 2$ = the smaller integer.
$$x(x - 2) = 99$$
$$x^2 - 2x = 99$$
$$x^2 - 2x + 1 = 99 + 1$$
$$(x - 1)^2 = 100$$
$$x - 1 = \pm\sqrt{100}$$
$$x - 1 = \pm 10$$
$$x = 1 \pm 10$$
$$x = 1 + 10 \text{ or } x = 1 - 10$$
$$x = 11 \qquad \text{ or } x = -9$$
Since the integer is positive, it is 11.

24. Let x = Shawn's age,
then $x - 4$ = Aaron's age.
$$x(x - 4) = 45$$
$$x^2 - 4x = 45$$
$$x^2 - 4x + 4 = 45 + 4$$
$$(x - 2)^2 = 49$$
$$x - 2 = \pm\sqrt{49}$$
$$x - 2 = \pm 7$$
$$x = 2 \pm 7$$
$$x = 2 + 7 \text{ or } x = 2 - 7$$
$$x = 9 \qquad \text{ or } x = -5$$
Since the age must be positive, Shawn is 9 years old.

25. $a = 3, b = -2, c = 6$

$$p = \frac{-b \pm \sqrt{b^2 - 4ac}}{2a}$$

$$= \frac{-(-2) \pm \sqrt{(-2)^2 - 4(3)(6)}}{2(3)}$$

$$= \frac{2 \pm \sqrt{4 - 72}}{6}$$

$$= \frac{2 \pm \sqrt{-68}}{6}$$

$$= \frac{2 \pm 2i\sqrt{17}}{6}$$

$$= \frac{2\left(1 + i\sqrt{17}\right)}{2(3)}$$

$$= \frac{1 + i\sqrt{17}}{3}$$

The solutions are $\dfrac{1 + i\sqrt{17}}{3}$ and $\dfrac{1 - i\sqrt{17}}{3}$.

Cumulative Review Test

1. $-5x^2y + 3y^2 - xy$

$= -5(4)^2(-3) + 3(-3)^2 - 4(-3)$

$= 240 + 27 + 12$

$= 279$

2.
$$\frac{1}{2}z - \frac{2}{7}z = \frac{1}{5}(3z - 1)$$

$$70\left[\frac{1}{2}z - \frac{2}{7}z\right] = 70\left[\frac{1}{5}(3z - 1)\right]$$

$$35z - 20z = 14(3z - 1)$$

$$15z = 42z - 14$$

$$-27z = -14$$

$$z = \frac{14}{27}$$

3. $\dfrac{x}{8} = \dfrac{2}{3}$

$3x = (8)(2)$

$3x = 16$

$x = \dfrac{16}{3}$ or $5\dfrac{1}{3}$

The length of side x is $5\dfrac{1}{3}$ inches.

4. $2(x - 3) \le 6x - 5$

$2x - 6 \le 6x - 5$

$2x - 1 \le 6x$

$-1 \le 4x$

$-\dfrac{1}{4} \le x$

$x \ge -\dfrac{1}{4}$

$-\dfrac{1}{4}$

5.
$$A = \frac{m + n + P}{3}$$

$$3A = m + n + P$$

$$3A - m - n = P$$

$$P = 3A - m - n$$

6. $(6a^4b^5)^3(3a^2b^5)^2$

$= 6^3 a^{4(3)} b^{5(3)} \cdot 3^2 a^{2(2)} b^{5(2)}$

$= 216a^{12}b^{15} \cdot 9a^4b^{10}$

$= 1944a^{12+4}b^{15+10}$

$= 1944a^{16}b^{25}$

7.

$$
\begin{array}{r}
x + 4 \\
x + 2 \overline{\smash{)}\ x^2 + 6x + 5} \\
\underline{x^2 + 2x} \\
4x + 5 \\
\underline{4x + 8} \\
-3
\end{array}
$$

$$\frac{x^2 + 6x + 5}{x + 2} = x + 4 - \frac{3}{x + 2}$$

8. $2x^2 - 3xy - 4xy + 6y^2$

$= x(2x - 3y) - 2y(2x - 3y)$

$= (x - 2y)(2x - 3y)$

9. $6x^2 - 27x + 54$

$= 3(2x^2 - 9x + 18)$

$= 3(2x + 3)(x - 6)$

10. $\dfrac{4}{a^2-16}+\dfrac{2}{(a-4)^2}$

$=\dfrac{4}{(a-4)(a+4)}+\dfrac{2}{(a-4)^2}$

$=\dfrac{4}{(a-4)(a+4)}\cdot\dfrac{a-4}{a-4}+\dfrac{2}{(a-4)^2}\cdot\dfrac{a+4}{a+4}$

$=\dfrac{4a-16}{(a+4)(a-4)^2}+\dfrac{2a+8}{(a+4)(a-4)^2}$

$=\dfrac{6a-8}{(a+4)(a-4)^2}$

11. $x+\dfrac{48}{x}=14$

$x\left[x+\dfrac{48}{x}\right]=14\cdot x$

$x^2+48=14x$

$x^2-14x+48=0$

$(x-6)(x-8)=0$

$x-6=0 \text{ or } x-8=0$

$x=6 \text{ or } \quad x=8$

The solutions are 6 and 8.

12. Write in standard form.

$y=4x-8$

$\qquad\qquad\qquad\qquad$ Ordered Pair

Let $x=0$, then $y=-8$ $\quad (0,-8)$

Let $x=2$, then $y=0$ $\quad\;\; (2,0)$

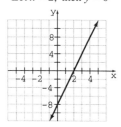

13. $5x-3y=12$

$4x-2y=6$

Multiply the first equation by 4 and the second equation by –5.

$4[5x-3y=12]$

$-5[4x-2y=6]$

gives

$20x-12y=48$

$\underline{-20x+10y=-30}$

$-2y=18$

$y=-9$

Substitute -9 for y in the first equation.

$5x-3y=12$

$5x-3(-9)=12$

$5x+27=12$

$5x=-15$

$x=-3$

The solution is (-3, -9)

14. $\sqrt{\dfrac{2x^2y^3}{12x}}=\sqrt{\dfrac{xy^3}{6}}$

$=\dfrac{\sqrt{xy^3}}{\sqrt{6}}$

$=\dfrac{\sqrt{y^2}\sqrt{xy}}{\sqrt{6}}$

$=\dfrac{y\sqrt{xy}}{\sqrt{6}}$

$=\dfrac{y\sqrt{xy}}{\sqrt{6}}\cdot\dfrac{\sqrt{6}}{\sqrt{6}}$

$=\dfrac{y\sqrt{6xy}}{6}$

15. $2\sqrt{28}-3\sqrt{7}+\sqrt{63}=2\sqrt{4}\sqrt{7}-3\sqrt{7}+\sqrt{9}\sqrt{7}$

$=2\cdot2\sqrt{7}-3\sqrt{7}+3\sqrt{7}$

$=4\sqrt{7}-3\sqrt{7}+3\sqrt{7}$

$=4\sqrt{7}$

16. $x-2=\sqrt{x^2-12}$

$(x-2)^2=\left(\sqrt{x^2-12}\right)^2$

$x^2-4x+4=x^2-12$

$-4x+4=-12$

$-4x=-16$

$x=4$

Check: $x-2=\sqrt{x^2-12}$

$4-2=\sqrt{4^2-12}$

$2=\sqrt{16-12}$

$2=\sqrt{4}$

$2=2$ True

17. $2x^2 + x - 8 = 0$

$a = 2, b = 1, c = -8$

$$x = \frac{-b \pm \sqrt{b^2 - 4ac}}{2a}$$

$$= \frac{-1 \pm \sqrt{(1)^2 - 4(2)(-8)}}{2(2)}$$

$$= \frac{-1 \pm \sqrt{1 + 64}}{4}$$

$$= \frac{-1 \pm \sqrt{65}}{4}$$

$$x = \frac{-1 + \sqrt{65}}{4} \text{ or } x = \frac{-1 - \sqrt{65}}{4}$$

The solutions are $\dfrac{-1 + \sqrt{65}}{4}$ and $\dfrac{-1 - \sqrt{65}}{4}$.

18. $\dfrac{500 \text{ square feet}}{4 \text{ pounds fertilizer}} = \dfrac{3200 \text{ square feet}}{x \text{ pounds fertilizer}}$

$$\frac{500}{4} = \frac{3200}{x}$$

$$500x = 4 \cdot 3200$$

$$500x = 12{,}800$$

$$x = 25.6$$

25.6 pounds of fertilizer are needed for 3200 square feet of lawn.

19. Let w = width of garden

Then $3w - 3$ = length of garden

$P = 2l + 2w$

$74 = 2(3w - 3) + 2w$

$74 = 6w - 6 + 2w$

$80 = 8w$

$10 = w$

The width is 10 feet and the length is $3(10) - 3 = 27$ feet.

20. Let w = walking speed

Then $w + 3$ = jogging speed

Time to walk 2 miles = $\dfrac{2}{w}$

Time to jog 2 miles = $\dfrac{2}{w + 3}$

Total time was 1 hour.

$$\frac{2}{w} + \frac{2}{w + 3} = 1$$

$$w(w + 3)\left[\frac{2}{w} + \frac{2}{w + 3}\right] = 1(w + 3)w$$

$$2(w + 3) + 2w = w^2 + 3w$$

$$2w + 6 + 2w = w^2 + 3w$$

$$4w + 6 = w^2 + 3w$$

$$0 = w^2 - w - 6$$

$$0 = (w - 3)(w + 2)$$

$$(w - 3)(w + 2) = 0$$

$$w - 3 = 0 \text{ or } w + 2 = 0$$

$$w = 3 \text{ or } \qquad w = -2$$

Since w must be positive, his walking speed is 3 mph and his jogging speed is $3 + 3 = 6$ mph.